Anthropology

The Biocultural View

Francis E. Johnston
University of Pennsylvania

Henry Selby
University of Texas at Austin

wcb
Wm. C. Brown Company
Publishers
Dubuque, Iowa

Book Team

Ed Bowers, Jr., *Publisher*

Bob Nash, *Editor*

David Corona, *Designer*

Marilyn Phelps, *Design Layout Assistant*

Patricia L. A. Hendricks, *Production Editor*

Wm. C. Brown Company Publishers

Wm. C. Brown, *President*

Larry W. Brown, *Executive Vice President*

Lawrence E. Cremer, *Vice President, Director, College Division*

Richard C. Crews, *Publisher*

Raymond C. Deveaux, *National Sales Manager*

John Graham, *National Marketing Manager*

Roger Meyer, *Director, Production/ Manufacturing*

John Carlisle, *Assistant Vice President, Production Division*

Ruth Richard, *Manager, Production-Editorial Department*

David Corona, *Design Director*

Credits appear on page 617.

Copyright © 1978 by Wm. C. Brown
Company Publishers
Library of Congress Catalog Card
Number: 77-77077
ISBN 0-697-07587-7

Printed in the United States of America

Contents

573
9719

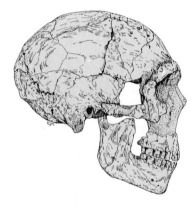

3-31-78   Published # 9

82085

Part 4
Human Culture

Part 5
Culture in Ecological
Perspective

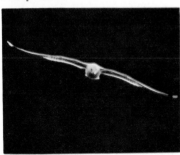

Insights

Preface

To study anthropology is to study human beings—as individuals and as groups of people who impose meaning on the world they live in. This involves a complex interaction between our biological selves, our environments, and the culture that allows us to survive in our world and give meaning to it. Human biology and human culture join in creating the network we have termed the *biocultural system*.

More than twenty years ago, each of the authors made the decision to become a professional anthropologist. Since then, as we have studied and worked in the field, we have become convinced that the perspective of the anthropologist is the one that combines all aspects of being human into a single unified view of humanity. It is from this point of view that *Anthropology: The Biocultural View* was written.

Student Audience

The book has been planned as an introductory text in general and cultural anthropology. While it is specifically intended for introductory anthropology courses, its point of view and broad perspective also make it an appropriate part of interdisciplinary programs in the social and behavioral sciences and the humanities.

We have assumed that students will come to this course without any prior knowledge of the field, and so we have explained essential ideas thoroughly as they are presented. The text is appropriate for students at both two-year and four-year schools.

Themes

The biocultural viewpoint provides the basis for the book's organization. We have focused on four main themes that are woven together as the book progresses.

The first theme is *you,* the individual—the things that make you human, that you share with other human beings everywhere, as well as the things that make you a unique person, different from other humans.

The second theme is *people*. You as an individual are also a member of a group of people—a community, a tribe, a nation. Your group influences you, and you in turn influence and change the group.

The third theme is *meaning*. As humankind evolved and human culture developed, humans asked searching questions about their world and their lives. They looked for meaning; they created meaning; and they altered their world to match the particular way they had defined it. This awareness of meaning is unique to humankind and so is crucial to being human.

Finally, the theme of the book is anthropology itself—the perspective from which anthropologists view individuals, groups, and meaning. We have drawn on our own experiences in anthropology and in the study of different peoples and systems of meaning in other countries and other environments. We try to convey to the reader what the anthropological experience is like. We help the reader see other peoples (or even ourselves) from the anthropological perspective. And we take from our own and others' field experience specific examples of other cultures, customs, and systems of meaning.

Organization

Anthropology: The Biocultural View is divided into six major parts, which present, develop, and weave together the major themes of the book.

The first part, "The Anthropological Context" (Chapters 1 to 3), sets the stage by describing the anthropological perspective, the particular way in which the anthropologist views and studies his or her fellow human beings. Chapter 3 examines specifically how humankind's place in the world has been seen and interpreted since ancient times and how these attitudes changed with the development of science and scientific thinking.

This leads into the second part, "Origin, Evolution, and Development" (Chapters 4 through 8), which looks at the evolution of the human species in the light of the most recent discoveries about early humans and hominids. This section also describes how human societies grew up from the simplest, earliest-known forms of organization to the dawn of historical civilization. We discuss not only the various stages through which our ancestors passed, but also the forces that brought about these stages. Biological evolution is seen as the unifying theory in all life sciences. We see how the interactions between human societies and their environments led to the development of agriculture, the settlement of cities, and the population explosion.

Another aspect of humankind in the anthropological perspective is introduced in the third part, "Human Biology" (Chapters 9 through 11). The emphasis here is on humans as physical beings who exist in environments that may threaten their existence. Physically adapting to such environments is mainly a function of our biological selves, and so this section introduces basic ideas of genetics, genetic adaptation, and biological variation among humans.

The fourth part of the book takes up a topic that, in the past, may have seemed to be the sole focus of anthropology—human culture (Chapters 12 through 18). Culture is those inner rules that determine the ways we look at, work in, and relate to our world. Culture gives meaning to our existence and, in turn, interprets our world consistent with that meaning. Aspects of culture including language, communication, symbolic systems, religious systems, and kinship and family relationships are explored here, as are cultural influences on social and political organization.

By this point in the book, the reader can see how our biology and our culture interweave and interact to form the network we call the biocultural system.

In the fifth part, "Culture in Ecological Perspective" (Chapters 19 through 21), the scope of human biocultural systems is widened to include the natural world. This section is especially relevant to current ecological concerns, as it points out how human environments and human beings interact. But we do not control our environments, and so there is uncertainty in these interactions. Human biocultural systems operate to permit people to get the best they can from their environment (which depends in part on how they define "the best") by reducing this uncertainty as much as they can.

All the themes of the book are drawn together in the examples that compose the sixth part, "Biocultural Integration." In three separate chapters, we look at three different examples of human biological sysstems in a particular mode of interaction with their environments: biocultural equilibrium (the Yanomamo of South America), unstable equilibrium (peoples of highland New Guinea), and biocultural disequilibrium or "the downward spiral" (the traditional Mesoamerican village). We show how each group derives its own definition of meaning from the world in which it lives—and how we who live in a modern industrialized society can learn from their experiences.

Special Features

—Each of the six parts of the book opens with a set of questions designed to guide the reader in looking for major points and themes in the chapters that follow.

—Featured "Insight" sections present anecdotes and interesting sidelights that further illuminate the themes of the chapter.

—Within the text, important and/or specialized terms are set in boldface type. These words are explained both in the end-of-chapter glossary and in the master glossary at the end of the book. In addition, unusual or difficult words are accompanied by a phonetic guide to pronunciation.

—Books and articles for students' outside reading are suggested at the end of each chapter.

—The graphic materials prepared especially for the book include maps of field areas and tribal locations and detailed renderings closely related to the text. Photographs from actual field situations bring drama and immediacy to the text they illustrate. Many of these photographs are from the author's own collection in the University of Pennsylvania (Philadelphia) museum. Many of the photographs in the section on biological evolution were provided by the San Diego (Cal.) Zoo.

Acknowledgments

This book could not have been written by the two of us working in isolation. Our families were supportive, our friends tolerant, and our students patient. We acknowledge the assistance of all of them, but mention particularly the contributions of certain other people. Larry Schell was the person just behind the scenes, keeping our lists straight and our pages numbered. Bob Nash reminded us, sometimes weekly, of the end that was in sight. Ginny Lathbury, Susan Howard, Linda Adair, and Michelle Lampl did more than their share, and we thank them for it. Bob Harding, Tom Patterson, Jim Flanagan, Wayne Kappel, and Morgan Maclachlan read individual chapters, and several anonymous reviewers endured the entire manuscript. We thank them all for their criticisms and suggestions.

We began this book thinking that we had a message to present. We still do. But we learned as we wrote and discussed and argued. In the end, we suspect that the book has taught us as much as it can teach you. If you learn as much from studying it as we did from writing it, we will be satisfied.

Francis E. Johnston   Henry Selby

The Anthropological Context

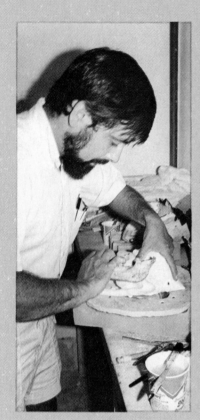

1. Why is it important to study anthropology?
2. Do anthropologists study humans in ways that are different from other scientists and humanists?
3. What are those features and characteristics that set anthropology apart as a science?
4. How are humans related to the rest of the living world?

Part **1**

1

The Anthropological Experience

Introduction

In this book and this course we do not aim to please—we aim to change you. We expect that this book and course will be your first exposure to anthropology, and we hope that it will affect your way of looking at you own world and the worlds of peoples who are, right now, alien and strange to you. One of our teachers told us a moving story about a young woman who was taking her first college course in statistics. The teacher wound up the second week of the course by stating that nothing was certain, but that all events were based on probability. He was very pleased with his oration. But as the class filed out, he noticed a young woman weeping in the back of the room. Concerned and distressed (for he was a kind person), he asked her whether he could help in any way. "No," she replied, "the damage is already done! I can never again believe in absolute truths and rules that made my world such a simple place to live in."

We believe that anthropology is like that.

After this course you will never again be able to talk or think (if, indeed, you ever did) the way some American soldiers in Vietnam did. They used to laugh about the fact that you couldn't tell one "slope," or "dink," or "gook" from another, just as British soldiers in the nineteenth century talked about "wogs." If a friendly village was destroyed, it didn't matter—the inhabitants were all gooks.

Figure 1.1
Making the best of life in traditional Australian society—Among the Arunta, a successful hunt is celebrated by a corroboree, which may last from a few days to a few weeks. These dancers are imitating the actions of animals.

Figure 1.2
Making the best of life in highland Guatemala—In Antigua, the old capital, Holy Week (the week before Easter) is marked by solemn rites depicting the last days of Jesus.

Figure 1.3
Making the best of life in the United States—Americans may take weekend trips to a crowded beach to play in the sand and water, to bask in the sun, and to socialize with friends.

But in anthropology there are no gooks or wogs. Or else we are all gooks and wogs. Anthropologists believe, and have proved, that there is a unity to the human condition. People are different, to be sure, but nobody is better than anyone else. All people everywhere and at all times have tried, and continue to try, to make the best out of their lives. What that "best" is depends on how they and fellow members of their community, tribe, or nation define it. Some Americans define "best" as enjoying good food (lots of red meat), good vacations (a few weeks of intensive activity that is not work), and a decent, secure job. The Yanomamo (*yah-no-MA-mo*), a group of Venezuelan Indians, define the best in life as keeping one's self and one's family safe from injury and disease at the hands of evil spirits and hostile neighbors, having good contacts with the spirits through the use of psychedelic drugs, maintaining one's reputation for ferocity through chest-pounding duels and fights, and having a lot of sex.

The Americans and the Yanomamo have different ways of defining what they want out of life. They have different **values,** as we say—different ideas of the desirable, for that is what a value is. When you have completed this course and you hear about some weird custom that a people has, we want to believe that you will *not* say, "That's weird!" We hope you will say, "That may sound weird, but if we knew more about what these people want out of life and the limited possibilities they have for achieving it, it probably wouldn't sound weird after all." Anthropologists try to make sense out of what people do, even though the people anthropologists study (including ourselves) do some apparently very strange things. Anthropologists don't try to be champion rationalizers. They merely try to show how apparently strange things fit into patterns and systems that do make sense.

We are also going to try to convince you that some of the most important things that affect your life are either unknown or only vaguely understood by you. There was a song in the sixties that some people identified with. The opening line went like this:

> "Cause something is happening,
> and you don't know what it is,
> do you, Mr. Jones?"*

Looking back, we can see some of those things that were "happening." When the atomic bomb was dropped on Hiroshima, the world's newspapers were full of phrases like "a new age is dawning" and "man has unleashed the most terrible force of all, nature's primal power." But buried in the back pages was the real sleeper—news about some new gadget called the computer, thought by most people to be a fancy super-quick adding machine. Now, thirty years later, the computer has altered our lives more drastically than even the atomic bomb. Dreams of the "Atomic Age"—whole cities being run by atomic power, artificial climates, and helicopters in every household—have not come true, but the information explosion made possible by high-speed computers is transforming our lives daily.

There are other things "happening" today of which we are only dimly aware. We know about the computer now and can imagine what it will do for us. Other things, however, are only nibbling at the fringes of our consciousness. Late in 1975, a research team showed that we are at the end of a three-century warming trend and that the periodic tilting of the earth's axis is causing average temperatures to drop. Since many of the marginal grain growing areas in North America, Europe, and Asia will be lost to production because of lowered temperatures, the world must change its eating habits or it will starve. In fact, an average drop of only 2 degrees in the summer temperature would bring about a new Ice Age.

Let us look to the immediate future. Recently the figures for the 1976 birthrate for the United States were announced. The birthrate is now 14.8 per thousand, which, when balanced against the death rate, means that we are approaching zero population growth. That sounds like good news, as it will decrease the pressure on our resources and ease the crowding of our cities and towns. But we only rarely think about and analyze the consequences of lower birthrates. The ramifications go far beyond the fact that the market for pediatricians and elementary school teachers is shrinking. People are living longer and working less, and babies born today are going to have the job of producing enough to sustain an ever-increasing proportion of older people. The postwar baby boom that the authors lived through provided jobs for them, and it will also provide jobs for today's babies. It is not too far-fetched to say that by the year 2000, when today's babies are entering their most productive years in the work force, there will be a very different attitude about the aged than there is today:

1. Older people will retain political power, and our society will become "old-people-centered," rather than child-centered as it is today.
2. The American ideal of youth as the best time of life and young people as the most attractive, vital part of society will change to a respect for the elderly and for their will and advice.
3. Since older people will have more influence, they will require the close support of their children. The family, instead of dying out, will change to a more traditional, extended form. Children will live with their parents and provide for them.
4. The country will become much more conservative than it is today, in the sense that it will not accept changes. Older people have a different sense of time than younger people. For an older person, a week or month is a much smaller fraction of life-lived-to-date than it is for a younger person, and so it seems like a shorter time. What feels like glacially slow change to a younger person feels like hurtling confusion to an older one because of their different senses of time. Since older people will have more influence than they have today, the rate of change in our civilization will slow.

You can supply many more ideas to fill out this scenario. What we hope is that this course and book will equip you to look for those important forces (such as population growth) that are affecting your lives without your realizing it.

The third and last thing we want you to learn is a respect for history and a certain humility about your own place in it. George Santayana, the philosopher, has reminded us that those who do not learn the lessons of history will be forced to relive them. Anthropological history, which stretches from tens of millions of years ago to the present day, tells us that we are a speck of experience in the life of this world. Alvin Toffler, author of *Future Shock,* puts our place in history into anthropological perspective in the passage on page 8.

It has been observed . . . that, if the last 50,000 years of man's existence were divided into lifetimes of approximately sixty-two years each, there have been about 800 such lifetimes. Of these 800, fully 650 were spent in caves.

Only during the last 75 lifetimes has it been possible to communicate effectively from one lifetime to another—as writing made it possible to do.

Only during the past six lifetimes did masses of men ever see a printed word. Only during the last four has it been possible to measure time with any precision. Only in the last two has anyone anywhere used an electric motor. And the overwhelming majority of all the material goods we use daily today have been developed within the present, 800th, lifetime. (Toffler 1970:15)

Toffler's perspective is short compared with that of anthropology. Anthropologists speak of the beginnings of human existence as occurring 5 million years ago. It was at that time that a foraging, short-statured, intelligent primate began to make its impact upon the earth. Sexually mature at the age of 12, with a life expectancy of 35 or so years, this humanoid creature, the first of the manlike hunters and the last of the manlike prey, lived a precarious existence on the grasslands of Africa.

That was 83,000 lifetimes ago. Yet the remains of that weak and improbable creature foreshadow all humankind.

What Is Anthropology?

With roots deep in the past, anthropology spans all the contemporary peoples of the earth. Seeking to discover universals and the patterns of human life, anthropologists study single groups of people in the past and the present with a careful, microscopic eye. It is an observational science, as is astronomy, yet it is also the broadest of the humanistic disciplines. Seeking meaning in individuals' lives all over the world, it imparts perspective and a deeper meaning to the everyday strivings of those who practice and study it.

We, speaking as anthropologists, do seek to change you. We were changed ourselves, and therefore we have a message to impart. We are not without our faults. We get "preachy," as you can tell from this first chapter. We cannot tolerate **ethnocentrism,** the assumption that all people make that their own ways are better, finer, and purer than the ways of other people. We are often as intolerant about intolerance as the most prejudiced.

We cannot tolerate ethnocentrism, the assumption that all people make that their own ways are better, finer, and purer than the ways of other people.

At heart we are often sentimentalists, jettisoning a scientific or philosophical objectivity in favor of defending "our people" or "our village." An old anthropological joke describes the typical Navajo family as comprising "parents, children, grandparents, and an anthropologist." We get so close to those we study that we become part of their social groups.

Anthropologists often talk as though we, the Americans, are the deviants, while that simple tribal man or woman whose beliefs we are studying is truly rational, sensible, and well adjusted. That is not true. There never was nor will be a pristine race of rational primitive people, close to nature, in touch with the spirits and the gods in a way that we ourselves have long since abandoned and forgotten. We are neither the worst nor the best of humankind. We are just another tribe of people trying to find our place in the sun according to our own beliefs.

The Field Experience

Anthropologists have been given a lot of half-humorous, half-derogatory names. We have called ourselves "marginal natives", because we are never truly a part of the society that we seek to understand. We are marginal in the bush, the outback, or the reservation, and we are marginal on our return when we cannot accept the assumptions that we took away with us. A sociologist once called anthropologists "people who reject their own culture . . . just before their own culture rejects them." Some businessmen regard us as perennial adolescents who cannot resist the lure of the field. Seemingly saner people cannot understand why anyone with any sense would choose to live for a year or more in a mud hut without running water or toilet facilities. "Why," they ask after listening to our stories, "would a person with a university education insist that her best friends were cannibals?" What pride these anthropologists seem to take in their ability to contract and compare strange tropical diseases! Among ourselves we dwell on these experiences—the fossil site, the archeological dig, or the out-of-the-way village.

It is a mark of our trade that we go to the primary sources to see firsthand the lives past and present, of the people we study. We go there because we believe we can better understand the peoples of the world by studying them in their own worlds rather than in a laboratory.

Though we try hard to generalize and to make statements about all of humankind, we are very wary of such statements as "everyone does this" or "everyone believes that" because we know that they simply are not true. We levy what is called the "ethnographic veto" on generalizations about the world that really apply only to modern industrialized nations.

We particularly abhor statements about what is "natural" for all human beings. Some people say that humans are naturally aggressive. This is not true. A human being is an animal with the ability to curtail aggression and to cooperate. From the earliest state our ancestors were cooperative animals. They hunted large animals for food. Since the hunted were far more powerful and better equipped for battle than the hunters, it was important for the hunters to work together. Today we can

Figure 1.4
Death is an event that all peoples incorporate into their systems of belief, but in different ways. In this scene from New Delhi, India we can see bodies burning and waiting to be burned at the cremation temple. Part of the cremation ceremony calls for the bodies to be dipped in the Ganges River.

see how the primodial meat-eaters caught their prey. There are fossilized footprints of many hunters around the stationary tracks of a mired animal. Geologists tell us that the site was originally a swamp, a million or so years ago. So we can see that these small-statured hunters, working together, drove their prey into the swamp where it was no match for their nimble minds, sharpened sticks, and rocks. To hunt, humans must cooperate. Our hunting legacy is a legacy not of aggression but of co-operation.

Being an anthropologist, and learning about anthropology, demands that you take a very long view of the human species from its beginnings to the present. It bids you to honor and understand the variety of human conduct and custom, even if it is abhorrent to you personally. And it bids you to see yourself as the outcome of a lengthy process of evolution, change, and development. You are a member of *just another* tribe or nation in a world that at last count accommodated more than 4,000 tribes.

Anthropology as a Discipline

A Definition of Anthropology

Anthropology is a discipline that studies human beings and their lives as they exist in their own worlds.

We can now define anthropology in a more formal way:

Anthropology is a discipline that studies human beings and their lives as they exist in their own worlds.

Figure 1.5
The Mataco Indians of the Chaco of northern Argentina bury their dead in trees.

Figure 1.6
The body of Grandfather has been smoked over a fire in the hut for two months and soon it will be placed on the mountain, but in the meantime the body is part of this highland New Guinea household.

"Anthropology is a discipline. . . ." Anthropology is a discipline because it has an organized body of thought, an organized way of looking at things, and an organized set of techniques—a methodology—for collecting data. All of these give it the formal structure of a science.

Anthropology was not always a formal discipline. In its early stages it was full of anecdote and story, and there was no attempt to be objective. For a long time Europeans could not believe that primitive people were more than savages. Bronislaw Malinowski (1884–1942) did the most to change this attitude. At first he was far from successful. Before leaving to study in the western Pacific, he told the local European experts that he would be studying the morals and manners of the Trobriand (*TROW-bree-and*) Islanders. But the experts told him: "They don't have any morals and their manners are vile." And perhaps this was so from the "experts'" point of view, because no one had tried to collect, using scientific techniques, a systematic body of knowledge about them.

Contemporary anthropologists go to the field to collect data systematically on a scientific problem. They know that they will be studying social organization and kinship, religion and ritual, economics and the natural setting, technology and demography, genetics and nutrition. They set this information out in a systematic way so that it will be not only useful to them, but also useful to and usable by others. The day has long since passed when an anthropologist would solicit funds to rent a raft to float down the Amazon and observe the local peoples. One has to have both a good scientific reason and a rigorous study plan.

Newly discovered peoples often arouse great interest in the press and magazines, and people are sometimes confused when they find that anthropologists are blasé about the new discovery. The fact is that 90 percent of the information that can be gathered from a new tribe is already known from studies carried out on its neighbors. When a new fossil is discovered in east Africa, anthropologists are most likely to say: "Yes, this confirms what we were already fairly certain about," since generally they already know what forms lived before and after the particular discovery. This "preknowledge" is a natural result of our prior efforts at the systematic collection and analysis of information as well as its publication in scientific journals.

"A discipline that studies human beings and their lives . . ." Anthropologists deal with people—not molecules, not laboratory rats, not chemical reactions. Since all people live in groups, we also study groups and the impact of groups upon the individual. If there is any word that catches all of what we do, it is "meaning." We study the meaning of peoples' lives as they live them. We follow them from the time they are in their mothers' wombs until they die—and even after death if they believe, as many do, that the dead are as important a part of the society as the living. Above all, meaning refers to the relationships between things and ideas that people create to give purpose to their lives. As much as possible, we try to recreate the experience of the "whole person." A psychologist might be interested in the relationship between two *variables,* such as social class and intelligence. The psychologist will take a statistical sample to ensure that she gets a good, laboratory-style, controlled measure of these two variables and then carry out observations or experiments. The part of the subjects' lives lived outside of the laboratory is not the concern of the psychologist.

The anthropologist has to care. Anthropologists are interested in people and their lives. Social class and intelligence are parts of those lives, as are making a living, choosing a spouse, or curing a disease. In other words, to the anthropologist, intelligence has no meaning if it isn't related to the rest of the person's life. People are never objects to anthropologists—they are sources of wisdom and knowledge, they are teachers, they are three-dimensional.

We do carry out experiments to deepen our knowledge of people and their lives. But more often we participate in those lives—we eat with our subjects, dance with them, get drunk with them, grieve with them,

Figure 1.7
The world of the Ainu, peoples of northern Japan, is related to the sea. The Ainu villages are close to the sea and the Ainu are skilled fishermen. Until recently they wore long, colorful robes with geometric designs.

and enter into their world of meaning. Sometimes our critics say: "Why don't you send a poet out there to study, if you are going to understand and communicate fully the meaning of peoples' lives? Poets and novelists can do better than you university types!" The critics have a point. The best recorders of non-Western experience are poets. The best record of the full measure of alien experience is given by novelists. Years ago, when anthropologists found it more necessary to justify their existence, Robert Redfield (1897–1958) was quick to note that the best anthropologists, in addition to being scientists, were also humanists (Redfield 1962).

The difference between the poet and the anthropologist is that the anthropologist tries to document, in a rigorous and objective way, conclusions about the meaning of peoples' lives. A poet would not systematically record daily rainfall, nor measure height, weight, and arm circumference, nor take a sample of blood. The poet would not analyze soil composition, crop yields, and energy outputs. A poet would not learn the language, carry out psychological tests and long interviews, or take samples of the population to find out what proportion of the people believe in heaven and hell. Finally, a poet would not punch his or her data onto computer cards and conduct sophisticated mathematical and statistical analyses of the results.

The anthropologist might do any or all of these things. What his or her account lacked in poetic intuition and in feeling would be made up in solid documentation that would provide the data for any conclusions.

Figure 1.8
The world of the Watusi dancers of east Africa is one of the aristocrat. Not only do these rigorously chosen persons, averaging well over six feet in height, perform for African royalty, they are also well trained in areas such as law, history, and the military sciences.

Figure 1.9
The world of these Borono dancers is in the Mato Grosso area of Brazil.

". . . A discipline that studies human beings and their lives as they exist in their own worlds." One of the reasons why anthropologists study the languages that are or were spoken is to make sure that they express the peoples' world *in the peoples' terms.* To anticipate an example we will expand upon in chapter 12, women in many Australian tribes of a century ago ate their babies if they had another baby that was still breast-feeding. Our typical reaction is: "How repugnant!" or "Imagine being so hungry as to want to eat baby flesh!" But these same Australians reported that baby flesh was delicious. Indeed, they spoke of feeling a special kind of hunger that could only be satisfied by baby meat. The anthropologist's job is to report the feelings, beliefs, and opinions of the people studied—not his or her own feelings.

All Zapotec (*ZAH-po-teck*) Indians of southern Mexico periodically have week-long drinking bouts, in which they drink to deep drunkenness every day. Starting in the early morning, they drink 60-proof distilled mescal (*mess-CAL*) (cactus juice) and are dead drunk by noon; but they arise by midafternoon and continue far into the night. "How destructive!" we might say, or "What a total waste of time," or "My God, they are losing all kinds of work time; no wonder they suffer from malnutrition." Not so. The anthropologist reports that the Zapotec drink with their kinfolk to convey respect and show trust. They drink because only by drinking can they ensure that their kinfolk will help them in times

of trouble. When the Zapotec Indians need help in planting or harvesting, or if they need to borrow money, they turn to those with whom they drink. In the very formal and controlled lives of the Zapotec, drinking with someone is the only way to acquire insurance. It is an economically rational thing to do.

Characteristics of Anthropology

Anthropology Is Both a Scientific and a Humanistic Discipline Anthropology is a science in that anthropologists use a rigorous set of methods and techniques to document observations that can be checked by others. This is the essence of science. "Doing good science" requires that you set out the problem you are investigating, along with your methods, your data, and your results, with sufficient clarity so that other people can say whether you are wrong or right.

Anthropologists try to do this, but since they deal with such complex matters as the meaning of peoples' lives, it is very difficult to do so. We might try to be as rigorous as possible, but often the truth emerges in startlingly accidental and unscientific ways. Here's one report.

We had been working hard on the area of belief. I had taken about a hundred pages of texts and had been going over them word-by-word with Abel, eight hours a day. We were exhausted. I had been badgering him to tell me why it was that old people could be buried in that part of the cemetery which was reserved for children. He had claimed that it was the custom, that's all. There was nothing more to say about it. He was hitting the rum by now and lay down on my cot. Suddenly he said, "You can't bury innocent people with sinners, can you?" I had one of those flashes of insight that sometime occur during field work. Earlier he had said that married people were sinners though he didn't know why. I realized that, even though he didn't, old people who were not married were considered children because they were innocent (and not sinners), and the whole system of categorizing people as adults and children, sinners and innocents in the village became clear.

From that point on, Fadwa el Guindi was able to explore systematically the world of sin and innocence, marriage and procreation, birth, baptism, and death. Not very scientific, you might say. No lab coat. No test tubes. No measurements. But she set out her results systematically and publicly in her book on *Religion in Culture,* and any scientifically minded person can check her results there.

Anthropology is not an experimental science. Anthropologists do not, as a rule, conduct experiments as would a biologist or a psychologist. Rather, anthropology is a *natural science.* This means that we are concerned with people in their worlds, living as they do from day to day in their natural settings.

Since anthropology is a natural science rather than an experimental one, its emphasis is on people in the world. The neatness of the experiment is not usually available to the anthropologist, and hypotheses must be tested by observing and analyzing humans as they are. In this way, anthropology is similar to astronomy. Astronomers cannot carry out experiments; they cannot say: "Let's see what happens when you move the moon 1,000 kilometers to the west," or "Let's destroy that galaxy to see what happens to the configurations of other galaxies in that region." Anthropologists and astronomers can observe and analyze the things they study, but they cannot experimentally control them.

Anthropology Is Scientific History   Anthropology is concerned with scientific history, too. This does not mean that we are interested in the history of science, but rather in the general historical processes that gave rise to towns, cities, and civilizations throughout the world. We emphasize *general* to differentiate ourselves from other historians. Most historians are interested in the *specific* chain of events that led to historical culminations. They ask questions like, "What were the events that led up to the U.S. Civil War?" or "What specific events gave rise to the crowning of Henry VIII?" Questions like this are the meat and potatoes of historical research. But anthropological historians and archeologists want to know, for instance, those relationships that led to the formation of cities, of *all* the cities in the world. Or they want to know what relationships they can discover to account for the decline of the Mayan civilization, because they want to understand why *all* civilizations rise and fall. Historians study the decline and fall of the Roman Empire because of their interest in Rome. Anthropological historians study the decline of the Mayan empire as an example of the decline of *all* civilizations.

Even though anthropologists studying the past are interested in processes and generalizations that are broadly applicable, they find themselves dealing, more often than not, with meticulously small bits of information. These fragments frequently hold the key to significant conclusions about the course and the meaning of human history.

Thus, fifty years ago, the scientific world believed that our ancestors had begun to think and to act as humans *after* their bodies had evolved to those of a modern human like ourselves. In particular, it was held that human thought and behavior required a large brain of the sort characteristic of living peoples. The implications of such a theory were critical: it meant that the complexities of our behavior were seen as being "laid upon" a developed (not a developing) biological and physical structure.

Then, in the 1920s, some small fragments of bone were discovered by workers in a South African limestone quarry. Bits of bone like this might very well have gone unnoticed or been attributed to some other animal, but Raymond Dart and his coworkers painstakingly recovered these pieces and cleaned off the inorganic material clinging to them. They then carefully studied the fragments to understand just what kind of animal they had come from and what its skeleton was really like. These studies, in which hours were devoted to analyzing a single fragment, revealed to the world that the early stages of human evolution saw creatures who walked upright almost as well as do we, who displayed enough creative thought and perception of the world to shape and manufacture tools out of river pebbles, yet who had brains only the size of those in modern apes! The impact of this realization, based not on theorizing in any library but on rigorous study of these few bony remains, was revolutionary. Instead of thinking, as before, that we had to look human in order to act human, we now know that we came to look human and to act human at the same time, in a process that took millions of years. To put it in more formal terms, our physical and behavioral traits evolved together and, since they were changing at the same time, each affected the other.

Anthropology Is Comparative   Anthropology is a comparative science. By comparing how belief and activities fit together in different societies, we achieve a global view of human ways. In so doing, we discover two things. First, we find that certain ideas we take for granted because they seem so self-evident are simply not true for all human societies.

For example, until Margaret Mead carried out her studies of male and female temperaments, we took for granted that women "naturally" were the weaker sex: unfit for executive and political power, passive, nurturant, mothering, unaggressive, and best fitted for the home, the

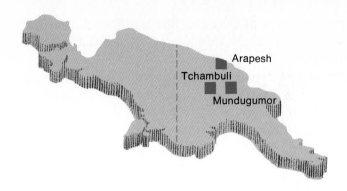

kitchen, and motherhood. (Disgracefully enough, an anthropologist in the early twentieth century wrote a scientific paper on the physical traits of "females and the lower races.")

But Margaret Mead studied masculinity and femininity as it was defined in three New Guinea societies: Arapesh, Mundugumor, and Tchambuli (Mead 1935). In Arapesh (*AIR-uh-pesh*), she found both men and women to be "feminine" by our standards. The Arapesh believe that men and women are naturally fitted for the nurturance and raising of children and yams. They do not believe that men are more sexually aggressive than women, nor the reverse. In Mead's words, both men and women are "naturally maternal, gentle, responsive and unaggressive." The Arapesh would not understand the notion that men and women are naturally different.

The Mundugumor (*mun-duh-guh-MOOR*) agree that men and women are identical in temperament, but the difference between the Mundugumor and the Arapesh is like night and day. The Mundugumor men and women are "masculine" by our standards. They both display aggressive boastfulness. They both are competitive, and neither is very nurturant. A Mundugumor child is as unlikely to receive nurturant mothering from its mother as it is from its father. When it cries the mother does not pick it up to comfort it, but scratches at the wicker basket in which the child is lying to distract it. The father does no more.

Men and women are natural rivals in Mundugumor, and both play a competitive marriage game to the hilt. The man wants to trade his daughter for another wife for himself, and he and the daughter work together against the mother. The mother wants to forestall her husband's marriage to a second wife, because she wants to trade off the daughter for a wife for her son. The son's wife will be subservient to her, unlike her husband's new wife, who would be her rival. The Mundugumor family, in this sense, sparks feuds and hostility. Neither side gives way to the other. Neither shows weakness. Men and women are equally strong, decisive, aggressive, scheming, and cunning.

Table 1.1
Sex and Temperament in Four Societies

Society	Masculine Temperaments	Feminine Temperaments
Americans	Men	Women
Arapesh	—	Men and women
Mundugumor	Men and women	—
Tchambuli	Women	Men

Based on Mead (1935); masculine and feminine temperaments are defined by what Americans traditionally believe.

The Tchambuli (*sham-BOO-lee*) again are different. Although they believe that men and women are different, by our standards, they believe that men are naturally "feminine" while women are naturally "masculine." Men, for example, live to dance, to perform rituals, to be artists—carving beautifully traced designs on dried gourds or human skulls. They live to dress well, to talk beautifully, to be graceful. They simper and chatter, and gossip, and are hopelessly impractical. They cannot arrange a feast, even though they would use the occasion to strut their beauty. The women have to do all the arranging. They are the competent executives. The men may rush out together and fish if a school of fish appears in a nearby lake. But the women, realizing that men are childish and "girlish" (in our terms), do the day-to-day gardening and fishing. If they left it to the men, all would starve to death. Men are naturally loving, but it is the women who give the men their security. In lovemaking, the women take the initiative; men are too passive, timid, and ashamed to initiate it. The dominant sculptured symbol of Tchambuli life is a female figure with a massive, scarlet painted vulva, which symbolizes the dominance of the female.

Mead was able to banish ideas about the "natural femininity" of women and the "natural masculinity" of males. Her results may be summarized in tabular form, as we have done in Table 1.1. If she sounds old-fashioned, it is because she has succeeded in bringing us to a comparative view where we can see that our ideas are not necessarily right or "natural."

Comparative research has such a broadening effect. You can't ask a fish what water is like because the fish doesn't know what a world without water is like: it has nothing to compare it with. Ask someone who has lived in the sea and on dry land. That person will be able to compare the two and tell you about them.

Another benefit of comparative research is that it tells us "what goes with what" all over the world. It tells us about universal relationships that hold across all societies. Here is an example.

John Whiting and his associates (1958) were interested in child growth and development, particularly in sexual identity. They were familiar with Western theory (i.e., Freudian) about sexual conflict in males and females and had studied the literature on the treatment of psychological disorders. In reviewing this literature they noted that there was a very high proportion of European boys who had conflicts about their sexuality; in particular, they had trouble identifying with their fathers and other adult men. Whiting noted that psychoanalysts had made this conflict central to an understanding of the psychological growth and maturation of boys, regarding it as a necessary consequence of being male.

However, such data on sexual conflict and identification were almost entirely from Europe and the United States. Whiting wondered just how widespread the problem of sexual conflict was and how other societies handled it. Reviewing the anthropological literature and accumulating information from published reports, he discovered, first, that sexual conflict was not so widespread as might have been thought, just as Margaret Mead had found out that our ideas of masculinity and femininity were far from universal. Whiting did learn that conflict in boys existed in about half the societies he surveyed. Furthermore, sexual conflicts were most severe in groups in which fathers were shadowy figures in their sons' lives, mothers slept with their small children, and there was a long taboo on sexual intercourse after birth. Boys in these societies became very close to their mothers and identified with them. To become men, the boys would have to be changed dramatically. And they were—through initiation rites involving a circumcision ceremony. Boys were changed from children into men by cutting their penis, thereby changing it from a child's nonsexual organ into a proper male organ. This was accompanied by rigorous training in the ways of men and by isolation from women. In one society included in their survey—the Tiwi of the Bathurst Islands just off the northern coast of Australia—the change was especially clear. Before initiation, the boys were carefree, giggling, playful, and close to their mothers and sisters. Afterwards, they were serious, somber, quiet and respectful to their fathers; they ignored their mothers and sisters.

It was only by comparing the relationships between mothers and children, husbands and wives, in more than fifty societies that Whiting and his colleagues were able to demonstrate this relationship. The comparative approach of the anthropologist enables us to study the structure of society in two ways. First, it allows us to broaden our ideas about what is natural or universal, just as Margaret Mead was able to show that our ideas of masculinity and femininity were far from universal. Second, we are better able to see what beliefs and activities go together. Whiting showed that close ties between mother and child in societies where the

Insight
Anthropological View—
Adolescence in American Society

Though John Whiting never claimed to have
demonstrated that his work was directly relevant to American society, it certainly helps us
understand our adolescent youth better.
Adolescence is a troubled period for most
American boys and girls. It is more troublesome for boys than girls because girls know
when they become women: they begin to
menstruate. Boys cannot mark their manhood
except by watching the signs of secondary
sexual characteristics, which are slow and
gradual. Neither boys nor girls in American
society have a dramatic ceremony in their
lives that states clearly and unambiguously,
"Now you are a man among men," or "Now
you are a woman of age and responsibility."
The complaint that American parents make
about their adolescents—that sometimes they
act as though they are 12 and at other times as
though they are 21—might well be eliminated
if we had a dramatic rite that identified the
children as adults. Neither the children nor
the adults would be able to mistake the proper
role for the child, then. But Americans lack
such a ritual.

father was a shadowy figure meant that boys were likely to have a sexual identity conflict, which was eliminated by an initiation ceremony making them men.

Summary

1. Anthropology is a discipline that tries to shock us out of a complacent acceptance of our own way of life. Anthropologists try to understand the ways of other peoples in the terms of those peoples. For example, read the following description of the ritual of a football game, as written by a non-Western observer.

In America they choose the largest males in the society for the ritual of /futbael/. They are dressed in ritual costumes that emphasize those parts of the anatomy that are defined as being sexually attractive. The shoulders are enlarged, and the genital area is fitted with special pads and cups to show off the sexual prowess of the warrior. Meanwhile, along the sidelines, there are special maidens called /cìrlidɔrz/ * who are similarly costumed. Their hips are fitted with special skirts that make them look round and well fit for the bearing of warriors' children. Their breasts are partially exposed, which is said to be sexually attractive to the warriors. They wave giant paper testicles which they call /paem paemz/ ** and the leader of the /cìrlidɔrz/ twirls a stick of wood that is shaped like a penis, throwing it in the air and catching it. Such is the most popular form of fertility rite among the Americans. It is unlike most fertility rites that we have witnessed in our travels, however, because it is held not once but repeatedly, and in the autumn rather than in spring.

This kind of description is written for humorous effect. Writers look at our customs with a comparative eye. Their reports are amusing, but they are *not* anthropology. The anthropologist would quickly find that his or her ethnocentric ideas about the nature of a football game as a fertility rite were simply wrong. The anthropologist would seek to understand the game in the way that Americans themselves understand it.

2. The central experienec of anthropologists is field work. We try to understand the totality of peoples' lives by living among them and sharing, as far as we can, the emotional depths of their lives. If we are interested in physiological or biological aspects of their lives, we still want to relate physiology and biology to the social and cultural data that we or our colleagues collect.

* cheerleaders
** pom poms

3. Being an anthropologist means being careful not to make untrue generalizations. Other kinds of professors, and just plain people, make general statements about human nature all the time, but we as anthropologists are very careful not to. We have seen, experienced, or read about such a variety of ways of living that we know there are very few universal statements that are true for all peoples, everywhere, at all times.

We must be careful here. In every community you find some people who best exemplify the values of that community. And everywhere they are lauded with respect. They have an abundance of that quality we call integrity. Equally, every community has its share of no-good deviants who are shunned, ignored, and treated with contempt. Good and evil, integrity and deviance are universal—but what conduct people think is deviant, and what conduct people think is admirable varies enormously from community to community.

4. Anthropology, then, is a discipline that studies people and their lives as they exist in their own worlds.

5. Anthropology is both a science and a humanistic discipline. There is room in anthropology for the poet, so long as he or she will count the sunsets and measure the rainfall. A poet catches the imponderables in people's lives, the subtle, the unspoken, the unconscious. The scientist studies the conscious, the concrete, the observable. Both skills are needed in anthropology.

6. Anthropologists are scientific historians as well. They are the detectives of prehistory. Archeologists are probably the best detectives of all, since they are able to take a tiny fragment of fossil or piece of pottery and reconstruct a fossil sequence or historical series from it. Anthropologists differ from historians in that we are *universal historians*. We are interested in the causes of historical processes everywhere and at all times—not just the fall of the Roman Empire, but the fall of all empires; not just the population growth and development of cities in ancient Greece, but the relationship between rates of population growth, population density, and the growth of urban places everywhere.

7. Last, as anthropologists we are interested in *comparative studies*. We want to know as much as we can about the variability in people's behavior. We want to testify to the range of the human experience. We want to stem the flow of ethnocentric generalizations by people who ultimately believe that if they cannot understand or imagine something, then it cannot be completely human.

As comparativists, we want to find out what institutions go together in all societies. Is it true that children who live in hunting societies are more independent than children who live in herding societies or farming communities? Yes, it is true. And it was found to be so by Herbert Barry, Margaret Bacon, and Irving Child, who surveyed the literature on more than 150 societies to see if it was true or not. Similarly, John Whiting found that initiation ceremonies were most likely to be found in those societies where mothers and their sons had established long, exclusive relationships in the absence of the father. The societies used the drama, ritual, and schooling of the initiation rituals to turn the boy into a man. By comparing ways of making a living (hunting, herding, farming) and ways of training children (for independence or dependence), the three anthropologists could establish the comparative generalizations that hunting societies train children for independence. John Whiting showed the purpose of initiation rites in the same way.

Suggested Readings

Boorstin, Daniel J. *The Americans.* New York: Random House, 1974.

Although written by an historian, this study of American life is as sensitive and searching as any in the contemporary literature.

Bowen, E. S. *Return to Laughter: An Anthropological Novel.* Garden City, N.Y.: Doubleday, 1964.

Probably the best fictionalized account of field work. Written by a well-known anthropologist, based on her work in Nigeria.

Chagnon, Napoleon. *Studying the Yanomamo.* New York: Holt, Rinehart, and Winston, 1974.

A first-rate account of how to go about doing difficult field work. Very good reading.

Spradley, James P., and Rynkiewich, Michael A. *The Nacirema.* Boston: Little Brown & Co., 1975.

A very good collection of readings on American life, written by anthropologists about their own culture. It gives a good feeling for the way anthropologists look at their own society. (Nacirema is "American" spelled backward.)

Glossary

value   The importance attached to an object or an idea by a society.

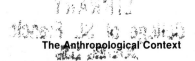

2

The Subject Matter of Anthropology

Introduction

If you ever wondered how any one scholar could possibly be an anthropologist and study *all* prehistory, archeology, human evolution, human biology, and *all* the world's contemporary peoples, you were right to wonder. The last anthropologist to encompass all of these fields was Alfred Kroeber, who died in 1960 at the age of 84.

Anthropologists today must specialize in one branch of the field. However, each one tries to keep a working knowledge of other fields, because all are dedicated to the study of human beings in their fullness. It is difficult.

Modern anthropology is divided into two major subdivisions, physical anthropology and cultural anthropology. Figure 2.1 is a diagram that shows the subdivisions of anthropology covered in this book.

The Subdivisions of Anthropology

Physical Anthropology

Evolutionary Biology   Physical anthropology also has two subdivisions: evolutionary biology and human biology. *Evolutionary biology* is the study of the evolution of the human species and of the ensuing relationship between ourselves and our relatives in the animal kingdom. Evolutionary biologists are interested in detailing the stages through which our ancestors passed as they were evolving into humans and in the implications of those events for our understanding of men and women today. The example given earlier about the evolution of the brain is one instance of such an implication because it says that all the behaviors that distinguish us as humans did not "appear" in some Garden of Eden; rather, each aspect of our humanity has its roots in the evolutionary stages through which our lineage has passed.

Evolutionary biologists may be subdivided further into *human paleontologists* and *primatologists*. Human paleontologists are the fossil hunters, who excavate the remains of our earliest ancestors from such places as an oasis in the Sahara Desert, a tar pit in Los Angeles, and the hills of northwestern India. Not only do they recover the fossils, but they also examine the myriad other things that are also found. Microscopic samples of pollen remaining at such sites give important information about the climate; animal bones say something about the animals who shared the habitat and were hunted. Tools found at a site allow us to reconstruct the way of life of peoples of the past. For example, we know that the Magdelenian (*mag-duh-LAY-nee-un*) people lived quite suc-

Evolutionary biology is the study of the evolution of the human species and of the ensuing relationship between ourselves and our relatives in the animal kingdom.

Human paleontologists are the fossil hunters.

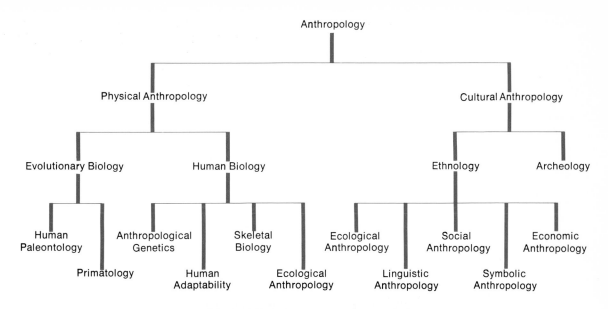

Anthropology

Physical Anthropology

Evolutionary Biology

Human Biology

Human Paleontology

Primatology

Anthropological Genetics

Human Adaptability

Skeletal Biology

Ecological Anthropology

Cultural Anthropology

Ethnology

Archeology

Ecological Anthropology

Linguistic Anthropology

Social Anthropology

Symbolic Anthropology

Economic Anthropology

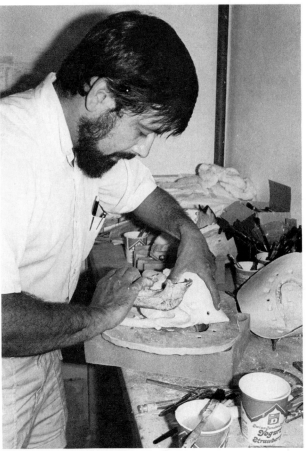

Figure 2.1
The subdivisions of anthropology.

Figure 2.2
A human paleontologist at work. Even though the paleontologist's work involves excavation in the field, considerable time is spent in the laboratory. There, plaster casts of the fossil find are made, so that the cast itself can be studied.

cessfully in the cold of northern Europe some 15,000 years ago. Anthropologists have excavated fishhooks and harpoons that demonstrate this people's exploitation of the rivers for fish. Awls and needles, also found, indicate that they sewed clothes.

Primatologists are physical anthropologists who study our evolutionary relationships by studying our closest animal relatives. Rather than excavating the remains of primates of the past, they observe the living ones in Africa, Asia, and the New World. Primatologists have shown us that many features thought to be uniquely human are, in fact, shared by these relatives of ours. In a sense, we share language; chimpanzees may be taught a varied vocabulary in sign language, which they use in appropriate situations. Like us, they cooperate in social groups. Monkeys and apes are not the ferocious "survival-of-the-fittest" animals we may imagine, nor are they the cute little creatures that amuse us at the zoo and on television. They are, in fact, intelligent social animals that live in groups, learn from observing each other as well as by experience, communicate effectively with each other, and are so like us biologically that our relationship is indisputable.

Primatologists have also shown us that many things attributed to humans as evidence of our animal nature simply aren't so. We have heard all too often that humans are aggressive because they have inherited this tendency: "We are killers because our ancestors were killers." Physical anthropologists who study primates have shown us that some groups of primates (though not very many) are indeed aggressive, though hardly killers. On the other hand, most primates are not aggressive and will defend themselves only if attacked by some predator. Gorillas, as an example, are peaceful animals and spend most of their time foraging among leaves and shoots for food.

Human Biology   Human biologists are physical anthropologists whose main concern is studying living populations rather than the evolutionary stages and relationships of the human species. They ask the question, "How do groups of humans differ, and what factors are responsible for these differences?" From their studies they draw conclusions about the nature and significance of human biological variation as well as its extent. Human biology may be subdivided into three areas: anthropological genetics, human adaptability, and skeletal biology.

Anthropological genetics is that branch of human biology concerned with genetic, or inherited, aspects of human variation. Anthropological geneticists are involved in determining just how variable humans are genetically and why this is so.

Anthropological geneticists also are involved in tracing the movements of groups of people, using inherited traits or "markers" that indi-

---

Primatologists are physical anthropologists who study our evolutionary relationships by studying our closest animal relatives.

Human biologists are physical anthropologists whose main concern is studying living populations rather than the evolutionary stages and relationships of the human species.

Anthropological genetics is that branch of human biology concerned with genetic, or inherited, aspects of human variation.

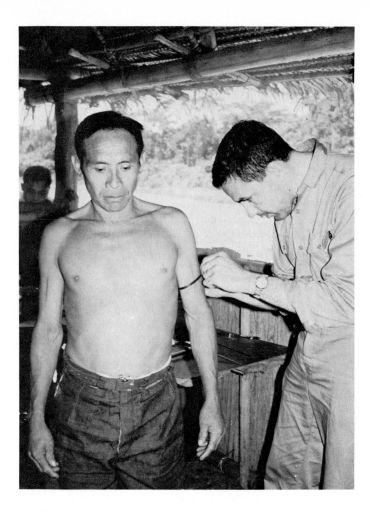

Figure 2.3
Human biologists collect detailed data from the people they study. By measuring the circumference of this South American Indian's upper arm the biologist obtains valuable data on the man's fat and muscle mass.

cate ancestry. Through these markers, the "genealogies" of groups of people can be determined and a great many problems of history solved. As an example, consider the origin of the gypsies, a distinct group of people found in many countries who travel from place to place. They are almost always isolated from the local inhabitants, and they may display different customs and even speak a different language. Frequently they are treated with suspicion.

Most of the gypsies of Europe (and of the United States) have migrated from Hungary. But is Hungary their homeland? The gypsies themselves have a tradition that India was their place of origin, and many anthropologists and historians have wondered if this were true or if they were instead Hungarians who somehow took up a "gypsy" way of life. Examining this problem, William Boyd (1963) demonstrated that, in fact, the Hungarian gypsies possess genetic markers indicating an Indian heritage, and so are the descendants of ancient migrants.

But is this true of all gypsies? Apparently not. Michael Crawford has studied the Tinkers, or Irish gypsies. Like other gypsies, the Tinkers speak a different language from the local Irish people and lead an itinerant life. However, they are not genetically different from other inhabitants of Ireland, and Crawford has concluded that they are not from India by way of Hungary, but instead are Irish by descent (Crawford 1973).

Human adaptability is the subdivision of human biology that deals with the way in which groups adapt to the rigors of their environment. The effects of climate, nutrition, and disease on biological variability are among their concerns. Human adaptability may also be concerned with inherited adaptations to environmental forces on and with human responses to the environment as we grow up or as our environment changes.

Skeletal biologists are distinguished from other human biologists by the special nature of their data—skeletons. Although they study remains from the past, they treat samples of skeletal remains in the same way that human biologists approach living populations. Since they are dealing with the recent past, usually within the last 10,000 years, they are able to amass large enough samples to allow them to ask many of the same questions as other human biologists do.

Cultural Anthropology

From the diagram you can see that cultural anthropology is broken into two major subdivisions: archeology and ethnology.

Archeology is the study of prehistory. It encompasses the story of humankind from the earliest period for which there is evidence of human existence on earth. We are as interested in pebble tools, or eoliths, which are barely distinguishable from rocks smoothed by natural processes, as we are in the remains of ancient civilizations high in the Andes or by the banks of the Euphrates. Equally, we are interested in contemporary history, that is, the remains of colonial Philadelphia or Fort Henry. Archeologists literally dig into our past. Generally, the deeper they dig, the earlier the remains that they find. They unearth pollen and seeds and analyze them genetically to find out what crops people grew. They examine coprolites, or fossilized feces, to find out about the diet. They unearth tools, living sites, floors, walls, and sacred places in an effort to determine whether there were social classes, advanced technologies, irrigation works, and established religions. Archeologists are the detectives of our past, able to reconstruct dramatic changes in our prehistory from the scantiest of details.

Ethnology is comparative cultural anthropology. It is done in the library by scholars who wish to study and distill the reports of ethnographers (writers about single cultures) and archeologists so that they can get a worldwide picture. John Whiting was doing ethnology when

Human adaptability is the subdivision of human biology that deals with the way in which groups adapt to the rigors of their environment.

Skeletal biologists are distinguished from other human biologists by the special nature of their data —skeletons.

Archeology is the study of prehistory.

Ethnology is comparative cultural anthropology.

Figure 2.4
Archeologists carefully uncover the remains of the past, including, as shown here, the dwellings of earlier inhabitants. The site is Hasanlu, a Bronze Age city in northern Iraq.

he compared more than fifty societies to solve the riddle of how male sexual conflicts were resolved. Perhaps the greatest living ethnologist is George Peter Murdock, who controls the data on more than 2,000 societies and can compare them at will. If you want to know what societies in the world have outrigger canoes, you can ask him, and without consulting a single book or article, he can tell you every society that has or once had such canoes. Ethnologists can consult computers where much of these data are stored and tell you, for example, whether the practice of a man marrying many wives is found more in societies that are run on patrilineal principles than in societies run on matrilineal principles (true); or whether drinking to a state of drunkenness more commonly occurs in societies such as our own, where there are not strong kinship ties (also true).

Sometimes we compare societies with a certain topic in mind, and so ethnology breaks down into many topical subheadings. We have included only those topics discussed in this book.

Linguistic Anthropology In anthropology, languages are studied for two reasons. Anthropologists study languages comparatively so that we can see how societies are related to each other. By examining the words and structure of a language, we can establish whether two languages are closely related or not. If they are, we can compare the ways they are different and discover the approximate time when the peoples went their separate way. Many linguists feel that languages become different at a constant rate, and therefore we are able to tell, within limits, how long ago they separated.

Anthropologists also learn languages for much more basic reasons. First, we have to learn the language in order to communicate to the people with whom we are living. This is a frustrating business unless one has a gift for languages. An anthropologist may feel like a perfect idiot-child when he or she is first doing field work and is only able to say things like, "Me fine, me happy, you happy, all happy, how fine." Since there are often no dictionaries or grammars of the language we are studying, we may have to create them.

Language is the royal road to understanding other people's thought processes and ideas. Our studies of unfamiliar peoples will only be as good as our ability to understand their language, their way of communicating, and their way of formulating ideas. Since anthropologists claim to present other peoples' worlds in the terms of those same peoples, we must learn the language. One cannot do good anthropology-in-translation. If we use an interpreter (as we sometimes must, particularly if time is short), we have to be sure that our mental picture is not a picture of other lives in our own terms, made up by the local teacher or informant to satisfy us.

When we write up an **ethnography,** an account of the lives of other peoples, we must be sure that we get the meanings correct. And we must also be sure beforehand, that we do not impose our ideas on the peoples' thoughts.

Here is an illustrative and moral story: Some cultural anthropologists were working on the beliefs of the Tzotzil (*zoat-ZEEL*) Indians in southeastern Mexico. The group received a questionnaire mailed by some agency wanting to know, among other things, what the Tzotzil word for "soul" was. Well, as you will discover in the discussion on Zinacanteco (*zin-ah-cahn-TAY-co*) souls in chapter 15, the only appropriate answer would have been to send back a two- or three-volume work on the subject. The idea of "soul" in Zinacantan (where the Tzotzil Indians live) is so complex and so important that there is effectively *no* one word for soul. In fact, there are more than forty. (The dilemma was solved by sending back the Spanish word. The questioner was not heard from afterward.) There is no point in hoping that important ideas can be directly translated

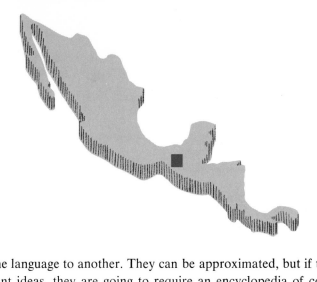

from one language to another. They can be approximated, but if they are important ideas, they are going to require an encyclopedia of comment along with them.

Anthropologists have to learn languages, and they have to study linguistics, which is the science of languages. Anthropologists who study language and culture are called *linguistic anthropologists*.

Anthropologists who study language and culture are called linguistic anthropologists.

Symbolic Anthropology Symbolic anthropology is a broadening and extending of linguistic anthropology. It is the study of how symbols and ideas are formed and gain meaning in other peoples' lives. In every society, certain activities and ideas stand for many things. For example, the cross is an important symbol to Christians. It stands for their belief in Christ, His suffering, His resurrection, and His redemption of humankind; it stands as well for the church, the Pope, the priesthood, and a blessed house. To some more scholarly people, it stands for the glorious humility of the early Christian martyrs, since the cross was used by the Romans for the excruciatingly painful execution of the lowest kind of criminals.

It is the study of how symbols and ideas are formed and gain meaning in other peoples' lives.

The kiss is another symbol in American culture. There are two kinds of kiss: the fraternal kiss (or "buss"), which is exchanged between relatives or friends, and the erotic kiss ("full on the lips"), which is exchanged between lovers. But a kiss between two criminals in organized crime can mean the premature termination of one party's life. It is literally the "kiss of death." A misdirected kiss aimed, metaphorically, at a person's rearmost parts indicates toadying. The kiss of a bishop's ring indicates love of God and obedience to His ministers. A kiss means many things, and an anthropologist coming to our culture would have to be aware of and understand all these meanings.

Figure 2.5
Symbols cause emotions in each of us beyond that which is pictured. These symbols, which are in American society, instill feelings of patriotism, protest, unAmericanism, plenty, and romance in us depending on who we are.

To understand another people's way of life, one has to learn the meanings of their symbols and the times and situations when they are appropriately used. Some years ago, Americans were surprised to see Soviet Premier Khrushchev embrace Premier Castro of Cuba. Khrushchev grabbed Castro, pounded him on the back, and kissed him repeatedly. The Russians in turn were astonished when some of them saw the film of the great Russian novel *Dr. Zhivago.* At one point in the film, Zhivago welcomed his stepparents and stepsister back to Moscow with an American-style peck. Hedrick Smith, the former Moscow Bureau Chief of the *New York Times,* reported in his book, *The Russians:*

It was abrupt and cool, a quick, flat, unemotional Western peck on the cheek and a handshake, obviously directed and acted by people unaware of the effusive, emotional outpouring that occurs when Russians greet or part at a railroad station. They immerse each other in endless hugs, embraces, warm kisses on both cheeks, three times, not just kissing in the air for show, but strong, firm kisses, often on the lips, and not only between men and women, or between women, but man-to-man as well. . . . So tame and out of character was the movie version [of Zhivago's welcome] that night the Russians were still chortling about it after the movie ended.

Hedrick Smith is a good anthropologist (as well as a Pulitzer Prizewinning journalist) and understands the context and background of the meaning of symbols in Russian life.

Symbols can be more abstract than kisses and crosses. In America, ideas such as "cleanliness," "progress," and "democracy" are powerful symbols. They stand for much more than the unadorned ideas they denote. The anthropologist's job is to understand the meaning and interpretation of symbols.

Social anthropology is the comparative study of society.

Social Anthropology Social anthropology is the comparative study of society. It embraces the study of all the ways in which people organize themselves to get the things done that have to be done to maintain a society and a way of life. Social anthropologists study the place and role of the individual within the group. Kinship is important to social anthropology because most of the people outside the industrialized world organize themselves into kin groups. It is hard to overemphasize the importance of kinship in traditional society.

Early in his career, one of the authors was doing a study on the importance of kinship because he didn't believe that is was nearly so important as older anthropologists had told him. He got his comeuppance one day when he was working with a local, Mexican teacher in the teacher's house and a stranger walked in. The stranger was very drunk, almost falling down. He seated himself and asked for a drink, which was produced. He then reached into his baggy, pajamalike trousers and fished out a pistol, which he began to wave about. The anthropologist was horrified, but his teacher seemed calm enough. The drunk tottered out into the yard, told both men how marvelous his pistol was, and pointed it in the direction of an embankment. The teacher's young daughter was standing in the direct line of fire. Before the anthropologist or the teacher could do anything, the drunk fired the pistol, narrowly missing the little girl. At that point the anthropologist lost his anthropological detachment and grabbed both drunk and pistol, disarming the former and unloading the latter. Afterward he asked the teacher, "Why on earth didn't you stop that drunk? He almost killed your daughter!" "I know," came the reply, "but what could I do? He is my brother-in-law." The study terminated at that point. Kinship *is* important.

Ecological Anthropology Anthropologists, no less than the people they study, must pay attention to the natural setting. We Americans ignored our own natural setting for too many years. When we began to see that we were polluting our own territory and the territory of others, the "**ecology** movement" was born. It was encouraged by the space program, for when the astronauts looked back at the beautiful green earth from the blackness of deep space, they made us more aware of the fact that we too are living on a spaceship—our planet. We came to realize that if we continued to abuse the earth's systems, it would no longer sustain us.

Human ecology is the study of the relationship between human beings and their environment. We have to distinguish between "ecological relations" and "the environment." The environment is the natural setting. Natural settings can be beautiful or dramatic or barren and desertlike, but ecology cannot. When people say, "I love Colorado because of the ecology," they are misusing the term. They mean that they like the environment. Human ecology is the study of how human beings affect and are affected by their environment.

Human ecology is the study of the relationship between human beings and their environment.

In Figure 2.1, ecological anthropology is shown as a subdivision of both human biology and ethnology. To subdivide anthropology is not easy since the subdivisions are not clear-cut. Ecological anthropology is one subdivision that belongs to both physical and cultural anthropology.

One of the problems in studying ecology is that the relationships get so complicated that no one can keep track of them. This is as true in traditional societies as it is in modern industrial ones. In this book we are discussing two plays or dramas that are taking place at the same time. One drama is taking place "on stage." It is the day-to-day drama of making a living, procreating, getting along in life, and satisfying our needs and wants. We are conscious of this drama.

But all too often there is another drama unfolding of which we are not aware. When the Americans and Canadians built steel factories and cities on the shores of Lake Erie, they thought they were making progress and creating a finer form of civilization and a better life for themselves.

Figure 2.6
Our relationships to the environment change as humans systematically alter their environments. In ancient Peru *right,* the Inca in the Andes built their communities amid spectacular scenes. At the Inca village of Machu Picchu, cultivation terraces are seen surrounding the habitation sites, all built on the edge of a deep valley. In the tropical rainforests *middle,* societies prepare gardens by a technique called slash-and-burn. Industrialized nations of the world harness water power to manufacture electricity, as seen in this view of the Hoover Dam *far right.*

But off-stage, unknown to them, the sewage that was pouring into Lake Erie was killing the lake. It was feeding the plant life in the lake such a rich diet of nitrogen and phosphates that the plant life began to grow at double, then triple, then many times its normal rate. This is called "eutrophication." First the fish died; then the lake started to get slimy, slick with green foam; then the microbic life began to change. Lake Erie has aged 150,000 years in the past half century, compared with how it would have aged had it been left alone. The lake died—a giant sewage disposal trap instead of one of our most pleasurable bodies of water. It wasn't until one of the feeder rivers to the lake actually caught fire spontaneously that this madness stopped.

When we spoke in the last chapter of the unseen processes that are going on because of the decline in the birthrate, we were referring to another process in the off-stage drama. Population growth and decline have powerful effects on the way humans affect and are affected by the environment. They are important aspects of a study of ecological relations.

The analysis of these relationships is especially complex among humans because the relationships involve so many things: the environment, our physical beings, our behavior, and the way in which we modify the environment.

Economic Anthropology People do not live on meanings alone. Our world of meaning and symbol makes us human and distinguishes us from

all other forms of animal life, but one cannot eat meanings. Perhaps the Greek gods on Olympus could subsist on the smoke of the fire of sacrifice, but human groups are used to and require more substantial fare.

The way people go about satisfying their wants is also a province of study for the anthropologist. An anthropologist who examines this is studying economics. All people have to satisfy their biological needs, or they will cease to exist. But since the world of needs is saturated with meaning, each group of people redefines these needs in terms of what they *want*. Anthropologists who study how people have organized to satisfy their wants are *anthropological economists*. For the economist, society is a system of organized appetite.

Anthropologists who study how people have organized to satisfy their wants are anthropological economists.

In ordinary life, Americans think of economics as the study of money, interest rates, securities, commodities, trade, ownership, production, and consumption. For many societies studied by anthropologists, however, there is no form of money as we understand it, and the concept of ownership is defined very differently. Consequently, anthropologists have to be very careful not to use common sense or even academic ideas about the economy when examining other people's lives.

In studying anthropological economics, we are interested in determining how wants are defined, what the means are for satisfying those wants, how scarce goods are divided up in the society, and how well-being (wealth) is defined and dealt with.

We learn that people we thought of as "primitive" because they had unsophisticated technologies are not nearly so badly off as we thought.

They work much less hard than Americans do despite our so-called "labor-saving devices." They live pretty well as they see it.

We learn that people are pretty intelligent in arranging their lives. They are clever and rational in making a decent life for themselves, as they define the "good life."

We learn that on the whole, traditional producers do not try to over-extend themselves. The idea of making as much money or producing as many goods as they can is quite foreign to their thinking.

We learn that other peoples do not take risks as readily as Americans do. They avoid taking chances because they realize that if they lose in some risky venture, they will either starve to death or be so far behind that they may never catch up.

Anthropological economists have a message for us about how to define our ideas of wealth and well-being so that we do not suffer the frustrations of never being able to satisfy our unsatiable appetites.

Putting Anthropology Back Together

What do anthropologists do? As the preceding sections have shown, we do lots of things—maybe, some have thought, too many things. It has been suggested on more than one occasion that anthropologists try to do so many different things that they don't do anything well. After all, not too many disciplines are so broad in their concerns as to deal with human genetics in South India, a religious ritual in Guatemala, and stone tools manufactured in Africa a million years ago. Periodically, anthropologists go through agonies of self-examination, asking ourselves whether we should get a divorce, or at least a trial separation, from each other. We could then associate with those scientists from other disciplines with whom we feel comfortable—biologists, sociologists, historians, system theorists, whoever they may be.

Fortunately, the answer comes back no. After all, in the final analysis anthropologists have more things in common with each other than we have things that separate us. In chapter 1, we presented the characteristics of anthropology, characteristics that hold whether we are studying nutrition in Malaysia or street gangs in Washington, D.C. These characteristics are as follows:

1. *Anthropology is the study of people.*
2. *Anthropology studies people in their own settings or habitats.*
3. *Anthropology interprets people and their lives in the context of the peoples' own worlds.*

It is these very characteristics that give anthropology its individual style and its unique approach to the same questions that other scientists also study. So, despite the differences that exist among anthropologists, we do share a set of common features that gives us an essential unity, a common orientation, and a similar way of viewing the world we study.

Because of the many concerns that fall within the domain of anthropology, it is necessary to subdivide the field into topics studied by individual anthropologists. In succeeding chapters we will examine these topics in detail, at times giving the impression of even more separation and division. You may very well wonder, at that point, just what keeps anthropology from bursting at the seams! We will then present three selected case studies designed to show the essence of the anthropological approach—that "it all hangs together."

More than anything else we are anthropologists because we realize that it does all hang together. Sociologists study society, psychologists study behavior, and physiologists study the workings of the body; but only anthropologists deal seriously with the fact that all of these and other elements operate in conjunction within an integrated system.

In putting anthropology "back together," return for a moment to Figure 2.1. The first time, the emphasis was on moving downward through the diagram in order to illustrate the subdivisions of anthropology. Now, begin at the bottom and move upward, assembling different aspects of anthropology into larger and larger units. Anthropologists do much the same thing in interpreting the meaning of their own data, analyses, or studies. When we speak of the "anthropological perspective," we mean that very process of placing our own work within the framework of Figure 2.1, evaluating its relationship to the other concerns of anthropologists.

Biology as a Unifying Concept

At the top of Figure 2.1 there is a division into two clusters: the physical and the cultural. Recognizing the existence of both and the importance of each to the other is crucial to the anthropological perspective and is at the core of "putting anthropology back together." Anthropologists do not ignore the biological side of humanity, but emphasize its role in interpreting the significance of being human. Humans are animals and manifest the same qualities of life as do monkeys, reptiles, and bacteria. Being human is being a biological organism.

In their book on conducting anthropological research in complex societies, Spradley and McCurdey (1972) present an account by W. D. Howard of bow-hunting groups in rural Minnesota. Howard describes the details of hunting as we would expect to find it described by someone doing ethnology. But because he is an anthropologist, Howard includes in his account the broader implications of hunting as an activity practiced by animals other than humans, and one senses that we are not just reading about man against deer, but about one mammal against another.

The hunters learn to walk quietly, keep from moving suddenly, and shoot from a secure position. . . . All hunters must keep a sharp lookout. . . . The hunters must learn to sense what the deer is most likely to do and be prepared to deal with its actions. If a drive succeeds in wounding a deer, the hunters must employ the skills necessary to follow it. . . . If the blood trail dries up, hoof-prints may be followed, although it takes a keener eye to see these. . . . Following a deer is a tiresome exercise, although the hunters profess to love it." (Howard 1972:205–206)

And in their introduction to this particular chapter, Spradley and Mc-Curdey draw the parallel between hunting as an activity seen in certain animal species and hunting as an activity seen in various human groups, and examine how the latter has been derived from the former over thousands of years of descent (Spradley and McCurdey 1972). This is the anthropological perspective, constantly relating the biological to the social and back again.

At the same time, anthropologists are quick to recognize that humans are unique creatures and, though animals, are a very special kind. Returning to the description of bow hunting, Howard, like Spradley and McCurdey, does not fall into the trap of assuming that human hunting behavior is simply "acting out" our animal instincts. As Howard notes,

Hunting . . . organizes social relations. . . . It is a mark of status . . . and it provides the hunters with a major source of fun and excitement. Hunting means more to them than the immediate challenge of outwitting and shooting game. . . . They hunt so often in the same general area that the land and its animals have become part of them. (Howard 1972:206)

The uniqueness of being human is found in the degree to which we can take an activity such as hunting, which is a characteristic activity of all carnivorous mammals, use it as do those mammals for obtaining food, and yet add another dimension to it. Hunting becomes a means of recognizing group identity: one hunts with friends or fellow members of a group. Hunting requires cooperation—some must lead, others must follow directions, all must interact with each other. Hunting a territory may also demonstrate to others that it is your land. Ann Fischer wrote of the Houma Indians of Louisiana, describing their status in the 1960s as a result of several hundred years of white contact. She noted that hunting, trapping, and fishing were still practiced but that their function had changed. They had become "territorial,": "the territory must be maintained and exploited or it will fall into other hands" (Fischer 1972:225).

Culture as a Unifying Concept

The other unifying concept in anthropology involves the fact that, as humans, we experience our environments in a way that differs from other animals, interpret that experience in terms of our previous experience, and modify our behavior accordingly. That is, we have a *set of rules* for interpreting our world. Anthropologists call this set of rules **culture.** In chapter 12 we deal extensively with the concept of culture as an attribute of being human. Here we will only mention it as a unifying concept crucial to anthropology and its understanding of humans and their groups.

We have a set of rules for interpreting our world. Anthropologists call this set of rules culture.

We are not born with a culture, but rather with the capacity for acquiring it, which we begin to do immediately. We learn the rules of the game from those around us as well as from our own experiences. We learn who and what we are and how we should behave in the presence of others, depending on who and what they are. We learn how to hunt, how to cook, how to say "my pencil is on the table" in French, and how to answer those important questions about the death of our friends and ultimately our own death. Certain rules are "fixed" in us very early and remain with us throughout our lives; others change continuously as we change and as our world is altered.

Whether or not humans are the only animals with culture is an issue to be discussed later; however, human culture is so elaborate and involved that it is uniquely human. It is so complex that individual anthropologists can devote their professional lives to a small part of it; and it is so important that it influences every aspect of our biological natures.

The Concept of Biocultural Integration

When anthropologists note that human activities hang together, they mean that our behavior and biology are integrated into a functioning unit. We are not beasts with savage natures that were inherited from our animal kin and must be kept under tight rein by culture. Nor are we simply the products of our culture. We use the term *biocultural integration* to refer to the way biology and culture mesh to create the human experience.

We use the term biocultural integration to refer to the way biology and culture mesh to create the human experience.

Neither culture nor biology is independent of the other; in fact, they are mutually interacting. Somewhere around midday, we become aware that our stomachs are making a most unpleasant noise, a growling sound. About that time we also become aware of a feeling of hunger. We are experiencing certain physiological reactions telling us that we need to eat. If we are in a group of people we will notice that several stomachs are growling; our culture schedules meals in such a way that we become hungry at about the same time and, in this case, we are ready for lunch. The stomach growling may produce embarrassed grins because middle-class American culture defines this physiological sound as rude.

Next we find ourselves in the lunchroom where we order "food," substances that contain certain nutrients needed by our bodies. However, our choice of food is based on a number of factors; some will eat a hamburger, others a salad, and others a much larger meal. Some of us eat ravenously while others pick at their food; but the meal is a social event, one where we relax with friends, exchange news, establish social bonds, and generally feel good. If we eat too much, the excess calories are deposited as fat and our bodies change physically, which can alter our interpretation of eating, what we eat, and with whom we share a meal.

Culture and biology are not separate phenomena but interacting and interdependent concepts; one affects the other, in some cases strongly, in other cases, only marginally. Some cultural decisions are idiosyncratic (i.e., they are the choices of individuals), while others are determined by the group or groups to which we belong. Whether we eat in a "bar–and–grill" will be determined by the social group to which we belong. That we do not eat horse meat reflects the fact that Americans do not define the horse as human food (except at the Harvard Faculty Club, where it is always on the menu).

Biocultural Integration and Adaptation Biocultural integration is seen most strikingly when we examine the relationships between a particular group and its natural environment. Some environments are harsher than others, but every environment exerts some stress upon those who inhabit it, requiring adjustments or adaptations to it. We will consider the concept and process of adaptation extensively throughout this book, but we will only introduce the term here as we demonstrate the idea of biocultural integration.

The Eskimos inhabit the coastal areas of the Arctic, living in Alaska, Canada, and Greenland. They are similar in many ways to their neighbors the Aleuts, who live in a similar environment along the Aleutian Island chain, which stretches out from southwestern Alaska. The Arctic environment is a harsh one with bitter cold, strong winds, and dangerous animals. The Eskimos and Aleuts, however, have adapted to these rigors through a series of biological and cultural mechanisms that are impressively integrated.

Biologically, they are adapted to the Arctic cold; their arms and legs are relatively short, cutting down the body's surface area from which heat is lost. Furthermore, they are physiologically superior, relative to

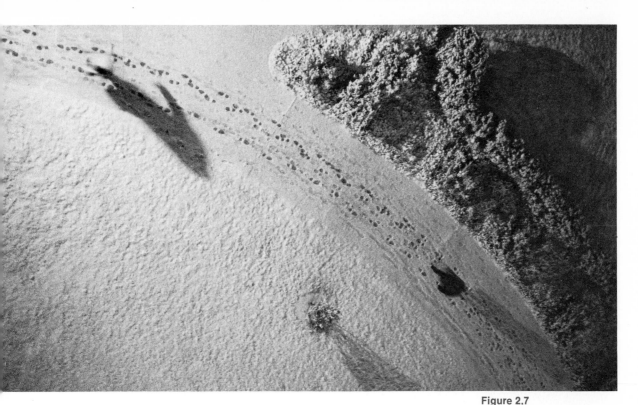

Figure 2.7
The Eskimos, who live in this sort of harsh environment, display a series of biological and cultural adaptations that enable them to survive.

non-Arctic groups, at keeping their hands and feet warm; they pump a greater amount of blood to their extremities, and this warmed blood carries the heat necessary to maintain body temperature almost to within essential limits.

These physiological adaptations are not enough, and they must be combined with cultural responses. Eskimos and Aleuts are skilled hunters, especially of water mammals, and they eat seals, walruses, and whales. These animals contain large amounts of fat, which when eaten provides the excess calories to be burned up by the Eskimos in the production of body heat. The tissues of these animals also contain relatively high amounts of vitamins A, C, and D, so the meat provides sufficient amounts of these essential nutrients too. Eskimo clothing provides protection against the cold; so do their snow houses. We might not think that a snow house is warm, but measurements of the temperatures within them show that they stay at 50 degrees F and more (A. Rappaport 1969).

This view of biocultural integration emphasizes the interaction of those aspects of biology and culture concerned with **subsistence** (obtaining food) and protection from the environment. Anthropologists also have shown that integration extends beyond this level to other domains of

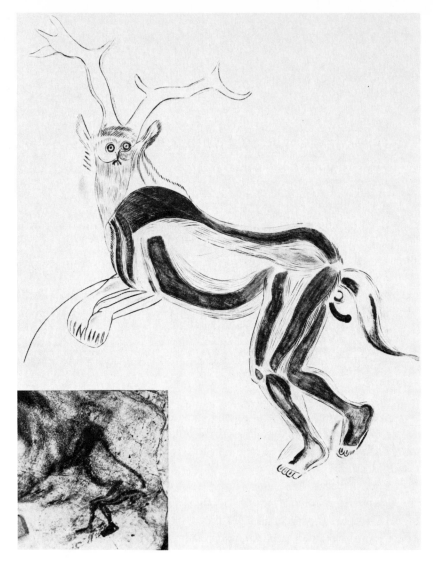

Figure 2.8
A reconstruction of the tens-of-thousands year-old work of art entitled "The Sorcerer." The inset *lower left* is the work of an artist from the Old Stone Age of what is now France.

culture. These may include ritual, art, religion, and other forms in which people "express" themselves in their world.

For example, in Europe we have found the remains of people who, 20,000 years ago, depended on hunting big game such as horses and bison. The importance of big game as a source of food was felt throughout their society, and we may imagine them mobilizing their biological and cultural resources to ensure hunting success. On the walls of caves at Les Eyzies in southern France, we find beautiful and realistic paintings of the animals these people hunted. It is logical to think that the paintings were ritualistic in style, picturing the animals from which the people derived their strength and which in turn took strength and skill to hunt and

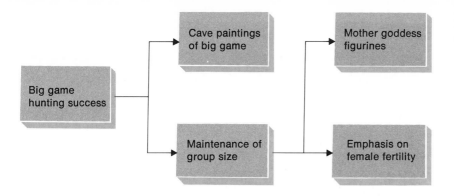

**Figure 2.9
Interrelationships in
Upper Paleolithic cultures.**

kill. Big game hunting with only spears and simple weapons requires a good-sized group of adults, and group fertility was valuable in ensuring enough individuals for the hunt. Throughout Europe and parts of Asia and Africa, archeologists find "fertility goddesses," figurines of females modeled in such a way as to represent a pregnant woman. We can postulate the existence of a big-game-hunting culture in which there was a tightly interacting network of biocultural integration.

We will see that as anthropologists put their discipline back together, they emphasize the interrelatedness of the various parts of human culture and biology. These parts, or components, are integrated into the structures that we study and that serve in adapting groups to their environments and giving meaning to people's lives.

Summary

1. Modern anthropology is divided into two major parts: physical anthropology and cultural anthropology. The former deals with biological aspects of being human and the latter with culture.

2. Physical anthropology may be subdivided into evolutionary biology, which studies aspects of the evolutionary process, and human biology, which is concerned with the significance of biological variation.

3. Cultural anthropology may be subdivided into archeology, the study of the past, and ethnology, the comparative study of culture of living peoples.

4. Humans are unique in the development of their culture, the set of rules acquired during one's life for interpreting the world.

5. Anthropology remains a unified discipline despite its subdivision into various parts. It is unified around the concept that biology and culture are integrated to create the human experience.

6. Biocultural integration is involved in the adaptation of a people to their environment. This may not only involve those components involved in day-to-day existence, but also frequently extends to the ritual and expressive aspects of a people.

Suggested Readings

Frantz, Charles. *The Student Anthropologist's Handbook*. Cambridge, Mass.: Schenkman Publishing Company, 1972.
> *This is an interesting book, which presents anthropology to the student as a profession and gives professional resources and insights.*

Hole, Frank, and Heizer, Robert F. *An Introduction to Prehistoric Archeology*. New York: Holt, Rinehart and Winston, 1969.
> *The authors do a good job of telling just what archeologists do and how they obtain data and analyze them.*

Naroll, Raoul, and Cohen, Donald, eds. *A Handbook of Method in Cultural Anthropology*. New York: Columbia University Press, 1973.
> *This is not for the casual reader. It is a detailed presentation of the methods cultural anthropologists use in their studies.*

Glossary

culture   The set of rules carried by each person that determines how he or she views and relates to the world.

ecology   The study of the relationship between human beings and their environment.

ethnography   The careful description of the culture and ways of life of human societies.

subsistence   The ways in which the members of a group make a living.

3

The Human Species in the Natural World

Introduction

All peoples wonder what they are, who they are, and how they relate to the other forms of life that they see around them. All peoples have "creation stories," tales that relate how humans came into existence and offer some sort of scheme that classifies forms of life into groups. Human beings are fascinated by the world around them and their relationship to it.

Peoples differ in the extent to which they regard themselves as members of the animal kingdom. Psalmists of the Old Testament clearly regarded human beings as unique—a view that anthropologists do not share. Read what one psalmist wrote:

> What is man, that thou art mindful of him?
> and the son of man, that thou visitest him?
> For thou hast made him a little lower than the angels,
> and hast crowned him with glory and honour.
> Thou madest him to have dominion over the works of
> thy hands;
> thou hast put all things under his feet.
>
> (Psalm 8)

This psalm was written sometime between 400 and 100 B.C. and expresses the views of people of that time. It was translated into this King James version in 1611 and was acceptable to people of that day too. There is no question that the psalmist felt that humans were endowed with privileges. This view is still very common today, not just among people of the Western world who waste energy, exterminate entire animal species, and decimate forests, but also among many people who live in technologically less developed societies. Such a view sees humans at the center of the world, with everything else "revolving" around our well-being; it is called *anthropocentric.*

Contrast the anthropocentric view with that of Ervin Laszlo, who tells us that:

The status of man is not lessened by admitting the amoeba as his kin. . . . Seeing himself as a connecting link in a complex natural hierarchy cancels man's anthropocentrism, but seeing the hierarchy itself as an expression of self-ordering and self-creating nature bolsters his self-esteem and encourages his humanism. (Laszlo 1972:118)

To Laszlo and those who share his ideas, we are a part of the natural world, and to realize this "bolsters" our self-esteem and makes us more not less human.

Neither view is entirely wrong or right; each one represents the particular way in which people see themselves as living creatures. Western scientists have studied the human species as a part of the natural world for centuries and have clearly established our place within it as part of a network of interacting living organisms. At the same time, philosophers, humanists, and religious writers have emphasized the uniqueness of human nature which, while displaying its roots within the living world, nevertheless is clearly different from any other form of life.

In studying humans, we must as anthropologists be aware of both aspects of our being. We are living "biological" beings, and understanding ourselves requires that we spend time considering the meaning and significance of that statement. We are also something more, and our capacity for culture gives us a uniqueness that also has meaning and significance.

In this chapter we ask four questions. (1) What is the place of human beings in the world of nature? (2) Upon what do we base that placement? (3) What features do we share in common with those organisms to which we are most closely related? (4) What is the significance of our sharing features in common with other organisms? The answers are crucial to understanding our biological nature and how this nature is interwoven with our cultural behavior.

Life

A Definition of Life

The most fundamental fact of our existence is that we are alive. But what is being alive? How do we define life? We know that we are alive and that rocks are not. Do we also know that the mold that appears on our shoes when they are damp or on our bread when it is kept too long is also alive? When does life begin? The issue of when and whether a woman has the right to have an abortion has stirred up conflicts and feelings as people have attempted to deal with the questions of rights and responsibilities. But it has also demonstrated our ignorance of a number of key issues. What is human life, and is it any different from other life? When is a human alive, and when is it human? Such questions are debated by politicians, legislators, and judges as well as ordinary people, and the debates stir up much controversy and feeling. Such questions are based in human biology and the relationship of humanity to other forms of life.

Unfortunately, there simply is no easy definition of life that will allow us to separate the world into the living and the nonliving. Rather, life is said to exist when something displays certain features and characteristics; we then say it is "alive." These characteristics may be summed up under five headings: (1) *organization*, (2) *metabolism*, (3) *growth*, (4) *sensitivity*, (5) *reproduction*. These characteristics divide the living

These characteristics may be summed up under five headings: (1) organization, (2) metabolism, (3) growth, (4) sensitivity, (5) reproduction.

from the nonliving world. Some organisms on the fringes of those worlds, intermediate between the two, do not show them all in equal completeness. Nevertheless this is the best science can do.

Characteristics of Life

Living things, regardless of their size or complexity, all display these five characteristics. Not only are these features "markers" to identify something that is alive, but they are also indicators of common processes essential to life, which serve to unify all living forms.

One of the basic characteristics of life is *organization*. If we look inside any organism we find that the inner contents are not just scattered about randomly; different sorts of structures can be clearly identified. At the chemical level are atoms, molecules, nucleic acids, and proteins. At higher levels there are blood vessels, bones, and internal organs. These structures are not found here and there; a pattern exists that is similar for related forms. In humans our legs are found at the lower extremes of our bodies, our hearts near our lungs.

There is a relationship between structure and function.

Furthermore, if we examine the organization, the patterns, and the structure that exist as a characteristic of life, we find an important principle that we will carry into our analysis of complex human society. There is a relationship between **structure** and **function.** Human hands function as they do because the structure of the bones, muscles, nerves, and blood vessels permits and facilitates that function. The structure of the human heart is a beautiful example of just how an intricate structure can display a design that is geared to carry out the function of pumping oxygenated blood to the body's tissues and unoxygenated blood to the lungs. The integration of structure and function is basic to life; it is a principle to which we will refer often in succeeding chapters.

Another characteristic of life is *metabolism*. The food we eat contains nutrients that the body uses as sources of energy in performing work. Oxygen is taken into the organism for use in these chemical reactions, through the process called respiration. Unused substances, as well as by-products of metabolism, are expelled, or excreted.

Life is also characterized by *growth,* whereby new substances are manufactured within the cells, utilizing the nutrients taken in. While metabolism refers to the breaking down of substances, growth refers to the *synthesis* of other substances. It also implies *differentiation,* the process of creating different kinds of structures. In all but single-cell organisms, growth also involves the manufacture of new cells.

Sensitivity as a characteristic of life means that organisms react to the environments surrounding them. In simple forms this reaction may be no more than a chemical change. In more complex organisms it may involve movement. In highly organized forms it means *behavior,* and in

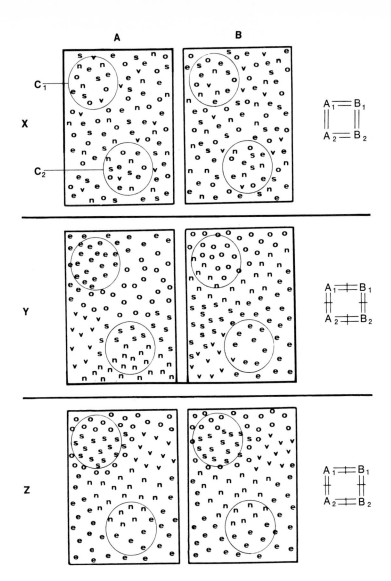

Figure 3.1
A schematic diagram of organization. A and B are two systems or individuals, and X, Y, and Z are three different states. The four circles are samples of the system. X shows no organization or pattern, since all are the same no matter where the sample is taken. Y shows no real organization or pattern; although the four samples differ, there is no pattern, and if we sample the two systems at the same sites, the samples differ. Z shows both organization and pattern. The samples differ from site to site within the same system. If we sample the same sites in two different systems (A and B), the patterns will be similar.

humans it means that we interpret our environment through a mutual interaction with it.

Finally, life involves *reproduction*. Living cells reproduce themselves and perpetuate their kind through time. They are "biologically related." In some organisms, reproduction is relatively simple and involves the process of self-copying. In others it is more complex and requires intercourse between two "sexes," each contributing to the new individual. Regardless of the process, reproduction ensures the continuity of life without its having to be re-created somehow each new generation.

Humans as Living Organisms

The Unity of Life

Life is difficult to define and can only be thought of in terms of a set of characteristics, as we have done. It refers to a vast number of diverse organisms ranging from simple to complex, from land-dwelling to sea-living, from common organisms found virtually everywhere to those found only in isolated pockets of the world. Yet there is a unity to life that identifies it as a single process wherever it is found; this unity places us as humans firmly within the framework of the living world, a part of it and not apart from it. It can be seen in three ways:

1. *Life is related structurally–functionally.* The same chemical constituents are found within the cells of every organism. Viruses and bacteria have cells whose nuclei are directed by the same chemicals as are the cells of birds, fish, and humans. The heart is an organ that serves a specific function. The hearts of many diverse organisms may be compared and, while they are not identical, they are similar and serve the same function in all.

2. *Life is related reproductively.* Living forms reproduce themselves so that there is a "line," or lineage, connecting organisms biologically through time. The life in each of us was not re-created but was received from our parents. We call this transmission-reception **heredity.**

3. *Life is related through evolution.* **Evolution** refers to a concept that will be discussed in some detail in succeeding chapters. However, it is so important to our understanding of the unity of life that we must mention it here, even though it may be only partly understood. One of the most significant implications of evolution is that the life we possess has been transmitted throughout the living world; that is, all life is the same and has the same biological source. Just as individuals are not re-created but have parents, humans have not been especially created but have evolutionary relatives throughout the animal world.

All life is the same and has the same biological source.

To the anthropologist, then, life is seen as a characteristic that humans possess and that is manifested in a series of processes identifiable throughout the spectrum of the living world. As we move from specific concerns of human biology into particular expressions of human behavior, we must never lose sight of the fact that we are studying elaborations of a common theme.

The Distinctiveness of Being Human

Despite the unity of life and the inclusion of humans within the biological world, we must not lose sight of the many traits and behaviors that distinguish us as human. We have already discussed this to some extent—the simple fact that anthropology exists as a discipline indicates that there is a distinctiveness to our species.

Our brains function like the central nervous systems of other living forms, directing the movements of our bodies, integrating reactions to stimuli into an appropriate response, directing the internal physiological processes that go on within us. But our brains are significantly more complex than those of our nearest relatives in the animal world. Their structure allows us to interact with the environment in a particular way, whereby we impose meaning upon that environment and react to it actively. Inanimate objects, natural events, and living creatures take on symbolic meanings growing out of our interactions.

Among various animals, reproduction, if **bisexual,** may involve elaborate courtship rites. This is certainly true among humans. In addition, human reproduction involves marriage, which is not only a biological union but also a social and economic one. We are biologically related to our parents and to our other kinfolk, but all groups may not recognize biological relationships in the same ways. As Sahlins points out, human kinship is not so much a set of biological relationships as it is a "system of meaningful categories" (Sahlins 1976:22). The consequences of reproduction—kinship—are interpreted in different ways in various human groups. This will be discussed fully in later chapters.

Living organisms display mobility, so that they can move in a way appropriate to their environments. In watery environments some simple forms have hairlike projections that wave in the fluid surrounding them, while more complex forms have fins enabling them to swim effectively. Land-dwelling animals have "limbs" to aid in movement over the ground or through the trees. Humans have a specialized form of locomotion in which the musculoskeletal system is structured as to facilitate **bipedal locomotion,** (movement on two limbs). This method of locomotion is so important at a symbolic level that we mark the beginning of childhood and the end of infancy by when an infant begins to walk.

There are many biological and behavioral traits that differentiate humans from the rest of the living world, just as there are traits that distinguish seals or rattlesnakes or koala bears. The anthropologist is interested in the features that humans share in common with the organic world; at the same time, the anthropologist is interested in the features that set us apart from that world.

Biological Determinism

Any discussion of humans as biological organisms must deal with the extent to which uniquely human characteristics are "determined" by our biological natures. Among scientists the issues reappear periodically, and new statements of old conclusions are made. To many such scientists, the problem is not directly relevant: sociologists study human society, especially the western European type; political scientists study governmental structures in nations; biochemists are concerned with chemical reactions; and human geneticists deal with the inheritance of traits. Only anthropologists deal with humans in all societies as biological beings who possess enormously complex cultural behaviors. Thus, it is largely anthropologists who must deal with the relationships between biology and behavior throughout our species.

The most recent expression of the concept of biological determinism is called **"sociobiology,"** a name derived largely from a book by E. O. Wilson (1975), although other authors have also contributed to the formulation of the theory (e.g., Alexander 1975). Essentially, sociobiology takes the position that human social behavior is an outcome of biological drives and processes. Sociobiologists claim that biological needs and drives are fulfilled by social institutions. The "aggressive" drive is satisfied by warfare. The biological drive to **territoriality,** or delineation of territory, is seen, according to sociobiologists, in human property rights. The family, as well as other social groups, is believed to be held together by sexual drives and the recognition of biological kinship.

What, then, does anthropology tell us about biological determinism? First of all, the evidence for much of the basic assumption is very shaky. Territoriality exists in many species of birds as well as in other animal species. But to say that the "turf" of a street gang or the "wide-open spaces" of a cattle baron are manifestations of a biological drive is to fall into the trap of hasty generalization. If territoriality were based in human biology, then it would be found in all human groups—it would be a universal. We know from the ethnographic record that many peoples have no real concept of "their" territory, or of the "rights" associated with land tenure.

The evidence is also shaky for the presumptions that human "aggressive" behavior and warfare are based on biology. Some sociobiologists picture humans as heirs to primitive savagery inherited from our immediate and remote ancestors. Warfare is seen as the outgrowth of this inheritance. Such theorizing overlooks the mass of data indicating that human groups are just as likely to be peaceful and quiet as they are to be warlike. Furthermore (as we shall see later), warfare takes many forms; in many small societies, it is more symbolic than real, involving posturing, shouted threats, and perhaps a brief skirmish between two or a few combatants. To be sure, in such situations, blood is often spilled and someone may be killed. However, the systematic destruction of another people is a recent invention of humans, coming into being with the rise of nations and states; it is more correctly understood in the context of economic and population pressures than as a result of innate biological drives.

The idea that kinship is based in biology and the family is held together by sexual attraction is more difficult to disprove. Certainly there are biological ties among some kinfolk, and the family does channel and focus sexual relations.

But the most fundamental fact about kinship is that it is *social*. A "father" is a father because he is defined as one, not because he contributed his genes to the baby. An adopted child can have as "fatherly" a father as any other child because to be a father is to behave like one in the socially appropriate way.

The most fundamental fact about kinship is that it is social.

The family channels sexual activity, but it is hardly maintained by biological/sexual drives. Sexual drives are satisfied outside of marriage, as well as within, in every society. As an institution, marriage exists apart from and independent of sexual intercourse. It is much more an economic coalition, a social bond, and a social group for raising and educating children than it is the means of satisfying sexual appetites.

Please note that when we say it is important to understand that humans are biological beings, we are in no way implying that biology directly determines culture. Each affects and interacts with the other, but neither determines the other.

When we say it is important to understand that humans are biological beings, we are in no way implying that biology directly determines culture.

The structure of society is not determined by biological needs. Humans are not free from their biology, but they are free to interpret and respond to biological needs in many ways. This is totally at odds with the simple-minded assumptions and analogies of much of sociobiological thinking.

Taxonomy

Method

Although our behavior and our society are not determined by biology, we are biological beings, a part of the world of nature. Just how do we fit into that world? Where is our place? We are closer to some animal groups than to others, but to which ones?

The living world has, on the one hand, diversity and variety; yet, on the other hand, it has a pattern. The pattern implies an underlying principle that, if discovered, would allow us to bring order out of the apparent chaos of variability. To do this we turn to the part of the natural sciences dealing with **taxonomy.**

Taxonomy has two phases. The first is categorizing and naming. Scientists survey the variation among organisms and separate the organisms into categories to which they give names. Second, these categories are arranged into a systematic scheme that expresses the underlying relationships among them.

Suppose you were assigned the task of constructing a taxonomy of pencils. What categories might you recognize? Initially, you would probably discriminate between wooden and mechanical pencils. But after that? Perhaps between wooden pencils with fixed or removable erasers, and then between different hardnesses of lead. Once you made your decisions you would have a taxonomy. It could be diagrammed like this:

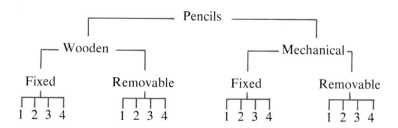

In your classification you have recognized sixteen kinds of pencils. This is not a scientific taxonomy because the characteristics you chose were convenient but arbitrary. They were not based on scientific principles.

Scientific Taxonomy

In science, taxonomy is based on a formal set of rules and procedures, as well as a formal underlying principle. The formal set of procedures is based on carefully comparing individuals and grouping similar ones into a common category. The successive comparison and combination of groups result in the construction of a formal taxonomy.

The principle underlying scientific taxonomy is biological relationship. By this we mean that all members of a particular group share a more common ancestry with each other than they do with members of other groups of the same level. The fact that we are humans means that we are more closely related to other humans than to any other animals. The fact that we are mammals means that our relationship to other mammals (e.g., cows, dogs, rats, dolphins) is closer than to nonmammals (e.g., birds, reptiles, amphibians). The fact that living organisms are descended from other living organisms provides a base for taxonomy not available to nonliving objects.

The Taxon   A **taxon** (plural, *taxa*) is any group that has been given a formal name as a specific category. These names are Latinized and recognized by the scientific community as referring to a specific group. *Rosales* (*row-SAH-lays*) is the name of the taxon that we usually call roses; another taxon, *Dibranchiformes* (*dye-branch-ee-FORM-ees*), consists of squids and octopuses; while *Homo* is the taxon to which all humans, past and present, belong.

Since a taxonomy indicates relationships, it is like a pedigree; and, like a pedigree, has families within families. We are members of the taxon *Homo,* which is combined with another, Pongidae (*PAHN-jid-ee*), the great apes, to form a higher order grouping called Hominoidea (*hah-mi-NOY-dee-ee*).

Taxonomic Nomenclature   The rules of scientific taxonomy have developed over centuries and have been formalized by a number of conferences. They involve principles for naming as well as for determining relationship.

The most famous taxonomist of all times was a Swedish naturalist, Carolus Linnaeus, who lived from 1707 to 1778. Linnaeus developed many of the formal rules that provide the basis for modern taxonomy; he published a series of editions of his book, *Systema Naturae* (*sis-TEM-ah nah-TUR-eye*), laying out the taxonomy of the animal kingdom, most of which is still accepted today.

Of all Linnaeus's many accomplishments, he is best known for giving us the scheme for naming plants and animals. In this scheme every living thing has two names: the first refers to its "group" and the second to its "kind." Used in this way, "kind" is a subcategory of "group." More formally, the first name (group) refers to the **genus** and the second to the **species** (kind). The lion, for instance, belongs to a genus called *Felis* (*FAY-lis*) and a species *leo*. (Note that the genus is spelled with an initial capital, but the species is not; both are italicized.) The formal name of

Figure 3.2
Different ways of categorizing living forms. *Top row:* These three species are from widely different living groups, yet all fly. *Middle row:* These three species are similar only in that they all live in the water. *Bottom row:* Even though these species differ in their habitats we categorize them as related because all are mammals.

Table 3.1

Taxonomy of *Homo sapiens*

Taxonomic Category	Group to Which Humans Belong	Other Members
Kingdom	Animalia	Vertebrata; all other animals such as bacteria, virus, shellfish, jellyfish.
Phylum	Vertebrata	Mammals; all other animals with backbones, such as fish, snakes, amphibians.
Class	Mammalia	Primates; all other warm-blooded animals that suckle their young, such as mice, whales, kangaroos, elephants.
Order	Primates	Anthropoidea; Prosimii (the lower primates: tarsiers, lorises, lemurs, etc.).
Suborder	Anthropoidea	Hominoidea; Old World monkeys; New World monkeys.
Superfamily	Hominoidea	Hominidae; Pongidae (orangutan, chimpanzee, gorilla); Hylobatidae (gibbon, siamang).
Family	Hominidae	*Homo* (man); *Australopithecus* (prehuman); *Ramapithecus* (early prehuman).
Genus	*Homo*	*Homo sapiens* (modern man); *Homo erectus* (early man).
Species	*sapiens*	All humans of the last 200,000 years.

the lion, therefore, is *Felis leo,* often abbreviated *F. leo.* To the genus also belong other species of cats, including the tiger and the leopard.

The formal name for humans is *Homo sapiens: Homo* is the genus and *sapiens* the species. All living humans today belong to *H. sapiens,* but some who lived hundreds of thousands of years ago are classified into another species, *H. erectus.* They will be described in the chapter dealing with human evolution.

Other Taxonomic Categories   Just as species are grouped into genera, so are related genera grouped into a *family,* and families into more general categories. The result is an elaborate system of classification of all life, with each species falling somewhere within the framework and, perhaps most importantly, placed in a scheme of relationships. The first person to describe a new species has the right to name it, and that name has priority; that is, the name remains no matter how inappropriate it may be. Sometimes this has strange results.

Some fifty years ago, Raymond Dart described a new genus, which lived in the distant past, that he related to humans. He named it *Australopithecus africanus.* The species name was all right, since it implied that the group came from Africa. However, if other skeletons of the same species are found on other continents, they will still have to be called *africanus.* However, the genus name *Australopithecus* (*aw-stral-oh-pith-EE-cus*) also has proved to be a poor descriptive term, since it means "southern ape." Subsequent discoveries have shown that Australopithecus was neither an ape nor was it exclusively from the south! Because of the rules of taxonomic naming, this name must remain. To an evolutionary biologist, this presents no problem since the name is only a label and doesn't have any other meaning. As a description, though, it has become rather inappropriate.

Table 3.1 presents the taxonomy of *H. sapiens* upwards through the highest taxon, *kingdom*. For comparative purposes, common names are given for some other animals belonging to various taxa. It is not possible to present the taxonomy of the entire animal kingdom in this book, since it is so incredibly diverse. The order Carnivora, which includes lions, foxes, dogs, and bears, contains 600 to 700 separate species. If we include all animal life, including microscopic bacteria, there are more than 700,000 species living on our Earth.

The Concept of the Species

When we consider humans from an anthropological point of view, or when a biologist studies or examines some living organism, one of two levels of organization is commonly involved. The first is the individual; these scientists are interested in the biology and the behavior of the person. However, they are also interested at another, higher, level of organization, that of the group. In the introductory chapters, we emphasized the role of the group in determining our culture. So far in this chapter, we have emphasized the notion of taxonomic groups as units. One of the characteristics of anthropology is that it deals with groups and, among other things, compares the differences among those groups; this is the comparative approach.

The basic group is the species. But the species is more than just the basic taxonomic unit; or, put in another way, the species is the basic taxonomic unit because it is much more than merely a convenient way of grouping animals together. The species is also the basic functional grouping in the natural world. Species is a "real-world" concept, denoting a specific group of animals that interbreed. Finally, the species is also an evolutionary unit. When we speak of evolutionary change, we are, more often than not, speaking of the transformation of one species into another. The species is the unit of evolutionary change. Thus its ultimate significance lies in the fact that the species is the basic group seen from three different perspectives: taxonomic, functional, and evolutionary.

We may define a species as a group of organisms that breed freely among themselves but are prevented from interbreeding with other species by isolating mechanisms (Geerking 1969). This definition is

A group of organisms that breed freely among themselves but are prevented from interbreeding with other species by isolating mechanisms.

acceptable to the biological world, indicating the meaning of the concept as currently understood by biologists. A species is a *reproductive* unit, and its members may breed among themselves but *not* with members of other species. Isolating mechanisms—the factors that prevent breeding between individuals of two species—are of several kinds. They may be mechanical, making copulation physically impossible, either because of size or the arrangement of the genitalia. Isolating mechanisms may be ecological, in that two species may occupy different environments and will not encounter each other except in zoos. Isolating mechanisms may be behavioral, in that the species' behavioral patterns may be so different as to preclude interbreeding. One species may be nocturnal (active at night), while another is diurnal (active during the day and sleeping at night). Finally, isolating mechanisms may be physiological. In this case, even if copulation is successful, conception will not occur. Or even if a hybrid is produced, as in the case of the mule (the offspring of a horse/donkey mating), that hybrid will be sterile and incapable of perpetuating its hybrid lineage.

The term "breed freely" refers not to fact but to potential. Individuals of the same species do not mate at random with all other individuals of the opposite sex. In the first place, animals tend to mate with those nearer to them, just as we have a greater probability of marrying someone living close to us than we do someone on the other side of the world. In the second place, mate selection among higher animals can be far more complicated than "free interbreeding." For example, dominant male baboons have greater access to females than do less dominant ones. Of all animals, humans through their culture have developed elaborate rules limiting the choice of a mate. These will be dealt with at length in a later chapter, so we will only note here their existence as well as their variety. In many states of the United States it is illegal to marry one's

Figure 3.3
Morphological variation within different species: adult human males and dogs.

first cousin, but in many other societies around the world, it is the ideal match. The Amish, one group of the Pennsylvania Dutch, are one of many groups that insist (not always successfully) on marriage within their faith.

Variability within a Species

Different animal species display more or less internal variability. That is, individuals differ considerably in some species, less so in others. *Homo sapiens* is one of the most variable—perhaps *the* most variable—of all species. Consider the height of adults; it can range from 135 to 215 centimeters (4½ to 7 feet). Other traits show equally impressive variability. Skin color ranges from the extreme darkness of African groups living in the upper Nile region of Sudan to the lightness of peoples of the northern regions of Europe, who show so little color that the redness of the blood vessels is clearly visible beneath the skin. Almost any observable human feature displays a wide range of variation.

The extent of human biological variability has proved difficult for anthropologists to deal with. In earlier years the practice was to reduce all variation to a series of averages, thus creating an "average-average-average" person, or a *type*. The notion of "the average man" is a great leveller, and we all know that there is no such thing. To say that all American males of European descent are 178 centimeters tall, weigh 77 kilograms, have light brown hair, and wear a size 15/33 shirt is to ignore the rich variation that characterizes not only white males, but any other single group.

Typology, or the study of types, is an erroneous approach to studying biological variability within our species because it ignores it. Ignoring individual variability leads to serious errors in understanding the differences between groups. This topic will be discussed in later chapters.

Insight
Human Variation—
A Problem in Typology

This story has been written for this chapter—and although it never happened, it might have. Since the Industrial Revolution, clothing manufacturers have been plagued with the problems of human variation as they attempted to make their products fit as many people as possible with as few sizes as possible. The error of typology exists whether one is designing clothes or studying the people of the central Australian desert, and just because anthropologists haven't had to make trousers for the Australian Aborigines does not mean that scientific typology hasn't committed the same kind of error. So read this story as an exercise in the dangers of treating a living, variable group of people as if they were a set of statistical averages.

A man decided to go into the business of manufacturing children's clothing and thought he would base his sizing on the latest scientific measurements. He hired an anthropologist to measure a wide range of children and to report these measurements to him in a way that he could use in making clothing. Being trained as a typologist, the anthropologist brought to the manufacturer a set of averages for children of different ages; it was decided to start slowly by making 500 pairs of jeans and shirts for boys, size 10. He based his sizing on these average measurements of 10-year-old boys:

Height	138 cm
Weight	32 kg
Arm length	50 cm
Leg length	80 cm
Chest circumference	66 cm
Waist circumference	59 cm
Hip circumference	72 cm
Shoulder-hip length	42 cm*

* this measurement used for shirt length

The 500 pairs of shirts and jeans were duly sold to retailers. At the end of the month, the manufacturer hired a consulting firm to check into the success of his sizing. The firm's report is summarized here:

1. 100 of the 10-year-old boys weighed more than 40 kg and found the jeans too tight around the hips and the shirts much too tight around the chest.
2. 175 of the boys were taller than 151 cm. The jeans were too short, as were the shirts. The shirt sleeves didn't come close to their wrists.
3. 125 boys weighed less than 58 kg. The shirts hung on them, and their mothers reported that they stepped on their jeans as they walked.
4. 80 boys were average in height and in weight. The shirts fit except that these boys had long arms (53–55 cm) and big hips (circumferences of 73–77 cm). The sleeves were too short, and they couldn't sit down in the jeans.
5. The mothers of these 480 boys had returned their purchases; the other 20 were purchased for boys who were built proportionally and a little small. Their mothers figured the boys would grow into the clothes and so they kept them.
6. The 480 pairs of shirts and jeans were put on sale at half price. All were purchased by mothers of 7- and 8-year-olds and put away until the following season.

Taxonomy consists of combining into groups organisms that are more similar to each other and hence related to each other. Organisms in the same category share features that, taken collectively, reveal something about the relationship of those organisms to the rest of the world (unlike the pencil taxonomy in the earlier example).

Consider the taxonomic class to which we belong, the Mammalia. The mammals are organisms that have four important traits in common:

1. The maintenance of a constant body temperature. All mammals maintain their internal body temperatures at a constant level (the level characteristic of each species) by means of physiological regulatory mechanisms.

2. Internal fertilization. The *ovum,* or egg, of the female mammal is fertilized by the male within her body, and the fertilized egg (*zygote*) is carried internally until it has developed enough to allow it to survive in the world. At that time, birth occurs.

3. Mammary glands. Female mammals nourish their young by means of their mammary glands, which secrete milk and serve as the source of nutrients during the early stages of life.

4. The ability to learn by experience. The brains of mammals are large and complex. These brains serve the usual function of controlling many physiological processes, such as hunger, but they also serve to interpret the surrounding environment to the animal. From this interaction with the environment comes changed behavior, or *learning.* As a group, mammals display a high degree of learning ability, and in fact, learning is usually crucial to proper development. If young mammals are deprived of interaction with the environment and do not learn, they fail to thrive. This happens even if they are provided with food and shelter.

These four traits characterize the class Mammalia. As with any taxonomic group there is variability, and the mammals show differences even in these traits. Some mammals lay eggs, others display relatively little learning ability, and so on. Nevertheless, allowing for such variations, we can say that these are features of this particular class.

The four criteria that define mammals are, in a sense, really one. Mammals can live independently of their environment to a much greater extent than other animals. They can survive in a variety of environments, reacting to different conditions by internal self-regulation and by learning. These four traits are the means whereby these animals attain their independence.

First, mammals maintain a constant internal state, called **homeostasis.** If the surrounding air temperature drops, mammals adjust their physiological functions to maintain body temperature. Thus they are more independent of changing environmental temperatures. Reptiles do not possess this ability, but must seek an environment where the temperature will permit their bodies to function properly.

Second, newly conceived mammals are protected from the rigors of the environment by being carried inside their mothers' bodies until they can withstand the environment on their own. In contrast, a female reptile must lay hundreds of eggs to ensure that a sufficient number of young will survive to perpetuate the species.

Third, mammals are fed by their mothers' milk. This nutrient is available to them regardless of the stresses of their environment.

Finally, mammals achieve independence because they are not just internally programmed organisms reacting to their environments by instinct. They interact with the environment, modifying their behavior as the environment changes. We call this potential for change in response to environmental changes the **plasticity** of the organism.

There is nothing magical about taxonomy. It is not, as scientists once thought, the aim of natural science, nor is any scientific taxonomy necessarily the correct one. Taxonomies change as we increase our knowledge, as the case of *Australopithecus* shows. Some taxonomists are "lumpers"; that is, they feel that there should be as few categories as possible, and they are quite willing to combine groups that may be rather different. Other taxonomists are "splitters"; they see the variation that exists and feel that the number of categories should be increased as a result.

Who is right? Neither one. Both views represent ways of looking at the natural world and both are compatible with the aims of science. As scientists refine their methods, increase their knowledge, and continue to communicate with each other, taxonomies become more rational and so have greater meaning.

Regardless of one's views about taxonomy, the place of *Homo sapiens* within the world of nature, as indicated by the taxonomy presented here, is secure. Our species is not only a part of the natural world, but is also placed within that world as a part of particular categories such as *primate, mammal,* and *vertebrate.* Each placement tells us something about where we fit into the living world and also tells us a great deal about ourselves as humans. To understand as fully as possible what it means to be human, and why all humans are not the same, we have to begin by understanding our placement among the three-quarters of a million species that inhabit the earth at this moment. Taxonomy is the way we discover that placement and, more importantly, is the initial step in understanding its significance.

Summary

1. The most fundamental fact of human existence is that we are alive. This places humans within the animal world and bids us examine our relationships to other organisms.

2. Life is characterized by five characteristics: organization, metabolism, growth, sensitivity, and reproduction.

3. All life is united as a single process, and this unity may be seen in three ways: structurally-functionally, reproductively, and through evolution. While humans share in this unity, they also display distinctive elaborations of each.

4. Sociobiology is a part of biology that supports biological determinism as the cause of many of our social institutions. However, sociobiologists have a simplistic view of society and tend to be guilty of hasty generalization from an inadequate analysis of anthropological data.

5. Humans are related to the rest of the animal world through taxonomy, the discipline that sorts organisms into categories that are given names. The categories are then arranged into a taxonomy relating one group to another. The principles by which this is done are formal rules agreed upon by scientists.

6. The basic grouping in the natural world is the species. It is basic when viewed from any of three perspectives: taxonomic, functional, or evolutionary.

7. In addition to describing a group, the features characteristic of a taxon reveal its relationship to the rest of the world. Thus, mammals are defined by four features: homeostasis; internal fertilization; feeding of the young by milk from the mother's mammary glands; and ability to learn. The traits combine to give mammals a high degree of independence of the environment.

8. Though arrived at by formal principles, taxonomies are subject to change as scientists refine their methods and collect more data.

Suggested Readings

Count, Earl. "The Biological Basis of Human Sociality," *American Anthropologist* 6(1958):1049–1085.

  A thoughtful presentation of the importance of our vertebrate biology to human social behavior.

Simpson, George G. *Principles of Animal Taxonomy*. New York: Columbia University Press, 1961.

  This basic book outlines the modern approach to taxonomy.

Glossary

bipedal locomotion   Moving about on two feet.

bisexual reproduction   Reproduction in which two sexes contribute equally to the genetic makeup of the offspring.

evolution   Biological change in a population through the process of heredity.

function   The contribution an object or a process makes to the operation of a system.

genus   A group of two or more related species.

heredity   The process by which the characteristics of parents are transmitted to those of offspring at the moment of fertilization.

homeostasis   The maintenance of a steady internal state by specific mechanisms of regulation.

plasticity   The extent to which the phenotype of an individual can be modified by the environment.

sociobiology   A school of biological scientists who believe that human social behavior is biologically rooted.

species   A group of organisms that breed freely among themselves but are prevented from breeding with other species.

structure   The arrangements of the parts of a system in relationship to each other.

taxonomy   The scientific naming of animal and plant populations. Also refers to a classification of living forms.

territoriality   The tendency of the populations of a species to defend a particular geographical range.

Origin, Evolution, and Development

1. What do we mean by evolution? Why is it so important?
2. What are the evolutionary stages through which our ancestors passed?
3. What do we know about the evolution of culture?
4. How have human societies developed to their present state?

Part **2**

4

An Introduction to Evolution

Introduction

For more than 500 years, natural scientists were occupied with the task of classifying the natural world. The result was the taxonomy of living forms discussed in the previous chapter. In this chapter, we discuss the natural processes that allow a taxonomy to be constructed—the processes leading to pattern and variability in living organisms—and the ways in which ideas about those natural processes developed in the world of science.

Taxonomy naturally poses questions to scientists who classify. Why do groups differ from each other? Why are certain groups more like each other than like another set of groups? Why do animals of the past differ from those of the present? Once the answer was: "God created the diversity of living forms according to his pleasures, placing them into the systematic relationships that we see." Since the taxonomy was God's handiwork, the scientists' duty was to seek to discover this classification, and then God's plan would be apparent. To state it another way, scientists developed the notion that order existed in nature and that by careful study, using logical procedures, this order would be discovered.

For a while, natural science proceeded in this manner. Linnaeus produced his massive works on taxonomy, and careful observation resulted in the accumulation of large amounts of data on the distribution and variety of life in the world. But out of this work came the slow, steady realization that the natural world wasn't the way it was thought to be. There was order, but there was also change. The order that had been documented by the taxonomists was, in fact, an indication of the stages through which organisms had passed.

This was explained by the development of the theory of **evolution,** a detailed, marvelously elegant theory of change in the living world, which has not only explained biological change but has shown how all life diverged from a single source.

Evolution is possibly the single most important theory ever developed in the world of science.

Evolution is possibly the single most important theory ever developed in the world of science. All other theories that explain living structure ultimately depend on evolutionary theory.

A Definition of Evolution

Evolution is such an important theory and concept that we will spend a significant part of this book discussing it and its consequences. There are many facets to evolution, many ways to consider it, and many consequences that follow from it. To begin our discussion, let us define evolution in a simple, yet straightforward, way: Evolution is the modification of a species, and the populations comprising it through time.

The *units* of evolution, therefore, are groups—species and the populations comprising them. At the same time the *material* of evolution is the hereditary material passed from parent to offspring, since the biological link through time is, after all, inheritance. Finally, the *mechanisms* of evolution are the forces that operate on populations in order to change the hereditary material from one generation to the next. In subsequent chapters we will deal with each of these areas. We will examine the changes that have occurred during the course of human evolution as the human species was successively transformed to its present form. We will examine the nature of the hereditary material as it is transformed through evolution, and, finally, we will examine the mechanisms operating in nature that bring about these changes, the mechanisms of evolution.

Evolution is the modification of a species, and the populations comprising it through time.

Cultural Evolution

Evolution is change through time, and while we have defined evolution in terms of the biological aspects of human nature, it is also true that culture and society change. In general terms, we may call this "cultural evolution." However, culture has not evolved in response to the same forces as biological evolution, nor is the material of cultural evolution the same. Cultural inheritance is not transmitted through the hereditary material, but through learning, experience, and observation.

In the past, anthropologists and other social scientists mistakenly concluded that cultural evolution and biological evolution were the same. The peoples of the industrialized nations of western Europe were seen as the "highest" products of both biological and cultural evolution, and other societies were arrayed below them. We now know that this viewpoint was wrong and that, while cultures change through time, the process cannot be equated in any way with biological evolution and must be studied as a separate topic.

The Development of a Theory of Evolution

Early Views of Species and their Origins

Throughout the Middle Ages, the Renaissance, and well into the nineteenth century, Western thinkers held the view of a divinely created and ordered natural world. Scientists recognized the order in nature, but saw it as reflecting a static universe created by God who had produced each species separately. Implicit in this notion was one of hierarchy, some "scale of being," along which living forms could be placed from

Figure 4.1
Nicholas Copernicus (1473-1543), a Polish astronomer, who demonstrated that, contrary to earlier ideas, the earth was not the center of the universe; instead, the earth revolved about the sun. He was harshly attacked by the church for these views.

lowest to highest. The place of humankind was clear: we were almost, but not quite, the highest, superseded only by angels!

This world view permeated the thinking of all, and the scientific community largely accepted it without question. Those who did not were attacked and ridiculed, and their ideas held up as contrary to God's laws. The Church played a dominant role in every aspect of life including the scientific, and the policy-making bodies of the church held views that were rigid and generally unyielding. To them it was clear that nature had a plan and that this plan had been formulated by God. Each group of animals had its place and all could be located along some fixed scale; life was seen as a "great chain of being."

Pre-Evolutionary Views of Variability

Natural scientists of this period tended to deal with variability in a very human way; when people are confronted with something that doesn't fit into their scheme of things, they often ignore it. The scientific world ignored variability and, in fact, discounted it. Baron Georges Cuvier (1769–1832) was a prominent French anatomist, who has been characterized by Loren Eiseley (1961) as the "wizard of the charnel house" because of his insistence on an anatomical pattern characteristic of each species. If one knew the pattern, one could reconstruct an entire skeleton from a single bone, and Cuvier delighted and mystified many observers by reconstructing skeletons under just such conditions.

The scientific world, however, could not completely ignore variability and, in particular, they were faced with the problem of variability in past forms of life. **Fossils** were recognized as the remains of dead organisms, but scientists were puzzled by the fact that they didn't resemble living forms. On the other hand, fossils weren't drastically different from the living, almost as if they were ancestors. How could this be reconciled? And how could one explain the discovery of fossils of now-extinct forms of life?

Natural scientists such as Cuvier explained such paradoxes by developing the theory of *catastrophism.* This idea was rooted in the then-current notion of separate creation. This theory held that an entire range of animal life had been created in the past, but for some reason, the Creator had then subsequently destroyed all life by means of some catastrophic event. The biblical Flood was seen as one such catastrophe. Following this destruction, He again created life in its various forms, but with species that differed from the ones He had destroyed. Some species were not created again and so could be thought of as extinct; others were changed slightly. The succession of species, then, resulted from a series of creations (and re-creations) through time.

Catastrophism provided an explanation for the differences seen between the animal world of the past and the present. A series of catastrophes was seen as the mechanism that led to these differences. This view persisted for some time, and Loring Brace (1964) has argued that it has not yet disappeared; he notes that some evolutionary biologists still refuse to accept certain fossil remains as ancestral to modern human species and all too quickly advocate that the older groups became extinct. Whether or not catastrophism is still prevalent to any degree, it offered the world of the eighteenth century a ready explanation for certain biological observations, when that explanation had to be made within the context of a static and unchanging universe.

Even while catastrophism represented mainstream thinking, some scientists did begin to interpret the world differently. Gradually there emerged the notions that species themselves could change slowly over time, that one species could give rise to another and, most revolutionary of all, that human beings were a product of this process. However, before such a radical idea could be formalized into a theory acceptable to the scientific world, several intermediate developments had to occur, developments that took decades of observation, analysis, thought, and controversy.

The Development of the Concept of Time

Eighteenth-century Europe was not ready to accept the notion of the transformation of one species into another. Even if the idea itself were admissible, it was clear that such a series of events would have had to have taken enormous periods of time and, to people living in the 1700s, the links to the past were recent ones. These links were not based on the scientific observations we so readily accept today but on biblical chronologies and pedigrees. After all, the Old Testament described the creation of the world and actually went through the generations that had occurred from the first "man" to biblical times. Obviously the world wasn't a very old place. In fact, Bishop James Ussher calculated from these pedigrees that God had created the earth in 4004 B.C. Dr. John Lightfoot pinpointed the timing at 9:00 A.M. on October 23rd of that year!

On the other hand, some individuals interpreted the world of nature in a different way. Among them was Johann Wolfgang von Goethe, the creator of *Faust,* the fictional character who sold his soul to the devil. Goethe had for some time refused to accept the catastrophic notions of creation though he offered no alternative. But his was only a single voice at a time when such theories were inadmissible.

The development of a modern concept of time and change received its greatest impetus from the works of Charles Lyell (1797–1875). Lyell, a British lawyer and member of the British Geological Society,

Figure 4.2
Aerial view of the Grande Ronde River in Washington state. The various layers, or strata, are clearly visible as they have accumulated on top of one another.

knew nothing of Goethe's views but was intensely interested in the formation of the earth's crust. Between 1830 and 1833, Lyell published three volumes of his *Principles of Geology,* which not only signaled the beginning of modern geology but which, once and for all, turned our concepts of time and of change inside out. The basic notion of Lyell's theory of **uniformitarianism** is that nature had worked continuously and uniformly on the earth's surface over incredibly long periods of time, through water, ice, volcanoes and other means. However, this had occurred so very slowly that humans, who had only observed the results, not the processes, erroneously inferred revolutions and catastrophes rather than gradual and cumulative change.

Lyell's theory not only upset all notions of change, but also drastically revised concepts of time. Changes in the earth could no longer be reckoned in a small number of Old Testament generations, but in epochs of millions of years. And, Lyell argued, such changes were not restricted to the inanimate material of the earth itself. On the contrary, if, over long periods of time, minor causes had produced such great changes in the earth, then similarly minor causes might very well have altered living forms. The long-term changes could have been interpreted as "new" creations.

Early Theories of Evolution: Lamarck

At the same time that Lyell was reshaping the world's idea of geological change, others were beginning to realize that one species might have changed, or evolved, into another. Jean Baptiste Lamarck (1744–1829), a professor of zoology in Paris, was one of these. Rejecting the catastrophic views of his colleague Cuvier, Lamarck argued strongly that evolution was a fact and that evolutionary change was brought about by the direct pressure of the environment. Changes occurred when there was a "need" for them, and the new structures were passed along from ancestor to descendant with successive modifications, again in response to need. Today we call Lamarck's theory that of the "inheritance of acquired characteristics," since it implies that modifications caused by the environment are passed along to one's descendants.

Lamarck pressed his ideas without hesitation. He wrote that humans had descended from the higher apes when certain of these animals had accustomed themselves to walk upright and had "raised their eyes to heaven." This new attitude had led to the development of the senses, the growth of the brain, and even the organization of society.

Lamarck was bitterly attacked by the scientists of the day, and his ideas were repudiated by those such as Cuvier, who held as strongly as ever to the doctrine of the fixity of species. Even today we find Lamarck's views far-fetched and naive, and perhaps it is understandable that he

Figure 4.3
Adaptations in animals.
A muskrat *left* lives in
shallow waters of North
America. Its feet act as
oars, enabling a swimming
speed of two to three mph.
Its eight-inch tail acts as a
rudder, and it can swim for
more than fifty yards under-
water. A walking stick *right*,
an insect that looks so
much like a stick, or stem,
that it is difficult to
distinguish it.

died a poor man, largely forgotten by his contemporaries. However, he should be remembered not only for his role as one of the first to advocate biological change, but also for another contribution. He was among the first to realize the importance of the environment in evolution. Lamarck was absolutely right when he saw the environment as a central feature in bringing about evolutionary change. He went wrong in interpreting this as resulting from direct environmental modifications that were transmitted to the next generation.

Adaptation: the Key to Evolution

Despite his contributions, Lamarck failed because this theory was neither logical nor adequate to explain known facts. This rests in the idea of **adaptation.** By this term we mean the tendency for organisms to have features that enhance their survival in the specific environments in which they live. Today we know of thousands of examples of specific ways in which animal species are adapted to their environments; and one of the major tasks occupying anthropologists is the study of the adaptations of human groups to their own worlds.

The concept of adaptation was worked into a theory of evolution out of the observations and experiments of Charles Darwin (1809–1882), the one person who finally put together a theory of evolution that was acceptable to the great majority of his scientific colleagues and, though more slowly, to the rest of the world. Darwin was a shy member of a well-known English family; he had tried, unsuccessfully, theology and then medicine, finally settling on natural science as his interest. He read the accounts of scientific explorers who described the exotic plants and animals they had discovered in their travels, and the habits of the "strange" human beings they encountered. He wondered just why certain forms were so fundamentally similar, yet so different. He translated this wonderment into action by enlisting as the scientist on an expedition to South America.

Figure 4.4
Giant tortoise from the Galapagos islands. Darwin's observations of these vegetarians contributed to his formation of the theory of natural selection.

This expedition left England in 1831 aboard the H.M.S. *Beagle,* and Darwin did not return until 1836. During those five years he observed firsthand the variety of life that existed in that area of the world, especially on the Galapagos Islands in the Pacific Ocean west of Ecuador. He found that, on the Galapagos, the animals and plants corresponded roughly to those found on the continent of South America, but were not identical. Each island possessed its own species, differing slightly from those of other islands as well as from the continental forms. These forms suggested a continuity of descent and led Darwin to ask "why?"

The twenty years of Darwin's life following his return were occupied with a series of experiments in which he bred various groups of animals and plants, demonstrating their flexibility and the modifications that came about as a result of descent. From his lifetime of observation, analysis, and interpretation, he developed a theory to explain just how lineages might be modified through time and how these modifications would lead to the adaptation of the lineages to their environments. He called this theory **natural selection.**

The theory of natural selection has been modified slightly by evolutionary biologists since that time, but it remains basically the same as that developed by Darwin. In studying the relationship between animals and their environments, Darwin had been influenced by the writings of the English economist T. R. Malthus, who had written of life as a "struggle for existence." Darwin saw that, in this struggle, those forms that were better adapted would be more successful and would survive to pass those adaptations to their offspring. Over time, adaptive variants within a species would be "selected" at the expense of less adapted forms, and the species would gradually become modified. These modifications would be advantageous, resulting in the adaptation of a species to its environment or to a series of changing environments.

Along with Lamarck, Darwin grasped the significance of the environment. But there the resemblance stopped. While Lamarck saw the environment as "causing" the change itself, Darwin theorized that the environment was "selecting" from among a set of variants the ones better adapted.

Alfred Russel Wallace: The Forgotten Evolutionist

The story of the development of the theory of evolution might very well stop here, except for the intriguing episode of Alfred Wallace. Wallace was an adventurer who had traveled over much of the world, making the same sorts of observations as had Darwin on the *Beagle.* Wallace developed the same theory as Darwin and wrote a manuscript describing his ideas during the twenty-year period when Darwin was still holding back the publication of his own work. Wallace had heard of Darwin as an eminent naturalist, and so he sent Darwin his manuscript asking him if publication could be arranged. We can easily imagine Darwin's reaction, seeing the very ideas that he had developed over many years of study now laid out in written form.

Fortunately, Darwin was an honorable person and did not throw Wallace's work away without telling anyone. In fact, he arranged for the joint publication of two papers; on July 1, 1858, the two were read before the Linnaean Society and subsequently published. After hundreds of years of slow and often controversial development, the final step in the formulation of a theory of evolution was made independently by two persons, Darwin and Wallace, working on opposite sides of the world!

The Post-Darwinian Era: The Science of Genetics

The reaction to Darwin and Wallace was immediate and heated; the first edition of Darwin's book *The Origin of Species,* published in 1859, sold out on the day it was published. By and large, opinions were quite positive, and the scientific world supported the notion of evolution through natural selection. But not completely—some prominent scientists still bitterly opposed the idea. Louis Henry Agassiz (1807–1873), a renowned American naturalist and geologist, rejected the idea of evolution until the day he died, holding that it was contrary to the orderliness of nature and the beauty of God's plan. Many members of the clergy were also outspoken in their criticism of evolution, and debates between scientists and bishops were held in many parts of England. The wife of one prelate is said to have remarked that "Charles Darwin has suggested that we are all descended from apes." She hoped it wasn't true, but if it was, she prayed that "no one would ever hear of it!"

Although there are those who still oppose evolution, the idea has become accepted by virtually all scientists and others who have taken the time to study objectively the theory and the supporting evidence. There is no question that the remarkable and continuing diversity of life upon the earth, past and present, is due not to the destructiveness and creative whims of God, but rather to the constructiveness and innovativeness of the process of evolution. Nearly all major religious bodies have accepted evolution as fact and have incorporated an evolutionary approach to life into their own theologies and beliefs.

The final refinement of evolutionary theory did not come from Darwin or Wallace. While each understood how certain variants might be selected by nature, neither knew how variation *originated,* how it was *maintained* from generation to generation, or how it was *transmitted* from parent to offspring. These things come within the realm of **genetics,** the science of heredity.

These things come within the realm of genetics, the science of heredity.

The understanding of the principles of heredity came from the work of an Austrian monk, Gregor Mendel (1822–1884), who deduced that they could be discovered by counting the offspring of parents who were different in certain aspects (i.e., by crossbreeding). In a series of brilliant experiments, Mendel crossed peas of various types and painstakingly recorded the results in terms of the ratios of offspring of different parental varieties. From these observations he deduced three "laws" of heredity:

1. If two varieties of one species are crossed, all the individuals of the first ensuing generation are similar to each other but different from the parents.
2. If the hybrids of this first generation are crossed with each other, the distinguishing characteristics of the original parents will reappear in a certain numerical proportion.
3. All characteristics are transmitted independently of each other.

We can understand the significance of these findings if we understand that prior to Mendel's work it was believed that the offspring were a "blend" of their parents. This was analogous to pouring together two liquids of different colors; the result would be intermediate between the two.

Instead, Mendel showed (law 1) that if the two parents are different, the offspring are similar to each other, yet different from either parent. He further demonstrated (law 2) that if these hybrids, resulting from the crossing of two different varieties, were crossed among themselves, then the parental characteristics would appear. But they would not just appear helter-skelter—they would do so in a particular proportion to each other.

Finally, Mendel showed (law 3) that the various traits are transmitted independently of each other, rather than as a cluster.

In other words, Mendel's experiments indicated that the hereditary characteristics were transmitted as individual units, or "particles," that appeared in offspring in proportion to the combinations that resulted. This was exactly the opposite of blending.

Mendel's laws constitute the basic principles of genetics as we know the science today, and are of great importance to students of evolution. However, when on February 8, 1865, Mendel presented his results to a scientific society in Brünn, Germany, this august body listened politely, thanked him for his presentation, and left, never knowing that they had heard laid out before them the rules of genetics that had eluded researchers for centuries. Mendel returned to his monastery, became engaged in administrative matters, and died in 1884, unknown at that time to the world except as one who had helped to expand the scope of the monastery.

Mendel's laws were "rediscovered" in the early part of the twentieth century through the work of three geneticists: Hugo de Vries (Holland), Thomas Hunt Morgan (U.S.), and Joseph Müller (U.S.). These three men rediscovered and enlarged upon the concepts of heredity formulated by Mendel and then went one enormous step further, demonstrating that variation within a species could arise spontaneously. While Darwin had shown how existing variability could be selected, he was unable to explain how variability arose. De Vries, Morgan, and Müller did just this, providing the basis for **population genetics,** that branch of the study of heredity dealing specifically with evolution.

Evolutionary theory continued to develop rapidly as biologists came to understand more and more about the relationships between a species and its environment, and as population geneticists refined their theories to explain the ways in which evolutionary change actually comes about.

Evolutionary Theory Today

By now evolutionary theory is highly developed, rational, and formalized. Countless books and papers have appeared on the subject, dealing with all aspects: philosophical, theoretical, empirical, and futuristic. Very little in our lives has not been affected in some way by the acceptance of evolution as fact. While we will, in a subsequent chapter, deal with evolution in specifics, we want now to discuss some of the ideas in a broader perspective.

Challenges to Evolutionary Theory

The great majority of persons accept evolution as fact and eagerly read newspaper accounts of new discoveries of human and humanlike fossils. Nevertheless, others continue to reject evolution as untrue, unscientific, and unreligious. They point to disputes among scientists and gaps in our knowledge, and they appeal to doubts that still may linger in the minds of some persons who have not seriously investigated the matter. Calling themselves "scientific creationists," such individuals continue to publish their own journals, which criticize evolution as theory and fact and convey a false impression of discord among evolutionary biologists.

What, then, of the current state of evolution and of its acceptance? The truth is straightforward: Well over 99.9 percent of scientists today accept evolution as a proven theory. While it is accepted by virtually all, it is still a theory undergoing some refinements. Evolutionary biologists may quibble and even argue over specifics, but none deny the fact. In particular, since much interest in evolution is centered upon "what happened," investigators spend much of their time reconstructing the evolu-

Well over 99.9 percent of scientists today accept evolution as a proven theory.

tionary past. And just as historians might not know the precise route taken by Christopher Columbus in reaching the New World, none but the foolhardy would ever doubt that he arrived! Gaps do remain to be filled in; and perhaps some discovery may cause scientists to alter a previously accepted sequence of events or even to modify some theory. So what? Science consists of objective explanations of events that may be tested and verified. If some changes are made in this process, so much the better.

Critics of evolution also have utilized religion as the basis of their rejection, arguing that one can't be religious and at the same time believe that humans evolved from another species. On the contrary, evolution is acceptable to almost every one of the major religious bodies. In fact, some leading evolutionists have at the same time been leading figures in their own denominations (for example, the Jesuit priest Teilhard de Chardin). Other leading theologians have incorporated an evolutionary way of thinking into their theological systems. The truth is that one may believe ardently in evolution and just as ardently in God without any necessary conflicts between the two.

The Units of Evolution

Beyond the individual, the basic unit of evolutionary biology is, as we have noted, the species. This has been emphasized in terms of both taxonomy and evolution. However, most species are too large to function as a single reproductive unit and so are subdivided into what natural scientists call **populations.**

A population is a subdivision of a species that exists at a moment in time as a reproductive unit.

A population is a subdivision of a species that exists at a moment in time as a reproductive unit. That is, individuals of a given population tend to mate within the group and not outside of it. Consequently, this type of population is also called a *breeding,* or *Mendelian,* population (a belated recognition of Mendel's contributions to the life sciences).

The main difference between a species and a population is that members of two different species are prevented from interbreeding by some fundamental biological reason; on the other hand, members of two populations of the same species do not mate because their populations are separated from each other. We will discuss the nature of the separation in a later chapter.

Populations are the units of evolutionary change within a species and, as such, are units of study. But populations exist within a particular set of environmental conditions, conditions that comprise the **ecosystem,** as discussed earlier. Evolutionary biologists must be extremely sensitive to the ecosystem and to its complexity. In particular, they must be sensitive to the fact that the interactions between all the various parts of the ecosystem are important in channelling evolutionary changes.

Although the natural environment is critical in determining the course of evolution, the ecosystem involves many other components. Humans share an ecosystem with countless other populations of living organisms: the animals we slaughter for food, the plants we grow and harvest, the disease organisms that attack us, the lice that infest us, the bacteria that live inside our bodies. Any human population, no matter how isolated it may be from other humans, interacts constantly with thousands of other populations of living organisms. Each population in the ecosystem is itself in the process of evolving, and all of us must reach some accommodation appropriate to all. For instance, the bacteria that live in our intestinal tracts are essential to the breakdown of food and to its absorption into our systems. Anyone who has been on prolonged antibiotic therapy knows of the diarrhea, constipation, and indigestion caused when these bacteria are killed. We need our colonies of bacteria, and those colonies need us as hosts. Evolution requires that each reach a state of accommodation, or mutual adaptation.

Mutation and Natural Selection

Darwin and his contemporaries lived in a world that saw nature as a struggle for existence: "red in tooth and claw." But to be human was to be above that struggle. Natural selection was conceived as the result of that struggle: those organisms within a group better adapted to the environment "won out." The prize awarded to the winners was to leave more descendants than the losers. Since offspring resembled parents, the proportion of individuals carrying the traits of the winners would gradually increase over time, resulting in better and better adaptation.

If all this sounds gory, it is the way the world was viewed by many influential scientists of the time. Malthus had written his "Essay on Population" (1798), in which he saw creatures, including humans, as having a tendency to multiply without restraint, with the ultimate results starvation and overpopulation. Malthusian thinking is quite evident today, as writers portray the future of the earth as bleak, because of overpopulation and a lack of enough food to go around. Whether they are right or wrong remains to be seen, but in any event, this struggling view of the universe pervaded the world of natural science much more completely in the nineteenth century.

Mutation   Despite the development of the theory of natural selection by Darwin and Wallace, there remained a major problem for evolutionary theorists of that day—how to explain the origin of variation. Scientists still did not know enough of cell chemistry to understand how minute changes could trigger large-scale changes in the organism. As we have noted earlier, it was not until after Darwin's time that the theory of **mutation** and the appreciation of its significance in evolution arose.

Mutation is recognized today as the basic source of variability for a species. In chapter 9 we will go more into the chemical aspect of mutation, but here we will only define it as a change arising in the hereditary material in response to some outside force or agent. This indicates that the hereditary material of a species may undergo alterations, and that these alterations are incorporated into the genetic structure of that species as variation.

Mutations may have one of two consequences. First, they may not produce any change in the way that an individual functions in his or her environment. In such an instance the mutation is called *neutral* and is recognized as a variant of no known importance to the individual or the species. As techniques improve, scientists develop new ways of studying how variable humans really are. The results of such studies have, in recent years, clearly indicated that humans, like all other species, possess a significant pool of hereditary variability that is neutral and is simply passed along from one generation to the next.

Second, mutations may produce a change in the way an individual functions. In this case, the mutation is not neutral but is of adaptive consequence. Such mutations may be *deleterious* (harmful) or *beneficial,* improving the individual's relationship to his or her environment.

Neutral mutations accumulate within a species and so bring about evolutionary change. Such change is very slow. Deleterious or beneficial mutations change the adaptive state of the individual, and hence the species or population, and so bring into play natural selection.

Natural Selection　Darwin's original concept of natural selection has been refined and modified somewhat as scientists have added to their knowledge. The notion of a struggle for existence has been tempered, and the problem of the origin of variability has been taken care of. We may therefore restate natural selection in modern terms, indicating its importance as the evolutionary mechanism bringing about adaptation to the environment.

The British evolutionist John Maynard Smith has presented three properties of natural selection (Smith 1969):

1. *Heredity*—there must exist a process of inheritance, since evolution is a change in the hereditary material transmitted between generations.
2. *Variation*—there must be variety within this hereditary material in the population.
3. *Population growth*—the population must have the capability and the propensity to grow in number.

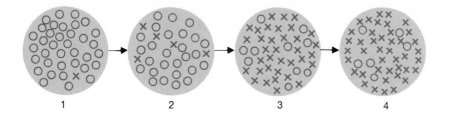

Figure 4.5
Schematic drawing of the effects of natural selection in a population through successive periods of time. The x, a rare variant at the beginning, gradually increases in frequency until it becomes predominant. The population still remains variable, however.

Where these three conditions are met, natural selection is the process by which a hereditary variant will contribute in greater proportion to the next generation, *if* that particular variant is adaptive. Growth in numbers is necessary because natural selection involves the selection or "culling" of a population. If enough individuals are prevented from reproducing, the population may be reduced in number and, if this continues for a long enough period, the population may become too small to survive. Such a process could hardly be called adaptive!

The process of culling, denoting the reduction of certain individuals' contribution to the next generation, is called the *cost of natural selection.* A population must be able to overcome that cost by its growth, or natural selection is not an advantage.

Since they make no difference in the adaptation of the species, neutral mutations are not involved in selection. However, they are extremely important as sources of variation. The population or species already possesses a pool of variation that may be called upon if the environment changes. Previously neutral mutations may then be adaptive, and selection can operate more rapidly as a result.

The measure of adaptation is reproduction. We call it *fitness.* The more offspring, the fitter the individual. The more offspring per individual, the fitter the group.

Natural selection requires *differential fitness* in order to operate. This may be expressed in either of two ways: (1) *differential mortality,* in which individuals possessing some variant die before having offspring or before they have completed their reproductive years; and (2) *differential fertility,* in which those possessing some variant live out a normal life span but do not have as many offspring as do those possessing another.

Natural selection may operate as Malthus and Darwin envisaged, as individuals carrying variants die in infancy from diseases to which they are susceptible. More often, natural selection is a very subtle process, detectable only if we analyze the fertility of large numbers of individuals and discover that certain ones have fewer offspring because of their inherited traits. In either case natural selection is the mechanism that brings about adaptation to the environment and thus has produced the amazing range of animal life as we have known it for hundreds of years.

The Evolutionary Process—England, the Industrial Revolution, and Natural Selection

Natural selection was the key that unlocked the door to an evolutionary view of the natural world. But natural selection is difficult to prove. It takes time, since it operates from generation to generation. The generation time for a fruit fly is two weeks, and so geneticists have experimented with countless numbers of these insects, simulating evolution in the laboratory.

But what of the natural world? Has anyone documented evolution by observing natural selection actually changing a species over time? Certainly not in humans. (After all, the length of our generations is twenty years. Even if we reproduced more quickly, it would be a difficult matter to demonstrate.) But we do have a well-documented case of natural selection. We know the stressing agent, the species, and the changes that resulted. Let us examine the case: industrial melanism.

There are about seventy species of moths, each with light and dark variants. The dark are called *melanic* (*mell-AN-ik*) because of the substance melanin, which is responsible for the color. In England, light-colored moths were common and melanic ones rare until the middle of the nineteenth century. At that time, the Industrial Revolution occurred, factories sprang up, and large-scale manufacturing processes were developed.

But the Industrial Revolution also caused pollution. The furnaces of the factories gave off clouds of black smoke that coated large areas of northern England with soot and turned the tree trunks to a dirty black color. The light-colored moths had been hidden from birds until then, since their coloration protected them. Now they were clearly visible against the sooty background and became easy prey.

The light-colored moths were at a selective disadvantage, while the melanic variety were selected because of their color. They were protectively colored against the black trees and hidden from the birds. The distribution of moths in northern England came to correspond closely to the degree of environmental pollution. In industrialized areas, the black variety became the common form, but away from the smokestacks, there was no selective pressure and the white variety remained, as in the past, the common form.

How do we know this has resulted from natural selection? Two lines of evidence substantiate this. First, scientists have shown, in the laboratory, that the survival of moths is related to the degree of protective coloration from birds. In addition, scientists released melanic forms in nonpolluted areas (with light tree trunks) and light-colored forms in polluted areas (with dark trunks). When they recaptured the moths, they found that those that were visible had disappeared, presumably eaten by birds.

The second line of evidence is based upon the efforts of the British people to clean up the pollution of their environment. Where they have been successful and the soot is no longer on the trees, the predominant color of the moths is changing back to light once again.

We can't demonstrate natural selection in humans for many reasons, but the case of industrial melanism is a striking example of the way that natural selection has worked. Better adapted (protectively colored) varieties were selected and, as a result, the species adapted to the stresses of the environment, the measure of adaptation being its survival.

Insight
The Development of a Theory—Evolutionary Theory and Psychosomatic Disease

What does evolutionary theory have to do with psychosomatic illness? Perhaps nothing, directly, but the development of the theory of natural selection may have been the cause of the long chronic illness of Charles Darwin.

After returning from his voyage on the H.M.S. *Beagle,* Darwin settled down to develop his ideas. But, in 1836, he began to develop the symptoms of a painful, chronic illness that troubled him from then until his death (from a heart attack) in 1882. The symptoms were those of a gastrointestinal disorder; he wrote of pain, weakness, and "palpitations" of the heart. He was treated with a variety of medicines, but none were successful in alleviating the pain, nausea, and vomiting that he endured.

Various authorities have speculated on the causes of Darwin's malady. Darwin's doctors suspected gout and performed several tests to establish this diagnosis. Medical historians have suggested chronic arsenic poisoning. At that time, arsenic was widely prescribed for headaches and a variety of symptoms. Darwin might have taken arsenic for many years and gradually brought his symptoms upon himself.

However, Dr. Ralph Colp, a psychiatrist, feels that Darwin's disease was psychosomatic, that is, caused by psychological stress (Colp 1977). Colp notes that Darwin's illness coincided with the writing of *The Origin of Species,* and the pain became the most intense as the book was completed. Darwin was often depressed by the picture of nature he was forming. At that time, he saw the world in the Malthusian mold of a struggle for existence. Natural selection was to be refined later into a subtle and elegant theory, but then he saw selection as the prize awarded to the

fittest who had survived the struggle for existence. In addition, Darwin knew the reception his book would have. He knew that he would be condemned by some people, laughed at by others.

Despite his illness, Darwin pushed on to the completion of his monumental work. We will never know if Colp is right, but it is a fascinating speculation. Natural selection may have been the one single theory responsible for modern natural science, but it may have brought fifty years of pain to the person who formulated it.

Varieties of the Evolutionary Process

There is but a single process that we call evolution. However, since this process operates at many levels, in many different kinds of organisms, and in response to many kinds of forces, it is convenient to speak of different varieties of evolutionary process. In mentioning them here, we start at the top, or the highest level, and work downward.

Phylogenesis   Phylogenesis (*fy-lo-GEN-is-is*), or *phyletic* evolution, refers to the transformation of one species into another. At an even higher level, we may speak of the evolution of more complex taxa. Thus, when we say that "fish evolved into amphibians," we are talking about a major evolutionary shift of the sort that comes under the term phylogenesis. As we shall see, the genus *Homo* evolved from an ancestral genus in a process that took millions of years of gradual evolution.

Anagenesis   Anagenesis (*an-uh-GEN-is-is*) is a term coined by Bernard Rensch, a German evolutionary biologist (Rensch 1960). Others have used the term *progressive* evolution, but not in the sense of "improvement." Rather, anagenesis, or progressive evolution, refers to evolution in a straight line without any side branches. In the development of *Homo,* the evolution of the brain is an example of anagenesis. There was a steady, though slow, trend toward increasing size and complexity of the brain that occurred in all populations of our ancestors living at the same time everywhere in the world. We do not see a series of variations—some big-brained, some with odd-shaped heads, or others with variations in proportion of parts of the brain. There is a straightforward increase in size and complexity. This is anagenesis.

Progressive evolution may also be seen in a related trait: intelligence. Again, human evolution may be described in terms of steady increases in problem-solving ability and in technology over millions of years. This increase in intelligence demonstrates one feature usually associated with progressive evolution: the development of independence of direct environmental regulation. Increasing intelligence has been associated with more and more reliance upon learning, changing our behavior in response to the environment, and changing the environment itself.

Cladogenesis   In contrast to anagenesis is *cladogenesis* (*klad-uh-GEN-is-is*), or *branching* evolution. We may visualize cladogenesis as the successive branching of a tree as we move upward and outward from the trunk. An example of this is in the evolution of the mammals, land-dwelling animals that have diversified as they have branched and now occupy a wide range of habitats. Though mammals as a group are land-dwelling, certain species (whales and dolphins) live in the sea and others (bats) fly.

When a cladogenic branching occurs relatively suddenly, as when an evolving line moves into a new and hitherto unoccupied ecosystem, it is said to undergo an evolutionary *radiation,* a rapid diversification of many forms. Each line may be thought of as a different mode of adaptation to that ecosystem, or as a different "evolutionary experiment." Those experiments that are successful will persist, while those that are unsuccessful in providing an adaptation will become extinct.

Microevolution At its basic level, *microevolution* is evolution of a single population, or a small group of populations, from one generation to the next. Microevolutionary changes are very minute and specific, occurring over the shortest possible unit of evolutionary time—the generation. Such changes are crucial to the understanding of all phases of evolution, since species are transformed, radiations occur, and lineages diversify, all as the results of the accumulation of microevolutionary changes.

Evolution and Adaptation

Darwin and Wallace made their contribution to evolution by demonstrating how evolution led to adaptation, thus explaining why there was such variety of living forms, each adapted to its own environment. While adaptation is the central process in evolution, we must understand that it is also a composite term, with several dimensions. Two particular types of adaptation may be distinguished here, since they are of special importance when we are considering phylogenetic changes.

Specialized Adaptation A specialized adaptation arises through natural selection when the structure of the organism is modified particularly for a specific natural setting and for none other or, at most, only a few. The implication of a specialized adaptation is a highly engineered and efficient structure, but one lacking the flexibility to be suited to another environment. Specialized forms usually do very well in their own environments so long as the environments remain generally stable. However, should they change, the specializations may become a hindrance and even lead to extinction.

In humans, our most obvious specialized adaptation is in the structure of our lower limbs and other parts of our bodies that are related to walking. In particular, our hips and the bones below them, along with the muscles, supporting nerves, and blood vessels, are adapted to our moving about on our lower extremities rather than on all fours. As a result, there are many anatomical peculiarities unique to humans. Human feet are quite distinct, and the shape of the bones is suited to bearing the weight of our bodies. Several hundred years ago, the Romans discovered

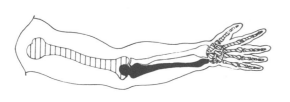
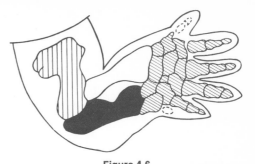

Figure 4.6
Generalized and specialized adaptations. The human forelimb *above* has retained the general structure of the early vertebrates. The feet of many modern mammals *below* have become drastically modified and specialized for locomotion.

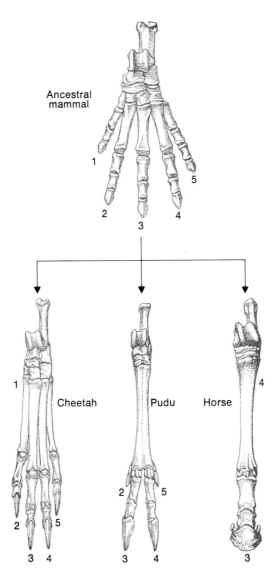

Figure 4.7
Bones of the human foot
form an arch. The arch is an
effective structure for
supporting the body's
weight.

that a doorway could be strengthened by arranging the stones over it in the form of an arch; the stone in the center was wedge-shaped and called the keystone. The Roman architects were simply duplicating a discovery that had been "made" during the course of evolution over 2 million years ago. As Figure 4.7 shows, the bones of the human foot are also shaped into an arch with three keystones to make it strong enough to carry the body's weight. This arch is held in place not by cement or mortar, but by a "sling" formed by a *tendon,* or extension of a muscle, which folds around these bones.

The evolution of the human foot and lower limb represents a specialized adaptation to a particular ecosystem characterized by our walking on our hind limbs.

Generalized Adaptation

In evolutionary terms, a generalized structure is one that has changed but little over time and does not display unique, particular features appropriate to a particular **habitat.** While our feet are specialized, our teeth are generalized. They possess many of the traits that are found in the fossils of the earliest mammals who lived over 75 million years ago.

A generalized structure is often better, in the long run, since it provides a greater range of future adaptive possibilities. Our behavior is an example of a very generalized adaptation in that we alter it in response to the particular environment we are encountering.

Anagenesis, as a process, tends to result in the retention of generalized traits, while cladogenesis tends to produce specialized traits.

Evolution and Taxonomy

In this and the preceding chapter, we have discussed two concepts: evolution and taxonomy. How are they related? Does one lead to or imply the other? Or are they simply different ways of studying life? Taxonomy deals with the ordering and classification of observations, while evolution deals with the process of change over time.

George Gaylord Simpson (Simpson 1963) has pointed out that taxonomy reflects evolution. In reality, a taxonomy is an "evolutionary tree," and species that are grouped into a common taxonomic category are closer in the evolutionary sense; that is, they share a more common heritage. We are placed among the Primates because of the common set of characteristics possessed by all Primates, but this also means that we have evolved as a primate and that the animals comprising that order are our closest relatives in the living world.

On the other hand, it is often difficult and even impossible to reconcile the notion of taxonomy with that of a single lineage evolving through time. This lineage undergoes a slow, steady alteration as it evolves and the changes accumulate, resulting in increasing differences from earlier stages. If we examine groups along a lineage that are widely separated in time, we probably will find that they are quite different from each other and may even be confidently classified into different species. However, groups that succeed each other are likely to be quite similar, and the morphology of one grades into the next. There is no "break," or discontinuity, between successive time periods. Where, then, do we draw the line and say that one species has "evolved" into another?

Species that succeed each other along a single lineage are called *chronospecies* to indicate that they are separated by time. We recognize that there is no valid demarcation between the two, but we also realize that we must indicate that considerable change has occurred throughout the lineage from past to present. By convention, we must set up some criteria that allow us to make a distinction, though we understand that this is a matter of convenience and not of true evolutionary significance.

The Significance of Evolution

Earlier in this chapter we mentioned the clergyman's wife who hoped that no one would hear of evolution if it were true. Our message here is that not only is it true, but that we must advertise it. As we understand evolution and study the processes by which humankind came to be, we cannot help but gain a deeper understanding of our world and our place in it. By placing ourselves within an evolutionary perspective, we place ourselves in a very special relationship to all life—always one of appreciation, frequently one of reverence. People of other societies commonly have this orientation, not because they understand the principles of evolution as a scientific theory, but because they have come to realize the close relationships among all life. Western scientists have placed this within a mechanistic and historical context and have called it "evolution."

Whether we accept or reject evolution, we all have benefitted from it. The realization of the unity of life has had tremendous practical implications, leading to the many breakthroughs in medical research. Furthermore, an evolutionary-centered view is crucial to the study of anthropology, whether we are biological or cultural anthropologists.

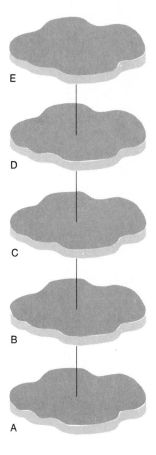

Figure 4.8
Five chronospecies in a single lineage. Although only one evolving line exists, it is convenient to delineate the appearance of successive species.

E

D

C

B

A

Summary

1. Before the mid-nineteenth century, scientists and others believed in a static and unchanging world, with each species having been created separately. A succession of species was explained by catastrophism—life was destroyed by God several times and then re-created.

2. The stage for the development of evolution was set when Lyell developed the theory of uniformitarianism, the gradual and uniform change of the earth's surface.

3. Charles Darwin and Alfred Wallace independently formulated the theory of natural selection as the mechanism bringing about adaptation to the environment.

4. Mendel's formulation of the laws of heredity set the stage for the development of the science of genetics.

5. Today, evolutionary change is seen as resulting from environmental selection of genetic variants through differential mortality and differential fertility. Selection is measured from reproductive fitness.

6. Evolution may be viewed as phylogenesis (change over long periods of time) or microevolution (change from one generation to the next).

7. Dimensions of evolution also include progressive, or straight-line, evolution (anagenesis) and branching (cladogenesis).

8. Evolution has produced adaptations that are either specialized or generalized. Specialized refers to adaptations to a specific habitat; generalized adaptations are adaptive to a wider range of natural settings.

9. Taxonomy and evolution are related. Taxonomies are representations of evolution.

10. Evolution is the most important theory ever developed in science. For humans, it places us in the context of the living world. For anthropologists, it provides an organizational scheme for viewing human biology.

Suggested Readings

Eiseley, Loren. *Darwin's Century: Evolution and the Men Who Discovered It.* Garden City, New York: Anchor Books, 1961.
An analysis of the history of the development of the theory of evolution, in terms of the people involved.

Mayer, Ernst. *Animal Species and Evolution.* Cambridge, Mass.: Harvard University Press, 1963.
A clear statement of the modern theory of evolution.

Volpe, E. Peter. *Understanding Evolution.* 3rd ed. Dubuque, Iowa: Wm. C. Brown Company Publishers, 1977.
A detailed presentation of the processes of evolution.

Glossary

adaptation   The process by which change leads to increased survival value of an individual or a population. Also refers to something resulting from this process.

ecosystem   A set of ecological relationships.

fossil   The hardened remains of an animal or plant after the organic material has disappeared.

genetics   The science of heredity.

habitat   The place or locale occupied by a population.

mutation   A change in the structure of a gene caused by some external agent.

natural selection   An evolutionary process in which those genetic variants that are better adapted are transmitted in greater proportion to the next generation.

population   A group of individuals that form a breeding unit.

population genetics   The part of genetics dealing with the study of population gene pools.

uniformitarianism   A geological theory holding that the earth's surfaces change slowly at a steady rate.

5

Primates: Taxonomy and Adaptation

Introduction

All humans, everywhere, have asked themselves the question, "Who are we?" The answers have been incredibly varied, frequently egocentric, and often incorrect, but they have always indicated the process of wonderment and analysis that is a part of human nature. Natural scientists have approached this question using techniques of observation and comparison, and their efforts have resulted in a taxonomy that includes humans as one species. For several hundred years we have been classified among that order of mammals called Primates, but the implications of that classification went unnoticed until Darwin demonstrated the way in which natural selection brought about adaptation, showing how one species evolved into another.

In the static, pre-Darwinian sense, being classified as with the Primates indicated that humans shared a broad set of anatomical, physiological, and even behavioral characteristics with the other animals placed within that order. But, from an evolutionary perspective, being classified a Primate also indicates that our evolutionary roots are to be found within that order. So we share those biological and behavioral characteristics with other Primates because we all have a common evolutionary heritage. The first step, therefore, in understanding our own evolution is to understand contemporary Primates. By doing this, we gain two perspectives. We can find out what it is that we share with other Primates and what it is about us that is distinctively human.

As we examine Primates, we will discuss the characteristics of the order from an evolutionary/adaptive point of view, since evolution is first of all adaptive. One of the most important aspects of this examination is to demonstrate that those very traits that indicate our distinctiveness have, in the final analysis, arisen from the modification of what many authorities have called the *primate pattern*.

Definition and Distribution

Those present-day mammals that nourish their unborn offspring by means of a placenta are customarily divided into 13 orders, which display a wide range of morphological variability. These orders are distributed over the entire face of the earth, and the Primates are one of them. They are perhaps best thought of as a group displaying an intriguing blend of generalized characteristics, which have evolved little since the earliest mammals, and evolutionary specializations that have set them apart from all other mammals.

General Physical Features

As a group, Primates are relatively unspecialized animals. While certain adaptive specializations are characteristic of individual species or even of some genera, most of the traits by which taxonomists define the order are generalized ones that have been retained since the earliest primates appeared in the fossil record. These have undergone relatively little modification. We refer to them as *primitive* traits, denoting not crudeness or simplicity but rather the antiquity of their origin and the fact that such traits are found among the earliest mammals.

The major primitive mammalian features that are used to define the order Primates are the following (remember that some species may vary with respect to particular features):

1. *Five digits on both pairs of limbs.* This trait, characteristic of the first placental mammals, has been retained throughout the order with few exceptions. Contrast this with other mammals whose digits have undergone considerable modification—the hooves of cattle, horses, rhinoceroses; the wings of bats; and the fins and flippers of dolphins.
2. *Two separate bones in the forearm and the lower leg.* In many mammals, these bones have fused into one, but Primates still have a *radius* and *ulna* in the forearm and a *tibia* and a *fibula* in the lower leg.
3. *A right and left clavicle.* The clavicle, or "collar bone," is a primitive structure found among reptiles, the ancestors of mammals. Clavicles function as "struts," bracing the upper extremity of the body of an animal that actively uses the upper body in moving about or in other functional activity.

In addition to these primitive mammalian traits, there are a number of specialized ones that further serve to define the order. These traits reflect the evolutionary developments within the Primates and are frequently referred to as trends, since there is a gradation in their expression from lower to higher forms. Some of the more primitive primates (again using primitive as above) do not display these features as completely as do others but, in general, all show them at least to some degree.

The five major specializations of Primates are:

1. *Forward direction of the eyes.* The eyes of Primates are close together and directed forward so that the line of vision is to the front. This is in contrast with most other mammals and especially with some, such as rabbits and hares, whose eyes face to the side in almost opposite directions.
2. *Opposable thumb and great toe.* The thumb and great toes of Primates do not lie alongside the other digits. Rather, they are "in opposition"

Figure 5.1
Right hands of adult primates that have been scaled to the same size. Note the similarities.

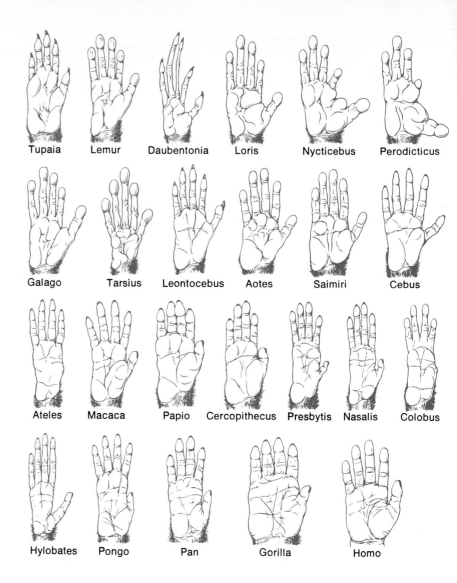

to those digits so that the thumb may touch the tip of each finger and (in most primates) the great toe may touch the other digits of the foot. This arrangement gives the Primates a particular ability to grasp objects. While opposability is characteristic of the order, the simpler primate species do not show it to the extent that the more complex species do. In addition, humans and our closest ancestors have undergone a secondary specialization associated with walking. As we described in chapter 4, human feet and lower extremities are specialized for our distinctive *bipedal* style of *locomotion*. As a result, we have lost the opposability of our great toes and they are not nearly so versatile as in other primates.

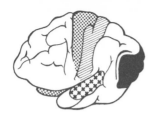

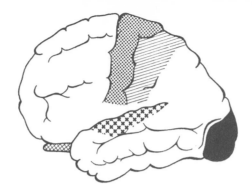

Figure 5.2
Cerebral cortex of ape and human brains. Note the general similarities, but also the differences in size as well as the areas associated with specific activities.

3. *Nails, instead of claws.* Even though several species among the simpler Primates display exceptions to this trait, the order as a whole is characterized by the evolution of fingernails and toenails in place of claws. Opposite to these are "pads" on the fingers and toes, displaying the ridges on the skin that we refer to as "fingerprints." These pads are *tactile,* important in touching and grasping.

4. *Large and complex brains.* Mammals have large brains, but primate brains are the largest of the mammals when considered in relation to the animal's total body size. Not only is the primate brain larger, an examination of the anatomy of the brain indicates that it is more complex than that of other orders. The most complex part of the primate brain is the outer layer, the **cerebral cortex,** which is much thicker and contains many cells. The cerebral cortex contains the cells responsible for memory, language, perception, and the other features we associate with humanness, intelligence, and the greater learning abilities of the Primates. Finally, this cortex has enlarged so much that it has folded inward (or invaginated) upon itself, leading to the brain's "wrinkles." The parts of the brain associated with vision have enlarged at the expense of those associated with the sense of smell.

5. *Longer period of maturation.* Primates are less mature at birth and develop over a longer period of time than other mammals. The amount of time taken to mature varies from primate species to species, but the trend is unmistakable. As a result, Primates are more dependent on the adults of their population, and during this period of development and dependence, they become *socialized.* They learn those behaviors, beliefs, and attitudes that are part of the society to which they belong and are transmitted socially and not biologically.

There are a number of other traits that distinguish Primates from other mammals and that, taken together, present us with a picture of the "primate pattern." For example, male primates have a *pendulous penis,*

Table 5.1

The Primate Pattern*

Primitive and generalized anatomy	Opposability of thumb to fingers
Erect and semierect postures and locomotor patterns	Power grip
	Precision grip
Emancipation of the forelimbs	Relatively large and complicated brains
Pentadactylism	Pendulous penis
Flattened nails	Two pectoral breasts
Less density of hair	Single births
Fewer special hairs	Unicornate uterus
Tropical and semitropical climates	Year-round fertility
Great variety of body sizes and weights	Prolonged physical and emotional dependence
Reduction of olfactory sense	
Reduction of snout	Reduction in number of teeth and lack of dental specialization
Expanded vision	
Arboreal environment	Omnivorous
Stereoscopic vision	Retention of the clavicle
Color vision	

* After Rosen, 1974

which is not attached to the abdomen by a flap of skin; male and female primates usually have only *two breasts*. These traits are not exclusive to Primates; a pendulous penis may also be seen in bears, bats, and hyenas, and two breasts characterize sea cows and elephants. What distinguishes any taxonomic group is not the presence of one or more features that are absent in another group; rather, we look for the *total morphological pattern* that, as a whole, distinguishes one group from another.

The notion of the total morphological pattern was developed by Sir Wilfred LeGros Clark, who was a pioneer in primate studies (Clark 1960). We may see the morphological pattern of Primates in Table 5.1 (from Rosen 1974), which indicates the breadth of traits that define the order.

Primate Taxonomy

Table 5.2 presents a simplified classification of the Primate order. We have included not only the formal taxonomic names but also the common names of the species, in addition to their geographical locales.

If we exclude the worldwide distribution of *H. sapiens,* we can see from the table and from Figure 5.3 that Primates are found throughout the tropical areas of the world, spilling over into adjacent subtropical and even temperate zones. We must remember that this distribution is that for today and the recent past. Throughout the millions of years of their evolutionary history, the Primates have ranged widely. In recent times, humans have drastically altered the ranges of other Primates, usually restricting them and in some instances eliminating species almost entirely.

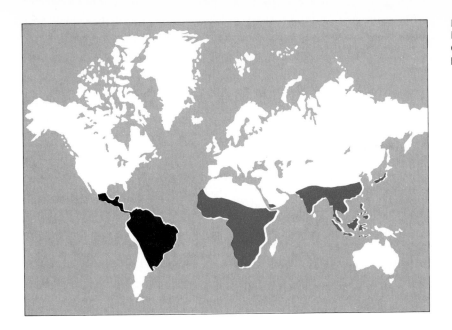

Figure 5.3
Map showing the world's distribution of nonhuman primates.

At the broadest level, Primates are divided into two suborders. The *Prosimii* (*pro-SIM-ee-ee*), or prosimians, are small animals (shown in Figures 5.4 through 5.8) that live today only in the Old World. Most prosimian species are nocturnal. As a group, the prosimians are extremely varied, and it is impossible to present a simple picture of their characteristics. They show a wide range of highly specialized adaptations to their habitats. Yet they still display those features that are part of the total primate pattern; look for those features in the figures.

The suborder Prosimii is divided into three infraorders.

1. Lemurs (*LEE-moorz*), or Lemuriformes (*lee-moor-ee-FOR-meez*). These are small animals ranging in size from the mouse lemur, weighing a few ounces, to larger species approaching the size of a dog. Today, they are found only in the forests on the island of Madagascar and a few islands near it.

2. Lorises (*LORE-is-is*), or Lorisiformes (*lore-is-ee-FOR-meez*). Lorises are, like lemurs, quite variable. Living in the forests of south and southeast Asia and of Africa, they are nocturnal and have developed specialized visual adaptations to this particular niche.

3. Tarsiers (*TAR-see-ers*), or Tarsiiformes (*tar-see-ee-FOR-meez*). Tarsiers are small prosimians living on the islands off the coast of southeast Asia. There is only one living genus, which is adapted to the tropical rain forest. Though no larger than squirrels, tarsiers are able to leap more than six feet. They are usually thought of as the most advanced of the prosimians.

Table 5.2

Simplified Classification of the Primate Order

Order	Suborder	Infraorder	Superfamily
Primates	Anthropoidea (Anthropoids) Monkeys and apes	Catarrhina (Catarrhines)	Hominoidea (Hominoids) Apes and humans
			Cercopithecoidea (Cercopithecoids) Old World monkeys
		Platyrrhina (Platyrrhines)	Ceboidea New World monkeys
	Prosimii (Prosimians)	Tarsiiformes (Tarsiers)	
		Lorisiformes (Lorises)	Lorisoidea (Lorisoids)
		Lemuriformes (Lemurs)	Lemuroidea (Lemuroids)
			Daubentonoidea

Family	Subfamily	Genus	Common Name
Hominidae		*Homo*	human
Pongidae	Ponginae	*Pan* *Pongo* *Gorilla*	chimpanzee orang-utan gorilla
	Hylobatinae	*Hylobates*	gibbon/siamang
Cercopithecidae	Cercopithecinae	*Cercopithecus* *Cerocebus* *Macaca* *Papio*	guenon (vervet) mangabey macaque baboon
	Colobinae	*Colobus* *Nasalis* *Presbytis* *Pygathrix* *Rhinopithecus* *Simias*	colobus proboscis monkey langur douc langur snubnosed langur Pagai Island langur
Cebidae	Cebinae	*Cebus* *Saimiri*	capuchin monkey squirrel monkey
	Alouattinae	*Alouatta*	howler monkey
	Aotinae	*Aotus* *Callicebus*	night monkey titis
	Atelinae	*Ateles* *Brachytelles* *Lagothrix*	spider monkey woolly spider monkey woolly monkey
	Pithecinae	*Pithecia* *Cacajao* *Chiropotes*	saki uakari bearded saki
Callithricidae		*Callithrix* *Callimico* *Cebuella* *Leontopithecus* *Sanguinus* *Tamarinus*	marmoset Goeldi's marmoset pygmy marmoset lion tamarin hairy-faced tamarin negro tamarin
		Tarsius	tarsier
Lorisidae	Lorisinae	*Loris* *Nycticebus* *Perodicticus* *Arctocebus*	slender loris slow loris potto golden potto
	Galaginae	*Galago*	galago, bushbaby
Lemuridae	Lemurinae	*Lemur* *Hapalemur* *Lepilemur*	lemur gentle lemur sportive lemur
	Cheirogaleinae	*Chierogaleus* *Microcebus* *Phaner*	dwarf lemur mouse lemur forked lemur
Indriidae		*Indri* *Avahi* *Propithecus*	indri woolly lemur sifakas
		Daubentonia	aye-aye

5.4

5.5

5.6

5.7

Figure 5.4
A ring-tailed lemur
(*L. catta*).

Figure 5.5
A slender loris (*L. tardigradus*).

Figure 5.6
The potto (*Periodicticus potto*) and offspring of the lorisoid primates.

Figure 5.7
Adult and young Mindanao tarsier.

Figure 5.8
Marmoset

Figure 5.9
A South American red-backed squirrel monkey.

The other suborder of the Primates is called the Anthropoideae, or the "higher" primates. This group is more numerous than the prosimians and typically more "primate" in terms of our own popular conceptions. They are usually grouped into three categories, or *grades*—monkeys, apes, and humans.

Monkeys

The word monkey is used to denote a large number of species, in fact, more than 25 genera, living in both the Old and the New World. Their ecosystems are varied, but the majority live in trees. In the forest, they are found from the highest part of the canopy to the lowest branches. All are agile as they move about from tree to tree.

Other species of monkeys spend all their waking hours on the ground. They are **terrestrial** and move about on the **savanna** (grassland) in groups as they forage for food.

Those monkeys living in the New World are grouped into the infraorder Platyrrhini (*plat-uh-REEN-ee*), while Old World monkeys are part of the infraorder Catarrhini (*cat-uh-REEN-ee*), to which also belongs the remaining primates: apes and humans. The separation of Old and New World monkeys at this fundamental taxonomic level indicates that the two groups evolved quite independently of each other. Furthermore, it suggests that many of the similarities between them have evolved through *parallel evolution,* which is the evolution of two related lines in a similar direction due to similar environmental pressures. Since Old World, but not New World, monkeys are placed in the same infraorder as apes and humans, this further suggests that those monkeys that evolved in the New World did so as a separate branch isolated from Old World primates.

5.8

5.9

5.10

5.11

5.12

5.13

5.14

Figure 5.10.
Leaf-eating monkey with offspring (*Colobus quereza*) of Africa.

Figure 5.11
Young African vervet monkey (*Cercopithecus aethiops*), which is found throughout the continent.

Figure 5.12
Rhesus monkey family (*Macacus rhesus*) of India.

Figure 5.13
Baboons—an adult male and female and their off-spring.

Figure 5.14
Grooming behavior in baboons.

Figure 5.15
A siamang gibbon (*Symphalangus syndactylus*); note the enlargement of the vocal sac.

Figure 5.16
Orang-utan (*Pongo*); note sexual dimorphism in size.

New World, or platyrrhine, monkeys have flat noses separated by a broad strip of tissue, and **prehensile** (*pree-HEN-sull*) tails, capable of grasping. Apart from these features, they are quite diverse and varied, though all are *arboreal* (they live in trees).

Old World monkeys span a wide range of environments, from the forests of Africa and Asia to the temperate climate of Japan. One species, the Hamadryas baboon, lives at altitudes in Ethiopia of up to 12,000 feet above sea level. Regardless of the diversity of habitat, they are classified into a single superfamily.

The Hominoidea

Apes and humans are also *Catarrhinae* but are further classified into a superfamily called the Hominoideae (or hominoids). The apes are grouped into the family Pongidae (pongids), while humans are the only living genus in the family Hominidae (*hah-MIN-ih-dee*), or hominids.

There are five genera of pongids. Two of these genera, *Hylobates* (*hy-low-BATE-eez*) and *Symphalangus* (*sim-fuh-LANG-us*), are the gibbon and the siamang. They are found in the forests of southeast Asia and the islands of Indonesia. They move through the trees by *brachiation,* holding their bodies erect as they swing from branch to branch hanging by their hands. The forelimbs of gibbons are extremely long, often more than twice the length of their trunks. Their thumbs are located nearer to their wrists than is usual for a primate, and their hands are "hooks" which aid in brachiation.

The other Asian ape is the orang-utan (*Pongo pygmaeus* [*PONG-oh pig-MAY-us*]), a solitary creature living in the forests of Borneo and Sumatra. Their orange-colored fur makes them very distinctive.

The African apes are the gorilla (genus *Gorilla*) and the chimpanzee (genus *Pan*), each with several species. There is some controversy over the taxonomy of the African apes. Certain authorities place them in the two separate genera mentioned, while others would make a single genus, *Pan,* with the gorilla as one species and the chimpanzee as the other.

Figure 5.17
Chimpanzee.

Figure 5.18
Chimpanzees grooming.

Figure 5.19
Gorilla.

Figure 5.20
Skeletons of gorilla and man.

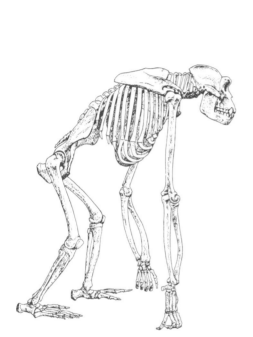
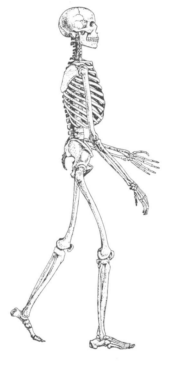

Regardless of the outcome of these matters, the African apes resemble humans rather closely, as Figure 5.20 shows. Chimpanzees live in the forests of Africa, though they spend much of their time moving about on the forest floor. Gorillas are found commonly in the highlands of east Africa, with a few remaining in the forested lowlands of west-central Africa. In general, gorillas are more terrestrial than chimpanzees.

The apes are a highly varied group of Primates, in terms of behavior, habitat, and morphology. Body sizes range from the gibbon, which weighs only about 20 pounds, to the male gorilla, which weighs up to 400 pounds (even more in captivity). They also vary in other features, for example, **sexual dimorphism.** This term refers to the extent that males and females of a species differ in traits other than those associated with their primary reproductive characteristics. Among Primates, it is particularly evident in body size. Gibbons show little if any differences in size between the sexes, while male gorillas and orang-utans may weigh twice as much as females.

The final group of hominoids are the Hominidae, or hominids. Humans are hominids—the only living ones, though, as we shall see, others existed in the past. Hominids are distributed over the entire world and, despite this widespread distribution among habitats and environments, all are members of a single genus and species, *Homo sapiens.*

Biochemical Relationships among the Primates

Biochemical reactions within the body's cells involve many molecules that can be compared. These molecules are part of the basic physiological reactions of the cell and so are intimately related to the way in which the individual is adapted to the environment.

Some molecular biologists who study these cells compare the biochemistry of various animals, from which they can develop a *molecular taxonomy*. Such a taxonomy is not based on similarity of morphology but on similarity of chemical reactions and of molecules.

When we compare primates, the results indicate that at the biochemical level, we are quite similar to the apes in general and especially to the African apes. Consider, for example, the red cells of our blood, which transport oxygen throughout our bodies by means of **hemoglobin.** Hemoglobin is made up of a chain of substances called **amino acids,** which occur in a distinctive sequence in each species. Human hemoglobin consists of 287 such amino acids, yet if we compare it to that of the gorilla, we find that there are differences at only two sites in the chain!

Now, this does not mean that humans are really the same as gorillas or that anyone would be unable to distinguish the two species. However, it does mean that at the basic level of cellular physiology, we are closer to our primate relatives than we might have imagined. The clearcut morphological differences indicate that the environment has, during the course of evolution, influenced hominoid morphology without differentiating the underlying biochemical processes from species to species.

Behavior

Primates are animals who have a highly developed and varied repertory of behavior. All mammals exhibit complex behaviors, but the Primates' behavior clearly stands out. The study of primate evolution is the study of the unfolding of a morphological pattern, but it is also the study of the unfolding of a behavioral pattern. Just as morphological changes in primate evolution have led to human biology as we know it today, so behavioral changes have led to human culture. And just as our understanding of human biological structure is enhanced by examining evolution, so is our understanding of human culture likewise enhanced by examining primate behavior.

Primate behavior may be viewed from two aspects, each of which is relevant to our understanding of humankind. The first is **intelligence,** the ability to solve problems and to display increasingly complex levels of thought. The second is *social behavior,* the fact that primates live in groups and act collectively. Both developments grow out of the increased sophistication of primate brains, and both have important implications for anthropologists who are interested in the dimensions of human culture.

One of the tasks of science is to generalize; that is, to proceed from specific observations of a particular situation to general conditions. In primate studies, the urge to generalize is there but, unfortunately, the data do not readily lend themselves to it. Primate behavior is *species-specific,* and just as a rule is developed out of one species, exceptions to it come from another.

As a result, it has been difficult (and often impossible) to make statements such as "Primates do this . . ." or "all Primates are characterized by that. . . ." If Primates are characterized by anything, it is an almost uncanny knack of knowing how to confound an experimenter or an observer just when he or she has settled on a new law or principle.

Primate Intelligence

Jolly (1972) notes that two aspects of intelligence may be considered apart from social behavior and are important in considering primate behavior. The first of these is adaptability to changed environments. Primates display an amazing ability to adapt their behaviors to different environments or to behave in accordance with their experience instead of some preprogrammed instincts. Thus primate behavior is not only adaptive, it is also *adaptable,* as animals take advantage of changes in their environment to exploit new or modified habitats. It is precisely this adaptability that accounts for much of our difficulty in generalizing from group to group.

This adaptability stems from the learning ability of primates, an ability that we are now only beginning to comprehend. In another chapter we will discuss the abilities of apes to learn a language. Here we will confine ourselves to noting the other kinds of behavior of which higher Primates have been found to be capable. Jolly (1972) has reviewed various studies of these abilities. For example, humans sort and classify. Developmental psychologists have studied the emergence of this ability in human children. When present, it indicates the intelligence necessary to recognize such categories as objects of the same color. Viki, a chimpanzee raised by two scientists named Hayes, was able to sort objects by classes, such as forks from spoons.

Experiments of this sort probe the ability that exists among species of Primates and clearly indicate a far greater capability than we might otherwise have imagined. These experiments do a great deal to reduce the "gap" that was thought to exist between human and nonhuman primates; they force us to rethink the meaning of culture.

Jolly also notes that Primates have been becoming more intelligent along with other mammals (Jolly 1972). As some predator becomes more intelligent in chasing down its prey, the prey itself becomes more intelligent at eluding the predator. Primates display complex abilities to learn from their experiences. For almost twenty years, Jane Goodall has observed a group of chimpanzees at the Gombe National Park in Tanzania (east Africa). Her studies have become widely known and have been reported in the scientific journals as well as in the press and other media. Goodall's descriptions of the chimps' abilities to use tools under various circumstances have done much to dispel the notion that we are distinguished as "man the toolmaker." Not only do chimpanzees use tools, they make them for a variety of purposes, learn techniques by observing other chimpanzees, and modify their tools as the occasion demands.

Primate intelligence is thus demonstrated in two ways. In laboratory situations, primates may be trained to do a variety of complex tasks, and the resulting experiments clearly indicate mental abilities at one time thought to be exclusively human. The other way is through observing primates in their natural setting, which is called *ethology*. In both instances, intelligence has been observed to be adaptive and utilized with a flexibility that is recognized as the primary characteristic of primate behavior.

Primate Social Behavior

The social behavior of Primates is equally species-specific, displaying considerable variability from group to group. In her review of primate social behavior, Jane Lancaster (1975) has identified five "themes" of social organization that "seem to represent behavioral potentials of most higher primates." These five themes are described in the sections following.

Dominance and Dominance Hierarchies   Dominance refers to the fact that one animal will give way to another under certain social situations. The second animal is then said to be dominant. Dominance in Primates is a function of the structure of the social group and reflects the roles played by the various individuals. The dominance hierarchy is the way in which dominance is expressed throughout a particular group. Males are usually dominant over females, and adults over young. Older males may be dominant over younger males and, if the hierarchy is clearly visible in a group, the dominant male may be the group leader.

Not all primate species have a dominance hierarchy, and in species in which hierarchies exist, dominance may be clearly evident and intense or almost casual in its observance. But, whenever found, dominance organizes social interactions and reduces uncertainty. If a new group of macaque monkeys is formed in a captive colony, there will be strong and intense interrelations among the animals until a dominance hierarchy emerges. At that time, the macaques will "relax" and spend more time in other kinds of behavior.

At one time, scientists believed that primate societies were held together by a dominance hierarchy that was maintained by fighting. We now know this isn't so. Dominance is species-specific. Where it exists, it is not maintained by fighting but is a feature implicitly recognized by the animals themselves and maintained by a set of subtle social mechanisms.

Finally, dominance is not the most important social feature of primates but is simply one theme of their social behavior. It is one way in which individuals relate to each other as they live their lives in a social group.

Mother-Infant Bond   The mother-infant bond is one of the most important social ties in primate society. This bond is based on the physical dependency of the young primate. Monkeys and apes do not leave their young in a nest at birth; rather, the newborn accompanies its mother. In monkeys, the infant clings to its mother's fur, while among apes, the newborn is unable to cling and the bond is even more intense, since the mother must assist in carrying her infant.

The mother-infant bond is one of the most important social ties in primate society.

Any number of studies have demonstrated that this bond is intense, enduring, and necessary for the normal development of the infant. Lancaster reports the research of Thelma Rowell, who investigated the nature of this bond among baboons:

In the course of some experiments she [Rowell] was doing with caged groups of baboons, she removed mothers from their infants when they were about six months old. The infants remained in their groups and were cared for by other females while their mothers were caged separately out of sight and hearing. Over half a year later the mothers were returned to their groups. As each mother was carried into sight of the cage, her infant, who had not seen her for over half its life, began to give 'lost infant' calls and, when each mother was put into the cage, her infant rushed to her arms and their former relationship was resumed. (Lancaster 1975:22)

Insight
The Mountain Gorilla— Method in the Madness

Scientists have studied the behavior of the nonhuman primates for decades, and many theories about the evolution of society were based on observations of the ways in which primates behaved. But there was something wrong with these early studies; they were made with animals in zoos or otherwise in captivity. How valid was this? One scientist remarked that it was as valid as an anthropologist making generalizations about human culture from studies of persons in concentration camps!

In the 1950s the science of ethology was born, and primatologists began to observe monkeys and apes in the animals' own habitats. But this takes time, and primate ethologists found themselves living in the field for months, even years, observing their subjects engaging in their day-to-day activities.

George Schaller was one of the first to conduct a systematic field study of a higher primate species in the field. Living in the field for over a year he carefully observed, recorded, and analyzed his results. He chose to observe the mountain gorilla, which live in the highlands of Uganda in east Africa. These animals, weighing several hundred pounds, have fascinated people for centuries. Roman chronicles from as long ago as 400 B.C. mention these creatures. In 1846, one missionary cautioned gorilla hunters to be wary and not let the animal get too close. "Should the gun fail to go off, the barrel is crushed between the gorilla's teeth, and the encounter soon proves fatal to the hunter."

But what did Schaller find during the year that he and his wife lived with the gorilla? The animals were large, strong, and ferocious-looking. But they frowned when annoyed, bit their lips when uncertain, and had temper tantrums when thwarted.

Schaller then described and analyzed one of the most striking acts of the behavior of any primate: the mammoth, silver-back male gorilla beating his chest. He divided this display into nine distinct acts for purposes of analysis. We won't describe all nine here but will summarize the sequence as given by Schaller:

"The male tips up his head and emits a series of soft, clear hoots that . . . fuse into a slurred growling sound. The gorillas have a look of great concentration on their faces when they hoot and [if disturbed] stop and look around as if annoyed." (Schaller 1964)

Just before the climax, the male rises on his legs, rips off some vegetation, throws it into the air, beats his chest two to twenty times, left and right hands alternating. He may run sideways for a few steps and may slash at anything in his path, including an unwary juvenile gorilla who has failed to get out of the way.

Pretty frightening, isn't it?

But we have left something out, something that gives us our first clue that this isn't some mindless act of violence. Just before the climax, the male stops hooting, plucks a single leaf from a plant, and places it between his lips—"an act of such daintiness that it never ceased to amaze [Schaller]."

Why does the gorilla do this? Schaller showed that the behavior wasn't directed at any other living creature because it happened when there wasn't anyone around to intimidate. In fact, the only relationship he found was that gorillas went into this display when they were excited. The chest-beating display releases accumulated tension. They are blowing off steam, and they are doing it in a standardized, almost ritualized, way so that their excitement is communicated. Placing the leaf between their lips may be a biologically controlled symbol of feeding. Other animals are observed to feed as a release for tension.

So, the fierce display of the mountain gorilla is a tension-releasing response, not a threatening one. It seems to be biologically based, yet not all males go through the same sequence when they beat their chests.

The gorillas' behavior offers fascinating insights into human behavior as well. Observe people at a sporting event. Do they sit quietly, observing the action as if they were reading a book? Far from it. As excitement builds, humans clap their hands, stamp their feet, throw things in the air, and eat. We even have cheerleaders to organize the release of our tensions. Imagine how some ethologists from another planet would describe the fearsome displays of human spectators at the Stanley Cup hockey finals!

This is hardly the kind of behavior one associates with animals that endure by "survival of the fittest!"

This emotional bond between mother and offspring is of positive adaptive value in providing a focus for early learning. Monkeys and apes deprived of certain social interactions exhibit deficits in exploratory and social behavior.

Furthermore, this bond is not simply one of infant dependence but persists into adulthood. Primates are well known for their tendencies to groom each other's bodies. Lancaster notes that one of the important determinants of grooming behavior is the previous existence of a mother-infant bond. Close relatives groom each other, and the grooming behavior shows itself most frequently between adults and their mothers. Lancaster interprets the data on mother-infant bonding and its persistence as indicating the existence of a **matrifocal,** or mother-centered, core in primate society.

Male-Female Bond   When we think of the male-female bond, we usually think of one based on sexual behavior and reproduction. This is, of course, true, and mature primates do form bonds on such a basis. In some species, there is no real "bond" in a social sense. Among monkeys, mating is usually promiscuous and casual. In higher primates, however, males and females often consort for longer periods of time, and ethologists observe that the attraction is more than a sexual one.

Among nonhuman primates, the male-female bond is strongest among gibbons. One male and one female will maintain, with their offspring, a familylike group for more than a year. However, to characterize this as a family is misleading, since many social interactions associated with a family are absent. For example, the male and female do not share food with each other, but feed as solitary animals.

In some species, a male possesses a "harem" of several females. This unit is of adaptive value in certain ecosystems. The hamadryas baboons are such a species, living in a semidesert habitat where food is widely scattered and must be obtained by foraging in small groups. These foraging groups are the harems, consisting of a male, several females, and their offspring. Several harems can disperse over an area searching for food. Each harem is protected from predators by a male. A male-female unit thus becomes an adaptive unit in the context of subsistence.

Separation of Roles by Age   In Primate society, animals of different ages take different roles. The young, with their prolonged years of development, are kept in a sheltered environment where they can grow up safely and, at the same time, learn adult roles by observation and experience. The play-wrestling of young male baboons previews the protective roles they will take as adults. Lancaster (1975) emphasizes that a protected environment with a virtual absence of fear and anxiety is optimal.

Separation of Roles by Sex   The degree to which male and female roles differ varies from species to species. All primates show more differences than just the female's taking the mother role. In some groups, males remain aloof from the young and have clear protective roles, while in others they will be joined by females in protecting the troop against predators. The greater the sexual dimorphism, the more distinct the roles.

Primate society is maintained by a social order based on bonds, roles, and predictability, not aggression. Such factors promote stability, peacefulness, and calm, rather than the Malthusian struggle still described by some.

Primate Traits in Evolutionary Perspective

Ecology vs. Phylogeny

Why do the Primates look and act as they do? This question is a basic one asked by researchers. They have found two answers.

First, some primate traits reflect phylogeny, or evolutionary relationships. We are similar to chimpanzees and gorillas because they are our closest relatives in the animal kingdom. A taxonomy reflects evolution and as a result reflects relationships. One principle of comparative studies is that forms that are more similar are more closely related, and on the basis of this principle we construct the evolutionary history of the Primates.

Second, other primate traits reflect pressures of the environment, as in the case of the hamadryas. Environmental pressure seems to have been a selective agent insofar as sexual dimorphism is concerned; where there is more threat from predators, males are relatively larger than females. So environment is another determinant of primate biology and behavior. Similar environmental pressures can produce similar characteristics in groups occupying similar habitats, even though the groups are not closely related in an evolutionary sense.

Arboreal Adaptation and Its Significance

The earliest Primates were mammals that moved into an arboreal habitat, adapting to it over the subsequent millions of years through the process of natural selection. This arboreal adaptation resulted in a core of primate characteristics that have persisted, making the primate pattern an arboreal one.

Figure 5.21
Grasp in primates showing
thumb opposability. The
drawing in the right-hand
corner demonstrates the
precision grip.

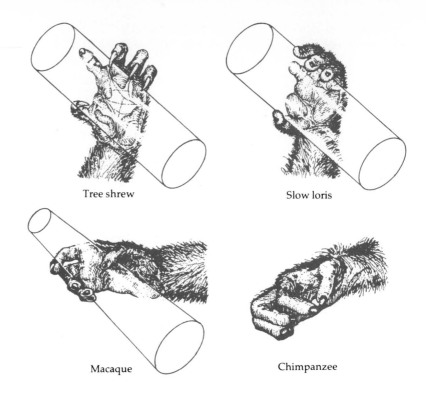

As Primates, humans also manifest this arboreal pattern. As we shall see, many of our traits may be related directly to our early ancestors who, as Primates, adapted to the trees. Furthermore, as we shall see, human culture itself evolved out of the arboreal pattern.

Grasp   The most obvious arboreal adaptation in Primates is the power of grasp. Opposability of the thumb and great toe represents an effective adaptation to the trees. The *power grip* made possible by this opposability (Napier and Napier 1967) allows an animal of considerable body size to support itself safely.

At the same time, opposability of the digits permits many fine and precise movements of the hand through the *precision grip*. Primates manipulate their environments with a high degree of manual dexterity, and in fact, hand use is a characteristic feature of primate behavior. We have already mentioned the social significance of grooming, which depends on the ability to make precision movements with the hand. Think of your own hands and how you depend on them. Try to write, tie your shoes, repair your wristwatch, or drive an automobile without using your thumbs! To be sure, many disabled persons have amply demonstrated the extent to which one can accommodate, but this is not the norm. We shall see in the next chapter that the ability to use our hands was translated in the early stages of hominid evolution into the manufacture of tools.

Vision One primate feature that is adaptive in an arboreal habitat is a well-developed sense of vision. We have previously noted the forward direction of the eyes and the overlapping of the fields of vision of the two eyes.

When eyes face forward, their sides are exposed and vulnerable to injury. Early primates adapted through the evolution of a bony *orbit* (Figure 5.22), a protective socket that encloses the eye on three sides. The presence of a closed orbit is an important diagnostic feature in recognizing the earliest primate fossils as primates.

The overlapping of the fields of vision is known as *binocular* vision (seeing with both eyes). As a result, primates have developed *stereoscopic* vision, the ability to see objects in three dimensions. Such an ability is a clear adaptation in an arboreal existence and also an important advantage where hand-eye coordination is important.

Other Evolutionary Trends

Besides these adaptations to an arboreal habitat, Primates display other evolutionary trends. Some of these trends are adaptive to life in the trees; others are not so related. All are important in the development of human characteristics and, in particular, the development of culture.

Diet Primates are *omnivorous;* they have a varied diet with nutrients supplied from a great many sources—fruits, leaves, insects, and other forms of meat. Chimpanzees even eat other primate species (monkeys) but, in general, there is greater flexibility in the diet as one moves from lower to higher species.

Meat-eating among primates is of evolutionary importance. While the inhabitants of affluent nations consume more meat than is good for them, nutritionists have known for many years that animal protein is higher quality protein for humans and their relatives than is vegetable protein. Animal protein provides "essential" amino acids (essential because they are necessary, not manufactured by the body, and unavailable from many plants). Meat-eating provides an adequate diet with less effort on the part of the animal. Meat-eating is also important in that cooperation is needed to hunt larger animals. Hunting requires some degree of organization and social interaction, and it is thought to have provided an important stimulus toward the development of social organization among humans.

Dentition The earliest placental mammals had forty-four teeth, eleven in each dental *quadrant* (upper/lower, left/right). Among the Primates, there has been a steady reduction in the number and size of the teeth as indicated by the fossil record. Most species of prosimians and New World monkeys have thirty-six teeth, though there is considerable variation,

Figure 5.22
Development of the orbit in primates.

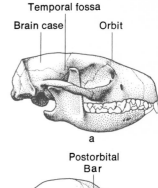

Temporal fossa
Brain case   Orbit

a

Postorbital
Bar

b

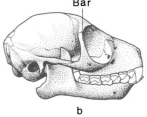

Postorbital
partition

c

Figure 5.23
Outlines of the lower molars and premolars of an orang, australopithecine specimens, *H. erectus,* an Australian aboriginal, and a European. Note the difference in overall size of the teeth from the lower to higher primates.

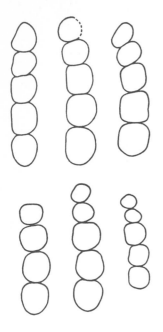

ranging from 18 up to 36. There is no variation in number among the Old World higher primates (catarrhines); each species has 32. These teeth are of four types: *incisors,* which cut; *canines,* which tear; *premolars* and *molars,* which grind. Teeth also serve defensive purposes and allow an animal to threaten a foe; if threatened, a baboon will open its mouth and show its long, daggerlike canines.

Posture and Locomotion   One of the most distinctive traits separating hominids from other primates, as well as from other mammals, is the human *upright posture.* Figure 5.20 shows the confrontation of a human skeleton and its relationship to posture. The head is balanced on the spinal column, not hanging from it; and the spinal column shows a distinct S-curve to accommodate the strain of weight-bearing. The human pelvis is shaped like a basin, so as to support the internal organs. The lower extremity, or foot, is drastically altered to support the weight of the body, and, as we have noted, our feet bear little resemblance to those of other primates. Throughout the body, the musculature has adapted to make upright posture the normal stance and *bipedal locomotion* more effortless.

This cluster of morphological features is among our most distinctive, and some scientists have defined hominids as "those primates who first stood erect." While erect posture does make our species different from others, we can see a steady trend in this direction from the prosimians upward.

The habitual postures of the various primate species reveal a clear trend toward increasing erectness of the trunk. Tarsiers are "vertical clingers," and many prosimians move from branch to branch with their bodies distinctly more upright than, say, cats.

Prosimians and monkeys are *quadrupedal* in their locomotion; they move about on all fours with the palms of their upper extremities flat on the ground. Apes are still quadrupedal even though their trunks are more upright; African apes have been observed to move about bipedally, though this is not the mode of locomotion to which they are best adapted. The African apes are "knuckle-walkers," supporting themselves on the knuckles of their hands and not their palms. Thus, there is a steady trend toward upright posture throughout the Primate order, culminating in the complex of adaptive changes seen among humans.

Primate Evolution and Human Culture: Interaction and Feedback

Now that we have gone through the evolutionary trends that have characterized the Primates as a group, we will discuss the trends as a set of adaptations, some related to an aboreal habitat, but all interrelated to each other and ultimately to the evolution of culture.

Figure 5.24
Different patterns of locomotion in higher primates.
The Gibbon *top* moves
through the trees with an
upright swinging motion.
Knuckle-walkers, like the
gorilla *middle,* support
themselves on the knuckles
of their hands and not their
palms. Man *bottom* com-
pletes the Primate trend
toward upright posture.

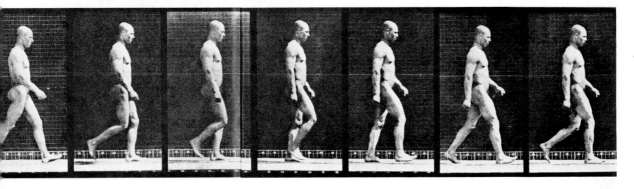

We may hypothesize the earliest primates moving into the trees and adapting to this new existence through a related series of changes. In particular, there was a progression of changes involving the hands, feet, and eyes. The hands and feet adapted to become grasping organs and the eyes adapted by developing stereoscopic vision. The two systems affected each other, with hand-eye coordination becoming fundamental to a way of life. At the same time, there was a decrease in the sense of smell and a replacement of smell by vision as a primary means of exploring the environment. Primates look at and feel objects in their environment rather than smell them.

Along with the reduction in the sense of smell came a reduction in olfactory tissues and structures and a reduction in the size of the snout. The teeth gradually became smaller in size and fewer in number, though with many species-specific adaptations to particular habitats. Nevertheless, teeth became generally less important as the hand-eye complex came to replace the nose-teeth complex.

With hand and eye development, grooming became an important mechanism of social interaction, emphasizing social bonds and, in some instances, dominance hierarchies. Primates came to interact with others as individuals, and bonding became an important part of this interaction.

Who were the Primates? They were social animals with strongly developed patterns of individual interactions and group behavior. They had hands capable of effectively and efficiently manipulating their environment with a variety of precision movements. They were intelligent animals with developed problem-solving abilities and learning capabilities enhanced by prolonged periods of learning. And they were animals that developed a more richly varied diet that did not require prolonged periods of foraging for vegetable materials; animals who added meat to their diet to improve protein intake; animals who, in addition, shared food—a significant form of cooperation.

These are the Primates—a group ripe for the evolution of that next stage of complex behavior: **culture.** One thing was lacking, and this was brought about by the final realization of a trend evident from the prosimians onward—upright posture. Upright posture implies terrestrial living, with an entirely new set of environmental pressures requiring further adaptation. And, just as important, it means freeing the hands from being locomotive organs to being organs that could be used to manufacture tools. Each step put a selective premium on bigger brains and more intelligence, to say nothing of more and more social organization.

The outcome was culture—a complex pattern of behaviors derived directly from biological structures and behaviors, yet a pattern of behavior that depended less and less upon biological factors and more and more upon learning. Inheritance took on a new dimension. Biological inheritance of the genetic material remained; but the cultural inheritance of learning and socialization was introduced and passed on from generation to generation just as directly as the hereditary material in body cells.

The study of Primates tells us of this series of evolutionary trends. Analysis demonstrates that these trends are not acting in isolation, but rather as a complex of interconnected changes. These changes are related to each other in a **feedback** system; a change in one directly and indirectly causes changes in a second and then a third, with the third affecting the first in a continuing cycle.

Evolution is full of feedbacks, since no system or structure evolves separately from others. In fact, evolution is best understood as a complex of feedback relationships. The evolution of the hand is of little consequence until it is related to changes in vision, grooming, social behavior, and the like. In the same vein, changes in vision related to hand use put a premium on further changes in the hand. The pattern of changes accelerates through feedback.

Summary

1. Primates constitute an order of mammals whose species have retained certain generalized mammalian features: five digits on each limb and two bones in the forearm and the lower leg.

2. As a group, Primates also show specialized adaptations to an arboreal habitat, including thumb and great toe opposability, forwardly directed eyes, and nails and tactile pads on fingers and toes.

3. The other primate features include large and complex brains and a relatively long period of maturation. These two traits confer the ability to learn from the environment and provide the time span during which socialization occurs.

4. Humans are classified as hominids and, along with the pongids, as hominoids. Hominoids are grouped along with Old and New World monkeys into the higher Primates.

5. One of the most distinctive features of the Primates is their behavior; this behavior is complex in two areas: intelligence and social behavior. Intelligence gives primates the ability to solve problems in the natural world and to learn from their experience in that world. Complex social behavior leads to cooperation, sharing, and to a society held together by a structure.

6. Primate social behavior is grouped into five themes: dominance, mother-infant bonding, male-female bonding, separation of roles by age, and separation of roles by sex.

7. From an evolutionary perspective, Primates are distinguished by having developed a series of adaptations to an arboreal habitat. These adaptations not only served to adapt these animals to the arboreal ecosystem but also were preconditions for culture.

8. When seen as a total complex of interrelated biological and behavioral features, primate characteristics demonstrate the development of human culture out of a series of evolutionary trends evident in the simplest primate species. These trends mutually affected each other in a feedback system that accelerated evolutionary developments.

Suggested Readings

Clark, W. E. Le Gros. *The Antecedents of Man*. Chicago: Quadrangle Books, 1961.

A classic description of primate morphology from an evolutionary point of view.

Eimerl, Sarel, and DeVore, Irven. *The Primates*. New York: Time-Life Books, 1974.

This profusely illustrated book presents a comprehensive view of the living primates.

Jay, Phyllis, ed. *Primate Behavior: Field Studies of Monkeys and Apes*. New York: Holt, Rinehart, and Winston, 1965.

This book contains reports by ethologists of their analyses of primate behavior.

Glossary

amino acid   A set of nitrogen-containing chemical compounds that combine to form proteins.

cerebral cortex   The outer layer of brain cells.

feedback   In a system, feedback refers to the effect that a change in one component will have on another component.

hemoglobin   The oxygen-carrying molecules of the blood.

intelligence   The ability to learn, to know, and to solve problems.

matrilocal   Referring to a society in which a married couple sets up residence with the woman's kinspeople.

savanna   A treeless, grassy plain.

sexual dimorphism   Differences between males and females in traits besides those of the primary reproductive system.

terrestrial   Living on the land.

6

Paleoanthropology and Hominid Evolution

Introduction

An aura of mystery surrounds our notions of the reconstruction of our evolutionary past. These notions are not without foundation. Many people have heard of the Leakey family, Louis, Mary, and their son Richard, who lived for years in Kenya, in east Africa, searching for fossils in the Olduvai Gorge. Others may know of Eugene Dubois, a Dutch adventurer who decided that the early ancestors of the human species were to be found in Indonesia, became a physician, and got himself posted there with the army. In an extraordinary piece of luck (or perhaps an uncanny sense of reasoning), Dubois, during one of his first tentative diggings, found what were to be among the most significant remains of the early members of the genus *Homo* yet uncovered.

Similar stories abound about other "fossil detectives" who have engaged in lifetimes of hunting for our earliest ancestors and who have produced the evidence that has captivated our minds as well as furnished the raw data for scientists analyzing the process of evolution.

But there is another side to the story. Those scraps of bone had to be brought into the laboratory to be cleaned, measured, and studied carefully and thoroughly. These studies involved analyzing the scrap of bone itself and comparing it with other specimens. They involved endless hours of discussion, reading, writing, and probably also controversy. The romanticism of the discovery has to be integrated with the objectivity and detail of the laboratory.

This chapter will present the result of that integration as it tells the story of hominid evolution, not from the observation of living primates (as we discussed in chapter 5), but from the analysis of the record of the past as it is preserved within the earth itself. While this story will not be presented as a romanticized version of what is hard and painstaking work, it will still retain an air of the unknown. As we have pointed out, the course of human evolution is not yet completely understood. We know the general stages through which our ancestors passed, but there are still gaps in the sequence—gaps that may be filled at any time, as some new fossil is discovered. Each new discovery carries with it an element of excitement, much like finding a piece that fits into a jigsaw puzzle.

The reconstruction of human evolution is exciting, it is romantic, it involves expeditions to out-of-the-way places, and it captures the imaginations of people everywhere. But always remember it is a science, subject to the same principles of objectivity, caution, verification, and simple technical expertise and knowledge to which all science must adhere.

Paleontology

Paleontology is the part of the study of the past that deals with the living world; *paleoanthropology,* or *human paleontology,* is that part of anthropology devoted to the study of our ancestors. It has four parts: (1) the reconstruction of the stages of human and primate evolution; (2) the development of taxonomies that include now-extinct species; (3) the study of **paleoecology,** the interactions between these ancient groups and their environments; and (4) the analysis of the development of culture through time, by examining those things that have been preserved over millions of years.

Paleontology is the part of the study of the past that deals with the living world; paleoanthropology, or human paleontology, is that part of anthropology devoted to the study of our ancestors.

Fossils, Fauna, and the Preservation of the Living World

Paleontologists study the remains of animal forms that lived in the past and have been preserved until the present time. When a living creature dies, various microorganisms begin to break down the tissues of the body, and we say that the tissues "decay." The organic parts are reduced to simpler compounds and returned to the ecosystem for recycling. Those parts of the body that contain a high proportion of nonorganic material (largely minerals such as calcium) may be preserved. If the conditions are right (i.e., if there is adequate drainage, if the remains are not crushed by the movements of the earth's crust, and so forth), the organic parts of such a structure will through time gradually be replaced by inorganic materials. It will become a fossil or, as people say, "be turned to stone." The process of fossilization is very slow and takes some 10,000 to 15,000 years.

Fossils are the "raw evidence" of evolution; when we hold one in our hands, we are holding the remains of some creature that once lived. No matter how elegant a theory a paleontologist may derive, it remains unproven until he or she has fossil evidence to back it up.

Establishing the human fossil record is made more difficult by the fact that it is rare to find the complete fossilized skeleton of any large mammal, hominids included. The more fragile bones are usually broken or decayed before fossilization occurs. The jaws and teeth are among the most likely parts to be preserved, along with the long bones of the limbs and the small bones of the wrists and ankles. On the other hand, the pelvis and the scapula (shoulder blade) are fragile and are not as a rule preserved. Usually, a "find" consists of only a few fragments of an individual. We seldom find more than a single person's bones at a time, though if we have some sort of "site" where members of a group lived or where they hunted and slaughtered animals, then we may find fossil remains from more than one person.

Because of the fragmentary nature of fossils, it is difficult to reach firm conclusions and dangerous to rush in with them prematurely. It is important to remember that a fossil is just a small sample of a population of once-living individuals. What could a paleontologist say about humans if he or she had only found five or six teeth? Variability among individuals also contributes to the dangers of hasty generalization. Given those five or six teeth, how well could someone characterize our whole group?

Because of this problem, different interpretations by different investigators are common, and disagreements frequent. One paleoanthropologist may conclude that, based on certain criteria, a particular specimen belonged to an apelike species; another investigator, studying the same specimen years later, may discover certain hominid features and reclassify the specimen into a new species, bringing about a major reinterpretation of evolutionary history. We have already made the analogy with a jigsaw puzzle; paleontology is similar to putting a puzzle together without having either the completed picture as a guide or even all the pieces. We shouldn't guess about the picture until we have a good notion of what it is.

Geological Time

Uniformitarianism was a major development in the history of earth sciences because, among other things, it laid the groundwork for the formation of sequences of gradual changes that occurred at a nearly constant rate. The concept of constancy was a major step because it provided the basis for *dating,* the assignment of an age (i.e., the age of formation) to a layer in a cross-section of the earth's crust.

The basic principle for establishing sequences and assigning ages is that of *stratigraphy,* the study of the *strata,* or layers of rock that have accumulated through time. Since the layers are formed on top of each other, deeper and deeper layers are successively older. A fossil found within a particular stratum is assigned the age of that layer.

Obviously stratigraphy isn't that simple, and careful study is required to develop sequences. Geologists who are concerned with this process are aware of the possibility of *inversions,* which occur when an upheaval of some sort causes older layers to rest on top of more recent ones. Geologists have developed techniques for detecting inversions, just as paleoanthropologists have developed ways to detect *intrusions,* the placement of a fossil into an older layer by some means. Years ago, a fossil was found in England and named the Galley Hill skull. This skull caused much consternation among human paleontologists because it was found in a layer some 200,000 years old, yet it resembled skulls that were like present-day humans or perhaps from the recent past. Why? Some interpreted Galley Hill as indicating that a lineage of modern-appearing individuals lived in what is now Great Britain at a time when

Table 6.1

Chart of geologic time

Era	Period	Duration (millions of years)	Beginning (millions of years ago)
Cenozoic	Quaternary	2.5	2.5
	Tertiary	63.5	65.0
Mesozoic	Cretaceous	71.0	136.0
	Jurassic	54.0	190.0
	Triassic	35.0	225.0
Paleozoic	Permian	55.0	280.0
	Pennsylvanian	45.0	325.0
	Mississippian	20.0	345.0
	Devonian	50.0	395.0
	Silurian	35.0	430.0
	Ordovician	70.0	500.0
	Cambrian	70.0	570.0

Precambrian (Begins over four billion years ago.)

Table 6.2

Divisions of Tertiary and Quaternary Periods

Era	Period	Epoch	Duration (millions of years)	Beginning (millions of years ago)
Cenozoic	Quaternary	Recent (approx. last 10,000 years		
		Pleistocene	2.5	2.5
	Tertiary	Pliocene	4.5	7.0
		Miocene	19.0	26.0
		Oligocene	12.0	38.0
		Eocene	16.0	54.0
		Paleocene	11.0	65.0

less advanced populations lived elsewhere. Others were more cautious and simply maintained an air of skepticism while awaiting additional evidence. The problem was solved when a reexamination of the *context* (i.e., the conditions of the stratum and the immediate area surrounding the find) indicated that the Galley Hill skull was, in fact, a relatively recent individual no more than 4,000 or 5,000 years old. He or she had been buried in a layer that dated far into the past.

Table 6.1 (from Eicher 1968) presents the major geological stages along with their estimated ages. The Cenozoic era is subdivided further in Table 6.2, since it is the period during which the Primates evolved and hence is of greatest interest to us. Later in this chapter we will present an even more detailed breakdown of this period as we focus on human evolution.

Radiometric Dating

Prior to 1950 dating was based on uniformitarian principles of a constant rate, even as it is today. However, at that time, geologists had no firm estimates of specific ages and were forced to rely heavily upon estimates with a large "plus-or-minus" factor. Since the mid-1950s, dating has advanced tremendously with the devising of **radiometric** techniques. Physicists and chemists have applied their knowledge of atomic structure to problems of dating, and scientists are now able to identify the age of various strata and their fossils with far greater precision and accuracy than ever before.

Radiometric dating is based on the study of radioactive elements. Some elements have alternate structures, or *isotopes,* that are radioactive, which means they are unstable and will emit particles or capture electrons. This process, radioactive *decay,* results in a changed atomic structure. By studying the rate of decay and measuring the amount of the radioactive isotope remaining in a specimen, scientists can estimate its age. If it is a fossil, the technique will tell us how many thousands or millions of years have passed since it died. If the sample is a rock or mineral from that layer, radiometric dating can provide an age for the layer. That age can be assigned to any fossils found within the layer.

The rate of radioactive decay varies widely, being very slow for uranium and very fast for carbon. In general, the slower the rate, the older the layer that can be dated by a particular element. Uranium decays so slowly that it is only useful for very early periods of the earth's history, long before Primates appeared.

For layers that contain fossil hominids, the most useful isotope is the radioactive form of potassium, K^{40} (K is the symbol for potassium and *40* indicates the isotope). K^{40} occurs in certain forms of igneous rocks and, under certain conditions, decays to Ar^{40} (the element argon). When a K–Ar date can be made, it is very valuable in dating layers containing hominid (and other primate) fossils from a few million to 25 or more million years old.

For more recent deposits, but especially for archeologists, the decay of the isotope of carbon C^{14} is often used. C^{14} is taken into an individual along with the other carbon he or she ingests until death. From then on, no new carbon is introduced (unless contamination occurs) and decay begins, with C^{14} converting to a form of nitrogen, N^{14}. As far as physicists are presently able to determine, one-half of the C^{14} present at any moment decays every 5,730 years (± 40 years), so that by measuring the ratio of C^{14} to C^{12} (the stable form) in a sample it is possible to estimate just how long ago the creature died.

One advantage of radiocarbon dating is that it can be done on the fossil itself, not on something else in the layer. Frequently, however, a layer is dated by using some other carbon-containing specimen: wood, shell, or the bone of another animal. Also, carbon is one of the earth's most abundant elements, so that specimens are often available.

Radiocarbon dating involves a number of problems as well. The remains of one specimen may become contaminated by another, and an outside amount of carbon, including C^{14}, may be introduced. The most serious limitation for paleontological purposes is that radiocarbon dating is inaccurate for older specimens, since the amount of C^{14} will diminish by half lives to such a small amount that it cannot be measured accurately. Various techniques have been developed to overcome this limitation. Hole and Heizer (1969) note that the older the specimen, the greater the error; originally the effective range of dating was about 30,000 years. New techniques have pushed the limit back to 50,000 years, and "for samples of great importance an elaborate, expensive, and time-consuming process" will provide age ascertainment back to 70,000 years.

Other techniques for dating, which use kinds of information other than radioactivity, are useful for archeologists rather than paleoanthropologists because of their effective ranges. We will cover them in a later chapter.

Paleoecology

A description of a fossil in terms of anatomical features is basic to the study of paleoanthropology, as is the placement of the group the fossil represents into some taxonomic scheme. However, this is not the end of the study. Anthropology is involved with understanding the meaning implied by human variability, and we have noted that much of this meaning is revealed by analyzing the interactions between a group and its ecosystem (i.e., the group's ecology). Consequently, paleoanthropologists also concern themselves with *paleoecology*. While this cannot be done with the degree of sophistication one can attain when studying the interactions of a living group, the study of paleoecology reveals much about the lifeways of a group that may have lived millions of years ago.

The first step is to reconstruct, as far as is possible, the environment itself. This is usually done by examining the **floral** (plant) and **faunal** (animal) assemblages found in the layer. Using microscopic techniques, it is possible to identify the pollen that may be recovered and characterize the vegetation. A knowledge of the vegetation and kinds of animal life will tell us about the climate of the time. One thing that studies of this sort have shown is that environments may have changed radically over the expanses of time during which hominids evolved. What is now a savanna or grassland may have been a tropical rain forest millions of years ago.

The faunal assemblage may be very informative since it indicates the activity of the hominids we are studying. Animal bones may indicate hunting activity, and the kinds of animals hunted may tell us a good deal of the abilities of the group. If the animals were slaughtered and dressed there, the techniques may be seen by examining the bones.

Putting together the ecosystem of a group of hominids whose fossils we are studying is time-consuming but essential work. The implications of human evolution are far richer if we do more than simply describe and, as far as our data will permit, treat our fossil material as if it were a living community, interacting with its environment and with each other. Obviously this is only possible to a degree in the fossil record, but it still is an ideal toward which paleoanthropologists strive.

Comparative Anatomy

Just as the reconstruction of the ecosystem is crucial in understanding a particular evolutionary stage, so is the comparison of structures among various organisms in such a way as to understand the significance of particular features of our fossils. Consider, for example, Figure 6.1, which compares certain anatomical traits of pongids and hominids. It should be immediately apparent that there is both similarity and difference. It is easy to recognize features that are *homologous* (i.e., they have the same origin and structure). For example, the arm and hand of the two species are easily recognizable. We know that embryos of the species develop in the same way, and the similarities are quite clear. Yet there are important differences. At a general level, the arms of the gorilla are longer than those of the human; this relative proportion of arm length to body length is one distinction between pongid and hominid that an anthropologist might make. More than that, these differences have functional significance. Apes use the arms in locomotion to move over the ground, while humans must bend over to touch the ground while standing.

Or again, note the differences in the pelvis. Even to the untrained eye, the differences and similarities are apparent. The comparative anatomist examines the specifics of these differences. The greater flare of the bone at the upper part of the human pelvis tells us that the muscles attached there are better adapted to upright posture.

It is sometimes dangerous to compare isolated traits, and so *functional complexes* are often used as units of comparison. A functional complex is a cluster of traits that are all involved in some particular function and, as a result, show some morphological association. When we speak of skeletal features associated with human locomotion, we refer to a complex of traits involving the feet, legs, and pelvis. As these are all interrelated and interdependent, they simply cannot change by themselves; any alteration in the configuration of one causes a change in another, either directly or indirectly. Using terminology already intro-

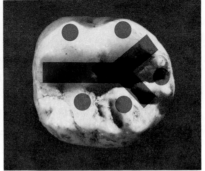

Figure 6.1
Comparison of certain skeletal and dental features in humans and apes. *Top* Lower molar of chimpanzee and human. Note the basic similarity of the cusps, indicated by dots. This is known as the Y-5 pattern. *Middle* Right hipbone of gorilla and of human, as viewed from the rear. *Bottom* Skeleton of the left hand of a gorilla and a human.

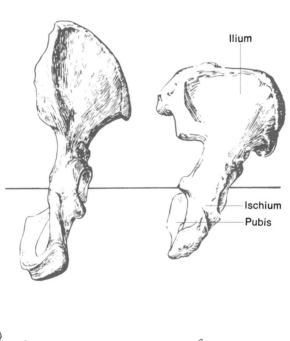

Ilium

Ischium

Pubis

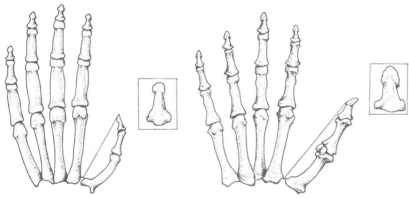

duced, we say that there is a *feedback* among the components of a functional complex.

Taxonomy

We have discussed taxonomy in chapter 3. Here, we emphasize that to the paleoanthropologist taxonomy is not just an exercise in ordering data. Rather, it is a graphic reconstruction of evolution, and decisions about taxonomy are interpretations of evolutionary processes and events. For example, there is always much interest in the question "When did humans appear?" When a paleoanthropologist analyzes a group of fossils and, as a result of comparisons and functional interpretations, decides to assign them to a new taxon within the genus *Homo,* he or she is effectively saying "It is my conclusion that the species represented by this fossil is morphologically and functionally so similar to ourselves that I assign it to a new taxon *within* the genus *Homo.* Therefore, it is human." This is an evolutionary statement, since it also says that at that time and in that place, humans had evolved.

The Evolution of the Hominidae

Pre-Hominid Evolution: The Primates

Since our concern is with humans, we shall focus on our closest ancestors. Yet, since our heritage is primate and since we have seen that much of our biology and behavior is derived from the Primates, we shall briefly review some of the major steps in primate evolution.

The earliest known Primate is represented by a single tooth from Cretaceous deposits in eastern Montana. While a tooth is hardly much evidence on which to base the beginning of an entire order, this tooth is unlike that of any other mammal and clearly shows primate traits. The genus and species is *Purgatorius ceratops,* and additional teeth of this same group have been recovered from the Paleocene (*PALE-ee-oh-seen*), the next later division of geologic time.

Table 6.2 presents the divisions of the Tertiary (*TERSH-ee-uh-ree*) and the Quaternary (*kwa-TURN-uh-ree*), the two geological periods during which the Primates evolved. Early in the Tertiary, in the earliest part of the Paleocene, mammals had appeared over much of the world. Among them were small rodentlike animals that were the first Primates. These animals moved into an arboreal habitat; their anatomy reveals the beginnings of those skeletal specializations that we identify with an arboreal way of life among the Primates.

The Paleocene and Eocene (*EE-oh-seen*) periods are known as the time of the prosimians, since more than 150 species have been described.

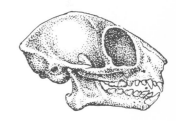

Figure 6.2
Reconstruction of the skeleton of *Plesiadapis*.

These species are unlike any primate living today, but they were pro-simianlike. Figure 6.2 shows the reconstruction of a member of the genus *Plesiadapis* (*plee-zee-ADD-a-puss*), a Paleocene prosimian found in France and in Colorado.

It is during the middle and late Eocene that fossils are found that resemble modern prosimians, and the ancestors of lemurs and tarsiers may be seen in the fossil record. Figure 6.3 shows the skull of *Necrolemur* (*nek-row-LEE-moor*), as reconstructed by the vertebrate paleontologist Elwyn Simons. *Necrolemur* may very well be ancestral to modern tarsiers.

Thus, by 50 million years ago, the basic features that characterize Primate skeletons are recognizable in fossils. These fossils are found in both the Old and New Worlds so that the actual beginnings of Primates extend back to the time when the continents now known as Europe, Africa, North and South America began to drift apart. Environmental conditions must have favored primate evolution, as shown by the great number of separate prosimian species. From that time on, the number of species has steadily declined, so that we may speculate that the forested area of the world has itself gradually declined.

Because of the basic differences between Old and New World monkeys, it appears that monkeys evolved from prosimians after the isolation of the Old from the New World. The earliest monkey fossils come from the Oligocene (*AH-lig-go-seen*) and the Miocene (*MY-oh-seen*), at about the same time as the first fossils classified as hominoids also appear.

These early hominoids are identified in fossil assemblages from Oligocene and Miocene strata in Africa, Asia, and Europe. Only the skulls and teeth are known. The earliest come from what is now the Fayum Oasis in the Egyptian Sahara Desert; they and the other fossils

Figure 6.3
Top Reconstruction of skull of *Necrolemur*.
Bottom Artist's conception of possible facial features of *Necrolemur*. Soft tissue is placed over the skull and other details are inferred.

indicate that these were small, apelike creatures. Though generally apelike, Oligocene/Miocene hominoids were not as specialized as today's apes (see Figure 6.4). A series of Miocene fossils from east Africa indicates a "generalized" ape morphology adapted to an arboreal niche, and presenting a morphology that could (and did) give rise to the living pongids and hominids.

In the Miocene, we see an evolutionary radiation of hominoids in Asia, Africa, and Europe, and a number of species have been described. One group seems so similar to the living gibbons that it is logical to conclude that before this time the line leading to that species split from the line leading to the great apes and hominids.

Pilbeam and Simons (1965) analyzed the Miocene hominoids (apart from those ancestral to the gibbon) and grouped them into a single genus, *Dryopithecus* (*dry-oh-pith-EE-cus*), or simply, the dryopithecines. The morphological patterns exhibited by this varied genus strongly suggests that the lines leading to orangs, gorillas, chimps, and hominids separated at about this time (Figure 6.5).

Pongid-Hominid Contrasts

Distributed across much of the Old World (Figure 6.6), the dryopithecines seem to be the best choice for the ancestors of the living apes and hominids: morphologically variable, adapted to a variety of habitats, and distributed across a wide geographical band. To understand the nature of the evolutionary processes that resulted in the differentiation of these two lineages, we should take a moment to consider those traits that paleontologists find useful in distinguishing hominids and pongids. They are listed in Table 6.3 and summarized below.

The pongid dental mechanism is characterized by a *U-shaped dental arch* into which are set large, pointed teeth. The canine teeth are especially large, projecting so that the lower two lock into the upper dentition. The space in the upper arch into which the lower canine fits is called the *canine diastema* (*dy-uh-STEEM-uh*). The upper and lower cheek teeth (premolars and molars) interlock as well, so that apes chew in an up-and-down fashion, shearing and crushing their food.

In contrast, the hominid dental mechanism is characterized by smaller teeth set into a *parabolic dental arch* (Figure 6.7). The canines are much smaller, and consequently there is no diastema. The chewing motion is a circular one, with the cheek teeth grinding the food rather than shearing it. The cusps of the molars and premolars are flatter and, with use, tend to wear down.

These morphological contrasts indicate differences in the type of foods consumed as well as the feeding behavior itself—in short, ecological differences between pongids and hominids. Since the teeth and jaws are

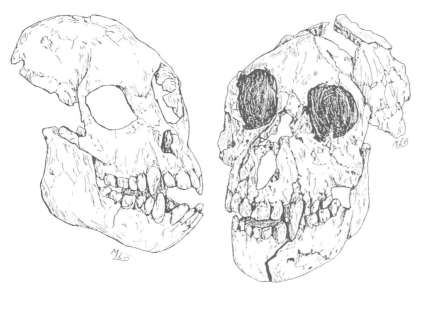

Figure 6.4
Skulls of *Aegyptopithecus* (right) and *Dryopithecus.* Note the generalized ape-like appearance.

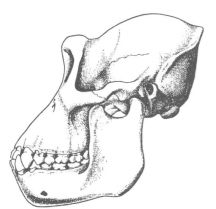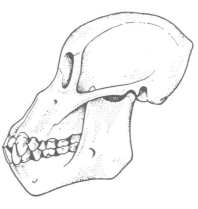

Figure 6.5
Side views of skulls of *Dryopithecus* (right) and *Gorilla.*

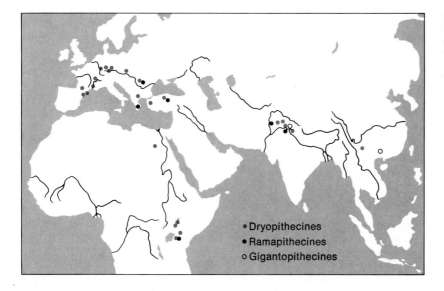

Figure 6.6
Map of Old World showing sites where dryopithecine fossils have been found and indicating known distribution of *Ramapithecus.*

- Dryopithecines
- Ramapithecines
- Gigantopithecines

Table 6.3
Hominid and Pongid Dental Traits

Hominid	Pongid
Dental arcade has parabolic, or elliptical form	Dental arcade U shaped
No diastemic interval	Diastema to accommodate canines
Incisors small	Incisors large
Canines relatively small, spatulate, bluntly pointed	Extremely large canines
Canines same length as other teeth	Canines longer than other teeth
No pronounced sexual dimorphism	Clear sexual dimorphism
Anterior lower premolar a bicuspid, non-sectorial type	Sectorial anterior lower premolar
Cusps of molars tend to be more rounded and more closely compacted	Cusps of molars less rounded
Canine teeth erupt early, usually before second molars	Canines erupt later relative to humans'
In deciduous dentition, lower milk canines are spatulate	Lower milk canines sharply pointed
Lower milk molars multicusped	Lower milk molars predominantly unicusped and conical

Figure 6.7
Dental arches of gorilla and human. Upper and lower jaw of man is at the top. Note differences in tooth size and the canine diastema in the gorilla.

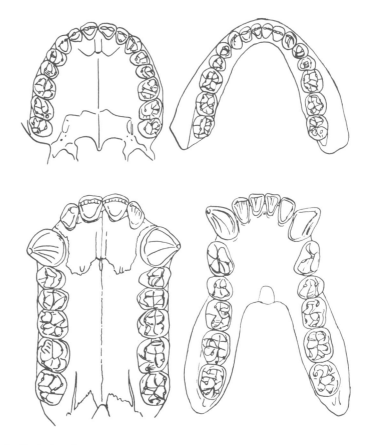

most often found fossilized, they are of prime importance to paleoanthropologists. There are, of course, other differences between pongids and hominids that must have existed in the Miocene, but the fossil record provides us with little evidence about them. In view of the adaptations of hominids to erect posture, we would particularly like to be able to document the origin of differences in that functional complex associated with locomotion, but such evidence does not yet exist.

The Earliest Hominids

In 1932, a paleontologist named G. E. Lewis, on an expedition in the hills of northern India, recovered the fragment of an upper left **maxilla** (upper jaw) of a higher Primate. He recognized that it was unlike the more apelike dryopithecines and established a new genus, *Ramapithecus* (*rah-muh-pith-EE-cus*), named after the Hindu god Rama (the suffix *-pithecus* means ape).

Over the next thirty years, other fossil jaws and teeth were found in India and in east Africa and were also assigned to this genus. Louis Leakey discovered some well-preserved maxillae in Kenya, which he named *Kenyapithecus wickeri* rather than *Ramapithecus*. He described them as being intriguingly hominidlike.

In the early 1960s Simons restudied all of this material and concluded that it could be grouped into a single genus, *Ramapithecus* (the first name given has priority). He demonstrated that there was but a single genus, which was distributed in both northern India and east Africa. While interesting, this was not nearly so significant as his second conclusion: that Ramapithecus was in fact a hominid. With this statement, Simons suggested that the hominid-pongid divergence had occurred during the Miocene and that the earliest known representative of the hominid lineage was *Ramapithecus*. K–Ar dates have established a range for this genus of 16 million years B.P. (before present) to 7 million years B.P., or from about the mid-Miocene to the Pliocene.

Simons's argument was based on two features. First, the morphology of the socket into which the canine tooth fit (the tooth unfortunately was missing) was smaller than in pongids, indicating a reduction in canine size, a hominid trait. In addition, Simons reconstructed the shape of the entire upper arch by following the curvature indicated by the part of the dental arch that was available in the fossil jawbone (Figure 6.8). Simons's reconstruction clearly suggests a parabolic arch, indicating the existence of hominids in India and Africa with dental mechanisms that were apparently adapted to the diets characteristic of later hominids, but not of pongids. Reduction in tooth size suggests that the hands might have been used more, and if the hands were used, then Ramapithecus may have had more upright posture. The feedback system between the

**Figure 6.8
Dentition of the upper jaw of chimpanzee *top* and human. In the center is the reconstruction by Simons of the dental arch of *Ramapithecus*.**

Chimpanzee

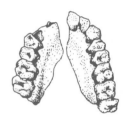

Ramapithecus

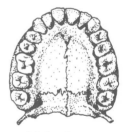

Modern human

teeth, the hands, and the pattern of locomotion could very well have been set in motion by this time.

Since Simons's publication, a number of additional fossils have been attributed to this genus, and its range has been extended northward into Europe. How correct are the assignments? Fossil fragments are just that, and interpretation is often very tentative. It may very well be that it is premature to assign too many fossils to *Ramapithecus,* since by so doing (remember, taxonomy = evolution) one is extending the geographical range of a genus represented so far only by incomplete fragments of bone.

Can we even be certain that *Ramapithecus* was a hominid? Not completely. While the majority of paleoanthropologists would agree with Simons, others would not. Many of the doubters note that we don't know enough to be sure, and that even if *Ramapithecus* was not a pongid, we still cannot say that this genus was on the lineage leading to the genus *Homo.* Still others argue that the diagnosis of *Ramapithecus* as a hominid is open to question. Walker and Andrews have questioned Simons's interpretation of the dental arch as rounded.

Such is the stuff that paleontological theories are made of! At this moment we can't be sure (and we will never be completely certain) that *Ramapithecus* was in fact a direct human ancestor. It may be a direct ancestor, it may be very close to it, it may be something in-between a hominid and a pongid, or it may simply be a variant of the dryopithecines. We can only make two conclusions at this time. First, the majority opinion is that *Ramapithecus* was a hominid. Second, even if *Ramapithecus* is far removed from human lineage, then the divergence among the dryopithecines, which is considerable, nevertheless suggests that the hominid line was soon to branch away from the pongid.

The Ecology of Early Hominids

In spite of the controversy about *Ramapithecus,* we have some ideas of the ecosystem to which the earliest hominids must have adapted as they gradually diverged from the apes. The evidence is scanty, and speculation is the rule; but using what evidence is available, our knowledge of living hominoids, and a little logic, we can paint a picture that is probably not far from wrong.

The evolution of the hominoids, evident by the Miocene, involved a radiation over much of the Old World. At the same time, the environmental changes that had led to the reduction in the number of primate species since the Eocene continued.

Some Old World primates evolved into well-adapted arboreal species. Certain species of monkeys became highly skilled at arboreal life; among the hominoids, so did the gibbon. Others—monkeys and pongids (the orang-utan and the chimpanzee)—also developed into arboreal species, though perhaps not as agile as the first group. Semiterrestrial species also appeared, probably representing groups living on the fringes of the forest who gradually spent more and more time on the ground, perhaps because the forests were shrinking.

Those hominoids that adapted to a terrestrial habitat diverged from the apes and became hominids. This new ecosystem led to environmental pressures that, through natural selection, produced dental changes in response to new diets, changes in the lower extremity in response to new patterns of locomotion, and changes in the mobility of the hands as they became freed for other uses.

Life on the ground exposed groups of animals to new threats from carnivorous predators, and social structures developed to cope with this threat. Some time ago, Washburn and Devore (1961) noted many similarities between the social lives of baboons and humans. These may very well reflect Miocene or Pliocene adaptations to a terrestrial existence.

Clifford Jolly has suggested that hominid differentiation might have come about as we have suggested here, but he has carried our ideas further (Jolly 1970) by suggesting that the early hominids changed their diets as they exploited a new environment. From a "fruit-centered diet [they changed] to one based upon cereals which would lead . . . to the complex of small-object-feeding, seed-eating terrestrial adaptations." These adaptations involve precisely those dental features that distinguish hominids from pongids.

Later Hominids: The Australopithecines

Despite the gaps in our knowledge of the differentiation of the earliest hominids, it is known that by the upper (later) Pliocene, 5 to 6 million years ago, there existed easily recognizable hominids who displayed the basic hominid morphological pattern. While there is some controversy about the taxonomy of various groups, and about the ancestral/descendant relationships, there is none about the existence of hominid populations.

The hominid fossils from this period, from 5 million to 1 million years B.P., are grouped into the australopithecines (after the genus name *Australopithecus,* assigned to the first find made by Raymond Dart and reported by him in 1925). In the decades following Dart's discovery, many more fossils have been recovered, so that we now know the australopithecines from the incomplete remains of over 300 individuals. The great majority come from sites in South Africa and east Africa, but many paleoanthropologists feel that certain fossils from Southeast Asia and China belong to the same group (Figure 6.9).

The oldest australopithecine material yet found comes from the east African country of Tanzania, in particular from its lake district. At the site named Lothogam, investigators have excavated a **mandible** (lower

Figure 6.9
Map showing areas where
Australopithecine fossils
have been found.

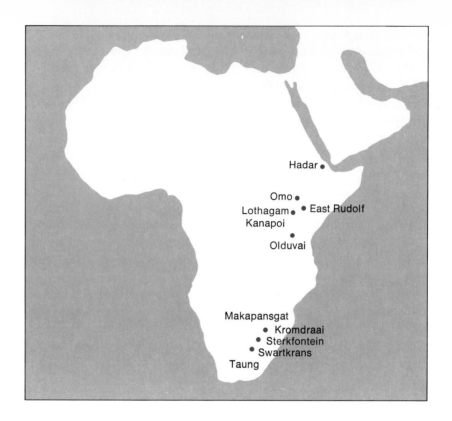

jaw) dated at approximately 5 million years B.P., while at Kanapoi a fragment of a *humerus* (the bone of the upper arm) has been assigned an age of 4 million years. From 3 million years onward, there exists a succession of fossils from east Africa. The most famous have come from the Olduvai Gorge, a rich source of fossils for over fifty years, worked for much of that time by Louis and Mary Leakey. More recently, their son Richard Leakey, as well as investigators from other countries, has worked to the north near the lakes of Kenya and Uganda and in the region around the Omo River in Ethiopia.

Many other australopithecine remains have come from South Africa, including the first, *Australopithecus africanus*. The South African fossils have provided a rich source of information for decades, but dating them has always been a problem. The sites were originally caves, and there is neither acceptable stratigraphy, nor materials appropriate for radiometric dating, nor other direct indicators of age. However, careful and painstaking studies over the years by Philip Tobias and his collaborators now suggest that the South African deposits are at least 3 million years old and generally contemporaneous with the east African material (Tobias 1975).

A few fossils from Java are similar to the African australopithecines and may tentatively be placed within that group (von Koenigswald 1976). However, the lack of fossils between the two ends of this geographic distribution presents a problem, and we cannot be certain at this time about the Southeast Asian material. The same is true for the "finds" from China. For centuries, "dragon's teeth" were used in treating diseases and could be bought at apothecary shops well into the twentieth century. Many of the "teeth" were in fact fossils, and paleontologists began to visit the shops in search of our early ancestors! Some of those that have been recovered display some features of australopithecine morphology and indicate that populations of this group might have been living in China. However, this conclusion is tentative, since there is no way to estimate age, nor is there any environmental context or other supporting information.

Australopithecines as Hominids   The morphology of the australopithecines is hominid. Figure 6.10 compares their dentition with that of *H. sapiens* and of a pongid, clearly revealing a functional and morphological complex similar to our own. In short, the basic hominid dental adaptations described above were well established by the late Pliocene and have persisted with relatively little change to the present day. The precise diet of the australopithecines is speculative, but we suspect that it was omnivorous. At Olduvai the remains of small and immature mammals clearly indicate meat-eating.

The australopithecines provide us with the first indication of posture and locomotion in Tertiary hominids, and there is no doubt that the skeletons of the members of this group were adapted to erect posture. Figure 6.11 compares the pelvises of various primate species, showing clearly that the hominid pattern is shared by the australopithecines.

How well adapted were the australopithecines to upright posture and bipedal locomotion? The answers are not yet clear, but there are some morphological differences between the pelvises of *Australopithecus* and of *Homo*. In a detailed study of pelvic morphology, Oxnard (1969) found that while the australopithecines demonstrated a hominid configuration, they nonetheless could be differentiated from *Homo* by sophisticated statistical techniques. Whether this means that they were less efficient at bipedal locomotion or at standing erect is unknown.

It is interesting that one area of the pelvis where the differences are most apparent is the *ischial tuberosity,* the lowest part of the pelvis and the part upon which one sits. For our purposes it is significant that the hamstring muscles (the *semimembranosis* and *semitendenosis*) attach at that point; these muscles are the primary extensors of the leg and are important in "straightening" the leg at the hip joint. Thus, they play a

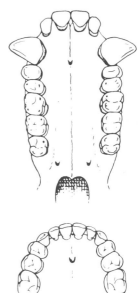
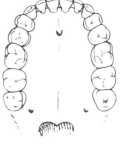
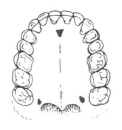

Figure 6.10
Upper dental arches of *Gorilla* top, *Australopithecus*, and *Homo sapiens*.

Figure 6.11
Pelvis *top* and right hip bones *bottom* of (left to right) chimpanzee, Australopithecine, and modern human.

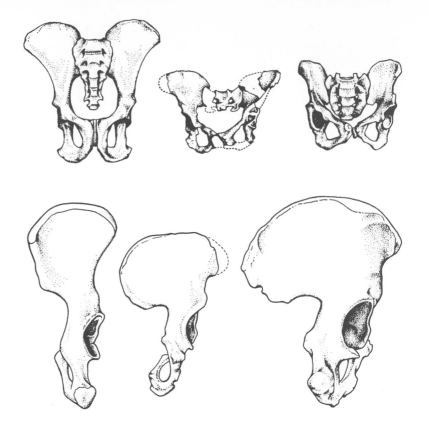

role in upright posture. Differences in bony morphology might indicate differences in the pattern of muscular attachment, which would relate to upright posture.

Nevertheless, we must again emphasize that, despite some differences, the australopithecine pelvis was a hominid one. In addition, an almost complete skeleton of a foot from the Olduvai Gorge was almost indistinguishable from that of a modern human.

Brains do not fossilize but brain cases do, and the analysis of skull size and shape provides important information on the evolution of the brain itself. Such studies are not simple, since the skull is rarely complete and the shape of the brain must be inferred from reconstructions. The results show a group whose brains were larger than those of the pongids, smaller than our own, and markedly variable in size from individual to individual.

The brains of modern adult humans tend to fall in the range of 1,300 to 1,400 cc in volume, though persons with normal intelligence may be found with brains ranging from 1,000 to 2,000 cc. The brains of the great apes are smaller—350 to 400 cc in chimpanzees and about 500 cc in gorillas—though these primates also show individual variation. The

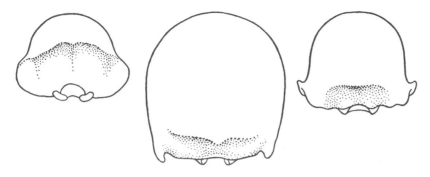

Figure 6.12
Drawings of the skulls of chimpanzee, and modern human and the robust forms of *Australopithecus.*

Figure 6.13
In textbooks, fossil skulls are usually shown as drawings of reconstructions. This figure shows the fragments, as they are more typically found.

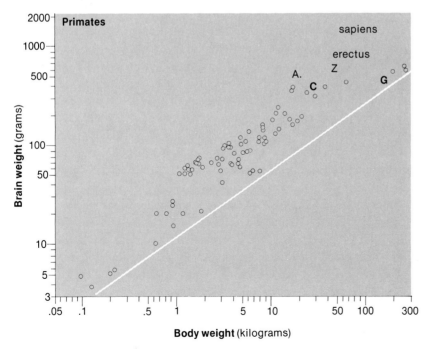

Figure 6.14
This graph shows the relationship between brain weight and body weight in primates. In general, the larger the body, the larger the brain. The human brain, however, is larger for a given body weight than the brain of other primates.

Figure 6.15
Artist's reconstruction of the possible appearance of *Australopithecus*, based upon the structure of the underlying skeleton.

hominid-pongid differences are even clearer when we consider brain size relative to body size, since the weight of the brain is somewhat dependent on the size of the body. When we take body size into account (Figure 6.14), our relative brain size is even larger than that characteristic of the pongids.

The brains of the australopithecines are estimated to have ranged from about 400 to over 800 cc—that is, they doubled in size from the smallest to the largest! This variability is quite significant. Such a wide range of difference suggests that rapid evolutionary change might have been occurring at this time, as natural selection operated at an intense level to bring about great changes in brain size over a rather short time.

Along with these similarities, there are other traits of the australopithecines that distinguish them from later hominids. Figure 6.12 indicates their protrusive faces, their heavy *brow ridges,* the prominent bony architecture of the facial skeleton, and the absence of the chin "button" characteristic of living humans. All these features are part of the functional complex associated with chewing; they provide sites for the attachment of muscles and buttress the face against the forces exerted by those muscles. These features indicate that the australopithecines used their teeth more forcibly than do modern humans, suggesting that there were still functional differences between *Australopithecus* and *Homo,* even though the basic hominid dental mechanism had evolved. We may speculate that their diet required heavier chewing forces and that still more strength would have been needed if they also used their teeth as a tool.

One interesting feature of australopithecine faces is the absence of a chin button. While the development of a chin in modern humans is related to chewing, it is also related to the broadening of the skull. DuBrul and Sicher (1954) have demonstrated that the chin as we know it evolved as a buttress against chewing forces, which became concentrated at that point as the mandible widened to fit into a progressively wider skull. By experimenting with the mechanical properties of mandibles, they were able to show that under these conditions the greatest stress point is at the chin. Australopithecines had narrow skulls and so did not require reinforcement, but in more recent hominids, natural selection resulted in the development of an increased mass of bone, which we call the chin. The wishbone of a chicken is analogous; it will never break in the center because of the mass of bone there.

We know nothing of the external features of the australopithecines— hair, skin color, amount of fat on their faces, and so forth. Nevertheless, artists can put soft tissue over the bony skeleton and give us a general idea. Figure 6.15 presents such a reconstruction.

Australopithecine Ecosystems　　As we indicated earlier, paleoecology is necessarily based on inference from incomplete data. Despite the problems, it is useful to infer the ecosystems of the australopithecines, though a great deal of speculation is included.

The australopithecines most likely lived in small bands, collecting and eating plants and other vegetable foods. They also ate meat, but their success as hunters is not known. Since the animals they are known to have killed were small, perhaps they were not as efficient as later hominids, yet meat was an important component of the diets of at least some groups.

On occasion, they may have been the hunted as well as the hunter! The South African remains, which come from caves, comprise both australopithecines and masses of other animal bones. Since such caves are often the lairs of predators, it may be that these South African sites are actually caves into which our hominid ancestors were dragged as part of another creature's meal.

It is impossible to estimate with any confidence the number of individuals living at any one site at a single moment in time; one site may span only a single day while another may have persisted for a million years. Alan Mann has carefully studied the South African remains and has concluded that the largest site, Swartkrans, has yielded fragments of 75 to 90 individuals, while at Kromdraii only 5 to 6 have been found (Mann 1975). Such information, considered in conjunction with data on present-day hunting and gathering peoples, indicates that we would expect to find these early hominids living in bands of perhaps 15 to 20 individuals.

During this period the African climate was warm, with wet and dry seasons. Speth and Davis (1976) have suggested that many of the living sites at Olduvai Gorge were occupied during the dry season. They further suggest that the australopithecines moved into other areas during the rainy season. Much of their time on the savanna must have been spent near beds of water. Lions, hyenas, and saber-tooth tigers were their predators and must have represented a constant threat.

The Evidence of Culture   One of the most important features of the australopithecines was their possession of culture. By this we mean that their "set of rules" included activities that could be preserved in the record of the past as evidence of culture—specifically, the manufacture of stone tools, which remain as evidence.

One of the most important features of the australo-pithecines was their possession of culture.

Higher primates use available objects such as sticks for tools; chimpanzees have been observed to break off sticks and form them into a tool for extracting termites from dead trees. But australopithecine tools differed from those of the other nonhuman Primates in three crucial respects that, when taken together, comprise a critical difference.

1. *Quantity.* The quantity of stone tools found indicates that tool-making was not just a response to an immediate need. Rather, it occupied a great proportion of their time (perhaps in place of foraging for food),

Figure 6.16
Australopithecine pebble
tools.

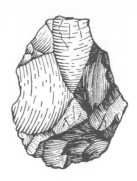

and presumably tools were made in advance of the time when they were needed.

2. *Quality*. No one would suggest that these tools were artistic or technological paragons compared with what we see later. They were simple and crude. But compared with anything ever produced by a pongid, they are considerably more sophisticated.

3. *Pattern*. These tools were made according to a preconceived idea of form, forming a *tradition*, that is, a form that spread throughout south and east Africa.

Australopithecine tools are called **pebble tools** and are at least 2.6 million years old (Figure 6.16). They were made by knocking the flakes off a "core" of rock to make a cutting edge. Archeologists have named this complex of tools the *Oldowan* tool industry. In characterizing this industry, Fagan has described the manufacturers as

adept stone toolmakers, using angular flakes and lumps of lava to make weapons, scrapers, and cutting tools. The tools themselves were probably used for cutting skin too tough for teeth to cut. In all probability, the hominids made extensive use of simple and untrimmed flakes for widely differing activities. (Fagan 1977:59)

Before the discovery of the Oldowan industry, anthropologists hypothesized that culture had suddenly "appeared" on the scene. Hominids were thought to have evolved a large brain, and when they were human-like, they had been endowed with the capacity for culture. At that instant, biological influences were thought to have disappeared and culture to have developed purely as a social phenomenon. We now know that these early hominids, standing upright imperfectly, weighing only 90–100 pounds, with protruding faces and with brains only half the size of those of modern humans, did possess a capacity for culture. The resulting expression, shown in the fossil record, is the Oldowan industry—simple by our standards, but culture nonetheless.

We now know that these early hominids, standing upright imperfectly, weighing only 90–100 pounds, with protruding faces and with brains only half the size of those of modern humans, did possess a capacity for culture.

Thus the hominids evolved to a stage of biological organization resulting in culture at a point when their morphology was still distinct from our own. We may hypothesize that the possession of culture conferred an important adaptive advantage upon a species. Natural selection acted on this advantage to produce, through continued progressive evolution, improved locomotor and grasping abilities, a decreased chewing mechanism, and most important, a rapidly increasing brain size. Bigger brains resulted in more intelligent individuals with greater technological expertise which, through feedback, made it more valuable to have even bigger brains. From the Australopithecines to their successors (a time span of perhaps a million years), the size of the brain doubled. Clearly, tools made humans as much as humans made tools!

Variability among the Australopithecines　The term "australopithecine" is a collective one, including a variety of fossils distributed over a wide geographical range and 4 or more million years of time. There is considerable variability, as might be expected in such a widespread group evolving rather rapidly. As more discoveries have been made, the extent of australopithecine variability has become more apparent, and the picture that has emerged is still unclear. No one argues any more that the australopithecines are not hominid, nor would anyone deny that among them are the ancestors of living humans. However, there are still important questions to be asked: How many species were there? And, assuming more than one, which were ancestral to ourselves? Growing out of these questions is another one: To what extent can we explain the mechanisms that were responsible for the variability observed?

In the past, paleoanthropologists, paying little attention to the rules of taxonomy, were too quick to give each new fossil a new genus name, so that among the australopithecines at least five genera have been suggested! Such an intolerable situation has eased and, since the 1960s, the practice has been to assign to each new fossil an ID number or "name" (e.g., the "Dear Boy" fossil found by the Leakeys) until agreement among authorities has been reached.

But even now there are different interpretations of the variability among australopithecines, amounting essentially to two viewpoints. The first holds that there are at least two species, while the other maintains that there is only one.

A number of paleoanthropologists have concluded that there are anywhere from two to five or even six species of australopithecines. This interpretation is based upon the existence of two "types" of morphologies, which are seen as representing two separate lineages. The first consists of populations displaying a "robust" skull morphology. Their dental/dietary

Figure 6.17
Comparison of skulls of
robust *top* and gracile
Australopithecines.

functional complex was adapted to a different ecosystem than the other line; the bones of the skull and face are more massive and the cheek teeth are relatively larger than in the other lineage. This group is given the name *Australopithecus robustus*. John Robinson has studied the morphology of the robust group and concluded that the dental mechanism suggests a vegetarian ecosystem, in which natural selection would favor a complex that emphasized crushing and grinding of vegetables, fruits, husks, etc. (Robinson 1963).

The other lineage has a more "gracile" facial skeleton, lacking the very heavy bones and large cheek teeth. They are given the name *Australopithecus africanus,* and Robinson has suggested that, unlike *A. robustus,* they might have been omnivorous.

Those who hold this view see hominid evolution at that time in terms of two evolving species within a single genus. Both species have been found in South Africa and east Africa, both manufactured pebble tools, and both spanned approximately the same range of time. Since they were contemporaneous and lived in the same area, they must have been adapted to differing ecosystems. Robinson's dietary hypothesis has been advanced to explain this difference. However, not all who accept two species also accept the notion of a vegetarian/omnivorous dichotomy.

Since *A. robustus* is less like what we would expect to find as our ancestor, there has been a tendency to assume that this line became extinct. However, there is no real evidence to support this, other than the logical argument of "greater morphological similarity = greater likelihood of ancestry." Such an argument, though possibly logical, is not in itself evidence and should not be applied blindly to the australopithecines.

In the 1960s, discoveries in east Africa led to the establishment of another species. In fact, even a new genus was proposed: *Homo habilis* (*HAB-ill-us*). The initial reaction to this proposal, made by Louis Leakey, was overwhelmingly negative, and *H. habilis* was seen as a variant of *A. africanus,* perhaps one that came somewhat later in time. However, the idea has received considerable support from the discovery in east Africa of a hominid skull from this period (known as KNM ER1470 or simply 1470) with a cranial capacity of 800 cc, which is twice the size of some other australopithecines. This would indeed suggest that a more modern variety of hominid existed at the same time as the australopithecines with more traditional morphology. If the name *Homo* is finally accepted, it would place the initial appearance of our genus at just under 3 million years ago, or 2 million years earlier than had been believed!

This interpretation of australopithecine evolution would go as follows: About 6 million years ago, the hominids entered an australopithecine phase of evolution. Two separate lineages appeared, adapted to different ecosystems. Considerable variability ensued, perhaps even a "mini-radiation." Cladogenic evolution can be seen in differences between east African and South African forms; while at the same time, progressive evolution is seen in both robust and gracile lineages with the evolution of upright posture and stone tools. In east Africa (and possibly in South Africa), a further differentiation occurred as a more advanced lineage, *H. habilis,* appeared, providing the link to more advanced hominids. Some *A. africanus* groups may have evolved into *H. habilis* while others may, along with *A. robustus,* have become extinct. At any one time the situation was complex and there might have been interaction, even perhaps exchange of mates among the different lineages.

Opposed to this view is the "single species hypothesis." Its proponents, chiefly C. L. Brace and M. H. Wolpoff, argue that the capacity for culture represents a major evolutionary step and constitutes a new ecosystem in itself—culture. "Although culture may have arisen as a defensive survival mechanism, once present it opened up a whole new range of environmental resources" (Wolpoff 1968). The accompanying adaptive advantages were not those of biology, but of learning, experience, and behavior. For this reason, it is highly unlikely that any species possessing culture would have become extinct, because of the adaptability, the capacity for change, that comes with culture.

Those who hold to this hypothesis interpret the australopithecines as a variable species through which evolution passed on the way to the genus *Homo.* Brace has argued that the analysis of australopithecine variability is considerably more complex than many investigators have made it out to be and that many factors besides differing dental adaptations could create an apparent species difference (Brace 1973).

Both views have their adherents, their theories, and their own methods of analysis. The fact that they differ reveals the problems of dealing with fragmentary material and indicates that different individuals, each approaching the same raw data objectively and scientifically, can come up with radically differing interpretations. Any final judgment of which interpretation is correct must unfortunately wait for more material.

The Significance of the Australopithecines   We have devoted more space to the australopithecines than we will give to the fossils of any other species, including ourselves. We have done so on purpose; the australopithecines offer us many insights into the evolutionary process in general and the history of the hominid lineage in particular. Questions of the origin of culture and the preconditions for it, the nature of evolutionary differentiation, and the interrelatedness of items of a functional complex may all be investigated by examining fossils from this period. Before the australopithecines, our knowledge is so fragmentary that we must speculate too much; after them, the hominid pattern is so firmly established that

But with the australo-pithecines we see the fossil evidence for the complexity of hominid evolution, inter-twined as it was with the development of culture— not culture as we know it from living humans, but culture that was far more dependent on and respon-sive to biological feedback. We may also refer to this as protoculture.

we can only recount what happened. But with the australopithecines we see the fossil evidence for the complexity of hominid evolution, intertwined as it was with the development of culture—not culture as we know it from living humans, but culture that was far more dependent on and responsive to biological feedback. We may also refer to this as **protoculture.**

The Final Stages of Human Evolution: The Genus *Homo*

Sometime around 1 million years ago, evolutionary change within the hominid lineage had proceeded to the level at which virtually all agree that the genus *Homo* had "appeared," or rather had emerged gradually to the point where it was to be formally recognized. Consequently, all fossils from then on are classified as *Homo*. The hominid line had enlarged its geographical range so that by 750,000 years B.P., fossils of this new genus are found in the south, east, and north of Africa (Morocco), in Europe as far north as Germany and Hungary, in southeast Asia (Java), and in China. Even though fossils have not been found, stone tools indicate that *Homo* also reached into other areas (e.g., England and Spain).

The morphology of these early humans is far enough removed from our own that they are grouped into a different species, *H. erectus*. Morphologically, they represent a continuation of trends seen among the australopithecines. Culturally, we see an elaboration of technical and social aspects. Geographically, we note a much wider distribution stretching into areas with a more temperate climate, which implies both biological and cultural adaptive mechanisms that would permit their existence away from the tropical savannas where earlier hominids lived.

The Geological Context *Homo erectus* appeared at the same general time that major changes began to occur in the physical world. For several hundred thousand years, the temperature of the earth's atmosphere had been dropping steadily, and more and more of the earth's moisture was becoming locked in the glaciers of the polar ice caps and certain mountain chains. As a result the glaciers enlarged, or advanced, covering larger and larger areas of the land.

These advances were not a single event but a succession of movements and retreats covering almost a million years; each cycle lasted tens or hundreds of thousands of years, radically changing the topography of the earth for long periods of time. For example, in North America the maximum glacial advance was as far south as the Ohio River; large boulders found today in southern Ohio are part of the glacial moraine left when the ice melted. In Europe, the Alpine glacier advanced and separated west from east more than once. Although Africa was not penetrated by glaciers, there was marked seasonality in rainfall, with clear-cut wet and dry periods.

These events signal the end of the Tertiary and the beginning of the Quaternary period (see Table 6.2). The first epoch within the Quaternary is the Pleistocene (*PLICE-tuh-seen*), or *Ice Age,* which is divided for convenience into three periods:

Lower Pleistocene, from somewhere between 5 and 1.5 million years B.P. to 1 million years B.P.

Middle Pleistocene, from 1 million to 200,000 years B.P.

Upper Pleistocene, from 200,000 to 10,000 years B.P.

Different geologists specify different times for the beginning of the Pleistocene. The cooling of the earth occurred gradually, and most see the Pleistocene as beginning with the first evidence of that cooling, usually a southward migration of cold-adapted life, as indicated by faunal assemblages.

The changes accompanying the movements of the glaciers were important for human evolution for two reasons:

1. The cyclic nature of the glacial advances and retreats caused major changes in temperature, vegetation, and animal life. Arctic conditions reached into central Europe, but in the interglacial periods the temperatures were warmer than they are now.

2. As more and more of the earth's water was accumulating in the glaciers, the level of the oceans dropped sharply and land bridges appeared between adjacent bodies of land where the water was shallow enough. England was joined to continental Europe at various times, and northeast Asia became connected to Alaska as the Bering Strait was bridged.

With major shifts in the environment and climate and with the appearance and disappearance of land bridges and corridors, evolving populations of humans were faced with new ecological possibilities as well as new environmental stresses. These required a number of evolutionary and cultural adaptations, some involving major population movements. The Pleistocene became a time of considerable evolutionary change as australopithecine-like forms became morphologically and culturally like modern humans.

Homo erectus From the end of the australopithecine phase, all hominid fossils until the middle Pleistocene are grouped into a single species: *H. erectus.* There is virtually unanimous agreement that evolution during the Pleistocene consisted of the progressive modification of the genus *Homo* from *H. erectus* to *H. sapiens.*

We know surprisingly little about the post-cranial morphology (i.e., the skeleton apart from the skull) of *H. erectus,* even though the fossils we possess indicate no basic differences from ourselves. Grasp, posture, and locomotion were all similar to what is seen in modern humans. The

Figure 6.18
Top Side view of skull from
China and back view of
H. erectus compared to
Australopithecus (top) and
modern human (bottom).

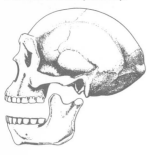

Nuchal crest

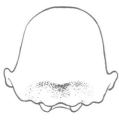

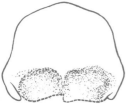

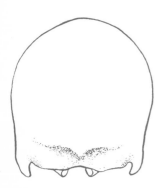

bones were somewhat sturdier and more robust, and the body size was smaller, but there are differences of degree rather than of kind.

The *H. erectus* skulls, however, were different from those of modern humans, and this difference is the basis for the species distinction. *H. erectus* brain sizes, while larger than the australopithecines, were smaller than *H. sapiens,* ranging between 800 and 1,200 cc. The *H. erectus* brain case was lower and, viewed from the back, shows that the parietal (*pah-RYE-uh-tull*) areas of the brain had not expanded as in *H. sapiens.* Since these areas are associated with memory, intellect, language, and the like, this implies biologically based behavioral differences between these species.

The culture of *H. erectus* will be covered in the next chapter, and here we need only note that it comprised a well-developed hunting and gathering system, which involved the killing of larger game, the manufacture of more sophisticated stone tools, and a need for greater social cooperation. The discovery of hearths at sites in Europe and China indicates the harnessing of fire at this time. Fire is important in influencing the diet and making a wider range of foods available. In addition, fire extended the habitation range by providing a source of heat in colder climates.

Homo sapiens   At the end of the middle Pleistocene, some 200,000 years B.P., the fossils indicate a gradual change in morphology in the direction of modern humans. This is called by some a "pre-sapiens" phase; by others, the appearance of our own species. Regardless of the terminology, the transition is clear and we see the emergence of *H. sapiens* as a species.

This transition is not documented to the same degree in all continents, and there are gaps in the record here and there. The oldest fossils placed within *H. sapiens* date to 200,000 B.P. and come from Swanscombe, England, and Steinheim, Germany. There are also finds from along the Solo River in Java and the Omo River in Ethiopia, although these are somewhat more recent, perhaps 100,000 B.P.

The available evidence indicates that *H. erectus* populations continued to expand in their range as they evolved, including all of Africa and Eurasia except for the Arctic and some sub-Arctic regions. By this time, brain sizes had reached those of modern humans, and stone tool technology and hunting skills had become quite elaborate.

The first populations of *H. sapiens* still did not resemble ourselves in facial morphology nor in the shape of the brain, and they are placed in a different subspecies.

Neanderthal   The differences between ourselves and the Neanderthal (*nee-ANN-der-tall*) may be seen in Figures 6.18 and 6.19. In comparison

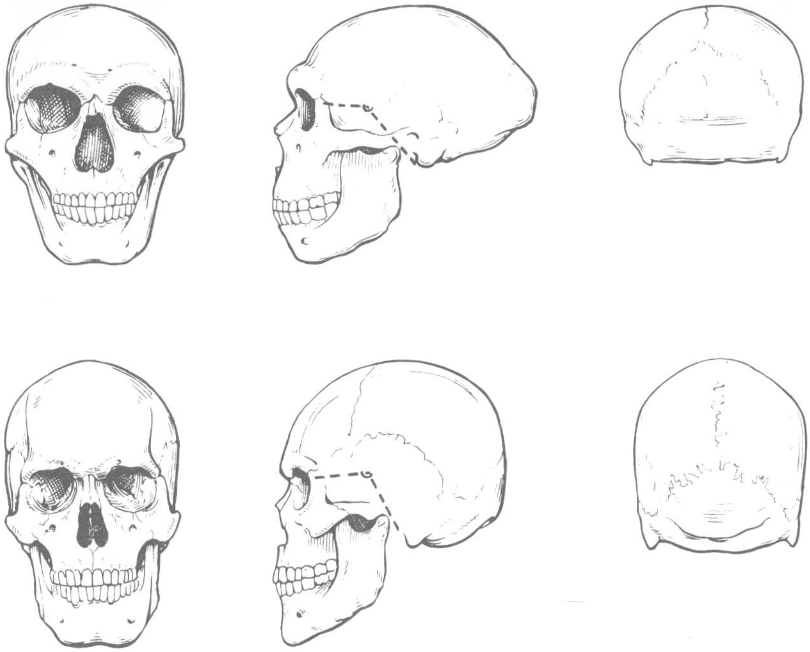

Figure 6.19
Front, side, and back views
of skulls of Neanderthal *top*
and modern human.

with modern humans, their faces were still massive and protrusive and the brow ridges large; nor had a chin button appeared. From the rear, the skull of Neanderthal, though as large as in modern humans and more rounded than in *H. erectus,* still differed from our own. The Neanderthal skull was circular, like a grapefruit, while ours is five-sided (Figure 6.19). A considerable amount of parietal expansion was still to come.

The culture of Neanderthal is referred to as **Mousterian** (*moo-STEER-ee-un*), which identifies it on the basis of kinds of tools and techniques of manufacture. We will only note in this chapter that this system was well adapted to the environments in which Neanderthals lived.

Distributed throughout the Old World, the Neanderthals present a picture of considerable geographical variability. However, the progression from Neanderthal to modern humans seems quite straightforward in general throughout Europe, Africa, and Asia. The only exception to this seems to be in western Europe where one variety, with particularly massive facial morphology, lived during the last advance of the glaciers, from 70,000 to 35,000 B.P. Paradoxically called "Classic" Neanderthal, this variety displays differences from all the others; in southwest Asia, eastern Europe, and the rest of the world. Since western Europe was cut off from the rest of the world during the last glacial period, F. C. Howell has suggested that these differences are due to evolution in isolation from other groups (Howell 1951). Some paleoanthropologists have suggested that the massive faces, distinctively shaped brow ridges, and other slight

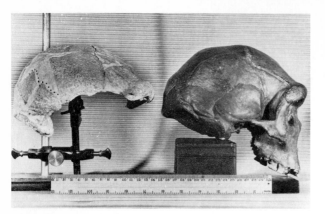

Figure 6.20
Neanderthaloid skulls from southern Africa.

differences in the morphology of western European Neanderthals might represent adaptive responses to the cold climate. However, A. T. Steegmann, in studying living humans (with, of course, modern facial morphologies), failed to find any relationship between variation in facial structure and ability to adapt to cold stress (Steegmann 1970).

At one time the issue of these western European Neanderthals was highly controversial. Why were they so different? They must have been a different species. If so, Neanderthals had become extinct and were a side issue in human evolution. In typical fashion, Western scientists had cast the problem in local terms and decided that what had happened in western Europe had, in fact, happened everywhere.

We now know that this isn't so. In all the world except western Europe, Neanderthals evolved into modern *H. sapiens* at about 40,000 to 35,000 B.P. (Figure 6.20). The situation in western Europe is admittedly less clear but not nearly as critical as once thought to be. There are two views. One school holds that with the retreat of the glaciers and the rapid climatic changes that occurred, Classic Neanderthals evolved rapidly into modern *H. sapiens* (Brace 1964b). The other interprets the rapid shift in morphology at this time as indicating the replacement of Classic Neanderthal by modern populations moving in from the east; a modification of this view sees assimilation, not replacement.

Regardless of the resolution of this rather local problem, modern *H. sapiens* appeared at the time of the retreat of the last glacier. Differing from ourselves morphologically in only minor details, they tend to be more robust and are often referred to as "archaic."

Modern Homo sapiens What do we mean by the term "modern" *Homo sapiens?* Paleoanthropologists use this term to refer to people whose morphology was not different from our own, except perhaps for some very minor details. We see people like this every day; we ourselves resemble our upper Pleistocene ancestors. The same range of variations is found in populations throughout the last 20,000 years. If we were to examine a single individual skeleton, we couldn't distinguish differences well enough to assign it to an early or a recent population. If we were to compare large samples of skeletons of the two groups, we would probably notice that, on the average, the upper Pleistocene group was a bit "heavier boned" than ourselves, and that would be all.

During the Pleistocene, *Homo sapiens* was, as we have noted, spreading over more and more of the earth's surface. The extent of this spread depended on several factors:

1. the numerical size of the species itself;
2. the ability of individual populations to adapt to the successively colder climates they encountered (these adaptations would have been both biological, through natural selection, and cultural, through change and innovation); and
3. the availability of open unglaciated land.

The third point is particularly important in examining population movements. The northern polar ice cap did not spread evenly southward to cover the world like a gigantic cap. It was directed and diverted by resistant geographical features so that even at the height of a glacial period, there were large open spaces in sub-Arctic regions and corridors between masses of ice. Primates are inquisitive animals, and humans, as primates, are curious about their environment. If there was a corridor, some groups undoubtedly traversed it just to see where it led! In addition, many of these groups may have depended on hunting large animals for food and so would have followed the animals as they moved through the corridors.

The spread of humans throughout the remainder of the world was dictated by a combination of factors. Obviously, some combinations required longer to surmount. For instance, people did not move into the islands of the Pacific until they were able to navigate over thousands of miles of open ocean—which probably didn't occur until after 3000 B.C. (Suggs 1960). Other ocean barriers were less foreboding and easier to cross. Even though there never seems to have been a land bridge connecting Australia to the islands, humans entered that continent as long ago as 30,000 to 40,000 years B.P.

Entry into the New World   How did the first Americans get into the New World? This question has fascinated people since the discovery of the Americas, and the answers have ranged from the scientific to the bizarre. (In the latter category are the theories that trace the American Indian back to the mythical continent of Atlantis or even to outer space!)

For decades, some scholars have attempted to demonstrate that the

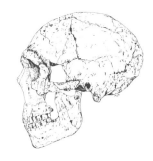

Figure 6.21
Skulls of fossils of modern *Homo sapiens*; Wadjak (Java) *top* and Amud (Israel). They are indistinguishable from the skulls of twentieth-century humans.

Figure 6.22
Map showing the route across Beringia into the New World followed by the earliest Americans. Ancestors of American Indians moved into the interior, following large animals. Ancestors of Eskimos and Aleuts (Bering Sea mongoloids) remained along the coast.

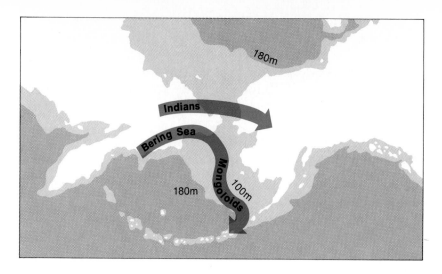

Native Americans came from the Old World across the Atlantic, perhaps from the early civilization of Egypt. The Mormon Church has conducted archeological research in an attempt to demonstrate that the American Indians were one of the lost tribes of Israel. However, taking all the evidence—historic and prehistoric, skeletal and cultural—the overwhelming majority of scientists agree that the first Americans entered the New World across a Pleistocene land bridge joining what are now Siberia and Alaska at the Bering Strait.

The Bering Strait was dry land at about 50,000 years B.P. and again later. Little is known about either period, but the evidence does suggest that the second bridge opened and closed periodically. David Hopkins has studied this region extensively, naming the rather vast area that became dry (i.e., the corridor) *Beringia* (Hopkins 1967).

There is controversy about when the first Americans entered the New World. Some anthropologists see this as quite early; Patterson (1973) suggests an entry at about 30,000–25,000 B.P., while McNeish would push this date much further back, perhaps even to 70,000 B.P. Various lines of evidence are given to support these dates, including C^{14} dates from South America as old as 20,000 years.

Others are more conservative and would place the time of entry no earlier than, and probably close to, 20,000 B.P. (Griffin 1978). Griffin stresses the uncertainty of much of the evidence presented to support an earlier crossing, and he especially stresses the possibility of error in the radiocarbon dating. Hopkins, from studies of Beringia itself, has suggested that corridors may have been open at 24,000 years, possibly at 20,000, and again at 16,000 (Hopkins 1978); there may have been closure in-between these years, but the evidence is scanty and difficult to interpret. Hopkins suggests 20,000 years as the most likely time.

Insight
Paleoanthropology— What Does a Fossil Say?

Fossils don't speak. They are only bits of bone that have been turned to stone. But hominid fossils are the remains of humans and their close ancestors. It is important to know when our evolutionary lineage developed its most distinctive features.

The most distinctive thing about us is our culture. And of all the parts of human culture, language is the main thing that sets us apart from other living forms. As we shall see in chapter 13, language molds the way in which we view our world. If we could decide what fossils could and could not speak, we would have made an important advance.

Evolutionary biologists have wrestled with this problem for the greater part of a century. Paul Broca, a nineteenth-century anatomist, maintained that there was a speech center in the brain that was visible as a point. "Broca's Point" was the name given to a particular impression made by that feature on the inside of the skull. If a skull had Broca's Point, that individual, when alive, could speak.

But this was shown to be unreliable. Variations in the presence of Broca's Point among the skulls of recent humans showed that this feature was unrelated to the ability to speak. Other attempts to find skeletal markers indicating speech have likewise failed.

The controversy goes on. Most paleoanthropologists feel that the australopithecines lacked speech because of the analysis of the brain as inferred from the size and shape of the skull. But what about the first *Homo sapiens?* Could the Neanderthals speak? Did they have a language?

The majority of anthropologists feel that the evidence of culture among Neanderthals indicates speech. They say that humans who

buried their dead and regularly placed a bear skull with the corpse must have had a world of symbolic meaning that required speech.

But others disagree. Lieberman and Crelin (1971) have analyzed the vocal tract of Neanderthal skulls using a series of elaborate methods. They have compared the Neanderthals with modern humans of various ages and with other primates. They conclude that, while the phonetic ability of Neanderthal was more advanced than that of other primates, Neanderthal could not produce the full range of modern human speech.

We will never know whether Neanderthals spoke. They certainly communicated, but with human speech? Carlisle and Siegel (1974) have criticized Lieberman and Crelin on several technical matters and have concluded that their analysis was invalid. The subject remains a matter of controversy.

Whatever the precise time, it seems that humans didn't simply "cross" into the New World, but in fact lived on the land bridge, which was several hundred miles wide at its maximum. They then spread eastward until they were in what is now Alaska and either followed large animals into central Canada or stayed along the coasts, living from the sea (Laughlin 1963). By 9,000 B.P. the land bridge was gone, and any further migrations had to cross some expanse of water.

Summary

1. The evolution of the hominid line begins with the first appearance of the Primates as small prosimian-like creatures in the Old and New Worlds during the Cretaceous and the subsequent Paleocene (early Tertiary). There followed a radiation that gave rise to the modern prosimians as well as the higher Primates.

2. During the Miocene, a varied genus of Old World anthropoids, *Dryopithecus,* lived in tropical and subtropical areas of Africa, Asia, and Europe. This genus gave rise to modern great apes, and some of its species also may have been among the earliest hominids. Probably in response to gradual deforestation, the early hominids adapted in their diets and locomotion, with accompanying morphological adaption. The earliest known hominid genus is called *Ramapithecus,* though it is not accepted as such by all authorities.

3. Hominid evolution during the late Pliocene (end of the Tertiary) and early Pleistocene is manifested by the australopithecines of Africa and possibly Asia. This stage of evolution is characterized by still small brains, though larger than those of great apes; upright posture, though not yet fully evolved; and a simple, though widespread, material culture.

4. Following the australopithecines, hominid evolution is represented by three trends: (1) rapid evolution of the brain; (2) a more gradual change in the morphology of the face and teeth; and (3) a steady increase in the complexity and efficiency of cultural adaptations.

5. *Homo erectus* was followed by *Homo sapiens* and the attainment of a modern skeletal morphology by 30,000 to 40,000 years ago. The cyclic advance and retreat of the glaciers during the Pleistocene imposed a varying set of environmental pressures and stimuli that accelerated the course of biological and cultural change.

6. The final movement of the hominids, into the New World and Australia, occurred just after the appearance of morphologically modern populations. Land bridges played an important role in these movements. The Americas, in particular, were peopled across the Bering Straits.

Suggested Readings

Gavan, James A. *Paleoanthropology and Primate Evolution*. Dubuque: William C. Brown Company Publishers, 1977.
  A readable survey of the major stages of hominid evolution.

Kennedy, Kenneth A.R. *Neanderthal Man*. Minneapolis: Burgess Publishing Co., 1975.
  A modern synthesis of the wide range of information available on this population. The author covers both the fossil evidence and its implications.

Pilbeam, David. *The Ascent of Man: An Introduction to Human Evolution*. New York: Macmillan, 1972.
  A detailed, factual account of the fossil evidence of hominid evolution.

Sarma, A. *Approaches to the Study of Paleoecology*. Dubuque: William C. Brown Company Publishers, 1977.
  The author covers the ways in which anthropologists date and reconstruct the past.

Simons, Elwyn L. *Primate Evolution: An Introduction to Man's Place in Nature*. New York: Macmillan, 1972.
  This analysis of evolutionary changes covers all of the Primates, but is especially good on the nonhominid ones.

Tobias, Phillip V. *The Brain in Hominid Evolution*. New York: Columbia University Press, 1971.
  The author covers, in a well-written book, the evidence for evolutionary changes in the hominid brain.

Glossary

fauna   A term referring collectively to animal life.

flora   A term referring collectively to plant life.

mandible   The lower jaw.

maxilla   The upper jaw.

Mousterian   A Middle Paleolithic tool tradition particularly identified with Neanderthal populations.

paleoecology   The science that seeks to determine the environments existing in the past.

paleontology   The science that studies the life that existed in the distant past.

pebble tools   The earliest recognizable stone tools made by hominids.

radiometric dating   The determination of the antiquity of some past fossil by means of the study of radioactive decay.

7

The Emergence of Culture

Introduction

The unfolding of human biological ancestry is a fascinating story of the interactions between an evolving lineage of primates who were to become hominids and finally human. It is the story of a series of responses to environmental stresses and to environmental opportunities. And it is a story of immense scientific import, for an understanding of our biological nature depends directly on an understanding of our evolutionary heritage.

But our biological evolutionary past is only half the story. As humans have evolved as physical beings, we have also changed as behavioral beings, developing a particular mode of behavior called "culture" and elaborating this into a complex of activities, understandings, and beliefs that define us as human. While the world of the twentieth century sets us apart from all other species with astonishing clarity, the record of evolution, with equal clarity, presents a picture of the gradual emergence of human culture over millions of years.

It is this emergence of culture that will concern us in this chapter, for just as forcefully as our biological evolution, it helps us to understand what it is to be human. In his book *The Problem of Life,* C. U. M. Smith tells us:

> On the one hand we are presented by the physical anthropologist and the primatologist with a mass of evidence indicating that man's lineage may be traced back to . . . the African Miocene. . . . On the other hand we are shown by the cultural anthropologist and the archeologist evidence—paintings in the Altamiran caves, the dwelling-places and utensils at Jarmo and Mount Carmel —which we instantly recognize as the work of people like ourselves. The first group of experts shows us the "exterior," the second the "interior." The first shows us skulls, bones, teeth—comparative anatomy; the second shows us "spirit." It is the latter we instantly recognize as human. (Smith 1976:10)

Those anthropologists who show us the "humanity" we share with the past are the archeologists, and it is their research that we will summarize in this chapter.

Archeology and the Study of Prehistory

All anthropologists have a knowledge of archeology, and many anthropologists were first attracted to the field through an interest in the societies of the past. To those who decide that the romance of archeology is irresistible, the test is immediate. One of the authors was drawn into the field this way and as a student soon found himself excavating a living site in the mountains of western Mexico not far from Durango. Those of us working at the site soon learned that, rather than romanticizing about the former inhabitants, we would literally dig into their past. But not with a pick and shovel. Hours were spent with a small brush and a tiny probe, uncovering

—without disturbing—some potentially important feature. More likely than not, this turned out to be a shard, or fragment of a pottery vessel. In fact, there were so many shards and so little else that we concluded that this site had been one where people spent their time breaking pots. The respite from this activity was hardly respite—it involved sifting everything that had been dug and discarded through a fine-mesh wire screen just in case anything (perhaps yet another potsherd) had been missed.

Why should anyone want to do this? For the same reasons that we have also suffered with dysentery further south in Mexico or brought 200 samples of saliva and urine out of the Amazon jungle. By painstaking observation of such improbable data as potsherds, archeologists have been able to piece together the structure of ancient societies, to reconstruct many of the ways in which societies have interacted with each other and with their environments, and to provide a perspective on culture from as broad a vantage point as possible.

Archeology as Anthropology

Archeology is similar to history in its delineation of sequences of past events and its interpretation of their importance. But there are differences as well. Most obvious to the casual observer is that historians deal with written records while archeologists focus on *prehistory:* the study of societies prior to their development of writing.

More important than this is the fact that archeologists are anthropologists and are studying culture. The differences are not in the objectives but in the nature of the data available for analysis. As Deetz notes, archeologists are "concerned with the way in which man's behavior is reflected in the objects he makes" (Deetz 1967).

Archeological Evidence

The archeologist studies "evidence" that usually is material recovered from archeological **sites,** places where human activity occurred. Sites often are where people lived, but they also may be where animals were slaughtered or where other activities occurred, such as a place where a particularly useful type of stone was quarried.

Archeological evidence is analyzed just as a paleontologist analyzes a fragment of bone. Sometimes this evidence is an **artifact,** something that was made by a person (though it now may be broken). The evidence is compared in order to ascertain relationships, similarities, and variations. It is also analyzed spatially; that is, in relation to its location and the locations of other artifacts or features.

But many archeologists go beyond this view of evidence and include other sources of information in their body of data. By observing or by utilizing others' observations of living people, archeologists can incorporate ethnographic information into their studies and broaden their scope. By observing how native peoples of today make clay pots, archeologists are able to infer a great deal about the techniques that were used in making the pots they excavate.

We cannot do justice here to the complexities and the sophistication of archeological analysis. We can only note that the range extends from the intensive study of a single shard—what is its composition? what is its temper (the substance added to the clay to strengthen it)? how was it decorated? what kind of vessel was it? how similar is it to other specimens? —to the analysis of an entire site. One such site is Tikal (*tee-KAHL*), a gigantic Mayan ceremonial center in the Peten, a district of Guatemala in the lowland jungles of the Yucatan peninsula. More than ten years of excavation and study by a large team of archeologists from the University Museum of the University of Pennsylvania has permitted the reconstruction of Tikal. At its center are huge, thousand-year-old temples and dwellings for priests and ceremonially important persons. On the periphery lived the thousands of common people whose energies went into supporting the emphasis upon ritual. Not only has the reconstruction of Tikal shown us the structure and arrangement of a major social and cultural complex, it has also helped in characterizing the Mayan civilization of Guatemala and Honduras as one in which ritual, belief in a supernatural, and the dominance of a priestly class were themes around which an entire society was organized.

Archeological Dating

Archeologists are faced with the same problems as human paleontologists in assigning ages to artifacts and sites. They use radiocarbon dating extensively to supplement and anchor in time the various sorts of sequences. These sequences may consist of the slow changes in the style of a particular type of pottery or the manufacture of particular types of stone tools. *Cross-dating* may be carried out by equating certain sites in the same region that contain the same artifacts or the same styles or design. Pleistocene archeologists, for instance, make use of geological information provided by changes in water level and beach lines; and all archeologists carefully study the fauna and flora excavated at sites.

Archeological Interpretation

In one sense there is very little to archeology. The archeologist has to deal with only two kinds of evidence—objects of all kinds and their associations with each other. In another sense, however, there is a great deal to archeology, particularly when it comes to interpreting the meaning and significance of archeological evidence. (Patterson 1973:12)

In this passage, Thomas Patterson succinctly sums up one of the central problems of archeology: that of placing the rather limited range of data within the broader perspective of anthropological study. The intensive study of artifacts and their location must somehow be combined with the broader implications of their meaning within society.

Louis Larson conducted just such an analysis in his study of a large earthen mound at Etowah (*ET-oh-wah*), in northwest Georgia. This site was dated in the period just prior to the voyage of Columbus (Larson 1971). Mound C was built in several phases and had periodically been used as a base for "temples" or structures placed on what was then its top. It was also used for burials, and over 350 individual skeletons were excavated.

These burials were not randomly scattered within the mound but occurred in two clusters. Most of the skeletons were of people buried during the construction phase of the mound. The second group were burials that were "intruded" into the mound after it had been constructed. This second cluster was carefully analyzed to determine what those individuals buried in the more restricted area had in common.

Larson's analysis showed no distinction by sex or age; there were children, adults, and the aged of both sexes. This suggested that the individuals were related to each other. Furthermore, more elaborate goods were buried with the individuals in this special group and, even more interesting, there was a "repetitive pattern" in the things that were found: "the same type of headdress, axe, ear ornament . . . appear with a monotonous regularity" (Larson 1971). Even the children seemed to wear items that were similar to the adults', but scaled down in size.

From this Larson concluded that this group represented a "descent family group" set apart from the others by special burial treatment. The grave goods indicated the use of valuable objects to show their rank. This trait suggested the existence of social stratification based on some hereditary criterion.

All of this information from an analysis of burials, associated objects, and location within the site! Basing his analysis upon hard evidence and without overreaching his data, Larson demonstrated the extent to which the "limited" data of the archeologist can in fact depict a range of behaviors and social practices.

Early Evidence of Culture

The earliest evidence of hominid culture comes, as we learned in the last chapter, from the stone tools excavated by paleoanthropologists. These tools show unquestioned evidence of being shaped by human hands. Undoubtedly, for a long period of time, early humans picked up stones and other objects and used them as tools, in the same way that other primates

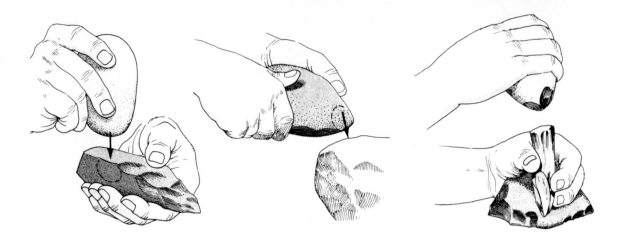

do. Furthermore, with the beginning of tool-making there must have been a long period of time in which the techniques were so simple, and perhaps experimental, that the tools cannot be distinguished from stones that are battered and "shaped" by natural agents, especially the action of water on rock. Archeologists cannot readily distinguish objects that were used without being reshaped. Nor can they study objects whose shaping was no different from that of natural forces. While this stage of human culture must have existed, it must go unstudied. If the use of an object somehow altered it in a recognizable fashion, then it can be studied. Certain kinds of abrasions, marking, or bevelling on a surface or an edge can suggest the regular use of that surface or edge and so may indicate periodic tool use. Whatever the ways in which they used the environment, these early humans were versatile in their approach to survival and must have utilized a broad range of objects and materials in nonspecific ways. While archeologists can speculate and hypothesize about such activity, we must restrict our analysis to more rigidly defined evidence: tools unquestionably made by human activity.

The Manufacture of Stone Tools

Early hominids must have manufactured tools from many materials, including the bones and horns of the animals they killed or scavenged. However, such tools are poorly preserved and cannot be studied systematically until much later in human evolution.

The earliest stone tools were produced by **percussion,** in which chips or flakes are knocked off to provide a cutting edge or a hammering surface. Percussion flaking, whose earliest known appearance is at Olduvai Gorge, persisted throughout the span of human prehistory and is still practiced among some societies today. A refinement of the percussion method involves the use of an intermediate tool such as a chisel, resulting

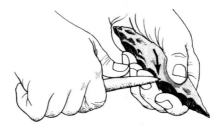

Figure 7.1
Demonstration of various techniques of making stone tools. *Left to right* The direct percussion method is shown in two drawings. Indirect percussion is exhibited in the middle drawing. A baton-like instrument is necessary for baton percussion tool making. Pressure flaking is another form of tool-making.

in *indirect percussion.* Blows may be directed with greater accuracy and a more concentrated force, resulting in a much straighter and sharper edge and a better tool.

The most sophisticated chipped stone technology is *pressure-flaking,* in which a piece of bone or antler is used to press off a tiny flake no larger than a nail-clipping. Extraordinarily beautiful and sharp tools may be made with the pressure-flaking technique. (As a graduate student, one of the authors had a professor who had mastered the art of making stone tools in this way. Each new semester, he would demonstrate the technique to his class, climaxing by shaving his face with the edge he had produced.)

Much, much later in the span of human evolution, there developed a new method of working stone—grinding. Ground stone tools, as we shall see, did not appear until a few thousand years ago. This method represented a major technological advance, since it became possible to make bowls, grinders, and other kinds of artifacts.

The selection of the proper material is important, and at first, humans made use of what they had. As their skills improved, they became more discriminating and learned the value of *flint,* or chert. This is a rock that fractures along a plane when struck, providing a smooth surface and making it possible to produce a razor-sharp cutting edge. We can readily imagine that a good tool-maker was an important person in early human societies. Good sources of flint were probably equally prized, and in fact, archeological sites show evidence of particular varieties of flint having been transported for hundreds of miles, perhaps being used as an item of trade along the way.

The Paleolithic and Its Divisions

Just as anthropologists divide an evolving lineage into species to recognize change and to create some usable categories, it is also convenient to construct *stages* of cultural development. The most widely used stages relate to the most widely distributed evidence of early culture: stone tool technology. The **Paleolithic** (*pay-lay-oh-LITH-ik*), or "Old Stone Age," covers that period from the beginning of tool-making, 2 million or more years into the past, until 10,000 B.P. During this time, flint and stone were worked only by percussion techniques, but from the beginning of this period to its end, there was a steady refinement in the technology and an increasing sophistication and specialization in the tools produced.

It is customary to subdivide the Paleolithic into three stages:

1. *Lower Paleolithic,* from the beginning of the period until 100,000 B.P. In terms of human evolution, this spans the period of the australopithecines and *H. erectus.*
2. *Middle Paleolithic,* from 100,000 to 35,000 B.P.—the period of the Neanderthals.
3. *Upper Paleolithic,* from 35,000 to 10,000 B.P.

In Europe, stone tools were recognized before the publication of Darwin's *Origin of Species.* The stages of the Paleolithic were conceived and developed in this part of the world. For decades afterward, scientists accepted the French sequence as the "human" one, and not until the middle of the twentieth century did archeologists begin to realize that certain features of it were local. In fact, as data began to accumulate from other parts of the world, it became apparent that while certain aspects seemed to be applicable across continents, cultural developments everywhere were characterized by regionalization, diversity, and adaptation to local environmental conditions. Because of this, it is important to realize that even though the following discussion may at times imply uniformity, Paleolithic artifacts show an impressive range of cultural variability. As much as possible, we will attempt to avoid giving any false sense of uniformity.

Hominid Culture of the Lower Paleolithic

The Australopithecines

The oldest recognizable stone tools were made by the australopithecines. As we have learned, these pebble tools were made from round, water-worn stones, generally as large as a hen's egg. The stones were smashed against something—a boulder or perhaps another pebble—knocking off a series of chips until a crude edge was formed. These tools were *unifacial,* or edged on one side only, which is a distinguishing feature of early hominid tools. They are called "choppers." (See Figure 7.2.)

The only sequence of tool development we have for this period is from the Olduvai Gorge, where the record spans more than 2 million years.

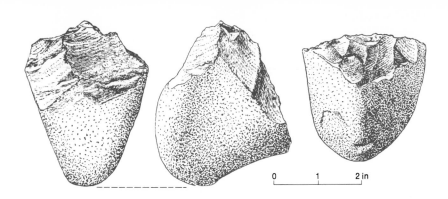

Figure 7.2
Oldowan pebble tools.

0   1   2 in

In summarizing this sequence, Fagan (1977) delineates three "types of tool kits" found successively there. The first, from the lower levels, is the Oldowan (*OLD-oh-wan*) tradition, which was discussed in chapter 6. The second is a bit more advanced and dates from about 1.5–1 million years ago; included in this second "tool kit," in addition to pebble tools, are some more pointed choppers as well as a rare, and not too well-made, new type of tool, called a hand axe. At about 1 million years B.P., or a little older, a third "tool kit" appears, which is more advanced and contains a larger proportion of hand axes.

Thus, Olduvai Gorge strongly suggests that, at least at that location, subsequent cultural stages associated with *Homo erectus* developed out of the australopithecine Oldowan tool kit.

Australopithecine sites have also yielded other tools, or stones showing evidence of hominid activity. They seem to have been used as hammerstones, chisels, scrapers, perhaps in a variety of ways by individuals slaughtering and preparing animals. The sites themselves are often a hardened level of earth indicating a continued usage: an occupation site or a living floor. These early hominids were not simply a horde of creatures wandering about but a group living for a short time at a recognizable site.

The final bit of archeological evidence relating to australopithecine culture is the discovery at one site of stones that do not occur naturally in the area. That is, individuals had the forethought to find a stone that was appropriately shaped, or of a desirable material, and carry it somewhere else to make it into a pebble tool or use it in some activity. This might not sound like much to us but, in terms of cultural beginnings, it indicates an impressive level of thought and planning.

To what extent can we reconstruct australopithecine culture? The data provided by archeologists present a picture of small family bands of individuals, following the movements of the animals they hunted and moving with them in conjunction with wet and dry seasons. Their tools were simple but well adapted to the needs of the group; having tools at all may very well have given them the ability to exploit fully the animals they hunted for food, using the bone and horn to make other tools, and perhaps even using the hides. Movement along the open savanna required cooperation to provide protection against predators. Butchering and tool-making suggest that a division of labor may have existed, which implies the possibility of roles and maybe even of social status.

The rules of behavior that comprise our culture require learning, much of which takes place during childhood. We have already discussed, in chapter 5, the bond that exists between a young primate and its mother. This bond establishes the essential condition for the transmission of culture: the relationship between an adult and an immature individual. Among higher primates, bonding is reinforced by an extended period of growth and development, with the young individual dependent on adults for longer periods of time. In living human groups, sexual maturity is attained, on the average, no younger that 12 years of age and as late as 18, providing a period of immaturity that may encompass 20 to 25 percent of the life span!

To what extent did the australopithecines display this extended developmental period? Answering this question necessitates an innovative approach, such as that developed by Alan Mann in his study of the South African australopithecines (Mann 1975). The molar teeth are the last to erupt. In living humans their eruption is spread over twelve or more years; the first molars begin to erupt at about 6 years of age and the third molars (or wisdom teeth) come in at about 18 years or even later. In pongids the molars erupt much more quickly over a much shorter span of time, as a consequence of their shorter period of development.

Mann examined the molar teeth of the immature South African australopithecines. Since the teeth of hominids begin to wear down as soon as they can function in chewing, especially if the diet is gritty and coarse, an extended period of molar development would result in a greater difference in tooth wear among the molars of a single individual. The molars of the australopithecines fit the pattern of differential wear expected of hominids. While we cannot be certain of just how long it took an australopithecine child to "grow up," we do know that the period of dependence was lengthened, as in a hominid, more than in the pre-hominid pattern. This clearly suggests that learning was an important means for transmitting culture among this group of early hominids.

Homo erectus

The appearance in the fossil record of skulls classed as *H. erectus* corresponds in time to the appearance of a new level of stone tool technology. At Olduvai Gorge can be seen the developmental sequence leading from the Oldowan to this new level called the Acheulian (*ah-shoo-LEE-un*) industry, the tool assemblage of *H. erectus*.

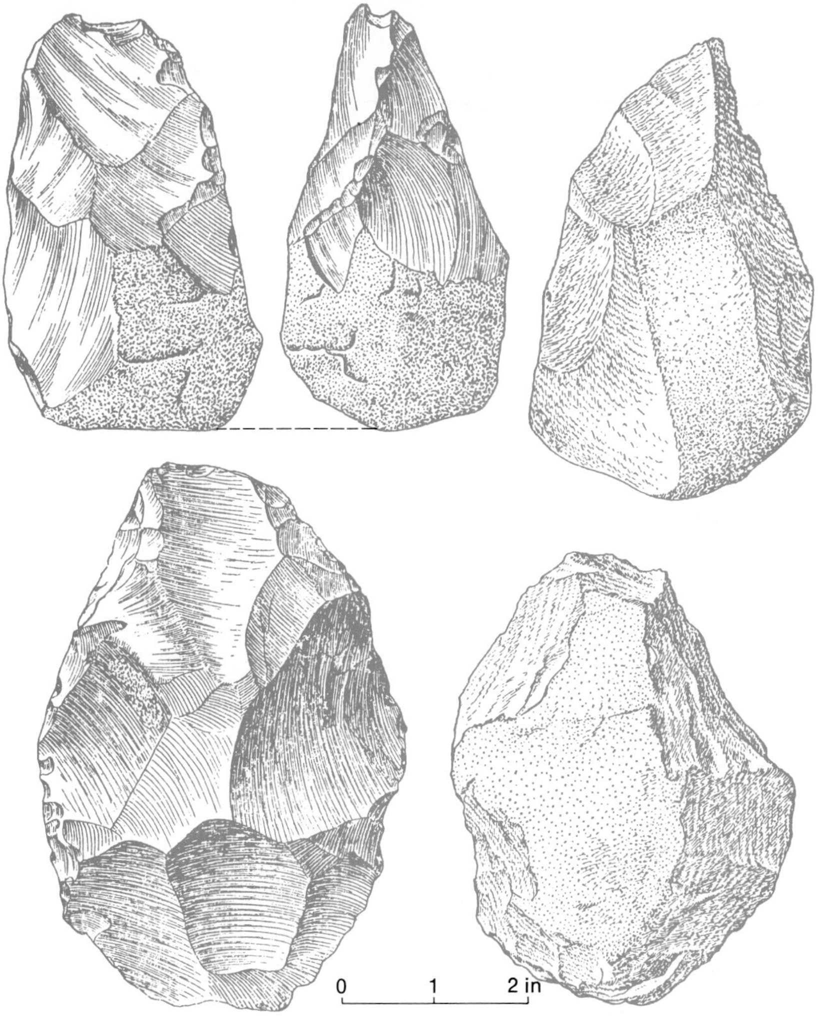

Figure 7.3
Early hand-axes from Africa
and Europe.

The most characteristic feature of the Acheulian tool kit is the *hand axe,* a bifacial (*by-FAY-shul*) tool shaped by blows on both sides. The result is a sharper and more efficient tool, and apparently an adaptive one—hand axes persist in the archeological record for over half a million years, with a steady record of improvement in their manufacture.

Hand axes (Figure 7.3) were general-purpose tools and could be used as hammers, to gouge or cut, or even as an awl. The earlier ones were larger than those that appeared later, but the similarity is both striking and impressive, indicating a tradition that not only lasted as long as it did but spread over much of the Old World.

Along with the appearance of a new species and a new level of stone tool technology, we find at this time additional evidence of more efficient

Figure 7.4
Acheulian tools from East
Africa.

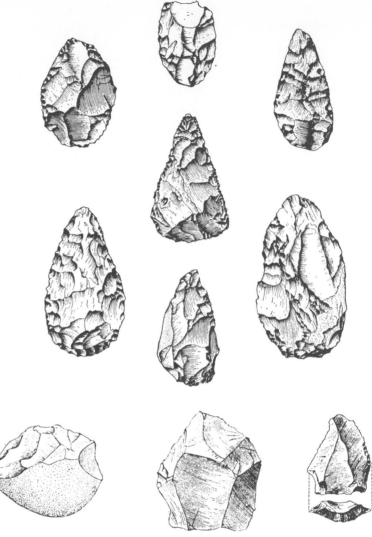

Figure 7.5
Soan chopping tools from
Asia.

0   1   2 in

cultural adaptations. The variety of animals killed for food, as well as the sizes of the animals, increases strikingly. The sites of Torralba (northeast of Madrid, Spain) and nearby Ambrona, were butchery sites where the remains of at least thirty elephants have been found along with dismembered skeletons of wild horses, deer, rhinoceros, and wild oxen! Traces of fire, artifacts or stone and even wood fragments all point to highly organized activities carried out by these Lower Paleolithic hunters.

Archeologists who have excavated at these sites have been able to reconstruct some of the butchering techniques. The meat was carefully stripped away from the bones and apparently taken elsewhere to eat. Some of the bones show burning, suggesting cooking and perhaps curing of the meat. At Torralba at least ten different occupations have been documented, indicating an important location with a succession of groups who worked there.

Hand axes from this time period have been excavated across Africa, Europe, and western Asia, although geographical variability begins to appear. Pebble tools persisted in parts of Europe. Quite possibly, Europe was a "cultural backwash," a peripheral area into which new traits spread later than elsewhere. Hand axes did not spread into east Asia. Instead, "chopping tools" characterized *H. erectus* populations living in what are now China, southeast Asia, and parts of north and central India. These Asian peoples are classified into the *Soan* culture. Their chopping tools (Figure 7.5) are simpler in design and in manufacture than the Acheulian hand axes.

Despite geographical variation in material culture, and despite the rather simpler chopping tools of the Soan people, there is no indication that either culture was superior or inferior in development. Fire also was used in east Asia. One of the most important sites is near the town of Choukoutien in China, not far from Peking, where a rich series of archeological remains, spanning tens of thousands of years, has been found. The evidence indicates humans who made use of their environments in much the same ways as did *H. erectus* of the Acheulian culture.

Culture of the Middle and Upper Paleolithic

As culture systems increased in complexity, they became more diverse, and archeologists working from the Middle Paleolithic onward must make distinctions between those changes that occurred everywhere and the localized traditions characterizing certain regions.

The most significant feature in the improving technology of stone tools was the increased emphasis on the use of flakes. At first, flakes had been removed to prepare a flint core for use as a hand axe. Now the

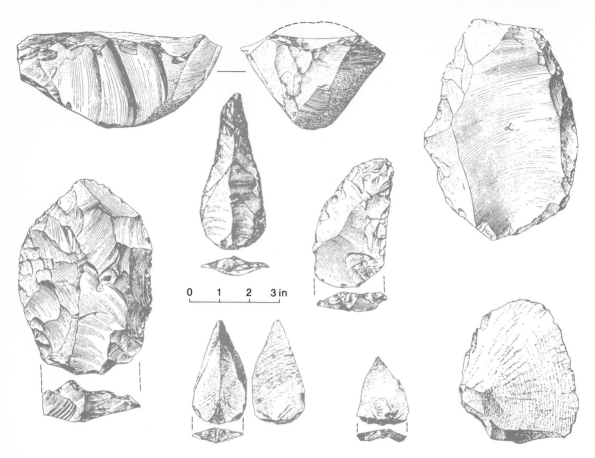

Figure 7.6
Levalloisian and Levallois-ian-like tools.

flakes themselves were used, and so new techniques were developed to allow more usable flakes to be removed from the core. One particular method, called the Levallois technique, is known from France southward into north Africa and eastward to southwest Asia (see Figure 7.6). This tradition, which dates from about 200,000 B.P., probably spread from group to group by the process of **diffusion,** the spread of ideas.

Tools in the Levalloisian tradition were made by carefully preparing a core, removing small flakes so as to produce a "striking platform." The platform was then struck a single crosswise blow, removing a large, sharp flake. This flake was often made sharper by later retouching or secondary flaking.

Mousterian Cultures

The best known of the Middle Paleolithic tool traditions is the Mousterian, which spread widely across much of the Old World. Hand axes persisted in the Mousterian tool kit, but they were made so carefully that it is easy

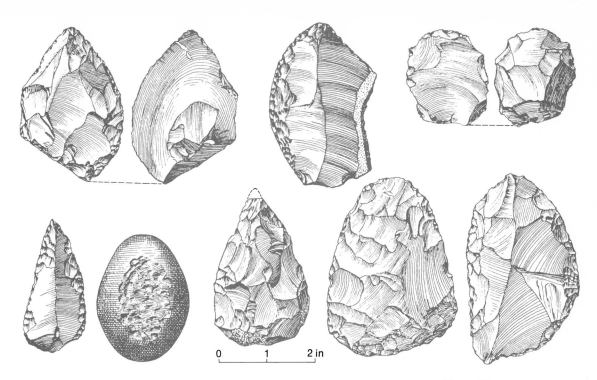

Figure 7.7
Mousterian tools.

0   1   2 in

to suppose that aesthetic considerations were becoming increasingly important. Tools were no longer "only something to get the job done," but began to take on a greater symbolic significance. "Beauty" and "style" may well have become important concepts.

Paleolithic archeologists recognize a specific cluster of traits as Mousterian and others as Levalloisian. Some traits are categorized as Levalloiso-Mousterian, as careful analysis demonstrates increasing variability. Both Mousterian and Mousterian-like traditions emphasized flake tools (Figure 7.7). Retouching the flakes produced scrapers as well as knives. The increase in the number of scraping tools indicates that these people wore some form of clothing, since hides must be carefully scraped as they are prepared.

Mousterian culture is identified with the Neanderthal stage of human evolution. By 75,000 B.P., Neanderthals had conquered and adapted to many different habitats: the tundra of glacial Europe, the forests of Africa, and the grasslands and mountains of Asia. By this time, not only were they skilled hunters, they were also expert at survival beyond the areas with rich natural resources. In the deserts of southwest Asia, archeologists have found ostrich eggs in association with Mousterian tools. Why an ostrich egg in a desert? The most logical answer is in the transport of water into and across an area where this vital resource was scarce.

The Evidence for Ritual and Belief We have stressed that archeologists are ultimately cultural anthropologists who study societies of the past. Because of this, they are involved with reconstructing as many aspects as possible of the lives of the people who inhabited a site. The inferences of high status groups at Etowah and of an emphasis on priestly ritual at Tikal are both examples of how the "stones-and-bones" of archeological data can be extrapolated to reveal beliefs, rituals, and customs.

What can we say about the Mousterian Neanderthals and their beliefs? Whatever we say must be rather more tentative and speculative—after all, Tikal, a massive center where perhaps 40,000 people lived, provides much more evidence for archeologists (Haviland 1970).

The first thing comes from the kinds of finds made during the Middle Paleolithic. Prior to that period, all finds fall into one of three classes: (1) isolated tools that were discovered somehow; (2) a skeleton of an individual killed in an accident or left where he or she died; (3) an occupation site associated with hunting. However, with the Mousterian culture of the Neanderthals, we find burials. The existence of burials indicates an awareness of death, and to be aware of death indicates a level of thought and perception beyond that which we all too often attribute to "simple cavemen."

Not only does burial indicate an awareness of death, it also indicates some relationship that existed in life. If we bury someone, it signifies that he or she has had some meaning in our lives.

Neanderthal burials frequently are found with the skulls of goats or bears surrounding the body. This has been interpreted as a "cult" based on some relationship to animals that were important as food sources. At the site of Shanidar Cave in Iraq, Ralph Solecki found the remains of a number of Neanderthals, some of whom had been buried. One individual was buried on what (upon analysis) turned out to be a bed of flowers. Another had had an arm amputated, the earliest known example of surgery.

Conclusions such as these are based on scattered bits of evidence, but they lead us to picture Neanderthals as culture-bearing peoples who had effectively adapted to a wide range of environmental conditions and had developed efficient techniques for chipping utilitarian stone implements for several different purposes. Interpersonal relationships had clearly gone beyond the level of cooperation for hunting or for defense against predators; the Neanderthals symbolized relationships in ritual acts of burial and the inclusion of grave goods that must have carried significant meaning in their lives.

The Upper Paleolithic

Upper Paleolithic cultures are associated with morphologically modern humans. Along with the scrapers, engravers, and knives of older periods,

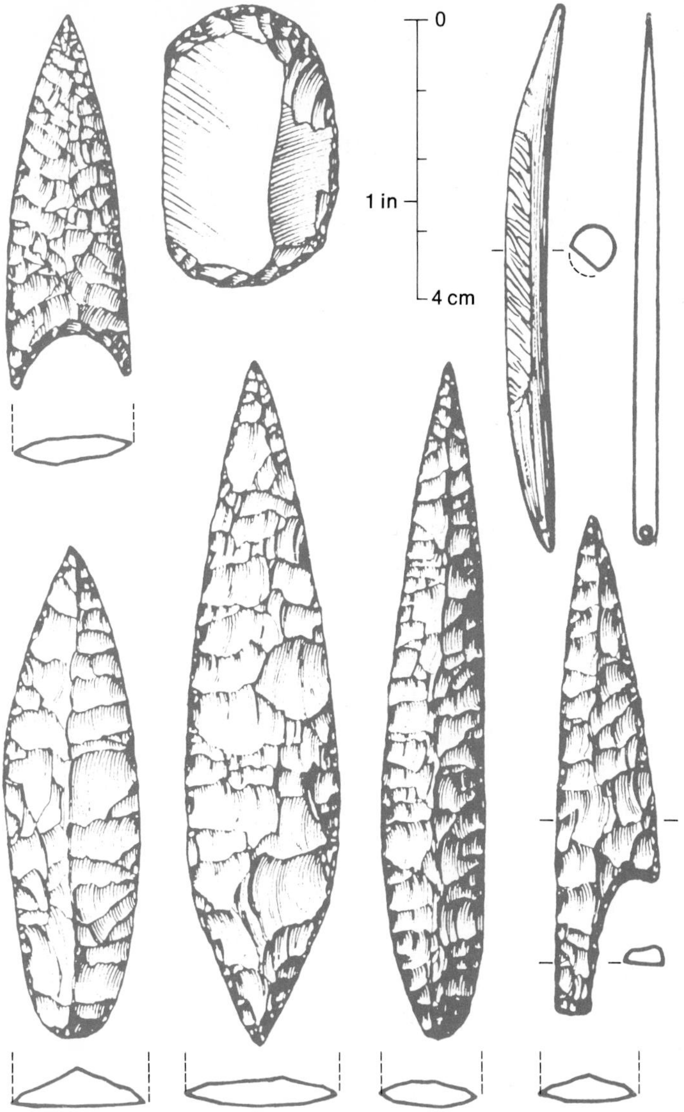

Figure 7.8
Upper Paleolithic tools.

there are superbly crafted stone blades, so elaborate and handsome that they must have been ceremonial. Some of them were more than 10 inches in length. (See Figure 7.8.)

Tools became more useful, with both more specialized tools and improvements in the older patterns. The first American Indians to penetrate into the Great Basin, the interior of western North America, were big game hunters who followed their quarry southward. One of their most characteristic stone tools was the *fluted point,* an exceptionally well-made projectile point with small flakes removed by pressure to form cutting edges. Down the center of the point ran a groove, or "flute." Besides mak-

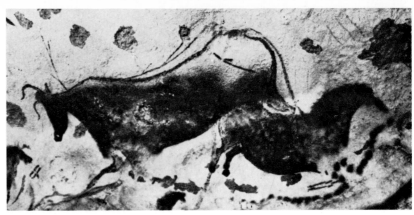

Figure 7.9
Venus figurine *below* from Europe, Hawte Gironne, France. Note the exaggerated abdominal and pelvic areas, which are suggestive of pregnancy.

Figure 7.10
Cave paintings, like the one at right, show the artistic style of early man.

ing the points distinctive, the flutes provided a channel for the blood of a wounded animal, hastening its death.

Throughout the Old and New World, local traditions proliferated, reflecting stylistic differences as well as adaptations to different kinds of environments. Ritualistic artifacts appeared—more than 60 *Venus figurines* (to which we referred in Chapter 2) have been found in Europe and Asia. These statuettes (Figure 7.9) represent female figures with the breasts and buttocks emphasized, and often with enlarged abdomens suggestive of pregnancy. They probably were fertility symbols, associated with some belief system that diffused across the area.

Other sculptured figures and bone carvings of animals were expertly executed by Upper Paleolithic artists. Most famous of all are the cave paintings (Figure 7.10), which depict animals that were hunted. Some are realistic while others show artistic style and even fantasy. The best known paintings are from the Dordogne River valley of southern France, but equally excellent ones come from the caves and rock shelters of Australia and South Africa.

The Transition to Food Production and Village Life

The Mesolithic

As the Pleistocene drew to a close, the topography of the earth began to change. Although this change was so gradual as to be almost imperceptible as a process, when viewed from the perspective of the twentieth century, it was as dramatic as almost anything that has happened in the long history of the earth. Along with changes in topography came changes in the distribution of animals and plants. As human groups adapted to these changes, culture entered a new phase. This phase began as a new strategy for exploiting food sources—farming and the domestication of animals.

This phase began as a new strategy for exploiting food sources—farming and the domestication of animals.

Communities became larger, people more sedentary, social structure more complex, and the rate of technological development faster.

As the glaciers retreated to about the positions they occupy today, climates throughout the world became milder and more regular, without the marked seasonality of the past. The ranges of many animal species that had been primary food sources were altered and, more often than not, reduced. Gone were the familiar animals of the Ice Age: the saber-tooth tiger and the mammoth. People developed new adaptive strategies less dependent on the huge herds of horses, reindeer, and bison. They took advantage of the new food base, utilizing as foods plants and animals that allowed the group to travel less and that could also support an increasingly populous human species. In fact, as the numbers of humans increased, the mobility of individual groups became more restricted, while the disappearance of the big game herds focused their attention more and more on the rivers and streams and the great variety of edible plants as sources of food. As people stayed in one place for longer and longer periods of time, they became more and more sedentary, until occupation sites became permanent settlements. This period immediately following the Paleolithic is called the Mesolithic.

Why Farming?

As scientists, anthropologists are interested in the causes of events or phenomena, and so archeologists are particularly interested in the causes of farming, in view of its far-reaching effects. Unfortunately, *cause* is not an easy concept to discuss, and even less easy to demonstrate from the record of the past. Several theories have been proposed (during three decades of analysis) to account for the development of this method of food exploitation throughout much of the world. We may think of these theories in terms of the "cause" each one hypothesizes: (1) the *environment;* (2) the *culture;* (3) the *population;* (4) the *system.*

The Environment The environment as a cause of the development of food production was the basis for the earliest theory on the subject, proposed by the British archeologist V. Gordon Childe (1936). Childe saw the rise of farming as a "revolution" and attributed it to changes in the environment, which were thought to have been relatively rapid at that time. According to Childe's "Oasis Theory," the Near East began to dry out (*dessicate*) at the end of the Pleistocene, causing both animals and humans to begin to congregate in clustered groups where water could be found (oases). An interrelationship developed, as humans depended on the animals and the animals came to depend on the humans for food. This led to the development of agriculture and to a dependence on animal domestication. The advantages of food production over hunting led to a rapid increase in population—to the settlement of towns and ultimately cities.

Childe and his colleagues located the center of plant and animal domestication in the "Fertile Crescent," a well-watered strip of land stretching from Egypt east and north into Iraq (Figure 7.11). Legend, of course, has it that the Garden of Eden was at the juncture of the Tigris and Euphrates rivers, within the Fertile Crescent.

To Childe, therefore, farming was a response of humans to environmental changes. This response was so successful that it diffused rapidly throughout the world and became the dominant mode of human cultural adaptation wherever the environment was suitable.

The Culture   In the 1950s, Braidwood proposed an alternate theory: that agriculture was a consequence of a diversified and elaborated cultural inventory (Braidwood and Howe 1962). Culture had developed more and more complex technologies, while people had become more and more innovative, responding to the potentials in their environment. Instead of the Fertile Crescent, Braidwood hypothesized that agriculture first developed on the overlooking hilly flanks of the mountains in the Near East. It was there, he argued, that grains and wild grasses grew, and so it was there that humans experimented with their environments.

The Population   The "environment" and "culture" theories were based upon the notion that agriculture was a "marvelous invention" that gave people the ability to exploit their environments in a new way, in a sense to "get more for less." But is this so? In the 1960s some archeologists began to look at just how much one puts into farming in return for what one gets out of it.

One of the incessant questions that plagues anthropologists when they discuss their work among various tribal groups is, "What do the people *do*?" Many of us have heard someone say, "I wouldn't want to be one of them! They must have a damned hard life scratching out a living in those little manioc gardens." The fact is that most people in preagricultural societies don't work very hard at all, and our answer to the question is, "They spend most of their time sitting around and talking!"

It is just such concerns that led archeologists to reevaluate the notion of the glorious advantages conferred by farming. Agriculture is certainly productive. After all, the United States and Canada could make up the world's food shortage through intensive agriculture. But what was it like initially? It has been shown (Price 1971) that farming is *labor-intensive*—a lot of energy is expended in relation to the return. Peasants must work very hard to obtain a sufficient yield from their plots.

Why, then, would people choose farming as a way of life? What would cause them to take up a way of obtaining food that meant more and

Insight
Archeological Analysis—
How Good Is Primitive Technology?

Threshing machines move through fields of grain at an amazing rate to one unfamiliar with modern farming. Modern technology has automated farming, increased productivity, and changed today's farmer from a worker to an administrator.

But what of the Natufians of the Mesolithic? Just how much more efficient was their technology at harvesting wild grasses than the methods that preceded them?

Dr. Jack R. Harlan answered this question for himself. Working in Turkey, he stripped the grain of wild wheat from its stalks, simulating the way it must have been done in the earliest stages of systematic collecting. Harlan found that he could pick 5½ pounds per hour this way. But he could not keep this up; his hands became raw and he couldn't use them.

Harlan next set a sickle blade that was 9,000 years old into a wooden handle and went about his chores in the same way as an early harvester of wild grain must have done. His yield went up by 20 percent, to 6½ pounds per hour. He calculated that a single family using this method could harvest more grain in a three-week season than they could eat in a year. Early technology, then, was effective and adaptive. It permitted a greater yield of food and must have been important in creating the conditions that led to a shift from hunting to farming and the settled way of life that accompanied it.

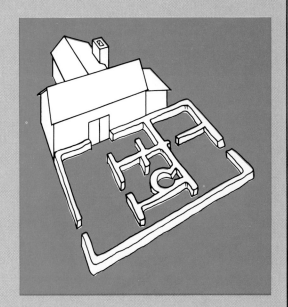

harder work? Esther Boserup has formulated a hypothesis (Boserup 1965) that at the end of the Pleistocene, the growth rate of the human species had begun to increase dramatically, causing increasing pressure of population on its resources. Lewis Binford (1968) has further developed this by postulating population increase as the cause of farming, which was a necessary response to population pressure.

The three theories discussed so far each imply a different cause for food production and animal domestication. In addition, they imply a different sequence of events following the initial stages of farming, events that led to towns and to urbanization. In this respect, Childe and Braidwood are generally similar in that they see farming as a "release"—people were released from their dependence on hunting and following animal herds. A few could feed many, and consequently others could develop their own means of expression, leading to art, to writing, to all of the things we associate with urbanization and civilization.

The population pressure theory, on the other hand, leads to the notion that farming required more labor and energy, which as the population increased, spiraled upward in a vicious cycle. The development of more complex social systems could therefore be viewed as a means whereby this upward cycle could be harnessed, regulated, and controlled.

The System   What if all the theorists were right? What if the development of farming was not based on a single cause, but on an interrelated network of factors that affected each other, exerted feedback on each other, and showed considerable local diversity? In other words, what if the development of food production resulted from the interactions of particular systems of populations and their environments?

Coe and Flannery (1964) emphasize that one should analyze the *microenvironments,* the immediate surroundings of social groups. Then one can postulate four different ways that agriculture could have been invented.

First, a group might have invented agriculture by inducing seasonal plants to give regular yields. Suppose the group had two food sources: one that was continuous the year round, and another that was only seasonal. Say also that they wanted to "regularize" the yields of the seasonal food. They could do so only by domesticating it, and thereby inventing agriculture.

A second group might not have a seasonal food supply that they regularized but a wild food that gave fluctuating yields. Sometimes the group went hungry, sometimes they had abundant food. Living in feast and famine for thousands of years may have led the people to control the yields at a satisfactory level. Again, the answer was *domestication = agriculture.*

Coe and Flannery point out that it wasn't just agrarian groups who invented agriculture. There is evidence that maritime groups also did so. Why? Because they were sedentary. They lived off a continuously available diet of shellfish and fish and gradually tamed the wild grasses in the natural setting. Agriculture was invented as a by-product of their settled way of life.

Finally, agriculture may have been invented under pressure as peoples tried to recreate an older way of life in a new environment. Perhaps a group moved away from its parent population and tried to exploit a poorer environment. Whereas the older population had lived in a relatively lush environment, the migratory group had to secure their food supply by increasing the yields of the wild grasses and cereals around them. How? Again, by taming and domesticating the plants and animals.

Coe and Flannery's hypothesis is attractive, as we see, because it doesn't force us to accept a single cause that operated everywhere. Instead, a range of causes may be seen for the range of appropriate environments. Nor does this hypothesis necessitate the "invention" of agriculture in a single nuclear area from which it rapidly diffused throughout the world. Where the environment was appropriate, the population sufficient, and the flow of ideas steady, food production became a natural developmental stage in the process that began back in the Pleistocene and continued to operate even after its development.

Summary

1. Archeologists study human prehistory using the evidence they excavate, inferring cultural and social behavior as they can.

2. The earliest evidence of material culture is the stone tools made by knocking chips off of flint cores. The earliest period is called Paleolithic (Old Stone Age), which lasted from 2 million to 10,000 years B.P.

3. Australopithecines made pebble tools, as part of the culture called Oldowan. Evidence indicates that their culture was transmitted to the young socially through an extended period of development, as it is among modern humans.

4. Hand axes are found in the last half of the lower Paleolithic in Europe, Africa, and west Asia. In east Asia, choppers are more commonly found.

5. Paleolithic hunters killed and butchered elephants and other large animals. Flakes were utilized as knives and scrapers in dressing the animals and perhaps in preparing the hides for clothing.

6. The culture of the Neanderthals is usually called Mousterian. During this time we find the first evidence of nonmaterial culture—burials and objects buried with the dead.

7. As the Pleistocene ended, the environment changed and humans cames to depend less upon large animals for food. They became sedentary and began to depend more on vegetable foods.

Along with a more settled life came the domestication of animals and the development of agriculture. Four theories have been advanced as to the causes of farming: environment, culture, population, the system. The most widely accepted one sees food production as a broad-spectrum event, growing out of the relationships of populations with their environments. The specifics of these relationships differed from place to place.

Suggested Readings

Braidwood, Robert. *Prehistoric Men*. 8th ed. Glenview, Ill.: Scott, Foresman and Company, 1975.

This widely known book provides an excellent overview of archeological changes from the earliest records of human activity.

Clark, Graham. *World Prehistory. A New Outline*. Cambridge: Cambridge University Press, 1969.

The author, a well-known British archeologist, focuses on technological developments.

Patterson, Thomas C. *America's Past: A New World Archeology*. Glenview, Ill.: Scott, Foresman and Company, 1973.

This small book is very well written. It is especially useful in that it focuses on the processes of change in populations.

Wood, W. Raymond, and McMillan, R. Bruce. *Prehistoric Man and His Environments. A Case Study in the Ozark Highland*. New York: Academic Press, 1976.

This book is unusual in its specific study of the adaptations of human groups to their environment in the Ozarks. The time period spans more than 10,000 years.

Glossary

artifact   Some object made by human activity.

diffusion   The spread of culture from group to group.

Paleolithic   The "Old Stone Age," beginning with the earliest evidence of tool-making and lasting until populations began to make the transition to a more sophisticated technology.

percussion   A technique of stone tool-making in which flakes are knocked off a flint core.

site   In archeological studies, a place where human activity occurred.

Cities, States, and Civilization

Introduction

With the domestication of plants and animals, the essential conditions were satisfied for the development of large and complex societies that could give rise to states and even nations. We know that a stable subsistence base was required, which came into existence with the processes of culture change that occurred during the Mesolithic (*mez-oh-LITH-ik*), the "Middle Stone Age." But we also know that these processes resulted from a variety of interactions between populations and their ecosystems and not, as was once believed, from a single cause. Different sequences of events in different areas led to civilization by different paths. Whereas, in the preceding chapter, we spoke of a process, we now turn to the history of cultures.

However, we will still examine the parallels that do exist in developments among the various regions. After all, one of the questions we have posed more than once in considering evolution and cultural development is to what extent there are general evolutionary changes as opposed to responses to local conditions.

As we consider larger and increasingly complex societies, we quickly find that the nature of the archeological evidence changes dramatically. While a Paleolithic archeologist might have as his or her data set an assemblage of stone tools and some animal bones, an archeologist studying a Bronze Age city is confronted with an entirely different range of objects. Still, the culture of the Paleolithic hunter and of the Bronze Age metallurgist both must be analyzed by careful and intensive techniques. Both sets of data must be used to interpret and reconstruct culture and to describe how and why it has changed.

The Neolithic

During the Mesolithic period, as we have noted, people began to interact with their environments in different ways, leading to a greater reliance on more stable foods and less mobile animals. Mesolithic peoples harvested plants, but they harvested wild varieties, gradually bringing them more and more under control until they were domesticated. In the same way, animals were domesticated and eventually kept constantly with the people as a steady source of meat, milk, and hides.

The three major centers were (1) the Far East (China and Thailand); (2) the Near East (Africa and Asia); (3) the New World (Mexico and Peru).

The change from harvesting wild plants and grasses to planting them occurred in several centers around the world in a relatively short period of time: 10,000 to 5000 B.P. The three major centers were (1) the Far East (China and Thailand); (2) the Near East (Africa and Asia); (3) the New World (Mexico and Peru). Developments in any one of the three

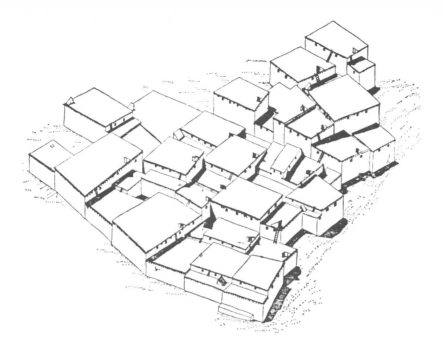

Figure 8.1
Schematic reconstruction of
a Paleolithic village in
Anatolia, *Catal Huyuk*.

major centers were independent of those in any other, so that food production and animal domestication occurred in various parts of the world as independent processes.

This period in which agriculture was developed and animals domesticated is called the *Neolithic,* or "New Stone Age." As we noted in the previous chapter, the major change in stone tool technology involved the introduction of ground stone implements, which were more efficient for grinding or pounding grains or other plants into flour and other edible forms.

Other significant changes also occurred in the Neolithic, signaling the changes made possible by the development of a stable subsistence base. These include (1) the invention of pottery; (2) permanent villages; and (3) the development of craft specializations and further divisions of labor.

The Far East: Thailand and China

One of the tasks of archeologists is to discover what happened, where, and when, but since all discoveries aren't made at one time, theories change and ideas are modified as new data are collected. The formulation of theories on the origin of agriculture, discussed in chapter 7, provide a ready example of such changes. The location of the earliest site of farming is another.

For decades archeologists have believed that the earliest known sites of agricultural communities were in the Near East. This belief persisted until only recently, when Chester Gorman excavated a site in northern

Figure 8.2
Asia showing early agri-
cultural centers.

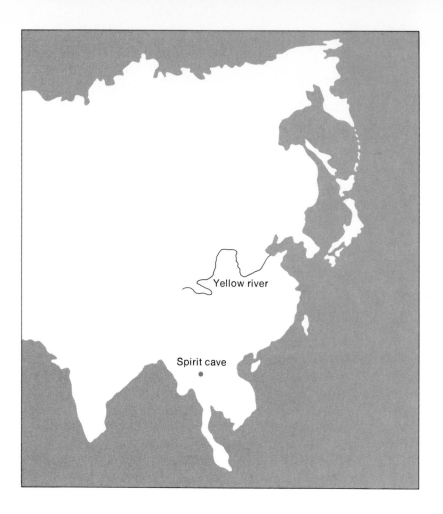

Thailand called Spirit Cave (Gorman 1971). At the lowest (i.e., the oldest) levels of Spirit Cave, Gorman was working with materials belonging to a tool assemblage called *Hoabinhian* (*ho-ah-BIN-ee-un*). At levels older than 11,000 years B.P., he found evidence of the utilization of a wide range of vegetable foods: nuts, beans, peas, peppers, and water chestnuts. This material indicates that as early as 11,000 B.P., there was a people who ate plants that seem likely to have been domesticated.

This finding is especially significant for two reasons. First, it demonstrates that food production in southeast Asia was considerably older than anywhere else in the world, by more than 2,000 years. The Spirit Cave discovery also is important because the people living at this level had not yet developed either ground stone or pottery, two other characteristics of the Neolithic. This reinforces our view that these important cultural developments did not come as a "package." Rather, they resulted from long processes growing out of interactions and adaptations of specific populations to specific environments. In our discussion of hominid evolution, we noted that culture itself evolved slowly in conjunction with morphological changes, the one providing feedback to the other. Apparently the same is true for the Neolithic. We do not suddenly find pottery-making farmers leading their domesticated animals to market—instead we find a picture of complex environmental interactions in which a change in one aspect of the environment or of the culture affected other cultural features and stimulated further change.

Spirit Cave is located in the hills of northern Thailand. If we hypothesize the development of agriculture in that region—perhaps at Spirit Cave—it then seems likely that either farmers, or the idea of farming, spread southward into the lowlands, along the well-watered river plains. People had been living there for some time in settled communities based mainly on fishing. By 8000 B.P., or perhaps even earlier, there is evidence for the development of agriculture in these lowlands with the beginning of rice cultivation.

The earliest agriculture in China has been found along the Yellow River, at about 6000 B.P., though these dates may be pushed further back with additional excavations. These groups domesticated a grass called *millet* which, though not widely used in the Western hemisphere, today feeds over 25 percent of the world's population.

We owe many items of our diet to foods domesticated in Asia. These include rice, millet, soybeans, yams, sugar cane, and bananas.

The Near East: North Africa and Southwest Asia

The transition to farming in the Near East occurred at about 9000 B.P. Before then, in the Mesolithic, a cultural assemblage known as *Natufian* (*nuh-TOO-fee-un*) stretched from southern Turkey into the Nile Valley of Egypt. The Natufians had a variety of living patterns—some lived in caves or rock shelters, while others lived in semipermanent settlements. One such site, in what is now Israel, was about half an acre in size.

Several kinds of evidence indicate that the Natufians were important in the transition to food production in this part of the world. First of all, the existence of large settlements indirectly indicates a more stable food supply than migrating herds of animals provide. But there is more. At 'Ain Mallaha in Israel, archeologists found large round pits dug into the floors of the houses—storage chambers, presumably for grains or seeds. Stone bowls and mortars indicate an increasing reliance on plant foods, and also indicate that, unlike the peoples studied in southeast Asia, the Natufians had developed ground stone implements prior to the invention of agriculture.

The final bit of evidence that the Natufians were a prefarming culture is their use of microliths—small triangular flints set into handles to form a

Figure 8.3
Map of Near East showing
Fertile Crescent.

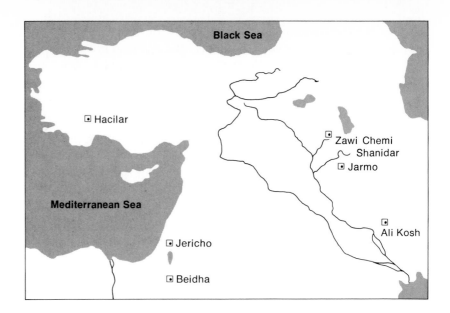

Figure 8.4
Implements from Ur, Meso
potamia; a gold cup and an
oil lamp belonging to the
Queen, 2500 B.C.

Figure 8.5
Implements from Gordion.

sickle. If one examines the edges of microliths closely, they have a patina, or shine, produced by their use in cutting and harvesting wild grains.

But the Natufians were not farmers, and the grasses they harvested were not domesticated. They were in that intermediate stage, harvesting wild plants, that precedes learning how to domesticate plants and bring them under control.

To find the earliest known evidence of farming in the Near East, we look to the important site of Jarmo, in Iraq, which was discovered and excavated by Robert Braidwood. Jarmo was occupied for thousands of years, even before farming developed there. Moving up from the lowest levels we can follow the steps taken in the transition from gathering wild plants and hunting wild animals to producing both plants and meat.

Seeds from wild wheat, charred from cooking in ancient hearths, have been found at levels from 10,000 B.P. and older, and domesticated varieties are seen at later periods. Those who dwelled in Jarmo gradually learned to bring this wild variety under control, to plant it in more convenient locations and at more convenient times, to care for it, and perhaps most important of all, to improve it so that it would yield more food for the people living there.

We owe, to these early Near Eastern farmers the cultivation of two grains that today feed much of the world's population: wheat and barley. Other foods domesticated there include olives, walnuts, almonds, dates, lentils, peas, chickpeas, and apricots.

The New World

The third center of plant and animal domestication was in the New World, where agriculture developed in two areas: Mesoamerica and highland South America. (Mesoamerica, or Middle America, includes Mexico and Central America as far south as the Isthmus of Panama.) The earliest evidence of the transition to food production has come from sites in the Tehuacán Valley, just south of Mexico City. A team of investigators headed by Richard MacNeish investigated a series of sites with occupations dating back to 12,000 B.P. As in other centers of farming, they found, for the early part of the period, a reliance on wild varieties of plants, with perhaps 65 percent of the food intake coming from plants (Patterson 1973). By 9000 B.P., the reliance upon wild plants increased and fewer and fewer bones of animals living in the area can be found at the sites.

By 7000 B.P., domesticated varieties of several food plants—corn (maize), beans, squash, chilies—are found, indicating that they were cultivated. From the remains though, it is estimated that these made up only 10 percent of the people's diet.

The major food contributed by Mesoamerican Indians is corn. Mangelsdorf, MacNeish, and Gallinat (1964) have documented the

Figure 8.6
Mesoamerica showing early
agricultural centers.

changes that occurred as varieties of wild corn, with cobs about 1-inch
long, were hybridized and gradually developed into a dietary staple for
Indians throughout this area.

Agriculture also developed in the Andes Mountains or Peru, a high
chain of mountains paralleling the Pacific coast. In the mountains, people
lived, and continue to live, at altitudes as high as 15,000 ft. above sea
level. The Andes slope precipitously to the ocean, and there human populations lived a rather sedentary existence, depending on fishing and shellfish for food. They gradually shifted to an agricultural diet about 5000
B.P., somewhat later than in Mexico.

The peoples of the New World contributed many foods to the rest of
the world. Among them are corn (maize), white potatoes, pumpkins,
squash, pinto beans, and lima beans.

The Domestication of Animals

Dogs have been domesticated since the Mesolithic, and their bones are
found at archeological sites in the Old and New World. Animal husbandry
came later, in conjunction with farming. As Table 8.1 shows, the majority
of domestic animal species have come from the Old World; the llama,
used only in Peru, was the major New World domestic animal. The earliest

Table 8.1

Selected domestic animals, with dates and locations of their earliest occurrence

sheep	Iraq	9000 B.P.
goat	Iran	8000
pig	Turkey	7500
cattle	Greece, Anatolia	7000
guinea pig	Peru	6500
llama	Peru	4000
camel	U.S.S.R.	4000
horse	U.S.S.R.	4000
water buffalo	Pakistan	4000
yak	Tibet	4000

From *The First Farmers* (Leonard 1973)

evidence comes from Iran and Iraq, where domestic varieties of sheep and goats have been found in deposits dating back to 9000 B.P. Changes in animal skeletons which show the process of domestication have been thoroughly studied.

Food Production Elsewhere

The three major centers just discussed were places where interactions among population size, environment, and human experimentation resulted in the development of agriculture. As far as we know, these developments were independent of each other. From these centers, farming techniques spread rapidly elsewhere in the world, with various peoples adapting the idea of farming and fitting it to their own environments.

In the New World, farming spread northward into North America. By the beginning of the Christian era, cultivation of corn (maize) was seen in New Mexico (the *Mogollon* peoples) and Arizona (*Hohokam*), later spreading further east and north. In the same manner, farming, especially the rice tradition, spread northward and westward in Asia.

In Africa, the technology and food production of Egypt spread southward and were adopted by the peoples of east Africa, who by 3000 B.P. had begun to cultivate the African yam. From there the technology spread westward into the central and west African forests.

Many peoples never developed farming. In some cases, the environment was simply not suitable and sufficient food could be obtained by hunting animals and collecting wild plants. This was true, for instance, of the Indians of the Northwest Coast of the United States and Canada, the Eskimos and Aleuts, and the Indians of the Great Basin of the western United States.

Consequences of Food Production and Animal Domestication

The domestication of plants and animals occurred as an outgrowth of the interactions between populations and their ecosystems. The immediate consequence was the development of a stable food base in areas where people could take advantage of growing seasons, soil types, and other considerations such as plant availability. The nature of the human-environment relationship took on a drastically new dimension when people were able actively to exploit and modify the landscape and the native plant and animal species. It is a long way from the first grains of domesticated wheat in Iraq to the grain elevators of Kansas and from the scattered remains of domestic sheep in the Near East to the Kansas City Stockyards. Nonetheless, the steady progression is graphic testimony to the ways in which human inventiveness and creativity not only produce change but at an ever-increasing pace.

There were equally drastic alterations in the biological, social, and population structure of human groups as a consequence of food production. Population increase accelerated dramatically, and a "population explosion" occurred at this time. We will discuss the *demography* of human groups in a later chapter; here we will note only that with the settling down of Neolithic peoples, the birthrates seem to have gone up markedly. This is based not only on the analysis of the sites themselves but on the observation of birthrates among simple farming and hunting and gathering groups of the present day.

Along with settled living came towns, settlements, communities, and people involved in new kinds of interaction with each other. Life was not organized around the hunt but around the day-to-day activities associated with village life. We may hypothesize the development of different kinds of social groups than had existed before. However important a family structure was to hunters, settling down permitted its extension and elaboration into larger groups.

One not so desirable consequence of village life was an increase in infectious disease.

One not so desirable consequence of village life was an increase in infectious disease, disease transmitted and spread by organisms. A mobile society of hunters does not stay in one place long enough to set up the cycle of infection and reinfection. As humans collect in settled villages, so do disease-carrying organisms. If, as is usually the case, sanitation is not ideal, organisms that are excreted from the body via the feces may be taken in orally once again, maintaining the disease through the "fecal-oral route." A larger and larger population size also provides more persons who can spread the disease. Finally, the presence of animals in close association with humans leads to another threat, the transmission of disease from animals to humans.

Thus, with settled living came greater control of the environment— but also a new set of environmental stresses. Infectious disease such as influenza, diarrhea, and tuberculosis did not become a persistent threat to humans before the Neolithic (Cockburn 1967).

Social Stratification

Social stratification refers to the organization of different groups within a society based on status. These status groups may reflect different roles, as mothers, hunters, and juveniles. In farming societies, additional categories may exist. With farming, only a segment of a group can feed the rest, and specialization and division of labor arise. Some people may be farmers, others potters, and still others serve as artists or as religious leaders.

Social stratification refers to the organization of different groups within a society based on status.

While an egalitarian society (every group valued equally) is an ideal, it seems that even early humans structured their society by status group. As more stratification developed, certain groups enjoyed more or less status, which gave them more or less access to food, to goods, or to the gods.

With stratification came the need for measures of control, for means of harnessing labor and energy, and for organizing for the common good. An old silver-back male may be the leader of a gorilla troop simply by virtue of his dominant role, but in a stratified human society considerably more complex systems must be constructed to regulate and control power.

These control systems are an outgrowth of settled village life and population increase, both of which depended initially upon the kind of food sources supplied by plant and animal domestication. Just as farming led to grain elevators and animal husbandry, so did increasing population size and density lead to complex societies, states, and nations.

The Neolithic Village

Before going on to the development of cities and civilizations, we will consider the structure and organization of the simpler Neolithic village. Anthropologists have studied villages since the beginning of the profession; frequently, the villages we study are built on the remains of earlier villages which, in turn, are on top of others, and so on downward through the earth and back in time until thousands of years have been spanned. The city of Jericho, renowned from the Old Testament, goes back in time to a Natufian settlement, dated to around 10,000 B.P. Hasanlu is a large archeological site in Iraq, excavated by Robert Dyson. Although it stretches back in time continuously for thousands of years, it is still occupied. Dyson's teams have excavated these earlier levels adjacent to the present-day village.

The earliest houses in the Near East were round huts, probably covered with animal hides. Shortly after, a rectangular form became widespread. The walls were mud, enclosing several rooms. The houses were located in clusters, which perhaps were occupied by related persons, perhaps an extended family or a lineage. Such is the case today in many parts of the world and, by analogy, we may presume the same thing for these first villages. Often the houses are grouped about an enclosure, or courtyard, in which animals could be penned.

In the New World, the same general pattern is seen: clusters of rectangular houses with mud walls, both with and without courtyards (Flannery 1976). They could be rather large; in the Oaxaca Valley of southern Mexico, early houses were typically 200 square feet or more in size. There may have been specialization of manufacturing skills in certain families, since different types of implements are found in different houses. This is significant in implying cooperation and exchange between households, which in turn would provide the foundation for larger social units.

In China, the earliest known houses were round with walls of mud and grass. As many as 600 persons may have lived at Pan-Po 6,000 years ago, in 18-by-18-foot houses constructed with below-ground floors reached by dirt ramps.

The potsherds found in these villages show evidence of the coming of decorative styles and, consequently, of more innovation in the *expressive* (rather than utilitarian) aspects of culture. The earliest decorations were made by pressing a piece of cloth into the wet clay; this pottery is called *cord-marked*. Other decorations were cut or punched into the vessel.

Civilization

The Neolithic village ultimately developed into urban civilization. Just as there was a transition from hunting and gathering to food production, so was there a transition from the mud-walled huts of Jericho and Pan-Po to the walled cities of the Near East and China. We are not speaking of an "invention" that diffused outward from some one location in all directions, like waves spreading when we throw a stone into a pool of water. We are speaking instead of a continuing complexity in the interaction of human groups with their environment.

Civilization was not—and is not—the special property of a few privileged peoples living here and there around the world. To be sure, there were centers where civilizations developed, but these centers only existed because of the people around them and, in fact, they were the focus of a huge support group. Civilizations sprang up around the world. Their cities were the cores of an entire complex of smaller groups, of villages, and of farmers who provided food for the cities, just as the American Midwest today feeds the urban centers of its east and west coasts.

So civilization is not an event, nor was it an invention. But, then, what is it? Quite simply, civilization is part of a process, a process that

Civilization is part of a process.

involves the same elements involved in the development of agriculture, but magnified and extended.

There is no single definition of civilization, and we will, in this section, indicate several ways in which the process has been defined and can be recognized. Perhaps the single most distinctive feature of civilization is the *harnessing of power*. There is control of people and control of the environment. Depending on our own interpretation of the word "control," we may view the control of people as involving their mobilization for the common good, pointing to the increasing sense of cooperation and collective activity displayed by humans over millions of years of evolution and cultural development. Or we may argue that control involves the subjugation of an entire class of persons who must work for those above them—a machine that exists only to run itself.

The State

The **state** is a unit, defined in social and political terms. Service (1975) has studied the state in relation to other levels of organization, both as a phenomenon and as an evolving entity. The state is distinguished by a strong, centralized government; that is, power is localized among a relatively small number of persons who make up the *ruling class*. This ruling class is a special, or elite, group that does not have kinship ties to the society as a whole—it is set apart.

Power is localized among a relatively small number of persons who make up the ruling class. This ruling class is a special, or elite, group that does not have kinship ties to the society as a whole—it is set apart.

The rulers have broad powers, including the power to tax, to regulate activities within the group, and even to make war on other peoples. This power requires a recognized code to define behavior and establish the existence of the rulers—a code of laws.

A state must have a large number of people interacting in ways that allow them to predict the behavior of others and to fit themselves into the pattern of the entire society. As we discussed earlier, this means social stratification. But the stratification of a state society is far more complex, more recognized, and even more formalized than in less complex societies. There are artisans who manufacture various objects for the society; farmers who plant, cultivate, and harvest food; religious leaders who interpret for the people and who intercede with higher beings; teachers who ensure the continued existence of the state by imparting "wisdom" to students. In short, if we think of a state society as an organism, it is a highly specialized one, with various parts performing well-defined and necessary functions.

States also require three other things. First, a large population is required to support such a specialized and centralized society. Accustomed to thinking of the large cities of the twentieth-century world, we tend to think that early civilizations were not very large. However, Patterson (1973) suggests that the Ancon-Chillon region, on the central coast of Peru, might have supported a population of more than 40,000 persons

First, a large population is required to support such a specialized and centralized society.

during the Huari Empire in 350 B.C., just before the rise of the Inca.

Second, states require a sophisticated technology.

Second, states require a sophisticated technology, capable of exploiting the environment in a variety of ways. Stone and pottery are not adequate as materials and so metallurgy develops. Mounds and houses are replaced by temples and by monumental architecture. Decorative designs and expressive elements become elaborate, and artistic concerns become just as important as straightforward function.

Third, states require access to a wide variety of materials and goods.

Third, states require access to a wide variety of materials and goods. Communication networks broaden and trade is widespread. Goods may be transported hundreds or thousands of miles, and regular channels of exchange become established.

The Development of Civilization

Archeologists have studied the sequences leading to the development of civilization in those places where it did occur. V. Gordon Childe argued that one of the primary prerequisites for civilization was a food surplus, since an ample, stable, and long-lasting food base was necessary to support so many specialized workers. Not only did civilization require harnessing of labor, it required the harnessing of natural resources as well. In a controversial monograph, Wittfogel (1957) has argued that irrigation was a necessity for civilization and that the control of irrigation was a major, if not *the* major, factor in the development of a stratified society. Water rights, the allocation of water resources, and the development of an irrigation technology are seen by Wittfogel as the stimuli leading to the rise of a centralized state society.

Irrigation is an important step in the continued exploitation of the environment. With it, crops are not limited to locations where they have developed and where there is sufficient moisture. Instead, crops may be cultivated in more arid regions, with water brought in by irrigation canals. In the Tehuacán Valley of Mexico, irrigation is associated with a quadrupling of population size from 1,000 to 4,000 in just a few thousand years. In the 1,500 years after this initial explosion, the population had expanded to an estimated 100,000 persons!

But was this *caused* by irrigation? Many anthropologists would answer no. For example, R. M. Adams (1960) has argued that irrigation agriculture is not a cause but a consequence of agriculture. This view is based on the wide variety of forms of irrigation found in the world of the past, from simple though extensive systems of canals to elaborate watercourses maintained by thousands of people. These elaborate systems seem not to have preceded the development of the state but to have come into being after the development of a socio-political structure that was capable of organizing the large numbers of people necessary to maintain them.

In some ways this is like the "chicken-or-egg" argument. Production of the stable food base and agricultural surplus that were needed to support a large, stratified, highly organized society demanded an efficient means of controlling water resources—hence irrigation. Rather than saying the one "caused" the other, it may be more correct to recognize the existence of a feedback network, as we have seen for other features of human development and organization. Irrigation agriculture and sociopolitical organization developed hand-in-hand, as mutually dependent processes rather than as cause-and-effect phenomena.

Metallurgy

One of the major technological innovations in the development of civilization was the perfection of metallurgy. Becoming able to make implements and other objects of hard, durable metal was an important step in exploiting the environment.

Metals found in nature were used widely by peoples from the end of the Paleolithic onward. Copper has been found at many sites and seems to have been a valuable item of trade among groups. Gold has likewise turned up among archeological assemblages.

Why these metals? Certainly not for their utilitarian qualities. Gold was too rare for widespread use and copper too soft to be of any real value as a tool. Evidently these earlier peoples stayed with the more familiar materials for their tools—stone, bone, wood—and were attracted to copper and gold more as objects of aesthetic value. Their glitter may have been responsible for their being traded.

Actual metallurgy, on the other hand, involves preparing a metal for use by a sophisticated multiphase process. First, the ore must be mined from the earth where it has been detected in deposits. Impurities must then be removed from the ore, by *smelting,* in which the ore is heated until it liquefies. Because the metal and the waste (slag) have different densities, the two can be separated. The pure metal is later melted and poured into molds, or cast, to be formed into the desired shape.

Human inventiveness is obvious in considering the steps of mining and smelting. First, there had to be the recognition of a deposit of ore and the realization of the usefulness, or perhaps simply the beauty, of the metal within it. Smelting must have taken a very long time to perfect. A very hot fire, 2,000° F or more, is needed, requiring an efficient and effective furnace.

Just as obvious as the inventiveness associated with metallurgy is the growing acceleration of technology. The stone-working of the Paleolithic lasted for 3 million years, while the development of metallurgy took but 6,000 years!

The stone-working of the Paleolithic lasted for 3 million years, while the development of metallurgy took but 6,000 years!

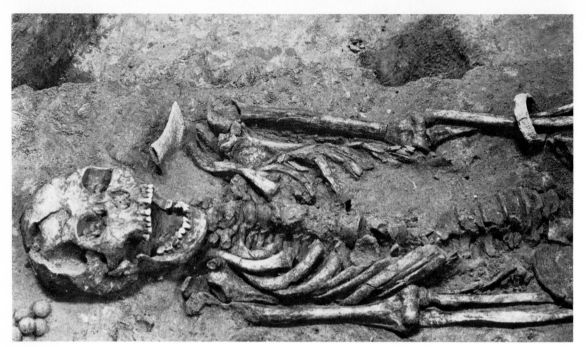

Figure 8.7
Burial from Ban Chiang, Thailand, 4500 B.C. Note the bronze bracelet still around the wrist and an axe head near the shoulder.

The Copper Age The first metal to be mined, smelted, and cast was copper. It is a soft metal, requiring a relatively low temperature for smelting. Copper also is plentiful in many areas and had been used in its natural state for some time. A pendant made from unworked copper was excavated at Shanidar Cave, in Iraq, dating to more than 11,000 B.P.

Copper smelting is known first, in the archeological record, in the Near East at about 6000 B.P., and it seems to have quickly become a major activity. Tools shortly appeared throughout the area, though they never seem to have been so widespread as to have been used by everyone. We may hypothesize that copper tools were limited to a special class or status group, perhaps as a symbol rather than as an efficient tool.

The earliest known smelting of copper is found at Tel-I-Iblis (*tell-ee-ib-LEES*), Iran. Since one stage of metalworking succeeded another, the entire sequence seems to have been earlier in the Near East than elsewhere in the world.

The Bronze Age The improvement of metallurgy resulted in the creation of the first *alloy,* or mixture of metals. About 5000 B.P., artisans began to mix copper and arsenic to form the alloy *bronze;* later tin was substituted for arsenic.

Bronze is much harder and more utilitarian and so was a marked improvement over copper as a material for tools. A broader range of tools could be made for use by more and more people.

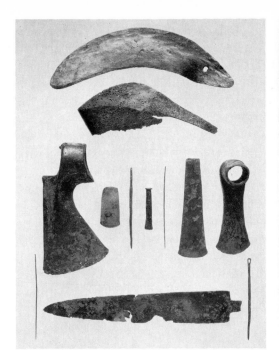

The Bronze Age in the Near East is the time in which there was a significant improvement in tool-making capability. It is also the time in which cities, true urban centers, appeared. These cities didn't "appear"— they developed from earlier settlements, towns that grew larger and more centralized, with more efficient means of agriculture, larger populations, and a metalworking technology that allowed greater efficiency and a broader range of tool types than before.

The Bronze Age lasted in the Near East until about 1500 B.C. (3500 B.P.) and is the period of many of the cities described in the Old Testament. Mesopotamia, at the head of the Persian Gulf and at the juncture of the Tigris and Euphrates rivers, is well known to most as the "cradle of civilization" for the Western world. Cities such as Uruk and Sumer flourished there through this period, and the networks among the cities of that time included trade, rivalry, and even warfare.

The Iron Age The attainment of an iron-smelting capability represented yet another major step in technology. Iron must be smelted at a temperature of 3,650° F and handled while hot to release impurities.

The extra work was worth it; ironworking spread widely throughout the Old World and provided the medium for the manufacture of a wide range of tools and weapons. Assyria, Babylon, and Persia were not just cities or states, but nations that competed—and sometimes warred— among themselves for economic wealth.

Metallurgy and Civilization   Archeologists of past decades placed a decided emphasis on metallurgy. One gains from reading their work the impression that "metals made civilization." Today it is possible to depict the sequence of culture change in the Near East without even mentioning the Copper, Bronze, and Iron ages. We note them here because they are still widely cited by many persons, particularly those more interested in studying and analyzing objects than the processes of culture change. The stages of metalworking are significant in indicating major technological innovations, but hardly the "cause" of cities, states, and nations.

Throughout this chapter we have presented the idea that development proceeded in a number of components of culture and society: sociopolitical organization, social stratification, food-producing systems, and technology. These components affected and exerted feedback on each other as societies in particular geographical areas became more complex. Metallurgy is useful as a way to characterize particular stages since it involves artifacts that are readily preserved. But remember that civilization is a far more complex process than just the transition from copper to bronze to iron.

Writing

If metallurgy provided the technological base for urbanization and the rise of states and nations, then writing provided the communication system for recording experience and transmitting it across space and time. Writing is certainly not the only means of recording and communicating; the oral tradition is far older and just as permanent. But writing provides a more effective and efficient method. Its value is seen in the fact that it was invented in as many as six separate areas.

How and when writing emerged cannot be completely reconstructed. Regular incisions on bones from a site in central Africa, dated to 8000 B.P., may indicate the development of a "photowriting" or introductory state.

A giant step in the development of writing was the notion of a symbol that would not represent an object, but the sound of its name. A picture of an eye and of a saw could represent the sentence "I saw." This **rebus** (*REE-bus*) **writing** led to the use of more and more symbols which came to be less and less like the object they might once have pictured.

Along with writing came mathematics and numerical recordkeeping. The Incas of Peru kept records by means of a knotted cord, a *quipu* (*Key-poo*), constructed to maintain "places," analogous to our decimals. In Asia, the *abacus,* still used today, provided an efficient means of arithmetic calculations. Along with other peoples, the Maya of Central America devised a calendar. Important events were carved into large stones (*stelae*) as pictures, along with the dates in which these occurred.

The earliest known *pictographic* writing is found in Sumer at 3500 B.C., with hieroglyphics in use at about 3000 B.C. Writing is found in the

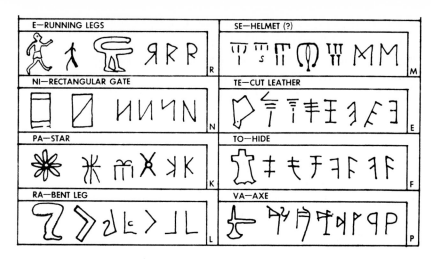

Figure 8.10
Top Steps in the development of writing: from a pictograph to an alphabet. *Bottom* Steps in the development of writing: a simple rebus.

sun   light   one   moon   light   night   house   hold

children   love   picture   books

Stop   rail   road   crossing   night   fall

Figure 8.11
Quipu, abacus, and a modern calculator—different ways of computation over the centuries.

Figure 8.12
Tikal, Temple 1.

Figure 8.13
Mayan calendar.

Figure 8.14
Mayan glyphs, carved in
stone *stela*, from Tikal.

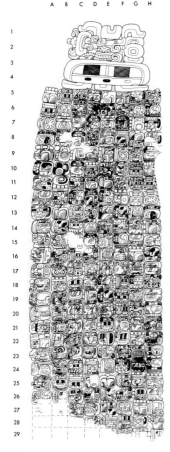

Indus Valley of western India by 2300 B.C. The Chinese developed *ideographs,* characters that represent ideas rather than sounds, by 2000 B.C.

Writing existed in the New World but cannot be studied. Unfortunately the *conquistadores* and their missionary colleagues believed the extensive written documents they found in Mexico and Central America to be "works of the devil." There are eyewitness accounts by these conquerors of the burning of huge piles of tablets and records. We will never be able to examine the written records of this civilization because of the activities of another civilization. Archeologists are able to reconstruct that writing existed in Mesoamerica by A.D. 500 but never seems to have been developed or even borrowed in Peru.

Civilization Outside the Near East

We have tended to focus on the Near East because the earliest records we have for the events and processes we have described come from there. However, there were other centers of civilization developing autonomously throughout the rest of the world.

The valley of the Indus River in western India was the site of important urban centers during the years 2500 to 1500 B.C. The cities of Mohenjo-Daro and Harappa were nuclear centers whose influence radiated throughout what is now the Indian subcontinent. Though these centers developed independently and displayed their own local flavor, trade goods from the Near East reveal their cosmopolitan nature.

Figure 8.15
Great Wall of China
completed in 221 B.C.

Figure 8.16
Chinese pictograph

Figure 8.17
Rock Temple of Ellora, India
7th-8th century A.D.

Figure 8.18
Chichen Itza, a major pre-Columbian ceremonial site from the Yucatan peninsula of Mexico.

In sub-Saharan Africa, there were not "city states," but large and prosperous states controlled by chieftains, whose authority was derived from their ruling skill as well as their religious prestige. Ironworking is seen throughout the area soon after 400 B.C. Particularly in the area just on the southern fringe of the Sahara Desert, trade was an important feature of the economy of these African states. In the first century A.D. Arab traders regularly crossed the desert to obtain gold, ivory, and salt. Large, complex, and efficiently organized states grew up in what are now Ghana and Mali. To the south, kingdoms also developed, as Bantu-speaking Africans spread steadily southward to displace the simpler Bushmen peoples.

Civilization in East Asia is usually described with reference to the areas where farming first developed: China and southeast Asia. In China the Shang Dynasty was established by 2000 B.C., when bronze and iron were in use. Later the Han Dynasty appears, and its rule extended in an unbroken line to the nineteenth century A.D.

Just as southeast Asia now seems to have been the site of the earliest domestication of plants, it is possible that subsequent development also occurred there somewhat earlier than in the Near East. We cannot yet be certain, but the site of Ban Chiang has yielded bronze artifacts that may be as old as 5000 B.P. or even older.

In the New World, we have mentioned the nuclear centers in Peru and in Mesoamerica. The great ceremonial centers in Mesoamerica indicate the rise of important religious sects, which in later times became interwoven with militarism. In Peru the Inca Empire stretched for almost 1,000 miles from north to south, connected by an efficient civil-religious administrative organization.

Figure 8.19
Angkor Wat 1113 A.D.

Figure 8.20
Close-up at Angkor Wat

Figure 8.21
Pyramid of the Sun
at Teotihuacan, near
Mexico City. This huge
complex of buildings and
pyramids was an important
ceremonial center for the
Aztecs, who lived in the
Valley of Mexico at the time
of the conquest of Mexico
by Spanish soldiers and
missionaries.

Figure 8.22
The site of Mohenjo-Daro
in the Indus Valley of western India.

Insight
Native American Civilization—Stereotypes, Myths, and Reality

This chapter deals mainly with civilizations that sprang up in nuclear centers of the world. But what of peoples living away from these nuclear areas? Were they civilized?

The answer to the second question is yes. There were many societies living around the core of each nuclear center, contributing to the center goods and materials, to say nothing of ideas. These supporting peoples received, in turn, the ideas and technology that had come together in the nuclear center. These surrounding peoples were as much a part of that civilization as a Maine lobsterman is part of the American civilization, despite the fact that he lives away from its urban centers.

We have developed the view of Native North Americans as being noble, harsh, warlike, uncivilized, and the tireless foes of white settlers. We have developed certain myths about the Indians, often endowing them with superhuman powers. We have narrowed their range of behavior in our own minds and reduced it to a *stereotype,* the assumption that all Indians behave in the same way at all times.

The record, however, is clearly different. The many societies and populations of North American Indians varied among themselves to a greater extent than did the peoples of Europe. We identify, in our own minds, the American Indians with the buffalo-hunters of the Great Plains. Yet these peoples of the Plains developed their use of horses and their dependence on the bison only after Europeans had pushed them into that area and after the horse was introduced by the Spanish from the south.

The Indians of the American Southwest were, for the most part, peaceful farmers who developed innovative means of irrigating their lands in the arid deserts. They successfully

exploited their environments for thousands of years. In Arizona and New Mexico, the Pueblo people lived in large communities of several thousand persons. Their houses were complex buildings with multiple stories containing hundreds of rooms. These were not unlike present-day apartments and condominiums. On the other hand, not all southwestern Indians were peaceful farmers. The Athabascan-speaking ancestors of modern Apache and Navajo Indians gradually spread southward from their Canadian homeland. They lived a nomadic existence, frequently raiding neighboring communities.

Complex societies existed along the northwest coast of North America and northward into southern Alaska. These Indians didn't become farmers; their natural environment was lush with salmon, other fish, and land animals. The food was so plentiful, and the technology used to obtain it so well developed, that large societies and elaborate social systems could be adequately supported.

Elsewhere in North America, Native Americans diversified their society as they exploited their environments. Not all groups found their environments so rich. Indians of the Great Basin, the deserts of California and Nevada, lived in an arid and rigorous environment, developing, as they did, techniques for survival.

Native North Americans offer us an example of a large, diversified group of peoples developing their ways of life as appropriate to their environments. White Americans have all too often thought of them as stereotypes, as uncivilized, and as "noble red men" somehow possessing mystical powers and properties and living in harmony with the world. In fact, they were, and still are, persons living so as to find meaning, as are we all.

Civilization, as we have defined it, never developed in North America, though large population centers were beginning to appear just at the time of Columbus's voyages. These centers were located along the large inland rivers—the Mississippi in particular—and were seemingly influenced by the diffusion of culture from Mesoamerica. The site of Cahokia, in Illinois, was a city with a population exceeding 20,000.

Metalworking was in its beginning stages in the New World when the Spaniards came to Mesoamerica and Peru. Some copper smelting and goldworking is seen in the archeological record from Peru, but it was not widespread.

Summary

1. The development of food production occurred in the Neolithic Period. At least three centers independently made the transition from hunting and gathering to agriculture and animal domestication between 10,000 and 5000 B.P. These centers were in the Far East, and Near East, and the New World.

2. Food production was associated with a radical change in the nature of human societies. They became more complex and increasingly socially stratified.

3. Civilization grew from Neolithic villages as population centers harnessed and regulated the energy of surrounding peoples. Strong centralized governments resulted in the rise of states with a ruling class, a sophisticated technology, and access to a wide range of goods and raw materials.

4. Developmental stages in the growth of civilizations are often described in terms of metallurgy. The sequence of metals used begins with the working of copper, going on to bronze and then iron.

5. Writing is another important characteristic of civilization. Writing was developed in at least six centers between 3500 B.C. (the Near East) and A.D. 500 (Central America).

Suggested Readings

Adams, Richard E. W. *Prehistoric Mesoamerica.* Boston: Little, Brown and Company, 1977.

The author synthesizes the archeological findings in this important area and offers an interpretation of their significance in understanding a single area.

Fagan, Brian M. *People of the Earth*. Boston: Little, Brown and Company, 1977.

> *A nicely written book that synthesizes the major features of prehistory on a worldwide basis, emphasizing the processes of change.*

Flannery, Kent V. "The Origins of Agriculture." *Annual Review of Anthropology* 2(1973):271–310. Palo Alto, Cal.: Annual Reviews, Inc.

> *The author presents a detailed analysis of the data relating to the origins of food production. It is an excellent summary of his own model.*

Flannery, Kent V., ed. *The Early Mesoamerican Village*. New York: Academic Press, 1976.

> *The chapters in this book focus on prehistoric settlement patterns in the area.*

Pfeiffer, John E. *The Emergence of Society. A Prehistory of the Establishment*. New York: McGraw-Hill, 1977.

> *Pfeiffer has produced a book that is a joy to read. It covers the rise of states and civilizations.*

Glossary

civilization   A stage of human society. Civilization is characterized by large cities, stratified societies, a state governed by a ruling class, and a sophisticated technology.

infectious disease   A disease caused by the presence of a specific organism.

rebus writing   An early type of writing in which the sounds of objects that are pictured suggest words and phrases.

social stratification   The existence in a society of different status groups.

state   A complex human society characterized by social stratification and governed by a ruling class.

Human Biology

Part 3

1. What is heredity? Why is it important to me?
2. What are the ways that humans adapt biologically to their environments?
3. Why are we so different biologically from each other?
4. What is a race? What is the true classification of races?

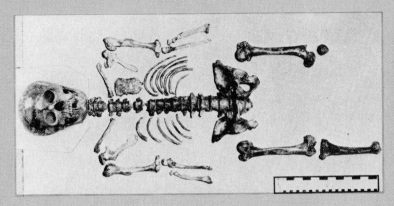

9

Genetics, Evolution, and Variation

Introduction

In previous chapters we have emphasized the "what" of the story of evolution, presenting it as a continuum of biological and cultural evolution. In this chapter we will emphasize the "how" of evolution, and the story will be one of how evolution is (and by extension, how it was) accomplished.

The characteristics of life are found in all organisms, but the way in which they are expressed varies widely. How a plant captures the oxygen needed for metabolism by converting light energy from the sun in photosynthesis; how a fish captures this oxygen from the water passing through its gills; and how we obtain the same oxygen from the air we take into our lungs—these are the concerns of the biological scientist. How these different functions have come to be is the concern of the evolutionary biologist, who studies the interactions between species and the natural world, in either the living or the fossil world. How the information and control system causing these functions to develop and operate is transmitted from one human generation to the next is the concern of the geneticist.

In this chapter we will consider one particular control system—the one received from one's parents, which we may think of as our *hereditary* system. This is the control system that we receive at the moment of our conception and whose units of control are **genes.** It is perhaps the basic control system, yet it is only one of several. We will consider it as a separate entity, but will also consider it in relation to other systems that are involved in the regulation of our life cycles. The hereditary, or genetic, system is of particular importance here since it is something that is altered during the course of biological evolution. We will, because of this, devote some time to considering the ways or *mechanisms* by which genes are altered in the process of evolution.

The Structure of the Gene

Imagine a spiral. It can be the spiral binding of a notebook, or a spiraled telephone cord, or a spiral staircase like those in towers and cupolas.

Now imagine another spiral running alongside the first one and linked to it by a series of connections, much as the rungs of a ladder connect the sides into a single structure. This structure is a double spiral or, in formal geometrical terms, a *double helix* (*HEE-licks*). If you have imagined a double helix, you will have visualized a schematic diagram of the shape of a gene, the thing that controls heredity.

Ever since the scientific world recognized the work of Gregor Mendel, it was realized that if you knew something about the physical characteristics of parents, you could predict something about their offspring's characteristics. The more you knew, the more you could predict. But just what was a gene? How did one "work"? And, perhaps most of all, how was this structure translated into one's offspring?

The discovery of the structure of the gene was one step in the discovery of the mechanisms that regulate life—but it may have been the most important step since Darwin formulated the concept of natural selection.

The Chemical Basis of the Gene   Almost all the cells of the body contain a central part, the *nucleus,* surrounded by the *cytoplasm,* which contains a number of different kinds of structures and compounds. The nucleus consists almost entirely of a protein/acid complex called **deoxyribonucleic acid,** or DNA (*day-ox-ee-rye-bo-new-CLAY-ik*). DNA is the hereditary material, shaped like a double helix and containing the genes.

DNA is the hereditary material, shaped like a double helix and containing the genes.

A spiral strand of DNA consists of a series of subunits called nucleotides, each of which is made up chemically of three parts: a phosphate, a sugar, and a base. There are only four different bases throughout the living world, and all four are found in all life. These bases are named *adenine, cytosine, guanine,* and *thymine* (*ADD-uh-neen; SY-tow-seen; GWA-neen; THY-meen*), or simply A, C, G, and T.

The DNA bases are important for two reasons. First, the sequence in which they appear determines the "message" carried by a particular gene. We may think of the bases as letters of the alphabet, whose sequence spells out words and sentences.

The second important fact about DNA bases is that the two strands of the double helix are joined at the bases. The bridge is a chemical bond formed by the element hydrogen at each base. The structure of the four DNA bases, however, is such that the chemical bonding can occur only when adenine is opposite thymine, and cytosine is opposite guanine.

Figure 9.1 diagrams a portion of a DNA spiral showing how one strand might consist of a string of bases; for example, on the left from the bottom, ACTG. Because of this structural relationship, called **complementarity,** we know exactly what the sequence will be along the other strand: TGAC.

In short, the gene consists of a strand of DNA whose base sequence spells out a particular message. Furthermore, one strand is joined to another at the bases, and the sequence of the bases on the first strand is the complement of the sequence on the other.

Genes, Codons, and Amino Acids   We have spoken of "letters" and "messages," but what are the words? Genetic "words" are called *codons* (*CO-donz*). The genetic alphabet is much simpler than the alphabet of any human language. Each codon contains only three bases, or each "word" contains only three letters.

Figure 9.1
Schematic diagram of the
double helical strands of
DNA. The letters refer to
the four bases, which are
joined by hydrogen bonds.

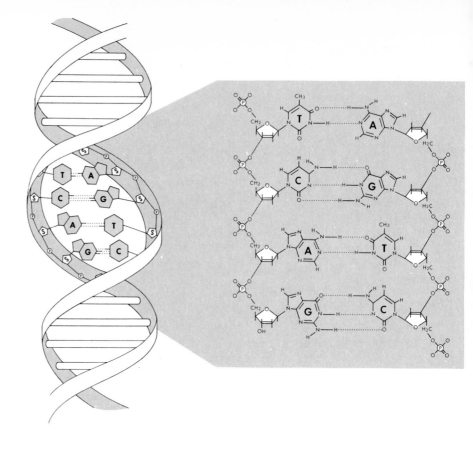

*The relationship between
a codon and amino acid is
called the genetic code.*

A codon has meaning because it specifies, or refers to, a specific compound called an *amino acid*. There are usually considered to be 20 amino acids, and each is specified by a particular codon. The relationship between a codon and amino acid is called the **genetic code.**

Genes act by transforming this message into the appropriate amino acid. This is illustrated schematically in Figure 9.2. The DNA strands separate at the bases and, still within the nucleus, each strand *synthesizes* a strand of material to which it can bond as it bonds to DNA. This material differs slightly from DNA, and is called **ribonucleic acid,** or **RNA** (*rye-bo-new-CLAY-ik*). Instead of the base thymine, RNA contains the base *uracil,* or U.

This form of RNA, *transfer RNA* (or tRNA), moves out into the cytoplasm and "collects" free amino acids that are present in the cell, having been transported there from the results of the digestion of food containing them. These amino acids are carried in the proper sequence and joined along a "template" of another form of RNA, *messenger RNA* (or mRNA), which has also been synthesized from that strand of DNA and hence contains bases in the same sequence.

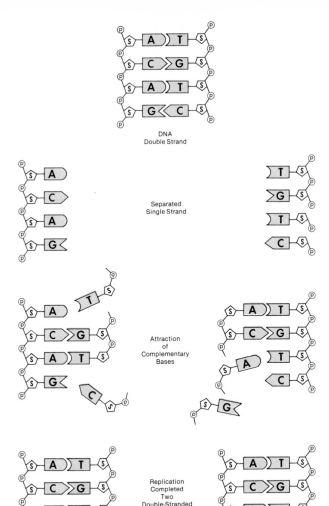

DNA
Double Strand

Separated
Single Strand

Attraction
of
Complementary
Bases

Replication
Completed
Two
Double-Stranded
Units

The result of these processes is to assemble strings of amino acids in a sequence specified, or coded, by the DNA, acting through the intermediate tRNA and mRNA. Chains of amino acids in specific sequence are, in fact, proteins. Table 9.1 presents the genetic code as carried by mRNA (since it is mRNA that attracts the appropriate amino acid). Returning to the language analogy, there are 20 words (amino acids), each containing three letters. Since there are more than 20 three-letter combinations, some codons are *redundant*—several will code the same amino acid. Some codons do not specify amino acids but are for "punctuation"—they tell the RNA to stop and hence signify the end of a gene.

Table 9.1

The Genetic Code: The RNA triplets for each amino acid.

Phenylalanine	Proline	Asparagine
UUU	CCU	AAU
UUC	CCC	AAC
Leucine	CCA	Lysine
UUA	CCG	AAA
UUG	Threonine	AAG
CUU	ACU	Aspartic Acid
CUC	ACC	GAU
CUA	ACA	GAC
CUG	ACG	Glutamic Acid
Isoleucine	Alanine	GAA
AUU	GCU	GAG
AUC	GCC	Cystine
AUA	GCA	UGU
Methionine	GCG	UGC
AUG	Tyrosine	Tryptophan
Valine	UAU	UGG
GUU	UAC	Arginine
GUC	Histidine	CGU
GUA	CAU	CGC
GUG	CAC	CGA
Serine	Glycine	CGG
UCU	CAA	AGA
UCC	CAG	AGG
UCA	GGU	
UCG	GGC	
AGU	GGG	
AGC	GGA	
	GGG	

The following triplets code the end-of-chain message:
UAA   UAG   UGA

Proteins and Enzymes   We now can say that the double helix of DNA and the genetic messages it carries result in the synthesis of proteins, which are the basic building blocks of the body. Some proteins are small, consisting of fewer than 100 amino acids, while others contain several hundred, all in a very specific sequence.

Certain proteins synthesized directly by genes are *structural;* that is, they function in some way as part of the body's structural material. For instance, hemoglobin is the major constituent of our red blood cells, giving the blood its color; in addition, hemoglobin transports oxygen through the bloodstream. It is a complex protein of 287 amino acids, the amino acid sequence being derived directly from the transfer of the genetic information through the DNA-RNA pathway.

Most of the genes, however, do not code structural protein, but *enzymes*. **Enzymes** are proteins that act as *catalysts*. That is, they must be present for most chemical reactions to take place, in a very specific way: one reaction requires one enzyme. Enzymes are plentiful—more than 1,000 may be synthesized within a particular cell, and each has its own reaction to catalyze. Some may be involved in reactions that lead to the synthesis of other structural proteins; some are important in the synthesis of other compounds such as fats and sugars, or in the breakdown of these compounds as sources of energy. All depend on the information carried by and received from the genes.

Enzymes are proteins that act as catalysts.

Each nucleus of every cell (except for the reproductive cells) contains a complete set of genes. But only a small part of the DNA in any one cell is active at any one time. After all, the enzymes manufactured by liver cells are not the same as those active within the red blood cells. So there are genes that inhibit, or block, other genes. *Inhibitor genes* are not well understood, but we do know that they allow those genes appropriate for a particular cell to be active. Furthermore, we know that certain inhibitor genes may suppress or block a particular strand of DNA until the proper time. In this way, cells begin to *differentiate* from each other and undergo the process we call development.

DNA in Perspective   The genetic material is complex and acts in ways that we still do not understand completely. It is, however, crucial to an individual's day-to-day functioning as well as to his or her functioning throughout an entire life cycle. Furthermore, since the genetic material is inherited, it is the link by which one generation passes, biologically, this information on to the next generation.

Genes are biological units located and operating within the restricted area of the cell. But they are hardly independent units. Were there no free amino acids in the cell, RNA could not assemble proteins in accordance with the sequence determined by the gene. Free amino acids come from the nutrients taken into the body, digested and transported throughout it, and carried into the cell. For a gene to carry out its function completely, it must receive certain materials from the environment. The individual's state of health must be such that cellular functions are in good order, and the products of the gene must be compatible with the world in which the individual lives. DNA is basic to biology, to evolution, and to being human, but only in the context of the other parts of the whole—including health, food, and the entire complex of cultural behavior (which in turn is equally basic to biology, to evolution, and to being human).

Figure 9.3
Photomicrograph of human
chromosomes of a normal
male.

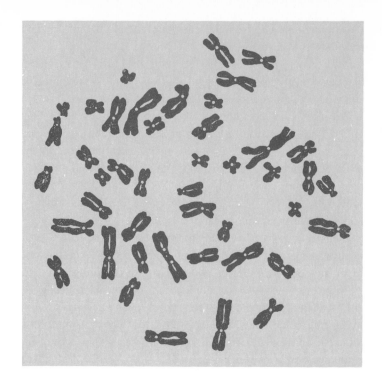

Genes and Chromosomes

Figure 9.3 is a photograph of the nucleus of a human white blood cell taken through the lens of a high-power microscope. The cell has been grown for a few days outside the individual's body in a culture medium and then treated in certain ways to allow us to see the threadlike structures.

These structures, called **chromosomes,** consist largely of DNA. In humans there is about 6 feet of DNA per cell in the coiled strands described earlier. Figure 9.4 shows these chromosomes in a special way, called a *karyotype (CARE-ee-oh-type)*, in which the individual chromosomes have been cut out from the picture and arranged from the largest to the smallest. The upper part of the figure is the karyotype of a normal human female; there are 23 pairs of chromosomes, numbered 1 through 22, plus a pair labeled *X*. The lower karyotype is of a male; the two are essentially the same except that the odd pair in the male has but one *X* chromosome and a small bit called the *Y*. Genetically, then, the only difference between males and females is that the female sex chromosomes are *XX* and the male are *XY* (they are called sex chromosomes simply because they are associated with gender).

The exact way in which the sex chromosomes determine gender is unknown. However, the study of prenatal development (embryology) has demonstrated that males and females do not differ in morphology during the first three weeks of their existence within the mother's womb. After the third week, males begin to develop external genitalia characteristic of their sex. Male genitalia are associated with the presence of the *Y* chromosome and female genitalia with its absence. It seems, therefore, that the structure of *Y*-chromosome DNA is responsible for the production of regular substances called *hormones,* which change a pattern of development from that producing a female to that which will become a male.

The human species has 46 chromosomes. Other species have their own characteristic numbers. While variations occur from person to person, they are rare. In most cases, some abnormality is found in persons with fewer or more than 46 chromosomes.

We know that the genes are located on the chromosomes as sections of DNA. Research has also shown that a particular gene will always be found at the same site on the same chromosome (unless there is, as in the odd rare case, some abnormality). This site is called the *locus* (plural, *loci*) of the gene.

Variability at a Locus   Chromosomes occur in pairs for a simple reason: one of each pair is inherited from one parent and one from the other. For the same reason, genes also occur in pairs. When the two genes (one from each parent) are the same, we say that the individual is a **homozygote** for that locus.

However, when a locus displays more than one form of the gene, the different forms are called **alleles** (*AL-eels*). When an individual has two different alleles, he or she is a **heterozygote** at that locus.

As we shall see, many (but not the majority) of our loci show alleles, throughout the human species. At some loci there may be two alleles, in others there may be 40 or more. Each person possesses two genes at a given locus; if the locus shows no variability within the species, then everyone will be homozygous. If there is allelic variability at a locus throughout the species, an individual may be either homozygous or heterozygous, depending on the genes received from his or her parents.

We must distinguish, then, between two levels of genetic variability: the individual and the population. We measure population variability by determining the amount of variability throughout the population; we measure individual variability by determining the individual's **genotype,** that is, the particular pair of genes at each locus.

Examples of Genetic Variability

(1) The ABO Locus   Let us consider two examples of loci with allelic variability among humans, beginning with the locus that determines our ABO blood type. "Type" here refers to a factor, or *antigen,* located on the surface of our red blood cells. This factor serves as a "label," so that our body can recognize some outside or foreign substance that has invaded it and may pose a threat to it. This particular red cell antigen is important in blood transfusions for that reason.

Our ABO blood type is genetically determined by the alleles that we have inherited at the ABO-locus. Viewed simply, there are three alleles present in humans, called A, B, and O.

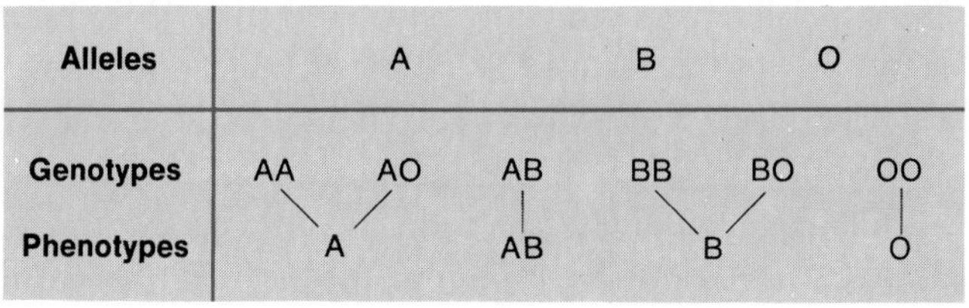

Alleles	A	B	O
Genotypes	AA AO	AB	BB BO	OO
Phenotypes	A	AB	B	O

Figure 9.5
Alleles, genotypes, and phenotypes at the ABO locus.

Since each person has two genes at the ABO locus, there are, as Figure 9.5 shows, six possible genotypes; three of them are homozygous and three are heterozygous. But there are four blood types—A, B, O, or AB. The figure shows that these four blood types are related to the six genotypes in a systematic way.

When the genotype is homozygous, the blood type corresponds directly to the genotype: an AA genotype determines type A blood. But when the genotype is heterozygous, the blood type is not obvious. Both A and B are **dominant** over O, which is **recessive.** Thus an AO genotype also results in blood type A.

The blood type is the **phenotype,** which means the result that we can observe. AA and AO are different genotypes, but both genotypes have the same phenotype (type A blood). So, for some genes and at some loci, the genotype corresponds directly to the phenotype while; in other instances, the genotype does not correspond so directly. We may say this in another way: In a heterozygotic genotype, the recessive allele is not expressed in the phenotype.

When the genotype is AB, so is the blood type. In this case, A and B are *codominant,* and the two alleles are both expressed in the phenotype.

The blood type is the phenotype, which means the result that we can observe.

(2) The Hemoglobin Locus Another example of human genetic variability is the hemoglobin locus where, as we have already noted, the code for the structure of the hemoglobin molecule is found. The genetic information at this locus is quite variable, and more than 100 different forms of hemoglobin have been identified among humans. Most of these are due to the presence of alleles for the different forms, and each form is characterized by some alteration of the amino acid sequence.

Most hemoglobin variants are quite rare, turning up here and there in individuals. The majority of humans have a type of hemoglobin abbreviated Hgb A—they are homozygous for the Hb^A allele. Some hemoglobin variants—Hgb S, Hgb C, Hgb E—are common in certain populations. For example, the abnormal variant Hgb S is called *sickle-cell hemoglobin.* When deprived of oxygen, the red blood cells of an individual with sickle-cell hemoglobin will become distorted and "sickle-shaped."

Hgb S is produced by an allele, Hb^S, which alters one of the amino acids of the 287 in sequence. At the sixth position from the end of the chain, the amino acid glutamic acid has been replaced by valine; an examination of the genetic code in Table 9.1 will show how the DNA base sequence itself might have been altered in the change from Hgb A to Hgb S.

Hemoglobin alleles are codominant. That is, a person who has the genotype Hb^AHb^S is heterozygous for the sickle-cell gene, and that person's phenotype can be distinguished from either homozygote. This genotype will produce two types of hemoglobin—normal and sickle-cell—since there is an allele for each type.

On the other hand, the homozygote Hb^SHb^S has the disease **sicklemia** (sickle-cell anemia), or sickle cells in the blood. This disease produces a very serious anemia as well as a cluster, or syndrome, of other symptoms. The life expectancy of a person with sicklemia is much shorter than normal, and without medical attention, the person is quite likely to die during childhood.

Genetic variability at the Hb locus is rich, with many alleles being known. Most of them are rare, but some of the variants are quite common. This locus has broadened our understanding of the nature of natural selection, and we will cover it in some detail later in this chapter.

Monogenic and Polygenic Inheritance

Blood type and hemoglobin structure are examples of traits determined by genes acting at a single locus—*monogenic* traits. There is one locus for our ABO type and another locus where the genes for our hemoglobin type are found, and no other loci are involved. By and large, biochemical traits such as these are monogenic since they are very specific and relatively simple.

On the other hand, many other traits are quite complex in terms of their genetic basis. A good example of this is stature; our height is composed of the lengths of the bones of the legs, the bones of the spinal column, as well as those in the head, pelvis, feet, and ankles. No one knows exactly how many loci are involved in the inheritance of stature.

Table 9.2 shows a hypothetical example of the way in which two loci might contribute to stature. At each locus there are two alleles, one adding one inch to the stature and the other adding nothing. At each locus there are three possible genotypes, and combining the two loci gives nine possible genotypes. There is no dominance, and the effects of each allele are simply added together.

This type of inheritance seems to be common for *polygenic* traits involving size. It is called *additive* for obvious reasons, and it is important in several ways. First, with polygenic inheritance there is a wide range of genotypes—with only two alleles at each of two loci, there are already

Table 9.2

A Hypothetical Example of Additive Inheritance

1) *Locus A*
   a) *Alleles* A^1—adds 1 inch to height
                    A^2—adds 2 inches to height
   b) *Genotypes* $A^1A^1 = +2$ inches
                    $A^1A^2 = +3$ inches
                    $A^2A^2 = +4$ inches

2) *Locus B*
   a) *Alleles* B^1—adds 1 inch to height
                    B^2—adds 2 inches to height
   b) *Genotype* $B^1B^1 = +2$ inches
                    $B^1B^2 = +3$ inches
                    $B^2B^2 = +4$ inches

3) *Combining both loci*

Genotype	Addition to Stature
$A^1A^1B^1B^1$	+4
$A^1A^1B^1B^2$	+5
$A^1A^1B^2B^2$	+6
$A^1A^2B^1B^1$	+5
$A^1A^2B^1B^2$	+6
$A^1A^2B^2B^2$	+7
$A^2A^2B^1B^1$	+6
$A^2A^2B^1B^2$	+7
$A^2A^2B^2B^2$	+8

nine genotypes. Add a third locus and you will see that the number of genotypes increases to 27 (i.e., 3^3)!

Second, as we have seen, more than one genotype can give rise to the same phenotype. In Table 9.2, three different genotypes each contribute two inches to the stature. Knowing the phenotype does not necessarily mean we know the genotypes.

Third, with so many different genotypes there are many more opportunities for the environment to have an effect. The very complexity of polygenic traits makes them more sensitive to the environment, and so the phenotype may be changed considerably because of the environment.

Heredity vs. Environment

Are you tall because your parents are tall, because you enjoyed a good environment, or because you were active at sports? This question has been asked many times by scientists and nonscientists. We could substitute for the word "tall" any of several others—smart, fat, sickly—and find ourselves instantly involved in controversy, argument, and even political issues.

In more general terms the question becomes: "Which is more important, heredity or environment?" Geneticists ask this question in a slightly different way. They want to know what the *heritability* of a certain trait is. By heritability is meant how much of the variability of a particular trait in a group is caused by genetic differences rather than the environment.

We know that all biological structures and processes depend to a degree on the control and regulation that is based within the DNA. If different alleles are involved, then they must contribute to the phenotypes. The greater the contribution, the greater the heritability. If the heritability of a trait were 1.00, then the environment would exercise no effect upon it. The only reason we would differ would be because we have different combinations of alleles.

The opposite of a high heritability is called *plasticity,* a term indicating that a particular trait is shaped by the environment and that people differ because they have experienced different environments.

What a simple concept! How nice it would be if we could determine the heritability and plasticity of particular traits. We would know so much more of human genetics and evolution, and we would know on which traits we ought to focus by improving environments. If intelligence is inherited (an often-discussed example), then our enrichment programs are doomed to failure; if it is determined by the environment, then we ought to plan our programs accordingly.

Unfortunately, the real world is not simple. The heritability of a polygenic trait varies from group to group as does the environment. Heritability estimates are valid *only* for the particular sample we are studying and cannot be generalized.

The Transmission of Genes

A person's genotype is not transmitted to his or her offspring, since human reproduction is bisexual. Instead we pass one half our genes, one of each pair at each locus. The genotype is divided so that we transmit individual alleles. Since each parent transmits half of his or her genes, the number of genes remains the same from generation to generation.

The *somatic,* or nonreproductive, cells of the body, replicate themselves by the process of *mitosis (my-TOW-sis)*, or cell division. The nucleus of a cell divides in half, and each separated strand of DNA makes a complement of itself. The DNA thus remains constant and complete in each new cell.

By heritability is meant how much of the variability of a particular trait in a group is caused by genetic differences rather than the environment.

The opposite of a high heritability is called plasticity.

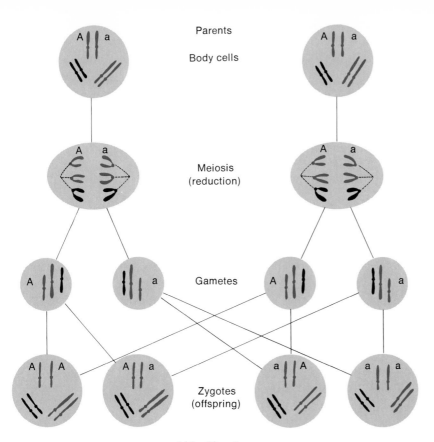

Figure 9.6
Schematic diagram of
chromosome replication
occurring during meiosis.

Parents

Body cells

Meiosis
(reduction)

Gametes

Zygotes
(offspring)

1AA : 2Aa : 1aa

The reproductive cells, or *gametes,* replicate themselves by the process of *meiosis (my-OH-sis).* Though initially similar to mitosis, meiosis differs in that there is a second "reduction division" in which only one chromosome of each pair is passed along to each of the two daughter cells. The number of chromosomes and genes is halved, to be restored at the moment of fertilization. If the fertilizing sperm cell happens to carry a Y chromosome, the new individual will be a male. If it carries an X chromosome, it will be a female, since the ovum always carries an X chromosome.

Segregation and Independent Assortment

As a result of meiosis, each pair of genes is halved, and either portion may be passed along to the offspring; the probability being 50:50, or ½, for each allele. This is called genetic segregation and means that from a single mating, with each parent contributing one of the two alleles at a locus, up to four genotypes may occur in an offspring.

Figure 9.7
Diagram of a 2x2 cross.

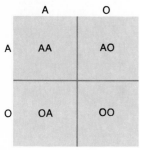

AO × AO
Proportions: 1 AA : 2 AO : 1 OO

Figure 9.7 diagrams a cross (a mating) between two AO heterozygotes for ABO blood type. Note that there are three genotypes. The ratio, or proportion, of these three genotypes is 1:2:1, but we will find this exact ratio only if we look at the offspring of a large number of such matings. It is entirely possible for two AO parents to have three children who each have the genotype OO.

Not only do the genes at one locus segregate, they also *assort* independently of those at any other locus. Consider, for example, an individual who is a double heterozygote at the ABO and Hb loci: AO/Hb^AHb^S. Such a person will produce four kinds of gametes:

$$A/Hb^A \qquad A/Hb^S \qquad O/Hb^A \qquad O/Hb^S$$

The law of independent assortment states that each of these gametes will be produced in equal proportions.

Segregation and independent assortment are important in promoting genetic variability. It doesn't take long to figure that with bisexual reproduction, segregation, and independent assortment all in effect, no two persons will have the same genotype at each of their loci unless they are identical twins.

Genes and Evolution

The Synthetic Theory of Evolution

Since the days of Charles Darwin, evolutionary theory has undergone considerable modification. The greatest refinements have come from *population genetics,* that branch of genetics that studies the genetic structure of populations. These populations are called *Mendelian,* or *breeding,* populations and are defined as populations because the individuals tend to mate within the group rather than outside it.

A Mendelian population is important in the study of evolution because it is an interacting unit—interacting in the genetic sense, individuals mating with each other.

A species is a major taxonomic category, as we have discussed. A Mendelian population is a subdivision of a species, a subdivision that comprises a reproductive unit. Among humans a population may exist for geographical reasons; for instance, a particular society or group may be so isolated geographically from others that it forms a population. A population may also exist for cultural reasons. In various parts of North America there are groups of people whose ancestors came to the New World in the eighteenth century for religious reasons. They are all called Anabaptists because they did not baptize infants, but older persons. In the United

Population genetics is that branch of genetics that studies the genetic structure of populations. These populations are called Mendelian, or breeding, populations and are defined as populations because the individuals tend to mate within the group rather than outside it.

States and Canada, there are several groups descended from these Anabaptists and still holding to their old beliefs: Mennonites, Amish, Hutter-
ites, and Dunkers. All of them are, genetically, Mendelian populations because persons are supposed to marry within the group, even though they
live adjacent to and interact socially with other people. In other words,
these populations are not defined geographically, but culturally.

A Mendelian population is a reproductive group. Parents come from
within the population and pass their genes to their offspring who remain in
the population. We may therefore say that the members of a population
share a *gene pool*. Offspring receive their genes from the gene pool by way
of their parents.

The *synthetic theory of evolution* states that evolution occurs as the
proportion, or frequency, of genes in the gene pool of a population changes
from generation to generation. These changes are caused by specific forces,
or *evolutionary mechanisms*. Anthropological geneticists study the changes
in gene frequency in Mendelian populations, as well as the evolutionary
mechanisms that cause them.

*We may therefore say that
the members of a population
share a gene pool.*

*The synthetic theory of
evolution states that
evolution occurs as the
genes in the gene pool of a
population changes from
generation to generation.*

Gene Frequency and the Hardy-Weinberg Theorem

Various alleles can exist in the gene pool of a population. The gene frequency of a particular allele is its frequency relative to others at that locus.

Table 9.3 presents an example of the calculation of the frequencies of
the alleles at the haptoglobin (or Hp) locus. The genes at this locus determine the structure of the haptoglobin molecule, a protein carried in the
blood serum (that part of the blood remaining when we remove the red
cells). In humans there are two haptoglobin alleles, Hp^1 and Hp^2. Thus
there are three genotypes: Hp (1-1), Hp (1-2), and Hp (2-2). Since
the alleles are codominant, there are three phenotypes. The table demonstrates how the calculation of the frequency of each allele is made.

Having calculated the gene frequency, we next want to know something about the changes in gene frequency from one generation to the
next. Before we can do this, let us assume certain things about the
population:

1. There is random mating. Since we are using as an example the Hp
   locus, this means that mates do not choose each other on the basis of
   their haptoglobin type.
2. No new Hp alleles are introduced into the population, either by mutation (to be discussed later) or by migration.
3. No one haptoglobin type is any better adapted than any other.
4. The population is large enough in size so that random events will not
   affect the frequency of haptoglobin alleles.

Table 9.3

Calculation of Gene Frequency

Individuals		Alleles		
Genotype	n	Hp¹	Hp²	Total
Hp¹/Hp¹	197	394	0	394
Hp¹/Hp²	131	131	131	262
Hp²/Hp²	22	0	44	44
	350	525	175	700

$$\text{Frequency of Hp}^1 = \frac{525}{700} = 0.75$$

$$\text{Frequency of Hp}^2 = \frac{175}{700} = 0.25$$

Where the heterozygote is not recognizable (i.e., where there is complete dominance), we may estimate the frequency of the recessive allele as the square root of the frequency of the homozygous recessive genotype. Thus

Hp², if recessive, could be estimated as

$$Hp^2 = \sqrt{0.0629} = 0.251$$
$$Hp^1 = 1.00 - 0.251 = 0.749$$

Table 9.4

The Hardy-Weinberg Theorem states that, given certain conditions, the distribution of genotypes among the offspring is determined by the frequency of genes among parents according to the binomial expansion.

Example: the haptoglobin locus

1) Alleles: Hp¹ and Hp²

2) Frequencies among parents:
   $$Hp^1 = .7 \qquad Hp^2 = .3$$

3) Binomial expansion
   $$(Hp^1 + Hp^2)^2 = Hp^1Hp^1 + 2Hp^1Hp^2 + Hp^2Hp^2$$

   substituting,
   $$(.7Hp^1 + .3Hp^2)^2 =$$
   $$.49\ Hp^1Hp^1 + .42\ Hp^1Hp^2 + .09\ Hp^2Hp^2,$$

   i.e., the frequencies among the offspring

If we know the gene frequencies of Hp^1 and Hp^2 in the population, and if we can make these assumptions for the population, then the frequency of the three genotypes among the offspring generation can be calculated from the frequencies of the two alleles among the parental generation. The method for doing this, called the *binomial expansion,* is illustrated in Table 9.4.

The calculation of genotypes by the binomial expansion is an extremely important theory in population (or evolutionary) genetics and is known as the *Hardy-Weinberg Theorem,* after the two scientists who first formulated it. It is important because it tells us that the genotype frequencies of the offspring generation can be predicted from the gene frequencies of the parents. That is, we can predict mathematically what will happen.

The Hardy-Weinberg Theorem is also important because, as Table 9.4 shows, the gene frequencies will not change from one generation to the next. We say that the frequencies will be in equilibrium (i.e., a steady state). Genetic variation will therefore not be lost; instead, any genetic variation will remain in the gene pool of the population from one generation to the next.

The frequency of the three genotypes among the offspring generation can be calculated from the frequencies of the two alleles among the parental generation.

The Mechanisms of Evolution

The above is all well and good, statistically neat and mathematically formal. But we know that gene frequencies do change, since the assumptions we noted cannot be met. Evolution does occur. We therefore turn our attention to those four assumptions—because if they are not met, then the population will not be in Hardy-Weinberg equilibrium and the frequencies will change: evolution will occur. Turning the idea around, we may say that because these assumptions are not met, they then become the mechanisms of evolution, the forces that bring about evolutionary change.

There are four evolutionary mechanisms. They are (1) *mutation,* (2) *gene flow,* (3) *natural selection,* and (4) *genetic drift.* The first two promote change by introducing variability into a population; the last two promote changes in the frequencies of alleles within the population itself.

The Introduction of Genetic Variability   The proportion of various alleles in a gene pool may be altered if the chemical structure of the gene itself is changed to a new form or if other alleles are introduced into the population by migration.

The first of these two mechanisms is called mutation. It may occur when the sequence of a particular codon is altered. For example, the base sequence of glutamic acid is GAG; if this were changed to GUG by some outside agent it would code valine. The hemoglobin type would be changed from the normal type A to the abnormal type S, or sickle-cell hemoglobin. Mutations are caused by many agents (mutagens). These are known to include radiation, both from natural sources such as the sun and from man-made agents such as X rays; along with drugs, chemicals, and possibly some of the pollutants that have invaded our air and food. The rate at which most mutations occur is low. Our best estimates indicate that, of every 1 million genes for a typical enzyme, 25 will mutate in a given generation, giving a rate of 25/1,000,000 or 1 in 40,000.

Since we are well-balanced organisms, many mutations are harmful in that they disturb this balance—often an enzyme that would have been produced by a gene is not produced and so its reaction is blocked. A large number of genetic diseases are caused in this way.

Other mutations may be *neutral,* so called because they don't seem to make any difference. Some mutations may be beneficial, improving the relationship of an individual to his or her environment.

Genetic variation may also be introduced into a population by means of **gene flow** or, as it is also called, *migration.* As individuals move into a population, choosing their mates within the new group, their genes become part of the gene pool. New alleles may be introduced in this way, and if there are enough migrants, the frequencies of existing alleles may be altered.

In chapter 8 we mentioned that archeologists trace contacts between groups by detecting objects that have been introduced into one from the other—a piece of obsidian, a distinctive projectile point, or a sudden flood of a new style of pottery decoration. Physical anthropologists trace contacts by detecting the presence of alleles introduced through mating from one population into another.

Random Change in Gene Frequency: Genetic Drift   Mutation and gene flow are evolutionary mechanisms that affect frequencies by introducing new alleles into a population. **Genetic drift** is a mechanism that alters the frequencies of alleles already present in the gene pool; no new ones are introduced, but existing variability is shuffled.

Drift is not a single mechanism but a group of mechanisms that operate in different ways—all, however, are random and unpredictable. They include all those processes, events, and disturbances of gene frequency that happen for unexplained reasons. Some people may die of accidents, or they may not marry, or they may choose to have no children.

Changes due to drift are of consequence only in the case of small populations. Chance fluctuations of various processes have a much greater impact upon groups of, say, less than 500 to 1,000 in total size. Under such conditions evolution can proceed rather rapidly.

Figure 9.8
Aerial photograph of the
South American tropical
rain forest. The major routes
of communication are by
means of the rivers. Shown
is the Ucayali River, a
tributary of the Amazon.

Table 9.5

Gene Frequencies in Samples from Populations of the Peruvian Rain Forest

Population	n Number of persons	Allele					
		P^1	Fy^a	Jk^a	L^M	L^S	Di^a
Cashinahua	113	.33	.75	.55	.72	.08	.19
Ticuna	122	.91	.62	.50	.81	.25	.20
Piro	90	.59	.61	.45	.70	.39	.20
Shipibo	142	.52	.83	.48	.70	.42	.40
Campa	89	.49	.82	.50	.78	.50	.24
Aguaruna	151	.73	.70	.25	.63	.48	.04

The best examples of genetic drift in living human populations are seen in the small populations living in the tropical rain forests of the world. Such populations are always small and tend to be isolated from each other. Hundreds of miles of impenetrable forest separate them and make contact possible only along the rivers that twist through the forest. Table 9.5 indicates the results of isolation of small groups. The table presents the frequencies of various alleles among selected groups of Peruvian Indians. These groups are closely related—all are forest-dwelling American Indians with close historical ties, and all are located a few hundred miles or less from each other. Yet note the considerable genetic diversity among them. Because of their genetic separation from each

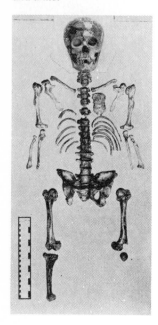

*Fitness means the relative
number of offspring pro-
duced by individuals carrying a particular allele.*

other for anywhere from 50 to perhaps 500 years, and because the populations number only a few hundred or more individuals, they have slowly
"drifted" apart in terms of gene frequencies. This drift has been random
and has resulted in the crazy-quilt picture of the alleles of their gene pools
that is shown in the table.

Genetic drift seems not to have been very important as an evolutionary mechanism among large national populations, and so many human
biologists have tended to discount it as an evolutionary mechanism of any
consequence. But on the other hand, hominid and human groups until the
Middle Pleistocene lived in widely scattered populations for millions of
years, with population (band) sizes numbering perhaps 50 and only
occasionally exceeding 100. The result of this could have been an incredible range of genetic diversity among the genus *Homo,* distributed in small
groups over much of the Old World.

Natural Selection: The Mechanism of Genetic Adaptation   Biological
scientists, human biologists, in fact, almost everyone with any knowledge
of evolutionary theory, all believe now that natural selection is the mechanism that has patterned diversity into an adaptive relationship with the
surrounding environment. Darwin first grasped the concept of evolution
when he observed the ways in which animal species, as well as subgroups
of species, were adapted to their environments. He saw this adaptation
as resulting from the selection by the environment of those variants that
were the best adapted to that given environment.

The basic theory of natural selection is today the same as it was
when developed by Darwin. Rather than modifications, we have refinements; and rather than speculation over the ways the process might be
carried out, we have as our basis the science of genetics as it has developed
over a century of research.

Darwin wrote of variants that are better adapted. Today we speak
of variants as "variation in the frequencies of alleles at a locus." We continue to use the concept of adaptation, but we measure it, for purposes of
analyzing natural selection, as the *fitness* of those variants. Used in this
sense, fitness means the relative number of offspring produced by individuals carrying a particular allele. If, on the average, such individuals produce only one half the number of offspring as do those with another gene,
we say that the fitness of the first allele is 0.5. Suppose that anyone who
inherits a particular allele is sterile; the fitness of that allele is then zero.

To avoid any confusion, let us differentiate between three "levels"
at which natural selection may be thought of as operating:

1. The *phenotype.* Natural selection operates on the phenotype because,
   in the final analysis, it is the phenotype, the expressed trait, that interacts with the environment. If a recessive allele is carried in a heterozy-

gous genotype, then selection cannot operate upon that allele since it will not be expressed.

2. The *genotype*. Natural selection also operates upon genotypes. A "gene pool" is only an imaginary construct; there are no genes "floating around in a pool." There are genotypes, and the fitness is determined by the particular genotype.

3. The *gene*. Natural selection may operate directly upon the phenotype and the genotype. But, after all, the gene is the unit of evolution—the unit that is transmitted from parent to offspring. The frequency of the gene is what evolution changes. Hence, any discussion of evolutionary change must finally focus on the gene itself and its frequency in the gene pool.

The environment "selects" from the pool of genetic variation those alleles that are better adapted to an environment, measuring adaptation in terms of the fitness associated with the gene. The frequencies of those alleles are consequently increased. Since the sum of all allele frequencies at any one locus must be 1.00, then if any one frequency is increased, the frequencies of the other alleles at that locus must be reduced correspondingly. Natural selection not only selects adapted genes, it lowers the frequency of nonadapted genes and, in the case of a dominant allele, may even eliminate them altogether.

Now it should be clear that natural selection is an involved process. Population geneticists recognize three "types" of natural selection, but there is really only a single process. When we refer to different types, we are really referring to the ways that natural selection is categorized by population geneticists.

Normalizing Selection   The first type of natural selection is *normalizing selection*. It occurs when harmful alleles are eliminated from a population. Diseases that are caused by genes result in selection against those genes.

The first type of natural selection is normalizing selection. It occurs when harmful alleles are eliminated from a population.

Normalizing selection keeps the gene pool "normal." It is conservative, since it maintains things as they are. If we think of mutation as that mechanism which puts harmful variants into a gene pool, than normalizing selection is the mechanism that eliminates them.

Normalizing selection is important in protecting the population from genes that are harmful to it. It preserves the population in its present state of adaptation and helps to ensure that the population will reproduce itself from generation to generation.

Normalizing selection is important in protecting the population from genes that are harmful to it.

Directional Selection   Directional selection is a form of selection that increases the frequency of an allele rather than eliminating it. It is selection in the Darwinian tradition of variants being "selected" by the environment so as to increase the level of adaptation of the population.

Directional selection is a form of selection that increases the frequency of an allele rather than eliminating it.

Since directional selection requires a long time perspective, and since our knowledge of much of human genetic variability is only a few decades old, we cannot point to any particular allele as having a high frequency because of directional selection. However, most evolutionary biologists believe that the long-term trends in evolution reflect this mechanism. The evolution of the brain and the evolution of upright posture are examples of trends that occurred because natural selection increased the frequencies of certain alleles in the hominid populations of that time.

Stabilizing Selection　If a variant is "bad," it is the object of normalizing selection. If it is "good," it is the object of directional selection. What if it is both good and bad? What will happen? Stabilizing selection is the form that operates when there are opposing selective forces working at a single locus. In humans, the best example of stabilizing selection is seen at the hemoglobin locus.

Stabilizing selection is the form that operates when there are opposing selective forces working at a single locus.

As we discussed above, the allele Hb^S, when homozygous, results in the inherited blood disease sickle-cell anemia (sicklemia). The severity of the disease means that the fitness of the Hb^SHb^S genotype is almost zero. But we are now talking about genotype—the heterozygote is a *carrier* of the allele, Hb^AHb^S, but his or her fitness is not affected.

Ordinarily selection would act against the Hb^S allele. Even though only the homozygote would be affected, it would still be deleterious and we would predict that normalizing selection would act to reduce its frequency. This is the case in the United States, where natural selection is reducing the frequency of this allele in black Americans, who have a relatively high frequency of Hb^S.

But there is another consideration. In those parts of Africa where falciparum malaria is found, the sickle cell enjoys a selective advantage. Falciparum malaria is a deadly disease of red blood cells in which a parasite carried by the *Anopheles* mosquito is injected into a person's bloodstream. The parasite lives within the cells and destroys them, bringing on malaria and often death.

Because sickle-cell hemoglobin is structurally different, the malaria parasite cannot live within these cells, and so the malaria does not run its full course in persons with this form of hemoglobin. The gene for sickle-cell anemia is therefore adaptive here because its presence in the gene pool of a population allows them to exist in a malarial environment.

If we consider the adaptations of the genotypes, we find the following:

Hb^AHb^A—Persons with this genotype are susceptible to falciparum malaria.

Hb^SHb^S—Persons with this genotype have sickle-cell anemia.

Hb^AHb^S—Persons with this genotype are normal.

Natural selection is directed at the two homozygotes. The heterozygote manufactures enough normal hemoglobin from the Hb^A allele to allow the body to carry out its normal functions of respiration. But enough sickle-cell hemoglobin is manufactured from the Hb^S allele to protect the individual against falciparum malaria and to allow immunity to be developed during childhood.

This is *stabilizing selection:* selection against the homozygote genotypes and selection in favor of the heterozygote. Geneticists also call this *heterozygote advantage.* Whatever the name, it results in the balanced equilibrium brought about by opposing selective forces. Since both alleles possess some selective advantage, they will be maintained in rather high frequencies; that is, they will be *polymorphic,* and we refer to stabilizing selection as producing a **balanced polymorphism.**

We refer to stabilizing selection as producing a balanced polymorphism.

An Overview of Evolutionary Genetics

The mechanisms of evolution that we have discussed do not work in isolation. They are all active at once, and the resulting course of evolution depends on how they interact with each other and with the environment of the population.

Earlier in this chapter we grouped the mechanisms of evolution into two categories: those responsible for the introduction of variation (mutation and gene flow) and those responsible for changes in the pattern of variation within a population (drift and selection). That is one way to view them, but in this section we will examine them in another way with another grouping. By doing this, we will demonstrate two different ways in which evolutionary changes may occur that could result in differing interpretations of the results of evolution.

Stochastic Mechanisms of Evolution

Suppose that you start out on a walk in some direction. Every time you must decide which of two or more paths to follow, you do so by tossing a coin. Where will you end up? You might visit some interesting places, but you won't have any idea about where you will be going in advance. Now extend this a little. Take twenty persons and group them into sets of four persons; put each set on one street corner so that the sets are separated by a single block. Now each individual should begin to walk, as before, and again when each person comes to a choice of routes, he or she should make the decision by coin-tossing. Now what will result? As each individual walks, he or she will begin to diverge from the other persons. But, in general, the four persons from any one set will tend to remain closer

Insight

Behavior Genetics—
Is Intelligence Inherited?

Few questions have inflamed human minds more than that of how much differences in intelligence reflect genetic factors. The scientific world has been torn by controversy on more than one occasion. Political systems have divided nations into groups that have espoused their philosophies to the point of violence.

But what do we know? What does it mean when the average IQ's for two samples of humans differ? Is one genetically the more intelligent? Are academic enrichment programs doomed because they cannot change the gene pool? The subject is complex and far too involved for us to go into it here. But one crucial point is too often overlooked: it is impossible for us to measure the genes for intelligence carried by any person. A little algebra will demonstrate that fact.

If our phenotype (P) is due to our heredity (H) and our environment (E), then we can say that our phenotypes are due to the effects of the two factors, or:

$$P = H + E$$

Now, the genetic component of intelligence in a group of persons may be thought of as that proportion of the group variation in intelligence that is due to genetic factors, or

$$Her = \frac{H}{H + E}$$

where *Her* is the heritability of intelligence.

The usual method is to compare twins. Identical twins are genetically identical; they differ only because of the environment (E). Fraternal twins differ in their genes as well as their environments (H + E). So if we compare the differences in intelligence between twins

who are identical and those who are fraternal, we have the following:

$$(Fraternal) - (Identical) = (H + E) - (E)$$

and, therefore,

$$Her = \frac{Frat - Iden}{Frat} = \frac{(H + E) - (E)}{H + E} = \frac{H}{H + E}$$

This looks imposing. We have designed a way to study the heritability of intelligence, since our equation ends with the original statement of what heritability equals. But does it? Look again. We really haven't measured heredity at all, have we? We have really only subtracted the environment of one set of twins from the environment of another set. Instead of measuring the genetic component, we have really measured the environment. We are really saying that what is left after we account for the environment is the heredity.

This is the paradox of trying to measure genetic differences in intelligence. It can't be done, and in fact, all we can do is measure the environment. So we really don't know if genes affect intelligence, how much they do so, or how much of the differences in intelligence we observe is due to that hidden genetic component.

to each other than they will to someone who started four or five blocks away.

We have just described evolution by **stochastic** mechanisms. If walking is a simulation of evolution, the paths these individuals took were determined by *stochastic,* or statistical, processes: tossing a coin. What causes the populations of the species (the individuals) to diverge from each other is genetic drift. What causes some to remain closer to each other is that they started from the same place. We could extend this example by noting that similarity would be maintained in a population through gene flow.

Many population geneticists see these as the primary mechanisms of evolutionary change in those alleles we can study at present. Populations are similar to each other because of *gene flow* between them, and they differ from each other because they have *drifted* apart. We cannot apply that principle blindly, since we have to take history into account as well. If a population in the South Pacific is genetically similar to one from northern Europe we don't assume that they have exchanged genes! It is interpreted as a result of *convergent evolution,* in which random processes by chance have caused this similarity.

This view of evolutionary change is called *non-Darwinian,* because change is interpreted as not happening by genetic adaptation but by random drift. Genetic variants are not seen as having adaptive significance (except where such significance can be demonstrated) but are neutral; hence this view is also called the view of the *neutralists.* Neutralists do recognize natural selection, but they see it as acting almost entirely as normalizing selection to eliminate deleterious variants, while neutral variants evolve in frequency through chance events.

This view of evolutionary change is called non-Darwinian.

Deterministic Mechanisms of Evolution

In contrast to this non-Darwinian evolution is *Darwinian evolution.* Such a view sees patterns of genetic variation as resulting from natural selection, not gene flow and drift. We call it a *deterministic* view, since it is held that selection "determines" evolution in a way that we can predict. It is also called a *selectionist* view.

To a selectionist, natural selection is primarily a directing or a stabilizing force—that is, it is innovative, shaping patterns of gene frequency in accordance with the pressures of the environment. Genetic variability results not from the "random-walking" analogy, but from specific adaptive forces. Genetic similarities do not result from populations' exchanging genes so much as from populations' adapting to similar evolutionary pressures.

Since this view of evolution represents an elaboration of Darwin's ideas, it is called *neo-Darwinian.* Neo-Darwinians feel that millions of years of evolution have produced a species with a "finely tuned" genetic structure interacting closely with its environment through natural selection. Variation that is not adaptive is seen as disturbing to this finely tuned relationship and, as a result, neo-Darwinians feel implicitly that neutral variation simply doesn't exist. Variation is equated with adaptation, and to study variation is to study adaptation.

Which view is right? Undoubtedly, both views share some part of the truth. In the last fifteen years, biochemical geneticists have uncovered much genetic variation in human populations and have been unable to demonstrate that it makes much difference to the individuals carrying the variants. It would seem, therefore, that a significant proportion of our genetic variation is neutral and has evolved by means of stochastic processes.

However, how much of our variation is neutral? No one knows, and so human biologists continue to study genetic variants in order to detect any that seem to be maintained by natural selection. Just as we can no longer ignore the existence of random stochastic evolution, neither can we ignore the steady directional trends in our evolutionary record that must have been caused by directional selection.

Summary

1. The gene is a double helical strand of DNA found in the nuclei of human cells. The four bases of this strand contain the genetic information.

2. Genetic information is transmitted from the gene by means of RNA, which is responsible for the synthesis of enzymes and other proteins.

3. Genes are carried on chromosomes, and a particular gene is located at a specific locus on a chromosome.

4. The genes at each locus are paired, one member of a pair coming from each parent. The genotype at that locus may be homozygous or heterozygous.

5. Heterozygous genotypes have different alleles. Alleles may be dominant, recessive, or codominant.

6. A Mendelian population is a group of persons who marry within that population. Its members share a common gene pool.

7. The synthetic theory of evolution defines evolution as changes in the frequency of alleles in a gene pool. The changes are caused by four evolutionary mechanisms: mutation, gene flow, genetic drift, and natural selection.

8. There are three types of natural selection: normalizing, directional, and stabilizing. [The hemoglobin locus provides, through the allele for sickle-cell anemia, an example of stabilizing selection.]

9. Non-Darwinian evolution sees evolutionary change as due to random factors. Gene frequencies are determined by genetic drift and gene flow.

10. Darwinian evolution views evolutionary change as a result of genetic adaptation. Gene frequencies are determined by natural selection.

Suggested Readings

Bodmer, Walter F., and Cavalli-Sforza, L. L. *Genetics, Evolution, and Man.* San Francisco: W. H. Freeman and Company, 1976.
> *This book may be heavy-going for a beginning student, nevertheless, it is authoritative and complete without being heavily mathematical.*

Crawford, Michael H., and Workman, Peter L., eds. *Methods and Theories of Anthropological Genetics.* Albuquerque: University of New Mexico Press, 1973.
> *A collection of papers relating human genetic variability to anthropological questions.*

Johnston, Francis E. *Microevolution of Human Populations.* Englewood Cliffs, N. J.: Prentice-Hall, 1973.
> *A simplified coverage of anthropological genetics focusing on evolutionary processes.*

McKusick, Victor A. *Human Genetics.* 2nd ed. Englewood Cliffs, N. J.: Prentice-Hall, 1969.
> *This is an excellent and thorough introduction to general human genetics.*

Watson, James D. *Molecular Biology of the Gene.* 2nd ed. New York: W. A. Benjamin, Inc., 1970.
> *A classic introduction to molecular genetics by one who won a Nobel Prize for work in the area.*

Glossary

allele An alternative form of a gene.

balanced polymorphism A genetic polymorphism that is maintained by selective pressures acting in opposite directions.

chromosome Strands of DNA found in the nucleus of each of the body's cells.

complementarity A principle stating that the base sequences of paired DNA strands are "complements." If one sequence is known, the other can be predicted.

deoxyribonucleic acid (DNA) A protein/acid compound found in the nucleus of cells; it is the hereditary material.

dominant An allele that will always be expressed in a heterozygous genotype, preventing the expression of the other allele of the pair.

enzymes   Proteins that act as catalysts in the thousands of chemical reactions that occur in the body's cells.

gene   The unit of heredity.

gene flow   The process by which genes enter and leave a gene pool as a result of migration.

genetic code   The amino acids determined by various triplets of RNA nucleotides.

genetic drift   A class of mechanisms that change gene frequency in a random, stochastic manner.

genotype   The combination of genes possessed by an organism.

heterozygote   A genotype in which different alleles of the gene are found at a locus on the two chromosomes of a pair.

homozygote   A genotype in which the same form of the gene is found at a locus on each chromosome of a pair.

phenotype   The expressed results of the interaction between one's genotype and the environment.

recessive   An allele that is not expressed in a heterozygous genotype.

ribonucleic acid (RNA)   A protein/acid compound that transfers genetic information from the cell nucleus into proteins.

sicklemia (sickle-cell anemia)   A disease in which the body's hemoglobin molecules are deficient in the capacity to carry oxygen, resulting in profound anemia.

stochastic evolution   Evolution by random, statistical change.

10

Adaptation, Adaptability, and Human Biology

Introduction

Making the ascent by train, one lightly touched by "seroche" [mountain sickness] experiences his first symptoms at an altitude of 10,000 feet or more. Subjectively lassitude, then headache, usually frontal growing in severity, and perhaps nausea are felt. One feels cold, particularly in the extremities, the pulse quickens, respiration becomes deeper and more frequent, the face is pallid, lips and nails are cyanotic [blue]. (Barrington 1968)

This is how one early traveler describes his experiences as he ascended into the South American Andes, outlining symptoms that are familiar to scientists and physicians as those of altitude sickness. Yet in South America, Asia, and Africa, hundreds of thousands of people live at those altitudes, as did their ancestors. How can they exist there? In studying the people who live in the world's many environments, we are interested in the adjustments people make that enable them to function in a world, to derive meaning from that world, and to persist in that world through time. In other words, how do people adapt to their environment?

Adaptation to the environment is not only a matter of the natives of high-altitude environments accommodating to the rigors of an oxygen-thin atmosphere. Far from it.

In his novel *Catch-22*, Joseph Heller demonstrates that stress and adaptation are features of everyday life.

The boy had black hair and needed a haircut and shoes and socks. His sickly face was pale and sad. His feet made grisly, soft, sucking sounds in the rain puddles on the wet pavement as he passed, and Yossarian was moved by such intense pity for his poverty that he wanted to smash his pale, sad, sickly face with his fist and knock him out of existence because he brought to mind all the pale, sad, sickly children in Italy that same night who needed haircuts and needed shoes and socks.

The concept of adaptation has been a major interest of natural scientists ever since Darwin first revealed the implications underlying it. Here we examine, in a broader perspective, the principles of biological adaptation. We also present some examples of the range of human adaptations and adaptability. Adaptation is a process that can involve all ranges of human biology and behavior. The very capacity to adapt has evolved, and humans possess a range of different kinds of adaptive mechanisms. An evolutionary perspective is central to our consideration of adaptation.

Adaptation as a Concept

We define adaptation as does Joseph Weiner, as "the adjustments necessary for successful existence in a particular habitat."

In general terms, we define adaptation as does Joseph Weiner, as "the adjustments necessary for successful existence in a particular habitat" (Weiner 1977: 389). Adaptation occurs at different levels of biological and cultural complexity. It consists of a series of responses that may be made by a single cell or by an entire society.

Different scientists see the concept of adaptation in different ways. Some argue that adaptation is an "all-or-none" process. To be alive is to be adapted, since anything that is nonadaptive will disappear. To them, no adaptation is better than any other (Stern 1970). Others see adaptation as an accommodation to opposing forces. They use stabilizing selection as a model; there are stresses that work in opposition to each other, and adaptation is the balance between these forces.

Most anthropologists agree that adaptation is a bit of both of these two views. It is correct (they feel) to say that any group that is not adapted to its environment is in trouble. Unless that group adjusts, its survival is unlikely. Therefore, being alive does indicate adaptation.

However, not all adaptations are equal in terms of efficiency. We discussed, in the previous chapter, the cost of selection. This idea can be extended to the cost of adaptation. If too many people must perish for a group to survive, then that adaptation is more costly than one necessitating fewer deaths. Adaptations can be compared so long as we make explicit the criteria we are using—whether deaths, energy expenditure, or population size increase.

Levels of Adaptation

Biological adaptations occur at three levels:

1. *Genetic*. A genetic adaptation occurs when an allele is adapted to a particular stress. For example, the sickle-cell gene is an adaptation to falciparum malaria. Genetic adaptations tend to be fixed; that is, a specific variant is adapted to a specific environmental stress. Genetic adaptations are the property of the gene pool of a population, and so the group as a whole is adapted. Even though everyone in a population does not carry the Hb^s allele, the population is adapted to malaria because the frequency of the allele is high enough to protect the entire group. Since they come about through natural selection, genetic adaptations require several, even many, generations.

2. *Physiological*. Physiological adaptations are adjustments made by individuals in response to short-term stress. Such responses are immediate, or nearly so, in contrast to the lengthy process of genetic adaptation. Physiological adaptations involve diverse responses to stresses due to nutritional intake, climate, altitude, and similar causes. Although such adaptations are not "controlled" by the genes, the capacity to make them has evolved.

3. *Developmental*. The term "developmental adaptation" (Baker 1969) refers to responses to stresses that occur over longer periods of time in the life of an individual; they reflect the *plasticity* of humans, that is,

the capability of the phenotype to alter in response to some chronic stress. Since this capability is greatest during the growing years, these changes are termed developmental adaptations. They persist into adulthood and result in efficient adaptations among adults.

Cultural responses to environmental stresses, which are equally as complex as biological changes, will be covered in subsequent chapters. In addition, cultural and biological factors may operate in response to the same stress. In fact, they generally do.

The Concept of Multiple Stresses

Ordinarily we think in terms of single stresses—say, temperature or disease or nutrition. This is largely because of the complexity of trying to think about a number of stresses all acting at the same time. Despite this, we must always realize that human populations live in ecosystems that contain many stressing agents. Take, for example, those Indians living in the Peruvian Andes at altitudes above 10,000 feet. To what stresses must they adapt? One obvious answer is, "The reduced oxygen in the air at that altitude, of course." This is right, as the stress of reduced oxygen pressure is considerable. But consider the other pressures faced by such groups. At altitudes this great it is cold, with temperatures falling into the 30s and 40s (Fahrenheit) every night. The crops that can be grown at this altitude are not nearly so nutritious as those grown lower, so the people also are exposed to nutritional stresses. Altitude, temperature, nutrition—all these are components of the system of stresses that can be identified in high-altitude Peruvians (Baker 1969).

An Adaptation May Become a Stress

An adaptation itself becomes a stress more commonly than one might think, especially from a long-term point of view. In an earlier chapter we discussed the development of farming as an adaptation, with the result that people could live in settled communities with larger populations. But what other results does a sedentary way of life bring? One has been the increase in infectious diseases, which became prevalent as people settled in villages, living in the midst of the parasites they once left behind them. Adaptations that become stresses require still further adaptations.

Biological Responses to Stress

In this section we will describe the human responses to various selected stresses. As we do so, we will demonstrate the range of stresses to which the human species has adapted, and still is adapting, during its evolution.

By focusing on stresses, we will emphasize the complexity of the responses, including to a limited degree those responses that are part of culture. Our main emphasis will be on genetic, physiological, and developmental responses to identifiable stresses.

Temperature

Temperature is one of the most variable features of human environments, for humans range from the cold of the Arctic to the heat of the world's deserts. Despite the great range of temperatures in these environments, humans, as mammals, are able to maintain a body temperature within a narrow range around 98.6° F (37° C). This is accomplished by an efficient "thermostat" in the brain, the hypothalamus, which senses changes in body temperature. If the difference between the heat produced by the body and the temperature of the air around it is too great, too much heat will be lost at the body's surface. If the difference is too little, then not enough heat will be lost, and it will accumulate.

Various physiological mechanisms are brought into play when the hypothalamus senses that heat is being lost too rapidly or too slowly. When the air is cold and heat is lost too rapidly, we speak of *cold stress*. In response, the blood vessels constrict, reducing the flow of warmed arterial blood to the surface where its heat would dissipate. If this is insufficient, we will begin to shiver, expending energy through work and thus producing heat.

If the air temperature is too high, the body will not lose heat rapidly enough, and there will be *heat stress*. One response is the dilation of the blood vessels, increasing the flow of warmed blood to the surface. Another is perspiration; as the sweat evaporates, the temperature of the air immediately surrounding the body is lowered, permitting the loss of heat.

These responses are universal, shown by all humans; they are the basic set of responses utilized to maintain **homeostasis,** or equilibrium, in temperature. In addition, our bodies can become acclimatized to chronic conditions we experience. Suppose we were to conduct an experiment on the day-to-day ability of humans to work in a controlled environment where the temperature is constantly high. On the first day, our subjects will be able to work for only about an hour without giving up. However, after five days of working in these conditions, they will be able to work for four or more hours. In addition, we find that the subjects are expending less energy as they work. Not only is their capacity to work increased, but their efficiency is also improved.

Considering this experiment, what about the peoples of the world who have lived in chronically hot or cold environments for thousands of years? Have anthropologists found adaptations in these populations that

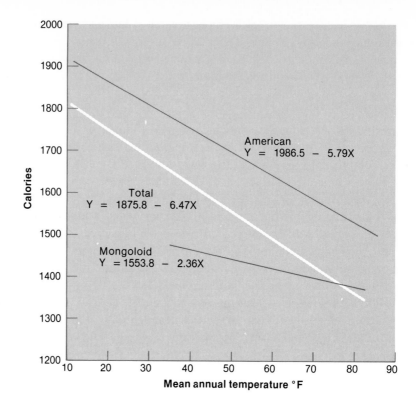

Figure 10.1
Relationship between average metabolic rate, expressed in calories expended, and annual temperature. Where the temperature is lower, individuals burn up more calories in the resting state.

American
$Y = 1986.5 - 5.79X$

Total
$Y = 1875.8 - 6.47X$

Mongoloid
$Y = 1553.8 - 2.36X$

Calories

Mean annual temperature °F

differentiate heat-stressed from cold-stressed groups? The answer is yes, and in fact, there is a wide range of adaptive variation characterizing populations living in different temperature conditions.

As an example, consider *basal metabolic rates* (BMR). This rate is a measure of the heat produced by the body under controlled, resting conditions. Derek Roberts has compared the metabolic rates of populations living in different parts of the world, analyzing the extent to which groups living in cold climates produce more body heat while at rest than those living in hot climates. The study is not concerned with heat produced while performing any activities; only that in the resting state—the heat the members of a given group "normally" produce.

Figure 10.1 is taken from Roberts's analysis (Roberts 1952). It shows clearly that people native to particular temperatures produce heat appropriate to that temperature. The lower the temperature, the higher the total heat production, expressed in the graph as calories. There are exceptions, as one might expect; after all, temperature cannot account for all the variation in human basal metabolic rates. Nevertheless the trend is clear and indicates an *adaptive gradient* relating heat production to temperature. (The term *gradient* means that as temperature gradually increases, BMR gradually decreases.)

Studies of specific populations have revealed two patterns of adaptation to cold temperatures:

1. *Metabolic acclimatization.* In this response, the adaptation to cold stress comes through an increase in body heat production, or metabolism. We may use the analogy of turning up the thermostat in a house to produce more warmth. Peoples with this adaptive mechanism show an increase in metabolic rate when they are experimentally exposed to cold stress. The *core* (inner) temperature of their bodies remains at or near 98.6° F (37° C). The extra heat produced is carried to the surface of the body where it is lost into the air. Consequently, peoples displaying this response have higher skin temperatures.

Metabolic acclimatization characterizes most of the populations of the world. Peoples who live in colder regions maintain their body temperatures more effectively than those in warmer regions. Eskimos are better adapted to cold than people in the lower 48 states. And people in the northern states are better adapted than people in the southern states.

Metabolic acclimatization is, in some ways, costly. Just as heating bills go up when the thermostat is set higher, so the body requires more energy (calories) when metabolism increases. In both cases, the extra heat is eventually lost, through the walls of the house or from the surface of the body.

2. *Insulative hypothermia.* The second pattern of adaptation to cold involves the conservation of the heat that is generated, rather than the production of extra heat. It is analogous to closing off unused rooms and insulating a house. The core temperature remains at 98.6° F (37° C) and there is no increase in metabolism; no more heat is produced. Instead, the surface temperature of the body becomes lower, dropping in some instances to below 60° F (16° C). This indicates that body heat is not being lost as readily; instead, it is conserved for the protection of the internal organs.

Insulative hypothermia is the response of some people living in the colder deserts of the world: the Aborigines of the central Australian desert and the Khoisan-speaking Bushmen of the Kalahari of South Africa. In one experiment, some Australian Aborigines were monitored as they slept, wearing only their usual minimal clothing, through the cold desert winter night. A control sample of Europeans not used to such temperatures slept under the same conditions. The whites produced more body heat than the Australians, but their responses were erratic and varied from one hour to the next. The Aborigines maintained a relatively low but constant heat production throughout the night. It was also observed that the whites slept fitfully while the Australian subjects slept quietly.

Heat loss is also prevented by the layer of fat surrounding the body. While this fat layer serves to store calories for energy, it also insulates the body like a blanket—the thicker the layer, the better the insulation. The

Figure 10.2
These two bodies are of equal volume. In addition, the radius of the sphere is equal to the base of the solid. However, their surface areas differ, as shown and, as a result, the ratio of mass/surface area is different. Heat loss would be facilitated more in the solid. Thus the solid is more "adapted" to hot climates and the sphere more "adapted" to cold climates.

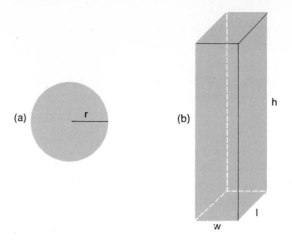

(a)

(b)

Volume = $\frac{4}{3}\pi r^3$ = 100
Surface Area = πd^2 = 104.2
Surface Area/Volume = 1.042

Volume = lwh = 100
Surface Area = 155.5
Surface Area/Volume = 1.555

Figure 10.3
Relationship between average body weight and annual temperature in various groups. Smaller people are found in warmer regions and larger people in colder regions.

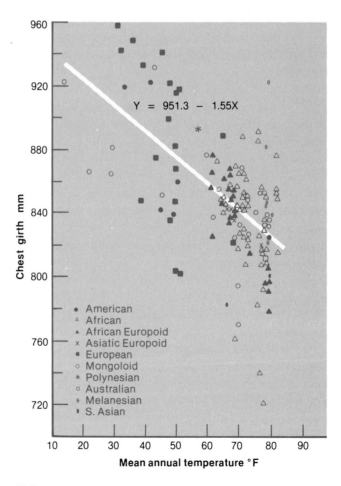

$Y = 951.3 - 1.55X$

- • American
- △ African
- ▲ African Europoid
- × Asiatic Europoid
- ■ European
- ○ Mongoloid
- * Polynesian
- ▫ Australian
- ⊖ Melanesian
- • S. Asian

Chest girth mm

Mean annual temperature °F

amount of fat carried by various groups differs widely, largely because of nutritional reasons. However, in any human group, females have more fat than males. An average white American male carries about 15 percent of his body weight as fat, while a female has about 25 percent. Americans of African ancestry have less fat, though the sex differences remain.

Tests of cold resistance between males and females show greater resistance among females. For example, one experiment placed subjects in a water bath in which the temperature was steadily lowered; the temperature at which each subject began to shiver was recorded. Male subjects consistently shivered before females, indicating less resistance to the cold. The most obvious explanation for this sex difference is the greater insulation provided by increased fat deposits in females.

A wide range of morphological features are associated with temperature, indicating that the differences recorded in body shapes and sizes among peoples of the world are of adaptive significance. A "bulkier" body is easier to keep warm than a slender one. Since heat is produced by the cell mass of the body, the greater that mass, the more heat produced. As Figure 10.2 shows, increasing the size of the body (or any object) increases its volume (and hence its mass) by an exponential factor of 3 (that is, x^3). But it increases the surface area of the body by only a factor of 2 (x^2). So by increasing size, we cube the volume, but only square the surface area.

The result is obvious: a larger body is adaptive in a colder climate since there is relatively more bulk to produce heat than there is surface area to dissipate it. If we examine the distribution of body size among peoples of the world relative to the climates in which they live, studying only populations living in environments where their ancestors have lived for generations, we find a clear association (Figure 10.3). Derek Roberts showed that larger body sizes are found among peoples living in colder regions and smaller sizes among people living in warmer regions.

Body size is not the only adaptive aspect of human morphology. There is also body shape, especially the length of the extremities. Figure 10.4 contrasts the physique of an Eskimo with that of an African from the very hot, dry climate of the upper Nile. The very long extremities of the Nilote are similar in function to the sections of a radiator—they provide maximal surface area for the loss of heat—while the shorter extremities of the Eskimo retain the heat more effectively.

A linear physique is especially adaptive to dry heat, where the humidity is low. Under such conditions, the sweat will evaporate more quickly, causing greater heat loss. Africans living in the hot, dry regions of the continent are tall and slender with elongated extremities, a physique "designed" for living in those conditions.

On the other hand, when the climate is humid, perspiration is less effective as a method of heat loss. It is more adaptive to be small and to

Figure 10.4
The differences recorded in body shapes and sizes among peoples of the world are of adaptive significance. Contrast the physiques of the Greenland Eskimo people with the African woman from the upper regions of the Nile and note how their bodies are adapted to the climates in which they live.

produce less heat—and such an adaptation characterizes the world's tropical forest dwellers.

Other morphological features have been suggested as being adaptive to temperature but the evidence is not conclusive. (See, for example, Weiner 1977.) Nose shape, for example, is related to climate in that peoples living in dry areas characteristically have long, narrow noses. Since one function of the nose is to moisten the air breathed in and remove dust particles from it, longer noses may be adaptive in such an environment.

Morphological responses to temperature stem from differential rates of growth during childhood. However, since growth is also affected by other factors such as nutrition, it is often difficult to make many statements about growth as a response to climatic stress, though the associations noted are strongly suggestive.

Are these adaptive features of morphology inherited or acquired? That is, are they genetic adaptations that have been selected through the processes of evolution, or are they adaptive responses to the environment that arise during growth? We cannot be certain of the answer. It seems difficult to attribute to the environment the many adaptive differences we may see in body size and shape. Furthermore, the people of African ancestry now living in North and South America continue to display relatively long legs despite having lived in new environments for centuries. Likewise, the descendants of Europeans living in the New World are more like other Europeans than like either American Indians or New World blacks.

On the other hand, experimenters have shown that if rats are raised from birth at either very high or very low temperatures, their growth patterns will be altered in an adaptive way (Harrison 1959; Lee 1969). Cold-stressed rats and mice will grow up with shorter tails and less elongated bodies than heat-stressed rats and mice. It is quite possible that genetic and environmental factors reinforce each other as mechanisms for climatic adaptation.

Disease

Of all the stresses to which human populations have been exposed, disease is one of the most severe. The term "disease" is difficult to define, representing simply an abnormal state of being. We may think of disease in three categories, each one having implications for the process of biological adaptation.

The first category is *inherited disease,* a disease caused by a genetic defect. Such diseases are usually rather rare, since natural selection may be directed against the responsible gene. They are usually impossible to cure since they are inherited and the defect is in the DNA. Treatment usually involves dealing with the symptoms.

The next category is *infectious disease,* which is caused by the presence of some organism—bacteria, viruses, and the like. These organisms are part of the environment to which humans have been chronically exposed, and mechanisms of resistance commonly have evolved by natural selection. Genetic variation in human populations may exist because natural selection is acting as a response to the stresses of different diseases.

The final category consists of *chronic diseases.* Chronic diseases are not caused by microorganisms but by agents such as environmental pollutants and overnutrition. They make up the bulk of the disease load borne by modern industrialized nations. While we have eradicated many infectious diseases through vaccination programs and other public health measures, we have created urban environments that create their own stresses and their own set of diseases.

Cancer is a disease of modern civilization. Michael Zimmerman, an anthropologist, has performed autopsies on many Egyptian mummies and found no malignancies among them. Contrast this with the United States today. Or consider our diets. We do not lack nutrients as the peoples of the Third World do, but we eat far too much sugar, salt, and animal fat. Obesity, high blood pressure, and heart disease—diseases that kill Americans of the twentieth century—are caused by malnutrition. Not the malnutrition of deficiency, but the malnutrition of excess and affluence.

In the United States, modern medicine has reduced the incidence of infectious disease to the lowest levels ever known. But many chronic diseases are on the increase, and we seem unable to control the social conditions responsible for them. Modern medicine can only attempt to prolong the lives of those who contract these diseases.

Genetic Adaptation to Disease   By now there is evidence that some of the so-called "normal" human genetic variants are in fact associated with certain diseases. In particular, different alleles at the ABO locus seem to indicate susceptibilities to particular diseases. Persons with the A allele show an increased susceptibility to some cancers: cancer of the stomach, pancreas, uterine cervix, and salivary glands. On the other hand, persons with blood type O (or OO homozygotes) show a higher incidence of gastric ulcers and possibly of plague and syphilis.

This may sound bizarre, but it really shouldn't. The substances responsible for the ABO blood types are closely tied into the body's immune system, which determines an individual's ability to defend himself or herself physiologically against infectious agents. It would seem logical that the widespread variation in the distribution of the ABO alleles would reflect thousands of years of natural selection. Certain alleles were selected against because, in a given environment they were susceptible to agents of disease.

Genetic Adaptation to Malaria Of all diseases that have affected the human species, malaria seems to have been one of the most potent. Falciparum malaria, an often-fatal form, is widespread in west and central Africa, south India, southeast and southwest Asia, and in earlier years, southern Europe, especially Italy and Greece and the Mediterranean islands. Modern medical technology has done much to arrest the spread of malaria, but it is highly resistant to eradication.

Where malaria is common, or was common in the recent past, several genetic variants also are common. Research has demonstrated that these variants have problably been selected as adaptive responses to the disease. We have already mentioned sickle-cell hemoglobin, which was shown to be resistant to malaria by Anthony Allison in the mid-1950s (Allison 1955). Shortly afterward, in one of the classics of biocultural research in anthropology, Frank Livingstone delineated the role of human activity in the interaction between malaria and human gene pools (Livingstone 1958).

Livingstone's research demonstrated that the Hb^S allele was associated with malaria in populations that practiced **swidden,** or **slash-and-burn,** agriculture. The trees of the tropical rain forest were felled and then the trees and underbrush burned off, making a garden in which crops could be raised. In central Africa, the adoption of root crops introduced from the east allowed people to penetrate the forests of central and west Africa by providing them with the subsistence base for exploiting a rain forest ecology.

However, swidden agriculture requires huge parcels of land. This particular food production system depletes the garden soil of nutrients in a few plantings, and the society must prepare new lands. There are always gardens in various stages of preparation, cultivation, and regrowth. In the last stage, when the land is fallow, or unused, it is a ready breeding ground for mosquitoes. The threat of malaria increases strikingly along with the mosquito population and the parasites they carry.

We may reason as follows: The rain forests were areas for hunting and some collecting until the development of root-cropping. Then the forest was penetrated and was increasingly exploited by agricultural groups practicing slash-and-burn farming. This farming technique led to the increase in the anopheles mosquito and so to an increase also in the incidence of falciparum malaria, carried by a parasite of the mosquito. Under those conditions, the allele Hb^S was at a selective advantage. Whereas normalizing selection had previously worked toward its elimination, now heterozygote advantage led to an increase in the frequency of the gene to its present high level in Africa.

Thus, human cultural activity altered the habitat and led to a new set of environmental conditions and disease agents. This resulted in a

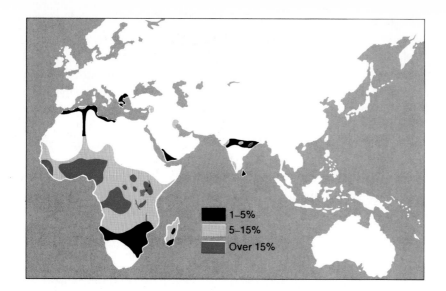

Figure 10.5
Distribution of hemoglobin
variants in Old World.

1–5%
5–15%
Over 15%

change in the action of natural selection and led to frequencies of .30 for Hb^S in some groups. When Africans were brought as slaves to the New World, the selective advantage was lost. (Falciparum malaria was not present in the New World until it was introduced by the explorers and has never been present in North America.) Therefore, all selection in Americans of African ancestry has been directed at the elimination of the allele, since it has no advantage in the western hemisphere. It protects against nothing and only causes sickle-cell anemia, the often-fatal disease we discussed in an earlier chapter.

The malaria story does not end with Hb^S. Although most of the hemoglobin variants are rare ones, apparently the result of recurrent mutations, two others are also common among groups living in the malaria belt of the Old World. Hemoglobin C, caused by the Hb^C allele, is common in central Africa and southwest Asia; in southeast Asia, Hb^E is found in groups exposed to malaria. Presumably, these represent variants that were selected because they conferred a resistance to the disease through their effects on hemoglobin structure.

Two other genetic variants complete the malaria story. One codes a red cell enzyme called glucose-6-phosphate-dehydrogenase, or *G6PD;* a deficient form of the enzyme seems to be malaria-resistant. It is found in Africa as well as in southwest Asia.

The other variant allele results in a red blood cell with a shortened life span. A normal red blood cell lives for some three months before it dies and is replaced by a new one. In the genetic disease *thalassemia,* the red cell lives only a few weeks, producing a severe anemia. The alleles for this disease are found in high frequency in Italy and in Greece (as well as in Italian- and Greek-Americans), especially in parts of those countries where malaria was a problem before the advent of modern medical technology.

Disease stress may have been an important selective agent in human evolution, especially in the past several thousand years since populations became large enough to support a disease. Before then, an infectious agent would move through a small, isolated population, infecting everyone and making those who survived immune. When it had infected everyone, there was no one left alive who had not been infected. In a larger population, however, by the time the infectious organism had spread through a population, a new generation had grown to a susceptible age and the disease could begin again (Cockburn 1967).

Nutrition

As DNA provides the instructions for the synthesis of substances vital to human life, the nutrients we take in with the food we eat provide the raw materials required by the DNA. These nutrients provide the cells with energy for carrying out various reactions, amino acids for manufacturing protein, and vitamins and minerals essential to the body's functioning.

Human diets must contain adequate amounts of these nutrients. Stini (1975) has argued that in areas where nutritional intake is limited, small body size is an effective adaptation, since a small person does not require as many calories or as much protein to support his or her body mass.

In one example, Brooke Thomas has analyzed the utilization of nutrient energy among high-altitude Peruvians. The growth spurt that occurs at adolescence results in a rapid addition of body mass as individuals grow in both height and weight. But in the Peruvian community of Nuñoa, the adolescent spurt is delayed, and when it occurs, is not intense. This modification of growth saves the Nuñoans 35,000,000 calories—corresponding to 31,000 pounds of potatoes (Thomas 1973).

Humans display a variety of physiological mechanisms that allow them to adapt to changing nutrient intakes. For example, calcium is a mineral essential to the body. When the intake of calcium is adequate, the body absorbs about only 30 percent of that taken in as part of the diet; the rest is excreted. However, when the calcium in the diet drops, the body adjusts. It absorbs a higher percentage and excretes less, providing an adequate supply in the face of a reduced diet.

Changing nutritional patterns associated with the development of agriculture have drastically altered the biological interactions of groups with their environments. The disease diabetes, for example, is caused by a deficiency in the production of the hormone insulin. A diet high in carbohydrates can trigger this disease. But human diets did not become so high in carbohydrates until the development of agriculture, when starchy vegetable products became much more common in human diets.

Many nutritional adaptations are cultural, involving practices that enhance the nutrient value of foods. In the Near East, wheat was domesticated as the primary plant food. But one substance in wheat, phytate, is difficult to digest and forms compounds that are excreted, causing a loss of some essential nutrients including the mineral zinc. Since there is little zinc in the Near Eastern diet, this loss produces deficiency symptoms in people who eat a high-wheat diet. The adaptation to this stress is to make the wheat into leavened bread; the yeast used in leavening reduces the amount of zinc lost from the wheat.

In Mesoamerica, the traditional Indian diet is rich in corn. In fact, corn is both the major source of energy and a source of protein. However, corn is deficient in one essential amino acid, lysine, and so the protein of the traditional maize diet is poor in quality. The Indians of the area, though knowing no formal biochemistry, nonetheless have adapted. They boil the corn in lime water, rich in calcium carbonate. As a result, the relative amount of lysine is increased threefold, and the amino acid balance of this dietary staple is much improved (Katz, Hediger, and Valleroy 1975).

Ultraviolet Radiation

Still another stress is the ultraviolet radiation of the sun. Sunlight is necessary, on the one hand, for the body to manufacture vitamin D, which is essential for the absorption of calcium into the system. But the radiation of the sun is also harmful, producing skin cancer in many persons. While this particular form of cancer is not so dangerous as others, nevertheless its prevalence in places such as Australia, Texas, and South Africa is several times that in more northerly latitudes.

Where the radiation of the sun is intense (i.e., near the Equator) native peoples have darker skins. It has been shown that this dark skin color is due to the deposition of granules of a pigment called **melanin** within the outer layer of the skin. In addition to giving the skin its characteristic color, melanin also acts as a barrier to the sun's rays; darker skin filters out more of this harmful radiation.

It has been suggested that dark skin is an adaptation to intense ultraviolet radiation. The geographical distribution of skin color confirms this idea, as does the fact that everyone tans in response to sunlight, no matter how dark their skin.

If dark skin protects against the sun's rays, what is the advantage of

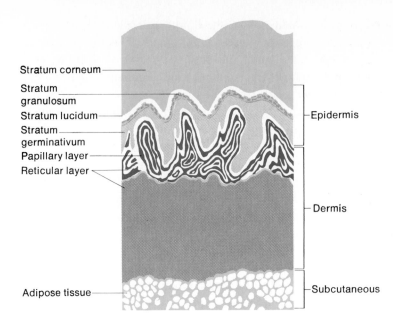

Figure 10.6
Schematic of cross-section of skin. Skin color is due to melanin, which arises from melanocytes located at the base of the epidermis.

Stratum corneum

Stratum granulosum

Stratum lucidum

Stratum germinativum

Papillary layer

Reticular layer

Epidermis

Dermis

Adipose tissue

Subcutaneous

light skin color? Loomis (1967) argues that light skin color is an adaptation for the northern latitudes, where the amount of sunlight and the direction of the rays result in far lower levels of radiation. In such environments, light skin color would facilitate the production of vitamin D and allow the absorption of adequate amounts of calcium.

There are exceptions to the hypothesized distribution of light and dark skin color as a response to sunlight. The American Indians do not vary a great deal in color, yet they are distributed from the Arctic Circle to and beyond the Equator. Likewise, the peoples of Tasmania (now extinct, having been eliminated by Europeans) lived in a temperate environment yet were dark-skinned. On the whole, though, the association seems to be a clear one despite these exceptions.

Altitude

Humans have lived at high altitudes for centuries, and as we suggested at the beginning of this chapter, the stress on the nonacclimatized can be considerable. On the other hand, the people who are indigenous to the area function well and work hard; in fact, the mighty Inca Empire of prehistoric times was centered in the highlands of Peru.

At high altitudes, stress derives from diminished oxygen pressure. Since every body function depends on a sufficient oxygen supply, it is obvious that an oxygen-deficient environment must produce a spectrum of adaptations. Such is the case. High-altitude natives display adaptations in four areas: blood, circulation, respiration, and morphology. Although hemoglobin is not structurally different from that of lowland natives, its level is considerably higher, providing more area for transporting oxygen. Other biochemical and cellular changes enhance the transport of oxygen through the circulatory system and into the tissues themselves.

High-altitude natives take in more air as they breathe, about 20 percent more than sea-level residents. High-altitude American Indians have developed large barrel chests to enhance oxygen intake.

Growth patterns also seem to be altered at high altitudes. In Peru, Frisancho and Baker (1970) have described a slowed pattern of growth with hardly any discernible adolescent spurt. Reproduction is affected. It was decades before a child was born to the immigrant Spanish parents; and birth weights are lower among high-altitude Indians than among their lowland relatives (McClung 1969).

Are these responses genetic or are they the result of human plasticity? After a decade of careful study, Baker (1969) and his colleagues have concluded that the majority of the responses noted are nongenetic and have arisen as a result of exposure to stressful conditions through the sensitive years of development.

Cultural Interactions

Despite this chapter's emphasis on biological adaptation, we cannot ignore the crucial role of culture in adaptation. There is no doubt that early hominids adapted biologically to the stresses they encountered in their original tropical homelands. As they spread throughout the world into different climates, zones, and ecosystems, the spectrum of adaptations increased further. There is no doubt that gene pools have been modified, and physiology and morphology shaped to adjust to the multiple stresses of environments. In other words, variation results from adaptation; and to study biological variation is to study the results of adaptive processes.

Culture, however, is that mechanism of adaptation, unique to humans, which has ultimately made the difference. While biological adaptation is evident among Arctic peoples, so are cultural adaptations to this acutely cold environment. Their clothing and houses protect them from the weather; their technology allows them successfully to exploit the animal and plant life. Without these cultural factors, Eskimos, Aleuts, and Indians could not have survived for thousands of years.

Culture, however, is that mechanism of adaptation, unique to humans, which has ultimately made the difference.

The same is true elsewhere. While the environmental stress may not be as dramatic as in the Arctic, culture is still central to the adaptive process, whether it is expressed in ways of ensuring an adequate diet, ways of protecting against disease, or ways of surviving in varying ranges of temperature.

Evolution and Adaptation— Are We Better on All Fours?

It is standard practice to extol the advantages of upright posture. "It distinguishes humans from apes!" we say, or "It freed the hands for making tools." Other reasons also are given for the evolution of this specialized means of carrying one's self and of the specialized means of locomotion that accompanied it. They all seem reasonable and logical, and they generally go unchallenged by evolutionary biologists.

But is upright posture all to the good? What are some of its *unfavorable* consequences? Or, as Wilton Krogman wrote in 1951, what are the "scars of human evolution"?

Look at our spinal columns. They are engineered to permit us to stand erect. The single curved arch of the backbone of the quadruped has evolved into the S-shaped curve of *H. sapiens.* Our spinal columns are flexible, and they twist and bend with ease. To accomplish this, however, our vertebrae (the individual bones of our spines) have become wedge-shaped, thicker in front and thinner in the back. They can pivot on each

other like hinges. But sudden strains may cause the lowest vertebrae to slip backward. Our backs ache because our ancestors stood erect.

Let us consider our internal organs. They are not suspended from our vertebrae as in quadrupeds; they hang straight down parallel to the spinal column. The wall of the abdomen has the task of supporting the internal organs that press downward and outward against it. Evolution has produced a reinforced wall with three sheets of muscles. But evolution hasn't finished the job; there is a triangular area in the wall where there is virtually no muscular support—a site where we are prone to hernia. A hernia is the result of the protrusion of abdominal organs through the wall, something which we can attribute to our evolution.

We could list other "scars," too. Fallen arches, impacted wisdom teeth, and varicose veins are all problems we encounter and burdens we bear. We bear these burdens because we stand erect as humans—by means of a skeletal system that has not solved this basic problem of human engineering.

Adaptation and the Unity of the Species

The consequence of the spread of humans throughout the entire world has been an incredible range of biological diversity brought on by adaptive responses to environmental stresses. One of the most important aspects of this is that humans have successfully adapted to so many environments, yet have remained a single species. The polar bear, the brown bear, and the grizzly bear are all different species adapted to different habitats, but the humans who live in those same environments are all members of one species, *H. sapiens.*

Human adaptive processes have more and more been transferred from the allele to the phenotype. Rather than specific, genetically determined responses to specific environmental stresses, humans have evolved the capacity to adapt through plasticity of the phenotype, through the accumulation of responses arising during the growing years, and through mechanisms learned as a result of culture.

The fact that we have remained a single species is important in studying human adaptation and adaptability. It is important as well in its implications for the diffusion of culture and the maintenance of a common core of humanity. Gene flow indicates that there is biological communication between populations. It also indicates that people are moving from group to group and, as they move, they communicate, spread ideas, and facilitate cultural innovation.

How this happened we can only speculate. Perhaps the natural inquisitiveness of our species caused individuals to communicate with their fellow humans. Perhaps population sizes were increasing so rapidly that there was constant out-migration from groups as they became too large for the ecosystem in which they lived. As out-migration occurred, relationships with parental groups were maintained, and gene flow kept enough homogeneity between the groups to prevent speciation—the separation into distinct species.

We only know that human groups did not become long-term isolates, separated for thousands of years from other groups and breeding only within the boundaries of their own population. This would have led to speciation. Instead, the human species evolved as a single species throughout the world, and this unity of the species was maintained even when the habitats differed radically.

In the past, anthropologists argued about differences in the mental processes of "primitive" peoples. If their mentalities and their temperaments differed biologically, then so might their needs. If all of this was true, then Europeans and their descendants were innately superior, not just because of accidents of history but because of biological evolution.

The human species evolved as a single species throughout the world, and this unity of the species was maintained even when the habitats differed radically.

In 1938, in one of the most influential books ever written by an anthropologist, *The Mind of Primitive Man,* Franz Boas (1858–1942) argued forcefully and convincingly that all humans displayed the same basic needs. Just as we are one species biologically, so are we one mentally.

Just as we are one species biologically, so are we one mentally.

Anthropologists have continued to make this theme central in their study of human diversity. Regardless of the environments, the adaptive responses, and the biological variability that we display, all of us are human.

Summary

1. The concept of adaptation is crucial in studying the relationships between populations and their environments.

2. Adaptations may be genetic, physiological, or developmental. *Genetic* adaptations arise from natural selection, while *physiological* and *developmental* adaptations refer to changes in the phenotype.

3. The two major types of physiological adaptations to temperature in human groups are metabolic acclimatization and insulative hypothermia. Insulation against the cold is also provided by the body's layer of fat.

4. Cold climates favor large individuals with short extremities. In hot dry climates, the best-adapted physique is a linear one, with long extremities and relatively small body mass. In hot wet climates, smaller individuals are at an adaptive advantage.

5. Human populations adapt to disease stresses. In sedentary farmers, infectious diseases are common, but in industrialized nations, the major stress comes from chronic disease.

6. The best example of the interaction of culture, biology, and disease is the evolutionary response to malaria.

7. Other stresses to which groups have adapted include nutrition, ultraviolet radiation, and altitude.

8. Culture is the mechanism of adaptation that has allowed humans to live successfully in so many environments. It has also resulted in the biological unity of the species: though we have adapted to many different stresses, we are still a single species.

Suggested Readings

Baker, Paul T., and Weiner, Joseph S. *The Biology of Human Adaptability.* Oxford: Clarendon Press, 1966.
  An excellent overview of the many facets of human adaptability.

Dubos, Rene. *Man Adapting.* New Haven, Conn.: Yale University Press, 1965.
  The author skillfully describes the interactions between humans and their environments, stressing health and disease.

Little, M. A., and Morren, George E. B., Jr. *Ecology, Energetics, and Human Variability.* Dubuque: William C. Brown Company Publishers, 1976.
  A well-done introduction to human ecology, stressing the concept of the ecosystem as a model for energy flow.

Stini, William A. *Ecology and Human Adaptation.* Dubuque: William C. Brown Company Publishers, 1975.
  The author presents the concept of adaptation in human biology, emphasizing the role of culture as a buffer.

Underwood, Jane H. *Biocultural Interactions and Human Variation.* Dubuque: William C. Brown Company Publishers, 1975.
  The author stresses the fact that biology and culture interact in the adaptive process.

Glossary

melanin   Granules of pigment just under the surface of skin that give the skin its characteristic color.

slash-and-burn   Swidden agriculture.

swidden   Slash-and-burn agriculture. The larger trees and undergrowth are cut down, and final clearance is done by burning everything.

11

Biological Variation in Living Human Populations

Introduction

Humans are an incredibly varied lot, spread over the entire earth, exposed to all kinds of environments, and displaying different ways of living in those environments. This we know from reading and looking at pictures and from our own travels and the travels of others.

But it is not enough to realize that we are different, and that the differences reflect important processes and mechanisms. We also have to be concerned with the nature, extent, and clustering of those differences. We need to know just *how* we differ, in what characteristics. We need to know *how much* we differ, what the range of variation is that we can observe. Finally, we need to know *how continuous* the differences are. That is, if we were to start from San Francisco and go around the world in a westerly direction, would we observe a gradual change in the physical characteristics of the people we encounter? Or would we note discontinuities, gaps, and other indications that the distribution of variability can be seen in terms of subgroups or, more formally, of subspecies?

In this chapter we will extend the "so what" question by examining the extent and distribution of human biological variability and by attempting to place it into some perspective.

Earlier Views of Biological Variability

The existence of biological variability has fascinated scientists and non-scientists for as long as we have records. We know many stories of the response—usually curiosity—to encounters with different peoples. Marco Polo is renowned because of his travels to the Far East, his reception there, and the news he brought back. Sir Walter Raleigh created a sensation when he took Native Americans to England. The Explorers Club is an organization of people who have traveled to out-of-the-way places and encountered different groups of people.

Nothing seems to have stimulated the development of the sciences of human biology and behavior as much as the discovery of variation among the world's peoples. Prior to that time, scientists were concerned with structure and function, but only within the narrow context of western Europe. Variability was limited. The discovery of fossils prodded investigators to explain them, providing a major force in the development of the theory of evolution. The recognition of the extent of physical variation among the living peoples of the world led to the search for an explanation and to the development of the science of human biology.

The first reaction to human biological variability was to deny humanity to other groups. The *polygenists* held that the different groups encountered were, in fact, different species. Acceptance of this view would, of course, have placed an entirely different perspective on the interpretation of human variation. In the pre-evolutionary world of the nineteenth century, different species would have meant different creations; and with different creations, the problem was solved. "They" simply were not human and therefore belonged to another world.

The Origin of the Race Concept

Gradually the *monogenist* view of human diversity—that all were one species—became accepted at least in principle. At the time, the controversy had moral overtones, since Christian missionaries were faced with the question of whether to attempt to convert peoples in these newly discovered lands—for if they weren't human, they didn't have souls. This problem was solved when the Pope stated that American Indians were human!

In accepting the monogenist view, the scientific world began to develop the concept of race. Since variability was seen in typological terms, races were thought of as types, or varieties, of humans. And since classification was then the basic task of science, physical anthropologists became involved with the development of a "correct" racial taxonomy. In the period between 1735 and the middle of the twentieth century, taxonomies appeared regularly, each based on its own set of traits and each having its own adherents.

Approaches to the Question of Race

The earliest anthropologists interpreted racial variation as arising out of a mixture of original "pure" types, identified as Caucasoid, Negroid, and Mongoloid. Each type was defined by a set of morphological criteria, while intermediate types were interpreted as having come from a mixture of the ancestral types. Studies of groups involved their measurement and description, followed by the identification of types, which were (as discussed in chapter 3) merely collections of statistical averages. The "racial history" of the group was then interpreted in terms of the types identified. For example, the inhabitants of Melanesia, the islands north of Australia including New Guinea, were shown to display a "Negroid element." This element was interpreted as indicating a common ancestry, and Melanesians were therefore considered to be Negroes whose ancestors had migrated to their present homeland. A category "Oceanic Negroes" was recognized and included as a racial subtype within the Negroid type.

Skeletal studies reconstructed history in this way. A physical anthropologist might analyze a collection of skeletons from a European archeological site, identifying the types from measurements of the bones.

In such an interpretation, each different type would represent a different migration, so that an entire site would be seen in terms of successive waves of migrations, one following the other over a period of a few thousand years.

What is the basis for this view of human biological variability? It is based on interpreting similarities as the results of common ancestry and differences as the results of, first, separation, and second, the successive admixture of types through time. To detect these admixtures and construct a taxonomy organized on such a principle, nonadaptive traits must be utilized. Adaptive traits change in response to environmental pressures and therefore are not valid indicators of group history.

As a result of this approach, early physical anthropologists focused on the detection of statistical types and the search for nonadaptive traits to be used in detecting these types. This resulted in the concept of *morphological races,* which were not groups of people, but sets of traits. You were a member of a particular race if you exhibited a certain morphology, regardless of who you were or where you lived. For example, "Nordics" were people with blue eyes, blond hair, light skin, and long heads. This led to problems. In 1948, Snow described the skeletons of Indian Knoll, a large site in southern Kentucky dating back to about 3,000 B.P. This site yielded over 1,000 skeletons, and Snow's analysis included the delineation of certain types as seen in the skulls. A number of skulls appeared Caucasoid in type, while several others were Negroid. Now, Snow never intimated that Europeans and Africans had crossed the Atlantic Ocean and penetrated the interior of North America 2,000 years before the voyage of Columbus! He recognized this discovery as simply indicating a problem with the concept of the morphological race. Within a few years, such problems led most anthropologists to reject this concept of classification.

Races as Populations　In the 1950s, population biology developed as the dominant approach to biological variation, and physical anthropology was profoundly affected by it. The approach was based upon the idea that the population, not the type, was the basic unit of study. A population existed as a reproductive unit and was to be studied as such. A part of that study involved describing biological variability in the population and comparing it with other populations. At the same time, population genetics developed, and the focus changed to the gene pool. In *Genetics and the Races of Man,* Boyd (1950) argued convincingly that since the phenotype was subject to environmental effects, one should study the genes and classify races according to gene frequencies.

The rise of population biology represented a major conceptual advancement. The unit of study shifted from the type to the population.

Individuals belonged to a race not because of their features or their genes, but because they were members of that population. Races were equated with Mendelian populations, and Mendelian populations changed and fluctuated as the conditions bringing them into existence changed. The key was to determine the existence of populations and then to describe them.

We follow this rule today. In assigning people to races (or today's more acceptable term, *ethnic group*), we ask, "What are you?" We don't take measurements or make observations and then ask; we accept a person's self-description.

Individuals belonged to a race not because of their features or their genes, but because they were members of that population.

Race and Adaptation   In 1950, during the period in which these developments were occurring, a book appeared that signaled yet another major advance in physical anthropology: *Races: A Study of the Problem of Race Formation in Man,* by Coon, Garn, and Birdsell. The ideas on which this book was based were radically different from those of earlier anthropologists. Coon, Garn, and Birdsell argued that the search for nonadaptive traits missed the point. In fact, they said, races existed because of natural selection; they were populations that had evolved in response to natural selection in their own environments. The long extremities of Africans, the flat faces of Asians, the straight noses of Europeans—these were not merely aspects of a type indicating ancestry, but genetic adaptations to the environment.

This view was revolutionary because it held that race differences were important because they indicated adaptation, *not* separation. Anthropologists began to search actively for adaptive differences between racial groups, and many of the biological systems mentioned in the previous chapter were first studied during this period. The term "race" suddenly took on a dynamic, evolutionary flavor instead of a static, taxonomic one. The rise of neo-Darwinism and the development of a mathematical theory of natural selection further stimulated such studies, and all these developments indicate the emerging emphasis on adaptation.

Geographical Races   While the view of races as adaptive units brought the concept of race into a more modern biological framework, it also dealt the concept a severe blow. The rejection of the idea of morphological race did away with the elegant mathematical theory that had been constructed to handle a complex of variables.

The equation of a race with a population did not help any. Did this mean that the Khoisan-speakers of the Kalahari Desert of South Africa, numbering at most a few thousand, were a race equivalent to the Mongoloids of Asia? What about black Americans? Were they a race separate from Africans because they were now different reproductive populations?

Figure 11.1
A north polar projection
map of the world showing
the distribution of Garn's 9
geographical races.

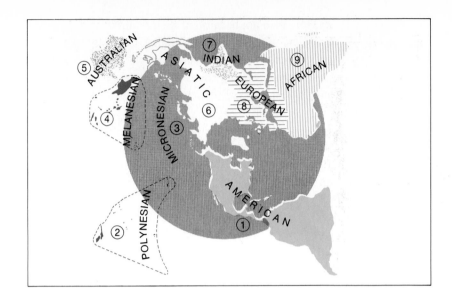

In other words, how many races are there? Are there only four, as Linnaeus suggested in the eighteenth century, or are there more as Dobzhansky suggested in the 1950s? Did racial differences reflect population history (admixture) or adaptation (natural selection)?

The concept of the geographical race represented an attempt to reconcile these views. A number of researchers (e.g., Garn and Coon 1955; Mayr 1963) noted that any racial taxonomy was subjective and that the number of races would ultimately depend on the opinions of the classifier. They introduced the notion of the **geographical race,** a concept that integrated race as population history and race as adaptive group. Mayr, noting that a race was really a subspecies, defined a race as "an aggregate of local populations of a species, inhabiting a geographical subdivision of the range of the species, and differing taxonomically from other populations of the species" (Mayr 1963:348).

How did this view close the gap between history and adaptation? First, it held that a race was a collection of populations inhabiting some definable geographical area. Populations living in one area would tend to resemble each other because they would have exchanged genes with each other more than with groups in other areas.

Second, this view recognized that the characteristics defining a particular race could have arisen within that geographical area by natural selection and spread to the limit of the group range. Obviously, the racial groups were not isolated from each other, but gene flow was constrained by geography. Where groups (i.e., races) came into contact with each other, genes would be exchanged and the characteristics of one race would "blend" into those of the other.

Mayr, noting that a race was really a subspecies, defined a race as "an aggregate of local populations of a species, inhabiting a geographical subdivision of the range of the species, and differing taxonomically from other populations of the species."

The concept of the geographical race is accepted by most anthropologists today as a principle for viewing racial classification. However, Garn (1971) has noted that we must recognize other levels as well. He suggests the term **local races** to define populations that become isolated from their neighbors and, as a result, develop distinctive physical or even genetic features, yet are numerically too small to be considered logically as a geographical race. Table 11.1 lists a racial classification suggested by Garn that includes both geographic and local races, while Figure 11.1 is a map indicating the distribution of his geographical races.

Challenges to the Concept of Race

Racism

The greatest stimulus for attacks upon the utility of race as a concept has been provided by **racism.** Racism is a doctrine that sees a population as biologically and culturally inferior because of its physical characteristics. These characteristics identify the population as being of another race; as a result, the people are prejudged.

Racism is wrong on three counts. First, biological inferiority is an incorrect term; all we can say about the merits of a variable is its adaptive efficiency relative to some other variable. "Superior" or "inferior" are not terms that have any meaning with regards to adaptive efficiency.

Second, racism is based upon the false premise that the biology of a group determines its culture. The capacity for culture evolved well over a million years ago, but differences in the cultural systems of various groups are unrelated to biological differences. Culture is learned through socialization and inherited through history.

Third, racism is based on the notion that race is a real category that exists in the world.

Race and Variability

Anthropologists have also attacked the concept of race as having no value on other grounds. First, some argue that human diversity is, in reality, distributed along **clines,** or gradients. Since the idea of races implies discrete units and variants, it presents the false impression that human biological variation exists in well-defined clusters, rather than in clines (Livingstone 1962). Brace suggests that far more information is gained by studying clines themselves and that using race as a unit at all obscures the significance of the relationships between a particular cline and a gradient in environmental stress (Brace 1964).

Other anthropologists have criticized the concept because it implies that traits are "clustered" together—this is also called the **con-**

Table 11.1
A Racial Classification—
Geographical and Selected
Local Races*

1. Amerindian geographical race
   a. North American
   b. Central American
   c. Caribbean
   d. South American
   e. Fuegian
2. Polynesian geographical race
3. Micronesian geographical race
4. Melanesian geographical race
5. Australian geographical race
   a. Murrayian
   b. Carpenterian
6. Asian geographical race
   a. Turkic
   b. Tibetan
   c. North Chinese
   d. Extreme Mongoloid
   e. Southeast Asian
7. Indian geographical race
   a. Hindu
   b. Dravidian
8. European geographical race
   a. Northwest European
   b. Northeast European
   c. Alpine
   d. Mediterranean
   e. Iranian
9. African geographical race
   a. East African
   b. Sudanese
   c. Forest Negro
   d. Bantu
10. Long isolated marginal local races
    a. Ainu
    b. South African Bushmen and Hottentots

* taken from Garn 1951

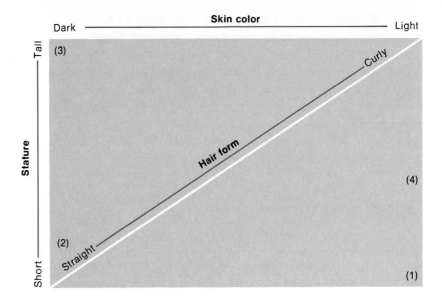

Figure 11.2
Schematic diagram of the effects of discordance in the distributions of traits. The diagram represents a geographical area, within which three traits are distributed along clines. Skin color runs from west (dark) to east (light), stature from tall (north) to short (south), and hair form from straight (southwest) to curly (northeast). Individuals at (1) would be short and light-skinned, with moderately curly hair. Individuals at (2) would be short and dark with straight hair. What traits would a person at (3) and at (4) show?

cordance of those traits. Take, for example, hair color within a group and assume that it is distributed in an east-west direction from light to dark. Now consider another trait—stature—and assume that in the same group it is distributed from tall to short. But stature is distributed in a northeast-southwest direction. It is not concordant with hair color, and there is no internal consistency within the group. With several traits, including gene frequencies if we wish, we will find that there is little taxonomic concordance within any single race (Hiernaux 1964). Figure 11.2 diagrams the effect of a lack of trait concordance.

Yet another criticism of race as a concept has come from the investigation of the distribution of variation. Greater variability is found within a race than between races. We may imagine a "pool" of variability that exists within the human species. Then we can assign various proportions of this variability to different "effects" or "causes." One cause would be *between-individuals* variability, the extent to which individuals differ from each other. We can also determine *between-groups* variability, the differences between the averages of various traits from one group to the next. If we find these proportions for genetic traits, we discover that about 75 percent of human variability is between individuals and only about 25 percent between groups. Another way of saying this is that the differences between individuals within a given race are greater than the differences between the races themselves. This being the case, we may overemphasize the differences between races if we don't consider these differences in relation to the greater amount of variability within the races.

Insight
Racial Variation—
The "Biomechanics" of Evolution

We speak of many ways that natural selection has altered the human body. We describe the environmental forces that are responsible for the selection. But in a provocative article, Alice Brues has suggested that weapon use may have been a potent force in selecting certain body builds (Brues 1959).

Biomechanics refers to the study of the human body as a mechanical system—a system of levers, links, and interconnecting vectors of force. Brues suggests that in spear-throwing, the greatest biomechanical efficiency is brought about when the individual has a linear physique, allowing maximum extension of the arm. When baseball pitchers throw the ball or cricket players bowl, they release the ball when it is farthest from their bodies and at the top of the motion. A linear physique presents us with a longer arm.

A bowman, on the other hand, needs to meet other demands. Strong shoulders and a broad back are needed to pull back the string against the pressure of the bow itself. Brues suggests that the development of the physique associated with Asians, which stresses body breadths, was related to these peoples' development of an efficient use of bows in hunting, more so than anywhere else in the world. She further suggests that the linear physique of east Africans was more suited to throwing a spear. In fact, they preferred the spear to the bow.

Brues further discusses this hypothesis by relating the development of agriculture to the need for a generalized heavy build capable of sustained labor. She suggests that the linear builds of east Africans were not adapted to such pursuits and that, as a result, at least some groups adopted herding instead of farming.

This idea is speculative but fascinating. It indicates the complexities that have gone into the process of natural selection and warns against the too quick acceptance of any single cause as *the* answer. Alice Brues has clearly showed us yet another way in which human biology and human cultural activities are interrelated and integrated.

The Race Concept in Anthropology Today

For anthropologists the concept of race isn't that important.

Is there any agreement among contemporary anthropologists over the term "race"? For anthropologists the concept of race isn't that important, except as a historical exercise that demonstrates the growth and decline of an idea. This exercise, however, may be important because to many people the term "race" represents a real category. To the public in general, racial differences exist and are easily recognizable; furthermore, these differences may, and in fact, do, carry great meaning. Adoption agencies have great problems in placing babies resulting from "interracial" matings because of the purported mixture of traits that is seen. Marriages between individuals may be determined first of all by skin color and then by mutual attraction. The lower IQ's of inner city children may be attributed to racial traits rather than to the quality of their education and other factors.

Racial classifications are only taxonomies of convenience.

Racial classifications are only taxonomies of convenience. They are merely statements about someone's ancestry that allow us to reduce biological variability to some more convenient category. To say that a person is Asian says very little about his or her biology. If we have an individual's skeleton, we cannot assign that person to a racial category with more than a 50 pecent chance of being right, even with the most up-to-date information available. The only reason we are more accurate with the living is because, to most people, race equals skin color.

Races are units of classification and populations are units of study.

Since racial taxonomies are matters of convenience, races are not units of study. Races are units of classification and populations are units of study. If we want to compare some aspect of Africans and Europeans, we really are not doing so unless we sample *all* Africans and *all* Europeans. We are actually making much more specific comparisons; for example, we may be comparing a population from the highlands of Uganda with one from the mountains of Greece. If that is so, then we should say so, since

our findings may not be relevant at all to other Africans—say, from the hot forests of Dahomey—or to other Europeans—say, from the Rhine valley.

We cannot outlaw the use of the term "race," but we can do our best to prevent its misuse. As a taxonomic term, it is valid and useful; as a term indicating ancestry and history, it may be just what we want. But as a term describing a specific population being studied or referring to an average or a type and ignoring individual variability, it is usually useless and often misleading.

The Distribution of Human Biological Variability

Human biological variation is, then, distributed according to patterns, not in a random fashion. These patterns result from the action of adaptation to the environment (genetic adaptation or phenotypic modification) and from the movements of groups and individuals. Consider, for example, the peoples of southern Europe, especially the eastern part of the Mediterranean. Their European ancestry is unmistakable, shown in a wide range of morphological and genetic traits. Biologically, they fall within a distribution of traits that we identify as being European.

At the same time, the people who live in Italy and Greece are not indistinguishable from other Europeans. Herein lies the problem with regard to types—on the average, we may differentiate between an Italian and a Norwegian on any number of traits. But given a series of persons of unknown ancestry and the task of guessing their backgrounds, we would find that we would be wrong almost as often as we were right. So we say that there is a *clinal distribution* of physical traits from north to south in Europe. The southern Europeans, while falling within the Euro-

Figure 11.3
Facial variability in European males. Adults from Germany, England, France, Italy, and Greece. Should they be classed into one race or several? Do the features of these gentlemen fit your preconceptions? How much of the variability is biological, and how much of the variability is really due to the different clothes, hair styles, or facial expressions?

pean range of variability, still may be "placed" within the cline, or gradient.

But other traits quite clearly distinguish southern Europeans as a group from the related populations to the north. The gene for the red blood cell disease thalassemia is absent among northern Europeans and, in fact, among all European groups except those of Italian or Greek ancestry. This trait cuts across ancestry, since it demarcates southern Europeans from those to the north. The gene exists because of adaptation to malaria by means of natural selection.

So while some traits place Italians and Greeks within a European "cluster," the allele for thalassemia does just the opposite. As if this weren't enough, the relatively high frequency of this allele also is characteristic of populations in southwestern Asia and north and north-central Africa. In other words, the "adaptive cluster" groups certain populations together, while the "historical cluster" groups others.

In this section we will discuss certain human biological traits in terms of their geographical patterns. We cannot do this in great detail because there are simply too many to cover, and others have written more extensively on the subject (e.g., Garn 1971; Molnar 1975; Brues 1977; Harrison et al. 1977). But we can indicate selectively just how traits are distributed and patterned and, where appropriate, suggest which trait distributions reflect ancestry and which reflect adaptation.

Genetic Traits

When we use the term "genetic traits" we mean those biological features that are under simple genetic control, usually monogenic, and that are affected little by the environment. We may group them into three classes:

1. *Antigens.* Antigens are substances that "identify" each of us. If an antigen that we do not possess enters the body, the body manufactures *antibodies* (as one of several defenses) specifically directed against it. In this way, our bodies are able to recognize and to react against dangerous organisms, such as infectious agents. Anthropologists who study genetic variation usually deal with those antigens that are coded by our genes and are located on the surface of the red blood cells. They are called *blood groups.*
2. *Protein variants.* Utilizing a variety of techniques, chemists have demonstrated a range of variation in the structure of various proteins that the body manufactures, including enzymes. Geneticists have demonstrated that many of the variants are due to different alleles, while anthropologists have shown that the frequencies of the alleles are quite variable in human groups.
3. *Other variants.* Genetic variants have also been detected by other means, although their underlying structural basis is not understood.

Table 11.2

Major Blood Group Systems*

System	Antigens	Genotypes	Phenotypes	Date of Discovery
ABO	A_1, A_2, B	OO, AA, BB, AB	O, A_1, A_2, B, AB	1900
Lewis	Le^a, Le^b	Le^aLe^a, Le^bLe^b, LeLe	Le (a+b−), Le (a−b+) Le (a−b−)	1946
Rh				
MNSs	M, N, S, s	MS/MS, MS/Ms, Ms/Ms, MS/NS, MS/Ns, Ms/NS, Ms/Ns, NS/NS, NS/Ns, Ns/Ns	M, N, MN, S, s, Ss	1927
P	P_1, P_2	P_1P_1, P_1P_2, P_2P_2, P_1p, P_2p, pp	P_1, P_2, p	1927
Lutheran	Lu^a, Lu^b	Lu^aLu^a, Lu^aLu^b, Lu^bLu^b	Lu (a+b−), Lu (a−b+)	1945
Kell	K (Kell) k (Cellano)	KK, Kk, kk	K+K−, k+k+, K−k+, (K−k−)	1946
Duffy	Fy^a, Fy^b	Fy^aFy^a, Fy^aFy^b, Fy^bFy^b, FyFy	Fy (a+b−), Fy (a+b+), Fy (a−b+), Fy (a−b−)	1950
Kidd	Jk^a, Jk^b	Jk^aJk^a, Jk^aJk^b, Jk^bJk^b	Jk (a+b−), Jk (a+b+) Jk (a−b+), Jk (a−b−)	1951
Diego	Di^a	Di^aDi^a, Di^aDi, DiDi	Di (a+), Di (a−)	1955
Sutter	Js^a	Js^aJs^a, Js^aJs, JsJs	Js (a+), Js (a−)	
Auberger	Au^a	Au^aAu^a, Au^aAu, AuAu	Au (a+), Au (a−)	1961
Xg	Xg^a	Xg^aY, XgY, Xg^aXg^a, Xg^aXg, XgXg	Xg (a+), Xg (a−)	1962

* from Molnar 1975

For example, the substance *phenylthiocarbamide* (PTC) has a very bitter taste for most people. However, some individuals, because of the genes they possess, are unable to taste it at all; they are "non-tasters" or have "taste blindness."

The Blood Groups   More than twenty blood groups are known to exist in humans; of these, between ten and fifteen vary from population to population (i.e., they are *polymorphic*). Each is controlled by a different locus, and in some cases, the inheritance is simple and well understood. An example of this is our ABO blood group system, which has already been discussed. Other systems are complex and not completely understood. Anyone whose blood has been "typed" knows whether he or she is "positive" or "negative." This refers to the Rh system, one antigen, or blood group, system that is genetically controlled.

Table 11.3 presents the frequencies of alleles for four blood groups in a number of populations. Where a value is not given, we have no information on that system. A pattern is readily discernible. For example, the O allele of the ABO system is universally present in American Indians of the South American rain forest; the presence of A or B indicates a history

Table 11.3

Allele frequencies of ABO, MN, Rh, Fy, and P*

	ABO system			MNS system				Rhesus system						Duffy		P system	
	A	B	O	MS	Ms	NS	Ns	CDE	CDe	cDE	cDe	Cde cdE	cde	Fy^a	Fy^b	P$_1$^{a}	P$_1$^{b}
South African Bantu	.19	.12	.69	.09	.49	.04	.38	00	.14	.01	.60	.02	.23	.06	.94	.72	.28
Nuer of Sudan	.16	.13	.71	.15	.42	.08	.35	00	00	.02	.81	00	.17	—	—	.69	.32
Hottentots	.21	.16	.62	.12	.62	.02	.24	00	.19	.06	.68	00	.07	.15	.85	.13	.87
Xavante Indians (Brazil)	00	00	1.00	.37	.41	.09	.13	.04	.59	.33	00	00	.04	.54	.46	.64	.36
Carib Indians	.04	.01	.95	.33	.43	.06	.18	.01	.55	.28	.16	00	00	.59	.41	.54	.46
Eskimo	.25	.02	.73	.19	.62	00	.19	.03	.73	.22	.02	00	00	.75	.25	.18	.82
Chinese	.20	.24	.56	.04	.57	.01	.38	00	.71	.18	.03	00	.08	.90	.10	.15	.85
Australian Aborigines	.37	00	.63	00	.46	.01	.53	00	.79	.18	.03	00	00	1.00	00	.36	.64
Micronesians	.20	.10	.70	00	.14	00	.86	00	.49	.47	.04	00	00	1.00	00	.55	.45
Brahmins (Uttar Pradesh)	.25	.20	.55	.31	.30	.08	.31	.03	.51	.12	.09	.04	.22	—	—	—	—
Afghanistans	.21	.25	.54	.17	.49	.10	.24	00	.60	.24	.02	00	.14	.58	.42	.39	.61
English	.25	.05	.70	.25	.28	.08	.39	00	.41	.16	.01	.02	.40	.43	.57	.49	.51
Bedouin	.17	00	.73	.37	.41	.07	.15	00	.41	.17	.14	00	.28	.26	.74	.42	.58

* from Weiner 1971

of European or African admixture. Among native North Americans, the frequency of O ranges between 0.7 and 1.0, but may be lower in the southeastern and northwestern United States.

While O is quite common in American Indians, its frequency is lower in Asia. There is an east-to-west cline from China into the fringes of eastern Europe, with gradually decreasing frequencies, all falling within the range of 0.5 to 0.6.

Similar patterns exist for other blood groups. The highest frequencies for the Rh-negative allele (r) occur among populations of European ancestry, ranging between 0.2 and 0.5. In Asians, American Indians, and Africans, the frequencies are quite low.

Enzymes and Other Proteins   Extensive data on other proteins and the body's enzymes are generally lacking because these systems have only been known for a relatively short time. Table 11.4 presents frequencies for selected groups to give some idea of the range of variation that does exist.

Other Genetic Systems   Table 11.5 shows frequencies for a genetic system that has been studied worldwide by anthropologists and geneticists. We have already mentioned the PTC locus; the table shows that there is a geographic pattern to the frequency. Europeans have a rather high frequency of nontasters (as high as 30 percent), while peoples of Asian, African, or Native American ancestry are almost all tasters.

Table 11.4

Examples of range of frequencies of serum proteins in human groups.[*]

	Haptoglobin[1] Hp1	Transferrin[2] TfC
Native Australians	.56	
Native North Americans	.3-.5	1.00
Native South Americans	.5-.8	1.00
Europeans	.3-.4	
Asians	.2-.3	.9-1.0
Africans	.5-.8	.8- .9
Black Americans	.5-.6	.9-1.0

1. Protein found in the serum; two alleles, Hp1 and Hp2, make up virtually all the genetic variation in humans.
2. Protein found in the serum that binds iron. Several variants are known, although many are rare.
* Data taken from Lerner and Libby (1976), Molnar (1975), and Workman, Blumberg, and Cooper (1963)

Table 11.5

PTC-tasting in various groups

	Number Tested	Nontasters (percent)
Hindus	489	33.7
Danish	251	32.7
English	441	31.5
Spanish	203	25.6
Portuguese	454	24.0
Negritos (Malaya)	50	18.0
Malays	237	16.0
Japanese	295	7.1
Lapps	140	6.4
West Africans	74	2.7
Chinese	50	2.0
South American Indians (Brazil)	163	1.2

* Frequency of nontasters of PTC in various populations

Red-green color blindness is a genetic trait caused by a recessive allele carried on the X-chromosome. Because a male who carries the allele always is color blind and a female is color blind only when she is homozygous for the allele, this trait is usually studied in males. Table 11.6 gives the frequency of red-green color blindness in males of various groups. Although there is considerable variation from group to group, there seems to be little geographic variation. The only noticeable pattern is a surprising one—groups who subsist largely through hunting and gathering show lower frequencies of color blindness than do peoples from agricultural societies or industrialized countries.

Table 11.6

Frequency Of Red- Green Color Blindness In Males Of Various Populations

Population	Sample size	Color-blind males (percent)
Arabs (Druse)	337	10.0
Norwegians	9,047	8.0
Swiss	2,000	8.0
Germans	6,863	7.7
Belgians	9,540	7.4
British	16,180	6.6
Iranians	947	4.5
Andra Pradesh (India)	292	7.5
Chinese (Peiping)	1,164	6.9
Chinese (all)	36,301	5.0
Tibetans	241	5.0
Japanese	259,000	4.0
Mexicans	571	2.3
Navajo Indians	535	1.1
Eskimos	297	2.5
Tswana	407	3.0
Hutu	1,000	2.9
Tutsi	1,000	2.5
Zairians	929	1.7
Australian Aborigines	4,455	1.9
Fiji Islanders	608	0.8

Why Are There Genetic Differences?   As we noted earlier, anthropologists have had little success in demonstrating adaptation in these genetic systems, except for traits related to malaria and possibly the ABO locus. The others remain a mystery. Many anthropologists feel that these frequencies result from population movements, that the patterns reflect ancestry. Some have attempted to use them to reconstruct relationships, relating populations to each other in terms of their genetic distance (Szathmary 1978, for example). Others have constructed **dendrograms,** treelike networks relating populations to each other. Figure 11.4 is an example of such a dendrogram. Although such attempts do reveal genetic relationships among groups known to have been in contact with each other or to have had a common ancestry, there are, as the figure shows, some strange and obviously incorrect clusterings. Such problems arise because populations evolve and change for several reasons, one of which is genetic drift. The random differentiation drift produces may have caused specific populations to develop atypical frequencies for certain genes.

Phenotypic Traits

There are countless traits that we can observe and measure in a living human. These traits may be averaged for a group, and two groups can

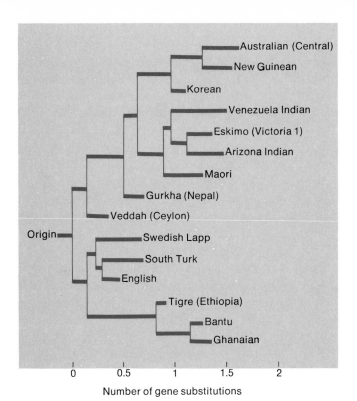

Figure 11.4
Dendrogram showing genetic distances among various human populations. Distances are indicated by placement and by connecting branches. Some genetically close groups are logical, as with Australia and New Guinea. Other close relationships seem strange. Thus, the Polynesian Maori are genetically closer to Eskimos than to the New Guinean group.

be compared in terms of stature, skin color, slope of the forehead, texture of hair, shape of eyes, and on and on. In recent decades anthropologists have avoided making comparisons of this sort of measurable trait because their results usually elicited a "So what?" from their audiences. Not only is the significance of such variables not understood, but the degree of genetic control is usually uncertain.

A good example is the shape of the head. For hundreds of years, anthropologists have classed people as longheaded, roundheaded, and intermediate. This seems funny and we can always get a laugh by discussing the subject. But geographical variation does exist, and in the 1920s Sir Roland Dixon constructed an entire racial taxonomy based solely on head shape. That he would want to do so is one thing, but that he could and did find correspondence to the recognized races is quite another.

We also should consider that from the Paleolithic to the recent present there has been a steady evolutionary trend toward roundheadedness. Why? Is this natural selection? No one knows. In fact, studies of twins indicate that the shape of the head shows little heritability, and Stanley Garn has suggested that roundheadedness may be the result of nutritional changes.

All this simply demonstrates that we know very little about the significance of phenotypic variation, let alone which variants are significant. Maybe it serves no purpose to study head shape at all. At the present time, anthropologists are avoiding the issue since they can do nothing except describe. The same is true for many other morphological variants whose significance is not understood. There are some, however, that are of more interest and seem to be of more biological significance.

Nose Shape   One feature all too frequently discussed as a "racial" trait is nose shape. Anthropologists have described a myriad of details about the nose: is the bridge "high" or "low"? is the nose concave, straight, or convex? is the nose high and narrow or short and broad? These aspects of shape are easily recognizable; if we think for a moment, we can visualize the range of variation that does exist. But—and this is the important question—are the variations distributed in some pattern and, if so, what?

In general, nose shape does not differentiate racial or ethnic groups very well. To be sure, there are stereotypes: the narrow nose of the Europeans, the broad nose of Africans, the convex nose of southwestern Asians. But these are just stereotypes. The nose shapes of east Africans can be just as high and narrow as those of any European, and the notion of a "Jewish nose" is simply a racial slur.

Nose shape does, however, seem to show a pattern of distribution when we take climate into account. Weiner (1977) has noted the significant relationship that exists between nose shape and the degree of humidity in the air. Among living peoples, long, narrow noses are found in groups inhabiting desert regions, both cold and hot. Short, broad noses characterize populations of the damp tropics. Weiner suggests that longer noses are more effective for moistening the excessively dry desert air, thereby avoiding the problems of infection that may occur when the respiratory tract is abnormally dried.

In her discussion of this issue, Brues (1977) feels that a longer nose may also filter dust more effectively. She, however, does not feel that any theory adequately explains the distribution of nose shape.

Despite the lack of suitable explanations, nose shape seems more related to environment and humidity than to race per se. As with skin color, it would seem to reflect adaptive mechanisms more than historical relationships.

Adaptation Plus Ancestry

Humans interact with their environments in a great many ways. It is simplistic to consider one trait at a time in one environment at a time. On the other hand, we cannot simultaneously think of all variables in all

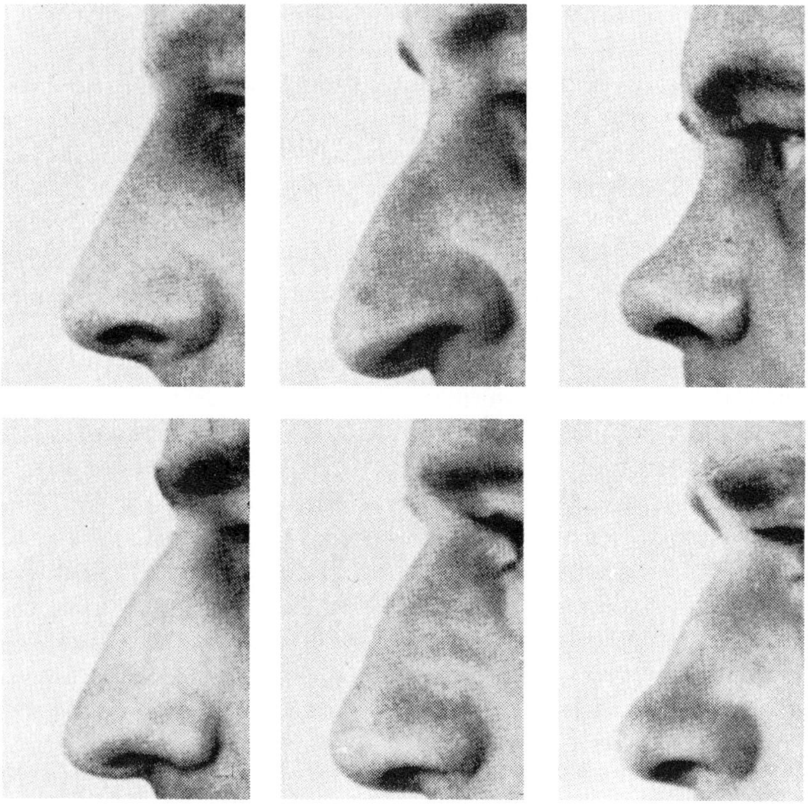

Figure 11.5
Nasal variation within and between human racial groups.

environments. We must somehow keep everything in mind, not falling victim to any "easy" explanation. And since there are so many causes and so many effects, we should beware of any explanation that "explains too well."

Some years ago, one of the authors came into contact with a student who wanted to write a master's thesis on the conservatism of peasant peoples. It is well known that poor farmers with small farms tend to be similar in many ways, even though they live in different societies. One trait of the so-called "peasants" is to be conservative, resistant to change, looking into their own worlds, and frequently guided by the past.

The student wanted to write a thesis based on the notion that peasants were that way because they were undernourished and had been intellectually impaired by chronic undernutrition. No doubt the student could have constructed such an argument based on certain measurements of intelligence, and could have tied the subject up in a neat package. But, as we quickly pointed out, he had overlooked the many other, and more important, determinants of the way people view their world. Peasants are exploited by the larger society, are poorer, and have a lower socioeconomic status. Many of their children grow up and move away, and they spend much of their existence coping with day-to-day problems. Any of these factors would act to make a group more conservative, inward-looking, and past-oriented.

The student never wrote this thesis. The lesson here has nothing to do with thesis writing; but it has everything to do with too pat explanations of complex phenomena. If anthropologists have been cautious about generalizing, it is because they understand the dangers of hasty generalization. If they criticize unwarranted conclusions, it is because they know the history of their own discipline and have read the unwarranted conclusions made by nineteenth-century anthropologists from inadequate data. And if they tend to be suspicious of schemes that explain too readily the distribution of human biological variation, it is because they realize two things. First, we do not really know very much about what causes specific groups to display certain biological structures. Second, hasty and simplistic explanations have been used too often as justifications for racial discrimination, warfare, and genocide.

All we can do is to indicate those traits and genes that seem to be distributed as they are because of adaptations to environments. We can then indicate those that are so distributed because they have been carried along by the movements of peoples. We can also point out that these two processes may act together. If we consider the continent of Africa as an example, we may easily point to certain features that, in a general way, characterize all black Africans. It is these features that were recognized by early anthropologists in their construction of a category called "Negro."

Some of these traits are adaptive in certain environments, but are also found outside those environments.

Africa is geographically large, containing a varied set of climates, temperatures, altitudes, and humidities. How can we explain, consistent with our scientific knowledge, how adaptive traits that we identify with black Africans spread over the whole continent? Let us consider the prehistoric and historic record.

We hypothesize that these adaptive features arose in west and central Africa as people began to make the transition from hunting to simple food production and ultimately to state societies. Remember that not only culture was changing, but also the morphology of the species. As this happened, Africans from the west central part of the continent became more and more numerous and began to spread out, not to the north, because of the Sahara Desert, but to the south. The record of prehistory and history indicates that peoples speaking Bantu (the language of central Africa) spread into the south central and southern areas of the continent, assimilating smaller groups and continually increasing in numbers and influence.

These Bantu speakers spread both their culture and themselves—for they introduced their genes and their physical traits into the new areas into which they moved. Although these traits were adapted to the forests of the north, they were not maladaptive in the south, where conditions may not have differed that greatly. Certainly the continued development of culture served to "buffer" the biological system from the direct effects of the environment.

Using this record as a model, we can explain the simultaneous roles of adaptation and population movement in the distribution of human biological traits. In some instances, the adaptive aspect is visible; in others, the aspect is related to ancestry. Anthropologists have given up attempting to explain biological variation solely in terms of race, evolution, adaptation, or history. While we examine the extent of the range of variation and the distributional patterns, we also must consider the complex of forces that act to create and to pattern variation.

Summary

1. Anthropologists have been concerned with the question of race since the beginning of the discipline. At first, the emphasis was upon classification and the delineation of morphological races.

2. In the 1950s, anthropologists began to visualize races as populations and not as types. In addition, racial variation was increasingly interpreted as adaptive.

3. The concept of geographical race is the one generally accepted today. It represents the integration of race as an adaptive group and race as an historical group.

4. Racism is wrong on three counts. First, biological inferiority or superiority cannot be assessed. Second, the biology of a group does not determine its culture. Finally, anthropologists do not even agree as to what races are or whether the term has any value in science.

5. Human biological variability does seem to fall into clusters that identify specific groups. These clusters reflect the similar adaptations and common ancestry of the groups classified together.

6. Races are only groups of populations classified together as a matter of convenience. A race is not a unit of study but a unit of taxonomic convenience.

7. The concept of race is not of great importance to anthropologists today.

Suggested Readings

Boyd, William C. *Genetics and the Races of Man.* Boston: Little, Brown and Company, 1950.

> *A classic work employing a genetic and population approach to race rather than a typological and morphological one.*

Brues, Alice M. *People and Races.* New York: Macmillan Publishing Co., 1977.

> *An up-to-date and comprehensive review of modern human variation, considering the implications for racial taxonomy and human adaptation.*

Garn, Stanley M. *Human Races.* 3rd ed. Springfield, Ill.: Charles C Thomas, 1971.

> *A human biologist looks carefully at human variation and racial classification.*

Kennedy, Kenneth A. R. *Human Variation in Space and Time.* Dubuque: Wm. C. Brown Company Publishers, 1976.

> *A compact consideration of human variation and of the development of racial studies. Identifies those elements that are retained in modern approaches to race that originated in the past.*

King, James C. *The Biology of Race.* New York: Harcourt Brace Jovanovich, 1971.

> *This brief work applies knowledge of modern human genetics to the study of biological and behavioral variation.*

Montagu, Ashley (Ed.). *The Concept of Race.* New York: Collier Books, 1964.

> *A collection of many of the best articles by scientists who have studied race and human variation.*

Glossary

cline A gradual change in the frequency of a gene or a trait across a geographical range.

concordance Agreement. Two variables are concordant if they change in similar fashion.

dendrogram A branching or treelike diagram. Populations on closer branches are more closely related to each other than are populations on distant branches.

geographical race A taxonomic group of populations occupying a certain geographical range and displaying similarities in their genetic structures.

local race A biologically identifiable population living in the midst of a geographical race, yet maintaining their distinctiveness by isolative mechanisms.

racism A false doctrine maintaining that, because of their biology, members of one race are superior to members of another.

Human Culture

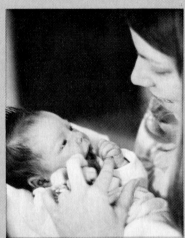

Part 4

1. What is culture?
2. Are there humans who do not have culture? Are there animals with culture?
3. How does one communicate meaning?
4. How do peoples symbolize meaning in their belief systems, their religion, and their social organizations?

12

Culture and the Definition of *Human*

Introduction

So far we have talked about human beings as animals, for the most part. We have been more concerned with the physiological, the genetic, and the historic, and with the ways that we can understand the adaptation of the individual and whole populations to the environment. It is important to start off by discussing human beings as animals, because we often forget that we are animals of the order Primates. On the other hand, it would be silly to suggest that we are *only* animals. There is something that distinguishes us from other animals. That "something" is called by anthropologists the *capacity for culture*. All human beings have the capacity for culture. No animals have the capacity for culture, even though human culture evolved out of animal protoculture. To define culture is to define humanness. We can define culture as follows: Culture is a set of rules for constructing the world, interpreting the world, and adapting to it.

"... Culture is a set of rules ..."

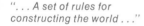

Culture is not something you can see or touch; it is a set of rules. You can see and touch tools and weapons, houses and canoes, but they are not culture. These things, or *material artifacts,* are the outcomes or products of the application of cultural rules. Culture can be thought of as a set of instructions for thinking up a world that makes sense, understanding that world, and living in it.

Cultural rules are deep within us, and usually we are not aware of them. Sometimes anthropologists talk about a "grammar of culture," because there is a set of rules for behavior and thought just as there is for language. These rules are difficult to discover. We have to be content to guess at them from observing people's behavior, thinking about our own, and asking about people's thoughts. We try to develop generalizations and laws about cultural rules from this kind of data.

"... A set of rules for constructing the world ..."

One world that we know, see, feel, and live in is thought up. Together with the other members of our society, we create it. In some ways our picture of society and the environment is pretty accurate (though never completely so). The representation that we have in our minds of the world corresponds pretty closely to what we would be able to see if we had perfect knowledge. But we are not free to construct just any picture at all, as we shall see in a moment when we talk about people who do just that.

There are two important restraints on our creation of a picture of the world. First, when we are born there is a picture of the world waiting for us. Our parents and other adults show us this picture. They teach us about the world that was constructed for them, which they modified during the course of their lives by talking and agreeing and disagreeing with others. These other people are the second restraint. We cannot go

"... Culture is a set of rules ..."

"... A set of rules for constructing the world ..."

Figure 12.1
A newborn baby has an interpretation of the world waiting for it.

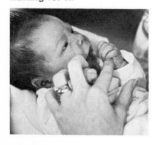

off on a tangent and make up our own individual world. If we do, we cease to be normal. We have to agree with others about our world. If we have a different vision or belief, we have to "negotiate" with others so that the picture of the world is shared. If we do this, and if the picture is reasonably consistent in itself, then we have an adequate picture and an adequate culture. This process of construction and negotiation is what makes baby human animals social and cultural humans. We call the process **socialization.**

". . . interpreting the world . . ."

We not only construct our world, but we also interpret it. Constructing and interpreting go hand in hand because we have to understand our own picture as well as other people's. We call this act of understanding "interpretation." There are rules for interpreting our experience of our world too. Once again, we have to agree on these rules.

Our cultural rules permit us both to construct and to interpret our world.

". . . and adapting to it . . ."

The rules that we use to construct and interpret our world also permit us to modify our behavior and the behavior of the social group so we can adapt to our environment. We see the environment through a cultural filter. We sometimes picture and interpret it wrongly, and we sometimes can change it so we can live in it more easily. In the end, however, we still have to adapt to it. Culture is a set of rules that channels this adaptation.

". . . interpreting the world . . ."

". . . and adapting to it . . ."

People Without Culture

Are there people who do not have culture? Surprisingly enough, yes. People can lose culture in two ways. The first is tragic and common. An individual can cease to construct and interpret the world in the way that it is constructed and interpreted by the others in the society. Such a person is labeled "crazy" or "psychotic" and is believed, often rightly, to be unable to adapt to the environment. Psychotic people cannot adapt to the environment because their picture of the world is usually completely false (not just partially false like that of the rest of us). They cannot communicate with other people because their rules of interpretation are completely different from those of others.

Psychotic people are still human, obviously. They have the capacity for culture. They are temporarily without it, however.

The second way that culture can be lost occurs very rarely in wild or "wolf" children. The best-documented account of a **wolf child** (or **feral child**) was that of Victor, a wolf child raised and studied by a French psychologist, Jean-Marc-Gaspard Itard. Itard wrote a careful account of his attempt to give culture to this child who had lost it. It is interesting to

Figure 12.2
Victor the Wolf Child.

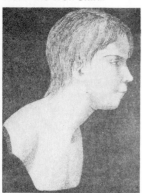

look at Victor, at the time of his capture, to see what a human being without culture is like.

Victor, the Wolf Child   Victor was eleven or twelve years old when he was captured in the forest by three hunters. The best estimate was that he had been abandoned for about seven years. When the news of his capture spread, people came enthusiastically to see him, hoping to see a noble creature of the woods and wilds, uncontaminated by corrupting civilization. But what greeted their eyes? Dr. Itard wrote:

. . . a disgusting, slovenly boy, affected with spasmodic and frequent convulsive motions, continually balancing himself like some of the animals in the zoo, biting and scratching those who contradicted him, expressing no kind of affection for those who attended upon him; and in short, indifferent to everybody, and paying no regard to anything. (Malson 1972:96)

One of Victor's more mysterious qualities was that he either could not or did not pay attention to things that we human beings think are important. The first time a gun was discharged behind his ear, he was startled. After the first time, he did not appear to hear it. But he would respond to the sound when chestnuts, his favorite food, were cracked, apparently able to hear this sound through the thickest of walls.

His mood swings were violent; so much so that under other circumstances he would have been described as mentally ill.

He has been observed, within his chamber . . . rocking backwards and forwards with a tiresome uniformity, directing his eyes constantly towards the window, and casting them in a melancholy manner on the external air. If, at any time, a boisterous wind arose; if the sun concealed behind a cloud suddenly burst forth, brilliantly illuminating the surrounding atmosphere, he expressed an almost convulsive joy by thundering peals of laughter; during which all his turnings backwards and forwards resembled very much a kind of leap which he wished to take, to throw himself out of the window into the garden. Sometimes, instead of joyful emotions, he exhibited a species of madness; he wrung his hands, applied his fists to his eyes, gnashed his teeth, and became formidable to persons about him. One morning, after a heavy fall of snow, as soon as he awakened, he uttered a cry of joy, leaped from his bed, ran to the window, and afterwards to the door, going backwards and forwards, from one to the other, with the greatest impatience, and at length, escaped half-dressed into the garden. There he exhibited the utmost emotions of pleasure; he ran, rolled himself in the snow and taking it up by handfuls devoured it with an incredible avidity. (Malson 1972:103–104)

Victor never did learn to speak. He became domesticated, however, devoted to his guardian, capable of simple tasks, and certainly capable of love and attentiveness; but equally certainly, he never developed the set of rules that allowed him to construct and interpret and adapt to the world that the people around him had constructed.

Dr. Itard tells us that Victor took an enormous pleasure in drinking spring water. But, one day Victor accidentally drank a glass of clear liquid that he thought was water but that, in fact, was alcohol. He screamed, leaped from the table, almost overturning it, and went running down the avenue as fast as his quick legs would take him. Now, the important thing is not that Victor did not like alcohol, but that no one could ever teach Victor the place of alcohol in a nineteenth-century Frenchman's diet. Victor could never know that alcohol could be part of something called a meal (nor would he ever know that what we eat has any meaning). But every Frenchman would. Here is the reason Victor cannot be said to have acquired culture. He failed to learn the rules that the human beings around him used to construct and interpret the world.

Some people think that Victor was retarded or, more likely, psychotic. They suggest that he was not a wolf child who had wandered in the forest for years but a schizophrenic who had run away from home or had been driven from it into the woods by his parents. The truth is that we will never know until we have more cases and better documentation on abandoned children. But for our argument here, *it doesn't matter*. If Victor was psychotic, then by our definition he had lost his culture. If he failed to acquire culture, then he was in a similar condition. In either case, Victor is an example of a person without culture. And since he apparently lacked the capacity for culture, we have to conclude that Victor was not human.

The Origins of Culture: Protoculture

Although we have said that all human beings and no animals have culture, this does not mean that we cannot seek the origins of culture in animal behavior. We are animals, and we should expect to find behavior among animals that is similar to, or an analogy of, cultured human behavior. In fact, we do. The more we learn about animal behavior the more we become convinced that *there is a difference in degree, but not in kind between human beings and other animals*. That is, in most ways we are not completely different from all other animals, but we are more developed in our cultural habits.

There is a difference in degree, but not in kind between human beings and other animals.

The Components of Culture

The four most important components of true human culture are (1) tools (and technology); (2) language (and the ability to use symbols); (3) conscience and morality (including religion and systems of belief); and (4) social organization based on moral rules. These four components evolved together, and all four must be present for us to say that *human* culture exists.

All four components are foreshadowed by animal activities that appear to be like human culture. A useful term for these animal activities is **protoculture.**

Figure 12.3
Neanderthal man was a
cooperative hunter.

Obviously it is very difficult to state when human culture emerged. We cannot be certain that early hominids possessed all four components, although, as we have seen, australopithecines had tools and some sort of social organization. Whether that social organization had a moral base or not, we will never know.

We doubt that australopithecines were capable of speech. The brain was too small, and the lateral differentiation in the brain that we associate with the growth of speech centers and the development of right-hand dominance is simply too underdeveloped.

We are less sure about *Homo erectus*. It is certainly possible that true culture was developed as long ago as 1 million years, during the period of *Homo erectus*. The cranial capacity of *Homo erectus* (about 1,000 cc.) is sufficiently large to make possible the elaboration of true human culture from protoculture. Brian Stross (1976) has recently reviewed the literature on the origin and evolution of language and thinks that it was possible, but not very probable, that *Homo erectus* had language. The earliest period when we are sure that language use prevailed was about 100,000 years ago during the Mousterian period. The Neanderthals most probably did have true human language. Their brains were adequate to the task, and they had well-developed speech centers. Their cooperative hunting techniques would seem, on the face of it, to have required the kind of detailed communication that is only readily possible through language. They not only made complex and well-crafted tools (Mousterian tradition), but they passed the knowledge of tool manufacturing down from generation to generation.

Figure 12.4
Other animals use tools.

By 100,000 years ago, then, we are talking about true human culture. Previous to that, and certainly previous to 1 million years ago, we can only talk with certainty about protoculture.

We gain a better idea of our place in the animal kingdom if we examine the analogues of the four components of culture as they appear among the animals in protoculture.

Tools For many years it was thought that only human beings manufactured and used tools.

As a result, everyone was quite surprised when Jane Goodall found that chimpanzees formed and used tools for specific purposes. She had gone to the Gombe preserve in Tanzania to study the behavior of chimpanzees in the wild. After nine months of observation, she made an astounding discovery—chimps both made and used tools in the wild.

David Graybeard [a chimpanzee—Goodall named all the chimps] was squatting beside the red earth mound of a termite nest and as I watched I saw him carefully push a long grass stem down into a hole in the mound. After a moment he withdrew it and picked something from the end of his mouth. I was too far away to make out what he was eating (it was termites) but it was obvious that he was actually using a grass stem as a tool. (Goodall 1972:50)

Perhaps we should have known better than to try to define man as "the animal that uses tools." Birds, chimps, and other animals use tools, too. The woodpecker finch, for example, regularly uses twigs and cactus spines to dig insects out of crevices in tree bark. The Egyptian vulture picks up rocks in its beak and hurls them to break open ostrich eggs. The

sea otter collects stones and shells from the ocean bottom, places them on its stomach while floating on its back on the surface, and then uses them as anvils against which to pound and crack open mussels and other hard-shelled mollusks.

It seems clear that many other animals besides *Homo sapiens* use tools and even make them. Tool use is well established in protoculture.

Animal Communication   The second important component of human culture is language. The basis for language in protoculture is animal communication through signs. We have known for a long time that animals communicate with *signs;* that is, signals that have a fixed meaning. These signs, communicated through odors, chemical means, and gestures, as well as vocal-auditory displays, can convey quite complex information. Birds warn other birds of the presence of predators. Bees do a "dance" that tells other bees the direction and distance of food sources. Animals can "lie," too. Konrad Lorenz, the ethologist, tells of a female chow dog that did not want to follow her owner on his bicycle and, when told to come along, limped badly. On the way back home, however, her limp mysteriously disappeared. This sort of "lying" should not be confused with the behavior of some birds, which feign injury in the presence of a predator in order to distract it away from the nest; such feigned behavior is general to whole species and is not the invention of one animal.

Many animals play. As Gregory Bateson has pointed out, play is an amazing accomplishment. Watch two dogs playing and think of the subtlety of communication that allows them to say to one another, "Look, the gesture, posture, and sounds I am making would normally mean fighting and aggression, but this is just a fake so that we can play and have fun." This is a complex idea requiring the dogs to be able to decode a growl and a bite and understand, "this is not the message it normally is."

Figure 12.5
Animals playing: think of
the complexity involved in
their communication.

Animals Learning Human Languages   One of the most exciting advances in our understanding of animal psychology and communication has come about in recent years as animals have been taught to understand and communicate in human language. As we mentioned, in the late 1940s Keith and Catherine Hayes first tried to teach a chimpanzee named Viki to speak English, but were not notably successful. The animal finally learned to pronounce (with help) four words: "mama," "papa," "cup," and "up." Apparently chimpanzees do not have the apparatus for spoken language.

Then R. A. and B. T. Gardner of the University of Nevada had a better idea. Since chimpanzees utilize many gestures in the wild, they decided to teach chimps to communicate in American Sign Language, a system of communication used by deaf-mutes. They taught it to Washoe, their first subject, and it worked! Washoe learned a vocabulary of over 130 signs in four years of training, and then was taken to the Institute of Primate Studies at the University of Oklahoma to see if she could teach some of the animals there. Washoe was putting words together properly (i.e., had good, if elementary, syntax) and could make such requests as "go in," "tickle Washoe," and "open blanket." She could invent new names for things: a watermelon became "red drink." She could apply new names to novel situations. When a macaque monkey attacked her at the primate center, she made the sign "Dirty monkey." Washoe and her current successors in the Gardners's laboratory in Reno do not only answer questions and respond to comments, they also commonly initiate conversations with questions and comments of their own. Recently Washoe had a baby that died. One of the saddest sights was to see her making the sign "Baby, baby, baby . . ." over and over again.

Sarah, an African-born female chimpanzee, began her "schooling" under David Premack at the age of six, learning to manipulate tokens

Insight

Human Culture—The Importance of Speech to Nonhuman Animals

There is a good deal of exciting research going on right now in teaching animals human language. Anything written now may be out of date in a few years—but that does not stop us from speculating about the issues.

Will animals that learn to speak react like feral children and forget entirely their animal background? Is their animal history (and biography) not capable of being expressed in speech, since it was never "coded" that way in the first place? (That is probably why feral children cannot recount in language their prelinguistic experience. Some people say the same about psychedelic drug trips and psychotic experiences: they are beyond words to express and cannot be coded in language. Imagine the disappointment of the scientist who first manages to convey the idea of introspection to a genius chimpanzee, only to find the chimp saying that she simply can't talk in human language about her previous experiences as an animal.

Our feeling is that this is most unlikely. Chimps obviously enjoy and are intrigued by the experiments in which they participate, but when put with other chimps who know human language, they do not appear spontaneously to make gestural conversation with each other.

So far, it appears that there are going to be no chimpanzee probings into the nature of reality, into the essential nature of chimpness, and into the separation of nature from culture. To skeptical observers, it seems that we have pierced the veil of animal consciousness, overleaped the barriers to communication with another species.

Disputes aside, compare the attitude of the chimp who is precociously acquiring language with that famous moment in the life of Helen Keller, the blind and deaf child who learned to speak. Like the chimps, Helen Keller learned signs, though more quickly. After a month of instruction she knew eighteen nouns and three verbs. Because she confused the words for "mug" and "water," her teacher took her out to the pump and splashed water over her hand, while spelling out the word in her palm. The idea blazed in Helen Keller's mind. In her own words:

We walked down the path to the well-house, attracted by the fragrance of the honeysuckle with which it was covered. Someone was drawing water and my teacher placed my hand under the spout.

As the cool stream gushed over one hand she spelled into the other the word *water,* first slowly, then rapidly. I stood still, my whole attention fixed upon the motion of her fingers. Suddenly I felt a misty consciousness as of something forgotten— a thrill of returning thought; and somehow the mystery of language was revealed to me. I knew then that "w-a-t-e-r" meant the wonderful cool something that was flowing over my hand. That living word awakened my soul, gave it light, and set it free.

This testament to the power of language in human beings seems different from what Sarah or Washoe are experiencing. One wonders why primates other than *Homo sapiens* have not shown the same kind of emotional turmoil and excitement at the opening up of the countless possibilities for experience that language alone affords.

As soon as the idea of language dawned upon Helen Keller, she could not stop asking questions, and her rate of learning sky-rocketed. Perhaps the chimpanzees have not yet reached that take-off point. But, more likely, they never will.

Figure 12.6
Chimpanzees are learning
how to solve problems as
well as learning to sign with
American Sign Language.

representing words on a magnetic board. She became very adept. Sarah
can recognize some complicated logical relations of the "if . . . then" sort,
responding to a sentence such as this: "If Sarah does such-and-such, then
Mary (the trainer) will give Sarah a banana." She can respond to compound commands where certain words have been left out and only implied. In one experiment, Premack found that she understood the sentence "Sarah, put the banana in the dish and the apple in the pail," even
though it contains two commands ("Put the banana in the dish, Sarah,"
and "Put the apple in the pail, Sarah") and the second "put the . . ." has
been left out. It looks as though Sarah has some idea about grammar, but
we cannot be sure, since she cannot perform the deletions when she
"speaks" (by manipulating the tokens). Perhaps Sarah's most impressive
achievement has been her ability to transfer the words "all," "none,"
"one," and "some" from the specific items used in teaching her (crackers
she could eat) to general use. These words are very important in formal
logic, and Sarah was able to use them properly with different classes of
things as soon as she had learned their meaning.

But Sarah, Washoe, and their other chimp colleagues still do not
have true language, because by "true language" we mean that the animal
has the ability to communicate and think in symbols. We contrast **symbol**
and **sign.** A *symbol* is something that stands for something else, just as
the color white as a symbol can stand for "cleanliness," "virginity,"
"saintliness," "spring," "light," "heaven," and many other things. A *sign*
is something that stands for only one thing—it has a fixed referent or set of
referents. The meaning of a sign is fixed and cannot be broadened or

*A symbol is something that
stands for something else.*

changed in the course of communication. A "Stop" sign means stop. A vocal call that means "Danger!" *always* means "Danger!" and nothing else.

Animals in the wild use signs. Chimpanzees, in the laboratory, are beginning to be able to use symbols. They are beginning to learn the rudiments of true language. None has acquired the skills of a human child . . . yet.

Conscience and Morality in Protoculture

The third important component of human culture is the belief in moral rules and the practice of altruism, or making sacrifices on behalf of the group. Conscience and morality imply believing in something beyond one's self. There is no evidence that animals do this, although one can see how it could have evolved from some apparently very unselfish behavior that animals do display.

Some sociobiologists have examined what they call **altruism** in animals. This word normally means "a disregard for one's own welfare for the sake of the welfare of others." If animals show altruism, we might regard it as a sign that they have consciences.

We note that sometimes animals will help other fellow species members when they are hurt, in danger, or injured. Porpoises will carry other porpoises to safety when one has been injured, and whales will support an injured companion in the water.* Birds will put themselves into jeopardy, betraying their own position by giving a danger signal to warn the flock. Perhaps we can see the beginnings of altruism in this kind of helpfulness.

Biologically, however, altruism in animal species other than humans is the highest form of selfishness. It is true that single insects will perform acts of self-sacrifice in order to save the group, and for many years biologists were unable to explain this non-Darwinian behavior. Recently an explanation has been found. It was noted that animals who did acts of self-sacrifice thus ensured the survival of many close relatives who bore identical or similar genes. One way that we all become immortal is to reproduce our genes in the next generation by having children. Another way (with a similar effect) is to reproduce ourselves through our brother's children, or our sister's children, or other close relatives. As Dawkins (1976) put it, it is as though the genes were selfish and used the animal as a temporary resting place, but shucked the animal off when it was

---

* Tales of porpoises helping shipwrecked sailors to shore are as old as the first century A.D., when Pliny the Younger described such an event in his *Letters*. Mother porpoises must push their newborn young to the surface to breathe, and so we might assume that porpoise behavior toward humans is simply an extension of a behavior highly adaptive for their own species.

convenient. So when the gene has a "choice" whether to preserve itself in one animal or another, it chooses to preserve itself in the maximum number of animals. If the sacrifice of one individual raises the probability of the survival and reproduction of another, that is fine with the gene.*

William D. Hamilton has calculated the conditions under which this "altruistic" behavior makes genetic sense, finding that on the whole animals are better off sacrificing themselves than not.

But one can still readily see the analogy of conscience in this selfish animal behavior. For with the invention of symbolism, and meaning, one can readily imagine that self-sacrifice would take on a cultural rather than a biological meaning, and be transformed into a human value, rather than an animal behavior.

The Incest Taboo   The fourth component of culture with which we are concerned is the formation of complex social groups based on moral rules.

Complex social organization is found among many kinds of animals. Whether we can talk about kinship in the sense of true human kinship among animals, is once again, very dubious. Certainly mothers of offspring in many animal societies look after their young. Certainly, also, there are some primate groups in which we find relatively stable consort pairs who live together in an arrangement that might look like marriage.

But the root of human social organization is the channeling of sexual drives and the prohibition of sexual relations between members of the nuclear family (father/daughter, mother/son, and brother/sister). This set of prohibitions is called the **incest taboo.**

There is evidence that some animals do not have sexual relations with their parents. Jane Goodall, in her studies of chimpanzees in the wild, twice saw a female in heat have sexual relations with every mature male in the troop except her own two sons. J. Itani (1972) has reported that many Old World monkeys and apes seldom mate with their mothers, even though they remain with the troop. Other animals, lions for example, leave the pride and search for mates among other bands.

Still, the evidence is inconclusive. It is not clear, for example, whether primates have an innate distaste for mating with their parents or whether they are excluded from mating with adults distant from them in the dominance ordering of the group.

In any case, the incest taboo among human groups is quite different from that in animal groups. It is true that in all human groups sexual relations between brother and sister, father and daughter, and mother and son are forbidden. But that is just a beginning. In some societies it is

---

* Please don't think that genes make decisions or think aloud to themselves. This is merely the simplest way of putting the argument.

Figure 12.7
Rules against incestuous
relations afford the moral
basis of ordered society.

taboo to have sexual relations with one's mother's sister but encouraged with one's father's sister (both aunts). Similarly, in other societies it would be a horrible crime to have sexual relations with one's mother's father's sister's son's daughter, while relations with one's mother's mother's brother's daughter's daughter would be fine (both cousins).* There is so much variability in human societies that biologists cannot explain it on biological grounds. The incest taboo is learned behavior. It is cultural behavior.

As we have said, there are four basic components of culture. *Tools* are basic because they are crucial to the way we adapt to our environment and extract energy from it for our own uses. They are crucial to ecological and economic relationships. *Language* is important because it frees our minds to speculate, to communicate, and to transmit our experience from one to another, and from one generation to another. Without language there can be no accumulation of skills, no building of a cultural inventory, no learning and transmittal of complex chains of thought. *Conscience and morality* are basic to the construction of moral and religious systems that channel our conduct and restrain our passions and greeds. An ordered human social and religious life is not possible without them. Finally, the *incest taboo* makes possible living in families

---

* In the United States, states vary in the way they prohibit marriage between close kin. Karl Heider (1969) shows that marriages with one's mother, daughter, granddaughter, sister, niece, and aunt are called "incestuous" in all states except Iowa (where marriage with a grandmother is not forbidden), Georgia (where marriage to a niece is not forbidden), and Rhode Island (where Jews may marry according to the Levitical laws that permit marriage to both a grandmother and a niece).

Chart 12.1
The Four Components Of Culture

The Four Most Important Components of Human Culture	Prototypes of These Components in Animal Behavior
1. Tools and technology	1. Tools, manufactured and used by chimpanzees observed in the wild by Jane Goodall.
2. Language and symbolic communication	2. Animal communication systems. The ability of chimpanzees to communicate, form sentences and do logic problems with counters, or use American sign language.
3. Conscience and morality	3. Mutual aid between animals. Altruism (which is really genetic selfishness) in insects.
4. Complex social organization based on moral rules (and the incest taboo)	4. Infrequent sexual relations between parents and children, and perhaps between siblings, in primate groups.

were disputes over sexual partners. The incest taboo forces the family to reach outside itself for mates and thereby creates the necessity and the opportunity for larger social bonds. Alliances can be formed and whole families joined together by the bonds of kinship. The building of a larger society can and must begin.

These four components are found universally, in all human societies everywhere. The roots for each, however, are found in the nonhuman animals and in their animal form fused into protoculture.

A Difference in Degree Rather than Kind

We may yet be a little lower than the angels and quite a bit higher than other primates, but we are not unique in the universe. This is what the statement "different in degree and not in kind" means. We do not have some unique faculty found nowhere else in the animal kingdom; rather, we do certain things more persistently than other animals. Can animals plan? Yes, but human beings plan *constantly,* if we mean "plan" in the sense of thinking out one's purposes ("ends") and the ways one can achieve them ("means"). Do animals communicate about abstract and displaced referents? Can they form new combinations of symbols for new meanings? Chimpanzees can. Human beings, however, do it *as a habit,* persistently. Can animals discriminate between classes of objects and events in the world? Can they, to use the proper word, *categorize?* Surely—Sarah could. But human beings play with categories. They make them up, try them out, exchange them back and forth, attach meanings to them, fight over them, put values on them; and no other animal is so obsessed with categories, meanings, and the interpretation of what is going on around them.

The difference between human beings and animals is not that humans have language or tools but rather that they formulate rules for putting things together and interpreting them. Attributing meaning to events means to set them in a context where they relate to other things.

Ethnocentrism and Cultural Relativism

"Culture" also has another meaning. We talk of "American culture," "Eskimo culture," or "Cheyenne culture." We distinguish among those ways that different groups have of interpreting and adapting to the world. Most people feel their own culture is superior to every other group's. This belief is called **ethnocentrism,** which means judging all other cultures in terms of one's own. Americans used to be very ethnocentric, thinking themselves to be superior to most people. After World War II, the U.S. government tried to tell peoples in Europe, Asia, and Latin America how to run their lives (that is, as we did), and people told us, "Yankee, go home!" Perhaps we began to learn during the Vietnam War that our culture was not superior. Perhaps we are a good deal less ethnocentric now, so that we can be proud of our culture and heritage without thinking less of anyone else's. At the heart of anthropology is the idea of **cultural relativism,** which states that cultures are different but that one is *not* better than another.

Most people feel their own culture is superior to every other group's. This belief is called ethnocentrism, which means judging all other cultures in terms of one's own.

The doctrine of cultural relativism states that all cultures must be evaluated in their own terms. Cultures, which are sets of rules, are like grammars, which are sets of rules for language. In the next chapter we shall see in how many ways cultures are like languages. Languages, of course, can be put to evil uses, as in crying "Fire!" in a crowded theatre when there is none, or in inciting a crowd to murder and lynching. But we do not say that language itself is evil, nor that some grammars are evil grammars. Neither do we say that some grammars are better than other grammars. Each grammar is adequate and sufficient for its language. Each culture is adequate and sufficient for its society.

The doctrine of cultural relativism states that all cultures must be evaluated in their own terms.

There are no bad cultures, just as there are no good ones. "Good" and "bad" are not ideas that apply to ways of constructing, interpreting, and adapting to the world.

There are bad societies, however. There are bad uses to which cultures may be put. And there certainly are evil nation states and evil governments.

Hitler's Nazi Germany was an evil society. Its leaders tried systematically to use political power to subvert German culture and destroy other peoples and nations. They tried to impose the Nazi way of constructing, interpreting, and adapting to the world on the German people, and they hoped to impose it on the rest of the European nations. The Nazi picture of the world embodied a plan for adaptation that could only end in its own destruction.

But German culture was not destroyed by World War II. Wars do not destroy culture. Meaning, traditions, symbols, languages, families, moral rules, and technological ideas all survive wars.

We Cannot Judge Cultures

We cannot judge cultures in the way we can and must judge societies and nation states. If we did, we would have to make up criteria for making that judgment, and these would necessarily be either ethnocentric or arbitrary.

For example, one tribe in New Guinea practices necrophilia with close female relatives (Berndt 1962). That is, when a woman dies, her sons have sexual intercourse with the corpse. During the course of the act, they disembowel the corpse and prepare it for a feast. This practice is certainly repugnant to us, but is it morally bad? Only in ethnocentric terms. The New Guinea tribesmen regard it as a way of doing honor to the corpse and ensuring its peace in the hereafter.

Another example concerns one of the most pitiable tribal groups in recent world history, the Australian Aborigines, who were systematically killed by European settlers. Aborigine society is fascinating, rich in lore, myth, and legend; famous for its kinship systems and for the way it created a world of harmonious kinfolk. Daisy Bates, who spent a lifetime among the Aborigines, reports the following:

Baby cannibalism was rife [common] among these central-western peoples, as it is west of the border in Central Australia. In one group, east of Murchison and Gascoyn Rivers, every woman who had a baby had killed and eaten it, dividing it with her sisters, who, in turn, killed their children at birth and returned the gift of food, so that the group had not preserved a single living child for some years. When the frightful hunger for baby meat overcame the mother before or at the birth of the baby, it was killed and cooked regardless of sex. Division was made according to the ancestral food laws. I cannot remember a case where the mother ate a child she had allowed, at the beginning, to live. (Bates 1967:107)

Later Bates writes:

I use the word "cannibalism" advisedly. Every one of these central natives was a cannibal. Cannibalism had its local name from Kimberley to Eucla, and through all the unoccupied territory east of it, and there were many grisly rites attached thereto. Human meat had always been their favorite food, and there were killing vendettas from time immemorial. In order that the killing should be safe, murder slippers or pads were made, emu feathers twisted and twined together, bound to the foot with human hair, on which the natives walk and run as easily as a white man in running shoes, their feet leaving no track. Dusk and dawn were the customary hours for raiding a camp. Victims were shared according to the law. The older men ate the soft and virile parts, and the brain; swift runners were given the thighs; hands, arms, or shoulders went to the best spear throwers, and so on. Those who received the skull, shoulder or arm kept the bones, which they polished and rounded, strung on hair, and kept on their person, either as pointing bones or magic pendants. (Bates 1967:195)

Mothers eating their babies? Planning raids to get human meat, and sharing it according to the law? Giving the genitals to the older, more prestigious men? How utterly repugnant to us!

But it is repugnant because it violates *our* rules for constructing and interpreting the world. It does not violate the Australian tribal people's rules.

On the other hand, were the ideas that formed the behavior of the German people during World War II valid and authentic expressions of their rules for constructing and interpreting the world? Were genocide, imperialist aggression, and virulent racism authentic expressions of German culture? Obviously not. The Germans tried to hide these things from themselves. They rationalized their aggressive imperialism as no more than rational defense of their homeland. They lied to themselves and hid from themselves knowledge of the concentration and slave labor camps. These expressions are seen clearly to be inauthentic because the people of the culture deemed them to be inauthentic. The aberration of Nazism was repugnant, not just to us but to the culture-bearers themselves.

Figure 12.8
Australian tribal peoples were as devoted to their children as we or any other peoples are.

Culture and Biology

Human beings are animals, but they are something else besides—they have a capacity for culture. Culture, though, does not release humans from the biological restraints or their biological heritage. Human beings are embedded individually and collectively in a matrix of biology and culture. This matrix is the **biocultural system.**

The biocultural system is made up of parts, or subsystems. The predominantly cultural subsystems that we have differentiated for this book are these:

1. The linguistic subsystem.
2. The subsystem of meaning.
3. The subsystem of religion.
4. The subsystem of cosmology.
5. The subsystem of kinship.
6. The subsystem of political organization.

We can call all these six subsystems the **cultural cluster.** The predominantly biological subsystems that we isolated earlier and discussed were:

1. The morphological and physiological subsystem.
2. The genetic subsystem.

These two subsystems are the **biological cluster.**

Two subsystems are both biological and cultural, to such an extent that we cannot say to which subheading they belong:

1. The ecological subsystem.
2. The economic subsystem.

These two subsystems are the **ecological cluster.** These are the subsystems that we have chosen for discussion in this book.

The rest of this book is devoted to explaining how subsystems of the biocultural system are related. We began with the biological cluster, now we deal with cultural cluster, and finally we will cover the ecological cluster. In the final section of the book we will give three examples of how the total biocultural system operates in three different societies to produce three quite distinct system types.

Summary

1. The first problem to be addressed when we consider human beings is how to define "being human." Being human is to have the capacity for true culture. All human beings have this capacity, but no other animal does.

There are examples of human beings who have either temporarily lost culture or have failed to acquire it: severe psychotics and feral children.

2. True human culture is unique, but it has its roots in animals. The analogues of the components of true human culture are to be found in animal behavior.

3. There are four components of true human culture: tools, language, conscience (and morality), and an ordered social life (as evidenced by the incest taboo). Each of these is foreshadowed in animal behavior.

4. We can therefore say that human beings are different from other animals in degree but not in kind.

5. Human beings are all one species, and human culture is all one entity. But just as we can talk about French people or Russian people, we can talk about different cultures. The first principle of the anthropological understanding of culture is cultural relativism—no culture can be judged except in its own terms.

6. There are no good cultures and no bad cultures. "Good" and "bad" are not ideas that apply to culture. There are good and bad societies, however; Nazi Germany was one recent example of a bad society. We can and must judge societies. We cannot judge cultures.

7. Human beings exist in a system that comprises ten major subsystems, divided into three groups: the biological cluster, the cultural cluster, and the ecological cluster. Taken together, they constitute the biocultural system. So far in this book we have been concerned with the biological cluster. Now we turn to the cultural.

Suggested Readings

Eibl-Eibesfeldt, Irenaus. *Ethology: The Biology of Behavior*. 2nd ed. New York: Holt, Rinehart and Winston, 1975.
> *This is about the best source to start with on animal communication.*

Goodall, Jane. *In the Shadow of Man*. New York: Dell Publishing, 1972.
> *For an account of the difficulties and excitement of studying primates in the wild, students should read this.*

Malson, Lucien. *Wolf Children and the Problem of Human Nature*. New York: Monthly Review Press, 1975.
> *This is a translation of Dr. Itard's account of Victor's upbringing, along with a list and brief discussion of other reported wolf children.*

Thompson, E. S. Whitney. *Sociocultural Systems*. Dubuque: Wm. C. Brown Company Publishers, 1977.
> *A book on the contemporary study of systems in social science. You do not need mathematics to read it, but it will require you to tune up your faculties.*

Glossary

altruism   Self-sacrificing behavior on behalf of the group.

biocultural system   The system that is made up of three clusters of subsystems: the cultural cluster, the biological cluster, and the ecological cluster.

biological cluster   A cluster of the biocultural system made up of two subsystems: the morphological and physiological subsystem, and the genetic subsystem.

cultural cluster   The cultural cluster of the biocultural system is made up of six subsystems: the linguistic subsystem, the subsystem of meaning, the subsystem of religion, the subsystem of cosmology, the subsystem of kinship, and the subsystem of political organization.

cultural relativism   The doctrine that all cultures have to be evaluated in their own terms.

ecological cluster   The ecological cluster of the biocultural system is made up of two subsystems: the ecological subsystem and the economic subsystem.

ethnocentrism   The belief that one's own culture provides an absolute standard for judging other cultures. *Cf.* cultural relativism

feral child   A child who has been abandoned by or isolated from human contact so that it grows up an "animal," without culture.

incest taboo   The cultural rule that prohibits sexual intercourse with certain classes of relatives.

protoculture   Those animal behaviors that foreshadow true human culture.

sign   The signal with a fixed referent; signs can refer to only one thing. *Cf.* symbol

socialization   The process whereby children are turned into social animals with culture.

symbol   Something that stands for something else.

wolf child   *See* feral child.

13

Language and Communication

Introduction

Anthropologists first arriving in the field usually suffer **culture shock.** The major reason for this is that we are regarded as "idiot children"—we cannot communicate, we are bad-mannered, we do not know how to do many of the most rudimentary things appropriately. In general (*in the eyes of the local people*), we act like ungainly clods. Before we can engage in any scientific research, we have to retrain ourselves. It is as though we had to go through growing up again. We start off by putting together elementary sentences that make us sound like children. There is nothing quite so frustrating for normally talkative, not to say literary, academics as being reduced to saying things like, "I like food. You like food, too? We like village. Village good." But the first thing we have to do is to learn the language. We start off this chapter by showing you how anthropologists go about doing that.

The study of language (all languages, the theory of language) also is important to anthropologists. Language is a subsystem of the biocultural system, one that we know quite a bit about and so should understand. But the theories that we use for learning languages and for understanding them are different. The first is a theory that a high school would use to teach you Spanish (or any other language). It is called **immediate constituent analysis** (I/C for short). The theory that the linguist learns to understand language is called **transformational-generative theory** (or TG for short). We will give you an introduction to TG theory, too.

Figure 13.1
Anthropologists work in difficult conditions to get their naturally occurring data.

Anthropologists are interested in all communicative codes, not just that one very important code we mentioned: language. There are many other ways that human beings communicate with one another, and if we are going to understand the meaning of peoples' lives as they live them, we have to monitor and understand all the messages they send each other. We call this the study of communicative codes.

We also study language and speech in communities because these give us clues as to how the community is organized, how people regard each other, and how people construct their world. Language conveys social meaning: it separates one part of the community from another and gives each group its special quality. The study of language and society is called *sociolinguistics*.

The I/C Model of Language

Learning to Communicate

You cannot understand what is happening in an alien culture unless you can understand what things people think and talk about and *how* they think and talk about these things. The first job of ethnographers is to immerse themselves completely in the community or tribe they have chosen to study and learn the language. Alan Beals, who worked in a traditional village in India, describes his experience:

In this learning process, regular language lessons seemed of little value, and I came to regret the time that I had spent learning Kanarese grammar. The grammar that I learned was that of Sanskrit and Latin and had little relevance to the way in which people actually formed sentences. The final breakthrough seemed to be due to two things: [my] isolation from persons who could speak English and [my] transcribing of field notes in Kanarese. If I had to do it over again, I would go alone to a place where nobody spoke English and I would arrange for the constant companionship of an uneducated man between the ages of nine and fifteen. As soon as I could ask simple questions like, "What is that?" I would begin asking them and carefully writing down both the questions and the answers. After each interview I would practice reading back the material to my companion and I would try to form simple sentences like, "That is a tree." Isolated in a strange place, unable to talk, unable to ask for food, one is placed under the same pressures that confront a child learning a language. There is no choice but to learn and to learn quickly. (Beals 1970: 48–49)

Not all anthropologists do it this way. Sometimes enough bilingual people are available in the community for us either to use a translater and interpreter or to talk to people in their second language. For example, when the local people in Latin America have a halting or passing fluency in Spanish or Portuguese, many anthropologists talk to them in that language rather than in the everyday language. This is almost always a mistake,

Figure 13.2
Learning a language is difficult but absolutely essential.

since these people do not think or talk habitually in Spanish or Portuguese and therefore do not explain themselves to themselves in that way.

Alan Beals's "total immersion" method is by far the best, though any successful way is a good way. The vast majority of anthropologists start off with a bilingual informant who knows the language we want to learn and who has also learned another language with which we are familiar—a contact language, such as French, Spanish, Arabic, Chinese, or English—at a mission school or in an urban center. Working through an interpreter is an unsatisfactory business at best, because it introduces another screen, or filter, between the anthropologist and the culture-bearers. So anthropologists try to learn the local language as soon as they can.

How to Learn a Language

You do not have to be a watchmaker in order to tell time, but it helps to know something about how a watch works if you are trying to construct one. Anthropologists need to know enough linguistics to know how languages in general are put together; but, although it would be helpful, they do not have to know current linguistic theory intimately. As we have said, the best form of analysis to use for learning a language is I/C (immediate constituent) analysis. It is based on an old-fashioned theory about language, which does not serve well as a guide to understanding the nature of language. But what it does better than modern formal theories of language is help one discover the grammar and vocabulary of a language and how to speak it. This is how I/C analysis works.

Phonology   When your first informant opens his or her mouth, you had better be prepared for a stream of unintelligible sound. One of the authors worked in a British secondary school and remembers the first days among *that* tribe. Once, in anger, he advanced upon one luckless school child, who leaped out of his seat and headed for the exits. When our author asked the class why the child had cut and run, he was presented with the reply, "/heeforteuwuzgunnafumpim/" all in one word. Only after five minutes of coaching by the natives could the "word" be decomposed into its constituent sound units as "He thought you was going to thump him."

We take for granted that streams of sound in a foreign language are *segmented* (i.e., cut up into sound units), because we can segment streams of sound in our own language, and we are in the habit of writing and reading words in separate (segmented) units. But the sound stream does not come in word-length segments. Rather, it flows in more natural, thought-mirroring segments, and one has to work hard to divide up the stream into its immediate *constituents* (or *constituent units*).

The human vocal apparatus can produce literally thousands of

320   **Human Culture**   **Part 4**

Figure 13.3
The acoustical stream as recorded on an oscillo-graph.

sounds, called **phones,** which can be distinguished by a *phonetician*— a person who studies sounds used in language (**phonology**). Each speaker learns to ignore some differences between phones and recognize others. English speakers recognize the sound difference between *bile* and *vile,* but the Zapotecs do not. They cannot hear the distinction between *b* and *v* and vary freely between them. A conversation that contained this confusion went as follows:

Selby: Well, which is it—*bela* or *vela?*
Zapotec: Yes.
Selby (In rising irritation): Come on, which one—*vela* or *bela?*
Zapotec: Very good, you seem to know our word for "brother" now.

To the Zapotec the *b* and *v* sounds were indistinguishable. He did not even hear the difference in the two phones (the *phonetic* distinction) that we hear.

Similarly, most people do not hear a difference between the *p*'s in the English words *pit* and *spit,* but a trained linguist can. The first is said with a puff of air after it (*aspirated*), while the second has no puff (*unaspirated*). That difference, which we do not recognize or even hear, is very important in some languages, such as Quechua, a language spoken in Bolivia. Quechua speakers can have two words with different meanings that are identical except that the *p* is aspirated in one and unaspirated in the other.

A linguist, like a phonetician, can recognize 700 to 800 different sounds that human beings use to distinguish different words. Not surprisingly, most of us are not able to distinguish that many. In fact, American English speakers lump all the sounds we regularly emit into 33 classes, or **phonemes.** Some languages have as few as 12 phonemes, while others have as many as 60 (Stross 1976: 6).

Morphology   What does *anti-* mean? What about *dis-*? They are not words, but they combine with other meaningful elements in language to form words. They are called **morphemes.** A morpheme is a minimal unit of meaning. It is minimal because you cannot break it down any further. *Anti-* and *dis-* have meaning, but they cannot be used alone in well-formed sentences; they are called **bound morphemes.** Most morphemes can be used by themselves and are therefore *words;* words and other morphemes can be put together to form *compound words.*

A morpheme is a minimal unit of meaning.

We can form huge words by piling up morphemes. For a long time the *Guinness Book of Records* stated that the largest word in the English language was one meaning "a belief that the queen of England should not be removed as the head of the official [established] church." The word is *antidisestablishmentarianism.* The way the meanings are piled up can be seen in Table 13.1.

In linguistics, **morphology** is the study of how morphemes go together to make up words and larger segments of meaning. *Anti-* and *dis-,* for example, are prefixes; they must come before the main word. Morphemes change the meaning of a word: *work-ed* is different from *work-ing,* which is different from *re-work* or *re-work-ed.* There are rules that one must discover before one realizes that *-ed* means "past tense" and *re-* means "to do something again." Sometimes the rules are obvious, but sometimes they are not.

Take the morpheme *as-* in the word *reassign.* Be your own informant. Which of the following words is the root word: *resign* or *assign?* It is quite obvious that the root word is *assign* and that *reassign* means "assign again." We feel or intuit this solution because the prefix *re-* occurs a good deal more in our language than the infix *as-.*

Traditional linguists recognize two major divisions of morphology. First is the study of **paradigms,** or the ways words change to yield new meanings. A Latin paradigm every student learns within a week of starting to learn this language shows how very slight changes in verb endings change the meanings of the word (Table 13.2).

The other branch of morphology is the study of the formation of words and stems in which rather larger changes take place. Plural formations, for example, are quite varied—so much so that it is hard to give *all* the rules for the formation of plurals in English. They are very compli-

Table 13.1
Piling Up Morphemes

Morpheme	Meaning
anti-	"being against"
dis-	"undoing something"
establish	"making the queen the official head of the church" [this is a technical meaning for *establish*]
-ment	"the act of (establishing)"
-arian	"a person who is all of those things said earlier"
-ism	"a belief that the above person holds"
Total: "a belief against removing the queen from the official leadership of a state religion," or "being against those who want to remove the queen as head of the church"	

Table 13.2
Paradigm of Latin Verb *ama-*

Singular		Plural	
amo	"I love"	amamus	"we love"
amas	"you love"	amatis	"you (pl.) love"
amat	"he, she, it loves"	amant	"they love"

Table 13.3
Some English Plurals

Example	Singular	Plural	Sound Change
(1)	boy	boys	Add the sound /z/ or /əz/
(2)	house	houses	
(3)	cat	cats	Add the sound /s/
(4)	ox	oxen	Add the sound /ən/ or /rən/
(5)	child	children	
(6)	sheep	sheep	Make no changes at all
(7)	foot	feet	Change the interior of the word

cated because one has to account for what our grade school teachers called "exceptions." (See Table 13.3.)

Pronunciation is important here, because we are interested in sound changes. Examples (1) and (2) in Table 13.3 show plural formation with /z/ or /əz/. Example (3) shows it with /s/. Examples (4) and (5) show a plural in /ən/ and /rən/. Example (6) is a *zero change,* sometimes shown as /ø/, whereas (7) shows a sound change in the interior of the word.

A linguist studying morphology would create a set of rules to predict these changes.

Morphophonemics Because sound changes can sometimes signal changes in meaning (as in *foot/feet*) and because sometimes affixes induce sound changes, one has to study them both. The study of sound changes that create meaning changes is called **morphophonemics,** that is, a combination of morphology and phonemics and is distinguished from morphology itself. The linguistic anthropologist finds the rules for sound and form changes so that he or she will not have to memorize endless lists of exceptions.

Syntax To learn a language, we not only have to know about sound and form changes that create meaning changes in single and compound words, but we also have to be able to string words together. The rules that govern the operation of "stringing together" are called *syntactic* rules, or the **syntax** of a language. Some sound sequences are appropriate and some are not. The appropriate ones are called *well-formed utterances*. One has to understand morphology to understand syntax, and so syntax includes the study of morphology.

A well-formed utterance need not be meaningful. Lewis Carroll specialized in writing nonsense verse that was meaningless. The trick lay in persuading people that the verse must mean something because it was well-formed. The famous verse:

> 'Twas brillig, and the slithy toves
> Did gyre and gimble in the wabe;
> All mimsy were the borogoves,
> And the mome raths outgrabe.

See if you agree with the interpretation we made as children:

'Twas = "It was"
brillig = adjective describing the kind of day it was—perhaps sunshiny or brilliant.
slithy = adjective that describes toves, perhaps meaning slimy or something like that.
toves = noun, perhaps a kind of animal, because in the second line we note that they perform two kinds of action—gyring and gimbleing. We assume that this is the plural.

Carroll uses the right kind of word in the right kind of place, which is why his verse has the illusion of meaning. For anthropologists and linguists, another "nonsense" sentence is even more famous than Carroll's verse; it is Noam Chomsky's "Colorless green ideas sleep furiously." We surely recognize and understand sentences formed just like it: "Frantic hungry schoolchildren scream angrily." Chomsky's sentence, too, is meaningless, even though it is well-formed.

When we say the proper words go in the proper places, we mean that the right **form classes** of words are in the right positions in the sentence. Being properly placed, they have the conventional relations to other words in the sentence so that the whole can make sense. Syntactic rules allocate words to form classes, position them properly in sentences, and permit us to make well-formed utterances that have meaning.

In I/C analysis, our language instructor educates us by taking sentences apart so that we can see what goes with what. We have to rely on the intuitions of the local informant as to what belongs together and what goes separately. Take the following sentence:

The old teacher lives happily in the house.

Our intuitions about the sentence tell us that *old* goes with *teacher,* that *happily* goes with *lives,* that the three words *in the house* go together. To check our intuitions, we get our informant to substitute single words for each of these, as follows:

The old teacher   lives happily   in the house.
The mechanic   works   inside.

An additional replacement yields:

He   works   inside.

This analysis tells us how larger units are made up of smaller ones to create well-formed sentences. Thus, we know that one never says "house the in." We find that word order is especially important in English because this language lacks word endings that tell us what role a word plays in the sentence. We learn that *concord,* or agreement, is important. One says "this duck" but "these ducks," "man walks" but "men walk," and so on. In general, one learns the regular features, or the rules of combination, so that one can produce well-formed utterances.

If one follows this plan rigorously, then, with a great deal of work, drill, elicitation, and memorization, one can learn a language.

The Transformational-Generative Model of Language

Surface and Depth

When all is said and done, we have learned a language and have found out how the language (and other communicative devices) are used creatively

Strangely, often the most important rules that govern our lives and to which we adhere most faithfully are those we are unaware of—the unconscious rules.

to form a distinctive word. We have not learned much about language itself, nor have we learned much about ideas that may be important to people but are unconscious and not coded in their language. Strangely, often the most important rules that govern our lives and to which we adhere most faithfully are those we are unaware of—the unconscious rules.

For instance, in the case of the complications of forming the English plural, we are all capable of applying the rules correctly, but we cannot explain what they are. We listen to children apply rules they have learned and smile when they misapply one. They may say, "Look, Mama, I have two foots"—applying the rule and getting the wrong answer.

One way to think about language is to imagine it exists on two levels —on the topmost, visible, surface level (*surface structure*) and on the level of *deep structure*. The well-formed utterance is audible, presenting to our senses something we can hear. It is analogous to the phenotype (the surface form, or appearance, of an organism), which we discussed earlier. But sometimes appearances are deceiving. For example, take the sentence:

> Murdering students can be dangerous.

There is an inherent ambiguity here. Are the students in the mood for bloodshed? Or is the act of murdering them likely to land one in trouble? How about this pair of sentences?

> I believe that American culture will survive.
> I believe in the survival of American culture.

They mean exactly the same thing (they are *synonymous*), but their surface appearances are different. In the case of the murdering students, we have one sentence with two meanings; while in the second example, we have two sentences with one meaning. The fact that the appearance of language can be deceiving provides one of many possible reasons why it is necessary to posit a deep structure for sentences we hear. The "murdering students" example has two deep structures, depending on whether it is the students or the act of killing them that is dangerous, while the "American culture" sentences have a single deep structure yielding two different but synonymous surface forms.

What we need is a model of language that accounts for both synonymy and ambiguity, as well as many other well-known facts about language. For example, languages (and grammars) are *productive;* that is, one can form new sentences that have never been formed before. This makes languages infinite. No sentence is ungrammatical because it is too long. (The hearer may not pay attention or may fall asleep, but that does not make the utterance ungrammatical.)

Because of these facts, the model for language must be a complex one, and it is only in its formative stages of development. To start developing a model, we must first imagine an ideal situation in which every member of the speech community speaks the same language, understands it perfectly, and speaks in grammatical sentences. This is what Noam Chomsky calls the "ideal speaker-hearer in a homogeneous environment." (Do not worry that no such group of people exists. In science we often make assumptions about idealized situations so we can study the laws that would hold under these ideal conditions.)

Let us assume our ideal speaker has a thought he or she wishes to communicate. First the thought is *coded* in deep structure. Next it is put into general syntactic form so that it can be transmitted. During this step emotions and thoughts that are untransmittable by language are filtered out and either not communicated or communicated through some other mode. Assume the speaker wishes to report some simple event—a man picking up his handkerchief. The thought can be broken down into three elements: *the man, picking up,* and *handkerchief.* These thoughts have to be put together in a proper form so that the surface structure of the utterance is grammatical. The following hypothetical attempt is clearly wrong:

> The man pick up handkerchief.

But it is close. Certain *obligatory changes* have to be made in order to make it grammatical. We call these obligatory changes *transformations.* First, the subject and the verb have to agree.

> The man picks up handkerchief.

That is still not quite right. A particle (*determiner*) is missing in the second noun phrase. It is obligatory to put it in.

> The man picks up the handkerchief.

Finally! But if the handkerchief had been mentioned earlier, perhaps one could say,

> The man picks up it.

The sentence would be understood but felt to be wrong, and the hearer could readily correct it. A particle (*up*) is in the wrong place, and an obligatory transformation requires one to change the order of the pronoun and the particle. The next is correct:

> The man picks it up.

How about the following sentence—does it mean the same thing?

> The handkerchief is picked up by the man.

The thought that first prompted the sentence is the same and so the sentence has the same meaning; but it has been changed by an *optional transformation* called the *passive transformation.*

On the other hand, how about this sentence—does it make sense?

The handkerchief was climbed by the man.

It does not make sense to us. One does not climb handkerchiefs.

It's surface is well-formed, but it has no meaning and so is not grammatical. To be grammatical a sentence must be both well-formed and have meaning.

Language and Culture

Language and Cultural Systems

You should remember the following three things about language. First, language is both productive and complex. Building a model that accurately represents language is an extremely difficult task that is now only in its earliest stages of development. Second, the base rules of language lie in its deep structure, and in the transformations of various kinds that are necessary to bring language to its surface structure. Third, because the appearance of language can be deceiving, one must look beneath its surface form to arrive at the underlying structure.

So it is with cultural systems. Their appearances are important to us because they are what we see and study. But the explanation of how they work has to go below the level of appearances. It has to get at the deep structure, or *infrastructure,* in order to see the more meaningful reality that "truly" explains.

If we understand language, we are well on the way to understanding culture. The structure of language and the structure of culture are not the same. That is, they are not *isomorphic.* But we believe they are analogous, or similar. They correspond to some degree.

Anthropologists study single languages so they can communicate with their informants. If we are going to get the inside view of other cultures, we must understand the way people *code* and *categorize* their world. We must first construct a **folk lexicography,** that is, a dictionary of the important categories and relations in a system of ideas (a single culture) and how they fit together. For the purposes of learning a language. it is often sufficient to do immediate constituent (I/C) analysis and let one's intuitions work with the surface appearance of the language.

But anthropologists study *language* (all languages) because they think it provides ideas about how cultural systems are put together. For this, one has to understand the generative model of language.

Language(s) and Culture(s)

We must distinguish between two usages for the word "language." Sometimes when we say "language," we mean all human language, as compared with the communicative systems of other species of animals. We call this "Language with a capital L." At other times, particularly when we are carrying out ethnographic studies of single cultural systems, we mean the language spoken by the culture-bearers of that particular system. This can be called "language with a lowercase *l*." The diagram below shows the relationship:

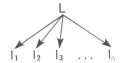

where L means all human or natural languages and l_1 could mean American English, l_2 could mean Chinese, l_3 could mean Zapotec.

Similarly, we must distinguish between culture in two senses. "Culture with a capital C" is all human culture, as opposed to animal protoculture. Just as there are many different languages spoken by the peoples of the earth, so there are many different "cultures with a lowercase *c*."

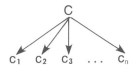

In the diagram, C means human culture, while c_1 could be American culture, c_2 could mean Chinese culture, c_3 Zapotec culture.

If we were studying Zapotec culture, we would spend a good deal of time studying l_3, Zapotec language, because it is a subsystem of c_3 (Zapotec culture). We study that language not just to be able to communicate with the Zapotecs, although that is important, but to find out more about the way they habitually think about and organize their world. (More on that later.)

In addition to studying particular cultures and their languages, anthropologists study L, natural human language (as opposed to computer languages, logical languages, or animal communicative systems), because it tells us about the structure of C, human culture.

Figure 13.4
Men at this European
sidewalk cafe converse
close to one another, closer
than is customary in the U.S.

We cannot be sure, but it may be that many other subsystems of the cultural system are constructed the way language is. Understanding the structure of l_1 (a particular language like American English, for example) will help us understand the structure of c_1 (the United States of America). Understanding the structure of L (all languages, any language) does help us understand C (culture, all human cultures, any culture).

Other Communicative Modes

Robots in science fiction movies speak strangely because their voices lack emotional expression. Human beings communicate through smell, body heat, tone of voice, pace of speech, emphasis, intonation, facial expression, body position, gestures, and a host of other ways. Two things should be noted about these communicative modes. First, they are very important, sometimes, in fact, the only important part of a message being communicated. Second, these modes are usually not under conscious control, and therefore the messages sent in these ways are truthful. (Lie detectors are based on this premise.)

The anthropologist Gregory Bateson used to drive home these two points in his lectures by posing the question of how a girl tells whether a boy really loves her or not. "Suppose," he would say, "the girl asks, 'Do you love me?' and the boy replies, 'Yes, I really love you!' " We all know that the girl is not concerned with the grammaticality of the sentence nor with decomposing it into its constituent units. She wants to know whether it is true or not. If the boy replies, "Argle, blurb glum bubble," it would probably convey the message because she is listening to the nonlinguistic apects of the communicative act. She attends (probably without knowing it, certainly without knowing all of it) to the boy's eyes, his bodily position, his movements during the utterance, and the intonation of his voice. If the emotion is truly felt and not bogus, the boy's eyes will glisten, because they will dilate and reflect more light. His body should be open and trustworthy-looking. If he hunches his shoulders, crosses his legs, and hugs himself with his arms, this would quickly be interpreted to mean he is protecting himself from his own remark, denying with his body what he is saying with his voice.

If his mouth is drawn, if his gaze wanders, if his skin is absolutely dry, then again the girl will know he is not telling the truth. For under strong emotional stress, the sweat glands release moisture and the blood rate surges, producing a flushed appearance on the surface of the skin. As for intonation, it should not be stagey or timid. It should not be too loud, either, nor should there be too much variability in the pitch of the phrases or words. If the tone is absolutely flat, it suggests that strong counter-emotions are being held in check; but if the voice goes up and down too much, it suggests that it is being consciously manipulated, that it is perhaps being used to deceive. "Saying something as though you mean it" is an important thing we all learn. Particularly we learn to decode other peoples' messages for truth value, utilizing information gleaned from attending to nonlinguistic communicative modes.

Proxemics

Proxemics is the study of the meaning and manipulation of space. Studies by Edward Hall, O. Michael Watson, and others have shown how human beings arrange their space to make themselves comfortable and to communicate ideas. Americans, for example, are uncomfortable speaking while standing so close together that they can smell each other, whereas Arabs feel uncomfortable speaking at what they regard as the large distances Americans habitually use. If we want to close in on someone, or "buttonhole" a person, we communicate this by moving in close and perhaps blocking the line of retreat. (To "buttonhole" originally meant to put your finger through the buttonhole in a man's jacket lapel in order to haul him toward you and hold him. The poet Coleridge, who used to talk for hours without ceasing, was a notorious buttonholer and made the term popular as a result.) In some way, we all manipulate the space between speaker and hearer to persuade and convince.

Navahos gaze at the ground while they speak to someone, because eye contact is embarrassing to them. Yet when Americans do not stare into people's eyes, holding their gaze in a candid fashion, we are accused of not being direct enough. Watson and Graves (1970) found that Arab males employ mutual direct eye contact during most of a conversation—two to two-and-a-half times as long as Britishers studied by Kendon.

Smell

We know that complex signals about territoriality, sexual state, or danger are transmitted in other animals through scent by means of compounds called pheromones. In our species, smell as a means of communication is less important relative to other senses. The extent to which humans use this sensory modality has not been thoroughly investigated. Nevertheless, we do know that people in psychotic or severe anxiety states emit characteristic smells that other psychotics recognize and use to find out their companion's inner state. "How do things smell tonight?" is a good question for a mental hospital attendant to ask if he or she wants to know whether it will be a quiet night. In addition, pheromonal communication may be responsible for the observed synchronization of menstrual cycles among women living in the same college dormitory. While we may

Figure 13.5
Actors can control their appearance and their voices in ways that we cannot.

Figure 13.6
Some people feel that the atmosphere of the back wards of mental hospitals can be understood by using smell.

not be aware of the function of smell on this biological level, we are certainly aware that, culturally, humans can communicate complex messages through scent. People in our culture go to great lengths to mask normal body odors and substitute those of soaps, deodorants, mouthwash, and perfumes to communicate complex messages regarding sexuality and social status.

Paralinguistics

Paralanguage, like proxemics, refers to nonlinguistic elements of communication. Tone of voice, pitch, loudness, voice quality, tempo, and register—all these are included under the heading of paralinguistic phenomena. Children learn paralinguistic features of speech before any others, and we all use our voices and communication channels strategically. For example, wheedling a favor from someone requires the strategic manipulation of both paralinguistic and proxemic factors: in our culture, the body is slightly bent over and forward in a gesture of submission; eyes are downcast as a measure of shame or obeisance; the voice is pitched high and childlike in a further gesture of submission. We try to make ourselves sound like spaniels in order to elicit some favor or other. Cross-culturally, paralinguistic features vary. The Tzotziles convey respect by acting in the same way we do when we are asking for a favor.

Sometimes paralinguistic features carry the whole load of communication. Adams (1957) reported that Egyptian villagers exchange conventional expressions that are always the same and therefore meaningless. Friendliness or enmity are conveyed entirely by qualities of pitch, tone, and melodiousness of the voice.

Sometimes paralinguistic features are obligatory for certain categories of people. According to Garbell (1965), many elderly female speakers of Urmi, a dialect spoken by Jews in Azerbaijan (north Persia), replace practically all "plain" words by "flat" ones. That is, they sound the words further back in the mouth, round their lips more, and pout as they speak.

Speech Surrogates

Just as we have Morse code and writing as substitutes for spoken language, other cultures use whistling, drumming, slit-gongs, flutes, or sea shells as communicative devices. The nature of a drum, whistle, or gong language depends on the kind of language ordinarily spoken by the people who use it. *Tonal* languages such as Chinese, in which the pitch of the word is phonemic (i.e., makes a difference in meaning), lend themselves fairly readily to whistle and gong languages. The sender can mimic the tones of the ordinary language, and fairly complex messages can be sent. Obviously, drums can be used to broadcast signals, just as the bugle was used for cavalry signals. Drummers can abridge the sound features of the ordinary language to mimic speech. As you would expect, many words that sound different in ordinary language sound the same in drum language, and sometimes (as in Kele, Congo) a whole sentence on the drums has to be substituted for a single spoken word. In Akan, the best-studied drum language (Nketia 1963, 1971), the drummer mimics the sound of whole sentences—the syllables, the stress, the duration of the syllable, the rhythm of the word group, the speed of the utterance, and the tone of the syllable.

Figure 13.7
Drum languages can be very efficient in places where tonal languages are spoken.

Sociolinguistics

Language and Society

Sociolinguistics is the study of the relationship between society and language. The way we speak reflects and constrains our position in society. If we want to change our position, we may have to change our manner of speaking. English schoolchildren with working-class backgrounds have to change their language habits when they get middle-class jobs. They sound differently (phonological change); they put sentences together differently (syntactic change); and they use different words (lexical change). Similarly, black Americans from the ghetto who get middle-class jobs have to drop black English, which is often incomprehensible to the average white American, and speak standard English.

The way we speak tells other people who we are, and who we are constrains the way we speak. Women and minorities are particularly aware of this. Every American girl knows it is difficult to end a telephone conversation with a boy. She has to wait until he makes "ending noises," and then she can wrap it up. "Shuckin' and jivin' " was a technique once used by American blacks to make whites feel they were in control of the situation. It involved a high-pitched voice, rolling eyes, a wheedling tone, and a downcast head—an act of exaggerated submission that whites could take for true submission.

We do not normally think of ourselves as being able to speak in a number of codes, but we all can and do constantly switch back and forth among them. Children do not talk to each other the way they talk to their parents. They learn at least two codes—one for peers and one for authority figures. Some bilingual people switch languages rather than codes. In Paraguay, where both Spanish and Guarani are spoken, Guarani expresses greater intimacy and Spanish, more distance and formality (Rubin 1968). The Kaska switch from their North American Indian language to English to curse. Many peasant and Indian groups use their Indian dialects to conceal information from outsiders. Denison (1968) studied a trilingual (three-language) community and noted that there were thirteen factors that one had to take into account to use the right language. These included the kind of situation one was in (at home or in a formal setting); the feeling one had when speaking (was one speaking spontaneously); and with whom one was speaking (were they older or younger? were they of the opposite sex?). Using the languages properly was an important part of being a good citizen of the community.

Sometimes words vary when one switches codes. We can see this historically in the paired words *pork* versus *pig* and *beef* versus *cattle*. The first in each pair is derived from Norman French and the second from Anglo-Saxon. Probably the Norman French conquerors of England were more used to seeing their meat cooked and served by their Saxon vassals, and so their words for pig (*porc*) and cattle (*boeuf*) became the words for the meat, while the Anglo-Saxon words came to stand for the living animals, raised by Saxon farmers.

Pronouns and Social Distance

Many languages make a distinction in the way a speaker says *you,* one form (in French and Spanish, the *tu*-form) being used for intimacy and solidarity and another (*vous* or *usted*) for distance, respect, and authority. Americans find this quite difficult to deal with when they are abroad. Both authors of this text work in rural villages and big cities in Latin America, for example, and find that a great deal of "*Usted*-ing" goes on in the villages, but little in the city. If we were to "Usted" our colleagues in the city, they would think of us as country bumpkins, because there is much more "*tu*-ing" there.

Titles and Kin Terms

Americans, as Burling (1970) and others have pointed out, are very strange about names. One of the authors was astonished to find that many American students called their professors by first names and vice versa. Being British, he had always been called by his last name by his professor (and his professor's wife), while he had always addressed his professor as "Professor Warmington." Many people are unsure at first what to call their in-laws. There is a story about the newly married man who would run up three flights of stairs to talk to his mother-in-law face to face so that he would not have to call her by her first name ("Joan" was too intimate, too presumptuous) or by a title and last name (you cannot call your own mother-in-law "Mrs. Smith") or by a kin term (how can you possibly ever call another woman what you have always called your own mother?). In answer to the question, "What do you call your mother-in-law?" young people often answer, "I don't know how to address her properly."

Europeans used to say that Americans were the kind of people who called you by your first name five minutes after they had met you and then forgot to say good-bye. This seemed odd to Europeans, because they only used first names of people whom they knew well, but would always acknowledge their parting. Saying goodbye to everybody was the polite and friendly thing to do.

Summary

1. Language and languages are very important to anthropologists. They have to learn languages even when there are no grammars, dictionaries, or systems of writing as learning aids. They must, therefore, be aware of the structure of languages. Since language is a subsystem of the total biocultural system, it is an intrinsic part of their study. That means they must understand the structure of all languages and learn some linguistic theory.

2. Often we find in studies of biocultural systems that different communicative modes are utilized in different ways from those we are used to. We know that proxemic, paralinguistic, olfactory (smell), and facial attitudes are important. Other people use these things to different degrees and in different combinations. To understand a foreign culture's communicative modes, we must understand how they utilize the communicative resources at their disposal.

3. Language is a social phenomenon. The way we speak reflects and constrains our social position. Many societies, like our own, have different dialects for different segments of the society. Some, like our own, have prestige dialects that must be learned if one is going to enter prestige occupations or positions.

Suggested Readings

Burling, Robbins. *Man's Many Voices*. New York: Holt, Rinehart, and Winston, 1970.

   This is a first-rate introduction to the study of language by a well-known anthropologist and linguist. It goes through all the subjects mentioned in this chapter in more detail and with good references.

Goodenough, Ward. *Language and Culture*. Reading, Pa.: Addison-Wesley, 1975.

   A short introduction to the subject of the relationships between language and culture.

Hymes, Dell, ed. *Language in Culture and Society*. New York: Harper and Row, 1964.

A book offering a tremendous collection of articles on language, sociolinguistics, anthropological linguistics, and language and culture. The classic article on practically every important topic is to be found here.

Stross, Brian. *The Origin and Evolution of Language*. Dubuque: Wm. C. Brown Company Publishers, 1976.

A gem of a primer on the origin and evolution of language. Up-to-date with all the most recent, fascinating findings on brain research and the fossil record. Highly recommended for a good read.

Glossary

bound morpheme   A morpheme that can appear only with another morpheme and cannot stand on its own.

culture shock   The feelings of malaise that everyone gets when they first enter and start to work in an alien culture.

folk lexicography   An encyclopedia of the important categories and relations in a biocultural system.

form class   A class of words that can be substituted in a sentence and still preserve grammaticality.

immediate constituent analysis (I/C)   Analysis of language by breaking it down into its constituent parts.

morpheme   A minimal unit of meaning.

morphology   In linguistics, morphology is the study of how morphemes go together to form words and compound words. (Do not confuse this with *morphology* as it is used to refer to the form of animals and humans.)

morphophonemics   The study of how sound changes create new meanings.

paradigms   (1) Paradigm can be used to refer to the systematic way that words change to give different meanings. The example was from Latin *ama-*. (2) The semantic structure that happens when every dimension partitions the whole semantic field. (3) The items of a commutable set (hat, toque, ski cap, etc.). (4) The associations that come with all the items of a set of symbols.

phone   A linguistic sound that can be discriminated by an expert.

phoneme   That bundle of sounds (phones) that are discriminated by the local people in their language.

phonology   The study of the sound system of a language.

syntax   The rules for stringing together morphemes to create well-formed utterances.

14

Meaning

Introduction

When one starts out to say something, one does not perform the operations in the way we have described them for learning a language in the last chapter. We do not ask ourselves first, "What phonemes do I have to work with?" and second, "How may I properly combine them into morphemes?" and third, "What rules do I have to remember to string morphemes together according to their form-classes so as to produce an utterance?" All that takes place quite unconsciously, and people only become conscious of it in special situations; for example, when they have a speech impediment or when they are speaking to a person who has a limited knowledge of their language.* Normally, what happens is that we have a thought, an image, or a vague feeling of some kind, and this gives rise to a more or less proper communication *if* we can put it into words.

Meaning and Experience

Language Classifies Events in the World

Meaning is the means by which we communicate about the *extra-linguistic* world, or as we often say, the "real world." What language does is segment the "real world" so we can talk and think about it. If the outside world were a great formless blob, as in some science fiction stories, we could not say too much about it: "How is the great formless blob today?" "Large and without form!" Language incorporates our version of what that outside world is like; it is our reality. It is perfectly true that the outside world may not be exactly the way our language classifies it for us. But it had better be a fairly good copy, or we will be going on some very improper assumptions about extralinguistic reality that could get us into a lot of trouble.

Language: The Royal Road to Good Ethnography

Anthropologists enter their subjects' world through language.

Anthropologists enter their subjects' world through language. By learning the system of meanings that their subjects use to construct and interpret their world, anthropologists learn about other people's worlds. The building blocks for constructing the world are the *categories of experi-*

* When speaking, for example, to a person who knows a Romance language (derived from Latin) but little English, English speakers tend to fall into a strange brand of English derived from Latin, because they know these Latin words will be represented in the person's language. We might say things like, "You are very reasonable," when we mean, "That's right," or "We were cogitating about a preprandial libation," which means, "We were thinking about having a drink before lunch." These events are rare. (Usually, we just shout to make ourselves understood.)

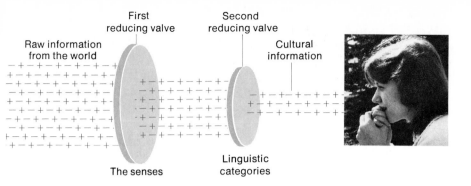

Figure 14.1
First our senses and then
our linguistic categories
reduce the amount of
information to which we
attend.

ence that are defined and labeled in the language of the people being studied.

Think about *experience* for a minute. The world is presented, via the perceptual faculties, in a constant stream of impressions. You hear, see, smell, feel, touch, taste, experience constantly. You are perceptually turned on all the time. An astonishing amount of information is available to us if we could take it in and process it. At the very most we can attend to about 1 percent of the available information, and, by generous estimate, we can process only about 50 percent of that. Our senses and our minds act as reducing valves, screening out that 99 percent and that 50 percent of the information that we can neither use nor handle.

The senses work in conjunction with a faculty we can call the "monitor" to pick up high-information events. High-information events are those that surprise us a great deal. If you are driving down a superhighway, your monitor is turned on all the time, checking on the cars around you. But it only demands your attention when some infrequent, surprising event takes place. Suddenly a tractor trailer pulls up close behind you. Immediately you attend to it. What our monitor permits us to do is to put most of the world "on hold" and ignore it until something unusual happens.

The monitor called up the attender for the tractor trailer not merely because it was a rare event, but because it was relevant to the situation of driving on the superhighway. It meant danger! That is where meaning comes in.

The monitor calls up the attender in this case when it picks out from the stream of impressions a class of events that appears dangerous. Under other conditions, it could pick out a class of events because it appears interesting, lovable, threatening, recognizable, and so on. One attends to events because they have been *classified*. They are classified because our language defines and labels them.

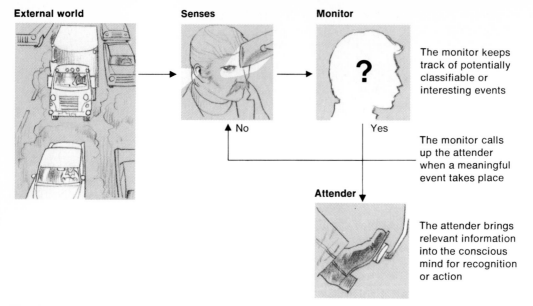

External world

Senses

Monitor

?

The monitor keeps track of potentially classifiable or interesting events

No

Yes

The monitor calls up the attender when a meaningful event takes place

Attender

The attender brings relevant information into the conscious mind for recognition or action

Figure 14.2
Our mode of monitoring and attending to events in the external world.

What language does, then, is give us a set of instructions for breaking up the continuous stream of impressions from experience, for classifying the bits, and then giving them labels. Categories and classes of meanings do for sense impressions what phonemes do for the streams of sound that strike our ear. The stream of experience and the acoustical stream are analogous. We *segment* the acoustical stream into meaningful sounds, or phonemes. We segment the stream of experience into meaningful units called categories.

Every cultural system has its own way of breaking up the world of experience into categories. An anthropologist tries to learn his or her informant-teacher's way of classifying experience and then translate it back to the readers. The best and easiest way to learn the informant-teacher's mode of classification is through language.

Field Work and Meaning

The field worker must first figure out the systems of meaning in the cultural system he or she is studying. The easiest part of the task is studying those categories of experience that are absent in one's own cultural system —for instance, "witchcraft" or "magical hair" or the "wedding fandango." It is rather more difficult, and usually more important, to understand ideas that are common to both cultural systems, but have different meanings: life, justice, love, envy, death. These must be studied carefully.

Rules for Doing Good Field Work in Meaning Few of the readers of this book will ever do any field work. But if you know some of the basic procedures that anthropologists follow, you will be better able to see what their results mean. The cardinal rule for doing good field work in the study of meaning is this:

Do not ask irrelevant questions!

Do not think that you know how to ask a relevant question of someone whose culture you do not share. People will almost always give you some answer to a question. It is important that the question make sense and that it be phrased in a way that the people themselves would ask it. Here is an example of an anthropologist's error in asking irrelevant questions.

One of the authors was interviewing when the topic of the "evil eye" came out in the conversation.

"And how" said the anthropologist, "do people give the evil eye to others?"

"It is 'thrown'," said the teacher.
"How far can you throw it?" the anthropologist asked.
"I beg your pardon?"
(Not getting the subtle hint) "How far can you throw it?"
"One hundred meters!"
"Ah, but what if it has to go through a mud wall or around a corner?"
"Seventy-five!"

At that point the two both burst into laughter, because the anthropologist realized that he had inadvertently translated the word "to throw" in the expression "to throw (i.e., give someone) the evil eye" as though it were the same as the English verb "to throw a baseball."

What the anthropologist should have said was this, cumbersome as it might appear:

"What question can I ask about the evil eye?"
"You may ask how it is thrown."
"How is it thrown?"
"It is thrown, usually inadvertently, by a person who passes it in the presence of a child or animal."
"Can I ask if people can throw it on purpose?"
"Yes."
"Can they throw it on purpose?"

"Yes, but when they do, they usually accompany it with a puff of breath or a surreptitious waving of their hat so as to blow deadly air at the child or the animal they want to harm."

"What can I ask about deadly air?" etc.

Now this is undoubtedly tedious, but one must do it at first to avoid treating evil eye stares like baseballs and importing all kinds of ideas into the belief system that were not there to start with. After a while, you gain enough knowledge of the language, your teachers, and your ignorance to enable you to go both quickly and carefully.

Do not think that local terms mean the same thing as the English words you translated them with.

Do not think that local terms mean the same thing as the English words you translated them with.

To implement the spirit of this rule one must put together a *folk encyclopedia,* a kind of super-dictionary for the local language. It tells you what the terms you have collected through elicitation *really* mean and what relationships any term has with all other important terms. Take the term "father" in American English in its genealogical sense. Webster's Dictionary states the following: **fa′ther** n. one who has begotten a child. . . .

A folk encyclopedia would give much more information than that. It would give in condensed form the genealogical relationship of the idea "father" with many other important ideas elicited in the course of formal questioning, such as "mother," "son," "daughter," "uncle," "aunt," "cousin," "brother-in-law," and so on. And this would be only one part of the entry under the heading "genealogical knowledge."

It is important to collect this kind of encyclopedic knowledge. In many cultural systems the father's brother is called "father" as are the father's father's brother's son and many other people. You cannot understand the meaning of "father" until you understand all the relationships it has with other terms. One must understand these in the same way that the people being studied do.

Two rules, then: (1) elicit the important ideas of the cultural system by asking relevant questions. (2) Form an encyclopedia of local knowledge that reflects the relationships of those terms to the other terms that serve to define them. Whatever happens, do not permit the following story to be told about you, as it was about a now-retired sociologist who worked on the subject of religion. "Why," the local people said, "he was so wise in our ways. He taught us many many things about our beliefs that we had never known before."

Denotative Meaning

One of the areas where we have a good idea of what words mean is in the area of **denotative meaning.** We distinguish between what a word *denotes* in the extralinguistic world and what it *connotes.* "Dog" *denotes* a special class of canine. It *connotes* "extra blanket on a cold night," "Rover whom we all love dearly," and other feelings about dogs. Connotation refers to all the emotional loading we put on events that are classified by words.

The Analysis of Denotative Meaning   Let us look at how to analyze denotative meaning. Kinship terms provide a good example. Consider the following list of kinship terms:

grandfather	grandmother	aunt
grandson	granddaughter	uncle
father	mother	niece
son	daughter	nephew
brother	sister	cousin

Our task is to find out what the denotative attributes of these terms are so we can define them. We are not worried about whether we love our own mother or grandfather; we merely want to know if these terms can be defined in some kind of field of meaning, or *semantic field*.

By using a technique that permitted them to exclude connotative meaning, two anthropologists, A. K. Romney and R. G. D'Andrade, came up with the picture shown in Chart 14.1 of the relations of similarity and contrast for these terms.

Chart 14.1
Semantic Relationships of American English Kin Terms

Generational Removal	Direct		Collateral	
	Male	*Female*	*Male*	*Female*
2	grandfather grandson	grandmother granddaughter	uncle	aunt
1	father son	mother daughter	nephew	niece
0	brother	sister	cousin	

They carried out psychological tests to see if people actually organized the terms in this way and found that they did. What in particular did they find? People classify kin terms according to the following attributes:

1. *Sex.*   With the exception of *cousin,* all kin terms in American English differentiate between males and females of the (otherwise) same category. We classify almost all relatives differently if they are males or females.

2. *Generational removal.*   We think of "grandfather" as being different from "grandson" (and therefore have different words for them), but not so different as "father." That is, grandfather and grandson share

one attribute—they are both two generations removed from the thinker/speaker (*Ego,* as she or he is called in anthropology). Similarly, father and son are different, but closer together than son/brother or father/brother. Why? Because father and son share the attribute of being one generation removed from Ego.

Note that there are three degrees of generational removal shown: 0 (zero), people of the same generation as Ego; 1, people one generation away; and 2, people two generations away, up or down.

3. *Polarity.* Look at the "two-generations-removed" cell (Chart 14.2). Grandfather and grandson are not the same in meaning, although they are quite close. They differ because one is "senior" generation and the other is "junior" (represented respectively by the "+" and the "–" to the left of the cell). They are similar because the person whom Ego calls "grandfather" calls him "grandson." Age is important in American English, and one has to distinguish between the older and younger persons in a pair. This is called *polarity,* indicating there are two poles to the relationship (i.e., older-younger). The same distinction is being made in the term pairs father/son and uncle/nephew. (We are not using the female terms here, but the same distinction holds for them, too.)

Chart 14.2
The Two–Generations–Removed Cell

	Direct	
	Male	*Female*
+	grandfather	grandmother
−	grandson	granddaughter

4. *Collaterality.* The last distinction we use to define the kin terms in Chart 14.1 is *collaterality*. That is, we distinguish between people related to us through a brother or sister (*collateral*) and those relatives who are our *direct* ancestors or descendants..

5. *Other distinctions* (not shown). What other distinctions do American English speakers make between different kinds of relatives? For one, they distinguish between *in-laws* and *blood relatives*. They code that distinction by using such terms as *father-in-law* or *brother-in-law*. But they are not thorough in this distinction; sometimes they ignore it. For example, they do not distinguish in terminology between a "blood aunt" and an "aunt by marriage." If they were going to be thorough about distinguishing between people related by blood from those related by marriage, they ought to make the distinction in their terminology. Sometimes they do, but sometimes they do not. Why this is so is not clear.

The Feature Model of Meaning Such a representation of the meaning of a sample of kin terms as that in Chart 14.1 is called a **feature model,** because it defines each kin term by its features, or values, on the distinctions we have been making. The feature model is useful for anthropologists, so we should explain it a little. First, we want you to understand the notion of *dimension*. Imagine a straight line as follows:

We represent dimensions by straight lines. Now imagine there are two words we want to compare—for example, *black* and *white*. One way to represent them would be to show that they contrast, or are at opposite poles of a single dimension. Now our problem is this: what is the name of the dimension? Answer: "lightness." This dimension runs from zero lightness (black) to complete lightness (white). If we want, we can say it runs from zero to one:

Lightness Dimension

How about *father/grandfather/me/son/grandson?* If we put them on a dimension, they would fall out like this:

Generation Level Dimension

$$0 \longrightarrow\hspace{5cm}\longrightarrow 1$$

grandson son me father grandfather

The dimension organizing the terms along the straight line is "generation." One discovers the name of the dimension by asking, "What attribute or idea would line the terms up this way, with grandfather at the opposite end from grandson, father and son closer together, and Ego in the middle?" "Age" would also be a good description; the dimension runs from youngest to oldest.

This placement of kin terms on a line says that there is a dimension of meaning that American English speakers use to sort their kin terms, and that I, the anthropologist, call it "generation." This is the way American English speakers actually think about their kin terms.

The Organization of American English Kin Terms Here are the features (or dimensions) for the list of kin terms: (1) sex of relative, (2) generational removal, (3) polarity, and (4) collaterality. How, then, are the terms defined? We can list them using the following symbol set:

1. Sex of the relative: δ (male); $\female$ (female).
2. Generational removal: 0, 1, 2.
3. Polarity: $+$ (senior); $-$ (junior)
4. Collaterality: $\overline{C}$ (not collateral); C (collateral)

We can now define these kin terms *denotatively,* as shown in Chart 14.3.

Chart 14.3
Definitions of American English Kin Terms (Males Only)

Kin Terms	Symbolic Definition	English Gloss of Symbolic Definitions
Grandfather	$\delta\,2+\overline{C}$	male up 2 generations from Ego, not collateral
Father	$\delta\,1+\overline{C}$	male up 1 generation from Ego, not collateral
Son	$\delta\,1-\overline{C}$	male down 1 generation from Ego, not collateral
Grandson	$\delta\,2-\overline{C}$	male down 2 generations from Ego, not collateral
Uncle	$\delta\,1+C$	male, up 1 generation from Ego, collateral
Nephew	$\delta\,1-C$	male down 1 generation from Ego, collateral
Cousin	$\delta\,0C$	male, same generation as Ego, collateral

Paradigm of Types of Furniture

	Bathroom Location	Living Room Location
Something to sit on	toilet	chair
Something to lie down in/on	bathtub	sofa

Paradigm of Kin Terms

	Male	Female
+1 Generation	father	mother
−1 Generation	son	daughter

Meaning Is Relational It was stated earlier that meaning is relational. Some evidence for this is given by the experiment every child tries, which is to repeat the same word over and over again and watch it lose all meaning whatsoever. Any word will do—say it long enough and it seems to cut itself off from other words and ideas that give it meaning and thereby become disembodied and meaningless.

For us to relate words to other words, we need a way of organizing them in our heads. We do not know all the ways that words and ideas are arranged in our heads so that they are in relation to other words, but we do know some. (We suspect there are not all that many.) Here are some of them.

A **paradigm** occurs when you partition a semantic field with dimensions that run through the whole field. Two simple paradigms might look like the examples above. Note how the partitions separate the terms. The dimension that distinguishes *father/mother* is "sex of relative." The dimension that distinguishes *father/son* is "polarity" (the senior/junior relation). But for the whole structure to be a paradigm, every word has to have a value on each dimension. Every word, then, is well defined in relation to every other. Nothing falls between the cracks. Paradigms are useful for storing information we need to use frequently and access easily, and for which contrasts are well defined and culturally important.

As you will recall from Chapter 3, taxonomies emphasize part-whole relations, or "kind-of" relations.

Here is a taxonomy of trees:

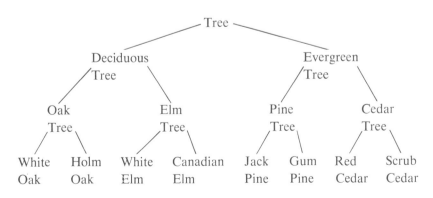

If you follow the terms up from the left-hand pair, you will see that *white oak* and *holm oak* are in a "kind-of" relation to *oak* (in better English, the white oak and the holm oak are "kinds of oak.") Similarly, oak and elm trees are both kinds of deciduous trees.

Taxonomies are useful to us because by using them we can store enormous amounts of information in our memories. Using taxonomies we can store up to 2^{11}, or 2048 categories along with their interrelations. Not surprisingly, then, in large and complex domains where fine distinctions are necessary, people tend to use taxonomies to store information. Plant domains are especially prone to being memorized as taxonomies. All mushrooms may look alike to you, but one of them, the *Amanita philoides,* is extremely poisonous; so you had better have a classification and storage device that not only tells you that it is a kind of mushroom, but also allows you to distinguish between it and other mushrooms.

Unidimensional Scales   Unidimensional (one-dimensional) scales are used to arrange things in order—just like the example we gave earlier of the generation-removal dimension of kinship. We shall see later that unidimensional scaling, or putting things in their order of preference, is a very powerful tool for organizing people and symbols. Basically, a unidimensional scale says that the elements you are arranging (or scaling) are all alike on some attribute but that some elements have more of the attribute than others. This type of ordering is familiar:

$$0 \rule{8cm}{0.4pt} 1$$

slave   beggar   yeoman   knight   prince   king

What can we say about these words or categories? We can say that a king is more powerful than a prince, who is more powerful than a knight, who is more powerful than a yeoman, who is more powerful than a beggar, who is more powerful than a slave. If we let the symbol ">" represent "is more powerful than," and letters represent the various categories, we could say:

$$F > E > D > C > B > A.$$

This is a principle very often used for ordering moral ideas or categories that have some intrinsic idea of "betterness" or "power" or "attractiveness." We will see many examples of this preference-ordering principle as we go along, particularly in the area of social organization.

Multidimensional Scaling   A final example of the way human beings store information in their memories is the *multidimensional scale*. Remember, we are only giving examples of the ways ideas or categories relate to one another so as to take on meaning. The most complex storing

Chart 14.4
Two Sets of Three Kinship Terms

Direct and Blood	Affine
Father	Father-in-law
Son	Son-in-law
Brother	Brother-in-law

method we can lay out with some degree of exactitude is the multi-dimensional ordering. Chart 14.4 shows six terms, the three on the left belonging to the set of blood and direct relatives, and the three on the right belonging to the *affine* set, the set of in-laws. A way of representing these terms (we would have to test to see whether it is the true way) would be the following:

Father-in-law

Father   Brother   Son

Brother-in-law

Son-in-law

If we draw the connecting lines, the figure looks familiar enough from our high school geometry days:

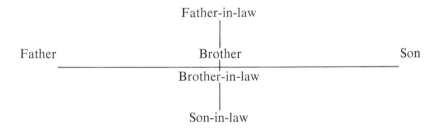

This is a two-dimensional space (or two-space), with an *x*-axis (or *abscissa,* the horizontal dimension) and a *y*-axis (or *ordinate,* the vertical dimension). Each category has (x,y) coordinates to define its position in the space, and we can measure the distance between them, just as in geometry, by using the theorem of Pythagoras.*

---

* Just to remind you: If you want to know the distance from a point (x,y) to a point (x',y'), you calculate $\sqrt{(x'-x)^2 + (y'-y)^2}$, which gives the length of the hypotenuse, or the direct distance between the two points. That is, the square of the hypotenuse is equal to the sum of the squares of the other two sides.

We live in a three-dimensional world, but we can imagine more dimensions (up to about six or seven for the purposes of storing information). When things get complicated and we want to make maximum effective use of our brains' computing power (that is, when we do not mind doing a good deal of work to make very fine discriminations), we use a multidimensional scale in five or six dimensions to store things. Habitually, however, we hardly ever go above four dimensions—and three is by far our favorite.

We have not gone into the ways that we find out what these semantic structures are. Nowadays we do most such work on the computer, but what we end up with is a model or representation of the *denotative meaning of a semantic domain*.

Connotative Meaning

Another kind of meaning we can study is the emotional "coloring" that words and ideas have in our minds. To use our previous example: *grandfather* does not mean just $\delta 2 + \overline{C}$, although that is a perfectly correct way of expressing the denotative meaning of the idea. *Grandfather* can mean "warmth," "love," "generosity," "old," "slow," and a host of other feelings and ideas that we may associate with the idea of "grandfather."

A method of tapping **connotative meaning** is the semantic differential test. In this test you have to judge a word as to where it fits on dimensions defined by two adjectives of opposite meaning. Here are some examples of the adjectives used.

0 ————————————————————————— 1
  fast   slow

0 ————————————————————————— 1
  hard   dull

0 ————————————————————————— 1
  good   bad

0 ————————————————————————— 1
  strong   weak

0 ————————————————————————— 1
  first   last

Charles Osgood, a psychologist who has used this technique widely, has made a remarkable finding. People seem mainly to use three dimensions to classify the emotional meaning of words and categories. These three dimensions are the following:

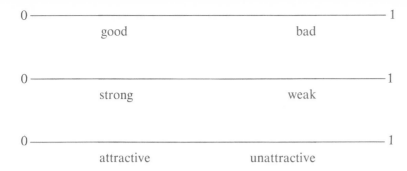

So the space we (and people in most cultures) use to relate one word to another is just like the world we live in—three-dimensional.

In our kinship lexicon, you can probably guess where "father," "mother," "uncle" and "daughter" would fit on these three dimensions.

Language and the External World

People have wondered for centuries whether the world that we construct or perceive is a faithful copy of the real world. Some philosophers believe that there is no real world at all. They think that the world that we know is entirely a construction of the mind. The mind working upon itself creates the world, they suggest. There are no real, palpable, observable, external entities "out there" in this view. Rather, the events and elements of the real world are products of our mind.

Dr. Samuel Johnson, the best-educated English speaker of the eighteenth century, had this position explained to him by his friend and biographer Boswell. Boswell asked, "Well, sir, how do you hold with these ideas?" Dr. Johnson replied by kicking a rock. To Johnson those concrete elements or events in the external world were not products of the mind. They were external to the mind, and they could be measured, observed, and kicked. You cannot kick an idea.

All of us are more or less in line with Dr. Johnson, but we also believe that language helps us construct and interpret that world "out there." Anthropologists do not feel that language *determines* the form of the outside world, but that it *affects* our representation of it. Those who go further than this and feel that our language determines or completely dictates the way we see the world are called **Whorfians** after Benjamin Lee Whorf (1897–1941), the foremost exponent of this view. At the other end of the pole are those who believe reality is the same for all people every-

Figure 14.4
The Hopi and the Eskimos
classify things differently
from us.

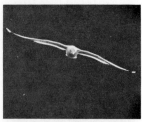

where, no matter how they think about or speak of it. These people are the **radical empiricists.**

Most of us are in between these two positions. We say, "Yes, language does affect the way we habitually think and construct our reality, but language does not *determine* the way we construct our world." To understand the argument, we should examine both positions.

The Sapir-Whorf Hypothesis

Benjamin Lee Whorf (an insurance investigator when he was not a linguist) developed the idea that language was a tyrant forcing us to see the world in a single way. In investigating the causes of industrial fires, Whorf noticed that apparently intelligent workers did some pretty dumb things. For example, although empty gas drums are a good deal more dangerous than full ones (because of the highly explosive vapors they contain), workers would smoke carelessly around the empty drums and not around the full ones. Why? Whorf thought it was because the workers associated the word *empty* with ideas like "safe," "unhazardous," or "null," "void," and "inert," and the word *full* with the concept "dangerous substance present." Whorf gave another example from his experience:

> In a wood distillation plant the metal stills were insulated with a composition prepared from limestone and called at the plant "spun limestone." No attempt was made to protect this covering from excessive heat or the contact of flame. After a period of use, the fire below one of the stills spread to the "limestone," which, to everyone's great surprise, burned vigorously. Exposure to acetic acid fumes from the stills had converted part of the limestone (calcium carbonate) to calcium acetate. This when heated in a fire decomposes, forming inflammable acetone. Behavior that tolerated fire close to the covering was induced by use of the name "limestone," which because it ends in "-stone" implies noncombustibility. (Whorf 1956:136)

This kind of observation led Whorf to explore the relationship between the way we habitually code reality in language and the way we think. He noted, for example, that some languages make very fine distinctions in areas where what he called "Standard Average European" languages like American English make few distinctions (and, of course, vice versa). He used Eskimo as an example:

> We have the same word for falling snow, snow on the ground, snow packed hard like ice, slushy snow, wind-driven flying snow—whatever the situation may be. To an Eskimo, this all-inclusive word would be almost unthinkable; he would say that falling snow, slushy snow, and so on, are sensuously and operationally different things to contend with; he uses different words for them and for other kinds of snow. The Aztecs go even farther than we in the opposite direction, with "cold," "ice," and "snow" all represented by the same basic word with different terminations; "ice" is the noun form; "cold" is the adjectival form; and for "snow," "ice mist." (Whorf 1956:216)

Whorf believed that the way we categorize events determines the way we think about them. He would argue that the Eskimo has a different idea of snow than the speaker of Standard Average European.

This is not so, but something like it is true. It is true that we tend to code events in familiar categories. As a general rule, it is sufficient for English speakers merely to point out that "it is snowing," but because Americans are so automobile-oriented, they make a distinction between "it is snowing," "freezing rain is coming down," "it is hailing," and other kinds of snow-related climatic conditions that bear on driving. People of every culture, so far as we know, make elaborate, fine distinctions among things (or events) important to them. Brent Berlin reports that the Tzeltal-speaking Mayan Indians have five different words for corn-on-the-cob. Why? Because corn is the most important article in their agriculture and diet, and different kinds of corn (speckled corn, wormy corn, etc.) are used for different things.

We use short, familiar words to do a preliminary sorting of events we are observing or reporting. If finer discriminations are required, we can also make those. "Don't bother to make a snowman," we say to our children, "It isn't good packing snow," thereby utilizing a local expression or inventing a new one because the child has to know about the quality of snow. If you are a nonskier, talk to one who knows about snow conditions: What is the difference between "corn," "boiler plate," and "powder snow"? What snow is good for schussing? Skiers can tell you and apparently know what they are talking about. They would be able to converse with Eskimos at cocktail parties. But most of the time we do not require ourselves to make exceedingly fine distinctions about snow and find our gross categorizations (compared with the Eskimos') perfectly adequate.

Whorf's ideas about vocabulary may seem a little oversimplified, but there is another side of the argument that is more complicated and perhaps more convincing. We will give you an example and ask you to make up your own mind.

An Example: Verb Aspects   When we speak of the tense and voice of a verb (as in future tense, passive voice), we are talking about the *aspect* of the verb. Think for a second about tense in English. We cannot make up a sentence that does not include a verb in some tense or other. Example:

She is running	She will run
She runs	She will have run
She was running	She had run
She ran	

All these include the idea of time and duration. *She is running* implies the activity is taking place at the moment. *She runs* is the same, but it

Figure 14.5
Eskimos classify different kinds of snow very finely.

Insight
Language and Judgments— Fallacies of Thinking Derived From Language

We should not misjudge the impact of language on our judgment—it can be very strong. In one area of thinking we make major errors that have major impacts on people's lives: judging other people's behavior. For example, we tend to think that if people are energetic, they are aggressive; if they are aggressive, they are hostile; and so on. On the other hand, if a person is deemed to be generous, he or she is deemed to be warm, caring, and helpful. These lines of reasoning are not true. If we observe behavior very closely, we do not find that people who are energetic are necessarily also aggressive or that people who are aggressive are also hostile. Videotape analyses of laboratory-controlled small groups carrying out all kinds of tasks have shown that this kind of thinking is wrong.

How do we make this mistake? Quite simply, we use a very powerful rule that has no basis in fact. We say to ourselves that if two ideas are similar—if two categories and their labels are *similar in meaning*—then they must go together in people's behavior. But we are wrong. Consistently wrong.

Table 1
Our Mode of Reasoning

A Summary of Our Mode of Reasoning
1. Our monitor picks up high-information behavior (i.e., the subject does something that he or she, or people in general, does not do very often —much surprise).
2. We categorize it linguistically: "Very energetic."
3. We ask ourselves: "What are energetic people like?"
4. Our language-meaning processor goes to work and comes up with the answer: "Energetic people are aggressive."
5. We feed this information into the monitor.
6. The monitor calls our attention to that person's behavior whenever that person behaves in a way that our linguistic meaning processor can categorize as "aggressive."
7. We find a class of behavior that can be classified as aggressive and we attend to it, process it, and remember it.
8. Thus we have proven that this person is not only energetic, but also aggressive, just as our implicit (linguistic) theory predicted.

contains the additional bit of information that she makes a habit of running. *She ran* means she did it in the past, and *she had run* means she had completed the act of running when something else happened in the past. *She will run* makes the prediction that this act will take place at some future time. Tense is an *obligatory distinction* that we have to make in order to say anything at all.

Dorothy Lee, in studying Wintu, a California Indian language, has found different verb aspects. In Wintu, *validity* is the important aspect of the verb. A Wintu woman uses one word for "he runs" if she actually saw the person run but a different word if she only heard about it. If

How can we be so stupid? Quite simply because we have a very powerful theory that leads us directly to wrong conclusions. First, when we learn our language we learn what words "go together," or are similar in meaning. Then we observe people behave. "Aha!" we say to ourselves, "George is being very energetic!" We input this information into our heads and look for predictions, as though we were to say to ourselves, "What else can I know about George?" At this point the meanings come into play, and we note (unconsciously) that *aggressive* is similar in meaning to *energetic,* and so we direct our attention (unconsciously) to instances of George's behavior that we might class as aggressive. Sooner or later George acts aggressively (we have ignored instances where he was acting calmly and tamely because we were not looking for them), and we say again, "Aha! Here is a confirmation of what we knew all along."

This is an example of our ability to set up a chain of reasoning based on language and then to confirm it in experience—when both the reasoning and the experience are wrong. This is called *systematic linguistic distortion,* and we should be aware of it in order to stop ourselves from being misled by it. In fact, if you have read and understood this passage, you have now made those unconscious operations more conscious and have stopped yourself from leaping to erroneous, linguistically derived conclusions.

he runs at the same time every day and she can more or less predict it, then she uses a third form. Other languages have similar ways of conjugating their verbs.

One thing seems certain: the Wintu should make good lawyers in our Western legal system. In court we are careful to distinguish between hearsay evidence and real evidence, just as the Wintu, in their everyday language, use different words to distinguish an event actually seen from one heard about from someone else. But a law professor would have to point out to a Wintu law student that he or she did make this distinction. The Wintu are unconscious of it. They might not automatically be able

Figure 14.6
Americans may be in a rush, and may like to be on time, but it is not because of their language.

to apply this distinction in a courtroom situation, even though they would be able to remember more clearly how they had learned about a situation than an English speaker would.

Now the question: Are English speakers comparatively obsessed with time and Wintu speakers with making sure that everyone knows the factual or empirical basis of their statements? In other words, are English speakers natural "schedulers"? Does the way they conjugate their verbs show how preoccupied they are with time? Can we go on to suggest that they economize time and say and believe things like "time is money" and "a stitch in time saves nine," because their language *forces* them to preoccupy themselves with time? Can we equally say that the Wintu are the world's natural lawyers—that they would have no need for a large body of laws of evidence admitting some kinds of statements as good evidence and excluding others as hearsay? Whorf thought so, but we do not.

Clearly, there are many languages where time is an important aspect of verbs even though the speakers do not show the English speaker's obsession with time. Zapotec is one. One of the authors worked in Zapotec and can assure you there is not the remotest possibility of considering the Zapotec good schedulers or obsessed with time. In Zapotec, as in most places where anthropologists work, getting people to "come on time" is a major problem.

Conclusions

When we speak of giving our lives meaning, we underscore the fact that human beings have an innate tendency to confer meaning on events in their individual and collective lives—to tie together and relate ideas. Therefore our sense of coherence and pattern is also inborn, or innate. It is part of being human.

The understanding of meaning is one of the most challenging subjects in anthropology and linguistics. People have been studying it continuously for at least two and a half millenia. Perhaps in our lifetimes it will be possible for us finally to state what we mean by "meaning." Since it is our window on the world and the necessity for us to understand our world and the worlds of others grows day by day, it is a topic that cannot be ignored.

Summary

1. To understand how people construct and interpret their worlds we must understand the system of meaning that they use. The royal road to understanding meaning is through the careful study of language, for it has an important effect on the way we think about the world. Language contains sets of *categories* that tell us in advance what events are important to us. These categories define our world in convenient classes. Language takes the continuous stream of messages that comes to us as experience from our environment, and segments it. Language does for experience what phonemes do for the continuous stream of sound that we decode into meaningful sound units.

2. To understand an alien people's system of meaning, careful field work and analysis are necessary. There are two fundamental rules that one must follow to do good field work. First, *never* ask irrelevant questions. Make sure the questions you ask are meaningful to the teacher-informant before you ask them. Make sure they are phrased in the way that people phrase questions to each other in that cultural system. Otherwise you will get answers that will be meaningless in terms of the people whose cultural system you are studying. Second, never forget that your shorthand translations of important ideas are not faithful representations of what those ideas mean to the people who use them. You must always put together a folk encyclopedia that tells you what *relationship* each of the terms you elicited has with the other important terms that go along with it.

3. There are two kinds of meaning with which we must be concerned in this chapter: denotative meaning and connotative meaning. Denotation refers to the way the object or event is defined in the cultural system, while connotation refers to the way we feel about the object or event.

4. If we take the domain of American English kin terms, we find that there are four attributes or components that partition this world. They are (1) generation, (2) sex of relative, (3) polarity, and (4) collaterality. We can define (denotatively) American English kin terms

on these four dimensions and can then give a formal definition of their meaning. Having done this, we can compare the meaning with the meanings that similar terms have in another culture.

5. This model of meaning, which seeks definitions of objects and events on the basis of their attributes or features, is called the feature model of meaning.

6. Does language determine our view of the world? Hardly. But it surely does affect it. People who believe that language determines the way we see the world are called Whorfians. People who believe that our view of the world is a faithful copy of that external reality are called radical empiricists. The authors of this text believe that the truth lies between these two positions. We can easily see, as could Benjamin Lee Whorf, that we are affected by language. We saw at the beginning of the chapter how language with its preset categories structures our experience and gives it meaning. We know that the world of experience is filtered through language, but we also believe that, with some important exceptions, language is a pretty faithful copy of the world. We discussed one of the exceptions: how we make very faulty inferences about people and how they behave.

7. Language and meaning are the royal road to the understanding of how people construct and interpret their world.

Suggested Readings

Berlin, Brent, and Kay, Paul. *The Evolution of Color Terms*. The Hague: Mouton, 1972.

> *This is the work that showed that there was a small number of systems for coding color in human culture. It is worth looking at as an example of experimental approaches in anthropology.*

Brown, Roger. *Words and Things*. Glencoe: Free Press, 1952.

> *Although this work is twenty years old, it is still sound and a good read.*

Burling, Robbins. *Man's Many Voices*. New York: Holt, Rinehart and Winston, 1970.

> *An excellent introduction to many of the issues raised in this chapter.*

Hoijer, H. H. "The Sapir-Whorf Hypothesis." In H. Hoijer (ed.), *Language in Culture*. Washington, D.C.: American Anthropological Association, 1954.

> *An excellent introduction to the work of the Whorfian hypothesis.*

Romney, A. K., and D'Andrade, R. G. *Transcultural Studies in Cognition*. Washington, D.C.: American Anthropological Association, 1964.

> *This is the source book for a lot of studies that have been cited in this chapter and throughout the book. It was a very influential publication when it appeared and is still important. Hard going, though. Read it to get a taste of the kind of work that is done in "semantic anthropology."*

Symbolic Systems and Cultural Logics

Figure 15.1
Natural symbols suggest the things they stand for.

Introduction

In the last chapter we discussed *meaning* in language. Here we are going to talk about the devices that people—all of us—use to construct a world of *symbols*. Anthropologists have to decode the symbolic systems of their subjects as well as their language. And the symbolic systems are often more abstruse, more difficult to get at, and harder to translate than the languages.

Translating Symbols

Natural and Artificial Symbols

Some symbols stand in an obvious relation to the things or events that they symbolize. A tuberous root may stand for a penis, or a spark struck from flint may stand for lightning, or the figure of a ship's helmsman may stand for the ruler or governor of a tribe or state. The relationship between the symbol and the thing symbolized is natural and easy here. There is a natural association between them.

Many symbols are not naturally associated with the things they symbolize. Symbols often act as though they were morphemes: they combine according to syntactic rules to form "sentences" of symbols, and the original natural association between the symbols and the thing symbolized is not present. As with strings of linguistic sounds, anthropologists have to decode these symbolic strings. That is the concern of this chapter: we are going to lay out some of the tricks and techniques that *we all use* in our everyday thinking and symbolizing. Note the emphasis on "we all use"! Many of the examples are going to be from exotic cultural systems, and we have chosen them because they are particularly clear examples of the technique in action. But every device is also in continuous use by all of us, all the time. We use them to construct and interpret our world.

The Problem of Double Translation

In decoding, or translating, these symbolic strings, anthropologists have to perform a two-stage process.

First, we have to understand what the local people are saying, doing, and thinking, and translate their activities, thoughts, and words into terms that our own imaginations can comprehend. Then we have to explain *our* understanding of the local people's thoughts, activities, and words to other people: to other anthropologists, to students, or to the public at large. This second act of translation is equally important and equally difficult. It means that we have to allow the local people to speak for themselves in their own terms, but in a way that the average reader will understand.

Figure 15.2
It is very difficult to decode the symbols of a ritual until you have studied the ways they are put into "sentences" in symbolic language.

The problem of double translation is particularly acute when it comes to translating symbols. First we have to explain what these symbols are, what they can mean in general, what they mean under such circumstances that are now being described, and finally, what they meant in this particular event. (Quite honestly, by the time ethnographers have done all that, they feel they have analyzed a symbol to death.)

Sometimes the anthropologist's task of translating is so close to being impossible that we give up. Or we fudge the description and try to make it sound like something much more familiar than it really is. Our first example is an account of one time when there was no fudging or dodging at all.

Carlos Castaneda Learns to Fly   Carlos Castaneda possesses more knowledge than any other contemporary about the witchcraft and sorcery beliefs of the people of Mesoamerica. He describes his first stumbling attempts to understand his own behavior under the influence of a drug taken ritually at his teacher's instructions. He had taken datura root mixed with the lard of a wild boar, removed his clothes, smeared himself with a special paste, and flown. He flew over the plains and the mountains, twisting here and there, directing his progress with his head, enjoying a freedom and swiftness he had never before enjoyed along with a sadness and longing he had never felt. He tells us what happened when he tried to understand his

experience in a conversation with his teacher, thirty-six hours after the flight:

Finally, before I left that evening, I had to ask him. "Did I really fly, Don Juan?"

"That is what you told me. Didn't you?"

"I know, Don Juan. I mean, did my body fly? Did I take off like a bird?"

"You always ask me questions I cannot answer. You flew. That is what the second portion of the devil's weed is for. As you take more of it, you will learn how to fly perfectly. It is not a simple matter. A man *flies* with the help of the second portion of the devil's weed. That is all I can tell you. What you want to know makes no sense. Birds fly like birds and a man who has taken the devil's weed flies as such."

"As birds do?"

"No, he flies as a man who has taken the weed."

"Then I didn't really fly, Don Juan. I flew in my imagination, in my mind alone. Where was my body?"

"In the bushes," he replied cuttingly, but immediately broke into laughter again. "The trouble with you is that you understand things in only one way. You don't think a man flies; and yet a [witch] can move a thousand miles in one second to see what is going on. He can deliver a blow to his enemies long distances away. So, does he or doesn't he fly?"

The argument goes on, and not for years does Castaneda realize that the flight that he has taken is the first sign of a power that will enable him to become a sorcerer of great power.

Did Carlos Fly?   Castaneda took here the first important step toward becoming a sorcerer. By the end of his studies he was able to transport himself at will from one part of the great market in Mexico City to another. He could ride the wind into a level of existence that no Westerner had ever visited. Whether you believe he flew or not is not important. Castaneda is a gifted writer and is employing his considerable gifts in translating the experience and symbols of sorcery to convey to his readers what the training for sorcery involved.

Castaneda accomplished the first step of anthropological under-standing probably better than any of his contemporaries. Whether he com-municates that knowledge to you is for you to decide. But the difficulty about "flying" illustrates the difficulty that all dedicated anthropologists have. The more they understand the culture they are studying, the less able they are to translate it into terms that others can understand because they know they will do violence to that tradition. If there is one problem that plagues social anthropology more than any other, it is this problem of double translation. The rest of this chapter will describe how anthropolo-gists go about solving this problem, by understanding the mechanisms that in turn enable us to understand alien worlds in the same matter-of-fact ways their own people experience them.

The more they understand the culture they are studying, the less able they are to translate it into terms that others can understand because they know they will do violence to that tradition.

Understanding the Logic of Symbolism

On the surface, the statement "Carlos flew across the marketplace" is grammatical. You can understand it. If you have never "flown" you can think of the idea as a metaphor for rapid transportation. Perhaps if you have had drug experiences, you will understand it more in the way that Carlos Castaneda understood it. The sentence makes sense to most people somehow, even if full comprehension of the meaning would require the reader to spend a good deal of time in the culture where such flying is experienced.

But there are other statements that do not appear to make sense at all to us, even when they are translated into perfectly clear sentences. They are ungrammatical in the same sense as the sentence in chapter 13: "The handkerchief was climbed by the man." There doesn't appear to be any context in which climbing up a handkerchief would make sense. So we fail to understand the sentence even though we know what all the words mean.

Anthropologists encounter sentences or statements like that all the time. It is essential that they understand them. In particular, anthropologists want to understand the logic and the context that make apparently ungrammatical, meaningless sentences have meaning.

In this section we are going to investigate some of the devices that anthropologists have discovered in people's thinking and try to show the logic of their thought.

"Mapping," The Logic of Totemism

Certain peoples around the world claim that they are animals or natural features of the landscape such as mountains or springs. If you interviewed them persistently, you would quickly find out that they do not think of themselves as having the appearance, or the abilities, or the habits of an animal (except on very special occasions). But, despite the fact that they have the appearance, the abilities, and the habits of a human being, they say, "I am a bear!"

The statement makes sense if you understand **mapping,** the logic of **totemism.**

What many groups do is create distinctions among themselves and name those distinctions. They draw their names (and identities) from the animal world. The logic goes: just as a beaver is different from a kingfisher in the natural world, so are the "Beaver people" different from the "Kingfisher people" in the cultural world.

A simple but not misleading analogy can be drawn from the world of sports. It doesn't matter that the Boston hockey team wears brown, and the Philadelphia team wears red. All that matters is that the colors are different. The message is *not* the following: "The Boston players are

The statement makes sense if you understand mapping, the logic of totemism.

**Figure 15.4
A totemic mapping (in text).**

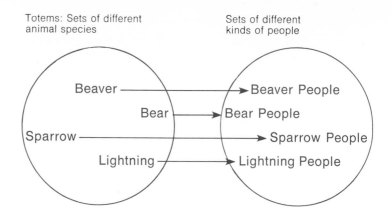

Totems: Sets of different animal species

Sets of different kinds of people

drab like Boston baked beans and brown bread, while the Philadelphia team is fiery, exciting, and dangerous. That is why Boston is brown and Philadelphia is red." No, the statement is:

Brown and Red are different colors
just as
Boston and Philadelphia are different teams.

So also, in totemism, you have two sets: a set of groups of people and a set of kinds of animals, and a *mapping* between the two sets. The mapping is the rule that associates the animal with the group. It is symbolized by the arrows in Figure 15.4. The animals are called the *totems*.

Once you map animals and natural features into groups and subgroups, then you can create logical structures based on the mapping.

Human beings are creative, and so they often develop this idea. Very often they have special ceremonies in which the animal totems are symbolized by the people. There might be a sacred dance in which the "Kangaroo people" imitate the kangaroo, and the "Emu people" the emu, while the "lightning people" make crackling noises, and the "peoples of the spring" bring water to the dancers. The ritual would emphasize the fact that all the totems were present and working together. The society's symbols and the society itself came together.

By mapping social groups into animals and natural features, the society can symbolize the way it is divided up into its parts while still remaining a whole.

Mapping is the simplest known device for making symbolic statements. All it does is take one set of ideas or entities (social groups) and relate it to another set (animals). It is useful and important when there is a need to symbolize the differences between ideas or entities that are outwardly very similar in appearance, such as social groups in the same society.

**Figure 15.5
A Ngat atgura man following a totemic Kangaroo Cykle dance.**

Opposition

Opposition is the logical device that divides up symbolic terms into pairs of opposites. In this way two sets, or classes, of symbols *in opposition* are created:

Q: What is the opposite of "left?"   A: "Right"
Q: What is the opposite of "woman?"   A: "Man"
Q: What is the opposite of "moon?"   A: "Sun"

In this way two sets are formed:

Set One	*Set Two*
left	right
woman	man
moon	sun

Like mapping, opposition is a very simple device used to define symbolic categories. We get a better idea of the meaning, or symbolism, of a category if we know what its opposite is, just as we knew more about the meaning of kin terms when we could see them contrasted (or opposed) on a dimension.

Oppositions are used widely in religious systems. Here are some familiar ones:

heaven	hell
God	Devil (or Satan)
lightness	darkness

We are unconscious of these orderings and do not realize what an impact they have on our thinking. These oppositions are deep within our system of meaning, however. Here are two characteristics of our own thinking resulting from such symbolic oppositions.

A Result from Psychology   The first characteristic was found by psychological testing. If people are shown a line of objects and asked which is best, they almost always pick the one on the right. If, as in one experiment, college students are asked to choose from a blackboard display of identical items of clothing in a line, they tend to pick the one (or ones) on the right. In American culture we feel that things on the right are somehow better, more reliable, and stronger than things on the left.

To understand why we feel this way involves going into the languages and traditions of Western culture and asking about the symbolic history of the ideas "right" and "left." The word for "left" in Latin is *sinister,* and the word for "right" is *dexter.* "Left" in our culture's history has been associated with "evil" or "anomalous" or "dangerous"; while "right" is associated with the law (*droit,* the word for "law" in French, is derived from

Chart 15.1

Oppositions in America

Left	Right
Sinister	Straightforward
Evil	Good
Anomalous	Regular
Illegal	Legal
Politically radical	Politically conservative

Latin *dexter* and means "law" or "right.") In politics, "left" means "change society to new (sinister) forms," while "right" means "keep things as they are," or "keep going straight ahead." Even recently, parents used to give their left-handed children pain, problems, and no end of moral misgiving over their "affliction." They would often make them change to being right-handed, doing considerable harm to the psychological well-being of the child. At the same time, it has been estimated that up to 10 percent of the people in America are naturally left-handed.

This system of logic by oppositions is by no means confined to our society or culture. It is found all over the world. In the chapters on social organization we will see whole societies being organized on this basis. Chart 15.1 summarizes some of the oppositions we have mentioned.

Man and Woman The second characteristic of our thinking in oppositions is related to the meaning of "man" and "woman." It explains why we say that men and women are different in areas of behavior where there is no reason to believe there is really any difference. Americans say that men are rational in their thinking, whereas women are intuitive. They say that men act in a cool and calculating fashion, whereas women act impulsively and emotionally.

In each case Americans say this because the feminine characteristic is associated with the "left" side of the opposition, while the masculine characteristic is associated with the "right" side. These habits of thought are very persistent in our thinking. Women in the feminist movement have learned that we do not know why we think these things and are always surprised to see our thinking drifting back to these deep "home truths," even after we have learned better. We drift back because the oppositions are deep in our symbolic system of meaning.

Opposition is the second means for constructing symbolic meanings, or sentences. Mapping was the first.

Mediation

The third way we have of creating symbolic meaning is by using **mediation.** (Do not read the term as "meditation" the way some readers have!) This is the process of putting some idea in between two others. We might say that the median strip on a turnpike or superhighway mediates between

Figure 15.6
A tryptych of Jesus Christ as
the Mediator between God
and Man.

the two lanes. The two lanes represent the terms of the opposition: the "east-bound" lane is one term, the "west-bound" lane the other, and the strip in the middle mediates them.

If a system of symbols is one of pure opposition, there are no mediating categories. More commonly, such categories do exist, and *when* they do, they are very important. When belief systems have a third term that is neither on one side nor the other of an opposition, but partly in both, people pay a great deal of attention to it. It becomes an area of elaborated belief, ritual, and philosophical thinking.

A familiar kind of mediation can be taken from Christian liturgy, where the priest or the people pray to "Jesus Christ, our only mediator and advocate" (in the words of the *Book of Common Prayer*). Jesus Christ mediates two opposed categories, "God" and "human beings." Without Jesus Christ these two categories would be in pure opposition. But Christ was "born of woman" (i.e., was a human being) and "conceived by the Holy Ghost" (i.e., was divine and God-like as well). He is the "Son of God" in the words of Matthew and the "Son of Man" in the words of John. He lived on the earth during His ministry, but was taken up into heaven after His crucifixion. The symbolism of His life consists in mediating the opposition between God and human beings.

Mediation and Transformation   Mediating categories are extremely important in belief systems, often serving to transform one pole of an opposition into the other. Anthropologists say that the opposition is "collapsed" via the mediating category. The Zapotec, who have been studied by El Guindi*, have a myth of the witch that shows how the graveyard in Zapotec cosmology mediates between the poles of the opposition "human beings"/"witches." Here is a shortened version of the myth of the witch:

There was once a witch who lived with her husband in the village. Every day during the "heavy hours" the witch goes out into the village, kidnaps the children, and takes them away with her to the field. After returning them the children die. The mothers do not notice that the children are gone, because the witch puts a grindstone pestle in their arms.

A neighbor warned the witch's husband that his wife was a witch and told him to be careful, because when the witch cannot find a child in another house to play with (and kill), she kills her own child.

It happened that one day the witch circled the village during the heavy hours and could not find any child that was not being carefully attended by a wakeful mother. When she came home at evening her husband was already in bed holding the child in his arms. She tried to lift the child out of her sleeping husband's arms but the husband woke up and she stopped. Later, when he was asleep, she tried again, but found that the child was tied to the father by arms, waist, and ankles. When she tried to loose the child, the husband woke up and heard a buzzard on the roof, which convinced him that his wife was a witch.

By this time the wife had left the house, and the husband hurried out to see where she had gone. He left the child at a neighbor's house with the warning that the mother was a witch and followed the wife.

He went to the cemetery. Just in front of the chapel he saw many heads. The witches leave their heads in front of the chapel and then go forth into the field to do their evil. So, the witch had left her head in front of the chapel and gone away. The husband immediately switched heads. He switched his wife's head with a man's head.

When the witch returned to the cemetery to put her head on, she couldn't find it, so she put on the male head and covered it with a shawl. She went home, but when she talked she spoke with a man's voice. She never could remove her shawl and eventually died of shame.

Here the graveyard mediates between the "house" on the one hand and the "field" on the other. Witches belong to the field and human beings to the house. There are many dualistic oppositions in Zapotec aligned in this way. Chart 15.2 lists some of them. Mediating categories link opposed categories and/or serve as the means of transforming them—just as the graveyard transformed a good woman with a spiritual life soul into a witch with an animal familiar.

* You may remember El Guindi's work on social distinctions in Zapotec from chapter 1. Remember how pleased she was to find the key to Zapotec social categories in the distinction (opposition) between "sinners" and "innocents"?

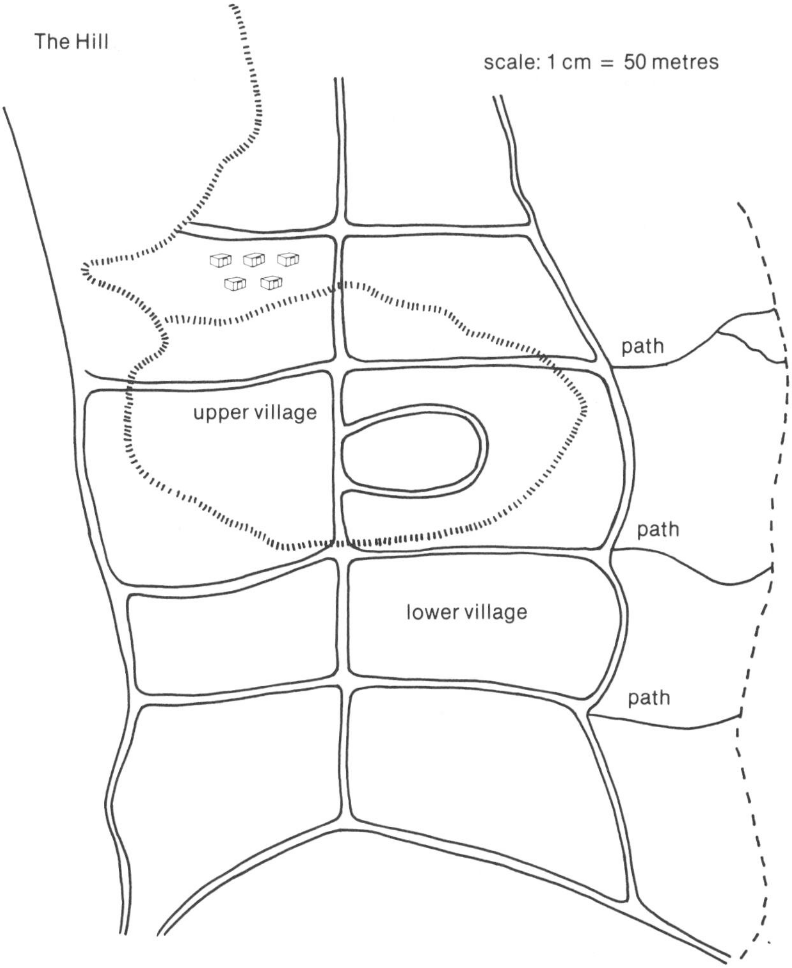

Figure 15.7
A schematic diagram of a
Zapotec village.

The Hill

scale: 1 cm = 50 metres

path

upper village

path

lower village

path

Chart 15.2
Dualistic Oppositions in Zapotec Culture

House	Field
Inside	Outside
Trust	Distrust
Good	Evil
Sacred	Not sacred
Safe	Dangerous
Edible food	Inedible food
Blessed water	Unblessed water
Licit sex	Illicit sex
Soul of life	Animal familiar
Jesus	Devil
Saints	Evil spirits
Human beings	Witches
Ritual	Profane

Mediating categories are important to belief systems because they stop the system from falling into two opposed halves. They pull it together. In Christian theology, God and Man would be locked into opposition and never be able to contact one another were it not for the mediation of Jesus Christ. In Zapotec myth, the field with its witches and the village with its houses and people would be locked into pure opposition and never be able to contact one another were it not for the mediation of the graveyard. Mediating categories act as the linch pin to hold systems of belief together.

Illegitimate Mediations   Sometimes there are events or phenomena that masquerade as mediating categories, but that cannot be true mediators because they are trying to mediate a system of pure oppositions. In our own system of belief, for example, there is a pure opposition between "man" and "woman." There are no creatures that mediate between them, being partly man and partly woman. There is no process, as there was for the Zapotec witch, of changing from one kind of person to another. When something happens to attack or break down a system of pure opposition, we become very nervous and anxious. If the phenomenon is real (not a fiction), we usually try to do something to rid ourselves of it, either by denying its existence or eliminating it.

Transsexuals make us nervous because they are people who mediate the opposition man : woman. Transsexuals have been brought up as members of the "wrong sex." Their gender identities (male or female), which are furnished and defined by the time they are two years of age, are opposed to the sex they feel themselves to be. They are women trapped in men's bodies, or men trapped in women's bodies. Americans feel uneasy about the idea of transsexuals.

One famous case of a woman trapped in a man's body was studied by medical and sociological personnel at the University of California at Los Angeles. "Agnes" repeatedly tried to convince her doctors that her male genitals were a mistake, an abnormal growth. She pointed out that at the age of twelve she had been enormously gratified to see her breasts grow and had felt that they were the essential signs of her true sex. After careful, thorough, and prolonged study, the doctors decided to amputate her penis and make an artificial vagina. She was pleased. After much suffering and complicated medical work, the operation was a success. She recovered and was able to establish her female identity to the point of having sexual relations with a man.

The doctors felt that this operation was justified by the fact that Agnes not only considered herself a female, but had at least some "true" female features (i.e., breasts). Later, however, they discovered that Agnes's breasts had not grown spontaneously, nor had her other feminine characteristics happened naturally. At the age of 12, just as puberty

Figure 15.8
Renee Richards, before and after the sex change operation.

began, at the time that her voice lowered and she began to develop pubic hair, she had secured female hormones from her mother, forged the prescription, and taken the medicine on her own.

What interests the anthropologist is the reaction of the doctors. When they found out that Agnes had used hormones, they felt that they had been deluded and had been induced to perform an unnatural operation. They felt that she was a fraud, a "freak of nature" who should be punished. Few people seemed to think that Agnes's determination to secure the help she needed to become what she knew she was should be applauded. Americans feel uneasy about voluntary crossing of the sex/gender lines. The male: female opposition is fundamental to our belief system, and Agnes tampered with it.

Science fiction is full of characters who are illegitimate mediations and "fall between the cracks" of the system of categories. Our enduring interest in the character of the "monster" created by Frankenstein comes from this source. In American culture we make a firm, distinct opposition between the artificial (that which is created by human skills) and the natural. It is one of our most general and important distinctions. Frankenstein's artificial creature was also a human being, a product of nature. The difference between Frankenstein's monster and Jesus Christ lies in the fact that the "monster" is an illegitimate mediator, whereas Christ is not. The illegitimate mediator is a freak, an oddity, a being that falls between the categories.

Things That Do Not Fit into the Classification

Opposition, mapping, and mediation are forms of classification. Often, however, there are creatures that do not fit into systems of classification. "Duck-billed platypuses are mammals?" we ask, surprised that this bird-like, egg-laying creature would be a member of our taxon. "A poisonous snake is a kind of clothing?" we ask, hearing that a famous Englishwoman used to wear one to debutante parties.

Some animals do not fit into the given linguistic classification. When Americans find out that there are people who wear snakes and that there are birdlike mammals that lay eggs, they express amazement and surprise. Many other peoples of the world would make them holy, or sacred, or taboo. In this way, other peoples emphasize the odd, anomalous place that these animals or events have in their scheme of meaning and belief.

Food Taboos in the Old Testament   Mary Douglas (1966) studied food taboos in the Old Testament and found that those creatures that are "abominations" are precisely those that do not fit into the animal classification of the ancient Semites. Animals were freaks if they did not belong in a proper category. "Every animal that parts the hoof, and has the hoof cloven in two, and chews the cud you may eat," states the Bible (Leviticus). That means that the camel, the rock badger, the hare, and the pig are all unclean and may not be eaten. Why? The camel because it chews the cud but does not part the hoof; the rock badger because it chews the cud but does not part the hoof; the hare because it chews the cud but does not part the hoof; and the swine because it parts the hoof (is cloven-footed) but does not chew the cud.

Why are some locusts edible and others not? According to Douglas (1966:71), "The case of the locusts is interesting and consistent. The test of whether it is a clean and therefore edible kind is how it moves upon the earth. If it crawls it is unclean. If it hops it is clean. In the Talmud it is noted that a frog is not listed with creeping things and conveys no uncleanness. I suggest that the frog's hop accounts for it not being listed. If penguins lived in the Near East I would expect them to be ruled unclean as wingless birds."

If an animal is an imperfect member of its class, then it is unclean and contact with it is taboo.

If an animal is an imperfect member of its class, then it is unclean and contact with it is taboo.

Animal Terms and Categories of Abuse   Frankenstein's monster and inedible penguins are examples of creatures that intuitively seem to us to be sacred or taboo either because they fall between categories of importance or because they lack some defining attribute of the class to which they properly should belong.

But consider the following: Why should we get angry when someone calls us a son of a bitch, but not become nearly so angry when they call us a polar bear or a skunk. Edmund Leach (1964) has pointed out that we *create* binary (two-valued) categories—men versus not man, animals versus not animal—and then we create a mediating category between them, loading this ambiguous intermediate category with taboo or sacredness. Pets and domesticated animals are an intermediate category, since they have attributes like humans (they live in the house, eat table scraps from the human's dinner, and are endowed with emotions like human beings), but they are still animals. Thus to call someone a bitch, cat, pig, swine, ass, goat, or cur (dog) is always insulting; whereas to call a person a tiger, a buffalo, or an elephant is only the mildest of allusions. Similarly, animals that are close to humans provide a vocabulary of obscenity and taboo for parts of the human anatomy, such as "cock" and "pussy" for penis and female pubic hair.

These examples are not linguistic flukes. We create the categories of our experience and then we think with them. And, as anthropologists and linguists are daily discovering, we think with them creatively and systematically. Just because the examples have been drawn from English, it should not be thought that the analysis only applies there. Leach's analysis (just cited) was carried out in Kachin, a Tibeto-Burman language.

Metaphor

A more familiar mechanism that people in other cultures use to say things that sound strange and ungrammatical is metaphor. Metaphors have a cultural logic, too, and however strange they sound to our ears as we are doing field work, we have to understand them if we are going to understand the way that people construct and interpret their world.

A metaphor is a statement that something *is* something else. "The camel is the ship of the desert" is a metaphor. It states that, in some way understood by the natives (Americans, in this case), a ship in its medium is equivalent to a camel in its medium. It doesn't say that the ship is *like* a camel; it states that it *is* a camel. It does not state in what particular way the ship is like a camel. An anthropologist from another culture would probably ask (in the same way we do, to the chagrin of our local teachers) "Does a camel have a rudder, sails, a bowsprit . . . ?" We would shake our heads to the ninny who asked this question and answer, "No, a ship is a self-contained, autonomous system for the conveyance of people and goods, capable of long journeys in an environment that can be assumed to be dangerous and hostile. The camel is the same as a ship in that sense, except that its environment is the desert, not the oceans." Then our anthropologist from afar might say, "Oh, then, how about this metaphor: 'The spaceship is the passenger train of the solar system.'" And we would shake our heads and tell him to stick to the text, leave the camel and the ship in metaphor, and not try to be creative until he learned the language and culture better. "It just isn't very witty or inventive. No one would say that!" A metaphor is a clever invention that in an interesting and provocative way, catches an identity that was until then unsuspected. Ships and camels qualify. Spaceships and passenger trains do not.

Metaphor and Association   Keith H. Basso (1976), who has studied the Western Apache for years, was interested in what the Apache call "wise words." These also are creative metaphors. He gives some examples:

> Lightning is a boy.
> Ravens are widows.
> Carrion beetle is a white man.
> Butterflies are girls.

The reason that ravens are widows is not that both wear black. The Apache laughed when Basso suggested that. Ravens are widows because (in Apache thinking) both are poor and have no one to provide for them. Widows stand about near one's camp and wait for one to give them food. In the same way, ravens stand near roads waiting for a car to hit some animals so that they can eat.

What about carrion beetles and white men? Carrion beetles remind Apache of white men because both waste too much food. When the carrion beetle is young, for example, it lives off leafy plants. It eats a hole in a leaf and then moves on to another, leaving plenty of good food behind. But that is not all. Carrion beetles are like white people because they only come out into the summer heat early in the morning and again late in the evening.

In other words, the bad behavioral characteristics of the animal is cojoined with the bad behavioral characteristics of the kind of person, and the metaphor is made by *association*.

But you cannot say that anything that stays in a cool place during the afternoon is a white man. You could not say, for example, that "a shaded spring is a white man," because a spring is too distant in meaning from a "living thing" to be a good analogy. That would be rather like the

(a)

Figure 15.9
An illustration of the idea
that ravens are widows, and
carrion beetle is white man
(according to the logic
given in the text).

(b)

small child who learns for the first time that the cushioned footrest around the fireplace is called a fender and then asks the conundrum: "Why is a fireplace like an automobile?" When the adults say they do not know, the child triumphantly replies, "Because they both have fenders!" True, but the comparison is not terribly creative nor amusing. There has to be some similarity between the classes of things to which two objects belong in order to have a good metaphor. Carrion beetles can be compared to white men because they are both "living things." Basso diagrams the relationship (Basso, 1976:102):

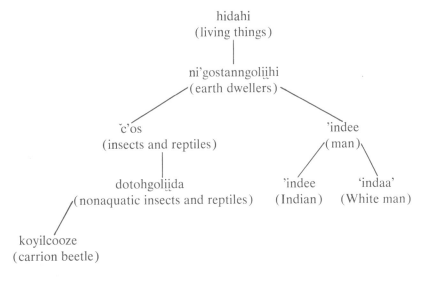

Analogy

The last mechanism that people everywhere use to construct and interpret their world is *analogy*. Analogies are not obvious when one is studying the worlds of other peoples. Sometimes, as in the following example,

**Figure 15.10
A Nuer tribesman.**

they strike one as very strange and impossible to interpret until you understand a good deal more about the whole system of belief.

E. E. Evans-Pritchard (1902–1973) noted that the Nuer, a tribe of the Nilotic Sudan, say that "twins are birds." Immediately he pointed out: "They are not saying that a twin has a beak, feathers and so forth. Nor in their everyday relations as twins do Nuer speak of them as birds, or act toward them as birds."

A clue as to why "twins are birds" can be discovered from the names that are given to twins: *gwong,* meaning guinea fowl, and *ngec,* meaning partridge. Guinea fowl and partridge are unusual birds because they are mostly earthbound. They rarely fly. They are *dit* ("birds") in Nuer classification, but they are the lowest order of birds. They just make it into the class.

Twins are regarded as sacred in many parts of the world, often because they are born in "litters" rather than singly the way most human beings are. Creatures that have offspring one at a time are called *monoparous,* while creatures that have many offspring at a time are called *polyparous.* Many animals are polyparous, but human beings usually are monoparous. So twins are like animals in being born in twos, unlike most human beings.

The reasoning that makes twins into birds is *analogical.* They are birds because in the classification of spirits they are an anomalous "in-between" category. The major classification of spirits in the Nuer world discriminates "spirits of the above" (heavens) and "spirits of the below" (earth). Birds, particularly the most lowly birds, like partridge and guinea fowl, are in a mediating position between "above" and "below." They walk upon the earth, but they belong to the sky as well.

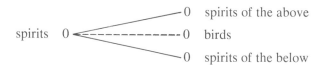

The world of living things, for the Nuer, is divided into human beings who are monoparous, and animal creatures who are polyparous. Therefore, twins are in the middle, halfway between humans and other animals.

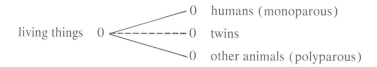

Just as birds mediate the categories of the spirit world, so do twins mediate the categories of the world of living things. Both are important, because they are mediating categories, and both draw out ideological comment from the Nuer, who identify them by analogy.

The Nuer carry out this logic in their behavior toward twins. When an infant twin dies, for example, the Nuer say "he has flown away." Twins who die are not buried the way single children are, but are placed in a reed basket or winnowing tray and put in trees. The Nuer believe that birds will not feed on them because the birds recognize their own kinfolk.

In Nuer thinking, twins are *analogous* to birds.

Paradigm and Syntagm   Mapping, mediation, transformation, opposition, metaphor, and analogy are all devices for forming "sentences" of symbols. In that sense, they are like grammatical rules. Some of the sentences that are formed can look very odd at first, but in fact make perfect sense if you understand those devices used to form them.

First, a word about *symbols*. Recall that a symbol is something that stands for something (or "some things") else. Symbols are ideas, categories, or events that are assigned multiple, conventional meanings. White is a color category, but it is also a symbol in American culture. Its symbolic meanings include "clean," "birth," "holy," "virgin" (the bride wears white), "life," "pure," and so on.

Symbols mean different things in different cultures. Victor Turner has done very detailed studies of the color symbolism of the Ndembu of central Africa. "White" in Ndembu can mean masculine, as in their expression "white river," which means semen. But it can also mean female, since white is the color of breast milk. "White" can also mean the *myudi* tree, which Turner calls the "milk tree" because it exudes a white latex sap; *myudi* means "breast milk." The *myudi* tree is very important

Figure 15.11
Sketch map showing where the Ndembu *left* and the Nuer are located.

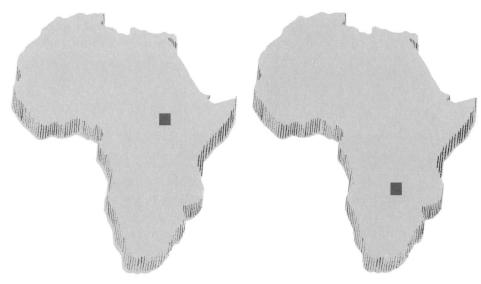

at girls' initiation rites and can stand for the social group as well, because it is the source of both males and females and *is* the matrilineage (the women who organize the social group).

The meaning of white is different in American and in Ndembu. But in both it is a symbol.

Symbols are defined, or get their particular meaning, in two ways. First, they take meaning from the context of opposition and association. That is to say, they take meaning because *they are compared with other symbols of the same type.* White is defined (in English) as opposite to black. People who see things as being in stark contrast with no intermediate stage are said to see things "in black and white." White is "life," black is "death." White is "purity," black is "sin." White is "happiness and gaiety," and black is "sorrow and mourning." White as a category and as a symbol takes its meaning from its relations with other categories. We call this mode of creating meaning *paradigmatic;* that is, we are saying a lot of things at the same time when we say "white" ("and not black").

When we form sentences with symbols as we do in ritual or in myth, we string them together. We are familiar with this "stringing together" in poetry and take it for granted. The poet e. e. cummings was very good at this. Here are some lines from Poem 117 of his *Collected Poems*:

117

I have seen her a stealthily frail
flower walking with its fellows in the death
of light, against whose enormous curve of flesh
exactly cubes of tiny fragrance try; . . .

The power of the lines lies in the use of the many meanings of the symbols joined together. "Flowers" do not "walk." A frail woman walks. But "flower" is a symbol with paradigmatic associations like the following:

$$
\begin{bmatrix}
\text{flower} \\
\text{sweet fragrance} \\
\text{frailty} \\
\text{death in its season} \\
\text{woman} \\
\text{brightly colored}
\end{bmatrix}
\quad
\begin{array}{l}
\text{A symbolic paradigm} \\
\text{"flower"}
\end{array}
$$

We know this column of associations. We learned it as we learned English. But a poet knows it better and can form sentences with the associations, choosing one value from the column to stand for all the others and carrying them along in the mind of the reader. Thus, when we read the last two lines and find that feminine, voluptuous softness is vying against ("trying") precise geometric forms of fragrance, we can imagine, among other things, that this frail woman is a paradox. She is partly female because softness is "female" and partly male since her fragrance is of the crystals or "exact cubes," which are "male."

Figure 15.12
Melodic line of "My Country 'Tis of Thee."

A myth, a ritual, or a creative act of symbolic thinking is in a way like a musical score, as Lévi-Strauss has suggested. There are two dimensions to a musical score, the harmonic and the melodic. The first bar of "My Country 'Tis of Thee" is shown in Figure 15.12. The figure shows the melodic line. If the musical notes were cultural symbols, the melodic line, heard through time, would represent the *syntagmatic* dimension. Once we add the harmony, we take musical tones that are associated with the melodic notes and form columns of associations. Each note in the melody is enriched by the addition of other notes. Proper harmonies are formed from the **paradigm** of notes that are associated with the melodic note in the right key. Filling in the partial paradigm of each note, we can write out these same bars with a paradigmatic as well as a syntagmatic axis, as shown in Figure 15.13.

Figure 15.13
Same melodic line, but with harmony added.

Once you get the idea, or the premise, of the music set and induce the listener to expect certain kinds of harmonies, you can become more inventive. You might write a theme and variations (as Beethoven did with this tune). Or you might have the bass sing his part as a solo. (It would only make sense if you knew that the listener knew the melody.) Or you might write out an orchestral score in which different instruments would add their sounds and meanings to individual notes, thus deepening the color and tonality of the piece.

We all learn to expect certain resolutions of musical passages. The composer may surprise us, but we still go on expecting them. There is a premise in the development of the musical ideas that leads us to expect

We know the rules without knowing we know them.

The paradigmatic units in the clothing code are the commutable, or substitutable, items of clothing that cannot be worn at the same time.

this resolution.* That expectation is a result of the composer's application of a set of **syntagmatic rules,** of which we are unconscious but which enable us to understand the music. We know the rules without knowing we know them.

Paradigmatic and Syntagmatic Rules in Clothing   Clothing provides another example of **paradigmatic** and **syntagmatic rules** of symbolism. It is a *code*—that is, a means of transmitting messages. A certain presentation of oneself transmits a determinable meaning, and we are all aware of the way we do this. The arguments parents have with their children over what to wear on social occasions concern the message to be transmitted. Some parents want their young teenage children to be independent and nonconformist, to wear clothes that reflect the message: "My child is a special person, out of the way, with intellectual interests and a taste for the aesthetic, prone to read poetry," and so on. The children, though, may want to send a different message: "I am *not* different, weird, and prone to do really stupid things like spend all day reading poetry; and I may be smart, but I am not some 'brain', so treat me like one of the gang." Thus, the argument.

What are the *paradigmatic* units in the clothing code? They are the commutable, or substitutable, items of clothing that cannot be worn at the same time. You can wear a top hat, a toque, no hat, or a ski cap, but not all at the same time, since they are all hats. So you lump them together as being substitutable units within the larger category "hat" or "head covering," and choose from among them. Similarly, you cannot wear trousers, jeans, shorts, and a kilt at the same time. These four items, then, form a commutable set, and you have to choose one or the other of them. The manner in which you lay out your wardrobe is the *syntagmatic* order. For example, you can wear a top hat with a morning coat (cutaway), grey trousers, spats, and black shoes. Although people may think you are a diplomat or on your way to a fancy dress ball, the ordering of those items is perfectly correct. However, you would not want to go out wearing a toque, starched shirt, four-in-hand tie, bikini shorts, long black stockings, and a pair of Keds. You will be stopped by the police for hostile questioning. Why? Because you have broken a number of very important rules about "what goes together with what." You did not appear indecently exposed in public. The law you broke was not a criminal law, but a social custom governing the way we dress. Your message was something very close to "I am nutty as a fruitcake," because your clothes were in violation of the syntagmatic rules. You dressed *ungrammatically*.

---

* The composer Wolfgang Amadeus Mozart did not like to get up in the morning. But there was one sure-fire way of getting him out of bed. A friend would come in and play the first seven notes of the scale, without playing the last note. Left "hanging," Mozart would leap out of bed to play the resolving note.

Figure 15.14
A really outlandish and incorrect get-up contrasted with an impeccably correct one.

Clothes, then, are powerful symbols. Anthropologists have to study the system of such symbols and the way they are strung together in order to understand the system of meanings in the cultural system they are studying. This means that, at a minimum, we must understand both the admissible substitutions (the paradigmatic aspect) and the rules for stringing symbols together (the syntagmatic aspect).

Symbols in Myths and Legends It may seem strange to think of ideas being strung together like notes in a musical composition, but that is what happens in those very important stories we call *myths*.

Say that in your cultural system there is a myth that begins with a barren wife murdering her husband. You know that, in the next part of the story, she is turned into something that something happens to. Could you guess what the "proper" or "appropriate" thing for her to turn into would be? Probably not. But would you know whether the "thing" that she turned into was a proper thing or not? Probably yes. As in listening to music, we have a strong feeling about proper resolutions to stories.

Let us suggest a myth that goes as follows. A barren wife murders her husband and leaves the village. Subsequently, she meets a sorcerer who is dressed all in white, and he turns her into a pregnant boy. The boy rests nine months and gives birth to a single bear cub, and dies in childbirth. You would not be able to predict his (her) death, but you would feel his death was a proper ending.

Now assume that this tale is part of an important myth in the culture you are studying. After all, it deals with *the* most important themes in all cultures: fertility, marriage, health, illness, deformity, life, death, the here-and-now versus the magical, the human versus the animal.

What can we make of this?

First think about the barren wife. Barren wives are anomalous in many cultures because to be a complete, "legitimate" wife, a woman has to bear children. This woman is somehow not a proper wife. "Barren" and "wife" are two ideas that do not go together; they are opposed to one another. We call this opposition an *unresolved opposition* in the sense that something has to happen to resolve it.

It does. She overcomes the unresolved opposition by murdering her husband. No longer is she a barren wife. She might have stopped being a barren wife (legitimately) by becoming pregnant. But she stopped being a barren wife (illegitimately) by murdering her husband. She is no longer a wife.

She leaves the community. That act is over.

She meets a magician who is good. We know he is good because he is dressed in white, and in this culture white is a symbol of good. The good magician transforms the woman into a pregnant boy. In this way he eliminates the "bad change" (the murder) by a "good change" (the only kind he can make). But what happens? The woman is now back in the position of an illegitimate, unresolved opposition: Boys do not get pregnant. But she (now he) did. The issue must be resolved, and so she gives birth. But since the pregnancy is unnatural, it must have an unnatural issue. On the other hand, since she/he is human, the offspring is going to be human too. So she gives birth to an animal, a *single* animal. She is monoparous like a human being, but still gives birth to an animal, a bear.

That is a sentence in a myth. We can diagram it:

	Barren wife		Murders husband	To become normal woman
Line One	−	+	−	+
			+	
	Pregnant boy		Gives birth to single cub	But dies
Line Two	+	−	−	−
			+	

The issue is resolved by changing the value of all the signs so that when you add Line One to Line Two the sum is zero.*

* Two notes for those who are really reading the argument closely. The "sum" is zero in the sense that if you add up the pluses and minuses in the columns they all cancel out.

The actions whereby the transformations are made are given values of both plus and minus because they are both "good" and "bad." The first (murders husband) is good because it resolves the opposition and bad because murder is morally evil. The second is good because it resolves the opposition and evil because it is morally wrong for human beings to bear animals in childbirth.

Another way of putting it would be as follows:

1. By murdering her husband a barren wife turns herself into a normal woman.

2. By giving birth to a single bear cub a pregnant boy becomes normal, but dies.

We are not suggesting that myths or rituals are the same as music or mathematics. We are only suggesting that there is a logic to paradigmatic and syntagmatic relations that we must decode in order to understand the uses of symbols in our own culture as well as in traditional cultures.

Summary

1. When anthropologists study the world of other peoples, their job is to understand and interpret that world in the way the people do. In chapter 14 we talked about the problems of understanding linguistic meaning, or semantic meaning. In this chapter we talked about the problems of translating other people's worlds into a form that we can understand. We have to perform an act of *double translation*. First, we translate the exotic world to ourselves. We acquire a "gut feeling" for the culture we are studying. We watch ourselves to see whether we are behaving appropriately and are understanding what is going on around us. We have learned the language well by this time. We understand the *content* of what people are saying. But do we understand the *nuance* and subtleties? Do we understand the jokes? Do we know when people are speaking well, as opposed to just speaking? If we can say yes to all these questions, then we have completed the first phase of translation.

2. The second phase of translation is equally important. The "gut feelings" we have must be translated into a form that the average intelligent student or reader will understand. We cannot translate directly, for if we do the life we describe will seem terribly exotic. But it isn't at all exotic for the people who live it, and it is *their* lives in *their* terms that we are trying to describe.

3. Next we must understand people's logic. Nowhere do everyday people use formal logic the way a logician or a mathematician does. But people do have a lot of techniques for constructing a world of meaning, even if mathematics is not one of them. We use mappings from one domain to another, saying, for example, that the world of human beings is, in important respects, of the same structure as the world of animals. Such mappings are called totemic.

4. Many cultures, our own in particular, make use of *oppositions*. We in the United States line up whole series of categories into opposed sets and construct our lives on that basis. We believe, for instance, that

women think intuitively and are emotional, while men think logically and are self-composed at all times, because women and men are symbolically opposed; and the ideas of "intuition" and "emotiveness" fall on the "female" side.

5. *Mediation* is an important logical device that people use. Mediating categories are very important in thinking, and we load them with a great deal of meaning and importance. Jesus Christ is an excellent example of a mediating category, mediating God and Man.

6. We worry a good deal about categories that fall "between the cracks" of our folk logical systems, and make them either sacred or taboo. In the Jewish food laws, for example, categories of animals that are "neither fish nor fowl" are forbidden. We find that animals that are humanlike (domesticated) are forbidden in the sense that they provide us with our vocabulary of obscenity. Ideas or categories that threaten sacred oppositions, as homosexuality or transsexuality do, are objects of taboo.

7. Humans can be creative with systems of categories, too. We can invent brilliant *metaphors,* saying with the Apache, for example, that "widows are ravens" or "white people are carrion beetles." Or we can construct logical theorems by using *analogy,* as do the Nuer in saying that "twins are birds."

And so it is with symbols. We endow concepts and categories with symbolic meaning and then string these symbolic categories together like a melody. Then we add harmony in the form of the *paradigm* of meanings associated with each concept. The melodic line reflects and is obedient to paradigmatic rules: the rules for stringing ideas together. The harmony reflects and is obedient to paradigmatic rules: the rules that determine all the associations of a symbol. It sounds complicated, but we are terribly quick to figure out when it is well done and when it is not.

These are the most important techniques we all use to construct our world of meaning. They are shared with all human beings. Our ability to be creative and imaginative in constructing our worlds is a measure of our humanity. It is fundamental to the definition of being human. No animal can do this. Every human being can.

Suggested Readings

Douglas, Mary. *Purity and Danger: An Analysis of the Concepts of Pollution and Taboo.* London: Routledge and Kegan Paul, 1963.
> *The book from which the analysis of the food taboos of the Old Testament was taken. A very good introduction to the fundamental anthropological thinking about beliefs.*

Leach, Edmund. *Culture and Communication.* Cambridge: Cambridge University Press, 1976.
> *A recent summary study of the logic by which symbols are connected. Leach has had a great impact on the thinking of the writers of this book.*

This little paperback is one of the most accessible introductions to contemporary thinking in this area.

Lévi-Strauss, Claude. *The Savage Mind.* Chicago: University of Chicago Press, 1966.

The thinking on totemism was taken from this book. It is difficult going, but has been a very influential book in modern anthropology. Try chapter 3 first.

Turner, Victor. *The Forest of Symbols.* Ithaca and London: Cornell University Press, 1967

A very good study of the logic of association in ritual symbolism.

Glossary

mapping   The rule in totemism that associates a particular animal or natural event with a particular subgroup or tribe.

mediation   Putting an idea or category between two opposed ideas or categories so that it acts as a go-between for the oppositions.

opposition   A logical device that creates a world of binary symbols (i.e., divided in two).

paradigmatic rules   The rules that identify the members of a paradigmatic set; similar to the rules for writing harmony in music.

syntagmatic rules   The rules for stringing symbols (and paradigms) together; similar to the rules for writing melody in music.

totemism   The belief that associates some animal or other "natural event" with a subgroup or tribe for the purposes of classification.

16

Religious Systems

387

Introduction

Every known society has religious beliefs. Sometimes the "atheistic Communists" are cited as counterexamples to this general truth, but it is hard to believe that Lenin (whose body has lain in state in the Kremlin since his death in 1924) and Mao Tse-tung do not have divine status. And certainly good Communists believe in the superhuman power of history to affect their lives and lead them ever closer to the socialist utopia.

Are People in Traditional Society More Religious?

On the other hand, not all people everywhere at all times are religious. There are plenty of atheists and agnostics in the traditional world, just as there are in the modern world. The difference between traditional peoples and modern Western peoples lies in the way they explain the world to themselves. In traditional systems of thought there simply is no other way than the religious way to express the human relation to the cosmos. Religion in traditional society is not just a set of beliefs about superhuman powers. It is an *idiom,* a manner of thought and speech that people must use to explain their world to themselves. Traditional peoples can no more avoid religious expressions than we can avoid using tenses in our verbs. Neither of us has any choice in the matter. For this reason travelers and anthropologists have sometimes felt that traditional peoples are more religious than those of us in modern societies. But they might as well say that we are obsessed by time because we are obliged to code it in all our verb forms.

Psychology and Religious Beliefs

Many anthropologists believe that the forms that any religion or belief system takes are determined by the psychological needs of the people, and that these needs are determined by psychological cravings (or conflicts) generated by the way children are brought up in the society. Years ago, Sigmund Freud suggested that the conflict within ourselves over our feelings of dependency on our parents, particularly those of boys toward their fathers, has led to the belief in a "super-father" extended in space (Freud 1939). For this reason, we believe in an all-powerful, benevolent, moral, judging God—who is no more and no less than the logical extension of our image of our own father when we have (supposedly) grown out of the need for a father in everyday life.

S. F. Nadel (1903–1956) once studied two African tribes that were very similar in their economic forms, their technology, and their way of

Figure 16.1
Red Square at night with Lenin's tomb in the foreground.

living in general, but very dissimilar in religion. One was the Otoro, the other the Heiban. This is how the religions of the groups differed.

The Religions of Heiban and Otoro

Though both peoples believe in the existence of a high god and other deities and invisible spirits, their pictures of the spirits are entirely different. The Otoro believe that the spirits look like ordinary human beings; the Heiban imagine them to be white-skinned, red-haired, and one-legged. The Heiban also believe that there are female spirits capable of killing any male who attempts to steal spirit wealth—crops or animals. The Otoro know nothing of these. Both peoples have magic rites that are performed through a special spear. The Heiban worry about the spear, hide it away, and permit only one per kin group; while the Otoro are comparatively relaxed about it. If they do not have a spear, a knife will do. The Heiban worry about the spear's owner. Has he sinned? Has he committed

some crime? Then the magic will not work. The Otoro do not believe that the morals of the spear owner matter. It will work in any case.

Both societies have a rainmaker. Once again, the Heiban worry about this. Since he carries out his rituals privately, they wonder, "Has he performed the ritual?" If the rains do not come, they fret and threaten the rainmaker, even shouting threats of violence. The Otoro relax—the rainmaker is not that important to them. He is only the intermediary between the people and God. The Heiban worry about too much rain; they also have a rain-stopper. The Otoro do not.

Both the Otoro and the Heiban believe that illnesses are caused by mystical means, by the insertion of some magically poisonous substance into the body. But the Heiban believe that anyone can be a sorcerer; they have more diseases than the Otoro and they worry more about them. In both societies, God is believed to send leprosy because of incest. But among the Heiban, leprosy is thought to be caused by sexual intercourse between any relatives. In Otoro, only the rare case of incest between parent and child will bring it.

In short, these societies which in other ways are almost identical differ greatly in the tone of their religious beliefs. The Heiban world, in Nadel's words, "is more sinister than that of the Otoro, and gives greater play to aggression, real or fancied (as for example in their attitude toward the rainmaker). For the Otoro, relatively few unexcited observances insure the desired normality of life and nature. In Heiban, one feels the need for repeated ritual interpretations . . . for excited interpretations, and for the coercion of the deity. The Heiban are more magically oriented, more aggressive, emotionally tense, coercive and pessimistic, and the Otoro are more religious, calm, dispassionate, submissive and optimistic" (Nadel 1955).

Why the Heiban and the Otoro Differ

Since they are so similar in so many other ways, why do the Heiban and the Otoro differ so much in their attitudes toward superhuman beings? There are two sets of reasons: psychological and sociological.

Psychologically the Heiban are more insecure, more full of conflicts than the Otoro. In the area of sexuality, for example, which is often important in belief systems, we find that the Otoro do not place much importance on sexual behavior. They do not seem to be overly interested or obsessed in any way about sex. The Heiban, on the other hand, boast about their sex lives and their adulterous affairs and complain about the frigidity of their wives and how their wives "tire so easily." For the Heiban, as well, male homosexuality is a problem—it is evil, abnormal. The Otoro permit homosexuality in men and give it a place in their society. Men can choose to dress like women and take women's

Table 16.1

Religious Differences: Heiban and Otoro

People in Heiban society have more sexual conflicts and more insecurity, conflict, and doubt about their sexuality than do the Otoro people. These psychological differences show up in the differences between their religions. Here is a summary:

Religious Characteristic	Heiban	Otoro
Appearance of spirits	Frightening: Red-haired, white-skinned, one-legged	Ordinary: Just like ordinary human beings
Killer female spirits	Present	Absent
People's feelings about the spear ritual	Anxious, nervous	Carefree
Anxiety about Rainmaker?	Yes; also have rain-stopper	No
Feelings about cause of leprosy	Easily caught. Sexual relations between any two relatives will cause it.	Only the very rare case of sexual relations between parent and child will cause it.

roles. Unlike the Heiban, the Otoro can take sexual differences in their stride.

Abram Kardiner (1891–19—) has showed how people's fears and anxieties could be mirrored in their religious beliefs. He studied Ralph Linton's reports on the Marquesan Islanders of Polynesia (Kardiner 1939) and noted that the Marquesan men grew up with a strong ambivalence (or "love and hate") toward their mothers. This was not surprising, since Marquesan mothers showed very little interest in their children, weaning them when they were six months old in order to preserve their breasts for their lovers. Kardiner also noted that there were more men than woman in the society and that men suffered from frustrated sexual needs. At the same time, women had to compete for men to gain prestige, and to compete they had to bear children.

Two religious beliefs stemmed from these experiences. The men believed in spirits with **vaginae dentatae,** that is, toothed vaginas that could emasculate them; while the women experienced **pseudocyesis,** or false pregnancy. Women also believed that there were female spirits who would rob them of their babies in the womb, reflecting their anxiety about other women robbing them of their prestige.

Many of the emphases of our religious beliefs can be traced to our psychological needs. Following Freud, many psychologists feel that American culture's stress on autonomy ("standing on your own two feet"), independence, and self-reliance has given rise to a secret desire on all our parts to have a father figure to lean on. We provide ourselves with a spirit to replace the father on whom we may not lean, in the form of the Judeo-Christian God. Our vision of God is one of a judicious, moral, sin-

Figure 16.3
The cult of the Virgin Mary is extremely important and popular in Latin America.

punishing, all-powerful spirit because, in our child's eye, our own fathers were like that. Equally, psychologists of religion believe that the rupture of the very close tie between a boy and his mother in Latin American cultures leads to the cult of the Virgin Mary, which is more highly developed there than in other Catholic countries.

Some of these arguments may be too speculative. But it is certain that religious beliefs both mirror and assuage our anxieties. They emanate from ourselves, from our own psyches and experiences.*

Society and Religion

The act of religious worship is collective. People get together to worship. Religious symbols are public, whether they be six-pointed stars, crucifixes, or stone tablets with cryptic inscriptions. The fact that symbols (and most acts of worship) are public has led many anthropologists to believe that religion and acts of worship embody and dramatize a society's symbolic unity. That unity derives from a common faith in

---

* We should be careful here. This is not to say that, because our culture's idea of God takes its form from our own anxieties, God does not exist. It doesn't necessarily follow. God can exist apart from our psychological conflicts and everyday anxieties.

the efficacy, importance, and shared meaning of the symbols of worship and the ideals that they represent. Émile Durkheim (1858–1917) stated:

Religious beliefs . . . are always common to a determined group, which makes a profession of adhering to them and of practicing the rites connected with them. They are not merely received individually by all the members of the group; they are something belonging to the group, and they make its unit. The individuals which compose it feel themselves united to each other by the simple fact that they have a common faith. A society whose members are united by the fact that they think in the same way in regard to the sacred world and its relations with the profane world, and by the fact that they translated these common ideas into common practice is what is called a church. In all history we do not find a single religion without a church. (Durkheim 1965)

Durkheim does not mean "church" in the sense of a building, nor "church" in the sense of a hierarchically organized priestly system. He is referring to the common bond of belief that unites all members of the society and differentiates them from others.

An American Example: Cleanliness as a "Religious" Idea

America is a secular society. Though many Americans—a majority—go to church, religious ideas are not universally believed and endorsed. But Americans do share certain public ideas (and symbols). These ideas and symbols are the important, shaping metaphors of the secular American religion. "Progress" is one idea. Nearly all Americans believe in the reality of progress and its inherent goodness. "The importance of the individual" is another idea that Americans believe in in a fundamental way. Still another is the idea of "cleanliness." Americans believe that cleanliness is a moral state—it is, as the old expression has it, "next to godliness." The opposite of clean is dirty, and dirt is immoral and sinful. Americans cannot abide "dirty people," and the idea of dirt extends from soiled appearance to spoiled (dirty) language, to sexual practices, to improper modes of thinking (a "dirty mind"), to criminal practices (a "dirty business" or "dirty work"). Dirt is sin and cleanliness is virtue.

Foreigners visiting America are always struck by this apparent obsession that Americans have with dirt. Americans, for example, believe that they "smell," in the sense of "stink." Now many other peoples believe that people *other than* themselves "stink," but since they are used to their own characteristic odor, they do not notice it and certainly would not characterize one of their own as having an unpleasant odor. Yet, since cleanliness is moral to Americans, while dirt is sinful, and since dirt and smell go together (they mark things that are rotten or spoiled), then our own smell must be repugnant as well. As a result, to the amusement of foreigners, we spend billions of dollars getting rid of this smell. We buy deodorants for our houses, our bodies, our baths, our cars, and our dogs,

Figure 16.4
Kitchens and bathrooms
are very important, almost
ritual places in American
culture. Above all they must
be gleaming and clean.
This is not true in other
countries and cultures.

and are bade to pay strict attention to the odor of sin where it appears most readily in the form of dirt. Bathrooms, where dirty people are converted into clean people, must be specially treated. The dirt that is stripped from people must be purged by using special substances ("Bathroom cleaners with extra strength"). Bathrooms are important ritual places in American homes because they are places where "that which best remains outside" (dirt) is brought inside. Dirt and excrement belong to the outside. Dogs, after all, defecate on our lawns with impunity. But people's dirt is much more dangerous and polluting than animal dirt; therefore, it must be kept inside, in the house, where it can be protected, kept private, and disposed of.

Americans also believe in things called germs.* Germs cause diseases. They are dirty and dangerous, all the more so because they are invisible. One of the authors was explaining to a modernizing Zapotec Indian that, as a Westerner, he found beliefs in witchcraft very hard to understand. He pointed out that the Zapotec believed that witches could float such objects as cactus spines, liquor, iron filings, and "air" into another person's body by blowing them. Once this had happened, the person who was the object of the "blowing" would sicken and die. During the course of the conversation, the Zapotec colleague asked how the anthropologist believed diseases were caused. "Why, by germs" was the reply and, in explanation: "Germs are invisible, small, substances that enter the body through the skin or through the mouth and other openings and work upon the bodily system so as to make us sick!" The Indian's reply was ready and obvious: "Why, then, we believe the same thing."

It is all very well for us to say that we are sold these deodorants, these cleaning agents, these depilatories (hair is dirty, too, if it is in the wrong place), these soaps. But that is the easy way out. The reason that we *can* be sold these products is because of our belief that cleanliness is a moral condition and that dirt and stench and sin are all the same—evil!

One cannot live in a society if one does not subscribe to its common, shared, symbolic meanings. Either one is driven to the margin of the society and not permitted access to the important, desired goods or symbols, or one is eliminated: jailed, executed, or exiled. Tramps, or "bums," are believed to wear dirt as an emblem, as part of their uniform, to de-

---

* Ideas like "germs," "viruses," "infections," and "resistance" have two meanings: the scientific meaning and the folk meaning. Whenever we talk about belief systems, cultural logics, and religious systems, we are talking about the *folk meaning* of a concept. This refers to the level of understanding of the idea held by the average person, not the medical researcher, or doctor, or microbiologist. The special kind of knowledge we call "scientific knowledge" is different from folk knowledge because it is systematically tested under controlled conditions and is never accepted as absolutely true for all times and places. Scientific knowledge is rigorously validated provisional knowledge that will change as soon as new tests change its value. Folk knowledge is not rigorously collected nor subject to change in the same way.

Figure 16.5
The Mesoamerican curer is particularly effective for diseases which are unknown to Western medical science.

clare their marginal status. They are outsiders and do not share in the important social symbols such as money, prestigeful occupation, and prideful possession. They are on the margin of the society, allocated special places (Skid Row) within our cities, and constantly harassed by police, courts, and jailers in order to ensure that their status remains marginal. The middle class majority has little sympathy for them because their badge ("dirt") proclaims that they have rejected one of the most important, shared symbols of our society ("cleanliness") and therefore do not deserve fully to participate in our "church" (as Durkheim used the word; that is, our society).

So, religion serves two social functions. As Durkheim said, it serves to provide a bond of unity for a whole society. Religion is the ideological basis for the formation of a church, and the "church" is the whole society collected in worship of its shared, public symbols. The second function of religion is to take those central organizing symbols of a society and give them a special place in people's consciousness. It makes them sacred. "Cleanliness" in American culture is a sacred value because it is set apart and given special moral meaning.

Religion as a System of Explanations

Religious beliefs provide explanations for important and enduring questions whose answers lie outside ordinary, everyday experience.

A third function of religious beliefs is equally important. *Religious beliefs provide explanations for important and enduring questions whose answers lie outside ordinary, everyday experience.* Some of these questions are universal: Why do people die? Where did society come from? Where did humankind originate? Why is there evil in the world? Why did this particular evil (say, an accident) just happen to me?

Rather than try to give a list of all the questions that can be answered by religious systems, let us concentrate on three questions that are nearly universal.

Identity: The Concept of the Soul

The first question is a complicated one that everyone has to answer: *Who am I?* It is posed in a complicated way. *"What is the relationship between the 'me' as I experience myself, and the 'me' as it is culturally defined?"*

"What is the relationship between the 'me' as I experience myself, and the 'me' as it is culturally defined?"

The "experienced you" is a very complex creature. You experience yourself in a tremendous variety of ways: through normal waking consciousness, dream states, sleep states, trance states, hypnotic states, intoxicated states, and many others. You have many kinds of knowledge about yourself and about the way you experience reality. You see things, feel things, touch and taste things, using your five senses, and you can easily talk about that. What you find difficult to talk about are the strange sensory combinations that you use to experience things in their fullness. You not only hear music, you "feel" it. Sometimes you convert music into visual patterns that bring associations of smell and touch. All your senses and your intuitions are working completely, together, to enable you to experience things in their fullness, in your many modes of consciousness.

But that is not what the cultural rules define as *proper experience*. Proper experience, as culturally defined, is usually based on experience felt through *one* mode of consciousness: normal waking consciousness. **Synesthesia,** the practice of using several senses at the same time (such as seeing colors in music), is severely restricted by most cultural systems. Yet you experience it all the time.

So everyone has this basic problem. Cultural rules stipulate that you can only experience reality in a proper (one-dimensional) fashion. And this proper fashion is always much narrower than your own experience. So how do you explain the discrepancy between the culturally defined "you" and the "you" that you experience? A universal means of explaining this discrepancy is to invent another "you"—one that is intrinsically a part of the culturally defined "you" but has greater ca-

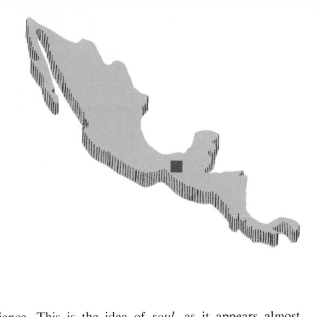

Figure 16.6
Sketch map of Mexico
showing where the
Zinacantan are.

pacities for experience. This is the idea of *soul,* as it appears almost universally around the world in religious and cosmological systems.

The World of the Zinacantecan Souls The Tzotzil-speaking Maya Indians of the *municipio* of Zinacantan in southern Mexico live between two worlds: the world of their social reality and the world of the spirits or souls. They have been studied by the members of the Harvard Chiapas Project under the direction of Evon Z. Vogt.

There are two souls in Zinacantan, the *chu'lel* and the *chanul,* which can be translated respectively as the "personal soul" and the "animal familiar."

The *chu'lel* is the inner soul of the person. It is composed of thirteen parts and must be carefully guarded, since death occurs when one loses one's inner soul. Mothers are particularly careful with their children's souls. They always sweep up the soul with their shawls when they leave a place where they have been sitting with their child, for fear that some parts of the inner soul will be left behind. Baptism is necessary to fix the soul of the child.

The animal familiar is the *chanul.* It is a wild animal: jaguar, coyote, puma, ocelot, anteater, opossum, fox, squirrel, weasel, raccoon, hawk, or owl. The animal souls are the familiars of the person to whom they are assigned at birth. They are watered, fed, and cared for by the ancestral gods under the guidance of the supernatural Señor Alcalde (that is, the supernatural president), who is the highest religious official in the community. The animal familiars live in corrals and are converted into sheep or cows by the ancestral gods so that they can leave the corral and graze in the hotter lands in the southern lowlands. The important thing about the *chanul,* or animal familiar, is that everything that happens to it also happens to the individual whose familiar it is.

The belief in souls is important to the Zinacantecos for two reasons: it allows them to explain the otherwise inexplicable; and it allows them to mediate between the world over which they have control (the house, the well, the village, the fields) and the world of the forested mountain.

Being both human beings and animal familiars adds an extra dimension to the Zinacantecos' experience. The person *is* the soul, and the soul is the person. Souls are what are called *alter egos* (the "other self"), just as we suggested in the earlier discussion on experience.

The Zinacantecos provide a good example of the human use of the idea of soul. Some peoples have a very wan notion of the soul—it is merely a puff of smoke or a dimly flickering light that symbolizes another life within the lived life. Other peoples let their imaginations run and develop the idea of soul to phantasmagoric proportions. In chapter 22 you will encounter the Yanomamo, who have elaborated the idea of soul much more than the Zinacantecos. The Yanomamo have shamans who engage in air-to-ground missilry, sending murdering souls to snuff out the lives of children in neighboring villages.

Religion Provides Explanations

Human beings everywhere need to understand their universe. But the universe, or cosmos, is full of uncertainty because of the incompleteness of human knowledge. Religion provides explanations for ultimate, unanswerable questions. It proves that the world is a predictable moral place rather than a random immoral one. It is better for human beings to believe that the world is well ordered and that sinless people will not be visited with sickness, death, and evil circumstances, than to believe that life is unfair and random and that, worst of all, people can do little to help themselves. We resist our ignorance and our feelings of inability to help ourselves by creating explanations and programs of action that will both explain and help.

Explaining Random Events: The Monsoon Fails

Consider this problem from the point of view of a village rice farmer in south India. He relies on the rain from the monsoons. He knows that the monsoon is sometimes early, sometimes late, and sometimes on time. But it always comes sooner or later, and he can devise a planting and harvesting strategy to cope with its irregularity. Then one year the mon-

soon fails to come. Not only do all the crops fail so that people are forced to endure famine conditions, but his whole world is turned upside down. Up to now he has believed that the monsoon *always* came. Had he not believed this, subsistence dry rice farming in this part of the world would be impossible. Yet this time the monsoon did not arrive. Either the south Indian villager finds an explanation for this or he is forced to the conclusion that the whole world is a wildly unpredictable place in which his existence is constantly threatened.

You will probably agree that finding an explanation is the better of the two solutions, particularly if one is found that will do some good for the community. And one is found: "There was too much sin in the village, and therefore we were punished by the gods for it. There was adultery in the village, and fornication, and disrespect toward the elders. For this reason the gods withheld the monsoon."

How much better to explain the catastrophic event this way than by saying: "The monsoon did not come. This is just another example of how we are at the mercy of random events we can neither understand or control. Lord have mercy upon us who can be struck down at any time, for no apparent reason whatsoever."

Religious ideas can solve the problems posed by catastrophic events.

Magic

Magic is an attempt by a human being (or human beings) to control events directly. Unlike prayer, which is a supplication to a spiritual entity to intercede for one in the course of events, magic tries to intervene *directly* to shape the course of events to one's advantage. Most of the interventions are aimed at preventing the preventable, expediting the inevitable, or focusing and directing the habitual. In other words, magicians do not try to stop natural or social processes that cannot be stopped. No magician would attempt to purge the village of illness for all time; but rather would expedite the inevitable, say, by moving up the date when the season for some class of diseases (say, intestinal disorders) concludes. The magician and the people know that the season will end sooner or later, but the magician helps bring the ending sooner. The magician also focuses and directs something that always happens so that it happens to his or her advantage. In the rainy season, let us say there are always thunderstorms with lightning. The wise magician (and only the wise ones stay in business) will not attempt to stop the thunderstorms or the lightning, but will try to direct the lightning toward the homesteads of his or her enemies. Magic is usually based on a shrewd notion of how the

**Figure 16.8
A South American witch
doctor.**

natural and social world operates. The techniques of magic are based on a premise that sooner or later the desired effect will be brought about by the inevitable workings of the social or natural world.

Sickness occurs with great frequency in traditional societies. The prediction that a person will sicken with or without magic is a good one, given a simple notion of probability.

The truth of magic is never jeopardized, for it is well-nigh impossible to disprove magical beliefs. If a spell is cast or a rite performed and the target does not cooperate by sickening and dying, explanations are readily available. First, the ritual may have been badly performed. One of the characteristics of magical performances is the exactitude with which they must be carried out. One word out of place, one symbol wrong, and the spell will not work. Second, the sorcerer may not be genuine. He or she may have claimed to be a powerful sorcerer, or may have the reputation of powerful sorcery, but either people are wrong or the sorcerer is a fake. In either case, the effectiveness of the magic (and magic in general) is not doubted, impugned, or disproved. People in many societies talk about sorcerers in the same way we talk about doctors: "I paid that quack all that money and the medicine didn't do a bit of good!"

Robin Horton (1962) explains a popular "escape clause" in magical thought, comparing scientific thinking with magical thinking. Scientific thinking sees a specific outcome in terms of a specific cause, and so a scientific theory may make the following causal connections:

This diagram states "A causes E, B causes F" and so forth. But traditional belief systems that incorporate magic are never set up in this scientific manner. Traditional systems' causal series can be diagrammed like this:

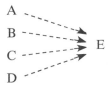

That is, "A or B or C or D or any combination can cause E."

Among the Kalabari, a people of west Africa where Horton worked, there is a clear system of causal factors of disease. If a "town law" has been broken, the "heroes" will bring disease. If an offense has been committed against kin, the "ancestors" will bring disease. "Water spirits" punish people who fail in their duties to friends and neighbors, while "medicine spirits" sicken one's enemies.

There is plenty of room here to explain illness on different grounds. If one diviner or curer states that the illness was caused by the ancestors, and the illness does not abate, then the next diviner can state that the offense against the ancestors that was thought to be so important by the first diagnostician was overemphasized. Perhaps the water spirits are causing the disease.

Another escape clause for the failure of magic derives from the fact that there is very often no statute of limitations on a magician's acts. Since the magician often works to bring illness and disease on enemies, it may take time, a lot of time, for the spell to work. When sooner or later the desired event occurs, the practitioner can claim credit for it.

Magical thought is so constructed that it always works. There is no room to question magic, because there are always escape clauses that can explain failure. But magic is not exotic and "primitive," the way we Westerners understand it. It is a form of religious thinking that, like all religious thought, yields answers to enduring and unanswerable questions. In this case the question is, "Why did this happen to me or to them?"

Witchcraft

Witchcraft is the practice of harming others at a distance through magical means.

Witchcraft is the practice of harming others at a distance through magical means. It is as old as humankind and absolutely universal. It is a part of the definition of being human. Witchcraft explains evil by stating that someone is out to "get" one—that is why evil befell one.

Beliefs in witchcraft persist even when there are no witches. The Zapotec firmly believe that there are two kinds of witches in their communities: "natural witches" and "self-educated witches." "Natural witches" have the misfortune to have been born with the soul of a supernatural oversize cat, or small mountain lion. They can transform themselves and fly from place to place to seek out the company of their fellow souls. But they cannot help it. They do not intentionally do harm to others. Self-educated witches, however, are the very stuff of malevolence. They transform themselves into cats (sometimes buzzards) and sit upon the housetops during the dead of night, or hover unseen at the crossroads during the heavy hours of day, to steal the Christian souls of the living so that they will sicken and die.

All Zapotec believe in the existence of witches. Everybody believes that some other people in the community are witches, and no one in the community is not a witch to someone. But the fact of the matter is, there are no witches among the Zapotec. No one practices witchcraft. No one does what witches are supposed to do: stick cactus thorns into images of people to puncture their bodies, blow iron filings through the air to poison another. No one even knows how to do these things, although everyone thinks that there are people who do know. But witchcraft does not require empirical proof. Were one so foolish as to try to convince the Zapotec that there were no witches, they would point out the effects of witchcraft everywhere, deducing the presence of witches from these effects. Protestant missionaries felt that dispelling the belief in witchcraft would lead to conversions, but the Zapotec shook their heads at such credulity. They converted to Protestantism but kept their belief in witchcraft.

Witchcraft Is Also a Social Phenomenon

A belief in witchcraft, like magic, does explain the occurrence of random events. It is also an explanation for the existence of evil. But we should not forget that it is a *social* process as well. That is, witches are fellow human beings, often fellow members of the village or tribe. Their malevolence is *not* random. In fact, rates of believed deaths from witchcraft vary with social conditions, and it is worth briefly considering witchcraft as a social process so that we can better understand it.

Figure 16.9
The Salem witch trials were among the last instances in this country when an attempt was made to purify the community by a witch hunt.

Insight
Religion—
Quesalid, The Unwilling Sorcerer

Traditional peoples are no less sensible than we are. They know that magic sometimes works and sometimes does not. Sometimes the anthropologists are just a little too quick to say that "the So-and-so people believe that witches come in the form of giant toothed vaginas to kill men in their sleep," when half the community in question does not believe anything of the sort. One of the authors had a local teacher who said, "I, of all people, should know what my alter ego soul is, because I was born down there where they come from. But to be honest, I haven't a clue."

We can understand this kind of statement and compare it with those of people in our own society who do not believe in God, or who do not believe in current medical theories. "People say that germs and viruses cause colds and flu, and I ought to know because I have plenty of them, but frankly I haven't got a clue what causes them!"

But what if a doctor said that? We would probably be rather more worried. What if a doctor said (as some have) that our whole theory of disease is wrong? And that he or she didn't believe in it? And what if this unbelieving doctor became very famous for his cures, yet never told a soul that he didn't believe the theory?

That is what happened to a sorcerer among the Kwakiutl Indians of the Northwest coast of Canada, who told his life story to Franz Boas.* Though Quesalid did not believe in the efficacy of shamanistic techniques, he was curious enough to want to learn when the opportunity was offered to him by an older shaman. He studied the magician's tricks, his

* This account is taken from Lévi-Strauss 1963.

techniques of ferreting out information about patients' social lives, and the techniques of spontaneous vomiting that shamans need to know. He learned how to hide a little bit of down in his mouth during the course of the cure, so that by biting his tongue or making his gums bleed, he could spit it out as a "bloody worm" at the critical moment when the sickness was withdrawn.

So much was intellectual curiosity. Quesalid had found out about curing techniques, and his skeptical fears had been confirmed.

But things have a habit of getting away from one. A critically ill patient sent for him. He went and performed a marvellous cure. His fame began to spread. While visiting a neighboring group, he saw their shamans perform a cure, and to his horror, they were even worse fakers since they proclaimed that the sickness was invisible and that when they held it in the palm of their hand, it could not even be seen! After one of their performances, he asked if he could perform a cure on a very ill patient. Granted permission, he performed as usual and withdrew the sickness in the form of a bloody worm. The local shamans were thrown into great consternation and begged him to tell them his secret. He refused on the proper grounds that he was not fully trained—he had never completed the full course required by the shaman who taught him.

He went home, but his fame spread. Other shamans, fearing for their livelihood (and their credibility), invited him along with many other of their colleagues to a shaman-istic contest. Quesalid triumphed with his bloody worm.

The beaten shaman came to him and begged to be told his secret. Quesalid was silent while the older man revealed all his tricks. But still he said nothing. The old man and his daughter, who had accompanied him, went home. They both went insane, and the old man died within three years.

Quesalid continued his profession, full of contempt for his own tricks, but very famous for his successes.

As he proceeded in his profession, a slow change took place in his attitude. He began to feel that there were real shamans in the world and claimed that he had actually met one. How did he know that this colleague alone was real? He took no money (like Quesalid) and never was seen to laugh! Quesalid never lost his contempt for the fakery of shamans who sold their services to suffering and gullible people, but neither did he deny the effect of his own technique, which he regarded as at least the best of the worst.

Quesalid probably had more intellectual honesty and moral integrity than the majority of us. How many of us could stand up to fame and success, even adulation and overwhelming gratitude, see the evidence of our great abilities before our eyes, and still maintain an attitude of skepticism about ourselves?

Economic Conditions   Rates of witchcraft generally rise in bad times. Did you know that the number of lynchings in the cotton-growing South during the early 1900s was tied to the price of cotton? The lower the price of cotton, the higher the number of lynchings! Witchcraft works in the same way: the more difficult times are, the more frequent the witchcraft accusations. Sometimes they reach epidemic proportions, threatening the fabric of a whole society.

One of the best studies of how economic conditions can affect people's beliefs in witches and in the frequency of witchcraft accusations was done in Bakweri (Cameroon). Among the Bakweri studied by Edwin Ardener (1961, 1970a, 1970b; Ardener, Ardener and Warmington 1960), witchcraft was generated by *inona,* or envy. When caught, witches were hanged, and each village had its hanging tree. Before World War I these beliefs served to control wealth, since the rich were careful to ward off envy by disposing of their possessions, killing off livestock and distributing the meat free among the villagers. But during the years after World War I, the Bakweri population dropped because of new migrants importing new diseases, particularly venereal disease. Ardener remarks that when he first entered the Bakweri villages, he was surprised by the absence of the hordes of small children that one usually meets in traditional villages. The villages were comparatively empty—except for the zombies! (Ardener 1970b:147).

The **zombies,** called *nyongo,* were new to the Bakweri. They had been imported from outside. Zombies were rich. They had supernatural ways of earning money, and that was how they could afford the tin-roofed houses that could be seen around the community during this period of extreme poverty. There were a lot of zombies in Bakweri during the early 1950s. The frustrations and hardships of the people encouraged ordinary poor folk to see every rich person as a zombie.

But then times changed. In 1958 the Bakweri formed a banana co-operative, and the market price for their crop rose dramatically on the world market. Each householder came into a windfall of about $250, an enormous sum in this economy. The zombies disappeared overnight. Since every householder was now comparatively "rich," clearly it could not be true that all "rich" Bakweri were zombies. The frustrations and discontents that had bred and fostered the belief in zombies disappeared with the improvements in economic conditions. (The Bakweri community also spent close to $5,000 on witchfinding secrets to ensure that the zombies stayed away. They saw it as a prudent investment in insurance.)

But by 1963 the world market conditions changed again. The price for bananas plunged, and economic conditions deteriorated. Rumors started up again. They sounded bizarre but ominous: "Frenchmen were

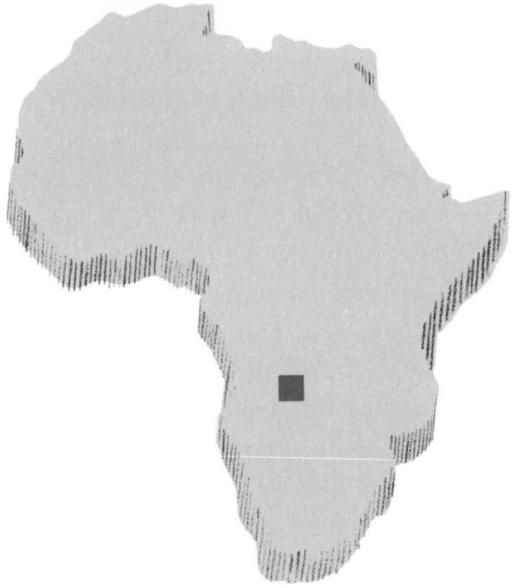

Figure 16.10
Sketch map of Africa,
showing where the Bakweri
live.

recruiting zombies to dig a deep-water port at the coast, and the zombies were soon going to take over the villages again. . . ."

The appearance and disappearance of the zombies is precisely correlated with the rise and fall in the price of bananas.

Social Control   Witchcraft does more than explain unpleasant and unexplained events to people and embody the suspicions and tensions that arise within a community or between communities. It is also a form of social control. In most societies, witches are punished if caught. The punishment may be mild—people may gossip about witches and treat them as outsiders. A witch may be unwelcome in social festivals and be discouraged from attending rituals.

In other societies the punishment may be much more severe. Lynchings of witches are not unknown. The life of a witch is perilous, lonely, and miserable in those many societies where they are not accorded special respect for their magical powers. Thus one social or political weapon at the disposal of members of a society is to accuse someone of being a witch. Unless witches have a special status of power, they will want to avoid being labeled a witch. They will divest themselves of the attributes of witchcraft, and conform to the standards and styles of those around them. A belief in witchcraft, then, can be a powerful and effective way of combating deviance.

Some societies believe that witches are the powerful, the rich, or the proud. This belief inhibits trying to rise in the social and economic system, for fear of being labeled a witch. Anthony Forge (1962, 1970)

Figure 16.11
A New Guinea "big man."

studied the Abelam of New Guinea, where there is great competition over becoming a "big man" in the community. "Big men" have many wives, and since women do most of the garden cultivation, they have increased food resources. They have more ritual objects, more followers in warfare, and can even hope, some day, to form their own villages. But they must always be on the lookout—they may be accused of sorcery, and their following will disappear.

Witchcraft accusations may also serve to stigmatize and control deviant behavior. The process usually goes like this. A person comes to be disliked or provokes the hostility of others. People begin to gossip. If the person or the family of kinfolk hear about the gossip, it serves as a warning; the accused can either start counter-gossip or change his or her behavior, defusing the hostility and thereby disproving the accusation.

If the person does not effectively counter the gossip, it will worsen, and all manner of imputations will be made about the purported witch. People will shun an accused witch and finally, even in a peaceful community, will drive him or her out.

Here is a moral tale told by the Baktaman people of New Guinea to the anthropologist Frederick Barth (1975:133). The lesson is clear: the Baktaman do not like difficult, bad-tempered, and cantankerous people. To get along in Baktaman, one must exercise control over one's behavior. The alleged witch's name was A.

A. was born among the Seltaman; he has always been a difficult and cantankerous person. When he finally got a wife he quarrelled with her all the time and finally beat her to death. Her kinsmen were angry and wanted to kill him in revenge, but nothing came of it. Having lost his wife, and alienated his affines, he became a wanderer and is constantly looking for a new wife. But no woman will have him, since he is vicious and old and known to be a sorcerer. A series of deaths are traced to him, in a repetitive pattern: He starts cultivating a man with a marriageable daughter, gives him taro and pig and sweet potato. Then he asks for the daughter. The parents are hesitant; the girl refuses. He then kills them by sorcery. One of the informants claimed to have escaped death under these circumstances because a friend saw A. put the food remains he had obtained into a fire with intent to kill; the friend managed to sneak in as soon as A. left and retrieved the food and threw it into the river, thus saving the informant's life. Several men have had similar narrow escapes. A. is arrogant and stops at nothing. For a while he was committing incest with his sister. When she finally categorically refused, he killed her with an arrow and threw her into the I river. He also copulates with dogs and pigs. The Baktaman finally became so incensed with him that he returned to Seltaman in the spring of 1968.

Witchcraft beliefs are as old as humanity. They explain why evil befalls innocent folk, and why there is social inequality and unfairness in the world. The operation of witchcraft defines friend and enemy, normal person and deviant. Witches are feared, but people also fear to be labeled

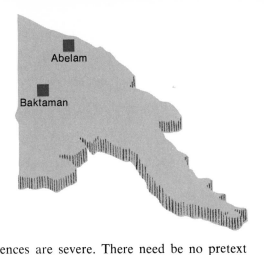

Abelam

Baktaman

as witches, for the consequences are severe. There need be no pretext for witchcraft, for sickness, death and misfortune occur all the time. They must be explained, and one's own people or one's neighbors will be held to account.

Beliefs in witchcraft are a two-edged sword. They give answers to unanswerable questions, and this provides comfort to the community. But they set people against one another and provide the basis for suspicions, even paranoia, which can sometimes be a heavy price to pay. Still, the price must not be too high for human groups, since witchcraft is found universally.

Summary

1. People in traditional societies are not more religious than people in modern societies. They appear that way because their religion is a way of talking and expressing themselves. It is an idiom, for them.

2. Religious beliefs are free to vary. They are not determined by other subsystems. They are strongly independent. The Otoro and Heiban live very close to each other in almost identical environments, with similar technologies and social systems. Yet their religions are very dissimilar.

3. Though the U.S. is a secular society, Americans believe in certain core ideas that are "religious" in tone. Cleanliness is one.

4. Religion is not just a set of beliefs. It is a system of explanations. The idea of the soul is an explanation of a universal human realization: the culturally defined self and the experienced self are not the same.

5. Religion provides explanations for unforeseeable and troublesome events in human experience, such as the failure of the monsoon to appear in south India. It is better to have a religious explanation than to have no explanation at all.

6. Magical thinking is as old as human culture and as widespread as the species. It is a means that people use to control events directly. Magic never fails because of the way it is constructed.

7. Witchcraft is the practice of harming other people at a distance through magical means. It, too, is as old as culture. It is a social phenomenon, linked to pressures in the social structure and to economic conditions.

8. Witchcraft serves as a mechanism of social control in two ways. It serves as a threatened punishment to those who are deviant in the community, and it keeps ordinary people in line as well.

Suggested Readings

Banton, Michael, ed. *Anthropological Approaches to the Study of Religion.* London: Tavistock, 1966.
> *An excellent collection of essays on the modern view of religion as a communicative and symbolic system.*

Goode, William J. *Religion Among the Primitives.* New York: Free Press, 1951.
> *Though over twenty-five years old, this still remains one of the most readable and comprehensive surveys of theories of religion.*

Lessa, William, and Vogt, Evon Z. *Reader in Comparative Religion: An Anthropological Approach.* 3rd ed. New York: Harper and Row, 1971.
> *Probably the best collection of readings ever published on any subject; has the classic article on every major topic of interest. Some of the longer-winded and prolix articles have been judiciously cut for a modern audience.*

Norbeck, Edward. *Religion in Primitive Society.* New York: Harper and Row, 1961.
> *A sensible book, comprehensive and well researched. Has an excellent bibliography too.*

Swanson, G. E. *The Birth of the Gods: The Origin of Primitive Beliefs.* Ann Arbor: University of Michigan Press, 1964.
> *A cross-cultural study of the origins of religion, in particular, the relationship between religion and the social order.*

Glossary

pseudocyesis   False pregnancy with all the signs of a normal pregnancy, without any fetus.

synesthesia—Experiencing with many senses at the same time, such as hearing, feeling, and seeing music.

vagina dentata   An emasculating spirit with a toothed vagina. Often associated with male hostility toward women.

zombie   A dead person who appears to be alive.

17

Kinship and Family

Introduction

In this chapter we will examine the logical beginnings, the underpinnings of human social organization. We first discuss the difference between society and culture, then social units and cultural units. Next we will look at what many anthropologists believe to be the essential ingredient without which human social organization as we know it could not exist—the **incest taboo.** This creates the basic distinction on which all organization is based: the *me/you* distinction, or the *my group/other group* distinction. The consequences of the incest taboo are seen in forms of kinship, family groupings, and marriage.

Society and Culture

First, some definitions. What is *society?* Very simply, it is the arrangement of warm bodies in space and time. What are *social units?* They are sometimes aggregations and sometimes groups of warm bodies that make up an organization larger than themselves. The warm bodies are an aggregation if they are an accidental gathering without any particular structure—a crowd at a football game or a swarm of moths circling a light bulb. A *group* has structure. An aggregation can turn into a group as, for example, when an aggregation of milling people turns into a lynch mob. As soon as a leader emerges, a set of ideas is transferred from one member to another, and the behavior of the aggregation takes on some *purpose,* it becomes a group.

We contrast society and social units with *culture* and **cultural units.** Culture is a set of ideas that is learned, patterned, and transmitted from generation to generation. Cultural units are ideas, often coded in language, that provide us with the raw material of cultural systems. A cultural unit is any category of events that we choose to recognize. Railroad trains, beauty, hippie, pine tree, autonomic nervous system, and poetry are all cultural units, fortunately coded in language (since if they were not they couldn't be written down).

When cultural units are coded in language, we call them *conscious cultural categories.* When they are not, we call them *unconscious* cultural categories. Unconscious cultural categories are often "differences that make a difference," to borrow a phrase from Gregory Bateson. For example, Berlin, Breedlove, and Raven (1968) found out that Tzeltal Indians sort out different kinds of corn because they know there is a difference that makes a difference, although they do not have any names for their groupings. Prison guards recognize a whole series of differences that make a difference between kinds of prisoners (or "residents"), but

Figure 17.1
Policemen, prison guards, and other people who deal with deviance have to make many decisions about categories of people based on a "seat-of-the-pants" feeling.

they cannot tell you what they are since they don't have names for them. They say (and the Tzeltal Indian would most likely echo their thoughts) that they have a "gut feeling" about certain kinds of prisoners that tells them either not to hassle them or, conversely, to give them a "write up" for the same kind of bad conduct. Judges and police officers report the same feelings, particularly police who must decide whether or not to make an arrest. All of these unconscious decisions reflect differences in cultural units.

The Incest Taboo in Human Society

The unique feature of human society that distinguishes it from any other society is the *incest taboo*—the existence of a rule that creates two classes of opposite-sex fellow species members: those with whom we may have sexual relations and, more importantly, those with whom we may not.

The incest taboo is universal in human society. It takes a variety of forms, but there is a universal human rule against sexual relations within the **nuclear family** (the elementary family composed of father, mother, and children). **Nuclear incest** is morally tabooed everywhere. There are examples of societies in which the rule against sexual relations extends to whole communities or large classes of relatives; and there is always an example, somewhere, of a society where sexual relations are permitted or even encouraged with every other close relative, perhaps the mother-in-law, a first cousin, a wife's sister, or an aunt. But the taboo on nuclear incest is universal.

The incest taboo—the existence of a rule that creates two classes of opposite-sex fellow species members: those with whom we may have sexual relations and, more importantly, those with whom we may not.

Figure 17.2
Sigmund Freud, one of the greatest minds of the 20th century, made the incest taboo a central idea in his theory of identification.

Causes of the Incest Taboo   The provocative question of *why* there is a prohibition on sexual relations between mother and son, father and daughter, and brother and sister has elicited a flood of comment and theorizing. Two psychological explanations are often given, and they are diametrically opposed.

The first explanation, which is Freud's, says that the incest taboo is to prevent boys' fulfilling a deep-seated, instinctual sexual urge to have sexual relations with their mothers or, secondarily, with their sisters in place of their mothers. Much of Freud's thinking was male-dominated, and his theory on maturation and the acquisition of a mature adult identity was linked to his views on mother-son incest. In his view, if the young boy is to arrive at a mature genital sexuality which includes the ability to form proper **object relations** (i.e., mature sexual relations with women outside his immediate family), he must somehow divest himself of the female identity acquired from his close childhood relationship with his mother and instead identify with his father. At first the child wants to dispose of the father and replace him. When the realization dawns that he cannot do this, he gets around it by identifying with the father, thereby possessing the mother through the father and establishing his male identity. The conflict he experiences during this period is called **Oedipal conflict,** after Oedipus, prince of Thebes, who unknowingly murdered his father and married his mother.

Freud's reasoning seems sound in broad outline, if not in detail. Clinical evidence from psychology has fairly well vindicated the existence of Oedipal conflict in Western society.

An opposing view, stated by Westermarck in his *History of Human Marriage* (1922), says that the incest taboo simply codifies the universal human feeling of uninterest, or lack of sexual arousal, toward members of the opposite sex with whom we are very familiar. There is also some interesting evidence for this conclusion drawn from experimental psychology and anthropology. Leslie Segner carried out an experiment measuring the level of sexual arousal among laboratory rats. She found that "distance lends enchantment": rats that were both brother-sister pairs and cage mates from birth showed less sexual arousal than rats who were cage mates from birth but not brother or sister. The latter in turn showed less interest than unrelated rats who were placed in the same cage close to the time of sexual maturity.

Some evidence that further supports Westermarck's position was gathered by Arthur Wolf, an anthropologist who studied in Taiwan, where the practice of arranged marriage persists in some families. When parents arrange marriages, the girl is brought to live in the husband's house when they are both very young, and they grow up like brother and sister. Wolf (1966) found that sexual relations were less satisfactory in these mar-

Figure 17.3
Arranged marriages are still found in the Far East, although the frequency is declining, particularly in Japan.

riages than in marriages between people who were not childhood associates. He measured sexual satisfaction by the frequency with which the men sought sex from prostitutes, the frequency of adultery among wives, divorce rates, and rates of sexual intercourse between spouses.

Just as the psychological evidence for the existence of the incest taboo is conflicting, the *sociological* evidence is also hard to evaluate. Malinowski made the sensible claim that if nuclear incest were permitted in the elementary family, sexual jealousy would tear the fabric of the family apart. The authority of the older generation, which is necessary for the transmission and preservation of the culture over time, would be destroyed, and societies that practiced nuclear incest would wipe themselves out. But the evidence is difficult and fragmentary. Now that people feel freer to report on their sexual behavior than they did in Malinowski's time more cases of "normal" incest are coming to light. A recent report in *New York* Magazine and other psychiatrists' reports in the press (hardly scientific sources, but scientific reports are hard to come by), indicate that brother-sister incest may be much more common than usually supposed.

Examples have been given of very close sexual relations between brother and sister that were carried on to the mutual satisfaction of the participants until such time as they grew out of it, that is, went off to college or found greater sexual satisfaction with partners outside the nuclear family. The case of father/daughter incest is less clear. In eleven cases studied by Kaufman, Peck and Tagiuri (1954), the family was very disorganized before the incest occurred; and in every case that was closely studied, the mother helped to arrange the relationship or condoned it by completely withdrawing. Very little is known about mother/son incest, and for that reason it is assumed to be much less frequent.

The biogenetic argument is clearest. It seems quite clear that hybridization or outbreeding is selectively advantageous in all breeding populations. One way we can account for the origin of the incest taboo is to assume that paleolithic man was as intelligent as we are and was able to observe the comparative disadvantages of inbreeding. Segner and Collins (1967) noted that roughly one-third of the myths involving incest recounted physical defects or sterility as a direct result. Much of the data on the deleterious genetic effects of incestuous unions has been collated by Lindzey (1967). He calculated that if inbreeding continued in a population for twenty generations, each member of the population would be genetically identical to every other, and therefore the adaptability of the population would be very low; if a change took place in the environmental conditions, the breeding population would have no resilience. Certainly the occurrence of lethal genes in inbred populations is higher than in outbreeding populations. Lindzey cites Adams and Neel's data comparing eighteen children of incestuous matings and eighteen children from similar homes and families without incest:

Adams and Neel (1957) . . . compared the children of 18 nuclear incest matings (12 brother-sister, and 6 father-daughter) with 18 control matings, rather closely matched with the incest group for age, weight, stature, intelligence, and socioeconomic status. At the end of 6 months they found that of the 18 children of incestuous union, five had died; two were severely mentally retarded, were subject to seizures and had to be institutionalized; one had a bilateral cleft palate; and three showed evidence of borderline intelligence (estimated IQ=70). Thus, only 7 of the 18 children were considered free of pathology and ready for adoption. On the other hand, none of the 18 control children had died or were institutionalized, none was severely mentally retarded and 15 were considered ready for adoption.

The problem is that such data look like plausible proof of the assertion that nuclear incest is so obviously harmful that cultured humans could hardly overlook the danger. But we cannot know whether the abnormalities of the children of the incestuous matings occurred because of genetic defects or because they were specially treated. Their parents were deviants, the children were abnormal as society defines abnormal, and we know enough about the relationship between people's feelings about themselves and illness (i.e., psychosomatic pathology) to know that we cannot disentangle the knot entirely. But if the effects are as dramatic as they appear to be, it does not seem likely to have escaped the notice of culture-bearing humans.

Effects of the Incest Taboo   Whatever brought about the incest taboo, it has one immediate result: the formation of alliances. If I cannot marry my sister but must marry yours, then I have to create a system of social classification that distinguishes my group from your group. The idea that our groups *exchange* women (or men—it doesn't matter) means that we are allied. Once the incest taboo is established, then it has a positive selective advantage that is not only genetic but also sociological, political, and evolutionary. Wolves are successful in the hunt because they can cooperate. Culture-bearing human beings are successful in the hunt because not only can they cooperate and communicate, but they also can call on the ties they have with those with whom they exchange spouses, thereby creating a web of alliances that gives them a selective advantage (other things being equal) over groups without this custom.

In short, the incest taboo, like other characteristics defining humanity, is deeply seated. The important thing is not to account for the origin of the incest taboo, but to examine its consequences so that we can come to understand the basis of human society.

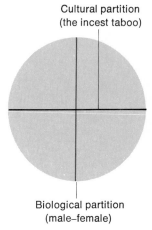

Figure 17.4
This Venn diagram shows how the world of human beings is partitioned first biologically (by sex distinctions) and then culturally (by the incest taboo).

Cultural partition
(the incest taboo)

Biological partition
(male–female)

The Family

The smallest society that can exist is two-person. The elementary social unit is the *dyad,* an interacting group of two persons. The elementary unit of social analysis is the *relation* between two people. Social analysis deals with relations.

The most elementary form of complex **dyadic relations** is *the family,* which in one form or another is almost universal. The family is a set of relations; the nuclear family consists of six such relations: father-son, father-daughter, mother-son, mother-daughter, husband-wife, and brother-sister. We call these elementary relationships *primary,* and we abbreviate them in the language of kinship as F, M, B, Z, S, D, H, W to indicate "father," "mother," "brother," "sister," "son," "daughter," "husband," and "wife." And we diagram the relationships in a genealogical plate as follows on page 418.

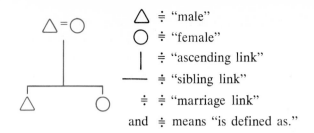

$\triangle \doteq$ "male"

$\bigcirc \doteq$ "female"

$| \doteq$ "ascending link"

$\underline{\quad} \doteq$ "sibling link"

$\doteq \doteq$ "marriage link"

and $\doteq$ means "is defined as."

We used to think that the nuclear family was universal, partly because we knew that kinship relations are universal. No known society lacks a kinship system, and kinship systems are made up of kinfolk, who are related to each other in *genealogical* ways. Genealogy is a way of analyzing our kinship relations by using the relationships of the nuclear family. For example, if I want to list all those relationships that qualify for the kin term "uncle" in my dialect of American English, we can write them out very simply as

$$\text{"Uncle"} = \left\{ \text{FB} \cup \text{MB} \cup \text{FZH} \cup \text{MZH} \right\}$$

which is a short way of saying that my uncle is one or all of the following sets of relations: "father's brother," "mother's brother," "father's sister's husband," "mother's sister's husband."

But although this logic may seem right, it doesn't hold up under extensive ethnographic examination. It is true that every society has a kinship system, that we can analyze kinship relations genealogically, and that our system of genealogical reckoning is based on the six primary relations that define the nuclear family. It seems logical to suppose that the Paleolithic peoples didn't pick these out of thin air, but based their system of reckoning on primary relationships. But so far as contemporary peoples are concerned, there are too many exceptions to the nuclear family to allow us to state categorically that it is universal.

The Nayar Do Not Have Nuclear Families

The best known exception is the Nayar people, a warrior subcaste of Malabar (India), who live in what Americans would call "absent-father" households. Kathleen Gough had to reconstruct the Nayars' ethnography, but it is clear that the family is made up of a woman and her children. In place of a "father," there is the mother's brother. A young Nayar girl is married after she reaches menarche, but she doesn't live with her husband, nor does he come to live with her. He might have sexual relations with her on their bridal night, but then again he might not. But his brothers and the fellow clan members of his generation would have rights of sexual access to her. Confusion over who is sleeping with the "wife" is avoided by leaving

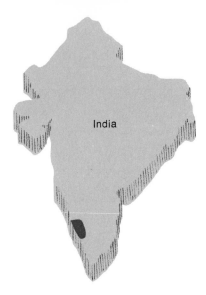

**Figure 17.5
India, showing where the
Nayar of Malabar live.**

a spear outside the door of the hut to indicate "occupied." The "wife" is permitted to take on lovers, while the men of her group are equally free to roam Nayar as visiting husbands or passing lovers in other clan groups.

Beside the Nayar, numerous other cases of **matrifocal households** are found throughout Latin America and parts of Africa, where the family unit is made up of a mother and her children. Thus it seems safe to conclude that the nuclear family is not universal.

The Sociological Basis of Kinship

When we use terms like "father" or "mother," or define uncle as "father's brother," it sounds as if we are talking about biological relations. We have a cultural belief, for example, that both the mother and the father contribute some "biogenetic material" to their offspring. We base this premise on routine statements that Americans make about kinship relations. Americans say things like, "Imagine if she gets her father's looks and her mother's brains!" which are supposed to be funny, but which can only be meaningful if we assume that both the father and the mother contribute. The fact of the matter is that kinship is sociological in nature.

Take the term "father." It is a kin term in American English. It implies that the male in question transmitted genetic materials to the child through a woman, usually the mother. But what if the mother had sexual relations with other men before or during the marriage? Can we be sure that the mother's husband is indeed the "father" of the child in

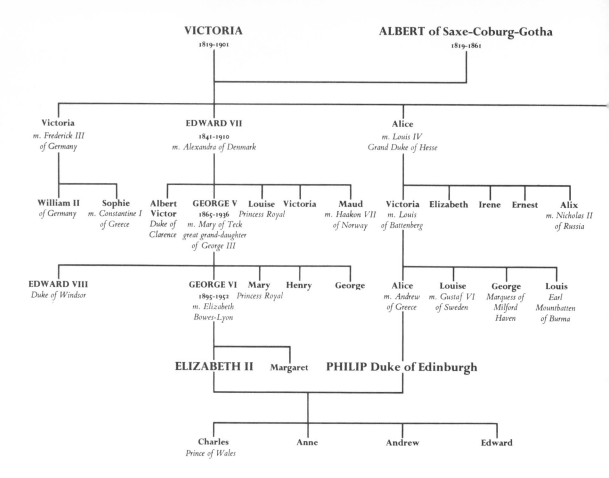

question? Obviously not. Paternity laws exist, but paternity is very hard to prove or disprove. That is why Roman law stated clearly: "The father is the mother's husband." This practice is generally followed in American society. All the trauma of telling a child that he or she was adopted derives from our notion that it is somehow unnatural to be brought up by people whom one regards as mother and father, but with whom one does not share this biogenetic substance. For the sake of analysis, we can distinguish between the *social father* (or *pater*) and the *genetic father,* the man whose identity may be known only to his confessor or psychiatrist, but who contributed the genes.

Some societies go further. In some parts of Australia, for example, there is a role for the "firestick father," a person designated by the society as the one who contributed the spirit essence that gave birth to the child.

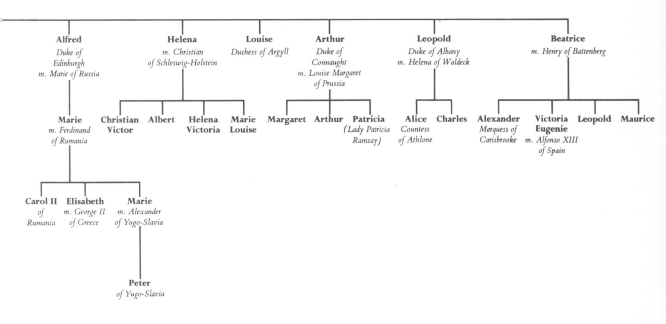

In this case, we call the "firestick father" the *genitor;* that is, the person who is socially recognized to have played a critical role in engendering the child. So now there are three terms: **pater, genitor,** and **genetic father.** The first two are socially recognized, and the third may or may not be known. The point is that for a biologically based theory of kinship, only the last would be important. In contrast, what we record on our kinship charts and genealogies is the *pater,* the socially defined father.

A little thought will indicate that the same ideas can be applied to the mother, yielding **mater, genetrix,** and **genetic mother.** If you think that the last two distinctions could never matter, you have not read your history and seen the great lengths to which royalty went to ensure that a baby wasn't smuggled into the royal bedchamber in a bed warmer, and that the queen was both *genetrix* and *genetic mother* of the royal heir.

Figure 17.6
Blood lines like these are very important in American and European society because people believe in heredity: the transmission of "essences" down the blood lines.

The genitor—that is, the person who is socially recognized to have played a critical role in engendering the child.

Consequences of Kinship Beliefs

Royal bed warmers seem quaint, but some of the other consequences of our beliefs about kinship are not so quaint. Americans believe that the same person should be *pater, genitor,* and *genetic father.* This is what causes the emotional scene when adopted parents reveal that their children are not quite "theirs," despite the clear fact that they have played the only important social roles of parents to the children.

Another consequence of our cultural belief is our definition of illegitimacy. How on earth, in a rational world, can a child be "illegitimate"? "Children are children," say most non-Western people, adding, "Some city people talk about 'children of the street,' meaning children whose mothers had sex with other men, but this is nonsense. Children need and always have the love of parents and kin: the father and mother will bring them up!" But Americans, with our cultural beliefs in the importance of biogenetic substances, say things like, "Genes will out," thereby endowing the child with a set of expectations about his or her behavior that can be at best confusing and at worst profoundly destructive.

Some people respond to any questioning of the whole idea of legitimacy versus illegitimacy by citing the problem of inheritance. Somehow (to them) it is wrong that inheritance not follow the "bloodline," from which the "illegitimate child" is excluded. But how can the inheritance of genes be equated with the inheritance of property? Rules of property transfer across generations presumably exist to minimize debate and conflict over valuables, not to prop up some biological theory. One might just as well say that the chairmanship of the board of General Motors should pass down some bloodline. Property can pass across generations in any number of ways, all of them sociologically defined. It can pass from mother's brother to sister's son (in a matrilineal society), or it can pass from father to father's younger brother (in some patrilineal societies), or it can revert to the state (as it partially does under our tax laws).

The notion of illegitimacy is important, say others (including some policymakers), for the maintenance of the family and the proper rearing of children. This is nonsense. True, if children are reared without any male closely affiliated with them, it may be damaging. But to say that a child "born out of wedlock" is somehow deprived of the companionship of senior-generation males is to assume that the mother belongs to some kind of cloistered all-female kin group. As we pointed out in the Nayar case (where the child never knows or sees his or her father), there are plenty of males around to relate to: all the males of the mother's matrilineal group, for starters.

But the notion persists. A hotly debated government report, the

Moynihan Report, indicated that the basis of the problems of black Americans lay in the illegitimacy rate, which was (in 1963) 23.6 percent for blacks compared with 3.1 percent for whites. As Jones and Ryan have pointed out, this may only mean that white society is so sick that it wants to rid itself of its most precious asset—its own children—through the use of abortion (then illegal), Enovid, or adoption, sentiments and mechanisms that are not precisely shared by the black community.

The anthropologist wonders why the argument arose in the first place. First, how do we know that the symbol "father" means precisely the same in white and black cultures? If the argument can be made that there is a black culture and a black kinship system that includes symbols such as "mother," "father," "son," and "daughter," who can say—without the appropriate culturally sensitive study—that the symbol "father" means the same in both? We would certainly not make the claim that *padre de familia* ("father of the family") means exactly the same to *chicanos* or Latin Americans as "father" means to North Americans. We know better than that!

"But," the argument proceeds, "we are not talking about symbols or meanings, we are talking about absent fathers and broken families." Consider the idea of "absent father." Who is more "absent"—the black male who visits his children, sees them in the street, recognizes them, and demands their respect, or the father whose family lives in the suburbs while he commutes to work and (in the cliché) drinks three martinis on his way home at night, arriving just in time to put the kids to bed and fall into the television set?

What about "broken families"? Possibly the family is somewhat differently defined among lower-class blacks (about whom these studies are written), and possibly they wouldn't know they were living in a broken family unless someone called it that. It could well be the case that the "broken family" is a middle-class white idea, appropriate only for middle-class white culture. Divorce that leaves a woman with small children stranded in a house in the suburbs, in a society that lives in couples and denies social lives to singles, is different from divorce or separation or even abandonment in a society where mothers with children are not seen to be impaired in any way, but rather strong, normal, competent, and not deviant in the slightest.

Variation in Family Form

Families in the rest of the world differ, for the most part, from our nuclear model. First of all, the preponderance of societies in the world (54 percent

Figure 17.7
Divorce can leave a nuclear
family isolated and desolate.
But in this (extended)
family the husband or wife
and children will have
plenty of company if there
is a divorce.

in Textor's *Cross-Cultural Summary*) live in **extended families,** families in which at least three generations are represented. An even greater preponderance (79 percent) live in societies where there is plural marriage (almost always polygyny, the practice that favors the marriage of a man with more than one wife). Even independent families, like our own, favor polygyny more than three to one over our practice of monogamy (having one spouse).

The single most frequent form of family organization is the **patrilineal extended family,** which consists of an older couple, their married sons and wives, their married sons' children, and their own unmarried children. Less frequently found, but still more common than our nuclear family, is the **matrilineal extended family,** which is made up of an older couple, their married daughters and their husbands, their married daughters' children, and their own unmarried children. Worldwide, by far the most societies seem to prefer extended families.

Compared with the nuclear family, the extended family has both advantages and drawbacks. Its advantages can best be seen from the point of view of the child, whose aunts and uncles are around (usually given "parentlike" status by being called "mother" and "father") along with the grandparents, with whom warm, close relationships are found worldwide. The child can turn to these people for support, love, comfort, and perhaps most important, help in understanding the parents. In our society it is a big step to go outside the nuclear family for such things.

There are drawbacks, too. Living in an extended family means having to get along with a lot of people. Privacy is at a minimum. To be sure, people who are brought up in extended families don't have the same feelings about privacy as we do. Anthropologists' children, for example, find it unnatural to come home from the field and go back to sleeping alone, after becoming used to sleeping five or six to a bed or a communal sleeping mat. There is a trade-off between a sense of security and a sense of privacy.

There can also be conflicts between the generations. The Irish family was notable for such conflicts: the son waiting around for the old man to die so that he could inherit and become a man in his own right. Some social scientists feel that the heavy drinking and brawling of Irish males arose from the frustrations involved. Sometimes, though, the children don't have to wait around for the father to die: there are societies where the rules state that the rights and obligations of full manhood pass to the heir when the heir comes of age. And that can bring trouble. In one African case (the people of the Nuba hills), there was a rule that the heir (in this case the sister's son, since the families were matrilineal) inherited before the elder was ready to give up the political, executive rights that he

had previously owned. Sometimes such "retirement" was required before the age of thirty. The result was witchcraft accusations (which are a symptom of tremendous hostility): each man accusing the other directly or indirectly of trying to commit murder, one to gain his rightful place, the other not to lose it.

Looking at family arrangements from the point of view of the individual, the choice between a nuclear family and an extended one depends on one's preference for privacy, independence, and mobility over security, dependence, and a sense of rootedness. Communes, rap groups, and ethnic, social, and political groups are attempts to rebuild the feeling of extended kinship in America; and the use of the terms "brother" and "sister" among group members reflects that feeling of lost kinship. We do not believe that the independent nuclear family is a capitalist plot to destroy the fabric of society and make labor as mobile, and thereby dependent on employers and capital, as possible. But it does seem true that industrialization and urbanization break down extended family arrangements. If kinship relationships are fundamental to the good life, and one is an optimist, one can take encouragement from the fact that extended family arrangements predominate throughout the world, and that only in the recent past have these arrangements broken down.

Marriage and the Family

Marriage is impossible to define, really. A traditional definition taken from *Notes and Queries* (a how-to-do-it anthropological field manual that tells you what-it-is-when-you-are-looking-at-it) states that marriage is a "union between a man and a woman such that the children born to the woman are recognized legitimate offspring of both parents." So marriage is the institution that provides the child with a *mater* and a *pater*. More importantly, it is an *alliance* between two groups. Recall, if you will, the discussion of incest, the rule that forbids certain classes of people from having sexual intercourse. There is another, quite different, rule found in every society that defines the group from whom one can draw a spouse (husband or wife). The rules of **exogamy** and **endogamy** vary widely from society to society. Americans are most sensitive to the rules of endogamy, if not entirely consciously so. Every American parent can tell his or her child the kind of spouse that is suitable for the family. In England (among the middle and upper classes) parents are explicit: "Are you sure he is of our class and background, my dear?" In the United States, except among certain ethnic groups, they are less explicit: "Are you sure he would make you happy, my dear; do you share enough interests and friends?" In both America and England, exogamous rules are invoked only when one petitions to marry one's first cousin.

In a word, the *endogamous* rules state how extensive the "spouse-pool" is. *Exogamous* rules state how close to the family you can get and not break the rule. In traditional south India, for example, both endogamous and exogamous rules were well defined. The rule of endogamy stated that you had to marry within your caste or sometimes your subcaste: Brahmins do not marry Sweepers. The rule further stated that you had to marry a certain class of relative: either a person from a kinship class of which one member was your mother's brother's daughter or your elder sister's daughter. The exogamous rule stated that you had to marry outside your own line.

Marriage, then, is constrained by exogamous and endogamous rules; it serves to legitimize the offspring and give them a *pater* and a *mater,* and to bring about an alliance between the groups that exchanged spouses. It should not be forgotten that in all societies marriage is an exchange between groups.

Plural Marriage and Its Problems   By plural marriage we mean cultural practices that favor marriage to multiple spouses. When one man marries a number of women, we call the practice **polygyny;** and when one woman marries a number of men, we call it **polyandry.** When a number of women marry a number of men, we call the practice *group marriage*. Polygyny is very common, polyandry extremely rare, and group marriage very doubtful, although we will describe the usual candidate case, and you can draw your own conclusions.

Since plural marriage ("bigamy") is a rare occurrence in American society—indeed a crime—we are not accustomed to thinking of its advantages and disadvantages. Yet the most common form of marriage in the world is polygyny (slightly over 50 percent). It is never the case that everyone in a polygynous society has more than one wife: if it were, then the birthrate would have to favor females over males in great disproportion, while in fact, in most societies, more boys than girls are born. Polygyny is achieved either by delaying the age of marriage for males, so that a relatively larger number of younger females are available for marriage, or by permitting sexual access to the wives of older men on a formal or informal basis to younger men. There is no society in the world where sexual access is regularly denied to any large class of people.

On a more mundane level, we might assume that since marriage and sex are so closely linked in our society (divorce, until relatively recently, was only possible on the grounds of adultery), there would be raging battles among the women over the man. Generally this is not the case, for there are a number of ways of handling the stresses involved. There may be a senior wife who is the executive officer of the domestic group. She indicates with whom the man will have sex (not excluding herself) and at what time, making sure that each wife shares sufficiently so that there is a degree of harmony and peace in the household. Or there may be a rule that the man will visit each wife in turn so that none is neglected. Or there may be some form of institutionalized adultery for the wives.

There are, however, societies in which there is co-wife hostility; our intuitions about the difficulties of having several wives are not totally in error.

One good example is the east African tribal group, the Gusii, which has been described by Robert LeVine (1963). The Gusii are patrilineal and practice polygyny. In Nyasongo, the community where LeVine did an important part of his work, fifteen men are monogamists, eleven men have two wives, and one has three wives. None of the precautionary rules just suggested is followed. The husband sleeps with whomever he pleases, usually the younger or youngest of his wives. Wives are not permitted to have extramarital relations, though husbands are. The wives fear the husband's rejection, for the only way they can achieve status in the society is by producing children. Husbands are not punished for refusing

Figure 17.9
Gusii

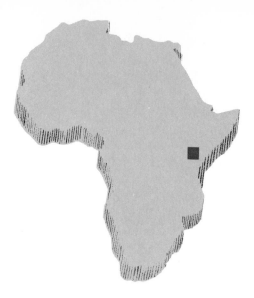

to sleep with their wives, and first wives are opposed to their husband's taking a second wife. LeVine reports:

Dissension among co-wives is one of the most common themes in Gusii folklore. One proverb is: "Another child-bearer is like an ancestor spirit at the outside wall." This is interpreted as meaning that secondary wives bring hatred which can result in murder and invoke the wrath of the spirits. There is a special word, *engareka,* which means "hatred between co-wives."

Dissension is particularly prevalent when the co-wives are close in age; when there is a great disparity in age, the younger accepts being ordered about by the older and in turn expects motherly treatment.

Generally, however, co-wives work together and, although they may be subordinate to the husband in male-dominated societies, often form coalitions against the husband to get what they want. In parts of west Africa, women do much of the trading. There polygyny is positively advantageous to the commercial success of the household, since the husband can be kept content, the children can be looked after, and one of the wives can easily be freed for trading trips and commercial activity.

We dwell on polygyny, not just because it is so common, but also because Americans and Westerners regard it as some kind of "peculiar" institution. Polygynists, particularly those who live in extended families, would regard our ways as being equally peculiar. If they learned anthropological jargon, they might call American society one characterized by

Figure 17.10
Two polygynous families,
one from the Mato Grasso
and the other from Mormon
Country, in Utah, three
generations ago.

"serial monogamy and matrifocality," since children (usually) stay with the mother after a divorce, and both men and women take on a number of spouses, one at a time. These polygynists might well comment on the family rows that occur over extramarital affairs, and wonder why we do not adopt polygyny also, since then the hostility is kept within the family, and "the other woman" (who pops up so regularly in advice columns) is at least married to the husband.

Polyandry   Polyandrous societies, where one woman has a number of husbands, practically never occur. (There are four recorded cases in Murdock's *Ethnographic Survey,* which is a sample of 862 of the world's cultures.)

Sometimes polyandry is almost a casual arrangement, as among the Kadar of south India. While there were two cases where one woman was married to two men, within the same society more men had plural wives. In addition, divorce rates were high, as were remarriages to previous spouses. Although we cannot judge directly, and the ethnographic data is bad, it does not seem too far-fetched to suggest that the Kadar were rather casual about all household, procreative, and sexual arrangements. Their society was small, and they lived in an abundant environment that did not require a tightly organized productive group. That is why they are sometimes cited as an example of group marriage.

The Toda, on the other hand, are probably the best known and best documented case of polyandry—but it was a special case of polyandry, since the wife shared a group of brothers. Thus the term **fraternal polyandry** is used for the Toda, versus **nonfraternal polyandry** among the Kadar. When a woman was married, she automatically became the wife of the group of brothers, born and unborn, to which her husband belonged. Jealousy seems not to have occurred, although one must always be suspicious of comments such as this, since ethnography tends to be male-biased. Sleeping arrangements were facilitated by having the brother who was engaged in sexual activity leave his cloak outside the door of the bamboo hut that served as dormitory and workplace during the day.

We have not discussed every family form, and type of marriage in the world because the number and variety of forms that anthropologists can define is so very large. If the social scientist wants to include every different wrinkle, then he or she is going to end up with an enormous number of types. Just to give one example: if you want to distinguish between patrilineal extended households where inheritance passes down the male line to all children, and patrilineal families where it passes only to one son, then you can use the term **famille souche** for the latter case. This is a definitional problem, and as a rule, we have been trying to stay out of arguments over definitions because we feel that if it is important

Figure 17.11
A Toda polyandrous family.

for your understanding and research to make fine distinctions and create a number of types, then you should go ahead and do it. If not, then do not. Sometimes anthropologists forget, when we get into arguments over whether the *X* people have extended families or not, that we are the ones who are making up these types. We should use them only to communicate our data accurately and, as a general rule, use as few definitions as allowable.

Summary

1. The incest taboo is the foundation of human society. It is a cultural distinction that creates the basis for a morally ordered social group.

2. No one knows why or how the incest taboo came to be. Freud believed that it was a powerful social rule that prevented us from doing what we dearly wished to do: have sexual relations with close relatives, our parents in particular. Other people, such as Wolf and Segner, think that our close relations with parents and siblings mute our sexual feelings for them.

3. However the incest taboo originated, and whatever sustains it, it is universal. Worldwide, it serves to make people form families and alliances.

4. One might think that the nuclear family (mother, father, children)

was universal, but it is not. The Nayar are the classic case of matrifocal households.

5. Kinship is based *not* on biology, but on sociology, or social relations and social definitions.

6. The most prevalent family form around the world is the extended family.

7. The most prevalent form of marriage around the world is polygyny. There are problems to plural marriages, but on the whole they work well.

Suggested Readings

Fox, Robin. *Kinship and Marriage*. New York: Penguin Books, 1967.
This is one of the best and simplest introductions to the study of social organization in anthropology that we have. Written in a delightful style, and clear as a bell.

Gearing, Fred. *The Face of the Fox*. Chicago: Aldine Publishing Co., 1970.
A fine and sensitive study of the Fox Indians. It does not deal with the family and social organization exclusively, but much of the material is relevant to the topics we have covered in this chapter.

Gough, Kathleen. "The Nayars and the Definition of Marriage." *Journal of the Royal Anthropological Institute* 89 (1959).
This was the article that forced people to change their minds about the universality of the nuclear family. It is reprinted in almost every book on marriage and the family.

Schneider, David M. *American Kinship: A Cultural Account*. Englewood Cliffs, N.J.: Prentice Hall, 1968.
American culture as seen by an anthropologist who has studied social organization around the world. It should give the reader the feeling that someone is peering over his or her shoulder and writing about everyone's life.

Turnbull, Colin. *The Mountain People*. New York: Simon and Schuster, 1972.
One of the most disturbing ethnographies we have had in years. The Ik, who are studied, seem to lack a kinship system in any meaningful sense. They are a thoroughly unpleasant people who may well not survive in their present form very long.

Glossary

cultural units   The ideas that a society has and uses to recognize events. They can be conscious or unconscious; they can be expressed in the spoken language, but need not be.

dyadic relation   A relationship between two people or two groups.

endogamous rule (or **rule of endogamy**)   The rule that states how distant or how different a person can be and still be a potential spouse.

engareka   A Gusii word meaning hatred between co-wives.

exogamous rule (or **rule of exogamy**)   The rule that states how close, or similar, a person can be and still be a potential spouse.

extended family   Family arrangement in which there are at least three generations of relatives living together.

famille souche   The family consisting of a couple with only one married child and their grandchildren by this child.

fraternal polyandry   The cultural practice of a woman marrying multiple husbands who are brothers.

genetic father   The man who actually engaged in the act of sexual intercourse that led to the conception of a particular child.

genetic mother   The woman who actually engaged in the act of sexual intercourse that led to the conception of a particular child.

genetrix   The woman who is socially recognized to have borne the child.

genitor   The man who is socially recognized to have engendered the child.

mater   One's social, not necessarily genetic, mother.

matrifocal household   A family made up of a mother and her children.

matrilineal extended family   A family made up of a couple, their married daughters (and grandchildren by these daughters) and their unmarried children of both sexes.

nonfraternal polyandry   The cultural practice of a woman marrying multiple husbands who are not brothers.

nuclear family   The family consisting of a socially defined mother, father, and children.

nuclear incest   Incest with a member of the nuclear family (mother-son, father-daughter, or brother-sister relations).

object relations   In Freudian theory, object relations mean mature sexual relations outside the family.

Oedipal conflict   In Freudian theory, Oedipal conflict refers to the ambivalence ("love/hate") that the maturing son feels toward his father. It peaks around age 4.

pater   The person who is socially defined to be the social father of the child.

patrilineal extended family   A family consisting of a couple, their married sons (and grandchildren by these sons) and their unmarried children of both sexes.

18

Symbolic and Sociopolitical Organizations

Introduction

Taken as a whole, human beings organize themselves in a surprisingly limited number of ways. Every individual is concerned with getting himself or herself a decent life and livelihood, and everywhere there are rules about how to do things properly.

But what is social organization? As we suggested in the last chapter, it is the shape, form, or configuration that warm bodies take in space and time, like the arrangement of chess pieces on a chess board. More importantly for anthropologists, social organization refers to the organization of social *symbols* and of *ideas* about social categories and how they fit together or conflict with each other. The most important thing about social symbols is that they are *exchanged* and that they have *value*. The study of social organization can be called the study of the exchange of social symbols, these being symbols that refer to people.

Marriage and the Exchange of Symbols

We often forget that we are engaged in the exchange of symbols because we take this process so much for granted that we can afford to ignore it. When we think of the idea of "mother," we can easily forget that we aren't talking about our flesh-and-blood mother who loved us, looked after us, and was unlike any other person in the world; we are speaking of a *class* of women, that is, an idea that has symbolic value. Or consider a wedding, which is a ritual in our society that is replete with symbolism. It is certainly true that our good friend Alice, who was our classmate at high school, is marrying George, the business major, and they are warm bodies in space, all right. More important to the anthropologist is the fact that a wedding is taking place. Instead of seeing George and Alice he sees two people kneeling together and is told that they are "bride" and "groom"; furthermore, he is immediately questioned as to whether he is "bride's side" or "groom's side," because they sit on different sides of a place called a "church" where this thing called a "wedding" is taking place. Afterwards the "bride" gives the "groom" a ring, and he reciprocates. The anthropologist's informants tell him that the ring symbolizes the perfect symmetric union of the pair, as symbolized by the circular form of the bauble. As the liturgy goes forward, the informant tells him that another exchange is taking place, which he cannot even see: it is the exchange of vows. He tape-records it and later, with the help of a trained informant, transcribes and translates it. He finds out that the bride is promising sexual and domestic services in return for sustenance and

Figure 18.1
American weddings are
organized into symbolic
categories.

maintenance. He hasn't even seen those functionless silver things that
are displayed in a nearby room, which represent the repayment of a
previous exchange from the newly married couple's parents to some other
"relative" or "friend" or a "social debt" that will be repaid at some
unspecified later date. These are the wedding gifts, and their symbolic
value is emphasized by the fact that they are rarely used, and then only
on ritual occasions. Later he will see the sharing and exchanging of food at
the "wedding breakfast," and will be told that people in this culture don't
all drink from the same glass, as in many others, but give a token of the
same act by clinking their glasses together.

These events, acts, and entities are symbols: food and sex being the
most powerful symbols in most cultures. This is not too surprising, since
they are the most basic prerequisites for the maintenance of the society
and the continuance of the culture.

One of the ways that the anthropologist would characterize American marriages is to use the word *homogamous,* meaning "like marries
like." The reason we can intuit that **homogamy** is a rule in American
culture is that nonhomogamous marriages make the newspapers, whether
they be January-September marriages of an older man with a younger
woman or, more rarely (and suspiciously), vice versa, or marriages across
caste or religious lines—"mixed marriages"—which, as Archie Bunker
and clucking dowagers know, "do not work out." One of the negotiations
that takes place before, during, and after marriages concerns the intri-
cacies of the "homogamy game," which is played by all parties to the
marriage: husband-wife, the immediate families of both, and the kindreds

on either side. Of course, one marries for love, but it's easier to love people like yourself than people who are very different. The "homogamy rule" is another way of stating the rule of *endogamy* and is never explicitly stated in American culture: there is no law requiring it, and laws that tried to (such as the miscegenation statutes) have been declared unconstitutional. It's a rule, nevertheless, implicit in the way that Americans, English, and western Europeans think, talk, and act when it comes to marriage.

Another thing that the anthropologist would inquire about is the relationship between husband and wife before marriage, and he would discover that they weren't relatives. Most Westerners believe that close relatives should not marry, even though they don't talk about the rules of *exogamy* the way the anthropologist does. The rule is so taken for granted that we practically never talk about it, except to counsel our children that they cannot marry their siblings (brothers and sisters) for reasons that are never really explained, except sometimes by saying that the babies would all be deformed. Exogamous proscriptions vary from state to state in North America; in some places they extend to first cousins, defined as the children of one's parents' full brothers or sisters.

Another rule for spouse choice in American culture is that there supposedly aren't any rules. One marries for love, and love is a powerful symbol in American culture, since it is the binding force that keeps families and marriages together and creates social stability at the domestic level. Men and women are free to decide to marry, and the only people who are immediately concerned (again supposedly) are the families of the marrying pair. American culture is unusual in the sense that the exchange that takes place in marriage is sharply limited. For example, no explicitly named kinship relationship is set up between the parents of the marrying pair: they refer to each other through **teknonymy,** that is, by tracing the relationship to each other through their children: Alice's folks talk about their affines as "George's family."

Another Homogamous Case

A very nice contrast with homogamous marriage in western European countries is seen in the marriage customs of the Middle East, where homogamy is also practiced. There the exogamous rule states that you cannot marry your full brother or sister (unless you are an ancient Pharaoh), but that you should marry—and are encouraged, induced, and pressured into marrying—a very close "brother" or "sister" who is a member of your own group and is drawn from a pool of spouses of whom one's father's brother's child is a member. This is called **patrilateral parallel-cousin marriage.** The marrying pair are partrilateral parallel cousins: *patrilateral,* because they trace their relationship through their respective fathers (if I marry my father's brother's daughter, then she is marrying her father's brother's son); *parallel,* because the person I marry is a child of a sibling of the same sex as my linking parent (my mother's sister's child and my father's brother's child are both my **parallel cousins).** If the person I married were the child of a sibling of the opposite sex of my linking parent, then I would be marrying my **cross cousin** (my mother's brother's child and my father's sister's child are my cross cousins). Parallel cousin marriage is as close as one can come in human society to marrying a sister. These marriages are often called "endogamous marriages," and the systems of group alignment that take place as a result of such marriages are called *endogamous systems.* This term could be confusing, because every system of marriage is endogamous (has boundaries), but the term is applied to the Middle Eastern case because marriage takes place *within* the group, and the group in this case is the **patrilineage.**

There seems to be a contradiction here. Recall, if you will, the dispute between Freud and Westermarck about the incest taboo. Westermarck's hypothesis, that we have a natural lack of sexual interest in our sisters and all people of the opposite sex with whom we were raised, seems to be invalidated by the practice of patrilateral parallel-cousin marriage. But in fact, a closer look seems to support Westermarck's thesis that distance lends enchantment, for Middle Eastern society takes great care to keep the sexes apart. In traditional communities, women are secluded, kept away from the men, and the novelty that was spoken of as being linked to sexual arousal is maintained artificially by a cultural ruse. Some work by Robert Fernea and one of the authors indicated that where women were very secluded, you would also find durable marriages. If seclusion was not so marked, you found either a reduction in the number of patrilateral parallel-cousin marriages or a rise in the frequency of divorce.

The Kinds of Groups that Exchange in Marriage

In describing the American wedding, we used two terms to refer to the groups involved: the immediate family and the kindred (or better, the "relatives on each side"). In the Middle East, there is a different way of defining the group, one that is found in a plurality of societies in the world—the *patrilineage.* This is a group of people who at birth are recruited to a well-defined group by emphasizing the tie between *men,* rather than women or both sexes. The use of the word "lineage" emphasizes the metaphor of a vertical line of men around whom the group is organized. In traditional genealogical diagrams, men are shown as triangles and women as circles, so we can diagram the "core" of the patrilineage as a line of men, like Figure 18.2.

**Figure 18.2
The "core" of the patrilineage.**

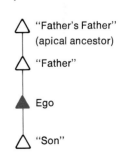

"Father's Father" (apical ancestor)

"Father"

Ego

"Son"

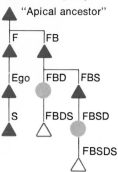

Figure 18.3
A patrilineal group.

"Apical ancestor"

F | FB

Ego | FBD | FBS

S | FBDS | FBSD

FBSDS

Symbolic essences are passed down the line of men: in this case it is that bundle of symbols which we can abbreviate as "membership in the group." This symbolic bundle passes through all men from an ancestor at the top of the line, the **apical ancestor,** and is transmitted *through* all men to their descendants, and *to* all women, where it stops. In the next diagram, the shaded symbols are members of the group who are in the lineage, while the unshaded are those who are not. You will notice immediately that membership passes through the lineage like electricity through an open circuit, but stops with the women (the circuit is closed).

The depth of patrilineages varies from society to society, and indeed from community to community. In some Arab societies the depth reaches up to fifteen generations before it fades off into mythical history; that is, people can trace all their patrilineal relatives going back fifteen generations. In other societies, New Guinea, for example, the patrilineages are only remembered going back four generations.

Dualism, Opposition, and Exchange

Anthropologists became fascinated by endogamous systems because they seemed anomalous, since they were not found anywhere else in the world. The rest of the world works on a *binary* principle of in-group versus out-group, and the solidarity of the society is based on the exchange of symbols between these groups. In Middle Eastern marriage systems there is most certainly an exchange of symbols: in tangible terms, bride wealth in the form of cattle, sheep, or goats is paid by the father of the groom to the bride's family, who in turn furnishes the bride's "trousseau" in the form of rugs, blankets, and a few other household items. Dualism is found throughout the system of symbolic meanings linked with the distinction between men and women. Take the symbolic layout of the Berber house, which Bordieu (1971) has described.

Berber Dualism

The Berber house is the world of all that is sacred and licit. The world outside of the house is the man's world: men who stay in the house are regarded as nonmen: they are like brood hens, staying at home during the day when they should be outside in the fields or at the assembly house. When boys mature, they must leave the world of women and so leave the house with the father.

The interior of the house is saturated in symbols relating to men and women. It is divided in two: the upper part (facing north), which is the domain of light, the fireplace, the loom, the place of women's activity; and the lower, dark part, the place of death, sexual activity, germination

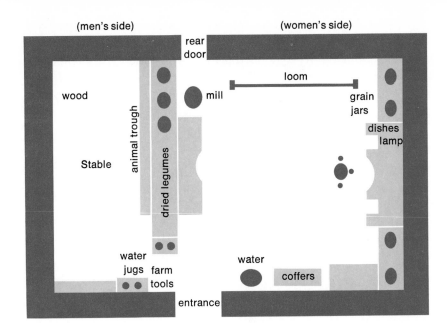

(men's side)   (women's side)

rear door

loom

wood

mill

grain jars

animal trough

dishes lamp

Stable

dried legumes

water jugs   farm tools

water

coffers

entrance

Figure 18.4
The Berber house is saturated with symbols relating to the lives of the men and women who live there.

of the seed, birth and rebirth. The weaving loom alone summarizes the way-stations of a woman's life; her umbilical cord is buried beneath it, and as a young girl she is made to pass through the warp of the loom magically to protect her virginity. At marriage she moves from behind the protection of the loom to be in front of it, symbolizing the passage of her honor from her father's and brother's keeping to that of her husband. In the fire burn the embers, which symbolize in their turn the womb of the mother with its secret hidden fire.

At the center of the dividing wall, male and female meet. The beam across the top of the main pillar, which is male, rests on the trunk, which is female. Around the beam is coiled the snake, the symbol of male fertility, but the pillar supports the beam.

The house is the place of women: "Woman has only two dwellings," says the proverb, "the house and the tomb." But although the house is "hers," it symbolizes the opposition between male and female, and their conjunction. The oppositions come in a series:

fire	water
cooked	raw
high	low
light	shadow
day	night
male	female
fertilizing	able to be fertilized
culture	nature

So in endogamous systems we find that although one may marry a brother or sister, the distinction between "my group" and "other group" that is denied in the system of marriage is re-created in the symbols of the house.

The Akwe-Shavante: Conscious, Society-wide Dualism

The Shavante of central Brazil, who have been studied by David Maybury-Lewis (1968), are thorough dualists. Maybury-Lewis's analysis of Shavante led him to postulate that there were symbolic oppositions that ran throughout Shavante thinking about Shavante sociology, to "keep things straight." He lists them:

HOUSEHOLD	Those married in	Dominant lineage
	Outsiders	Insiders
	Subordinate	Superordinate
COMMUNITY	They	We
	Opposite faction	My faction
RELATIONSHIP	They	We
TERMINOLOGY	Marriageable	Nonmarriageable
COSMOLOGY	Wazepari'wa	Spirits of the dead (da hiebá)
	Affines	Kin
	Wasi're'wa	Waniwihã

These social oppositions can be explained most easily if we look at them in order.

Household Boys marry into their wives' households. Because of polygyny, there is a wide disparity in the ages of the husband and wife, the boy marrying a girl who may still be an infant when he enters the age-grade that leaves the bachelor's hut. The boy is embarrassed by any suggestion that he might be having sexual intercourse with his wife. This is not because she is so young, for defloration can take place as early as the age of 8—rather he is embarrassed because sexual interest in his wife would be an admission that is he committing himself to permanent residence with his in-laws, in a house where he is a stranger and a member of the patrilineal out-group. The more he is married, the more he must come under the authority of his father-in-law and work for him. In his own father's house, he is a member of the in-group. Maybury-Lewis describes a time when the chief's family moved in with him because the chief was building a house. Two things struck Maybury-Lewis: first, how fast the young

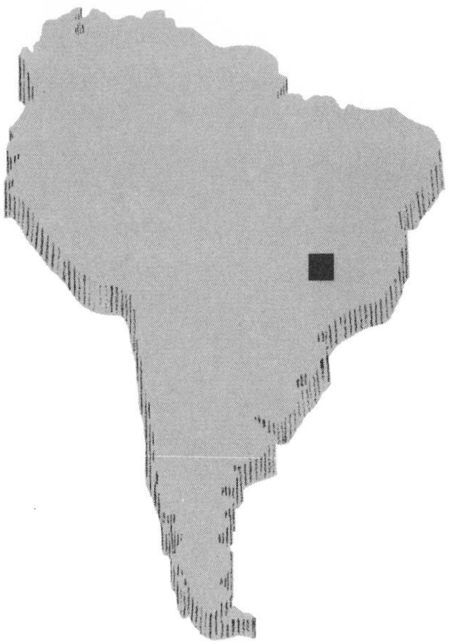

Figure 18.5
South America showing the
region of the Akwe
Shavante.

married couple moved out to get away from the in-laws and establish a
proper distance (normally older and younger couples are separated by a
screen); and second, how the patrilineal kinsmen of the bride lounged
about, helping little if at all, since they would have to work in their wives'
fathers' houses, while they were very much at home here in their own
house. These are some of the symbols that Maybury-Lewis sums up by
contrasting "those married in" vs. "dominant lineage," "outsiders" vs.
"insiders," "subordinate" vs. "superordinate."

Community The community is divided into two sides, called *waniwihā*
and *wasi're'wa*. These two words are hard to translate but are probably
best rendered "kin" and "affine," respectively. Shavante patrilineages
divide up their community. The lineages are well defined and are named.
Lineages are formed into factions, creating the distinction between "my
faction" and "opposite faction." People of the speaker's faction are called
wasiwasdi, to distinguish them from people of his own lineage, who are
addressed by appropriate kinship terms.

Kin Terminology The kinship terminology reflects the underlying binary
division of the world into two, and the distinction between *waniwihā*
and *wasi're'wa*. The terminological system of the Shavante consciously includes the separation of kinsmen into "them" and "us." "We" marry
"them."

Cosmology Dyadic relationships turn up in society but they also turn up in heaven as well. The system of opposed meanings that is found in the categories of social organization extends quite readily into other symbolic arenas, just as it did in Berber houses. In the cosmological system, the major distinction is between the *wazepari'wa,* who are dangerous spirits associated with one's affines, and the *da hiebá,* who are the benevolent spirits of the dead. Maybury-Lewis summarizes the opposed characteristics in the cosmological system:

wazepari'wa	da hiebá
malevolence	benevolence
taking	giving
terrifying	consoling
ending	beginning
west	east
affinal place	kin place
affines	kin
wasi're'wa	waniwihã

Each symbol is defined by the other and opposed to it, just as black is defined by white and opposed to it in the Western scheme of color categories. Symbols cannot stand alone: they are arranged in orders and structures, the simplest one being binary opposition.

Reciprocal Dualism: The Kariera System

The epitome of systems of dualistic reciprocity is found in Australia. We can briefly describe one simple case—the Kariera.

There are three ways that one can describe the Kariera system, depending on what one wants to emphasize. One can call it a system of restricted *exchange,* emphasizing that there are only two sides that make up the whole society, "our skin" (our side) and "other skin." Or one can call them systems of **symmetric alliance,** emphasizing that symbols of the same value are exchanged back and forth between the two sides. Or one can emphasize the terminological code (the names for important social categories) and the system of marriage and so call it a system of **bilateral cross-cousin marriage:** *bilateral,* meaning that there is a category of people who are cousins on both my father's and my mother's side simultaneously; and *cross-cousin* because this bilateral cousin is simultaneously my father's sister's child *and* my mother's brother's child.

Try to draw a diagram of the relationships that would have to obtain between people who were arranged in two sides. Do it in patrilineages for the sake of both simplicity and ethnographic accuracy. Remember that bilateral cross-cousin marriage is when a man marries someone who is simultaneously his mother's brother's child and his father's sister's child. To save you hours, it is all shown in Figure 18.6. Remember that this is a diagram of *positions,* not people. Students always ask, "What happens if Ego doesn't have a person who is simultaneously his FZD/MBD and can become his "W?" He'll still get married; the system is much more flexible than it looks, because what the diagram displays are the *rules* of the system—the "skins" or sides, the relationships of sister-exchange (my group gives your group a woman [or a man], and your group gives one to my group), and the kinship terminology. Since a lot of these systems were polygynous, a ruse commonly was utilized to guarantee that every man got a wife—just as in Shavante, the man married a woman who was much younger that he was.

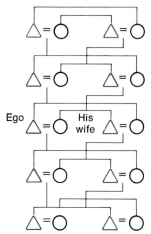

Figure 18.6
A Kariera kinship diagram.

Preference-Ordered Social Groups and Exchange

Keeping Things Straight When the Population Grows

Human beings expend a lot of time "keeping things straight." One method that we have discussed is to set up a system of related oppositions: black-white, holy-unholy, male-female, inside-outside, and so on. This is the kind of binary reckoning that computers do fairly well, but that human beings can do much better with their infinite capacity for extending meaning through metaphor, metonymy, association, and imagination. But it is not the only way of keeping things straight. A form of measure very commonly used in ordering social groups and categories is the "preference order." It is a kind of unidimensional order you studied in chapter 14.

Every schoolchild knows that if $A > B$ and $B > C$, then $A > C$. When this property holds true of three or more elements (social categories, in this case), it is called a *transitive* relationship, or a relationship of *transitivity.* If, on the other hand, the statement $A > B$, $B > C$, $C > A$ is true, we say that the relationship is *intransitive,* or characterized by *intransitivity.* Intransitivity is not rare in human thinking, even though it is just like saying "10 is larger than 8, 8 is larger than 5, and 5 is larger than 10."

Intransitive Preference Orders

The beauty of intransitivity in ordering human societies is that there is no bottom, no **pariah group** that is lower than any other group, just as there is no person or group who is top dog, clearly dominant over all. Imagine a system of occupations in which a brain surgeon was preferred to a college professor, a college professor to a sanitation worker, and a sanitation worker to a brain surgeon. All three groups would concur in this judgment. Think what it would do to a marriage system if there were a rule of **hypergamy,** that is, a rule that a woman should marry into a higher status group. No sanitation worker would ever let his daughter marry a brain surgeon, just as no brain surgeon would let his daughter marry a college professor, and so on. Similarly, if there were a rule of **hypogamy,** that is, a rule that a woman should marry into a lower status group, the cycle would be reversed. In neither case would we find a bottom or a top to the system, but rather a set of cycles of exchange that incorporate the very powerful sorting device of preference-ordering and avoid the creation of a hierarchical class or caste structure.

This kind of marriage system is found all over the world, particularly in Asia, and it can get very complicated indeed. Just as with dualistic systems, we can refer to these systems of marriage in three ways: (1) *systems of generalized exchange;* (2) *systems of asymmetric alliance;* and (3) *systems of matrilateral cross-cousin marriage.* If we focus on the fact that more than two groups (in fact, any number of groups) can be incorporated into the marriage cycles of symbolic exchange, then we use the term *generalized exchange.* If we want to focus on the fact that instead of reciprocity (*A* gives a sister or brother to *B,* who returns in kind), we have *A* giving a brother or sister to *B,* who gives a brother or sister to *C,* who gives in kind to *A* (in the simplest formulation), then we use the term *asymmetric alliance.* If we want to emphasize the kinship category from which the wife is drawn, then we use the expression *matrilateral cross-cousin marriage,* because a man marries a woman from a class defined by the letter for MBD.

The simplest example of such a system would incorporate three lineages (we shall use patrilineages, since they are more common in these systems, but any kind of social category or local group can serve). We get a simplified schematic chart of the various positions as follows:

Figure 18.7
Schematic of a matrilateral cross-cousin marriage.

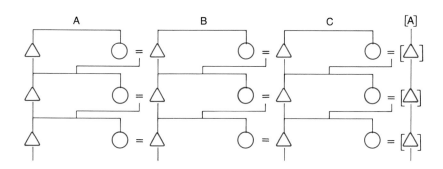

where "=" means "is married to," the wavy descending lines are lines from parents to children, and the horizontal lines link brother and sister. Note that every man on the second and third horizontal line is married to his "mother's brother's daughter," and every woman (conversely) to her "father's sister's son."

Notice also that women "flow" in the same direction, from left to right: *A* gives a woman to *B,* who gives a woman to *C,* who gives a woman to *A,* and the circle is complete. (For this reason some people call these systems "marriage in a circle," or *circular connubium.*) In the Kariera example, *A* gave to *B* who gave back to *A;* there was neither circle nor cycle, just reciprocity.

Systems of this kind, particularly when they utilize preference orderings, can keep a lot of people straight, many more than the 500-or-so upper limit that is imposed by dualistic systems. The upper limit for an intransitive preference-ordered system is certainly above 100,000. It is important to remember that you don't have to marry your mother's brother's daughter, you have to marry a "proper woman," a "potential spouse," which can mean a lot of different things depending on the differing ethnographic circumstances. If every man really had to marry his mother's brother's daughter, then there would be a lot of unmarried people, since it is very hard, on biological principles, to guarantee that each mother's brother's daughter will be available for every father's sister's son. Differential fertility, child mortality, and the laws of probability will take care of that. Any tribe that insisted on strict adherence to the rule of marrying the *true* mother's brother's daughter would lose out in the evolutionary scramble for reproductive success.

There are a lot of marriageable women. They are all called by the same term as the MBD. So the anthropologist imitates the way the local people talk about marriage and call it MBD-marriage.

The system works out well because it keeps groups ordered (related and in place) and creates stable alliances together with constant cycles of symbolic exchange.

Matrilateral Marriage and the System of Meaning Marriage systems often give rise to a system of meanings in which dualism appears, as though the whole world were arranged into oppositional sets along the lines of "wife-givers" versus "wife-receivers." Thus, just as asymmetries were embedded in dualistic systems that supposedly were characterized by reciprocity, so dualism is embedded in these asymmetric systems—a dualism that pervades local thinking. As Needham (1962) has shown using data from Purum, the Berber house and the Purum house are analogous to one another, divided dualistically but with different symbols, transformed into the social division that accords with wife-givers and wife-takers. A brief summary of this dualistic symbolism can be adapted from Needham (1962:96), and compared with the Shavante data of Maybury-Lewis.

Dualistic Classification Scheme of Purum

Wife-takers	Wife-givers
Front	Back
Affines	Kin
Strangers	Family
Inferior	Superior
Female	Male
Mortals	Gods, ancestral spirits
Sun	Moon
Bad death	Good death
Profane	Sacred
Forest	Village
Evil spirits	Beneficial spirits

Human beings play with ideas about the cosmological world, illness, sorcery, marriage, and the animal world in a consistent and complicated way. They are all tied together, and if we have given the impression that social symbols take precedence over other kinds of symbols, that is simply an artificial by-product of the fact that this chapter is about social organization. "Keeping things straight" does not mean simply keeping social categories straight, important as that is; it means keeping the world straight. Some of the ways that human beings do this are reciprocity, preference ordering, restricted exchange between two groups, generalized exchange between a number of groups, and opposition versus ranked symbols. Lévi-Strauss (1969) has called all the systems we have so far discussed in this chapter "elementary systems" because they are closed up, things are well-ordered, and there are positive rules that attach to marriage and to symbolic exchange in general. They can be compared to the systems we next consider, where the world is not so well-ordered, where "probability" rather than determinate rule systems operate. Here we will find that preference ordering is carried out to its fullest extent, transitivity reigns, as it were, and as a result, human beings are capable of organizing themselves to the full, using their most powerful device and its properties of ordering and transitivity. We give two examples: *segmentary lineage systems and caste/class systems*.

Transitive Preference Orders

Segmentary Lineage Systems

When the Sunday school teacher asked whether all the children in the study group liked the Bible, everyone dutifully agreed except one child who

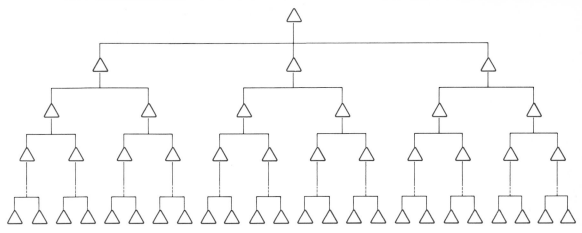

**Figure 18.8
Segmentary lineage
systems.**

stated flatly that it was okay, "but I didn't like all the 'begats'." "Begats"
may be tiresome reading to American children, but in many societies in
the world they are of primary importance in keeping things straight.

Ben Blount, a linguistic anthropologist, became interested in the
"begats," found two elderly Luo (east African) men who were renowned
for their knowledge in such matters, and set them to sorting things out with
a tape recorder. It took about two days to sort the genealogies, but when
the two Luo came to an agreement, it became apparent that the model
they were working with was a kind of pyramid. "In the beginning there
was the founding ancestor of the tribe, and he had three brothers, and they
begat . . . who begat . . . who begat . . . until today we can see the children
of the founding father, their living descendants, in our villages." The
notion of an *apical ancestor,* a founding father from whom the tribe is
descended and for whom the tribe is sometimes named, and the tracing of
relationships through his sons and his sons' sons down the generations
produces an arrangement of households in which everyone traces their
relationship to everyone else through males. This is called **agnatic descent**
and is distinguished from **uterine descent,** the less common form of reckoning descent through females.

A pyramid of descent groups can be easily diagrammed and understood if we remember that each male (triangle) represents a number of
generations of "begats," and that those two Luo gentlemen were not
performing mnemonic feats, but rather were arguing how things *ought* to
have been so that things would be politically, socially, and economically
where they are today, consistent with an agnatic ideology.

In the Middle East, where lineages are patrilineal, endogamous, and
important, they talk about the oppositions between segments (the living,

Figure 18.9
European royal lineages, such as ones for the family of Edward VIII *above* and Czar Nicholas *right* of Russia, were characterized by primogeniture.

flesh and blood triangles in the bottom level) and about building alliances in this way: "It's me and my brothers against my close cousins" and "me and my brothers and my close cousins against my distant cousins" and "all of us against the outsider."

To get back to our principles: transitive preference ordering is weaker in segmentary systems than it is in caste/class systems, unless there is *primogeniture* (privileges or greater prestige accorded to the first-born son), in which case the preference-ordering principle is very strong. This principle of primogeniture held in the Marquesan Islands, according to Ralph Linton, where informants told about the arrogance of a 5-year-old first-born child who ordered his parents out of the house and kept them out for most of the day. In some systems there is an idea of a royal lineage with cadet (younger son) lines. The closer you are to the royal lineage, the higher your prestige, with the highest prestige accorded to the person who is the first-born of the royal lineage.

Even where primogeniture is not important, there is preference ordering based on the individual. Every individual has to marry outside his

own lineage (and usually his mother's lineage, too). In marriage he takes distant blood relatives (consanguines) and converts them into close affines ("in-laws"). Every child born to the marriage will have matrilateral relatives under agnatic descent, just as a child born into a group that uses *uterine* descent will have patrilateral relatives.

Preference ordering is based on closeness. There is an implicit moral scale underlying segmentary systems whereby obligations recede with distance from the group. If my brother's son won't help me, then I am a real political nonentity, because he is about as close as one can get. But if even my fourth cousin will help me, then I have obviously manipulated the social system so as to put myself in a powerful position. *Blood money* is a nice instance of the moral scale. If you murder someone within your immediate family (including brothers and brothers' sons), then you are guilty of a "special crime" that does not involve revenge or the payment of blood money; it is settled within the close family. Once outside the arena of immediate kinfolk, blood money is paid in inverse proportion to the distance between the groups. This kind of ego-centered preference ordering

Figure 18.10

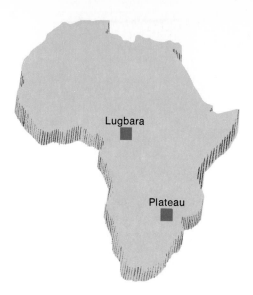

is a powerful moral principle that can serve to activate political alliances. Pity the poor tribesman from another group who murders a member of a segmentary system and finds the victim's whole clan after him! It can keep very large numbers (up to a million) people ordered.

The social order of heaven is a reflection of that on earth. There is a high god, for example, just as there is an apical, or senior, ancestor. The high god stands in the same relationship to the lesser spirits as the apical ancestor stands to the younger ancestor. The apical ancestor stands for the whole tribe. The lesser ancestor stands for segments of the tribe, that is, the lineages and sublineages.

At the lowest level of the hierarchy we find the local familiar spirits. They correspond to and belong to the places where the people of the tribe live. Each patrilineal extended family has its own ancestor and the ancestor its own shrine, but just as the living patriarch is surrounded by his junior brothers, unmarried sisters, children, and grandchildren so too the ancestor presides over his spiritual family. They are often mischievous junior spirits who make their presence known by playing tricks on people—occasionally serious ones—just like the grandchildren.

The same is true for matrilineal groups. Elizabeth Colson, who studied the Plateau Tonga, notes that the beliefs in *muzimu* ("ancestral spirits") reproduce the social order. Each person in Tonga is affiliated with a matrilineal group and receives an ancestral spirit from it. Because inheritance goes down the matriline, so does the ancestral spirit when one dies. And since the members of the same matrilineal group are considered to be equivalent, the *mizimu* of anyone in the line can affect the lives of anyone else. The importance of the household is reflected in the belief that one cannot become an ancestral spirit when one dies unless one has formed a proper household; and the husband's authority over the wife turns up as the dominance of his *mizimu* over hers in ritual invocations. The absence of local shrines attests to the dispersal of the matrilineal kinfolk in different villages.

Caste/Class Systems

In segmentary systems, transitive preference ordering occurs in the form of rules that relate social segments. There is a profound difference between this sort of preference ordering and that in caste/class systems: the first is ego-centered, or symmetrical, while the second is society-wide and asymmetrical. In the segmentary system, if you are my fourth cousin, then I am obligated to aid and assist you in a fourth-cousinly way and pay a comparatively small amount of blood money to your kinfolk when I murder you; the same holds for your actions toward me.

But when preference ordering is society-wide, pariah groups (that is, low class or low caste groups) are created. Because the orderings are both transitive and agreed to by all members of society, if $A > B$ and $B > C$, then $A > C$, and that's that—none of this business of the brain surgeon's son being honored to marry the sanitation man's daughter. In the words of the old English hymn:

> The rich man in his castle,
> The poor man at his gate,
> God made the high and lowly,
> And ordered their estate.

Class Systems Little need be said about class systems. Every reader of English has participated in them. It seems strange that when Lloyd Warner pointed out some fifty years ago that democratic America had a class system, there were some people who were shocked or a least feigned shock, but the pretense was rather like that of the Victorian woman who was shocked to hear the word "leg" spoken in a drawing room instead of the proper form "limb." Even Victorian drawing-room ladies were aware of the existence of legs, and it requires very upper class status in the United States and England to be unaware of the workings of the class system.

The United States has a class/caste system, the caste aspects of which seem to be slowly breaking down. This process is relatively recent.

Figure 18.11
As recently as fifteen years ago evidences of castes in America were as public as these.

As recently as 1959, Gerald Berreman was able to write an article in which he substituted "low-caste" or "untouchable" into paragraphs about black-white relations in the American South and found them to be true statements about Indian caste society. Here is an example of how Berreman could "translate" John Dollard's (1937) work on *Caste and Class in a Southern Town,* changing references to race to references to caste:

> In simplest terms, we mean by "a sexual gain" the fact that the (high-caste) men, by virtue of their caste position, have access to two classes of women, those of the (high) and (low) castes. The same condition is somewhat true of the (low-caste) women, except that they are rather the objects of the gain than the choosers, though it is a fact that they have some degree of access to (high-caste) men as well as men of their own caste. (Low-caste) men and (high-caste) women, on the other hand are limited to their own castes in sexual choices.

Berreman was able to make a point-by-point comparison between the caste system of village India and black-white relations in the United States, even to the point of showing that the high-caste rationalizations of the system ("the Negro is happy in his place") coincided with the statements of twice-born, upper-caste Brahmin Indians. Similarly, he noted that low-caste Indian villagers were able to describe "shucking and jiving for The Man" and what that did to one's self-esteem.

Hierarchy runs throughout Western and American thinking. Life is a ladder to be scaled and one doesn't want to be left behind. America is famous for its "progress," which is forward, onward, and upward. The importance of intelligence and IQ tests in particular reflects the compelling need that Americans have to produce a single scale on which they can preference-order their whole society.

An inevitable consequence of transitive preference ordering is that pariah groups (or untouchables, or low-class people) are created and endowed with all manner of bad characteristics. People in transitive systems think it is normal for low-class people to be criminal, as it is normal for outsiders to be witches among the Zapotec. During our research in prisons, this point was made by a black rehabilitation officer who said that one of the things he has to teach young prisoners is that they are not necessarily forever evil because they are in jail. The American "ladder" system has put them into a pariah group, imputing to them all manner of evil characteristics that are not necessarily true at all.

Transitive preference orderings are powerful devices for organizing large numbers of people into complex relations. But this system overrides complexity too, in the sense that it demands a single measuring stick for the whole society. One of the motives behind the slogan "do your own thing" was to attack the transitivity principle. If you are doing your own thing and valuing it highly and are content with it, and I can honestly respect you for it, then I am rejecting preference ordering in favor of reciprocity and rejecting a single dimension of judgment for multiple dimensions. I am rejecting the model of caste and class in favor of the model of kinship.

Caste in India Preference ordering is carried to its logical extreme in the caste system of south India. Every person is born into the caste, or **jati,** of his father, and jatis are ranked. The relative rankings of jatis vary from community to community, but there is general consensus about the major categories. From Brahmin to Untouchable, all persons have their place and their duty (*karma*). Even though today all people are living in the age of Kali Yuga, when impurity, disorder, and sin occur and the rains do not come on time, every person has a place in the society and achieves *dharma,* perfect orderliness in the universe, through the medium of perfect service (karma).

The whole universe is ranked. Animals are ranked: first the cow, the repository of the spirits, then tigers and lions, and finally, sheep and dogs. Each jati is associated with ranked gods in the universe: the high-caste, twice-born Brahmin is associated with the high gods Shiva and Parvati, while the lower castes are associated with more bumptious and less spiritual gods.

Figure 18.12
In Hindu India caste is a fact of life for all and everyone, including these Hindu women, knows their ranking and *karma*.

Food also is ranked and linked with pollution and purity. High jatis are vegetarian, low ones are meat-eaters, and the very low even eat beef. At the bottom of the hierarchy are the Untouchable castes.

The hierarchy is saturated with symbols, which are exchanged. The most tangible form of exchange is the exchange of services. The Barber caste is responsible for shaving and cutting the hair of all people, the Goldworker subcaste is an itinerant caste who goes from place to place carrying out its karma. The Brahmin caste has the high duty of keeping the temples and maintaining purity in the community.

One symbol that is *not* exchanged is spouses. One marries within one's own jati, preferably a person who is known not to be a "brother" or "sister" (that is, not a person of one's own patrilineage), but still one whose status as "potential spouse" is well known: a close relative such as father's sister's daughter (not one's own lineage, but that of one's father's sister's husband), mother's brother's daughter, or, perhaps best of all, elder sister's daughter. And even where one would most expect to find reciprocity and equality—marriage—hypergamous marriage rules are found. A man should marry a woman of lower status than himself. In south

India, hierarchy pervades every aspect of the social and symbolic order. Everything in its place, and a place for everything; this is dharma and will be reestablished at the end of the age of Kali Yuga, just as it was before.

Summary

1. Human beings organize themselves in a surprisingly limited number of ways. This chapter examines the symbolism and meanings that attach to different forms of social organization.

2. The institution that is most important to the anthropological study of social organization is marriage. Marriage creates the exchanges between social groups that must occur as a result of the incest taboo.

3. A surprising number of peoples around the world marry their relatives. In the Middle East we find bint 'amm marriage—marriage to a clan sister, or patrilateral parallel cousin.

4. This form of marriage sets up a series of dualistic oppositions between man and woman. Men and women are clearly segregated in Middle Eastern society and culture. More commonly found forms of dualism, which oppose consanguines and affines, is to be found among the Akwe-Shavante, who have a Kariera system of reciprocal exchange.

5. Systems of dualism and reciprocity are unable to handle large numbers of people in complex relationships. In this case, a new principle has to be introduced: preference ordering. There are two kinds of preference orderings found in human groups: transitive and intransitive. Intransitive preference orderings are found in systems of matrilateral cross-cousin marriage.

6. Transitive preference orderings are found in three kinds of groups: segmentary lineage systems (which sometimes have primogeniture), class systems (such as in modern America), and caste systems (such as in India). In transitive systems there is always the problem of the pariah group.

Suggested Readings

Bordieu, P. "The Berber House or the World Reversed." In *Mélanges Offerts à Claude Lévi-Strauss*, edited by J. Pouillon and P. Maranda. Paris: Mouton, 1971.

This article is briefly summarized in this chapter, but it is worth reading in full. A fine piece of symbolic analysis.

Leach, Edmund. *Political Systems of Highland Burma.* Cambridge: Cambridge University Press, 1954.

> *Somehow it seems appropriate that the best ethnography on power and its relationships with systems of asymmetric alliance should be done in an area that we know more familiarly as the "Golden Triangle," from which most of the world's opium supply comes. No mention of opium here, though, merely what many think is the best and richest study we have of a system of matrilateral alliance.*

Legesse, Asmaram. *Gada: Three Approaches to the Study of African Society.* New York: Free Press, 1974.

> *A symbolic, a structural-functional, and an ecological approach to one of the most fascinating ethnological riddles. In Gada people were "born dead" in the sense that they were assigned at birth to an age set that belonged properly to the ancestors. Legesse has figured out why and how.*

Maybury-Lewis, David. *The Savage and the Innocent.* Boston: Beacon Books, 1968.

> *Who was the savage and who the innocent? Find out by reading this candid and realistic account of what it is like to do field work among a difficult, inaccessible tribe. If you ever wondered how anthropologists got that data on those exotic societies, here is a delightful and honest account.*

Selby, Henry A. *Zapotec Deviance.* Austin: University of Texas Press, 1974.

> *Zapotec dualism as discovered by one of the authors. Here you will find even more material on the Zapotecs, who have been popping up in this book quite a bit. A study of crime and deviance turns into a study of social organization.*

Glossary

agnatic descent   Descent of all persons from some common male ancestor, so that everyone is related to everyone else.

apical ancestor   The "founding parent" of a lineage.

bilateral cross-cousin marriage   A system of marriage in which one chooses a spouse from a class that is defined as both mother's brother's daughter and father's sister's daughter.

bint 'amm marriage   *See* patrilateral parallel-cousin marriage.

cross cousin   The child of a sibling of the opposite sex from one's linking parent. (That is, one's mother's brother's child, or one's father's sister's child.)

homogamy   The cultural practice of marrying someone like yourself: from your own group, class or caste.

hypergamy   The practice of women marrying men who are of higher status (and, conversely, of men marrying women of lower status).

hypogamy   The practice of women marrying men who are of lower status than themselves (and, conversely, of men marrying women who are higher).

jati   A caste in India.

matrilineage   A group recruited on the basis of their ties through women.

parallel cousin   The child of the sibling of the same sex as the linking parent. (That is, father's brother's child, or mother's sister's child.)

pariah group   The lowest group in a society.

patrilateral parallel-cousin marriage   The cultural practice that favors the marriage of a person to his or her father's brother's child.

patrilineage   A social group recruited on the basis of one's relationships through males.

symmetric alliance   A system of exchange where each side reciprocates with the other.

Culture in Ecological Perspective

1. How do biocultural systems deal with the uncertainty that exists in the environment?
2. What is anthropological demography?
3. How do demographic processes relate to the biocultural system?
4. How do people define what they want from life and how do they go about attaining those things?

19

Cultural Ecology

Introduction

Cultural adaptation refers to the ways that peoples change their ideas and techniques for making a living so that they can get the "best" out of life, as they define it.

Human beings have to make a living. We cannot live on symbols and meanings only, although without them we would not be human. To earn a living we have to fit, or adapt, ourselves to the environment. We do this culturally as well as biologically. Cultural adaptation refers to the ways that peoples change their ideas and techniques for making a living so that they can get the "best" out of life, as they define it.

What "the best life" is varies enormously from culture to culture. Before one can understand cultural adaptation, one has to understand what people want. For example, not all people want material abundance; nomadic peoples, for instance, place very little emphasis on it. Eskimo hunters do not want to acquire a large number of possessions that will only encumber their movement, make it harder for them to find game, and seriously impair their ability to make a living. They, and people like them, deemphasize material goods.

Not all people want a rich, steady diet, either. The !Kung of the Kalahari desert work when they need to, but they work about half as much as we do. They are well enough nourished, but they can withstand hunger for a few days if they have to. They may not like it. But they apparently see little point in scurrying around a barren hunting land just to provide three meals, on time, each day. They take what the environment provides. To them, the best means neither material possessions nor a stable, predictable, varied diet.

Figure 19.1
Nomadic desert people, such as these, do not want to encumber themselves with a large number of possessions.

Not all people think of material goals as the most important ones. Most people feel that once one has satisfied one's bodily requirements, the emphasis should be on social or spiritual goals. Once the body's needs are met, they devote their efforts to developing a rich social life, enjoying relationships with kinfolk and other members of the community. Or to carrying out rituals and religious rites so that the community is at peace with the spirit world. Or to just taking it easy, substituting leisure for work in a way that we would regard as lazy or inefficient.

So to find out whether a population is efficiently adapted, one has to find out what the people's goals and values are in life. Then one can inquire as to whether they are meeting their goals and satisfying their desires in the best way they can.

The Two Dramas of Human Groups

Human beings are engaged in two plays or dramas at the same time. One play—the one of which we are aware—takes place on the social and cultural stage of everyday life. People go to work in the field or office, make love, strive for their children, cleave to their families, enjoy happiness, and endure despair. This is the **on-stage drama.** As observers just like the people whose lives we observe, we can see, talk about, enjoy, or despise this play. The way the drama is defined is a cultural matter. Meanings are negotiated and agreed on in every culture, and events are interpreted in the light of those meanings. A person is not happy or content because of some absolute good; happiness is not decreed by God to be the same for all peoples. We ourselves, given our cultural traditions, define happiness for ourselves.

Cultural symbols give meaning to the drama of everyday life. Events are defined in language and symbol and given importance in accord with those values. This is the daily, conscious, on-stage drama of life.

The Off-Stage Drama

An important **off-stage drama** also is taking place, of which we are often only dimly aware, if not utterly unconscious. This drama is often more important for the long-run survival of the group or species because sometimes human groups, who must think in the language and rhetoric of the on-stage drama, initiate irreversible processes that turn out to destroy them or impair their lives in the long run. A single death or a plague may mean personal misfortune, bitterness, loneliness, and grief for the actors in the on-stage drama. But it might mean the survival of the healthier gene pool for those who live. It might mean that overpopulation, which, unknown to the on-stage actors, is threatening the very resource base of their society, has been averted. The on-stage actors know nothing of aversion.

Sometimes the two processes work together, the on-stage motives

Figure 19.2
When Americans and Canadians were rebuilding after World War II they never dreamed that they would "kill" Lake Erie. But off-stage processes were going on that they were unaware of.

and feelings of the people bringing about changes that increase their adaptive fitness. We can take as an example the migration from the Valley of Oaxaca. People are leaving the villages of this valley because they think they can get a better job, better income, and better opportunities for their children in Mexico City. One can talk to them about their motives for leaving, and they are conscious of them.

But Wayne Kappel (1977) has studied this migration and found that had it not taken place, the rich valley which has sustained civilizations and culture for thousands of years would be turned into a rocky desert. The population would make inroads on the mountainous lands and deplete the water supply, thereby creating erosion and crop failures. Migration has saved the valley and the culture as a whole. But each family has decided to move for quite different reasons: they were going to join a relative in the capital city; they wanted to go to secondary school, to find a good job, to flee a murder charge. The on-stage actors were unaware of their act of salvation.

Cultural Ecology: The Study of the Two Dramas When anthropologists turn to the study of the relationship between human beings and their environment, they are concerned with both the on-stage and the off-stage dramas. For the purposes of survival and the maintenance of culture, the

Figure 19.3
Rain dancers like these
from the Zuni tribe believe
that they can bring rain.
However, there is no
scientific evidence that they
can.

off-stage drama is probably more important, despite the fact that both scientists and ordinary people understand it poorly. If it does not rain, the crops will not grow. That is a truth, discoverable and known to people and scientists alike. But people believe that they can intervene in the meteorological process and bring about conditions that will cause the rain to fall. In a village in India, people believe that the monsoon will come on time if the village is in a proper moral state. Therefore, ritual precautions must be taken before the onset of the all-important monsoon season to ensure that the village is ritually pure. Southwestern Indian groups in the United States believe that rain can be caused to fall through the rain dance. Central African groups have a rainmaker who has magical powers to cause the rain to fall. Some of them have rain-stoppers, too, so that the crops will not be flooded out. Americans have cloud-seeders who also claim that they can cause the rain to fall.

So far as scientists know, the rain-dancers, the rainmakers and rain-stoppers, and the cloud-seeders have no impact upon the rain. So far as we know, ritual purity and the onset of the monsoon are independent of each other.

But cultural ecologists study both dramas. They have to understand how environmental processes are believed to affect crop growth as well as how these processes *do* affect crop growth. When we say "do affect crop growth," we are assuming that our scientific theory of meteorological and agronomic processes is superior to other peoples' theories, and that we can explain why people are good or bad farmers better than they can themselves. Despite the fact that this is a tenuous assumption, we have to make it. If we don't, we will not be able to translate the practices of traditional rice or millet farmers into a language that we understand. We will not be able to deepen our understanding of ourselves or our fellow human beings.

Uncertainty in the Environment

Uncertainty refers to variability in ecological outputs over time.

The most important environmental variable to which a cultural ecologist must pay attention is **uncertainty.** Uncertainty refers to variability in ecological outputs over time. The more variability there is, the greater the amount of uncertainty. If, for example, the society gets a bumper harvest one year and practically nothing at all the next year, and this pattern is repeated (with variations) over a number of years, we would say the environment has a high degree of uncertainty. If, on the hand, the ecological outputs are the same year after year—if, that is, there is no variability in output—then we say that there is a very low degree of uncertainty in the environment. If we knew exactly what to expect every year and it never changed, we would be certain of the ecological output. So uncertainty runs from zero to 1.0, or from complete certainty (or no uncertainty) (0) to complete uncertainty (1.0).

Figure 19.4
The dimension of uncertainty.

0 _____ 1.0

Complete   Complete
Certainty   Uncertainty

More than two decades of anthropological fieldwork and analysis has gone into proving that the fundamental problem of design of biocultural systems is closely related to uncertainty.

Biocultural systems are designed to weather the extremes of ecological processes.

Biocultural systems are designed to weather the extremes of ecological processes. If, for example, all crops depend on rainfall, and there are periodic, randomly occurring droughts, the biocultural system will have to be designed so that it can weather these periodic droughts. A biocultural system that could only survive placid times or good times would be badly designed, would fail to thrive, and would ultimately go under. All surviving systems, therefore, have to have this built-in feature.

One way of looking at biocultural systems, then, is to see how they handle the fundamental problem of uncertainty.

The first way of handling uncertainty is to design feeding habits so that the people will consume the widest possible variety of foods. This means that the biocultural system has a wide ecological niche.

Insight
Human Ecology—Cow Love in India

Hindu India is noted for two things: periodic famines and sacred cows. Marvin Harris has carried out an intriguing analysis of "cow love" in India. The Hindu are vegetarians and accord sacred status to the cow. They have "old-age homes" for their cows. They permit them to wander on the byways of their land, eating food that would seemingly be better reserved for human beings. There are millions of these animals, and every Western agronomist has recommended that they be eaten up. These experts have been perplexed and dismayed at the unwillingness of the Hindu to be rational about these beasts.

Harris has shown that it is the Western expert who is being irrational. The Indian lovers of cows are practicing cultural ecological principles. In particular they are aware of the basic principle of design—that all biocultural systems must be designed so as to survive environmental uncertainties in the long run.

First, the cows are not denuding the countryside and taking food from children's mouths as the experts thought. They are eating wastes and marginal products that people would not eat anyway.

Second, the cows are extremely important to Indian agriculture, not because they contribute anything themselves but because they contribute *bullocks,* draft animals to pull plows and haul carts. The bullocks are absolutely essential to Indian agriculture. Every family must have one—and only cows can provide them. If the Indians were to try to imitate our energy-intensive, mechanized form of farming, the investments that would be required, not to mention the staggering costs for energy, would bankrupt the country.

Farming with bullocks is much more efficient than our method of farming, in any case. Mechanized modernized farming would drive down yields, compared with what the farmer gets now, as well as creating massive unemployment and disruption.

The bullock is essential to India. The cow is essential to the bullock. It would be a terrible tragedy and knock-out blow economically if the supply of bullocks were interrupted. What better way to assure a constant supply of these invaluable animals than to make their genetrixes sacred!

Reducing Uncertainty by Adapting to a Wide Ecological Niche

When a population has its own way of exploiting and adapting to the environment, we call this way its **ecological niche.** *Ecological niche for a human population refers to its feeding habits.*

Figure 19.5
Feeding habits and ecological niche width.

Feeding habits	
specialized	**generalized**

Ecological niche width	Narrow	Wide

Niches have width: they can be wide or narrow. One population may occupy a narrow niche; that is, it exploits only a small fraction of the available resources in its environment. Another population might exploit many resources in the same environment. The width of the niche has important consequences for the population. If it occupies a narrow niche, then the food supply derived from that narrow selection had better be safe, assured, and adequate, because if the supply runs out, so will the population. Here is a calculation of niche width developed by Hardesty (1975) from data by Rogers (1972) for a group of North American Indians in Canada.

Table 19.1

Niche Width of Mistassini Cree

Food Type	Amount/Year	Percent of Diet
Moose	4000 lb.	45
Caribou	1500 lb.	17
Bear	210 lb.	2
Beaver	2120 lb.	24
Hare	114 lb.	1
Muskrat	240 lb.	3
Porcupine	60 lb.	1
Mink	33 lb.	.5
Squirrel	8 lb.	—
Marten	5 lb.	—
Otter	110 lb.	1
Loon	44 lb.	.5
Geese	67 lb.	.5
Ducks	231 lb.	3
Ptarmigan	150 lb.	2
Spruce grouse	38 lb.	.5
Ruffled grouse	1 lb.	—
Owl	1 lb.	—

These Cree Indians have a problem. If both the moose and the beaver were to disappear, they could not survive. Their feeding habits are quite specialized, and if one or two of their major foods disappeared, they might well starve. We do not know whether they would change their food preferences or not. We would have to study the range of foods that they will accept, and we do not have that data.

Compare these hunters with some Australian tribal peoples that Birdsell (1953) studied. The percentages are not available, but look at the range of foods consumed, the *width* of the ecological niche!

A. Animal Foods

6 sorts of kangaroos
5 marsupials
2 species of opossum
9 species of marsupial rats and mice
Dingo
1 type of whale
2 species of seal
Birds of every kind including emus
    and wild turkeys
3 types of turtle
11 kinds of frog
7 types of iguanas and lizards
8 sorts of snakes
Eggs of every species of bird or lizard
29 kinds of fish
All saltwater shellfish except oysters
4 kinds of freshwater shellfish
4 kinds of grubs

B. Plant Foods

29 kinds of roots
4 kinds of fruit
2 species of cycad nut
2 other types of nut
Seeds of various species of
    leguminous plants
2 kinds of mesembranthum
2 types of fungus
4 sorts of gum
2 kinds of manna
Flowers of several species of *Banksia*

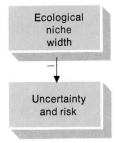

Figure 19.6
The first method of reducing uncertainty is to widen the niche width. The minus sign indicates that the relationship is inverse; as niche width increases, uncertainty decreases.

These Australian groups use the potential resources of their environment fully. They are unlikely to starve to death if one or two foods are unavailable. The first method for reducing uncertainty is to widen the ecological niche. The minus sign indicates that the relationship is inverse: as niche width *increases,* uncertainty *decreases.*

Reducing Uncertainty by Taking Advantage of a Varied Environment

Variability in the environment is referred to by ecologists as its **grain,** as in **fine-grained** or **coarse-grained** environments. A fine-grained environment is one in which variability is equally distributed over the landscape. Different plants, animal species, soil conditions, and climatic conditions occur evenly spread out over the whole space. If you think of the environment as a checkerboard, each square of the board is about the

Figure 19.7
The amber waves of grain
on this American farm
illustrate how human beings
can convert a fine-grained
environment into a mono-
crop regime.

same as every other square. So far as human populations are concerned, *pure* (single-minded) strategies are appropriate to fine-grained environments. What works in one square will work in another, and ecological relations will be very stable.

Coarse-grained environments, in contrast, are often referred to as patchy environments since, when mapped, they look like a patchwork quilt. As one moves from square to square over the landscape, conditions alter. In one patch one combination of plants is in equilibrium with its environment, while a short distance away, a completely different combination is established. Where the patches are small, people are better off with mixed food-procurement strategies. For example, producers should grow a little rice in the wet lowlands, millet in the higher and drier piedmont, and garden vegetables in plots near the houses where manure is available from animal droppings; they should hunt in the mountain areas where wild game abounds. If they were to adopt a pure strategy, they could exploit one patch in the environment but not the others. The Australian tribal peoples of the interior, studied by Birdsell, with their wide niche and generalized feeding habits, inhabited a fine-grained environment. They were browsers, eating those things that nature provided. The Kofyar of Nigeria, on the other hand, inhabit a patchy environment and have adopted a wide mix of production strategies to take advantage of it. Here is how the Kofyar cope.

The Kofyar of Nigeria The Kofyar tribe lives in a very patchy environment and takes advantage of it to reduce uncertainty. Altitude varies up to 1,500 feet, terrain varies from level to precipitous, and variable rainfall, bringing water surpluses and scarcities, contributes to a high degree of uncertainty. The Kofyar have three agricultural techniques. The first is **intensive agriculture** on the fields around the house, to which they can easily carry the manure and compost from the goat and cow corral. Here they grow coco yams, peppers and spices, millet, sorghum, cowpeas, pumpkin, okra, gourds, and some corn.

In the outlying fields they use several methods to prevent erosion from water run-off. They either dam up fields to turn them into rice paddies or build ridges in them and plant above the water level. Failing this, they build terraces of dry stone and plant sorghum, millet, and wet or dry rice.

On the hilly fields where the soil is less rich, they practice **extensive agriculture.** That is, instead of using the same fields every year, they use a field for up to four years and then leave it fallow for ten to fifteen. They fertilize these hilly fields not with compost and manure, which would be too heavy to carry from the house to the distant hills, but with wood ash. They not only bring the wood ash from their hearths, but also burn off the bush in the dry season and dig the ashes in with a hoe. Sometimes they can get the nomadic Fulani herdsmen to pasture their cattle in these fields,

Figure 19.8
The Kofyar hill farmer exploits his patchy environment with an ingeniously mixed food production strategy.

Figure 19.9
The first two principles of cultural ecology.

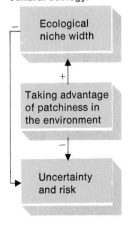

Ecological niche width

+

Taking advantage of patchiness in the environment

−

Uncertainty and risk

thus getting a supply of manure. If the field is flat enough so that the cattle can manure it regularly, the farmer does not have to let it fallow. In these fields, they grow groundnuts, sweet potatoes, maize, early millet, and dry ("hungry") rice.

In addition to their field crops, they cultivate palm trees. They also keep cattle and goats. They rotate crops to make sure that the soils stay fertile, and they maintain a flexible schedule of plantings to take advantage of the rains when they come. As soon as the ditches beside the roads fill with water, the Kofyar turn them into rice paddies.

Small wonder that agricultural professionals have said that the Kofyar exploit their environment in the best imaginable way. Hog butchers in the United States used to boast that they used everything in the pig except the squeal—Kofyar farmers could almost say the same.

This illustrates the second principle of cultural ecology: Other things being equal, taking advantage of patchiness in the environment reduces uncertainty.

Other things being equal, taking advantage of patchiness in the environment reduces uncertainty.

Reducing Uncertainty by Adapting a Resource in Constant, Abundant Supply

Another way of reducing risk is to "put all your eggs in one basket." By this we mean that you adopt a **pure production strategy.** The "basket," however, had better be very secure so as to ensure that it will always have some eggs in it. One population that is fortunate in having access to a resource in constant and abundant supply is the !Kung Bushmen studied by Richard Lee (1968, 1969, 1972). They live off the hard-shelled, easily stored, protein-rich nuts of the mongongo tree. Even though the !Kung live in a harsh desert terrain, the mongongo trees are old reliables: they give nuts aplenty every year, except under inconceivably dry conditions. The !Kung may not have any animals to hunt, and the moisture-bearing roots and tubers they usually eat may desiccate and yield little, but the mongongo trees always bear nuts. No matter how much uncertainty there is about the weather, the !Kung need pay little attention. There is little uncertainty attached to this aspect of their ecological relations.

Figure 19.10
The !Kung Bushmen eat a lot of mongongo nuts when they are not hunting giraffe.

The Chinampa Another example of how to assure supplies of scarce resources in an uncertain environment can be drawn from the "swamp gardeners" of ancient Mesoamerica. In Mexico and Guatemala, before the Spanish conquest in the sixteenth century, there were many empires with more populous cities than those of Europe at the time. The Spanish conquerors were astonished to find these large cities. Their broad avenues, teeming markets, magnificent temples, and crowded, ordered streets contrasted starkly with the dingy, ill-planned, ill-organized, disease-breeding European capitals like Madrid or London.

But the concentration of population in these Mesoamerican cities led to a problem of feeding all the inhabitants. Importing great quantities of food was impossible without draught animals and carts. Before the Spanish there were no draught animals in ancient Mesoamerica, and the wheel was used on children's toys, but never employed on carriages or carts. All burdens were carried on people's backs with a tump line. The carriers were very strong by our standards—able to carry as much as 150 pounds up and down mountainsides in elevated terrain where the air is thin and fatigue comes quickly. But despite their strength and endurance, they could not import enough to feed the city.

The answer to the problem of food procurement for Tenochtitlan, the capital of the Aztec empire, was the invention of one of the most productive, ingenious, and intensive forms of agriculture the world has seen. Since inadequate rainfall was the problem, the ancient Aztecs took their cornfields down to the lake (Lake Texcoco, now the site of Mexico City) and grew their plants in the water. This kind of field is called a *chinampa,* and remains of the ancient *chinampas* can still be seen just outside Mexico City. Pedro Armillas (1971) has studied the sixteenth-century reports describing how the Aztecs carried sod to the shores of Lake Texcoco and built eight-foot-wide ridges two feet above the water. They heaped up the mud from the lagoon and cultivated these tiny peninsulas from their canoes. Nursling plants were cultivated in special floating plots, about 30 feet long, at the shore. The whole plot was towed to the shore for replanting. For this reason, *chinampas* were sometimes called "floating gardens." *Chinampas* were truly ingenious—easily tended, easily fertilized with muck from the lagoon bottom, and sited so that moisture could penetrate where it was most needed, at the roots of the plants. Whatever the rainfall, they yielded what observers of the time called a "glorious harvest."

The *chinampa* illustrates the third method for the reduction of environmental uncertainty. Environmental uncertainty can be reduced by replacing a variable resource with a constant one by technological means.

Reducing Uncertainty by Expanding the Resource Base through Trade

Just after World War I, the Zapotec Indians endured a terrible period of famine and disease. The worldwide influenza attack, combined with two severely wet years that ruined their harvests, had brought them to starvation. Old people committed suicide by abstaining from meals. Children's bellies swelled up and the number of child deaths soared. "We were so poor," they told one of the authors, "that all we had to eat was meat!" This meant they were reduced to eating their draft animals, oxen and burros, and had no staple foods (corn tortillas) at all.

This situation is unthinkable today simply because the web of communications is so very much improved. The Pan-American highway runs

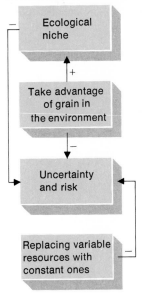

Figure 19.11
Three variables are now present in the uncertainty reduction model: (1) width of the ecological niche, (2) the environmental grain, and (3) resource replacement strategies.

Environmental uncertainty can be reduced by replacing a varible resource with a constant one by technological means.

through the Zapotec territories, and trucks can bring corn shipments up from the more productive southern regions. Because we take communication for granted, we forget that trade is yet another means to reduce uncertainty. Trade is a set of economic arrangements that permit communities and consumers to exploit environments far beyond their physical control. It is a means for energy extraction at a distance and, as such, is one of the means that human societies can adopt for reducing uncertainty in the environment.

Trade is a set of economic arrangements that permit communities and consumers to exploit environments far beyond their physical control.

Trade can be added to the uncertainty reduction model.

Population Pressure Increases Uncertainty

The ability of a society to withstand uncertainty is closely related to *population pressure*. A very uncertain environment cannot sustain a large, dense population except at great risk. If the number of people and animals that inhabit an environment exceeds the capacity of that environment, **environmental degradation** sets in. That is, the environment loses its ability to respond to repeated or random shocks, and the quality and the quantity of the resources it supplies to the animals and people who exploit it are sharply reduced. The width of the ecological niche also is reduced, since people and animals can no longer carry out their habitual activities in the environment. The results can be tragic. The modern world has not managed the problem of population pressure well, if we can judge by the problems that we have with pollution, waste control, and periodic famine. But before we consider the problem of population pressure and demographic controls, we have to understand how one calculates the maximum population that any given natural setting can sustain. This involves our understanding the idea of **carrying capacity.**

Carrying Capacity

The carrying capacity of any environment is the density of an ecological population at equilibrium, or at balance, with its environment.

The carrying capacity of any environment is the *density* of an ecological population at equilibrium, or at balance, with its environment. So, carrying capacity depends on the knowledge and techniques the population possesses for the exploitation of the environment. This is its *technology*. Carrying capacity also depends on the niche width of the population, since a population with a wider niche can be denser than one with a narrow niche in the same environment.

How do you figure out the carrying capacity of an environment? One way is to figure out how effective and efficient people are in exploiting the environment with their technology, and then determine how many people could be supported, in a balanced way, if their efficiency were 100 percent.

First, how much energy are people expending in food production and collection and the like? This is simple to ask, but hard to find out. You have to find out the rate of energy expenditure for different kinds of work, measure how far people have to travel, their strength, the basal metabolic rate and its variations under stress. In fact, you have to carry a portable laboratory into the field with you and measure with thermometers, sphygmomanometers, pedometers, and a host of other devices.

When you have completed your survey of how much energy is expended in the food quest, you have to figure out how much energy is brought in. That means measuring the caloric content of all the foods (meats, cereals, vegetable foods, sweets) that are consumed. It is hard enough to do this when people eat regularly and you can weigh all the food and get a laboratory to evaluate its content. But most people eat irregularly and either do not remember what they ate or distort the amount. You have to hover over them (particularly the children) and watch every morsel that passes their mouths. They (and you) can usually stand this for at most a week at a time.

Having completed these tasks, you can calculate your *output/input* ratio, or *measure of technological efficiency*.

$$\text{Technological efficiency} = \frac{\text{Energy output}}{\text{Energy input}}$$

Little and Morren (1976) have compared the output/input ratios for different technologies in different societies and have found that in order of efficiency they are (1) cultivation, (2) herding, (3) collection of wild foods, and (4) hunting. Table 19.2 gives their figures.

Table 19.2
Output-Input Ratios of Energetic Efficiency for Different Kinds of Technology

Indians of Highland Peru		
Energetic Efficiency for:		
Cultivation	11.5	These figures tell you how
Herding	7.5	many calories they get for each
		one they expend.
Tribal Peoples of Highland New Guinea		
Minyanmin		
Energetic Efficiency for:		
Cultivation	7.5	
Hunting & Collecting	8.9	
Pig Herding	6.4	
Maring		
Energetic Efficiency for:		
Cultivation	18.0	
Pig Herding	1.5	

Next you have to calculate the energy requirements of the population. This depends on the size, stature, age, and sex of the members of the population and their respective requirements for balanced nutrition. You convert women, old people and children into consumption units, based on 1.00 units for an adult man.

Thus, given the width of the ecological niche, the technological efficiency of the society, and estimates of the potential of the environment to sustain humans, crops, and animals, you have the carrying capacity.

What do you find when you have calculated all this? You find that very few societies yet studied come close to living up to their carrying capacity. The less efficient the technology, the less dense the population compared with what the environment *could* carry. Very few societies carry more than 50 percent of the capacity of their environment.

The less efficient the technology, the less dense the population compared with what the environment could carry.

Population Density and the Limiting Factor

There is one kind of society where population densities are very sensitive to the environment. Where a *limiting factor*—a scarce but needed resource —is threatened by population density, then the population is closely controlled by the environment. The limiting factor can be water (as it was for the Aztecs before they started growing their corn in the lake). Or it may be disease-free cattle or some nutrient in wild or collected foods. The limiting factor, then, threatens the balance between the nutritional requirements of the population and the ecological outputs. The Australian tribal peoples studied by Birdsell (1953) provide a good example.

The Australians   One of the best analyses of population control in conditions where resources are very scarce was done by Joseph Birdsell (1953) on tribal peoples of Australia.

Australia is a continental land mass with a great deal of variety in its ecological circumstances. The people who lived there prior to the European occupation had very simple technologies, but their niche width was impressive, as the list on page 471 showed. The Australians were close to being omnivores; they made our diet look boring and restricted by comparison.

Since the Australians deployed a simple technology *and* exploited their environment to the limit, they would be expected to be in ecological equilibrium with the environment. Rainfall prevented them from increasing in population density, such that they were indeed in equilibrium.

Birdsell plotted mean annual rainfall against population density, as well as other factors, and found a very strong relationship. Knowing the rainfall for the area, you could tell the size of the group. He also found, as we would predict, that areas where the uncertainty of the limiting factor

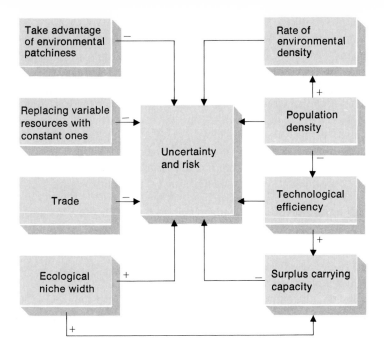

Figure 19.12

was greater were underpopulated, while areas where there was greater than average certainty were (comparatively) overpopulated.

Birdsell's example relates four variables: (1) a uniform (low) level of technological efficiency; (2) a wide ecological niche; (3) high degrees of uncertainty of the environment; and (4) an easily observed and well-defined limiting factor (rainfall).

The major problem posed by ecological relations is uncertainty. Ecological systems have to be designed to assure the system's survival during the periods of greatest variability. Therefore human beings have devised a host of ways of meeting the challenges posed by extreme conditions. They utilize cultural means to dampen the swings back and forth of important environmental variables. These methods have been studied in this chapter.

Summary

1. First we have to distinguish between *ecology* and *environment*. The environment is the natural setting in which a group lives. *Ecology* refers to the relations that the human group has with its living and non-living environment.

2. The main problem of designing a biocultural system is to make sure that it will survive all of the ecological conditions that it is going to

encounter. Ecological systems are characterized by *uncertainty,* which is defined as *variability in ecological outputs.* A more familiar way of talking about this variability is to talk about wide swings in environmental conditions as they affect human beings. The biocultural system has to be able to withstand severe droughts, or floods, or extreme cold or heat, plagues of locusts, epidemics of disease, and so on. Marvin Harris sees cow love as a good example of a design feature that enables the subsistence Indian farmer to survive the bad years of extreme conditions.

3. Human beings try to control the effects of environmental uncertainty. In this chapter we discussed the more important methods that they use to control uncertainty, and effects that these controls have.

There are seven ways that societies reduce environmental uncertainty so as to improve their survival chances.

1. They design their feeding habits and food preferences in such a way that they can substitute for foods in scarce supply. In other words, they widen their ecological niche.
2. They take advantage of patchiness in the environment by adopting a mixed production strategy. This means that they can substitute one production strategy for another if the environmental conditions alter temporarily.
3. They replace a variable resource with one in constant abundant supply. They can do this through manipulation of the diet, as do the !Kung, or they create an artificial environment, as did the Aztecs with their *chinampas,* or swamp gardens.
4. They expand their resource base culturally by engaging in trade.
5. They reduce population density, which in turn decreases the rate of environmental degradation.
6. They increase their technological efficiency.
7. They increase their surplus carrying capacity.

No society does all of these things. No society has to. The more closely, however, a biocultural system approaches its limit of carrying capacity, the more these controls have to be activated.

The best way to summarize the biocultural controls on uncertainty and risk is through a diagram. In this diagram the arrows are marked with either a plus ($+$) or a minus ($-$). If the arrow is marked *plus,* it means that the relationship between the two variables is *direct;* that is, they change in the same direction. If the first variable increases, the second variable increases. A minus sign indicates an inverse relationship. If the first variable increases, the second variable decreases, and vice versa. The head of the arrow indicates the direction of causality. The following diagram would mean "A causes B".

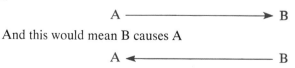

And this would mean B causes A

Insight
Productivity—Energetic Efficiency and American Agriculture

Americans sometimes think of themselves as being the most efficient people in the world. One of the glories of the American society is its ability to put people to work productively and efficiently. And it is true that the ratio of farmers to the number of people they feed is the highest in the world. Our intensive, monocultural farming system is the envy of the world, and our food-procurement strategy is being imitated everywhere.

But the fact of the matter is that we are *not* very efficient. What we are good at is "borrowing" energy from other sources and using it to raise our levels of agricultural productivity. To maintain the continual productivity of our fields we do not rotate crops as we should, but artificially raise their fertility levels by dumping fertilizer containing phosphates and nitrogen on them. We extend human energies by using tractors and labor-saving devices, at the expense of fueling, repairing, and paying for them. We store enormous quantities of food by constructing storage depots such as grain elevators, or by techniques such as fast freezing, drying, concentrating, or fabricating them into snack foods. When you calculate all the energy expenditures that go into preparing the ground, maintaining the technology of food production and food processing, as well as the energy expenditures of all the people who are involved in the distribution of food, we are not very efficient at all. As oil supplies tighten, the present energy-drenched technology is going to appear more and more like an albatross around our necks.

Suggested Readings

Geertz, Clifford. *Agricultural Involution*. Berkeley: University of California Press, 1963.

> *This splendid book contrasts two forms of cultural ecological adaptation in Indonesia: the sawah rice paddy (intensive) form of agriculture, and the swidden (slash-and-burn) form. Geertz shows how the recent history of Indonesia has favored the development of paddy agriculture and how this has permitted both colonial exploitation as well as great population growth.*

Hardesty, Donald. *Ecological Anthropology*. New York: John Wiley & Sons, 1976.

> *This is an excellent book to read after you have studied this chapter and the next one. It is the first solid book that introduces, systematically and for the beginning student, the whole subject of ecological anthropology.*

Levins, Richard. *Evolution in Changing Environments*. Princeton, N.J.: Princeton University Press, 1968.

> *This is a good book for those of you who have had training in biology or premedicine. It is an intermediate book that has stimulated a good deal of thought on the part of anthropologists, even though it is concerned with animal ecology.*

Netting, Robert MacC. *Cultural Ecology*. Reading, Mass.: Addison Wesley, 1972.

> *An excellent introduction to the subject by the person who wrote the books and articles on the Kofyar of Nigeria.*

Rappaport, Roy A. *Pigs for the Ancestors*. New Haven: Yale University Press, 1968.

> *A marvelous, detailed ecological study of a New Guinea people (the Maring). Rappaport shows how their rituals control problems brought about by overpopulation that threatens environmental design because of reduced surplus carrying capacity.*

Zubrow, Ezra. *Prehistoric Carrying Capacity*. Menlo Park, Cal.: Cummings, 1977.

> *This book is recommended for students who have had training in computer science. Here you will see how anthropologists try to determine carrying capacity, as well as how they try to prove their arguments through computer simulation. Not for beginners, and not for people who have had no background in computer science.*

Glossary

carrying capacity   The density of the human and animal population in some well-defined environment when it is at equilibrium (i.e., in balance with the environment).

coarse-grained environment   An environment that displays a lot of variety in its ecological outputs. (Sometimes referred to as a "patchy" environment.)

ecological niche   The feeding habits of a human population. Niches can be wide or narrow, depending on the range of foods consumed and the degree of strictness of the food preferences.

environmental degradation   The process whereby the ecological outputs of the environment decline.

extensive agriculture   Agricultural practices that use a lot of land instead of a lot of labor. Swidden agriculture is extensive, for example. *See also* intensive agriculture.

fine-grained environment   An environment that displays a low degree of variety in its ecological outputs.

grain   The degree of variegation of ecological outputs in a specified habitat.

intensive agriculture   Agricultural practices in which the same land is used over and over again, and much labor is expended in preparing it and keeping it fertile. *See also* extensive agriculture.

off-stage drama   The processes in the social and physical environment that are going on without our realizing it. Slow undetectable environmental degradation is an example of an off-stage process.

on-stage drama   The drama of everyday life, of which we are conscious and aware. It includes our own view of what we are doing, in our own terms and opinions. *See also* off-stage drama.

pure production strategy   In agriculture, an agricultural practice in which only one technique is used and very few crops are grown; (in general) the use of a single technique for food-getting.

uncertainty   The degree of variability in ecological outputs.

20

Anthropological Demography

Introduction

We have seen that the population itself is an important component of the biocultural system. Population means people and people mean numbers. The number of people in a population is a significant determinant of the nature of the adaptive relationship of the group to the environment. Too few persons may mean that a given habitat cannot be exploited efficiently, while too many will create pressures on the resource base of the ecosystem.

The analysis of the numerical features of a population constitutes the discipline of **demography.** Demographers study the size of a population as well as its structure. They analyze the changes in the size and structure of the population from year to year, but focus their efforts on the populations of nations and states.

The size, composition, and rate of change of a population also are important to an anthropologist studying a group. Throughout this book, we have been mentioning the role of group size and structure in determining the adaptation and adaptability of a population. In discussing the transition to food production, we discussed the interaction of techniques of subsistence with population size. When dealing with population genetics, we emphasized the differences in population size and how it affected evolutionary change.

In this chapter we will cover anthropological demography. Whereas demographers usually deal with large populations, anthropologists study small groups. Whereas demographers are usually interested in broad, long-range questions, anthropologists are interested in intensive, microscopic analysis of a whole society. And where demographers utilize elegant mathematical techniques, anthropologists rarely have the large sample sizes that such techniques require. So while the aim of the two disciplines may be the same, the approaches and methods are likely to differ.

Demographic Parameters

Anthropologists utilize three basic demographic parameters. First is *size;* that is, how many people make up the population? In a small hunting and gathering society, we may know this number precisely and are quite likely to know everyone by name. If the group is larger, we may have to estimate population size in some way, employing a sampling technique. Or we may be interested in the size of particular subgroups within the society; if there is social stratification, we will need to know the size of the various social or economic status groups.

The second parameter is *composition.* What is the structure of the population in terms of age? Or what is the *sex ratio?* This measure relates the number of males to females, using the formula:

$$\frac{\text{number of males}}{\text{number of females}} \times 100$$

This expresses the number of males per 100 females: if the sex ratio is 100, there is an equal number of each.

The third parameter is population *growth*. What is the rate at which the population is growing? Usually this is expressed as a percentage of the population size—we might determine that a population is growing at the rate of 3 percent per year. Don't be fooled by such an apparently low figure, which is a rate that characterizes the growth of the world's developing countries. A growth rate of 3 percent per year really means that the population will double in size every 23 years; a modest rate can mean an enormous growth!

A Population Pyramid

Figure 20.1, taken from *Demographic Anthropology* by Alan Swedlund and George Armelagos (1976), shows one way to visualize the age and sex structure of a population, a *population pyramid*. Males are grouped to the left of the vertical line and females to the right in each pyramid, and each sex is grouped by age, usually by five- or ten-year categories.

The first pyramid represents the population of a modern developed country. The numbers in each age category vary, but not by much until one reaches old age, when obviously they drop. Even though the proportion in the older age categories falls, there is still a large number of aged compared with the other two pyramids.

This contrasts with the second pyramid, one typical of a developing country. The number of older persons is drastically reduced and the number of children and youth is correspondingly increased. In fact, this pyramid looks like a pyramid!

The third pyramid is one derived from the Yanomamo Indians of the Venezuelan rain forest. It is of interest because it shows what many small, remote societies display—a disproportionate number of males. A number of mechanisms have been suggested to account for this, some of which we will discuss in the following pages; but in truth, no one knows exactly why this occurs.

Sex Ratio

The sex ratio is not a fixed number but varies widely. Demographers know that more males are born than females, the sex ratio at birth being on the order of 105. Biologists tell us that the ratio at conception may be even

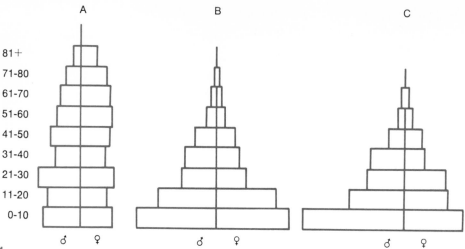

Figure 20.1
Age structure pyramids of three populations. Each horizontal bar represents ten years of age. The wider the bar the greater the percentage of the population represented. Pyramid A shows a modern "developed" pattern with low mortality rates and low fertility rates. Pyramid B depicts the "developing" pattern where fertility is quite high and mortality is relatively high. Pyramid C is an "anthropological" population based on two villages of the Yanomamo Indians.

higher, perhaps 120. In other words, more males die during fetal life than females, and in fact, more males die at any age throughout the life cycle until near the limits of longevity. Females are the hardier of the sexes; at birth in the United States, the life expectancy of a female is now eight years longer than that of a male.

Fertility and Mortality

New individuals enter a population in two ways: they are born into it or immigrate into it. The term *fertility* refers to births, and the **fertility rate** refers to the average number of births to women in specific age groups.

People may leave a population by emigration. They also die, and *mortality* is a measure of death. **Mortality rates** are calculated for particular ages, for infants or preschool children, for women of childbearing age, and so forth.

Because fertility and mortality vary widely from population to population, they are of interest in anthropology. Table 20.1 presents fertility estimates for various groups, taken from the survey of James Spuhler (1963). Fertility is given for females who have completed their reproductive years, normally women beyond age 45. This ensures that the number of births is not just a function of mother's age.

The fertilities given in the table show a pattern. The highest average number of births is found in sedentary populations, intensive farmers from developing countries; the lowest is found among women from the developed countries of the world. Tribal societies—smaller, often hunting-gathering populations—have moderate fertilities. In other words, tribal societies are able to maintain their populations without the excessively high fertility rates that we might imagine necessary.

Table 20.1

Fertility of Women in Various Groups.

Group	Mean Number of Offspring
Tribal	
Lesu (New Hebrides)	1.7
Peri (New Guinea)	1.3
Ramah Navajo (U.S.A.)	2.1
State	
Hutterites (Canada)	7.8
Maori (New Zealand)	5.2
Nations	
Japan	3.7
Czechoslovakia	2.3
Switzerland	1.8
Bengal (India)	4.8

Table 20.2

Estimated Annual Number of Infant Deaths Per 1,000 Live Births for Various Countries.

Sweden	13.0[1]	Germany F.R.	22.8[1]
Netherlands	13.6[1]	Israel	24.8[2]
Norway	13.7[1]	U.S.S.R.	26.4[2]
Iceland	14.1[1]	Italy	32.7[1]
Finland	14.5[1]	Jordan	36.3[2]
Japan	15.3[1]	Argentina	58.3[2]
Denmark	16.4[1]	Burma	66.5[2]
Switzerland	16.7[1]	Nigeria	78.9[2]
France	17.0[1]	Columbia	80.0[2]
Australia	17.8[1]	U.A.R.	83.2[2]
England & Wales	18.3[1]	Guatemala	91.5[2]
Canada	20.8[1]	Chile	99.7[2]
Belgium	21.7[1]	India	139.0[2]
U.S.A.	21.8[1]	Pakistan	142.0[2]
		Chad	160.0[2]

Sources:

1. Doll, R. "Monitoring the National Health Service." *Proc. Roy. Soc. Med.* 66:729–740 (1973).

2. Chase, A. *The Biological Imperatives. Health, Politics and Human Survival.* New York: Holt, Rinehart and Winston, 1971.

Table 20.2 presents estimates of infant mortality for a number of countries. Infant mortality is defined as the number of infants dying between the ages of one month and one year, expressed in terms of 1,000 infants. The range of variation is very high—in fact, twelvefold from the lowest to highest. The poorer nations of the world, as we would expect, have the highest infant mortality.

However, it might be surprising to note that the United States ranks fourteenth in infant mortality among these 29 countries! In fact, our infant mortality is higher than almost every country of western Europe except Italy and West Germany. In view of the fact that infant mortality is a sen-

Table 20.3

Estimated Annual Number of Infant Deaths, Per 1,000 Live Births, by Family Income, U.S.A. (All races combined.)

Family Income	Male	Female
Under $3,000	36.2	27.9
$3,000—4,999	28.1	21.9
$5,000—6,999	20.3	15.9
$7,000—9,999	21.3	18.2
$10,000 and over	22.1	17.6

Source: McMahon, B.; Kovar, M. G.; and Feldman, J. J. "Infant mortality rates: socioeconomic factor," *Vital and Health Statistics*, Ser. 22, No. 14. Washington, D.C.: U.S. Government Printing Office, 1972.

sitive measure of the health level of a group, this statistic has caused many health planners to question aspects of our health care system.

Further evidence for the sensitivity of infant mortality to environmental conditions is given by Table 20.3, which shows infant mortality in the United States in the early 1970s by family income. Income, while not a perfect measure, is still one of the best indicators we have of environmental quality among Americans. It is clear that income is related to mortality of infants. In poor families earning less than $3,000 per year, the mortality rate among infants is 60 percent higher than that found in the most affluent families.

Demography and Adaptation

The basic demographic parameters tell us a great deal about human populations. People constitute a stress—the more people, the more mouths to feed. Age is an important variable, since the greater the proportion of young persons, the greater the proportion of dependents in a group.

So, people constitute a demonstrable stress in any system. Anyone who has driven in a city's rush-hour traffic knows that. But people also constitute an adaptive mechanism. A variety of people can perform a variety of tasks. A large population affords a variety of occupational and craft specialists, to an extent not enjoyed by the small societies of the world.

Population Control

Now we are in a position to explore in more detail the role of demographic variables in the design of biocultural systems. Today it is not necessary to point out that unlimited population increase leads to environmental degra-

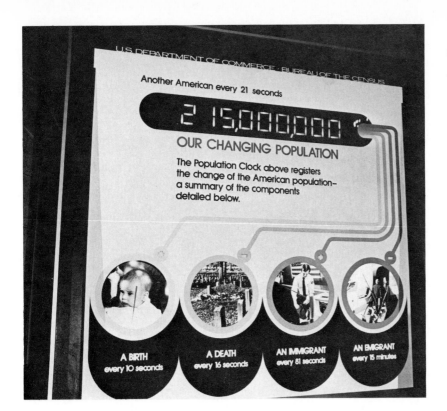

dation, and the resulting increase in environmental uncertainty in turn places the biocultural system in jeopardy. Everybody is conscious of the need to control population increase. But this is a recent preoccupation. Human groups have been much more concerned with keeping fertility high to ensure that the group survived. The notion of "limits to growth" did not exist in the past, and besides, if the group became too large, it could splinter into two or more new populations that simply moved into an unoccupied area. Even in the recent past, European societies (France and Germany, for example) encouraged fertility in their populations for economic and political reasons.

On-stage then, traditional societies encouraged fertility. But all societies have built-in checks on population growth as well; some are voluntary (and conscious) and others are involuntary (and unconscious). These checks helped to keep population size under control in the early periods of human history, yet they didn't have to be extremely efficient. After all, the human species was not very large and growth was not the problem that it is today. Yet these checks served to limit population growth to a moderate rate. Desmond (1962) has estimated that during the last 600,000 years of the Paleolithic, on the order of 12 billion people

Figure 20.3
Many countries are now beginning to control birthrates. India under Indira Gandhi made an especially hard attempt at control. It is very difficult to convince people that they will be better off if they have fewer children.

were born. Yet in only the last 6,000 years of human existence, 23 billion persons have been born.

Remember the formula:

$$\text{Population increase} = (\text{Fertility} + \text{Immigration}) - (\text{Mortality} + \text{Emigration})$$

To control population increase, fertility, mortality, and migration must be controlled. Let us start with fertility.

Controlling Fertility

There are two important involuntary means of fertility control: *lactation* and *malnutrition.*

Lactation (milk production by a nursing mother) may very well be the major mechanism by which groups unconsciously limit their fertility. It is now known that while a woman is nursing her infant, the lactation process adversely affects her ability to conceive. The effect is called **lactational amenorrhea,** or infertile menstrual cycles caused by lactation.

The extent to which lactation regulates fertility has been shown in Potter et al. (1963) in a study of a village in India. There the average interval between births was 30 months. By a statistical analysis of factors affecting this interval, Potter was able to show that 11 months of it could be accounted for by nursing; of all the factors that increased the birth interval, lactation was the most significant. He also analyzed a number of women who lost their infants in the first two months after birth and so did not lactate. Among these women, the average birth interval was much less; in fact it was 18 months, a reduction of 12 months.

Malnutrition is also a significant check on fertility. Women who are chronically undernourished conceive less readily since the shortage of essential nutrients affects their bodies, while the excess energy they expended in obtaining even a minimum amount of food reduces their sex drives.

Yet in many societies where women are chronically undernourished, they display high fertility rates. Imagine how high their fertility rates would be if lactational amenorrhea and malnutrition were absent!

A third mechanism of involuntary fertility control has been called, by Ashley Montagu, "adolescent sterility" (Montagu 1960). If we observe the sexual behavior of peoples around the world, we find that sexual intercourse begins with the onset of biological maturation. In some societies, for example, the Samoans, there is virtually no restriction on premarital intercourse.

Despite the high frequency in some groups of early sexual intercourse, birthrates remain low until women enter their twenties, even in societies with no reliable knowledge of contraceptives. Why? In 1960, Ashley Montagu brought together a body of information indicating clearly that the onset of menstruation in a female does not signal full sexual maturity. The female menstrual cycle is physiologically complex, and for a woman to conceive, several hormonal systems must all be working together. This may not happen until five to ten years after *menarche,* the first menstruation; it may take that long for everything to mature to proper working order.

Of course, teenagers can and do conceive. But a regular cycle of potential fertility is the exception rather than the rule. Although adolescent sterility isn't a reliable means of birth control, it is effective in reducing the overall fertility of women in a society.

There are four important modes of voluntary control over fertility that all involve depressing the frequency of sexual intercourse. All societies place some check on sexual intercourse, if only through the imposition of the incest taboo. But many forbid sexual intercourse at different times of the year or at different periods of the woman's life cycle. Sometimes beliefs about the body and about the spirits are invoked to prevent sexual intercourse. These on-stage beliefs may have little off-stage effect, as when they taboo sexual intercourse during the woman's menstrual period. But sometimes they have great off-stage effect, as in the case of a New Guinea tribal group. Lorraine Sexton calculated that over 200 days a year were tabooed for sexual intercourse. In this group, contact with women was felt to be defiling and weakening for men and so was kept to a minimum. All periods of warfare or war rituals, all important occasions when men had to be pure, were occasions when sex was tabooed. Clearly these on-stage beliefs had off-stage effects of diminishing fertility.

A very common taboo on sexual intercourse is to be found when a woman has just delivered a baby. This is called the *post-partum sex taboo.* It can last for as little as a month or two or as long as five years. In the latter case, husbands are permitted sexual satisfaction with other women, but the woman is effectively deleted from the roster of potential reproducers, and the taboo has a strong off-stage effect. Frequently, this custom is tied to lactation—it is felt that if a man has intercourse with a woman while she is nursing, it will damage her milk.

Late marriage and celibacy inhibit sexual intercourse and thereby drive down fertility. We are all aware of the great upsurge in population in the nineteenth century in Europe. Most of us believe that it was caused by improved public health conditions, but we may not realize that an additional boost was given to fertility rates by the declining age at marriage. Age at marriage declined from the Elizabethan period onwards. During the sixteenth and seventeenth centuries, people married in their twenties. During the late nineteenth century, people married in their teens. And even though marriage and sex are two different things, it is a fact that women who marry earlier will, on the average, have more children than those who marry later.

Marriage customs that encourage older and less fertile adults to mate with younger people reduce fertility as well. The Tiwi of Australia are accustomed to arrange marriages between young girls and prestigeful older men who are jealous of their sexual rights. Sometimes girls are even pledged at birth. We cannot be sure that these girls do not have frequent sexual contact outside of marriage with younger and more potent males. Still, the penalities for adultery are sufficient to deter such contact and drive down the fertility rate of the group as a whole.

To summarize, there are seven ways of reducing fertility, of which three are involuntary—lactation, malnutrition and adolescent sterility; and four are voluntary, involving taboos on sexual intercourse through (1) beliefs in pollution or harm from sex, (2) post-partum sex taboo, (3) late marriage and celibacy, and (4) marriage customs that mandate large age differences between men and women in marriage. Of course, modern contraceptive methods are spreading and will increasingly have to be added to the list. So perhaps we should add: (5) the pill.

Controlling Mortality

Mortality is the second variable that controls population increase. The most important source of high mortality in the population is *child mortality*. It is high in sedentary groups, low in hunting and gathering groups as well as in industrialized societies. Where it is high, 50 percent of all children will die by age 5. Therefore it is the most important mechanism of population control among the settled peasant populations of Asia, Latin America, and parts of Africa.

A second involuntary mode of population control through mortality may be called *predation*. In the animal kingdom the weaker and more vulnerable animals fall prey to predators. Human societies, however, put whole classes of people at *risk* of predation, often the most fertile in the population. Typically, young adult men are sent to war, thus eliminating their procreative potential through absence, death, or disablement.

Three voluntary mechanisms for population control through increased mortality rates are found: infanticide, abortion, and altruistic suicide.

Infanticide is the killing of children. There are two kinds of infanticide: overt and covert. Overt infanticide is institutionalized; that is, it is a public act, approved in custom and law and carried out by an authorized person in the society. Acts of infanticide carried out by ancient Roman fathers who told a slave to expose a child whom they did not wish to recognize were overt. Indians of the Amazon Basin will kill a malformed infant at birth, out of the belief that the infant is a "spirit" child; a god is its father. There is no punishment for infanticide if it is overt, because it is a recognized institution in the society.

Much commoner than overt infanticide is covert infanticide, whereby infants die from being abused, abandoned, or badly fed. Americans practice covert infanticide in the form of child abuse. In areas of the world where there are very high fertility rates and where women can expect to have an average of seven live births in their lifetime, it is certain that covert infanticide takes place. (It is hidden in the terribly high infant mortality rates: 50 percent of the children die before the age of 5.)

Female babies are killed more often then males. This makes sense in terms of population control, since the elimination of a female from a breeding population ensures that she will produce no offspring, while killing a male in a sex-balanced population carries no such assurance.

Abortion is the second voluntary means of raising mortality rates. Most societies practice abortion, sometimes with rather crude but effective methods. The legalization of abortion in the United States during certain phases of pregnancy has had a marked effect upon fertility. Kramer (1975) analyzed the impact of abortion on female fertility during 1970 and 1971 in New York City. Prior to the liberalization of the law regulating abortion, the fertility of white women averaged 2.15 births and black women, 2.85. In the course of 18 months, fertility rates fell to 1.84 and 2.11 respectively, slightly below the level necessary for replacement. Kramer concludes that abortion has accelerated the trend toward lower fertility (Kramer 1975).

Altruistic suicide is the final mechanism for controlling population increase through mortality. We used to think of it as being bizarre or primitive, but it is a part of the national debate about life, death, and terminal illness. The family member who chooses to die rather than live through the final stages of a terminal illness is no less committing altruistic suicide than the Eskimo elder who leaves the family hunting group and goes out on the ice alone to die of exposure. In times of crisis and stress, older people may choose to die to let the younger have their chance at life.

Five mechanisms are found, then, for population control through increased mortality rates: two of them are involuntary—infant mortality and predation; and three voluntary—infanticide, abortion, and altruistic suicide.

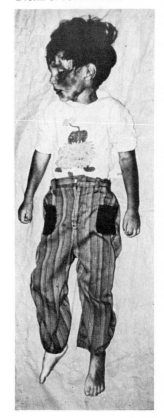

Figure 20.4
The problem of battered children is only now beginning to get the attention the problem deserves. Child abuse is a form of covert infanticide.

Population Pressure on Resources

The size or rate of growth of a population does not present problems all by itself. If a population has a large habitat into which it can expand, the population densities will not rise, even though the size of the population increases. **Population density** *is the number of people per unit of area,* conventionally calculated as the number per square mile.

Population density is the number of people per unit of area.

Population densities vary all over the world, from a low one-half person per square mile among hunting and gathering groups in marginal lands, to 915 per square mile in the densely populated urban areas of New Jersey.

Population pressure *refers to the pressure that is placed on resources when population density increases.* It was included in the general model of environmental uncertainty under the title "surplus carrying capacity." The more surplus carrying capacity a population enjoys, the less the population pressure on resources. But when the population density increases to the point where the surplus starts to get small, then controls in the biocultural system must be activated either to increase carrying capacity or decrease population density.

Biocultural systems do not wait for the surplus to go to zero. If they did, then there would be no resilience in the system, no latitude. Remember the fundamental problem of design: all biocultural systems have to survive in the long term, given environmental fluctuations. If the surplus went to zero during a favorable period for the system, then as soon as a bad period occurred, the system would be wiped out. That is what would have happened if the Indian rice and millet farmer had eaten his sacred cows.

Since all long-term survivors among biocultural systems have managed to activate controls before the surplus capacity went to zero, it is hard to point out instances where such controls did not work. There is one example, however, of a contemporary system in which disaster occurred and which at present is threatened with extinction. The people are the pastoral nomads of northern Africa, a part of the world called the Sahel. *The problem they failed to solve, which must be solved by all biocultural systems, is called the Tragedy of the Commons.* It bears careful study, because much of the subsequent discussion in demography and economics is going to be concerned with it.

The Tragedy of the Commons

A particular ecological problem originating from the relationship between population pressure and carrying capacity has dogged humankind for centuries and has become particularly acute in recent years. Garrett Hardin (1968) has called it the "tragedy of the commons." He means tragedy in the old-fashioned sense of a drama in which the spectator can see, in the off-stage drama, the remorseless working of events to bring about the destruction of the hero. In this case, Hardin means the remorseless working of population growth, combined with the pursuit of a decent life, bringing about the destruction of the environment that sustains a

Population pressure refers to the pressure that is placed on resources when population density increases.

The problem they failed to solve, which must be solved by all biocultural systems, is called the Tragedy of the Commons.

society. His example is hypothetical but, tragically, the Sahel exactly fits his imaginary scheme.

Imagine a group of herdsmen who are trying to do the best they can by pasturing their animals on the common land. "Common land" is land owned by the group as a whole and used by any and all members. Each herdsman has an interest in putting as many animals as he can on the common. This is because the benefits of the extra animal come to him, while the cost to him (in consumed pasture) is very small indeed. He adds another animal to his herd, and another, and another. Hardin states, "Therein is the tragedy. Each man is locked into a system that compels him to increase his herd without limit—in a world that is limited. Ruin is the destination toward which all men rush, each pursuing his own best interest in a society that believes in the freedom of the commons. Freedom in a commons brings ruin to all."

Pollution is the opposite side of the same coin. But rather than subtracting something from the commons, like pasture grass, we add something. To each polluter, the increase in costs (or the subtraction from social benefit) is a very small fraction of the gain received from being able to dispose of wastes cheaply or at no cost at all. So, we ourselves are locked into a system "of fouling our own nest so long as we behave only as independent, rational free-enterprisers."

The consequences of this thinking for population control are rather shocking. If it is the case that the tragedy of the commons inevitably occurs under conditions of freedom and, in particular, under conditions of freedom to breed, then that freedom has to be limited.

The Tragedy of the Sahel   To most of us pollution is an irritant rather than a tragedy. The spoilage of our national parks and open spaces is sad, and we hope reversible, but it does not have the impact of a natural disaster. In the Sahel, in Africa, the tragedy of the commons has had the force of a terrible sustained natural disaster. The nomadic Fulani and Tuareg herdsmen of this desert area have suffered a long drought that has left between 50 and 80 percent of their livestock dead, and their people starving and destitute in refugee camps. Computer analysis carried out by Picardi and Siefert (1976) has shown that the terrible drought of 1973–74 was *not* the root of the problem of starvation. Population growth that began in the 1920s was inexorably leading to the spoilage of the environment. Aid programs were worsening the situation. In fact, the institution of herd management techniques, breeding programs, well-digging and securing of water supplies, restocking programs, reforestation and reseeding programs designed to halt the deterioration only hastened the process of turning the pasture land into desert. The villain was not the

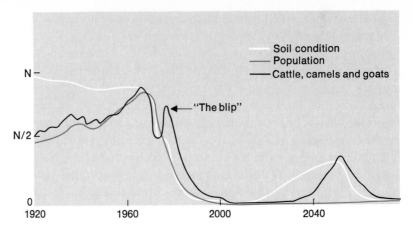

Figure 20.5
A computer simulation of the processes creating the tragedy of the Sahel.

drought at all, but a *deceptive* prosperity during the middle 1960s brought on by greater than average rainfall. The good rains came, the scrublands bloomed, the herdsmen increased herd sizes, and the scene was set. When the droughts came, the herdsmen had to retain more of their animals on the range land to get enough milk to feed themselves and their families. The range land became overgrazed to the point where it could not recuperate. The deserts took over as the inevitable result of individual families trying to keep up an adequate diet without regard for the welfare of all.

Picardi and Siefert (1976), in their computer simulation, showed that aid programs were more harmful than beneficial. Look at Figure 20.5. You can see that with all the well-intended aid from collaborating governments, by 1980 the Sahel will begin its inexorable progress toward death. As the ability of the environment to sustain a population declines, the remaining herders have one last "fling," increasing their herds dramatically. (See the arrow in the diagram.) That "blip" finishes the environment, and by the year 2000, a scarce twenty years after the temporary times of plenty, the Sahel is no longer capable of sustaining any herdsmen at all. A true tragedy of the commons will have occurred.

There are three ways that the tragedy of the commons can be avoided. First, *economically,* by restricting production and/or restricting access to the means of production (the commons). Second, *technologically,* by increasing the efficiency of one's means of production, thereby increasing carrying capacity. And third, *demographically,* by reducing population pressure on resources.

Since technology and economics are the subject of the next chapter, here we will concentrate on demographic solutions to the tragedy of the commons, or how to relieve population pressure on resources before it extinguishes the biocultural system.

Demographic Mechanisms to Control Population Pressure

Cyclic Management

We tend to think of societies as settled and continuous. If we are told, for example, that the population density of such and such a group is 100 persons per square mile, we assume that it stays around that figure. But this is not the case with all societies. Some human groups have a population-pressure control policy based on cyclical variation in the population density. During part of the year their societies have high population densities, while at other times they are quite low. Figure 20.6 shows just how a population can fluctuate in size—in this case, the population of the island of Tristan da Cunha in the mid-Atlantic (Roberts 1968).

The Plains Indians of North America were another group of tribes whose population sizes fluctuated strikingly, as Oliver (1962) has shown. They did not all live together during most of the year. Their life-support system was based on the bison who roamed together in great herds only in the summer when grass was comparatively plentiful. During the winter the bison herd fragmented and expanded its grazing territory north and south to survive the winter. The Indians not only followed the movements of the bison herds but also imitated their growth and decline in numbers. During the summer the tribes gathered in the south central plains to scout and kill among the great herds. This was the time when the great communal hunts took place, as well as tribal festivals such as the Sun Dance which attracted and required many people. When winter

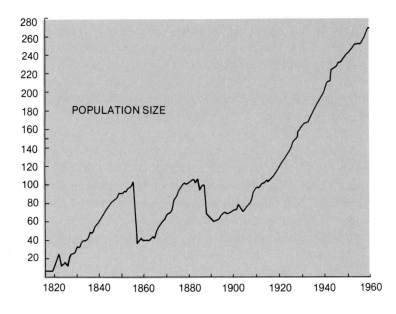

Figure 20.6
The size of the population of Tristan da Cunha on December 31 of each year from 1816 to 1960.

came, the bison split up and so did the tribe, breaking down into small multifamily bands.

If the tribes had never come together, they would have been defenseless against their enemies. They would have lacked the ability to come together for common defense. There would have been no tribal identity or common feeling—or, for that matter, any common language. Fortunately the fluctuating bison population permitted the periodic integration of the tribe, as well as providing the food for the maintenance of the larger group.

A Formal On-Stage Means of Redistributing Population

The Plains Indians followed the bison. It is not at all likely that they thought of the consequences of breaking up their groups every year, even though this dispersal and reunion alone permitted their technology to thrive and their system to survive.

Still other societies have conscious means at their disposal to bring about favorable population/resource ratios. These means are built into their social systems. Each family that tries to make a decent life for itself is presented a set of alternatives, one of which it chooses, and thereby redistributes the population so as to maintain favorable ratios.

One of the best studied of such systems is the Gilbertese, who were studied by Ward Goodenough (1955). To understand the Gilbertese population-pressure policy, one has to understand their system of kin groups, because the kin groups control access to the most important resource: land.

There are three kinds of kin groups that have something to do with the land: the *oo,* the *bwoti* and the *kainga.* The *oo* is a group of people who are all descended from a common ancestor. All the members of the *oo* have the right to claim land that belonged to the ancestral group, and land rights descend to both sons and daughters through fathers and mothers. As you can imagine, the number of claims on the ancestral territory increases with each generation, so that were everyone to claim their rights, the plots of land would be very small and uneconomical indeed.

Each piece of land is symbolized and represented by a "seat" or *bwoti* in the meeting house of that territory. The problem for each Gilbertese household head is to decide which *bwoti* belongs to him or which he may claim. Since he has rights to many plots of land by virtue of being a descendant from an ancestor and so belonging to that *oo,* he automatically has the right to be a member of many *bwoti.* He has to choose one.

The process of sorting people over the landscape is further complicated by the existence of a formally recognized grouping called the *kainga.* One belonged to the *kainga* if one's ancestor had resided there.

One could reside patrilocally or matrilocally, but if one chose the latter, one's children were debarred from membership in the father's *kainga*.

Goodenough (1955) says:

> Normally each member of the *kainga* had a plot in a tract of land associated with it. If this tract had a corresponding *bwoti* in the meeting house, all the *kainga*'s members would be eligible to sit there. The plots of those members of the *kainga* who moved away after marriage, however, went to their children, who belonged to other *kainga*. These children thus became eligible for membership in a *bwoti* other than that to which most of their *kainga* mates belonged. By this process members of the same *bwoti* could and did belong to different *kainga,* even though both types of groups were founded by the same ancestors. While each *kainga* tends to be associated with a specific *bwoti,* their respective personnel are not congruent.

Complicated, no? Think of it this way. Let's assume that Grandfather Northway owned a large, county-sized plantation in Virginia. All his descendants through his sons and daughters owned a part of it. All these people would be his *oo*. All the living household heads would have the right to a seat as a county commissioner (*bwoti*) and, as a county commissioner, a right to some land. Now Grandfather Northway was only one of your four grandparents and therefore you also had rights to other plantations throughout the state of Virginia. You, however, decide to live on Grandfather Northway's plantation and help work it. So, naturally, you have a seat as county commissioner in Northway County. But your brother decided that he could do better if he went to live on land that he claimed through Grandfather Huggins, your mother's father. So he becomes a member of the county commissioners in County Huggins. Your children can decide to change residence and so can your brother's children. Your other brother was a calculating fellow and married a rich wife and went to live on the lands that she had rights to. Now he is still your brother and still a descendant of both Grandfather Northway and Grandfather Huggins, but he is living with his in-laws and is, therefore, on that board of commissioners. Your children belong to the *kainga* of Northway County, your first brother's children to the *kainga* of Huggins County, and your other brother's children to the *kainga* of his in-laws. Their children will belong to the same *kainga* as their father.

That helps a little. But how on earth would things get so complicated? Well, in fact they are not. What we have discussed is complicated because we are trying to talk about the distribution of people in a landscape using the local ideas about inheritance, residence and descent. What we are really talking about is a system of open options, whereby people can take up residence and work for a living in different places. There is a tremendous amount of freedom of choice.

And in these systems there has to be. You see, the land-owning groups are small enough to be subject to the **law of small numbers,*** which means that there is going to be a good deal of fluctuation over time in the number of people in any *bwoti,* or land-using group. Some groups will be short-handed and others will be oversupplied with labor. So the rules of residence, inheritance, and descent work together to ensure that everyone can make a living and that the population can be distributed in a balanced way to spread population pressures evenly over the landscape.

Goodenough noted that on the island of Truk, where similar rules were followed, the groups readily double or halve their membership over the space of two generations. A rational household head will choose to live with that group where he can best make a living. The rules are sufficiently flexible to make this possible.

What Happens When Population Increases and Resources Are Fixed?

The Gilbertese are able to maintain an equilibrium between resources and population by moving people around. The carrying capacity of their environment is sufficient if people stay spread out. But there is another way to keep populations in balance. Instead of keeping the rules and moving the people about, you change the rules.

In highland New Guinea among the Mae Enga, there are similar, flexible choice rules, except that different communities interpret the rules according to how severe the population pressure is.

Meggitt (1965) has found that all the Highland groups have a "patrilineal ideology"; that is, if you ask them how people come to be affiliated with groups, they talk about the importance of ties down the male line. But if you take a census and genealogies in the villages, you can find lots of relatives living and working there who are not members of the patrilineal group. They are called *nonagnates* (agnatic means "patrilineal"). When population pressures become severe, the number of nonagnates diminishes sharply. Highland New Guinea people do not pay much attention to their ideology until they start running into shortages of land, and then they remember how patrilineal they are and exclude nonagnates from village lands. The open society closes its doors.

Flexible rules allow choice so long as the people do not feel that they are being crowded or that the process of environmental degradation

* The law of small numbers refers to the fact that statistical fluctuations are greatest when the group is numerically small. If I flip a coin ten times, what is the chance of getting seven heads? What then if I flip it a thousand times, what is the chance of getting 700 heads? The chances are much higher for getting a 7:3 split in ten tosses than in a thousand.

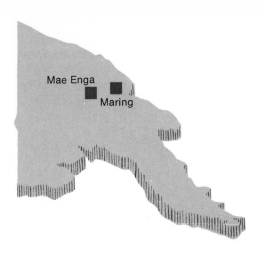

Figure 20.7
**New Guinea showing the
locations of the Maring and
the Mae Enga peoples.**

and creeping starvation is near. When that happens, they close their doors by reinterpreting the rules.

The United States used to receive immigrants from all over the world. But when people felt that their livelihoods were being threatened by the newcomers, they changed the immigration laws to slow the flood to a trickle. There is no evidence, as we now know, that our livelihoods were threatened, but our grandfathers felt there was and so they changed the rules, just like the Mae Enga.

Population Pressure and Warfare

Modern warfare, with its strategies of attrition (wearing the enemy down by inflicting maximum casualties) and unconditional surrender (forcing the enemy to forgo all rights after surrender), is unknown in traditional society. Warfare exists for a purpose, even though the purposes may not be entirely clear to the warriors. Andrew P. Vayda (1961) has studied warfare in New Guinea, and his data can be used to show how warfare can be a means of redistributing populations as well as maintaining a balance with resources.

New Guinea Warfare   Although warfare is endemic to the New Guinea highlands, its consequences insofar as the destruction of human life is concerned are usually very small. The initiation of warfare is ritually controlled. No party to a dispute may start fighting unless the group's own spirits are propitiated with pig sacrifice. Therefore, fights tend to break out only after major pig feasts have been held. There are always excuses for a fight: insults that have gone unchallenged, killings that have taken

Figure 20.8
New Guinea warriors, safe on a rocky perch, watch the battle below them.

place, illegal encroachments on the groups' lands, and many other slights, fancied or real.

Fighting can start with either "nothing fights" or raids. In "nothing fights" the villagers sally forth onto the fighting ground and shout insults at the other side, being careful to stay out of range of the enemies' spears or arrows. Raids, which are rarer, and only carried out by the stronger, more numerous clans against the weaker, are more vicious. Members of the more powerful clan infiltrate the weaker's village during the night and, at first light, stealthily creep up to the huts and poke their spears through in the hopes of wounding the inhabitants. Should the unfortunate house-holders try to escape, they are picked off with arrows.

After this first stage, the fight may well be over. The losing side, seeing in the "nothing fight" that they are inferior in numbers and spirit, will quit the battlefield; in the typical raid of the stronger against the weaker, the losers will abandon their village.

The "nothing fight," however, can escalate into a true fight where the enemies come to close quarters and do real damage. Though the warriors are cautious, dueling from behind heavy shields and darting out only when

Figure 20.9
Crouching New Guinea
warriors make their way
toward the front of the
battle lines.

it is apparently safe, deaths do occur. But the escalation is not irrevocable at this point. Just as with raids, the two parties can then agree that the issue has been solved and return to peaceful relations, without conquest or land redistribution.

However, if the enemy flees the field and is *routed*,* then it is possible for the fighting to proceed to the point where the losers are driven from their homeland and cease to compete with the conquerors for the mastery of the territory. This happens only occasionally, but when it does, it is instigated by groups who are suffering from population pressure on resources. The two Maring-speaking groups that Vayda noted had driven their enemies into refuge were those two populations who suffered from population pressure and whose environment showed either significant signs of degradation or shortage of forest lands. Vayda diagrams the stages of warfare as shown in Figure 20.10.

---

* *Routing* consists of going to the enemy settlements, burning the houses there, killing indiscriminately any men, women, or children found in the settlements and, after having put the survivors to flight, destroying gardens, fences, and pandanus groves, and defiling the burial places. Any survivors then go into refuge.

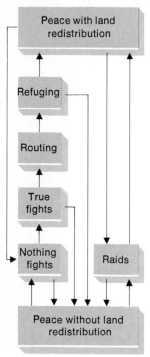

**Figure 20.10
The stages of warfare.**

Peace with land redistribution

Refuging

Routing

True fights

Nothing fights

Raids

Peace without land redistribution

Population Pressure and Technological Innovation

We should now consider one final issue that concerns population pressure and its control. During our discussion of the Neolithic period of cultural change, a chicken-and-egg problem was raised. We asked, "Did technological change increase food resources and thereby induce larger populations to take advantage of the opportunity? Or did population growth occur first and then bring about technological change to support it?" This is an old debate but nonetheless important. If technological change brings about population growth, then in this century we are surely bringing about a crisis of unprecedented proportions. World population is increasing so fast that we will have six billion inhabitants on this planet by the year 2000. By creating a technology that has reduced mortality rates and thereby increased population size, we have created a monster: unchecked population growth. People have to be fed; they will be fed or else we will see famine and pestilence that could remind us of the years of the Black Death in Europe. And with electronic communications girdling the globe, with transistor radios bringing news from all the world to all the world, we cannot expect starving peoples to rest peacefully while the rich of the world live in luxury.

On the other hand, if population pressure elicits or generates food technology, then we can rest more peaceably in the knowledge that a new equilibrium will be struck and that our present period of alarming growth will be checked in time, before we degrade our environment beyond repair.

There are arguments to be made on both sides, and the fact of the matter is, we simply do not know which position is true. If ever there was an unfortunate gap in our knowledge of archaeology and prehistory, it is this.

The Malthusian Position People who believe that population growth is brought about by technological change are called **Malthusians** after Thomas Malthus, the English economist whose *First Essay on Population* appeared in 1798. Malthus believed that there was an upper limit to the amount of food that could be squeezed from the land, and that population levels would rapidly rise to this upper limit from natural increase. He realized the implications of the fact that population rises *exponentially*—that is, each generation's females, being more numerous, provide doubly more numerous offspring. (Compound interest works the same way.)

Malthus believed that populations would inevitably push up against this upper boundary unless positive or preventive checks intervened to stop them. All the positive and preventive checks that we mentioned earlier are known to have existed in traditional societies, though never all in one. Population growth, fueled by the "passion between the sexes"

(Malthus's expression) inexorably pushes populations up to the point where the environment and food supplies are threatened. This is true, *if* (a very big "if") the technological level remains the same.

The Boserup Position We have already mentioned the proposition of Ester Boserup (1965), an agricultural economist. Boserup argues that population pressure does not force people to adopt more intensive methods of cultivation, although it gives them the opportunity to. She looks at the major methods of cultivation and finds that the most "primitive" are the most efficient technologically. That is, the output from slash-and-burn agriculture is not very high, but so little work has to be done that it is extremely efficient.*

No society would willingly shift to a less efficient but more productive system, like hoe or plow agriculture, because of the tremendous increase in labor that is required. Slash-and-burn cultivators are regularly reported to work no more than two to two-and-a-half hours per day, except in the busy season when time spent working increases by 50 percent. Time requirements rise for hoe, and again for plow agriculture, and double for intensive multicropped irrigated farming.

Each step of this agricultural process generates more food on the same amount of land but requires much more labor. Therefore, people do not take up these relatively inefficient (but more productive) forms of agriculture until they have to and until it makes sense to. They have to when their population expands to a point where their homeland cannot sustain it. It makes sense to convert to a more intensive form of cultivation when there is surplus labor.

Both these conditions are satisfied when population density increases.

Even our modern "advanced" society is not free of this problem. The machine-age technology we have developed has not resulted in savings of labor. Considering the manufacturing process, the costs involved, and the energy required to operate our appliances, it can be shown that they don't, overall, save work. Their contribution is in supporting a larger population or increasing the carrying capacity.

So, whereas Malthus proposed that all populations would rise until the Four Horsemen of the Apocalypse (Famine, War, Pestilence, and Death) cut them down, Boserup disagrees. She feels that with increasing

---

* Remember that technological efficiency is defined as:

$$\frac{\text{Energy Output}}{\text{Energy Input}}$$

There are two ways you can raise your level of efficiency: increase output or decrease input. Obviously, slash-and-burn farming maintains high efficiency by reducing the energy (or labor) input.

Insight
Does Crowding Lower Fertility In Humans?

Nonhuman animals who have adapted genetically to a habitat and are ecologically highly specialized are subject to environmental controls of the population. In a famous experiment by Calhoun (1962), rats were observed under progressively more crowded conditions. The rate of increase of the population was not just halted, but actually declined as a result of the action of the rats' endocrine glands. In the final, highly crowded condition, the rats started exhibiting a number of perversions: they failed to copulate, neglected their young, reabsorbed the embryos, and ate their own pups, while some of the females became infertile.

Despite the feelings of some observers at the time the experiments (and others like them) were reported, there is no evidence that similar effects occur in human populations. There is some evidence that fertility decreases as cities become more dense, but there could be so many reasons for this that we cannot state that it is because of the physiological effects of crowding. Judging from the preference people seem to have for city life, human beings enjoy crowded situations. Aside from the social insects, we seem to be the most social animals on earth. To preserve a population equilibrium, we have to use cultural means. There is a good deal of evidence that we are doing that at the present time.

populations, the labor input to farming sensibly and inevitably increases to produce more food. She notes, however, that everyone has to work harder to do it.

There is not sufficient evidence to say whether Malthus or Boserup is correct. But the authors, who have examined the evidence, believe that Boserup is right.

Summary

1. Anthropological demography deals with smaller populations than does demography proper. That means that we cannot use some of the more elegant mathematical models that demographers have developed. Nevertheless, we still have to study the size and composition of populations because they are very important to understanding adaptation.

2. The form of the population pyramid is different for industrialized nations, for sedentary agriculturalists, and for hunting-gathering societies. The different shapes of the pyramids reflect differences in fertility and mortality.

3. There are seven ways of controlling fertility, eight if modern contraceptive devices are included. Three are involuntary—lactation, malnutrition and adolescent sterility. Four are voluntary, involving beliefs in pollution or harm from sexual intercourse, a taboo on sexual contact after childbirth, late marriage and celibacy, and finally, marriage customs that mandate large age differences between men and women in marriage.

4. Five mechanisms are found for population control through increased mortality rates. Two of them are involuntary—infant mortality and predation—and three are voluntary—infanticide, abortion, and altruistic suicide.

5. We are concerned with more than population size and composition. Population pressure, arising from high population density, is our concern as well. It can lead to irreversible environmental degradation. All societies must solve the "tragedy of the commons." All societies must avoid the problems and tragedy that face the Fulani and Tuareg tribesmen in the Sahel.

6. Cyclic management is one means of controlling population pressure on resources. The Plains Indians used it.

7. Population redistribution to maintain favorable resource/people ratios is another way of controlling population pressure. The Gilbertese have an elaborate system of social rules of residence that enables them to redistribute property.

8. The Mae Enga (New Guinea) manipulate their rules of descent. They use rules of descent group formation as we use immigration laws:

tightening them when population pressure is perceived and loosening them when it is not.

9. Warfare is another means of redistributing population so that resource/people ratios do not slide to the point where irreversible off-stage processes can take hold.

10. There are two positions that can be taken on the problem of expanding populations on a finite planet. The Malthusian position states that all populations expand to the point where most of the people live in misery, only barely able to support themselves. Malthusians think that technological innovation only encourages higher population, and that populations always rise to the carrying capacity of their environments. The followers of Ester Boserup believe that population pressure induces technological innovation, which almost always proves sufficient to support the increased population.

Suggested Readings

Boserup, Ester. *The Conditions of Agricultural Growth.* Chicago: Aldine Publishing Co., 1965.
> *The book is short, the lesson is clear, and it is an important one.*

Brookfield, H. C., and Brown, Paula. *Struggle for Land: Agriculture and Group Territories among the Chimbu of the New Guinea Highlands.* Melbourne: Oxford University Press.
> *An excellent book on land and the rules for its use among a traditional Highland New Guinea people.*

Oliver, S. C. *Ecology and Cultural Continuity as Contributing Factors in the Social Organization of the Plains Indians.* University of California Publications in American Archeology and Ethnology 48(1) (1962).
> *This is the book from which we took the example on resource management by the Plains Indians. Well worth reading and finding out more about a fascinating people.*

Swedlund, Alan C., and Armelagos, George J. *Demographic Anthropology.* Dubuque: Wm. C. Brown Company Publishers, 1976.
> *An ideal place to begin to expand your knowledge of demography. A short, general book, with a good bibliography.*

Wrigley, E. A. *Population and History.* New York: McGraw-Hill, 1969.
> *An excellent introduction to the role of demography in history.*

Glossary

altruistic suicide   The rare cultural practice for individuals of some social group (often the elderly) to release that group from the obligation of feeding and caring for them.

demography   The analysis of the size, composition, and rate of change of a population.

fertility rate   The average number of births to women of specific age groups.

infanticide   The practice of killing children at birth. It may be overt and institutionalized in the society, or it may be covert and punishable.

lactation   The process of milk production by a nursing mother.

lactational amenorrhea   Infertile menstrual cycles caused by lactation.

law of small numbers   The law that states that there will be greater statistical variability in small populations than in large.

malnutrition   A state of dietary deficiency that leads to nutritional stress (not just a lack of food).

Malthusians   People who believe that population will inevitably rise to the carrying capacity of the biocultural system.

mortality rate   The average number of deaths for people of a certain age group.

nonagnates   People who are not members of the patrilineage.

population density   The number of people per unit of area (square mile, or square kilometer).

population pressure   The pressure that is placed on resources when population density increases.

21

Economic Systems

Introduction

An environment affords *possibilities* to a population. When we study what the population does with those possibilities by exploiting them to serve their needs and culturally determined wants, we are studying **economics.** Economic activities are carried out on-stage for the most part, although their outputs have consequences for the off-stage drama. Economics can be defined as the study of the way people make use of the scarce means at their disposal to attain culturally defined goals. As soon as we turn from cultural ecology to economics, we turn our attention away from the environmental system to the human system. Society, for the purposes of the economist, can now be redefined as "organized appetite."

A biologist and an economist can observe the same activities and understand them quite differently. The biologist sees the organism satisfying its *biological needs* and doing it sufficiently well to maintain the organism and the population. The economist sees people satisfying their *wants.* The economist assumes that the organism is satisfying its necessities and focuses attention on the way wants, or desires, are culturally organized, and how activities are organized to satisfy these wants. A **need** is something that one has to satisfy. A **want** is something one desires to satisfy. The organism has to satisfy its needs while satisfying its wants, but its wants may well exceed its needs. The human organism *needs* periodic intake of high quality protein, but most Americans *want* beef steak and pork chops, not the lamb or soybeans that would provide the protein just as well.

Economics is the study of the way people make use of the scarce means at their disposal to attain culturally defined goals.

Preferences

We use the term "preferences" to describe people's wants. We assume, first, that people know what they want out of life and that they are consistent in their choices. We assume they order their wants and give them priorities.

Second, we assume that people everywhere "do the best they can in getting what they want," or to use the proper phrase, they *maximize* (do the best they can with) their preferences. Preferences vary from society to society, from group to group, and from person to person. One society's meat is another society's poison, and one of the things that the anthropologist has to find out is what the people's preferences are, in order to know whether and how they go about maximizing them. Since people have to decide their preferences for themselves, preferences are *subjective*—decided by one's own feelings and opinions. The term *utility* refers to the satisfaction that one gets from the prospect of acquiring some goal. So, we assume that people **maximize subjective utility** when they allocate their scarce resources to get the best they can out of their lives. Since it has not been proven that people maximize subjective utility, we refer to the idea as a hypothesis. But for research in economic anthropology, we can think of no better place to start than by assuming that people are trying to maximize subjective utility and then see how close they come. If they do not come at all close, then this usually means that they are being stopped, or *constrained,* by the scarcity of some critical resource in getting the best they can, and we want to know what that resource is.

Some Properties of Our Preferences

Common sense can tell us some things about preferences, although common sense is not always a good guide to people's behavior. We assume that preferences are known, or knowable. We assume that a person being interviewed is able to tell the interviewer what he or she wants in words the interviewer is going to understand. Neither the interviewer nor the subject need know *why* the person wants some good, only that he or she wants it.

Preferences must be knowable and codable for people to be able to talk about them. And since they are coded, we have to learn the language of preferences just as we have to learn any other system of meaning. Because part of the cultural code bears on preferences, preference schedules (lists) are culturally defined. One of the Zapotec preferences is for "respect." They will expend a year's earnings, mortgage their lands, and use a month of their time in order to pay the expenses of the fiesta of their patron saint. This act has utility for them because it gains the respect of others and social power in the community. It also prevents their being bewitched and, therefore, seriously sickened or injured, while at the same time, it enables them to ask for the help of their kinfolk in communal projects. One must do careful ethnographic work to discern people's preferences.

You Can Get Too Much of a Good Thing

A second property of people's preferences is called **diminishing marginal utility,** which means that the satisfaction that people receive from some category of good (utility) diminishes with each extra unit of it that they acquire. There was a popular short story written during the Depression about the rich man and the poor man who both died on the same day. The poor man, who had been on relief, had found a hundred-dollar bill in the street, spent it on liquor, and got so drunk that he died of alcohol poisoning. The rich man, the same day, had gone into his broker's office and found that his total resources had fallen to one hundred dollars; in despair, he threw himself out the window and committed suicide. The

Preference schedules (lists) are culturally defined.

hundred dollars meant different things to the two men. Similarly, the extra hundred dollars that the millionaire adds to his riches yields much less satisfaction than the same hundred dollars means to a person who is broke. The utility to the poor person is much higher than to the rich. This is the principle of diminishing marginal utility.

This is the principle of diminishing marginal utility.

Risk Aversion

Except on rare occasions, most people do not like (we are "averse to") taking risks: we practice **risk aversion.** In the following gamble, imagine you are playing with real money, convince yourself that the money is real, and think what you would do. The diagram in Figure 21.2 is a picture of a lottery in which you have two choices at first—to play or not to play. If you decide not to play, you neither win nor lose. If you decide to play, you have a 50/50 chance of winning or losing one hundred dollars.

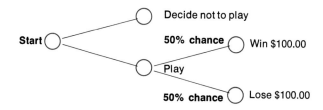

Figure 21.2
A fifty/fifty gamble.

What do you think most people decide? They usually decide not to play.

Risk aversion increases with the size of the stake and with the capital position of the player. For example, if you are rich you might accept the gamble in Figure 21.3, but if you were poor, you would not.

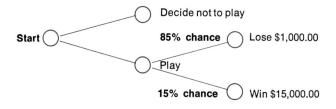

Figure 21.3
A rich man's risky gamble.

Now, if you played this game over and over again, you would stand to gain $400 per play over the long haul. But the stakes are so large that most people would avoid the game. They might even pay to get out of playing it. In fact, when we buy insurance we are paying to get out of gambles. Insurance companies are providing us with security, capitalizing on our aversion to risk.

People in traditional society, because they are generally poor, are highly risk averse. They avoid gambles.

Aversion   The first principle of economics in traditional society is based upon this finding: People in traditional society, because they are generally poor, are highly risk averse. They avoid gambles. If you think of entire societies as playing a game against nature, and think of nature as being a random or capricious player, you can then conclude that most people in traditional society are conservative in their strategy. Another way of putting it is to say that their economic strategies are arranged to minimize the uncertainty in the environment, to beat nature when it is doing its worst.

The Jamaican fishermen studied by William Davenport (1960) are an example of this conservativeness. Nature presents these folk with a gamble: they can fish either inside the lagoon where it is peaceful or outside the lagoon where they have to take a chance with the current. When the current is running outside, they lose their fishing pots, waste their time and energy, and come home a loser. But if they were calculating maximizers, they would still take their chances and fish on the "outside" all the time, because their profits would be larger, an average of 12 percent a month. But they choose not to do that. Instead, they play a conservative strategy based on their knowledge that the current runs one day out of four, and try to beat nature and stay in the game. As a result, their profits are lowered but they never go broke. They never have a run of bad luck that would put them out of the game.

Ownership

We saw earlier that an answer to the tragedy of the commons was the institution of restricted rights of access to public goods. One way of restricting access to public goods is to define a category of goods called private goods. When a single corporation, a person, a household, a lineage or clan, or a tribe has restricted access to some public good, we call this **private ownership.**

Peoples the world over vary enormously in what they define as public and private goods, and one job of the anthropologist is to find out how exclusive rights are coded in the society, and the degree to which categories of property are regarded as being the exclusive property of individuals, groups, or the whole tribe.

No right to private property is absolutely exclusive. If an American owns a farm in the Middle West, he or she cannot sell it to the Russians for a missile base, even though Americans generally have the right to sell their property as they see fit.

Americans tend to think of ownership as the right to dispose of property as they will. Most peoples around the world, particularly traditional peoples, are not as concerned about the rights of disposal of property. They are concerned with the rights to *use* the property, called **usufruct.** Herskovits (1952: 373) notes that the Eskimo rule of ownership is that

When a single corporation, a person, a household, a lineage or clan, or a tribe has restricted access to some public good, we call this private ownership.

Figure 21.4
American Indians signed
treaties the meanings of
which were uninterpretable
since the Indians recognize
ownership by usufruct.

possession is what counts: "A fox-trap lying idle may be taken by anyone who will use it; in Greenland a man already owning a tent or large boat does not inherit another's, since it is assumed that one person can never use more than one possession of this type."

Rights within the group are apportioned differently in different societies. George Spindler, who worked with the Menominee Indians of Wisconsin, reported that he was astonished to find that a 5-year-old child had the right to sell to a tourist a beautifully beaded costume made for him by his mother. When the mother was asked whether the boy was allowed to dispose of it, she said, "It is his. He can do with it as he wishes!"

The usual mode of ownership in traditional society is usufruct. This is why rents are so rarely charged for lands. The land has no value if it is not used; therefore no one has the right to charge for its use. This also explains why so many treaties with the North American Indians were so easily made by the U.S. government and then broken in anger by the Indians. It never occurred to the treaty-makers on the Indian side that they were abrogating their rights to hunting territory. Since the land had only use-value, it was absurd to suggest that any treaty could deny them access to it. In fact, all they thought they were doing was permitting the white man access to their hunting grounds—and then the white man stole the land itself!

Primitive Communism Never Happened

For a long time Westerners thought that some traditional peoples held all their resources in common. It was this belief in primeval communism that led anarchists to proclaim that "private property is theft!" Later studies showed that this was an exaggeration. For one thing, in every known society some goods are restricted in access. Goods that are manufactured by an individual, or by his or her group, usually are not public but private goods. We should not confuse the widespread practice of sharing with primitive communism. If a Nama Bushman, for example, makes a beautiful knife, everyone can admire his work. He will keep the knife for a while and then give it to someone else. The Bushmen, by their own account and by their actions, abhor the envy that accrues to someone who has something perfectly beautiful. Such goods are not kept for long, but quickly passed from member to member. But there is no question of where the knife originates nor whose generosity is being honored in the giving. If the knife belonged to all by right, then there would be no value in bestowing it on another person, since it would be giving to another what was already his or her due. Ownership implies the right of bestowal.

The definition of what can be owned is important in an anthropologist's understanding of the concept of property. We may think of Americans as obsessed by private ownership, but they are not. The Zapotec regard as private property goods that we would not even consider goods at all, such as empty bottles, corn gleanings, animal droppings, bits of cloth, and old torn clothing. But at the same time, the delicious fruit that grows on the cactus fences around their houses is a free good.

Among many slash-and-burn agriculturalists, land that is not in use can be claimed by one who needs it. Sometimes the tribal territory is divided up into sections reserved for clans, lineages, or extended family groupings, and the person in want may choose from within this territory.

We can state the principles of ownership as the second principle of traditional economics: Ownership in all societies is culturally and socially defined so as to restrict access to strategic and symbolic resources.

Ownership in all societies is culturally and socially defined so as to restrict access to strategic and symbolic resources.

Production and Consumption

The unit of production and consumption in traditional society is usually the individual household. We will examine production first.

Production in Traditional Society

Fixed Production Goals One of the most important aspects of production in traditional society is that people do not produce all they can. Most traditional peoples have **fixed production goals.** They produce what they need and stop when they have what they consider enough.

Household units of producers in traditional society have fixed production goals.

This is the third principle of traditional economics: Household units of producers in traditional society have fixed production goals.

What is considered *enough* varies from society to society. Though in many traditional societies, diets are monotonous and vary only slightly between rich and poor, the amount of production in a single community can vary widely. It is not just that some people are richer than others—a necessary consequence of different levels of production—but that the rate at which household heads will trade off units of food for units of leisure varies according to the utility for each.

Hungry Societies

The food procurement strategies of whole societies may guarantee them less food than they require. Such societies have hungry periods. There are, after all, two ways of combating food scarcity: one can produce more, or one can eat less. If people eat less, then they have to cut down on their activities. To Americans this may seem strange, since we are comparatively overfed. But other people around the world reject the idea of greater production, preferring reduced consumption. In times of hardship, they retire to their huts, drink coffee or water, fast, and rest.

The Bemba of Central Africa   The Bemba of central Africa, studied by Audrey Richards (1932), are a people who have a high utility for leisure and will substitute it for food production on a regular basis. They live in a difficult environment. Because of the tsetse fly which infects cattle with the deadly disease trypanosomiasis, they cannot keep cattle. There are no streams for fish, and game is very scarce. Their staple crop is finger millet, which is ground and then boiled into a lumpy porridge, which they consider the only "true" food. They eat it until their bellies are groaning and distended. In fact, Richards reports that we would think we had a stomach ache at the point when they think of themselves as being just nicely full.

For nine months the Bemba are well fed, for the millet lasts this long. But the other three months are "hungry months," as they call them. They serve only one meal a day. Sometimes there is not enough food for this one meal, and they take to their huts, drink water, and take snuff. Whatever food they have is likely to be eaten by relatives who will descend upon them if the word gets out that they have food. Since the Bemba housewife cannot know how many people are going to present themselves for dinner —it could be just the family, but it could include double the number of relatives—she cooks the same amount every day. When the relatives descend, everyone eats less, particularly the children, who live from table scraps and really feel the pangs of hunger.

Figure 21.5
Pollarding trees is far from easy. First you have to burn off the ground cover and let the sunlight in to the crops. Then you have to climb high into the trees and chop down the highest branches. Obviously, getting sunlight to the crops is not an easy task in tropical forests.

All Bemba know hunger well. They have all experienced starvation. They survive because they share, and as a result, the worst fate that can befall a Bemba is to live alone, isolated from his or her relatives. When an isolated family has food, it does not have to share. But when it has none, it cannot visit relatives, and the situation can become desperate.

The curious thing is that the Bemba need not go hungry! There is comparatively rich land available that they could plant in cassava and maize, crops with which they are familiar. But they say that the flours made from these crops (which other neighbor groups find edible and nourishing) do not fill one up; they "melt quicker inside" and therefore are not proper food. And besides, it is not proper work, raising cassava and maize—real work, "Bemba work," is performed when the tall trees of their forest lands are stripped of leaves and branches to let the sunlight in. (This is called *pollarding* the trees.) Men vie with each other in daring feats of climbing and in clever axe work high above the ground. Plowing or using a digging stick in the open lands, which we would find easier and more productive, is not "Bemba work" at all.

So they reduce their intake, reduce their activity, bear their hunger, and share what little they have with one another until the hungry season passes. Are they rational? Yes, by their own beliefs. We who have never known regular, periodic starvation would move heaven and earth to avoid it. We would change our family form, our government and our whole society, and give up all manner of other pleasures to avoid it. The Bemba will not even cultivate potentially rich lands within their own territories.

Low-Risk Production Strategies

With fixed production goals and a tendency to be highly risk averse, it is not surprising that most traditional societies around the world adopt low-risk strategies with consequent low payoffs, rather than strategies that would be more chancy but would yield them higher rewards. This principle of traditional economics is an extension of the first principle of high risk aversion. The fourth principle can be stated as follows: In traditional economies, producers overwhelmingly adopt low-risk strategies that have low payoffs for them.

In traditional economies, producers overwhelmingly adopt low-risk strategies that have low payoffs for them.

According to economic theory, farmers should allocate their labor, seed, and technology so that, under risk, they will receive the highest payoff either in the short or the long term. If a farmer is very cautious, he will probably get some crop each year, but in no year will he get a bumper crop, and over the long haul his average crop will be lower. People in traditional society often know that they are getting low outputs, but they prefer to trade off their utility for greater yields to ensure a secure, fixed output that will get them and their families through every year.

If there is no risk, the farmer can adopt a single strategy. This single strategy will probably be close to the theoretical maximum (optimum) because it will have been tried over centuries or millennia and will have been adopted because it gives the required amount for the least work. This is the fifth principle of traditional economics, the principle of least work: Other things being equal, people will do less rather than more work.

Other things being equal, people will do less rather than more work.

The Kapauku Horticulturalists   The Kapauku of New Guinea work hard and efficiently and apparently try to cultivate as rationally as they can. The uncertainty in their environment comes from flooding. If the rains are heavy, all the crops that they grow on the bottom lands of their mountain valleys are rotted out. The payoff is high if they plant on the bottom land, but the risk is also high. The yields from planting on the mountain sides are much smaller, but they are much safer too. Heavy rains will not wash the crop away nor rot it out.

Leopold Pospisil (1963), an anthropological economist who studied their production system, noted that they planted enough on the hillsides to ensure a sufficient crop of yams and sweet potatoes, their staple foods. He also noted that one village had tried to optimize by adopting the high-risk, valley-planting strategy. They were almost wiped out by the rains. Had they not been on very good terms with neighbors and so able to borrow enough to get them through the next season, they would have starved to death.

The Kapauku are a case of a society that adopts low-risk strategies with low payoff.

Figure 21.6
Kapauku farmers *top* burning off the ground cover in swidden, or "slash and burn," agriculture. The results *bottom* of the technique, which, according to Boserup, is the most efficient form of agriculture. Remember, efficiency is the ratio of (energy) inputs to (energy) outputs. Consider the American farmer who reaps a good amount but works so hard.

Labor Inputs to Production

When we were discussing the ecology of production in chapter 19, we were concerned with the energy efficiency of a particular productive strategy. When we turn to the study of economics, there is an analogous kind of relationship that we should explore in order to compare different societies and their forms of economic organization. The analogous relationship is the *efficiency,* or rate of output, given a certain level of labor input.

Figure 21.7
The optimal level of
production.

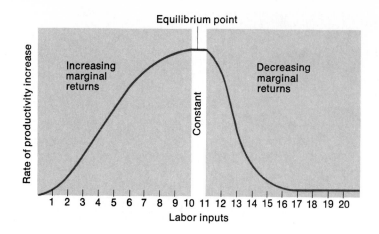

In discussing energy efficiency, we were concerned with the ratio of calories consumed in production to number of calories produced. In economics we are concerned with the rate of return to labor inputs. To use the correct term, we are interested in **marginal returns** to labor. "Marginal" is an important idea in economics. It refers to the return that one gets (in energy, or food, or production) when one inputs another, or *one more,* unit of labor into the productive process. There are three kinds of marginal returns. **Increasing marginal returns** refers to a situation where an extra unit of labor input (a man-day or man-hour) yields *more* than the previous man-day or man-hour. **Constant marginal returns** occur when the *same* amount of output is generated by the additional unit of labor as the last increase generated. **Decreasing returns** refers to the situation in which the added unit of labor yields less than the last one did. Economic theory tells the producer to stop adding labor input at the time when the marginal rate of return starts decreasing. The point just before this happens is called the *optimal level of production.* It is diagrammed in Figure 21.7. In this diagram marginal returns increase with the addition of each unit of labor up to the addition of the tenth unit. The addition of the eleventh unit increases total production, but by the same amount as the addition of the tenth unit increased it. Then the curve marking the rate of increase goes down. The twelfth unit increases total production all right, but it doesn't increase it as much as the tenth or eleventh unit did. The equilibrium point in this production system is between the tenth and the eleventh labor input unit.

Most of the traditional production systems that have been studied show *increasing* marginal returns. That is, the production system could absorb more labor profitably, but either there is a shortage of workers or people are not working as hard as they could in food production. Often both these things are true. Most traditional peoples do not share the

Figure 21.8
This American commune
depicts Chayanov's Rule:
the more efficient the household collective the less hard
work people put in.

"Puritan ethic" about hard work having its own reward. Instead, they favor the *principle of least work*. This principle states that at equilibrium, no one should put any more work into the productive process than he or she has to in order to maintain the culturally determined levels of satisfactory consumption.

Chayanov's Rule   An example of the principle of least work in action has been given by the economist A. V. Chayanov, who studied the Russian farming family (Chayanov 1966). This special formulation is called **Chayanov's Rule,** and is the sixth principle of traditional economics. Chayanov's Rule: the more efficient the household collective, the less hard work people put in. If the household produces only for itself and has only so many mouths to feed, one would expect its labor input to fall once its productivity is increased. In this sense, a well-organized household that contains the proper ratio of males to females and dependents to producers is truly a labor-saving device. By creating large, cooperative working groups, usually of kinfolk, the household can achieve together what it cannot achieve if it is small: **economies of scale.** We are all familiar with the idea that mass production lowers prices by spreading fixed costs over a large number of units. Similarly, by dividing up tasks among adult working members of the extended family and increasing total amount of land worked, efficiency is increased. Large extended families take ad-

Chayanov's Rule: the more efficient the household collective, the less hard work people put in.

vantage of economies of scale. They can maintain both output per working member and low labor inputs; that is, they work less hard.

The Problem of Free Ridership

If people have a preference for less work rather than more, and if they can achieve their goal of less work through enlarging the work force and specializing to some degree, then one would think that all societies would favor large work groups. But as the group gets bigger, the problem of keeping incentives high enough to reward extra members who join becomes harder and harder. In particular, expanding groups run up against the problem of **free ridership.**

The problem of free ridership is this. A person who is rational and calculating is bound to discover that he (or she) can feed his (or her) part of the large family grouping (say, a spouse and small child) and contribute very little labor to the collective. If the jobs are not divided up according to specialties, then that fraction of output due to one person's labor alone is not likely to be that large. If this person withdraws his (or her) labor, output will be maintained, and he (or she) will get a "free ride." The problem is that other people will see one member being maintained in idleness, and one of two things will occur. Either they also will withdraw their labor and there will be no output, or they will try to expel the nonworking member. If they do the latter, and the process continues, then the collective will disappear too. The labor management problem is to keep the group small enough so that the labor of each member is important and the rewards are sufficient to keep his or her loyalty. Mancur Olson (1965) has calculated that the largest a group can be under these conditions is between five and seven working members. Once the group gets bigger than this, free ridership becomes a problem. If the group is smaller than five members, it is more difficult to achieve economies of scale. When groups who pool their labor and apportion their consumption by shares get numerous, then the problem of keeping the group together is political and requires coercion. But the family is held together and organized by bonds of kinship. And the principles of kinship everywhere speak against coercion. Kinfolk are instead bound by love, respect, and reciprocity in willing association. Since work groups in traditional societies are constituted of and by kinfolk, the problem of free ridership does not permit the formation of effective large groups. This gives us the seventh principle of traditional economics: Household production groups, if they are to avoid coercion, can have no more than five to seven producers in the same collective.

Household production groups, if they are to avoid coercion, can have no more than five to seven producers in the same collective.

Calculating a Traditional Worker's Output   Earlier in this section we pointed out that, according to the economists, we ought to be very atten-

Figure 21.9
This South Indian farmer is
attentive to average returns.

tive to *marginal returns,* calculating whether an added unit of labor will yield at least as much as the last unit. If we have three people working in a group, for example, we should be able to calculate the extra amount of output produced by the second person and then the third person, and consider in the light of our experience whether the addition of a fourth person will add at least as much as the third did.

Without the benefit of input/output analysis, it is very hard to do this. T. Scarlett Epstein (1962, 1967) has noted that Indian subsistence agriculturalists do not pay attention to marginal returns. They pay attention to *average returns.* They can calculate the average product per person of a three- or four-person working group. But they cannot calculate the marginal product: how much *extra* each person *added* to the rate of return. They simply do not know. This is the eighth principle of traditional economics. People in traditional economic systems are concerned with average output rather than marginal output. This principle is important because it leads to some surprising results. Let us put some of these economic principles together.

Principle 1: People in traditional society, because they are generally poor, are highly risk averse. They avoid gambles.

Principle 3: Household units of producers in traditional society have fixed production goals.

Principle 4: In traditional economies producers overwhelmingly adopt low-risk strategies that have low payoffs for them. (But we should note that the strategies are constructed so that there will always be some payoff, even under high uncertainty.)

People in traditional economic systems are concerned with average output rather than marginal output.

Principle 8: People in traditional economic systems are concerned with average output, rather than marginal output.

How high does the average output have to be? High enough to cover them in bad years, given their culturally determined levels of consumption and satisfaction. What is going to happen in a good year? They are going to utilize the same strategies, figuring on reaching the same fixed production goals as they do in bad years—and they are going to have a surplus. This generally occurs.

Allan (1965) wrote a book called *The African Husbandman,* in which he recounts the astonishment of the Rhodesian (now Zimbabwe) government when they set up a corn marketing board and were swamped by surplus corn that they had not even suspected existed! The corn marketing board based their estimates of production on the years 1938 to 1944. These had been fair to bad years, and the amount of surplus was low, averaging about 34,000 tons. But during the late 1950s the African farmers had good years, and the surplus doubled to an average of 70,000 tons. Where did all that corn come from? From farmers who employed the same safe strategies, with fixed production goals, under uncertainty and generated a bumper crop in good years.

Epstein (1962) in her studies of South Indian traditional economies discovered that the economic philosophy based on these four principles guaranteed that the poorest villagers could never climb out of poverty. All the villagers were risk averse in the way we described. The poorer they were, the less willing they were to take gambles. So the very poorest low-caste villagers ("Untouchables," as they were called in those days) obtained a guarantee from the landowners of a fixed, customary payment for their work in good years and bad. No matter what happened to the crop, they would get a fixed amount. Not a proportion or a percentage—a fixed amount. When the traditional agricultural practices generated surpluses in good years (and we now know why they do), the low-caste workers received none of it. They received only their fixed payments. The landowners kept the surplus and used it for feasts, weddings, religious festivals, or cash. If the Untouchables had accepted a proportion of the crop (as a sharecropper does), they would have been better off in good years. But because of the greater power of the landowners, the low-caste workers would have received a smaller share of the crop than the landowners. And in bad years they would have starved. Under the fixed payment system, when the crop is bad, the landowners are no better off than the low-caste workers. They split the product about 50:50. Imagine what would happen to the low-caste worker if the split were 70:30. They would experience a reduction of 40 percent, which in bad years would finish them off.

So what the low-caste workers do is trade off a chance to have savings, accumulate capital, and better their situation in favor of a guaranteed subsisting poverty.

Population Pressure and Decreasing Returns

In the last chapter we discussed Boserup's hypothesis about the development of more intensive agricultural practices as a response to increasing population pressure. Boserup took the position that increasing population pressure forces people to cultivate the land more intensively and to raise their levels of output to feed the population.

She did not foresee that this process of intensification could be carried too far. Sometimes traditional societies achieve such economies of scale and productive efficiency that their population increases to the point where they must support a larger population than the apparent capacity of their environment. This happened in Java, Indonesia, under very special conditions of *sawah* irrigated wet rice agriculture.

Sawah Rice Agriculture in Indonesia The **sawah** is an irrigated rice terrace, which is constructed to control the flow of water into and out of the field. The soils of the rice terrace are thin and tropical, not at all productive. But if water that is rich in nutrients and warm enough to encourage the growth of blue-green, nitrogen-fixing algae is brought into the paddy, it provides nutrients for the rice crop. Water is more important than the soil for the growth of irrigated rice.

One of the many interesting things about *sawah* rice terraces is that they respond to what Geertz (1963) calls "loving care" by increasing yields. In fact, the rice paddy is capable of absorbing additional labor more than any other known system of agriculture. In some parts of Java, for example, the rice terraces are able to support up to 3,200 people per square mile. (Compare this with the carrying capacity of a hunting territory in the Paleolithic period, which has been estimated to be able to carry one person per square mile.) Geertz states,

. . . the output of most terraces can be almost indefinitely increased by more careful fine-comb cultivation techniques! It seems almost always possible somehow to squeeze just a little more out of even a mediocre sawah by working it just a little bit harder. Seeds can be sown in nurseries and then transplanted instead of broadcast; they can even be pregerminated in the house. Yield can be increased by planting shoots in exactly spaced rows, more frequent and complete weeding, periodic draining of the terrace during the growing season for the purposes of aeration, more thorough plowing, raking and leveling of the muddy soil before planting, placing selected organic debris on the plot, and so on; harvesting techniques can be similarly perfected both to reap the fullest percentage of the yield and leave the greatest amount of the harvested crop on

Figure 21.10
The terraced levels of a rice paddy *left* **and workers in an Indonesian paddy.**

the field to refertilize it, such as the technique of using the razor-like hand blade found over most of inner Indonesia; double-cropping and, in some favorable areas, perhaps triple cropping can be instituted. The capacity of most terraces to respond to loving care is amazing. . . . A whole series of such labor absorbing improvements in cultivation methods have played a central role in permitting the Javanese rural economy to soak up the bulk of the island's exploding population.

But even the *sawah* paddy is subject to the rule of diminishing marginal returns to labor. Geertz does not say at precisely what point increased labor yields less rice than the previous added unit. Clearly it varies from community to community. But it seems clear that the *sawah* paddy will absorb labor almost indefinitely, yielding decreasing returns. Thus the paddy gets tenderer and tenderer devotion from more and more loving hands. But the people become systematically more impoverished as every extra child is born.

Here then is a case where additional labor yields increasing impoverishment. Human technology has succeeded in producing a wonder of agricultural productivity. But nature, in the end, has its say. The natural rate of increase of the population and the wondrous productivity of the rice terrace have combined to ensure a life of back-breaking devotion to the paddy, and of progressively impoverished living.

We can state this as the ninth principle: Population pressure, when severe, will compel producers to add labor inputs past the point of zero marginal returns.

Population pressure, when severe, will compel producers to add labor inputs past the point of zero marginal returns.

The Division of Labor

Division of Labor by Sex

In every society we find that different jobs are given to women than to men. This does not mean that women are the "weaker sex" or that men are always given the tasks that require physical strength. With two exceptions —warfare and the hunting of big game—there is no task that is so demanding of strength that women *somewhere* in some culture do not carry it out.

Men, however, always are allotted the more physically dangerous tasks, according to a recent study by Burton, Brudner, and White (1976). Women always look after infants and small children. One can see the reason for this by reasoning from the theory of natural selection. The society that best protects its infants and nourishes its young has a better chance of reproducing into the next generation. Since women everywhere breast-feed their infants, the absence of the woman from the home territory would have a deleterious effect on infant nutrition. If women were to work far from the home territory, infant mortality rates would rise and the survivors into the next generation would be fewer. So, in the struggle for procreative success, the societies that best protect their offspring are going to have a selective advantage over those that do not.

Even though women are capable of doing all kinds of tasks that require physical strength, Murdock and Provost (1963) have shown that there are statistical trends in the way tasks are allocated by sex. In a study of 185 societies, they found that there was a strong tendency for men to take over not just the tasks of warfare and the hunting of large animals, but also such tasks as lumbering, mining, fowling, boatbuilding, stone-working, butchering, land clearance, and fishing. Women, on the other hand, much more frequently were responsible for gathering wild vegetable foods, dairy production, spinning, laundering, water fetching, and cooking. Table 21.1 is an abbreviated version of the division of labor in 185 societies, taken from Murdock and Provost (1973:207).

Table 21.1

Allocation of Activities by Sex in 185 Societies*

Task	Predominantly Male	Assigned to Both	Predominantly Female
1. Hunting of large sea animals	48	0	0
2. Metalworking	86	0	0
3. Stoneworking	67	6	0
4. Mining and quarrying	32	2	1
5. Land clearance	129	6	4
6. Tending large animals	78	14	6
7. Soil preparation	93	14	27
8. Generation of fire	46	16	24
9. Crop planting	62	33	46
10. Crop tending	45	24	62
11. Burden carrying	30	46	70
12. Loom weaving	24	6	58
13. Manufacture of clothing	20	11	91
14. Dairy production	4	0	24
15. Cooking	2	2	170

* The rows do not add up to 185 for two reasons: Either the task did not occur in the society, or the data were incomplete.

Specialization and Complexity

In most small-scale societies, we do not find further specialization of tasks beyond the division of labor by sex. However, with the growth of the scale of society, it becomes both easier and more important to introduce specialization of tasks. Culturally defined categories of "expert" can be invented and utilized by larger scale societies. If, however, people are taken out of the food procurement sphere of society, then they have to be supported by the labor of others. This requires an economic surplus. If the society is incapable for technological or ecological reasons of producing a surplus, then no full-time specialization can take place.

Specialization and the growth of scale go together for the reasons we have outlined. Specialization, up to a point, increases the efficiency of production. Therefore it creates its own surplus if the production goals of the society are raised accordingly. At the same time, specialization solves the problem of free ridership. When tasks are broken down, responsibility for their completion is allocated to social categories who become accountable for them. This means that the task group can be effectively made small enough to increase incentives and so control free ridership. So, as societies increase in size, and as production units increase in size and complexity, specialization must occur so that the production units will break down into groups small enough to control the problem of free ridership.

This is not to say that there are not densely populated societies with little division of labor. There are. We call them, after Durkheim, societies bound together by **mechanical solidarity.** In these societies the production units all are the same: usually the household. Each household is pretty much self-sufficient, and there is no hierarchy of production. It is as though the society were made up of a large number of atoms with very tenuous bonds between them. Little exchange is required, because each household is a copy of every other and is self-sufficient.

Such societies have enormous problems of **integration.** There are no good reasons for the units to hang together as a social or political unit. Public goods are rare, since there is no easy way to control access to them. The problem of the commons is severe. Problems of common defense and of fission are severe also. If any household unit wishes to withdraw its support of common defense, for example, it can do so and feel few consequences. Societies of this kind are organized into larger entities by kinship bonds, but quarreling and feuding are often endemic, and the social fabric is generally frail.

There is an enormous advantage, then, in bringing about a situation in which the society is well integrated. A complex division of labor can bring this about. When the division of labor is complex, household units are not independent, but *interdependent.* Since my own household does not make shoes or pottery, carry out religious rituals, or produce dairy products, I have to get these products from other units. I therefore establish ties of exchange with other units. These ties spread throughout the society so that the whole economic and social system depends on all the units doing their jobs and contributing their special skills and products to the common good. Durkheim called this state of affairs **organic solidarity.**

In a society with a complex division of labor, everyone has to be able to rely on everyone else's providing their service or product, or else the whole society ceases to exist. Such societies can deal with greater numbers of people at the expense of giving up household independence. The idea of *contract,* voluntarily entered into and legally binding, is necessary for such societies to function. But the gains are great: they can organize on a much larger scale, provide a greater range of products and services than autonomous households, and better provide for the common defense and the creation and maintenance of other public, indivisible goods. Therefore, in the long run, societies with *organic* solidarity will outproduce those with *mechanical* solidarity. Their success in integrating themselves, along with their comparatively greater scale, will ensure higher reproduction success than the simpler society; and they will therefore have the competitive edge.

Systems of Exchange

Exchange is the means of binding a society together, the recognition of interdependence. It is the fulfillment of contract. It indebts both parties

Figure 21.11
Coins such as these were
an integral part of exchange
in primitive societies.

to the exchange and makes them both better off. There is an intrinsic power or value to the symbols that are exchanged that transcends the utilitarian or practical value of the goods themselves. The more that exchanges are based on trust and negotiation, the more valuable they are in binding a relationship together.

Trust implies that the relationship between the two parties will continue into the future. It implies credit. When two people trust each other, they are prepared to become mutually indebted and to keep a running account through the period of the relationship, which may last all their lives. *Negotiation* is another kind of exchange: the exchange of values and sentiments. It implies that the two parties can agree on the relative values of the symbols that are being exchanged and that, therefore, they subscribe to similar values. Their commitment to these common values is evidence of their solidarity. Friendship, kinship, and good social relations are created and sustained by the exchange of symbols. That is why we emphasized exchange as the basis for social organization in chapters 17 and 18.

Exchange can take place without money. What matters is whether each party to the exchange feels that he or she is getting something out of the relationship. The dividend they get may reside in the relationship itself. One party may be willing to exchange with another for the psychological benefit of knowing that a close relationship has been established.

Not every exchange relationship is a close, binding, personal relationship. Often I need products that are not available in my neighborhood or among my kinfolk, and therefore I am willing to exchange what I have in comparative abundance for what some other party has in relative abundance. The first step in depersonalizing this form of personal negotiation and trust is the creation of *conventional rates of exchange.* If my kinfolk and I live by the sea, then we will have an abundance of fish. But we lack yams. So my kinfolk and I trade with the yam people, and we establish a rough equivalence of so many fish for so many baskets of yams.

In this case we say that the *utility* to each party is roughly equivalent. Both traders are about equally better off than they would have been if they had not traded.

A second development (but not in the evolutionary sense) is the development of a special-purpose accounting device, or **numeraire,** for keeping track of the various goods that are exchanged. Different peoples have used brass rods, dog's teeth, and cowrie shells as such accounting devices. This special-purpose money cannot be used for just any transaction. The sphere in which it can be used for transactions is usually well defined— perhaps only as an accounting device to keep track of cattle payments, or for the sale and purchase of foodstuffs (as opposed to ritual goods).

Special-purpose money may begin to generalize. But people usually resist such a move. In a case studied by Bohannon and his students, special-purpose money that had been used for the accounting, purchase, and sale of subsistence and capital goods began to be used for the payment of bride price. There was an outcry: it was felt to be totally inappropriate to use "thing-money" for paying the obligations between groups when they exchanged wives. It was analogous to treating a person like an animal or an object.

But in a changing and increasingly commercialized world, the idea and lure of a general-purpose exchange *numeraire* is very great. It permits exchange of the most general sort, and enables groups to convert goods and services of very different kinds into a common denominator, exchanging, say, a basket of yams for a piglet, a choice piece of cloth, or a day's labor. General-purpose money (such as the dollar) has three functions: it serves as an accounting device (a *numeraire* that allows one to set a price on, or evaluate, different goods and services); it serves also as a store of value and as a medium of exchange.

Money as a store of value has several advantages. Many people store value in tangible forms: livestock and vegetable products are common forms. But vegetable products are perishable, and livestock is vulnerable to disease and pestilence, so that one can lose all one's accumulated savings in a wet, sickly year. Money does not suffer from these disadvantages. Commercial economies are, of course, based on the existence of a general-purpose money.

With the advent of general-purpose money, two related developments take place. First, it becomes possible to establish relationships at a distance. That is, I can use my general-purpose exchange medium for trading relationships and not even know the people with whom I am exchanging. Exchange rates are not set by personal negotiation, but rather by the forces of the marketplace. They *externalize* the exchange relationship, subjecting it to forces outside my control. And they generalize it. Traders gain the advantage of increased scope but lose the personal touch.

This is what we mean when we say that commercialization begets depersonalization. The symbolic value of the exchange is lost, and utilitarian considerations become the most important. We move from the domain of kin relations, which are dominated by the ideals of amity, reciprocity, and mutual benefit, to the domain of instrumental relations, where each person seeks to maximize his or her own benefit at the expense of those who are unknown, unknowable, impersonal objects.

As a result, those petty exchanges of the symbols of everyday living, which create and sustain social relations and a sense of community in a nonmonetarized economy, cease. In their place we substitute ritualistic symbols in the form of wedding gifts or personal luxury items such as leather wallets and designer ties. We deny that the relationship is commercial by utilizing for exchange symbolic gifts that are valuable symboli-

Insight
The Formalist/Substantivist Dispute

One of the biggest arguments in economic anthropology was the dispute between those who felt that Western economic theory applied to economic behavior in all societies—ancient and modern, traditional and commercial—and those who felt that it was misapplied to ancient and traditional society. Those who felt it was misapplied were called **substantivists,** because they believed one had to analyze the *substance* or content of people's behavior to see if they were economically rational. The people who believed that modern economic theory applied to all societies were called **formalists** because they felt that the formal (mathematical) methods of modern economics could be used to find out whether people were economically rational. Do all people everywhere in every period of history allocate their energies efficiently so as to secure the greatest benefit to themselves and their families? If the answer to that question is affirmative, then the methods of modern economics do apply. If the answer is negative, then they do not.

Substantivists point out that the most important idea in modern economics was the *market.* A market is not a place or a group of people; it is a *means of setting a price,* and in particular what is called an *equilibrium price.* In economic theory, the equilibrium price is that price which balances supply and demand. If the price is too high, then the producers send too many goods to market, and supply exceeds demand. People will not buy at such a high price. If the price is too low, the producers withhold goods from the market until consumer demand pushes the price up. Both producers and consumers are sensitive to prices. They do not have to be physically at the market, but must be sensitive to prices from the market and act accordingly. Consumers are rational if they adjust their demand according to prices, choosing those goods that yield them the highest satisfaction, that is, maximize subjective utility.

In formal theory, consumers have to be able to compare bundles of commodities. They have to compare one bundle of, say, [8 oranges, 6 apples, 2 shirts, and a hoe] with a bundle of [4 oranges, 8 apples, 3 shirts, and 2 hoes]. Our arithmetic teachers told us that such different items were incommensurable, that "you couldn't add apples and oranges." But in fact we do. We measure them all in terms of a common measuring device called *money*. So if traditional societies have no means of measuring incommensurables, no money or equivalent yardstick of value, then the substantivists have won the argument, because there can be no prices and, therefore, no market.

Do they? We do not know! Certainly money as we think of it is rare enough in traditional societies. At least, it was rare before those societies became affected by the commercial, industrial West that introduces the ideas of money, price, and the market all at the same time. But anthropologists have discovered that people act in an economically rational fashion even in the absence of money. The Siane, for example, a tribe of New Guinea studied by Salisbury (1962), received a technological push from the introduction of steel axes that raised their productive efficiency. They did not invest their new output in cheaper and more abundant goods, but according to *their* demand schedule, which gave priority to ceremonial goods, warfare, and increased leisure. Were they rational? Yes, because their utility was increased more by manufacturing and enjoying ceremonial goods and by using their extra time for warfare and leisure.

The problem is that we do not know enough about measurement in general, and about culturally defined and possibly implicit measures that people use over the world. The formalist/substantivist dispute simply cannot be settled until we have more knowledge. It is best left alone for the moment. Certainly people act differently, given different opportunities. Whether the nuances of their decisions can be caught by modern economic theory remains an open question.

cally precisely because they are not items of daily use. But in so doing, most of us restrict the personal social relationships to a small group of kinfolk and close friends. Herein lies the irony: With the advent of the opportunity to conduct trade and exchange with a very large number of people, we in turn, break down the personal, the intimate, and the truly social bonds that give meaning to the lives of people of traditional communities.

Summary

1. When we study economics we are studying the way people make use of their scarce means to attain culturally defined goals. The goals are expressed in their preferences. We assume that people are trying to get the most satisfaction they can out of their lives, given the way they define satisfaction. This is what is meant by "maximizing subjective utility."

2. People everywhere undergo risk, but most people are risk averse. Poorer people are more risk averse than richer people, and since the people of traditional societies are generally poor, they tend to be more risk averse than people in modern societies. This "conservative" behavior is economically rational for them. It permits them to survive over the long term, whereas a higher risk-taking strategy set would not.

3. Every society has a concept of ownership, or the restricted access to public goods. There never was a society of "primitive communists" in which the idea of private property was absent.

4. Production in traditional societies is restricted in a number of ways:

People tend to have fixed production goals. They do not work unless they have to.

People can stop eating if the effort required is deemed to be too great, or if the work is demeaning. This happens rarely, but shows us a strategy that we find unusual.

People adopt low-risk production strategies because they can assure themselves of some crop every year that way. High-risk production strategies would raise yields, but would yield nothing in some years and so put people under severe nutritional stress.

5. People are careful about working, in traditional society. Though they cannot make very fine economic calculations, such as the marginal return to labor, they resolutely refuse to work when they do not have to. Chayanov found that more efficient peasant households used their greater efficiency for more leisure, not for greater production.

6. Sometimes intense population pressure compels greater and greater labor input. This is the case with the Indonesian rice paddy.

7. Labor is divided in all societies; the simplest and universal form of division of labor is by sex.

8. As societies become more complex and populous, personal ties and reciprocity are replaced by contract, impersonal (monetary) exchange, and asymmetry. We saw this in the study of social organization. We see it again in economic organization in the development of the market and social stratification.

Suggested Readings

Dalton, George, ed. *Tribal and Peasant Economies: Readings in Economic Anthropology*. New York: Natural History Press, 1967.

> *A very good book to use to expose yourself to different anthropological theories about economics in traditional life. Both theoretical and substantive articles are included.*

LeClair, E. E., Jr., and Schneider, Harold, eds. *Economic Anthropology: Readings in Theory and Analysis*. New York: Holt, Rinehart and Winston, 1968.

> *An excellent survey of economic thinking by anthropologists. Particularly complete on the formalist/substantivist debate. All the original documents are there.*

Sahlins, Marshall. *Stone Age Economics*. Chicago: Aldine Publishing Co., 1972.

> *Sahlins is about our best writer on these subjects. This is a very influential book and delightful to read.*

Schneider, Harold. *Economic Man*. New York: Free Press, 1975.

> *A very good, if somewhat uncritical, review of formalist writing in economic anthropology by one of the most eminent contributors.*

Glossary

Chayanov's Rule The more efficient a household collective, the less hard work people put into it.

constant marginal returns The situation in which the increase in output is the same for each added unit of input.

decreasing marginal returns The situation in which a smaller extra amount of output is given by each added unit of input.

diminishing marginal utility The rule that states that the more of something you get, the less you want the next unit.

economics The study of the way people make use of scarce means at their disposal to attain culturally defined goals.

economies of scale The increased efficiency that comes from the division of labor in the production of many goods rather than fewer.

fixed production goals The third principle of traditional economics: people will produce what they consider "enough," but no more.

formalists People who believe that you can analyze traditional economies with mathematical (formal) economic methods, just like market economies.

free ridership The problem in groups larger than seven members that one or more of the members will fail to contribute his or her share and thereby get a "free ride."

increasing marginal returns The situation in which more and more output results from each additional unit of input.

integration The manner and degree to which social units in a larger system are dependent or tied together by exchange.

marginal return The extra production that results from adding one *more* unit of input (say, labor).

maximization of subjective utility Getting the most of the things that you want.

mechanical solidarity Durkheim's phrase to describe the kind of solidarity that exists in a society where very little exchange takes place because the household firms are self-sufficient.

need A biologically based requirement for life itself. *Cf.* want.

numeraire An accountant's scale to measure the value of different "bundles" of commodities.

organic solidarity Durkheim's word to describe the social solidarity that comes about when there are both considerable exchange between social units and a complex division of labor.

ownership The restriction of rights of access to the means of production to one individual (or corporation); same as private ownership.

private ownership Restricted ownership—to a person or group.

risk aversion
1. When the risk gets large, we become more unwilling to play the game.
2. When the stakes get bigger, we are more unwilling to play the game.

sawah The Indonesian rice paddy.

substantivists People who believe that you cannot analyze traditional economic systems with modern (formal) methods.

usufruct
1. The right to use or enjoy the produce from some productive resource.
2. Ownership derived from the fact that the owner is using some resource.

want A culturally defined desire. *Cf.* need.

Biocultural Integration

Part 6

1. What modes of biocultural interaction can we see in human societies?
2. What is the reason for examining biocultural integration in living peoples?

22

The Yanomamo: An Example of Biocultural Equilibrium

Introduction

In the next three chapters we are going to introduce and explore the **mode of biocultural integration** of three biocultural systems that we have especially chosen for the purpose. By "mode of biocultural integration" we mean the way that the ecological, cultural, and biological clusters fit together so as to provide solutions to the problems faced by each social group.

We have chosen to illustrate three modes:

1. Biocultural equilibrium.
2. Unstable biocultural equilibrium.
3. The destructive downward spiral (or just "downward spiral").

We use the Yanomamo Indians of Venezuela as an example of a people and a biocultural system in equilibrium with the environment. The Yanomamo have been disturbed by encroaching Western traditions only in the past decade and a half. We peg our discussion to the *ethnographic present* of the time of contact. We show that the Yanomamo, in the period that they were ignored by Western peoples and ideas, had evolved a system in which cultural, ecological, and biological clusters were designed to fit together so that there were no long-term off-stage processes "ticking away" to undermine them. The clusters were tied together, or integrated, so that stresses induced by one subsystem or one cluster were never so great that they could not be handled by another subsystem or cluster.

As a result, the Yanomamo biocultural system was in equilibrium, or harmony, with its environment. If Westerners had not introduced new diseases, the Yanomamo could have existed into the indefinite future with their system unchanged and intact.

The second example is one of an *unstable equilibrium,* as exemplified in the peoples of highland New Guinea. An unstable equilibrium is the kind of a system in which every so often (usually quite regularly and predictably) the whole biocultural system has to be "shaken up" and rearranged to get all the parts properly integrated again. It's as though the system ticked along as time passed, getting more and more out of kilter until some trigger set off an upheaval that reshuffled all the parts so as to get it back into proper shape.

To illustrate biocultural equilibrium, the textbooks often use the example of a house heating system controlled by a thermostat. Once the thermostat is set, the temperature in the house is maintained around that temperature. The furnace is shut off and turned on to change the temperature every time the room temperature gets too far away from where it is set. The desired temperature is the equilibrium point in this heating system. Actual room temperature oscillates around the equilibrium point, but the whole heating system is designed to be *equilibrium-seeking.*

To illustrate unstable equilibrium, the textbooks sometimes use the example of an earthquake. Before an earthquake the tectonic plates under the earth's surface get more and more out of kilter. They build up pressures, stressing the system more and more. Finally the pressure gets unbearable, the plates shift, and the whole system is shaken up and rearranges itself. We experience this reshuffling as an earthquake. After the quake the pressure between the plates goes back to normal.

The last example is that of a society on the wane. This mode is exemplified here by the traditional Mesoamerican village. This biocultural system has been stressed to the point where it has lost its resiliency and can no longer activate the controls on its systems to bring them back into line. The biocultural system has gone into a kind of "tailspin." Just as an aircraft that has gone into a spin cannot restore the aerodynamic qualities of flight, so these biocultural systems have been exposed to such stress that they cannot maintain their historical trajectory.

The Biocultural System of the Yanomamo

Deep in the Amazon jungles, far from the major rivers that serve as traditional highways of communication for others, live the Yanomamo. By-passed by the migrations of Europeans into South America, they have been isolated from all but their nearest neighbors for thousands of years. They were contacted only in this century.

The Yanomamo are a fortunate people in the sense that they are stressed only slightly by their natural environment. Their technology is

Figure 22.1
Map of South America showing the homeland of the Yanomamos.

Figure 22.2
Woman with plantains, a
bananalike fruit that is the
staple food of the
Yanomamos.

simple, but adequate for the maintenance of a slash-and-burn horticultural production system that provides them with ample supplies of plantain, a foodstuff similar to bananas. Plantains are their staple food, making up 70 percent of their diet (Neel 1971).

Infectious diseases do not ravage the Yanomamo as they do the world's more sedentary communities. This freedom from infectious disease, however, has not resulted from natural selection selecting resistant genes. Western doctors were present when a measles epidemic hit them in the mid-1960s. Almost everyone, young and old, came down with measles, indicating a lack of previous exposure. But the Yanomamo did not die from the disease at an unusually high rate. With simple nursing care, the death rate was about 4 percent, a figure not too different from Western nations at the turn of this century (Centerwall 1968).

The Yanomamo are free of infectious disease such as measles because of their small numbers. They live in small, widely scattered villages. Over the entire area, population density averages but one person per two square miles. Infectious organisms cannot maintain themselves in small groups like the Yanomamo. When an epidemic occurs, everyone contracts the disease; some die, but all develop an immunity. In larger groups, by the time the disease has run its course through the population, previously uninfected individuals have grown to a susceptible age.

The Yanomamo are also largely free of such disease because they move frequently. They are not so likely to reinfect themselves by the oral-fecal route or in other ways. Hookworm, for example, is more common in sedentary people since it enters the body through the soles of the feet.

Because of the low incidence of serious diseases, they have very few native cures. None involves the use of curing techniques as we understand them, utilizing herbs, local remedies, and medicines.

The Yanomamo number about 10,000 and live in villages of between 40 and 250 people, spread out over a comparatively fine-grained environment. Their horticultural production system does little violence to nature: in fact, it *imitates* nature in the varied composition of their gardens. They plant the shoots of the plantain, along with bananas, yams, and occasionally some sweet manioc, in gardens which they have first burned and cleared (Neel 1971). Their environment and technology provide conditions of *low uncertainty and risk*. Despite the fact that they rely on a few foods for a large proportion of their diet ("put all their eggs in one basket," the way the !Kung Bushmen did with mongongo nuts), they are assured of adequate supplies because their territory is extensive and their numbers are low. Even though rainfall varies, there is never such a wet year that they cannot plant. Napoleon Chagnon (1968), who has studied them

Their environment and technology provide conditions of low uncertainty and risk.

Figure 22.4
Woman with wild palm
fruits.

for 12 years, calls them "pioneer" cultivators. It only takes ten months for a cutting to bear fruit (Smole 1976). And in emergencies, this time can be drastically cut by transplanting more mature plantains weighing ten to fifteen pounds.

In dire emergencies, when they are driven out of the villages and gardens by hostile enemies and spirits, and are unable to transport more mature plants, the Yanomamo plant maize (even though they do not eat it regularly), because it is a very quick-growing plant that gives them enough to eat until the plantains come in.

The Yanomamo are said to live under conditions of low uncertainty because they have many environmental options and few environmental pressures. Their ecological niche is surprisingly wide, despite their reliance on garden produce. (Chagnon has estimated that up to 80 percent of their food intake comes out of the garden.) They delight in varying their diet and will eat wild palm fruits even when there are ample supplies of plantain still available. They hunt when they feel "meat hunger," a condition for which they have a special word. Tapir, agouti, wild pig, birds, monkeys, capybara, armadillo, and red squirrel are all eaten. Anteaters and two-toed and three-toed sloths are also hunted, but their flesh has a strong odor and acid taste that the Yanomamo feel leaves something to be desired. Insects are consumed, especially termites, grasshoppers, locusts, caterpillars, and silkworms; these are a rich and important source of protein in the Yanomamo diet (Smole 1976).

Wild foods are also collected in the forest. A hunting expedition is a snacking expedition. Other journeys offer similar opportunities. A trip for firewood is a time for women to collect wild foods on the way: wild guava, various fruits and nuts, cacao pods, and especially honey, which the Yanomamo crave and for which they will search half a day.

Despite this varied diet, their food preferences are strict. Tomatoes, beans, and squash were introduced into parts of the Yanomamo country by outsiders, but the Yanamamo turned up their noses. They raise them only for trade. Yanamamo adults are **neophobic** about food (i.e., they dislike new foods) and will only consume something new if they see children or monkeys eating it.

Although there are no good estimates of current population levels, they are low enough that population pressure is unimportant among the Yanomamo. Computer simulations show that the population is expanding in numbers, as it may have in the past, but cultural means ensure that fertility is kept comparatively low. The absence of effective medical techniques results in a child mortality rate that, while higher than the industrialized nations of the world, is considerably lower than among the developing countries. As far as natality is concerned, in the United States a woman will average, during her reproductive years, about 2½ live births, while in

West Africa or in Bangladesh, the number will be closer to 7. Among the Yanomamo, the average number of live births is slightly under 4 (Neel and Chagnon 1968).

Child mortality is comparatively low for the Yanomamo. In Africa or Bangladesh, 40 percent of the children die before they reach 15 years of age. Among the Yanomamo, only 18 percent die. (In the United States, 4 percent die before the age of 15.)

The most frequent cause of death is malaria, the only infectious disease prevalent enough to cause stress. In Chagnon's (1968b:140) sample of 240 deaths, malaria and other epidemic diseases accounted for 54.2 percent of the deaths. The next most frequent cause was warfare (15.4 percent) and the third was sorcery (10.4 percent). Men suffer the majority of deaths in warfare (31 killed compared with 6 women), but the sex ratio is kept in balance by female deaths in childbirth (1.2 percent) as well as by female infanticide. Malaria is new to the region, so we can assume that under previous, more stable conditions, the rate of increase of the population was restrained by the practice of warfare, about which we shall have more to say in a minute.

Fertility is kept low by prohibiting sexual intercourse during the period that a child is nursing. Polygyny also reduces fertility by insuring that younger men have little access to women during the men's prime. Adultery occurs frequently enough to be a source of friction and feuding within villages. But it is illicit and is kept under control by the senior males who have tremendous power over their women.

Since fertility and mortality are moderate and balanced, we can see that population pressure on the resource base is kept down. The pattern of feuding, fighting, and warfare that elevates male mortality also ensures that villages do not exhaust the virgin forest around them. Villages frequently split up.

Alliances between villages are fragile, and treachery is constant. Chagnon describes the men of an allied village coming to the village in which he lived and forming an allied force which then attacked an enemy village. The women of Chagnon's village huddled in fear in his hut. But they did not fear those in the enemy village—rather they feared that the whole thing was only a ruse. The women were afraid that the men left behind in the allied village would descend upon them and abduct them while their husbands and kinsmen were off fighting.

Since alliances are constantly shifting, and since villages can change from being very large (250) to very small (50) in a short time, the Yanomamo are always on the move. They are constantly shifting their garden sites, and the landscape is dotted with old, worn-out gardens (or "barren old women," as the Yanomamo say). Yet environmental degradation does not occur. Tropical forests are very fragile and can turn to barren savannas or grasslands very easily once the forest cover is removed. Such degradation can pose serious problems as it has for similar cultivators in southeast Asia. But not among the Yanomamo. Low population pressure, virgin forest cultivation, and constant movement spread the Yanomamo over their territory, keeping population densities low and maintaining the environment.

When you put all these data together—good nutrition, low mortality from infectious disease, low uncertainty in the environment, a wide ecological niche (although with strict food preferences), and low population pressure—you have the conditions for an ecological equilibrium. The equilibrium is not threatened by an exploitative technology: the production system creates gardens that imitate nature.

The Yanomamo show us one kind of biocultural-environmental mode: the off-stage drama does not affect the Yanomamo way of life. Yanomamo culture is stable and does not sow the seeds of its own destruction. It is in equilibrium, at peace with nature, as it were. The study of the Yanomamo is the study of the drama that is taking place *on-stage*.

Equilibrium state

Were it not for the fact that there is severe competition over women, constant splitting of villages, and shifting alliances, the equilibrium could not be maintained. That it is maintained is due to on-stage beliefs and pressures that are finely adjusted to the demographic conditions in the various parts of the Yanomamo territory. It so happens that in those areas where population pressure is comparatively greater, the belief system ensures that female infanticide is at its highest, and warfare frequent. Mortality rates are also relatively high for both adult males and infant females, so that fertility does not rise to a dangerous level. The Yanomamo are, of course, completely unaware of the unintended consequence of their beliefs. As on-stage actors they see it in quite a different way.

The On-Stage Drama

The Actors' View   Warfare is chronic among the Yanomamo. They are active in politics and establish social and political ties with the villages around them. They invite neighboring villages to trade with them so that a political tie can be established. They enter into feasting relationships and they intermarry. In fact, if you were a Yanomamo headman, teaching some young tribesman how best to create a political coalition that would enable him to survive, you would teach him a step-by-step procedure for establishing relations. "First you make sure that you make or trade for some goods that the prospective allies need. Then you establish trading relations with them. You invite them to come to the village to trade with you, being careful to hide valuable things that you do not want to trade. Your prospective allies will be greedy and will ask for what they want. You will be forced to give it to them. (They know why you are inviting them, too!). If you can establish good trading relations, then try to involve them in a feast. This will mean that you will have to work hard, collecting more plantains than normal and sending out hunting expeditions to shoot wild animals (particularly monkey). This is hard work, but if they accept your invitation, you are one step closer to a political alliance."

A feast is often the trigger for violence. Visiting parties may become aggrieved at the treatment they are receiving. Or they may rake up some old insult and demand recompense. Then all hell can break loose. What starts as an innocent chest-pounding duel—in which two men alternately pummel each other until one of the pounders gives in—may escalate to a full-blown axe fight with serious injuries on both sides. Hardly a way of making political allies!

Trading, fighting, and finally, the reciprocal exchange of women are rungs on the ladder one scales to gain an ally.

But how does one gain enemies? First, the enemies of your allies are your own enemies. Second, the village you just split from is the worst enemy of all. Village splits create an unusual amount of hostility. Quarrels over witchcraft or women are the most frequent source of a split.

In many ways, splitting a village is the last resort. To do so puts everyone in danger, reducing village size from 200 to 100 or even 50 people. All this causes trouble. Individuals are vulnerable and weak and are prey to others. The forging of alliances is difficult. A potential ally may well pretend to enter into preliminary relationships, but have his eyes set on stealing women and children. One cannot be too careful.

To a Yanomamo, it is a hostile world out there. Allies cannot be trusted. The most violent kind of revenge sometimes occurs when one's group is invited to a feast with two other groups. It might appear on the surface that a grand political coalition, guaranteeing everyone's safety, is being forged. Not so. Unknown to the visitor, the two inviting parties are planning a *nomohoni*. They intend to kill all the men and abduct the women and children. Imagine that your group makes such a visit, and during the feast you are betrayed. The two conspiratorial groups fall upon you, and a great fight starts. As your men rush out of the village to escape the carnage, archers in ambush pick off the fugitives. You and your kinfolk are coolly killed, and the women are kept by the hosts.

Yanomamo Beliefs about Themselves There is a strong dependency between Yanomamo beliefs about themselves and their patterns of warfare. The Yanomamo believe that they are the only true human beings. They refer to members of other groups as "subhuman." They even de-

Insight
The Yanomamö Chest-Pounding Duel

Napoleon Chagnon describes the chest-pounding duel in his book on the Yanomamö (1968b:113–114):

"Two men from each side would step into the center of the milling belligerent crowd of weapon-wielding partisans, urged on by their comrades. One would step up, spread his legs apart, bare his chest, and hold his arms behind his back, daring the other to hit him. The opponent would size him up, adjust the man's chest or arms so as to give him the greatest advantage when he struck, and then step back to deliver his close-fisted blow. The striker would painstakingly adjust his own distance from the victim by measuring his arm's length to the man's chest, taking several dry runs before delivering his blow. He would then wind up like a baseball pitcher, but keeping both feet on the ground, and deliver a tremendous wallop with his fist to the man's left pectoral muscle, putting all his weight into the blow. The victim's knees would often buckle and he would stagger around a few moments, shaking his head to clear the stars, but remain silent. The blow inevitably raised a "frog" on the recipient's pectoral muscle where the striker's knuckles bit into his flesh. After each blow, the comrades of the deliverer would cheer and bounce up and down from the knees, waving and clacking their weapons over their heads. The victim's supporters, meanwhile, would urge their champion on frantically, insisting that he take another blow. If the delivery were made with sufficient force to knock the recipient to the ground, the man who delivered it would throw his arms above his head, roll his eyes back, and prance victoriously in a circle around his victim, growling and screaming, his feet almost a blur from his excited dance. The recipient would stand poised and take as many as four blows before demanding to hit his adversary. He would be permitted to strike his opponent as many times as the latter struck him, provided the opponent could take it. If not, he would be forced to retire, much to the dismay of his comrades and the delirious joy of their opponents. No fighter could retire after delivering a blow. If he attempted to do so, his adversary would plunge into the crowd and roughly haul him back out, sometimes being aided by the man's own supporters. Only after receiving his just dues could he retire. If he had delivered three blows, he had to receive three or be proved a poor fighter. He could retire with less than three only if he were injured. Then, one of his comrades would replace him and demand to hit the victorious opponent. The injured man's remaining blows would be canceled, and the man who delivered the victorious blow would have to receive more blows than he delivered. Thus, good fighters are at a disadvantage, since they receive disproportionately more punishment than they deliver. Their only reward is status: they can earn the reputation of being fierce."

grade other Yanomamo groups that are the slightest bit different. The difference is discovered by listening to others talk. If they display the slightest dialectal difference, or "mispronunciation," they are categorized as "not-quite-proper-Yanomamo."

The Yanomamo believe that the proper way for a man to act is "ferociously." They train their children in ferocity, baiting them until they strike back, and then applauding them. They have training exercises in which all the children in the village from ages 8 to 15 are forced to fight each other. The more fiercely they fight, the more they gain applause from their elders.

The Yanomamo also believe that there is constant warfare going on between the spirits of one village and the spirits of another. Evil spirits are sent by one village against another, and only the shamans can combat them. The shamans take psychedelic drugs and send their spirits forth to do combat against the evil spirits sent by the opposing villages. Under the influence of the drugs, the shamans believe that they leave their villages, travel into the villages of their enemies, and eat the souls of the children, who perish as a result. As soon as a group becomes convinced that village deaths are being caused by another village, they prepare to go to war.

The Biology of the Yanomamo: A Description

Now that you know something about the life and customs of the Yanomamo, we can now return to their biological aspects. We are interested in the ways the Yanomamo resemble or differ from other American Indians as well as their immediate Indian neighbors. We also want to know how much variation there is among Yanomamo villages. Finally, we want to know why any of these differences exist.

The Yanomamo display many characteristics that are due to their being South American Indian. They are small with broad faces and short arms and legs. They have the Diego blood factor, an inherited trait that is absent in whites and blacks and has its highest frequencies among Indians of the Amazon Basin. Their "Indianness" is clear and straightforward, and they are not different from other lowland South American groups.

At the same time, the Yanomamo do show some differences from their neighbors. Most of these traits, which are genetic, are very specific and not well known except to anthropological geneticists. These genetic features, which can be detected in the blood, are valuable because they indicate the degree to which the Yanomamo and their neighbors have exchanged genes with each other. Studies of these traits reveal that the boundaries between the Yanomamo and their neighbors are readily discernible. One way to analyze boundaries is in terms of "distance." Just as

Figure 22.6
Yanomamo man decorated with body paint.

Figure 22.7
Young mother with her son,
who is gripping a frog.

geographical distance is a measure of closeness, anthropological geneticists use the term **genetic distance.** Genetic distances between populations are large if the frequencies of the alleles of the two gene pools are markedly different. If the differences are small, the genetic distance is small.

The genetic distances between the Yanomamo and neighboring populations are considerable. In general, all Indian populations of the Amazon jungle show marked group differences. There is both diversity and heterogeneity. The heterogeneity reflects the isolation of populations that occurs in the rain forest. As we have discussed, small, isolated populations will gradually drift apart genetically through **stochastic evolution.**

Thus the Yanomamo differ from other Indians of the rain forest because of their isolation. However, the Yanomamo subgroups also differ from each other; they also are heterogeneous. The genetic distances between Yanomamo villages are the same as genetic distances between the Yanomamo and their nearest neighbors (Neel and Ward 1975). That is, the Yanomamo differ almost as much among themselves as they do from other Indian groups.

The distances we have been discussing are genetic ones, based on the analysis of biochemical traits such as the blood group. Interestingly, however, we find similar patterns in the distances calculated from measurements of the body itself. Morphologically, the Yanomamo show the effects of isolation from other Indians of the rain forest as well as isolation of the various Yanomamo subgroups from each other. Where groups are small and isolated from each other, morphology can "drift" as much as can alleles (Spielman et al. 1972).

Why Are the Yanomamo Subgroups Biologically So Unlike Each Other?
Having discovered that the Yanomamo are biologically heterogeneous, we may ask the next question: Why? What is producing this heterogeneity? Since there seems to be little in the way of acute environmental stress, we may postulate that the heterogeneity does not represent the effects of natural selection.

There are two factors that determine the biological structure of the Yanomamo: geography and culture.

Geography is important because villages that are farther apart are more isolated from each other, and, as a result, their biological distance is greater. A clear relationship exists between biological distance and geographical distance (Ward 1972; Spielman 1974). Geographically closer villages are biologically closer to each other.

In addition to geography, cultural factors are important determinants of biological relationships. In one analysis, investigators arranged the villages into seven dialect groups. By comparing 750 words and 38 rules of grammar and phonology, they could determine the "linguistic distances" among the dialects. Next they compared these linguistic distances with the genetic distances, based on analysis of various biochemical traits, and with biological distances based on anthropometric measurements. They found that the distances indicated by language, genetics, and morphology agreed quite well (Spielman et al. 1974).

In another analysis, Richard Ward (1972) studied the genetic distances among clusters of 37 villages that shared common histories. He found that historically related villages were more similar genetically. Furthermore, Ward analyzed more closely the 19 villages that were geographically part of the western subgroup and found the same thing there.

Figure 22.8
Guests drinking plantain
soup at a feast.

Where there were exceptions to this finding, there were specific social events that explained the exceptions. For example, three of the villages from the Namoweitari of the western subgroup were unexpectedly more similar to two from the Wanaboweitari than they were to other Namoweitari. An examination of the recent history of the area revealed that, in 1950, there was a treacherous feast, and a number of Namoweitari were forced to seek refuge among the Wanaboweitari. In return for this temporary shelter, they were forced to give the Wanaboweitari access to their women, and a number of pregnancies occurred. So several Namoweitari trace their ancestry to the Wanaboweitari.

The distributional patterns of Yanomamo biological traits, then, result not so much from the operation of natural selection and adaptation as they do from culture, migrations, population movement, and drift.

The Biological Off-Stage Drama

There is no threatening biological off-stage drama either. Because of the cultural characteristics of the Yanomamo and their way of life, not only

Figure 22.9
Fights over women may
escalate into violence
between groups of men.
Here such a fight is in the
beginning stages. The man
in the foreground, second
from the left, has been
struck on the head with
a club and is bleeding.

are environmental stresses minimized, but random genetic heterogeneity
is enhanced.

Genetic heterogeneity in small populations is important. It enhances
the flexibility of the gene pool. The more variability there is in the gene
pool, the less likely it is that some genetic disease can wipe out the whole
population. Think what would have happened in West African history
had there been no sickle-cell hemoglobin when the anopheles mosquito
took root in areas of heavy population. Falciparum malaria would have
swept through the population and decimated it. But in the West African
story, there was sufficient variability in the gene pool to include an apparently useless and even harmful trait—the sickle cell. This trait became
very useful indeed, once the conditions for the deadly variant of malaria
became prevalent.

Insight
Cultural Relativism, Anthropological Sentimentality, and the Yanomamo

It is worth pausing for a minute to remember that, as anthropologists, it is not our duty nor our calling to judge and evaluate other cultures and other people's ways. It is hard not to do this. Almost without exception, Westerners who have studied and lived with the Yanomamo have come away with the feeling that they were an unpleasant people leading a repugnant way of life. It is hard to get away from this feeling when one is constantly being shouted at, cursed, treated as a meal ticket, wheedled, threatened, pinched, snarled at, and cajoled. As if this were not bad enough, there are cultural rules that prevent the investigator from getting one absolutely essential data set: genealogical information that lays bare the ties between and among groups. Every time one tries to trace relationships between people via a dead person, there are howls of indignation. Every time one pronounces the name of a living adult male, tantrums ensue. It is difficult for an anthropologist (for he or she is also a human being) to silently watch violence, butchery, the brutal treatment of women, and the schooling of children in ways of violent death.

Chagnon reports that a woman was shot and killed because she was having an affair with her husband's brother. The husband was afraid of his brother, so rather than challenge him directly, he took the easier course and killed his wife. The Yanomamo felt that this action was entirely appropriate. Judith Shapiro, who studied the lot of Yanomamo women, believing perhaps that the earlier reports had been male-slanted and had therefore exaggerated the weakness and deprived condition of the Yanomamo women, found that the earlier reports had been accurate on the whole.

Perhaps the best testimony on the Yanomamo can be obtained from Helena Valero, a woman of Spanish blood who was abducted by the Yanomamo Indians and lived for twenty years with them. She was in the worst possible position—not only a woman, but also a stranger. Her life was constantly threatened, for she had no kinfolk to protect her. She was forced to flee into the forest to protect herself. She took refuge among different groups until she reached the age when she could be married. Her husband was not cruel, by Yanomamo standards, but one of the low points in her life was the day he broke her arm. She tells it in her own words (Biocca 1971:161–162).

"I was preparing Fusiwe's food; it seems that, at that moment, my child went up to his uncle who gave him a piece of meat from the crocodile's foot. Near the child was a black and white dog, very beautiful, of which Fusiwe was very fond. The dog snatched the meat from the child's hands, and the boy began to shout. The dog quickly swallowed the meat and choked itself; in two minutes it was dead. While the child came crying towards me, I heard them saying: 'Napagnuma [Helena's Yanomamo name] the dog is dead!'

"I saw nothing; I only felt a very heavy blow on my arm; I fell and lost my senses. It was Fusiwe who had struck me, because, he said, afterwards, I had not kept the child near me and that was why the dog was dead. The arm broke completely. Slowly I opened my eyes: I had that cold feeling in my body. I sighed and saw Fusiwe's old mother weeping near me, while the tushaua's daughter held my arm which was completely folded over and very swollen; I felt almost no pain, but it seemed to have gone to sleep. The daughter said to me: 'He has broken your arm, because your son has caused the dog to choke to death with the meat.' The old woman said: 'But why has he broken your arm?' Then she went up to Fusiwe and repeated, 'She has no father and no mother here: why have you broken her arm rather than anyone else's?' "

Helena eventually recovered. But her fear of her husband never quite died. The women thought it was wrong that he had broken her arm. But the Yanomamo live in a man's world, where men make the rules and also decide how those rules are to be enforced.

A miserable existence—hopelessly cut off from her kind and having no kinfolk to provide for her in a hostile and bleak environment. Eventually she was contacted by white missionaries and made her way to civilization. She was saved from "a fate worse than death."

Do you think so? She didn't. Her parents could not understand her. Her brothers blamed the Indians for everything that had happened and would not recognize her children as their nieces and nephews. They showed no understanding of her past or of her problems in dealing with two cultures, nor could they appreciate any of the subtleties of her life among the Indians. They were as ignorant and as ethnocentric as any Yanomamo. She was devastated, and lonelier than she had ever been under the forest canopy. Her unforgettable account of her experiences, which is detailed in a book called *Yanomamo*, ends with this pathetic note: "I thought that everything would be different with the white people."

Helena cannot be accused of sentimentality, that abiding sin of anthropologists and explorers who extol the virtues of "their tribe" or "their village," suggesting that primitive mankind lives in some kind of paradise. Nor can she be accused of ethnocentrism, that spurious doctrine that insists that one's own way of life is the canon by which one judges everyone else's. She emerges from her experience into a cold, white world a thorough relativist: seeing that the value that one places on an alien people's life is meaningless, and that other people can be evaluated only in their own terms.

You may recall our discussion of the dangers of pure production strategies (also called *monoculture,* or growing one crop). When plant breeders select a certain genetic strain of grain for its productive and disease-resistant qualities, the harvests start off being very good indeed. But these crops are very vulnerable. Once a disease or rust mutates and succeeds in attacking one plant, it can attack all of them. This is what happened in Ireland during the 1840s. The Irish had bred what Alan Beals has called a "super-potato," and their diet improved greatly from the giant tuber. But once the potato blight struck, it struck all the plants equally. The Irish began to starve to death. All their crops were wiped out, and they were forced to emigrate or die.

Human populations are the same. Genetic heterogeneity means that the population is preadapted to potential threats from new pressures from the environment just as they are to new diseases.

The Yanomamo are not unique in having no biological or ecological off-stage drama threatening their on-stage existence. All societies that are at equilibrium share their good fortune. But in the modern world, they are very unusual. That is why we picked them for our first example of the mode of biocultural integration called homeostatic equilibrium.

Why the Yanomamo?

We have selected the Yanomamo to demonstrate a particular mode of biocultural integration—stable equilibrium. The Yanomamo are not constrained by many of the things that constrain other societies. Their population sizes are small and their environment is adequate to meet their needs. They do not need to worry about diseases, harvests, or college educations. They can enter into elaborate political alliances, they can engage in warfare and feasting, and they can move about without too much worry about the present or the future.

The Yanomamo are not "noble savages" nor are they people living in a primitive Garden of Eden. They are people who, because of the combination of a series of factors of environment, society, demography, and biology, are in a state of equilibrium.

Summary

1. The purpose of the next three chapters is to introduce you to three modes of biocultural integration: biocultural equilibrium, unstable biocultural equilibrium, and the downward spiral.

2. The three biocultural systems that have been chosen to exemplify these three modes are (respectively) the Yanomamo Indians of Venezuela, the highland New Guinea peoples, and the traditional Mesoamerican village.

3. The Yanomamo Indians are free of biological stresses, if we ignore those that have recently been imported by Europeans in the form of infectious disease. Fertility levels are kept low by female infanticide and child mortality so that the average Yanomamo woman has about 4 births (compared with 7 in sedentary, developing countries).

4. The Yanomamo are not particularly stressed by disease either.

5. Their production mode is mainly swidden agriculture which does no harm to the tropical forest regime. They have no land shortage, and they move their villages and gardens regularly, thus avoiding pollution from human wastes and degradation of the environment through overexploitation.

6. Their on-stage beliefs about themselves and their tribe serve offstage purposes. Constant warfare, feuding, and shifting alliances ensure that population concentrations do not build to the point of threatening environmental degradation through excessive population pressure.

7. Their belief that all other groups are subhuman inhibits interbreeding and thereby maintains the group as a Mendelian population. Their beliefs that other Yanomamo are a little subhuman as well creates the conditions for genetic diversity. This in turn ensures plasticity and adaptive potential in the genome.

8. One of the reasons the Yanomamo were chosen as examples was to show that biocultural equilibrium does not mean a "harmonic paradise." The Yanomamo are very hard for us to like. To many of us (as people, not as anthropologists) their way of life is repugnant. Yet the lesson of Helena Valero is important: White people pose just as many problems as the Yanomamo.

Suggested Readings

Chagnon, Napoleon. *Yanomamo, The Fierce People.* 2nd ed. New York: Holt, Rinehart, and Winston, 1977.
   A well-known ethnography based on nineteen months of field work among the Yanomamo.

Neel, J. V. "Lessons From a Primitive People." *Science* 170(1970):815–822.
   A summary of Yanomamo biology, with discussion of its implications for modern medicine and human biology.

Smole, William J. *The Yanomamo Indians.* Austin: University of Texas Press, 1976.
   A detailed account of Yanomamo lifeways, especially good in accounts of their subsistence patterns.

Glossary

genetic distance   The dissimilarity or "distance" between two groups as measured by the different frequencies of the alleles of the two gene pools.

mode of biocultural integration   The way that the cultural, biological, and ecological clusters (and their subsystems) are tied together to handle stress. There are three modes:
1. biocultural equilibrium
2. unstable biocultural equilibrium
3. the downward spiral

neophobia   Fear of something new.

Highland New Guinea: A Case of Unstable Equilibrium

Introduction

The peoples of the New Guinea highlands are our second example. Their mode of biocultural integration is complex and is regulated by a complex control system. The shifts in the system are quite dramatic and considerably longer term than those of the Yanomamo. They have occurred systematically for as far back into the past as we can document, involving marked perturbations, or shifts, and including whole tribes or subtribal groups.

In highland New Guinea societies, internal pressures build up gradually, as we shall see. Every ten or twenty years the cultural system changes dramatically in the symbolic and social domains. These changes are widespread throughout the system and climax as warfare erupts between groups. A series of escalating encounters is followed by the reestablishment of the equilibrium.

Figure 23.1 diagrams this mode. The stresses build continuously but go unattended until a *catastrophic* response occurs. During the catastrophic response, relationships are rearranged so that the system can return to its equilibrium state. People/land, people/animal, male/female, group/group relations—all are renegotiated and reestablished.

On stage, people are living out their lives in their social and cultural settings on a day-to-day basis—they go to war, they have a feast. Offstage, however, the entire system is going awry until it has to be brought under control and restored.

First, let us look at the setting in which this mode of biocultural integration is carried out.

The Environmental Setting

New Guinea is the second largest island in the world, lying just to the south of the Equator. Politically, it is divided into two parts. West Irian, the western half, is administered by Indonesia; the eastern half, Papua, has only recently become independent. Papua presents a wide variety of landscapes, from low swamps, grasslands, and marshes in the south to mountains in the northern half, where peaks rise to nearly 15,000 feet above sea level.

Our focus in this chapter is on the highest part of the country, usually called the Central Cordillera, a series of east-west mountain ranges running parallel to each other and separated by grass-covered highland valleys. These valleys are among the most densely populated areas in New Guinea.

Figure 23.1
Schematic diagram of a
catastrophic response. The
system gradually moves
away from the equilibrium
position until it returns
suddenly to this position.

Equilibrium state

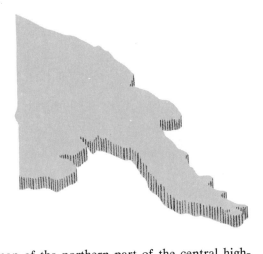

Figure 23.2
Map of the Papua New
Guinea highlands.

Figure 23.2 shows a map of the northern part of the central highlands. There are five districts: the West Highlands, South Highlands, East Highlands, Chimbu, and Madang. In these five districts, at altitudes of 5,000 feet and above, live the highlanders, often in dense clusters. Their valleys are cut off from the rest of the world by the mountains and are accessible primarily by airplane. The people were not contacted by outsiders until 1927, and it was 1933 before extensive visits were made by explorers (Lea and Irwin 1967).

The rainfall is high in these highlands, averaging between 85 and 110 inches per year. Water is no problem. Despite the steep slopes, erosion is not severe since violent storms are uncommon.

The climate is equatorial, but because of the altitude, temperatures are not extreme. At the post of Goroka, the average monthly high remains in the 75–80°F (23–27°C) range while the low averages 55–60°F (13–16°C). Higher up the slopes, lower temperatures are encountered.

Figure 23.3
View facing north across a highland valley. The light-colored areas on the opposite slope are gardens. The cleared space below the house in the foreground is used for dancing.

Figure 23.3 shows the general landscape and vegetation common to the area. While the area is heavily forested, there are extensive grasslands resulting from centuries of intensive slash-and-burn cultivation by the people living there (Howlett 1967).

Population Size and Density

As might be expected, accurate census data are not readily available, and it was not until the mid-1960s that an attempt at systematic enumeration was carried out by the Australian government. The 1966 census estimated slightly more than 2,000,000 people in Papuan New Guinea, with approximately 44 percent of the total living in the Central Cordillera. Because of the mountainous nature of the Cordilleran area, however, settlement is spotty. Although many areas have very low population densities, high densities also are found. In the Chimbu, as an example, the average density is 300 people per square mile. In some especially crowded areas, density is over 400 (Lea and Irwin 1967). (Compare this with 0.5 for the Yanomamo.) The settlement pattern is one of dispersed communities, which are themselves densely populated.

Sources of Stress in the Central Highlands

There are three sources of stress in this area. The first is *disease*. The incidence of disease is high and typical of people living in crowded conditions with poor sanitation and hygiene. Diarrhea, respiratory diseases (especially pneumonia), and malaria are all common. Malcolm (1970) found that 21 percent of the admissions to the Bundi hospital in the highlands of southern Madang were for malaria.

The prevalence of malaria strongly affects the settlement pattern. People are, as a rule, not found living in lower altitudes (below 4,500 feet) because malaria is prevalent there. Above 4,500 feet malaria occurs only during the wet season, when the rains create breeding grounds for the mosquito that carries the parasite. This is the reason for the high population densities at higher altitudes. People live there rather than at lower altitudes where the malaria parasite is common. However, Howlett (1967) reports that population pressure at higher altitudes has forced some people downward into malarial regions, where they suffer from this disease the year round.

The second environmental stress is *poor nutrition*. The people of the highlands cultivate small gardens and rely heavily on sweet potatoes as their staple food. Other vegetable foods that are occassionally eaten include taro (in the lower altitudes), fruits, a few peanuts, and the nut of the pandanus. As we will discuss later, pigs are common throughout the highlands and, when eaten, provide protein. However, one of the most pressing problems among these people is their protein and energy deficiency. Sweet potatoes are only about 1.1 percent protein and, because of their high starch content, are mostly calories. Sweet potatoes provide about 90 percent of the calories and 50 percent of the protein consumed (Baily 1966). It has been estimated that adults eat, on the average, four pounds of potatoes daily, and young children one-half pound. Because so much of the sweet potato is fibrous and indigestible, eating this much does not provide sufficient energy. The stomach simply cannot hold enough sweet potato to furnish an adequate caloric intake. As a result of this poor diet, malnutrition is common among highland people. Their estimated protein intakes are only 50 percent of what they require, and evidence of protein deficiency is widespread at all ages.

The third environmental stress is *population density*. Although the population density varies from group to group and area to area, the highlands as a whole are heavily populated. There are problems in finding an adequate food supply in such a rugged terrain, and this is complicated by the dense population. The population size is increasing, and there is a greater proportion of infants and children, who not only require more food because they are growing, but who are unable to contribute effectively to subsistence activities.

To summarize, highland people of central Papuan New Guinea live in widely scattered, though densely populated, settlements. They are intensive horticulturalists, depending heavily on the sweet potato for 90 percent of their calories and 50 percent of their protein. Their food is markedly deficient in protein content, and malnutrition is common. Population density places an increased load on the subsistence base, while infectious disease is common. In particular, they are exposed to malaria. Given all of this, how does their biocultural system help to alleviate this stress, bring about adaptation to this environment, and permit population survival?

Biocultural Integration in Madang

In describing biocultural integration of the New Guinea highlanders, we have selected the people of the Madang district. The northern part of this district stretches downward to sea level (see Figure 23.1) but the southern part is well within the Central Cordillera, with groups living at altitudes higher than 4,000 feet. One of these groups, representative of Papuan highlanders generally, are the Tsembaga, a Maring-speaking people living on the northern slopes of the Bismark mountain range. The Tsembaga have been intensively studied by Rappaport (1968, 1969, 1971, and 1974), who analyzed the relationships between their culture and their environment. The Tsembaga are a small group of 200 people, but they are nonetheless typical of highland populations throughout the Cordillera.

Additional information can be gained from the Bundi, a group living to the east of the Tsembaga but still in the same area. The Bundi are more numerous than the Tsembaga, with a population in excess of 6,700, and are more modernized since there are a mission station and government health facilities in their territory. However, Malcolm (1970) has described their human biological characteristics as well as their nutritional and health status, and his data fit quite well with Rappaport's. This allows us to include his analysis in our description.

The range of foods consumed by the highland peoples is quite narrow. Though they have access to a large number of different varieties of foods, their food preferences are strict. As we mentioned, their staple is the sweet potato. Rappaport (1968) counted 24 different nonanimal foods that they consumed, but his data show that most of them contributed only a negligible amount to the diet.

The highlanders are known as "pig-eaters." Yet pigs, along with marsupials, rats, insect larvae, eels, and snakes, make up only 1 percent

Figure 23.4
Members of two Tsembaga
clans feast on a wild pig.

of their total food consumption. Any of these would be an admirable source of the protein that is lacking in their diet.

Among highland Papuan groups, the biological and cultural systems are tightly interwoven in order to adapt the people to the stresses described above. One way a people adapts to scarce food resources is through small body size, for a small person requires less protein and fewer calories than a large one. Native Papuans are small people, males averaging 58 to 59 inches (147–149 cm.) and females 55 to 57 inches (139–144 cm.) in height. Body weights average around 100 pounds (45 kilos). The Bundi seem to be somewhat taller and heavier than the Tsembaga, but this may be due to the fact that the Bundi have had access to western medical care since 1958, while the Tsembaga are much more isolated.

New Guineans have a longer period of growth than almost any other people. They do not reach their full growth until between the ages of 21 and 24 years, compared with 15 to 17 years for Americans. Females do not begin to menstruate until 18 years, on the average, almost six years later than in the United States. A longer growth period conserves nutrients. Rather than the sudden burst of protein and calories needed for adolescents in industralized nations, this stretching-out of growth saves these nutrients and hence is adaptive.

Figure 23.5
Sacrificing a pig to the
Red Spirits.

Figure 23.6
Highland men dressed and
adorned for dancing.

The genetic systems of these people do not indicate any specific alleles that seem to be genetic adaptations, though extensive studies have not been conducted. Despite the malaria, sickle-cell hemoglobin is unknown. The available data suggest that the isolation of the various communities from each other is more important than natural selection in determining frequencies of the various polymorphisms. Thus the genetic situation is similar to what we have seen in the Amazon Basin.

Biological heterogeneity among villages is as high as it is in lowland South America. Studies of genetic traits and of the size and shape of the body (McHenry and Giles 1971; W. W. Howells 1973) indicate that highland New Guinea villages show considerable differentiation from each other despite the fact that they are related historically, culturally, and linguistically. Genetic drift seems to be an important evolutionary mechanism.

But it is in the cultural domain that we find the most striking instances of the integration of the biological and cultural subsystems. The ritual system of the Tsembaga facilitates adaptation and maintenance of the population. Rappaport has called their ritual cycle a "complex homeostatic mechanism," since it helps to maintain an undegraded environment, to keep fighting to manageable levels, to facilitate trade, to distribute surplus pork throughout the population, and to make this protein source available when it is "most needed" (Rappaport 1968). In other words, the ritual cycle is the mechanism that restores equilibrium when conditions threaten it.

Rearranging the System: The "Catastrophe"

In studying this system, let us analyze the events that lead up to the catastrophe: warfare. Tensions build up as disputes flare among neighboring groups. Because of population density, groups are in much closer contact with each other than were the Yanomamo. The reasons given for disputes include such things as rape, stealing crops, or sorcery. But Rappaport notes that population pressure is a frequent underlying off-stage cause even though it is not recognized by the people. Where population pressure does result from high density, such disputes disperse the groups over an area and is adaptive in holding down the density at any one location.

At the same time as the group tensions are building, and *not* coincidentally, the women have begun to complain to the men about the pigs. The pig population has grown to the point where it is a nuisance. They are getting into the sweet potato patches and uprooting the sweet potatoes. More than that, the women are having to work excessively hard just to feed the pigs. At the height of the pig population, over a third of the gardens that are tended are used to grow food for the pigs.

Complaints from the women and the flare-up of disputes between groups are the on-stage components of the growing friction. Off-stage, the competition between pigs and people for food, and the scarcity of forest cover contribute to the threat of ecological disequilibrium. Maring hogs are castrated, and the sows can only be impregnated by feral (or wild) boars that live in the forest. When the human population expands, the forest is turned into bush gardens. The increasing number of gardens reduces the amount of forest available for feral boars, thus bringing them into closer contact with the people and their domestic pigs and resulting in a further pig population explosion.

As tensions build up to the point of a fight, the ritual cycle becomes important. The Maring ideology recognizes two kinds of spirits: spirits of the high ground (Red Spirits) and spirits of the low ground (Spirits of Rot). The Red Spirits are the spirits of people killed in warfare, and their qualities are associated with martial values: hardness, strength, anger. The Spirits of Rot are the spirits of all those not killed in warfare. They are associated with being female, and their qualities are in opposition to those qualities of the Red Spirits. Spirits of Rot have qualities favoring fertility and growth: coldness, softness, wetness.

As hostilities escalate, the Tsembaga "segregate" the two sets of spirits. The community becomes identified with the Red Spirits and their qualities and moves away from qualities associated with the Spirits of Rot. They accomplish this by rituals that "bring" the Red Spirits into the bodies of the men of the village and by a taboo on activities associated with the Spirits of Rot. Sexual intercourse is forbidden since femaleness

Figure 23.7
New Guinea man with bow and arrows.

Figure 23.8
Tsembaga woman
renouncing a taboo.

is associated with fertility and hence with the Spirits of Rot; intercourse would drive out the Red Spirits.

Food taboos are activated. Marsupials are the "pigs" of the Red Spirits, while eels and pandanus are foods of the Spirits of Rot. Eels may not be eaten at all, while pandanus and marsupials may not be cooked together. The village is split apart symbolically. Women are separated from men, and contact between them is forbidden—thus the prohibition of sexual intercourse. This follows from the segregation of the Red Spirits (Men = hardness, strength, anger) from the Spirits of Rot (Women = wetness, coldness, fertility, softness). Moist foods, soft foods, foods cooked by women, and foods brought from the lower altitudes are forbidden to the men.

The on-stage reasoning is that the "femaleness" or the "soft-wet-ness" of the foods would diffuse the martial spirits from the warriors. Off-stage, changing the diet infuses it with high quality protein and enhances the warriors' rations, while the women are kept on regular, high starch foods.

During the elaborate ritualistic preparations for fighting, pigs are cooked and eaten, especially by the warriors. Allies are fed when they come to the village to assist. In this way, meat is distributed throughout the group, symbolizing alliances in addition to providing protein. Fighting may go on for weeks or even months, and meat is consumed throughout the period.

The Tsembaga distinguish "small" and "big" fights, the first being the initial stage which escalates to the second. Each group usually stands in a loose formation, several ranks deep, firing arrows at the other group. When a fatality occurs, fighting is discontinued and the victim mourned. Mourning ritual requires killing and eating of pigs.

Rappaport (1972:255) reports that the "fighting sometimes ends in the rout of one of the parties, and in such cases the victors despoiled the territory of their opponents, then retired to their own ground. Usually, however, warfare terminates by agreement between the antagonists that there has been enough fighting and injury and death for the time being." When a truce is arranged, all taboos are lifted, and a wholesale slaughter of pigs takes place. There are rituals that once again reintegrate the spirits of the high and the low ground. There is now a "debt" to the spirits because of the warfare, and sufficient pigs must be raised to repay them.

Back to Equilibrium

With the arrangement of the truce, we start to come down from the peak of the catastrophe and begin the return to normal.

The segregation of the Red Spirits from the Spirits of Rot is no longer necessary. Men and women can come into close contact and sexual intercourse is again permissible.

Taboos on the mixing and eating of the forbidden foods are lifted. Marsupials, snakes, lizards, frogs, rats, insects, grubs, birds, and even forbidden edible ferns are once more eaten. Foods that are *ordinarily* forbidden are also eaten during this period to mark it off as taking place in ritual time. The occasion is marked as special.

The *rumbin* is a hard, masculine plant associated with war. The pre-fight rituals commenced with the uprooting of the sacred *rumbin*. When it is planted, following the war, each man in the group clasps it, symbolically becoming a member of the patrilineal group. In this way allies who stay on, as well as outsiders who have been marginal to the society, are incorporated within the group. The integrity and strength of the patrilineal group are thereby emphasized and symbolized. The debt to the Red Spirits is partially paid off. With the planting of the *rumbin,* the Red Spirits are thanked for their help and are asked to care for the plant (symbolically, for the patrilineal group) and promised more pork in the future.

An oven is made, and a plant called the *amame* is planted all around it. Now the oven is a symbol of fertility. "As human children emerge from vaginas, so the fruits of the earth emerge from the oven" (Buchbinder and Rappaport 1976:29). The Spirits of Rot care for the oven and will in turn ensure that the pigs will be fertile and that the women will be healthy and bear many children.

But the *amame* is a male plant and will eventually overgrow and displace the oven, which will crumble and rot. So, too, the men will take over the spiritual and executive functions in the group, subordinating the women in the "natural" (for the Maring) order of things.

Buchbinder and Rappaport suggest a beautiful off-stage interpretation of the rituals that give symbolic meaning to sexuality (male/female distinctions), warfare, territory, and the spirit world. In the spirit world too, there is an off-stage cycling process. The fertility of women and pigs is associated with peace and the Spirits of Rot. Warfare and hardness are associated with the Red Spirits. The two spirit sets are in opposition to each other. As the Red Spirits decline in importance, the Spirits of Rot increase. You will recall that this corresponds to the increasing population pressure from pigs and people that started the whole process (off-stage) in the first place. Warfare reduces fertility temporarily by interrupting sexual activity; it also increases mortality through fighting. But the Red Spirits dominate warfare and are appeased (debts are paid) by sacrificing great numbers of pigs. They are at their zenith during the last phases of a war and the subsequent settling of the truce. At that time the Spirits of Rot are at their nadir (lowest point). The balance between the two sets of spirits is restored by the building of the oven, the resumption of normal rations, and the inception of sexual activity. Women, whose position had been lowered during the fighting and whose contribution was a passive one, now attain, ritually, their proper position in the society. The Spirits of Rot are revived and strengthened, and the society reunites into a normal state.

Conclusion

Now the catastrophe is past. The pig population has been reduced and the spirits appeased. The patrilineal group has been strengthened, and (sometimes) whole populations shifted to ensure that people/land ratios are once more favorable. The system is back to equilibrium and will remain there until the pressures once again begin to build.

But, almost immediately, the build-up begins. Because of the debt to the Red Spirits, the pig population must be rebuilt. As we know, the increase will lead to pressures, to problems, and to stresses. As inter-group tensions also increase, the system will ultimately be driven further and further from equilibrium until the catastrophic phase of the cycle is repeated.

It was the study of these processes that led us to think about the Maring (and the subgroup, the Tsembaga) as existing in a state of un-stable equilibrium that is kept stable in the long run by the periodic catas-trophes that, both on-stage and off-stage, serve to eliminate the conditions for instability.

Summary

1. The second mode of biocultural integration examined is the un-stable equilibrium. The peoples of highland New Guinea live in this mode. In an unstable equilibrium, off-stage processes create pressures on the system that build continuously until the system undergoes a sudden, wrenching realignment and reorganization.

2. There are three sources of stress in the biocultural system: dis-ease (particularly malaria), poor nutrition (from overdependence on the sweet potato), and population density.

3. The people adapt to these stresses through small body size, not by occupying a wide ecological niche. They mature more slowly than we do, and this longer growth period saves on nutrients.

4. The ritual cycle is the key to understanding the catastrophe and rearrangement of the biocultural system. As population pressure on re-sources builds off-stage, on-stage the women begin to complain bitterly about the pig population, and disputes flare with neighboring groups. As the pressure builds, a ritual reorganization of the spirits takes place so that the people can prepare for war. Dietary changes accompany the ritual reorganization, improving the diets of the fighting forces at the expense of the dependents. During the fighting there are many occasions for the killing and eating of the pigs in great pig feasts.

5. When the pig population has been decreased to where it no longer puts pressure on available land resources, the fighting trails off. Relations are restored to their former status, and the society goes back to its normal (equilibrium) state.

6. If the tensions have been particularly severe, and if the fighting escalates to the point of a "rout," then population pressure in the region is relieved by the device of scattering the losers over the landscape and driving them out of the territory.

Suggested Readings

Malcolm, Laurence A. *Growth and Development in New Guinea—A Study of the Bundi People of the Madang District*. Madang: Institute of Human Biology, 1970.

> *A description and analysis of the interaction between nutrition and physical development.*

Rappaport, Roy A. *Pigs for the Ancestors: Ritual in the Ecology of a New Guinea People*. New Haven: Yale University Press, 1968.

> *A classic study of cultural ecology, outlining the close interactions between components of the biocultural system.*

Vayda, Andrew P. "Expansion and warfare among swidden agriculturalists." *American Anthropologist* 63(1961):346–358.

> *An analysis of the role of warfare among slash-and-burn agriculturalists.*

Glossary

homeostatic   A system that oscillates around an equilibrium point and is equilibrium-seeking.

24

Traditional Mesoamerica: Biocultural Disequilibrium, or the Downward Spiral

Introduction

So far we have described biocultural integration in terms of two modes. Both modes keep the system in a state of equilibrium—the first a stable equilibrium, and the second an equilibrium that is attained after a series of events leading up to some catastrophic replacement. The important thing is that both modes act as regulators to restore the system to equilibrium.

But sometimes systems get out of equilibrium to such an extent that they cannot restore themselves by available control mechanisms. They go into a "downward spiral." Two things can happen. First, the system may change to such an extent that it is no longer recognizable as the system it was. Second, the system may destroy itself.

A familiar example of a downward spiral in the chemical world is an explosion. A chain of reactions is triggered in a compound. Ordinarily some control process would either stop the chain or bring the compound back to its original state; but the process is either lacking or too weak to stop the chain. As a result, the system goes out of control. It gains such intensity and momentum that the original compound changes suddenly and dramatically: there is an explosion.

We speak of changes that get out of control in this way as *exponential*. This means that the response of such a system is one of *acceleration*. Figure 24.1 diagrams an exponential change, illustrating that as time

Figure 24.1
Diagram of an exponential process. The curve keeps accelerating until it runs off the page.

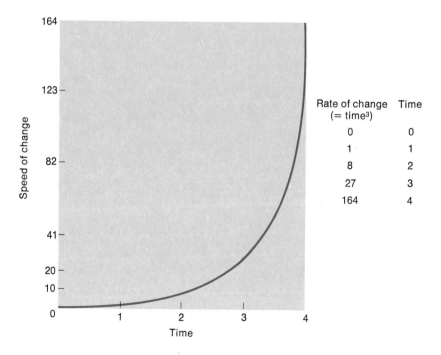

Rate of change (= time³)	Time
0	0
1	1
8	2
27	3
164	4

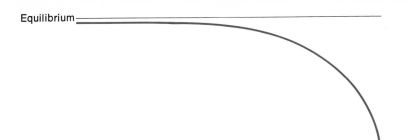

**Figure 24.2
Exponential change, down-
ward spiral.**

changes, the rate of system output changes by the cube of time. The line gets steeper and steeper until it flies off the page.

The downward spiral is the same process. (See figure 24.2) It is just another way to say that things are "going bad."

In this chapter we will describe a downward-spiraling biocultural system—the traditional Mesoamerican Indian village. The truth is that they are in bad shape. Things are out of control and the system will soon become changed dramatically. Even today the villages are kept going only by outside forces. Internal control forces are no longer functioning in any kind of control system to keep them in any equilibrium. Whatever equilibrium there is is not of the peoples' own doing; their worlds are not their own and their systems are not self-regulated.

The Traditional Mesoamerican Indian Village

Mesoamerica is the name given to the culture area of the old high civilizations of the Aztecs and the Maya. It extends southward from Mexico, through Guatemala to the Isthmus of Panama. Since both of the authors have done research there, many of the case materials are drawn from our own work, although we include the work of others where our own data are insufficient.

The reason we pick Mesoamerica as our third case is because there we can see the operation of biocultural stresses to a marked degree. The Mesoamerican village as we know it is a product of Spanish conquest and colonization as it has extended into the twentieth century. The conditions of these villages have worsened as the surrounding economy of the industrial world increased the strains.

These villages are not healthy places to live, and the poorer the village, the poorer the conditions. Your first night in a village will convince you of one thing: you are living in a barnyard. The villages are often *nucleated;* that is, the houses are built close to each other. Animal manure is found in every patio, and when the rainy season comes, clouds of house-flies descend. The houses are not screened, so the flies get in everywhere.

Figure 24.3
Map of Mesoamerica, where Aztecan and Mayan civilizations once flourished.

Each house is usually a well-built, well-ventilated adobe dwelling. But people don't live in them. Their houses are ritual centers, places where family rites occur. Funerals, marriages, baptisms, and saint's day festivals will always be held there. But most people live in the kitchens—bamboo structures, set apart from the main houses, with stick walls daubed with mud up to a height of about four feet. People live, eat, and sleep in their kitchens, along with the dogs, chickens, and turkeys that wander in and out despite half-hearted attempts to shoo them away. Mesoamerican villagers believe that domestic animals are part of the household, and these animals, with the exception of dogs, are treated with a good deal of care and attention. Dogs absorb the aggression, hostility, and other punitive impulses of the people. One would never strike a child and never hit a neighbor. But dogs are popular targets for rocks, sticks, blows, and well-aimed kicks.

The flimsy housing is no great problem. Mesoamerica falls almost entirely within the tropics, and the daily temperature and rainfall depend on the altitude of the village. Down on the coast, the "hot country" as the highlanders call it, it is hot and rainy, while above 7,000 feet it is cool the year round. At 10,000 feet it is cold, but the people wear heavier clothing, wrap themselves in their blankets, sleep in family groups, and rarely complain.

Our data are drawn from the highland areas. There the rainfall is seasonal. Ethnographers often feel that they will go crazy if anyone mentions the rain one more time, since it is the most common topic of conversation for six months of the year during the rainy season, supplanting even such perennial topics as sex and witchcraft. The on-stage actors are right about the rain. If it comes in the right time and in the right amounts, then the crops will be good. It must come before planting. When the corn

Figure 24.4
View of Chichicastenango, a highland Guatemalan community.

crop sprouts it is needed again. When the corn flowers, another heavy shower is needed, and finally just before the corn has completed its growth cycle, a final dousing is needed. If it rains too much, the corn will be green and tall, but the cobs will be small and diseased. If it rains too little, the corn plants will be yellow and pale, and the cobs will not have fat kernels.

Off-stage, the rain poses other problems. Generation after generation has chopped down the forests for firewood, exposing the top soil to the elements. If the rains are heavy, the topsoil will be stripped away, carving deep gullies (*barrancas*) in the hillsides and making the area unsuitable for growing corn. The people seem to be unaware of the effects of stripping off the forest cover. They accept erosion as a fact of life and take few preventive measures against it.

To understand the pressures on the traditional Mesoamerican village and its life support systems, one has to understand the history of the area. For centuries, before the coming of the Europeans, Mesoamerica was a channel through which cultural innovations, migrating groups, and items of trade all flowed freely. Rich and influential civilizations developed that affected the development of other Native American societies as far north as Illinois. The population was large enough and productive enough to support an affluent ruling class with monumental temples and impressive government buildings.

But times change. In the sixteenth century the New World was conquered by Europeans, and Mesoamerica came under the domination of Spanish rulers and Roman Catholic missionaries. The indigenous ruling classes were replaced by Spaniards who took over the administration of the older empires. The lands of Mesoamerica were split up among the Spanish conquerors and soldiers, and the missionaries were set loose to convert the heathen.

Figure 24.5
Church at Chichicasten-
ango, Guatemala. The
smoke comes from incense
burned on the steps; the
church is braced because
of damage inflicted by the
earthquake of 1976.

The missionaries were, in some respects, quite successful in their efforts, but in other respects they failed. Mesoamerican society is today Roman Catholic, and large churches may be seen even in small communities. But the Roman Catholic religion of the people displays elements perpetuated from their pre-Columbian belief system. The saints of the Catholic church have been eagerly adopted and blended with the deities they have worshipped for thousands of years. Catholic feast days are celebrated, but the celebrations contain elements not characteristic of Catholics elsewhere. The incense they have burned for centuries, symbolizing their prayers to the gods, is still burned on the steps of Catholic churches, but by men who are members of the traditional religious system, not priests of the church.

The Spanish soldiers also introduced change, particularly in the system of production. They introduced large domesticated animals: oxen, sheep, goats, cattle, and donkeys and horses. They also introduced the plow and new varieties of grain, principally wheat. They created a system of forced labor and organized farming similar to our own plantation system. It was called the *hacienda*.

Figure 24.6
Head of *cofradia* (civil-religious brotherhood) burning incense (*copal*) on the steps of the church at Chichicastenango. Religious rituals are blends of Roman Catholic and Mayan elements.

The conquerors also introduced infectious diseases. With the people brought together into the *haciendas,* disease organisms had the necessary conditions for being maintained. The Indian populations were decimated and the survivors forced into labor for Spanish landlords (*padrones*).

Despite all this, the Indians retained their indigenous village organizations. The central and most important institution in the village was, and still is, the **civil-religious hierarchy.** This is a ladder of political and religious offices that ambitious people climb during their lives so that they can earn the title of "respected elder" in the community. A respected elder will have donated his time, effort, and resources to fulfilling political and religious offices during his lifetime. Starting off life as a lowly ritual official, or as a policeman in the village, the ambitious man will try to become the sponsor of the festival of the patron saint, or the president of the village by the end of his years.

The production unit in the Mesoamerican village is the household. Most young people join the household of the groom's parents; thus we speak of residence as being *patrilocal.* Marriage and residence are the most important decisions that a young couple will ever make in their lives, because by marrying into a household one becomes a sharer in its wealth. Patrilocal residence is enforced by the people's beliefs. In some parts of Mesoamerica, people say that a person brings honor to his house by bringing his wife to live there. (He also provides free labor to the household.) They also say that if a man goes to live with his wife's family, there must be something wrong with him. He cannot, as they say, be a true man. If he were, he would not allow himself to be bossed around by his wife's kinfolk.

Similarly there is something wrong with a woman who attracts or seduces a man into her household. She must be an incontinent "pig" who is so sexually driven that she cannot wait for the proper time to marry and join her husband's family. She is so overcome by desire that she proposes to a man and brings him to live with her. Nevertheless, a substantial number of men do jeopardize their manhood and their wives' reputations by moving in with their wives' families. They do so because they themselves are poor, and their wives are better off. They endure the gossip and innuendo so that they can better themselves.

This system in which poor men marry richer women to better themselves means that there are always "circulating elites" in the village. Sol Tax has pointed out that, in the Guatemalan Indian village of Panajachel, people are rich in one generation, middling in the next, and perhaps poor in the third. It all depends on their choice of spouse and mode of residence (Tax 1952).

Along with the civil-religious hierarchy, the marriage rules keep social classes from forming in the village. "Everyone is poor in the village," they say. "Everyone is humble and knows want!" They are right. The premise of equality is borne out, ensuring that no one becomes rich, or if they do, no one stays rich.

The Production System

Each household is a unit of production and consumption. A man and his sons will till the family lands and raise corn, beans, and squash in what is called *milpa* agriculture. In *milpa* agriculture the three crops are raised together. If the household is of middling-to-rich economic status, it will have its own **yunta,** or yoke of oxen, provided that there is flat land where a *yunta* can be used. In the most mountainous areas *yuntas* are useless, and the householder raises corn by using a digging stick or a hoe. Even in those villages where there is flat arable land, people who are very poor or who wish to expand their holdings work the common land in the mountains. Here they must use a hoe, and though the yields are good, the work is backbreaking. In the mountains the ground cover is burned, just as among the Yanomamo, and the corn planted seed by seed.

The villagers work long hours. They do not rush, working slowly and patiently. They pride themselves on their endurance, on being able to withstand the exertion of inefficient, labor-intensive agriculture. In good years they will grow enough so that, except for the very poorest, everyone has sufficient to eat. But in average years, they will start to run out of food around May or June, and they will have to expend their scarce cash buying corn. This practice is dreaded because wages are between 50¢ and $1.00 a day, and corn costs about 10¢ a pound. During the hungry period, poor people have to eat "tortillas and salt"—a very inadequate diet indeed.

Environmental Stress

Mesoamerican communities are under a heavy load of environmental stress. They provide us with a clear picture of a tightly constrained bio-cultural system. The stressful elements are so tightly interwoven and mutually supporting that they give us a classic picture of a "vicious circle" of downward-spiraling poverty, suffering, and disease.

Population pressure is intense. The rate of population increase is among the world's highest: 3.5 percent a year, or a doubling of the population every 17 years. In the past, population growth was kept down by high mortality rates. Mortality was particularly high during the years of infancy and early childhood, and only half the persons born survived to a marriageable age. So despite a relatively high birthrate, not enough people lived long enough to marry and have children to cause rapid population increase.

In more recent times, several things have happened. First of all, Western medical care has had an impact on the lives of the people. While mortality is still high, it is lower than in the years after the Spanish conquest. The reduction in mortality has been most striking in the young, so that now more are living into the teenage years, the age when they normally marry. The number of births goes up as a result.

Second, individuals are having more children than in the past. This seems to reflect, as much as anything, a lower age at marriage. In the community of San Antonio Ilotenango in the highlands of Guatemala, the average age at marriage in women born between 1910 and 1925 was 17.4 years; women of the same community born between 1945 and 1954 were married, on the average, at 14.2 years. As a result, the average age of a woman at the birth of her first child has decreased from 20.9 years to 15.9 years. This means that the number of births per woman is increasing as the fertility of the community itself is rising (Scholl, Odell, and Johnston 1976).

Mesoamerican villagers are caught in a population explosion for these two reasons: Fewer infant and child deaths mean more adults who will have children. Lower ages at marriage result in greater fertility.

The increased fertility results in larger numbers of children, leading

Table 24.1

Typical Diet of a Guatemalan Family (taken from Nash, 1958)

Food item	Pounds per week
Corn	50
Black beans	3
Salt	1
Coffee	1
Bread	13
Meat	1½
Tomatoes	2
Onions	12
Sugar	6
	Other amounts (wkly)
Chile	8 oz.
Eggs	½ doz.
Bananas	10

to a population pyramid that is bottom-heavy (chapter 20). Because there are so many more "dependents," pressure on population resources is increased even more.

Food Production

The resources available to the community are severely limited. Through the centuries, the people have come to rely more and more on fewer and fewer food sources, until they are now referred to as a "monocrop" society, heavily dependent upon maize (corn). Table 24.1 (Nash 1957) is an example of a typical diet, in this case from a Guatemalan family. Their diets are deficient in both protein and calories, both derived mainly from corn (with beans as a supplementary source). Corn, however, is not a good source of protein since it is incomplete, lacking the essential amino acid lysine, which our bodies need but cannot manufacture themselves.

The peasant landholder, intensively working his small plot of land and depending on a relatively poor source of food to feed himself and his large family, is deep in poverty. He cannot purchase food to supplement the family's diet. In an attempt to obtain money, he may convert land that does not grow food into a cash crop, such as coffee, that can be sold. But he now grows less food because of cash-cropping. More money is required, and more land must be converted. As an alternative, men may migrate seasonally to places where there is work, harvesting sugarcane or cotton in the lowlands and along the coast. The change from the cool and temperate highland climate to the tropical one of the lowlands exposes them to stress. Many diseases are caused by a change of climate. The men who go to the coast frequently contract malaria.

In such a system one would expect to find malnutrition, and this is perhaps the single most pressing problem encountered in Mesoamerica. Between 5 and 10 percent of the children develop severe protein-calorie malnutrition, and as many as 75 percent of the remainder will display various signs of chronic mild-to-moderate malnutrion. The most susceptible age is between 1 and 3 years, when breast-feeding ceases. Until that time, the child does reasonably well since mothers are able to manufacture breast milk of sufficient quality even though their own nutrition is suboptimal. But when the child is weaned, he or she is subject to the mercies of the food-production system. Children are usually weaned by means of some sort of corn broth or sugar water, a poor diet for a rapidly growing child. They are then at a serious risk of becoming malnourished.

This situation is made worse by the high prevalence of infectious disease. Mesoamerican villages display substandard levels of sanitation and hygiene, and infectious organisms are widespread. Diarrhea is common, and children may have this disease for as much as 50 percent of their early years. Outbreaks of respiratory disease are frequent and, because of

Figure 24.7
A *pila* in San Antonio
Aguascalientes, Guatemala.
Pilas are areas of communal
water supply for the homes
as well as basins for
washing clothes.

the crowded living conditions, are readily transmitted from one person to another.

One might think that the rainy season would be beneficial since it supplies the water necessary for their crops. This is true, but as Wayne Kappel (1977) has shown, these people are "damned if it rains, and damned if it doesn't." While the rains provide the water for farming, they also overload and contaminate the already questionable water and sewage systems and cause an even higher frequency of diarrhea and dysentery. (In other parts of the world where they have been studied, the effects of the rainy season are so severe as to delay the growth of children during that period.) If it doesn't rain, there isn't enough food.

Not only do malnutrition and disease each have a serious effect on the health of the Mesoamerican community, but they also reinforce each other. We say that there is a *synergism* between them: one affects and increases the strength of the other. In a community where there is widespread malnutrition, there is reduced resistance to disease; the body simply doesn't have the resources to mobilize to fight the disease organism. Therefore, malnutrition increases the severity of disease. But there is more. When a child is ill, nutritional requirements increase. Now, when one contracts diarrhea, what is a common treatment? The individual is taken off solid food and placed on a reduced diet. In Mesoamerica this diet is usually non-nutritious, gruel and sugar water. The change in diets may cause the development of acute protein-calorie malnutrition in children already on the borderline. So, the relationship between malnutrition and disease is synergistic: the first causes the second which causes the first and so on. . . .

Figure 24.8
Market in Totonicapan, where a woman is weighing corn.

Figure 24.9
Street in Totonicapan, in the Guatemalan highlands.

Biocultural Disequilibrium

How do these conditions interact with the cultural system of the people? First of all, there is an association between malnutrition and mental development. The most current research indicates that children who are malnourished are deprived of the opportunities for learning and socialization so crucial to human development. As a result, children as well as older persons from societies such as these score lower on tests of intellectual performance. While they may function very well within their own particular social system, their academic achievement and potential are lowered, making it all the more difficult for them to improve their standard of living in a world that increasingly emphasizes schooling.

Now, why the impairment in intellectual performance? This is not an easy question to answer despite years of research, and in fact, there is no single answer. It seems certain that malnourished children, who are constantly fighting the physical effects of nutritional deprivation as well as episodes of disease, do not have the energy to learn as effectively as children from more privileged groups. And since future learning is always based upon previous experience, the deficits suffered at the crucial ages of 1 to 3 years may carry over into adult years unless counteracted by specific enrichment programs. Another factor seems to be that, in such communities, the parents and other adults are themselves so heavily occupied with the difficulties of their own existence that they can't afford to provide the enrichment that would result in increased learning and stimulation. Perhaps the parents themselves were the victims of malnu-

Figure 24.10
Market in San Martin
Jilotepeque, Guatemala.
Traditionally, Guatemalan
women wear *huipiles*
instead of blouses. The
huipil is typical of the
community from which each
woman has come to this
market.

trition, leading to what the Mexican nutritionist Joaquin Cravioto has called the "spiraling effect" of malnutrition. One final factor is undoubtedly rooted in the generalized poverty that typifies these communities. Where there is such poverty there is also a lack of good schools, innovative programs, and just opportunities for academic achievement.

Fortunately, this situation is not irreversible. Contrary to what once was thought, malnutrition does not necessarily damage the brain organically and prevent adequate biological development. Although such damage may occur in extremely severe cases, there has not been enough research to indicate whether, given the proper learning environment, the malnourished child has the capability of developing to an intellectual level comparable to his or her peers in more privileged societies.

Cultural factors may contribute directly to the problems of Mesoamerican communities. Knowledge about sanitation and hygiene is as important in reducing disease as is knowledge about nutrition. The poverty and living conditions characteristic of the community make it difficult, if not impossible, to maintain an adequate diet and an acceptable level of health.

Other factors within the cultural domain contribute to malnutrition. Modernization of the parents is a significant determinant of child health; "modernization" here is defined in terms of variables such as contact with the outside world and education.

Another important variable is the way in which food is distributed within a family. Ethnographic studies of Mesoamerican families have shown that food is diverted from noncontributors to those members who contribute most to its economic state. Parents say "meat is not good for children." If there is plenty of food, everybody can get enough; if food is in short supply, it will be channelled wherever it is perceived it will do the most good. Adults, especially males, will get more than their share; children get less than their share. (The nutritional disease *kwashiorkor* is named after an African word meaning the disease one gets when displaced at the breast by a new baby.)

This does not mean that the introduction of our own cultural values and food preferences will automatically alleviate such problems. A graphic example is those women who have given up breast-feeding in favor of bottle feeding as a result of Western influence. There is ample evidence from many societies, including our own, of the nutritional advantages to the child of breast-feeding. In Mesoamerica, the changeover may be disastrous. We have noted that a mother can manufacture high quality breast milk even if her diet is lower in protein and higher in carbohydrates than desirable. To produce an equivalent amount of cow's milk requires a society with enough wealth to feed and care for a large herd of cows. Wealth like this is not available in Mesoamerican communities. In American society, we take advantage of the various powdered supplements to infants' diets. These cannot be fully utilized in Mesoamerica since it is estimated their cost alone would take about 70 percent of the average family's income. As a result, the diets of infants who are bottle fed are, in these villages, deficient.

Low energy levels are characteristic of Mesoamericans, as with all people who suffer from dysentery, tuberculosis, and intestinal disorders. The people themselves recognize low energy levels. They justify them by saying that the best workers are the plodders, who work slowly but surely to get things done. "Plodders" do not maximize their production levels by taking advantage of the common lands in the mountains. That land goes unused, or abandoned, even though it would give good yields if a family group could work it diligently with a digging stick. But diligence requires energy, and 1,500 calories per day depletes, rather than restores, energy.

Mesoamericans do not take risks, either. They are sufficiently close to the margin of survival that they play safe agricultural strategies. In the community where one of the authors has worked, it was noticed that long-run production could be raised dramatically if people planted all their land early in the rainy season and take their chances that the rains would follow. In fact, there was one person who followed this "high-risk/high payoff" strategy. The other villagers regarded him as crazy. The rest of them spread their planting over the period from March through June and always got some harvest, but they were never able to take advantage of good years the way the high-risk planter was.

This depressing picture of Mesoamerican society is one of a tightly

Figure 24.11
San Antonio Aguascalientes, Guatemala. The cane fences screen living compounds from the road.

constrained ecosystem in which there is a circular effect, each component directly increasing the effects of another. There are no known instances of genetic adaptation. Nutrient intake, disease, population pressure, and cultural factors all mutually affect each other; and only the excessive mortality rates keep the whole system from running away with itself. While the people employ adaptive strategies to make the most out of what they have, the system cannot be called adapted. They do not maintain equilibrium by means of self-regulation and internal control. They do not "engage" their environment in an active process of adaptation and adjustment. They are, in fact, at the mercy of their environment: the natural world in which they live and the industrialized world which surrounds them. The people do not regulate their system; the environment determines it for them.

If you think that the situation in the Mesoamerican village is intolerable, then you agree with the villagers themselves. They are leaving their villages and going to the cities and towns of Mexico and Guatemala. What started as a trickle of migration before and just after World War II has turned into a flood. People are voting with their feet against the unhealthy poverty of the traditional village. The villages will most likely survive into the year 2000. Many villagers think so. But they will have been saved by passing their surplus population along to the cities.

Insight
Traditional Mesoamerica-The Civil-Religious Hierarchy in a Mesoamerican Village

The civil-religious hierarchy is important in Mesoamerican villages. Although it bestows prestige on the office holder, it requires him to expend the profits, or surplus, from years of labor in giving feasts for the village. People will spend as much as the equivalent of $800 on the festival of the patron saint. In a village of 1,200 people, the sponsor may slaughter four oxen, twelve turkeys, and a dozen goats to feed the entire village. The village orchestra will be hired for a week. Thousands of tortillas will be prepared (and paid for). A huge fireworks display will be purchased from the fireworks-maker. Most important of all, gallons of either distilled cactus juice or a local rum will be purchased. The priest (or better, two priests) will be brought in to celebrate mass. After mass, the whole village will come to the house of the sponsor and will feast sumptuously. They will drink until they are very very drunk. The men will dance far into the night. Turkey and tortillas, coffee, cacao, fermented drinks, soft drinks, and soups will be downed by the whole village. That is the end of the first day.

The second day is the "day of the bottle." Drinking proceeds in earnest now. Any man who fails to become deeply drunk will be insulting the patron saint as well as the sponsor. Beef is served.

The third day is the "day of the cure." Hangovers are banished by the heavy ingestion of distilled liquors. Those who attended the fiesta but failed to make it back to their own homes on the "night of the day of the bottle" are handed an "eye-opener"— a glass of distilled liquor and a bottle of warm local beer. (More recently, a third item has been added to the cure: a bottle of soda water laced with Alka Seltzer!) Beans are served.

Households have been known to put themselves so far into debt that up to ten years was required for the repayment of the debt. As Ira Buchler has said, this system is designed to convert material goods into prestige. It also is a leveling device ensuring that no person becomes significantly richer than the rest. Should a person seem to be getting ahead economically, he will be subtly (and not so subtly) asked to volunteer to sponsor a festival. Should he refuse, envy will be directed at him. And every villager knows that envy is the precursor of witchcraft, and that one can pay for witchcraft with one's life or the life of one's children and animals.

Insight
Birth Control- A Cultural Device for Checking Population Growth

With the improvements in diet and medical care that have come about since World War II, people are living longer and more children are surviving to adulthood. The villagers complain about the large number of children they have and frequently ask anthropologists why they have so few children. "Your wife is fat," they will tell us, meaning that she is healthy. "Why is it that you have so few children?" Anthropologists used to be able to say the formula, "God simply has not sent us any more children than the two we have now!" But the villagers are wiser now and ask: "Are you sure you are not on the pill?"

Despite their knowledge of the pill, they are not enthusiastic about using it. Nor are they eager to use intrauterine devices or other forms of artificial birth control.

The only cultural means that Mesoamericans use to control fertility are (1) a very short taboo on sexual intercourse after a baby is born, and (2) abortion. The sexual taboo is, as we said, short, and it is not highly institutionalized. Women report that they do not want to have sex with their husbands after giving birth, but that the men insist on it. They realize that if they defer too long, their husbands will find another woman. Since most men need few excuses to go hunting anyway, the women tend to give in to their husband's desires.

Abortion is widely practiced, but only when the woman is getting close to completed fertility, around the age of 40. And the methods are crude indeed. Since abortion is felt to be a very grave crime (and a sin), it must be done in secret. A woman will turn to her sister or her sister-in-law, and ask her to assist. The assistant may take stones and pound upon the fetus. Sticks are inserted up the vaginal canal to rupture the amniotic sac. Or potions of

limited effectiveness are drunk to abort the fetus.

The riddle of why women will take these drastic measures to stop the bearing of children and show no great enthusiasm for the practice of artificial birth control, despite their interest in and knowledge about it, remains precisely that: a riddle.

Figure 24.12
Tepoztlan, a village in southern Mexico that has been studied extensively by cultural anthropologists.

One cannot blame the villagers for being resentful. Living in a community that was the creation of the Spanish conquest, villagers have seen their traditional way of life threatened, changed, and rendered hopeless by the events of the twentieth century. The roads that provide escape from the villages today made that escape necessary by introducing into the villages Western ideas, values, and technology that forced a population explosion upon them. The same roads and buses that modern villagers use to go down to the hot country as wage laborers made that wage labor necessary by introducing cash-cropping and robbing them of their subsistence base.

From our scientific perspective, we see the traditional Mesoamerican Indian village as an example of an adaptive system of biocultural integration that has failed because of internal stresses initiated by forces from the outside. The system is out of control. It cannot bring itself back to equilibrium. The only thing that could restore this system would be a reversal, or at least an alleviation, of the pressures from the outside. But this is unlikely to happen. The surge of Western culture is relentless and unyielding. Before the situation equilibrates there will be drastic change. Earlier, we said that the Mesoamerican village will persist into the twenty-first century. But the structure of the village, the society, and the culture of the inhabitants are all variables still to be determined.

Summary

1. In this chapter we look at the third mode of biocultural integration: the downward spiral. In cases like the traditional Mesoamerican village, the control mechanisms that have held the system under control have been overwhelmed by pressures from the outside.

2. The most important feature of the climate is rainfall. Most farming is dry farming and requires adequate rainfall. But rainfall has decreased in recent years because of changes that have been brought about in the convectional wind currents by chopping down all the trees in the mountainous areas.

3. The villages today are a blend of Hispanic and indigenous elements. They are essentially unchanged from the seventeenth century.

4. The social system, particularly the civil-religious hierarchy and the system of marriage, are residence acts to ensure that nobody becomes rich in these communities. The villagers believe themselves to be living in a democracy, and by and large, they are—a democracy of extreme poverty.

5. The production system is based on *milpa* agriculture: the raising of corn, beans, and squash in the same field.

6. There are two very important areas of environmental stress: population pressure and nutritional pressure. The latter is so severe that it has caused a lowering of intellectual functioning. It also inhibits the speeding up of the work pace which would permit greater cultivation: endurance and plodding are rightly emphasized by the villagers since this is the best style of working, given their diet.

7. The villagers are very poor. They therefore take very few risks, again lowering their production levels.

8. The traditional Mesoamerican village is slowly slipping away. The only reason it has survived the last twenty years is because it has been able to ship off its surplus population to the cities. The system will most likely fail completely in the next thirty years and be replaced by one that is quite different. Thus will the twentieth century, at its close, see the end of a system that has endured for more than a thousand years.

Suggested Readings

Cravioto, Joaquin; Birch, H. G.; De Licardie, E.; Rosales, L.; and Vega, L.
The Ecology of Growth and Development in a Mexican Preindustrial Community. Monographs of the Society for Research in Child Development 34:5 (1969).
The authors describe the design and analysis of a study of growth and nutrition in a Mesoamerican community.

Nash, Manning. *Machine Age Maya. The Industrialization of a Guatemalan Community*. Chicago: University of Chicago Press, 1958.

An ethnographic analysis of the impact of the industrialized world on a traditional Mesoamerican community.

Reina, Ruben E. *The Law of the Saints*. Indianapolis: Bobbs-Merrill, 1966.

A description and analysis of the response of a Guatemalan community to changes in the world about them—they have turned against that world.

Selby, Henry A. *Zapotec Deviance. The Convergence of Folk and Modern Sociology*. Austin: University of Texas Press, 1974.

A comparison of the belief system of a people and the analysis of that system as analyzed by modern theory.

Tax, Sol. *Penny Capitalism: A Guatemalan Indian Economy*. Washington, D.C.: Smithsonian Institution, 1953.

A classic ethnography of traditional Mesoamerican culture.

Glossary

civil-religious hierarchy   A ladder of civil and religious offices found in the traditional villages of Mesoamerica.

yunta   A yoke of oxen (the word is Spanish).

Biocultural Integration: An Epilogue

By now, you have seen that humans are incredibly diverse in what they are, how they behave, and how they have organized themselves into groups in order to live in the world around them. We see, in others, ways of life, systems of meaning, and economic strategies that are often totally alien to us. Some of these things have attracted us, while others repulse us.

We see peoples who live in their worlds in ways that imitate nature, and we see others who so transform their environments that the new environments bear little resemblance to nature. We see societies that interpret their worlds in many ways and whose entire lives symbolize those interpretations.

We see societies that live on-stage, able to devote their time and energy to the elaboration of the meanings the individuals of each group share with one another. But we see societies who, though they do not realize it, are driven by the off-stage dramas that surround them. We can see societies that weave their systems of meaning into their on-stage lives, yet whose off-stage lives, in the long run, may drastically change those very systems.

Our first tendency is to judge, to want to "tamper." We may say, "Why don't those people do it this way?" Or, "That's silly—everyone knows that isn't true."

The science of anthropology, however, has shown, over and over again, that the systems of others are just as logical to them as our own is to us. Anthropologists have shown that all people, everywhere, have the same wants and needs. The difference is in the ways that people go about defining and achieving those needs.

Anthropologists have shown that our biocultural systems are just as illogical in many ways as the systems of others. We display maladaptations and incongruous behavior, and we are also affected by an off-stage drama of which we are not aware. But anthropologists can also compare societies in terms of specific features. Science has given us a scheme for making specific comparisons without imposing our own ideas of right and wrong as a result. We have the criteria for concluding that the people of Mesoamerica are in a downward spiral, but we have no reason for calling them stupid for not doing anything more about it than they are.

We cannot be certain where we will be in the future. We cannot predict what forms the societies of the world will have taken by the twenty-second century. Scientific futurists and fortune-tellers make predictions, but we can only judge how accurate they are when we have or have not experienced what they are predicting.

So anthropologists study what is and what has happened. We, as anthropologists, analyze human biocultural systems where we can, using the methods and techniques that our colleagues have developed.

One thing is certain. Humanity runs deeper than any of us can comprehend. The depth of our evolutionary past has been transferred into the biological and cultural world of our present. It is the transfer of that heritage that makes us human and that allows us to construct a world of meaning in a world that is all too often filled with uncertainty.

We conclude on a note of optimism. For centuries, wise men, scholars, writers, and scientists have all grappled with the interpretation of what it means to be human. Anthropologists have given to the world a unique and particular perspective. But all perspectives are only partial. Regardless of the perspective, the fact remains that humans have demonstrated, and will continue to demonstrate, that the world is not a hostile place, that it does have meaning, and that the worlds of biology, of meaning, and of nature will continue to be integrated into the biocultural system that we have described here.

Glossary

a

adaptation
The process by which change leads to increased survival value of an individual or a population. Also refers to something that has resulted from the process.

agnatic descent
Descent of all persons from some common ancestor, so that everyone is related to everyone else.

allele
An alternative form of a gene.

altruism
The behavior of self-sacrifice on behalf of the group.

altruistic suicide
The rare cultural practice for individuals of some social group (often the elderly) to release that group from the obligation of feeding and caring for them.

amino acid
A set of nitrogen-containing chemical compounds that combine to form proteins.

apical ancestor
The "founding parent" of a lineage.

arbitrary symbol
A symbol that is unrelated in appearance to the class of objects or events that it stands for.

artifact
Something made by human activity.

b

balanced polymorphism
A genetic polymorphism that is maintained by selective pressures acting in opposite directions.

bilateral cross-cousin marriage
A system of marriage in which one chooses a spouse from a class that is defined as both mother's brother's daughter and father's sister's daughter.

bint 'amm marriage
See patrilateral parallel-cousin marriage.

biocultural system
The system made up by three clusters: the cultural cluster, the biological cluster, and the ecological cluster.

biological cluster
The biological cluster of the biocultural system is made up of two subsystems: the morphological and physiological subsystem, and the genetic subsystem.
See ecological cluster, cultural cluster.

bipedal locomotion
Moving about on two feet.

bisexual reproduction
Reproduction in which two sexes contribute equally to the genetic makeup of the offspring.

bound morpheme
In linguistics, a morpheme that can only appear with another morpheme and cannot stand on its own.

c

carrying capacity
The density of the human and animal population in some well-defined environment when it is at equilibrium (i.e., at balance with the environment).

cerebral cortex
The outer layer of brain cells.

Chayanov's Rule
The more efficient a household collective, the less hard work people put in.

chromosome
Strands of DNA that are found in the nucleus of each of the body's cells.

civil-religious hierarchy
A ladder of civil and religious offices found in the traditional villages of Mesoamerica.

civilization
A stage of human society. Civilization is characterized by large cities, stratified societies, a state governed by a ruling class, and a sophisticated technology.

cline
A gradual change in the frequency of a gene or a trait across a geographical range.

coarse-grained environment
An environment that displays a lot of variety in its ecological outputs. (Sometimes referred to as a "patchy" environment.)

complementarity
A principle stating that the base sequences of paired DNA strands are "complements." If one sequence is known, the other can be predicted.

concordance
Agreement or harmony. Two variables are concordant if they change in similar fashion.

connotative meaning
That part of the meaning of a word that is emotional.

constant marginal returns
The situation in which the increase in output remains the same for each added unit of input.

cross cousin
The child of a sibling of the opposite sex from one's linking parent (in other words, one's mother's brother's child, or one's father's sister's child).

cultural cluster
The cultural cluster of the biocultural system is made up of six subsystems: the linguistic subsystem, the subsys-

tem of meaning, the subsystem of religion, the subsystem of cosmology, the subsystem of kinship, and the subsystem of political organization. *See* biological cluster, ecological cluster.

cultural relativism
The belief that all cultures have to be evaluated on their own terms.

cultural units
The ideas that a society has and uses to recognize events. They can be conscious or unconscious; they can be expressed in the spoken language, but need not be.

culture
The set of rules carried by each person that determines how he or she views and relates to the world.

culture shock
The feelings of malaise that everyone gets when he or she first enters and starts to work in an alien culture.

d

decreasing marginal returns
The situation in which a smaller extra amount of output is returned for each added unit of input.

demography
The analysis of the size, composition, and rate of change of a population.

dendrogram
A branching, or tree-like, diagram. Populations on closer branches are more closely related to each other than are populations on distant branches.

denotative meaning
The class of objects or events to which a word refers. *Cf.* connotative meaning.

deoxyribonucleic acid (DNA)
A protein/acid compound found in the nucleus of cells; it is the hereditary material.

dependency
A system is said to exhibit strict dependency when all its subsystems communicate. A change in one element or one subsystem will bring about a change in all the others.

diffusion
The spread of culture from group to group.

diminishing marginal utility
The rule stating that the more of something you get, the less you want the next unit.

dominant
Describing an allele that will always be expressed in a heterozygous genotype, and that will prevent the expression of the other allele of the pair.

dyadic relation
A relationship between two people or two groups.

e

ecological cluster
The ecological cluster of the biocultural system is made up of two subsystems: the ecological subsystem and the economic subsystem. *See* biological cluster, cultural cluster.

ecological niche
The feeding habits of a human population. Niches can be broad or narrow, depending on the range of foods consumed and the strictness of food preferences.

ecology
The study of the relationship between human beings and their environment.

economics
The study of the way people make use of scarce means at their disposal to attain culturally defined goals.

economies of scale
The increased efficiency that comes from the division of labor in the production of many goods rather than fewer.

ecosystem
A set of ecological relationships.

endogamous rule (or rule of endogamy)
The rule that states how distant or how different a person can be and still be a potential spouse.

engareka
A Gusii word meaning hatred between co-wives.

environmental degradation
The process whereby the ecological outputs of the environment decline, usually irreversibly.

enzymes
Proteins that act as catalysts in the thousands of chemical reactions that occur in the body's cells.

equilibrium-seeking
See homeostatic.

ethnocentrism
The belief that one's own culture provides an absolute standard for judging other cultures. *Cf.* cultural relativism.

ethnography
The careful description of the culture and ways of life of human societies.

evolution
Hereditary biological change through time in a population.

exogamous rule (or rule of exogamy)
The rule that states how close, or similar, a person can be and still be a potential spouse.

extended family
Family in which there are at least three generations of relatives living together.

extensive agriculture
Agricultural practices that use a lot of land instead of a lot of labor. Swidden agriculture is extensive, for example. *Cf.* intensive agriculture

f

famille souche
The family consisting of a couple with only one married child and their grandchildren by this child.

fauna
A term referring collectively to animal life.

feature model of meaning
That model of meaning in language that defines each word by its attributes or distinctive features.

feedback
In a system, feedback refers to the effect that a change in one component will have on another component.

feral child
A child who has been abandoned by or isolated from human contact so that it grows up an "animal," without culture.

fertility rate
The average number of births by women, usually of specific age groups.

fine-grained environment
An environment that displays a low degree of variety in its ecological outputs.

fixed production goals
The third principle of traditional economics: people will produce what they consider "enough" but no more.

flora
A term referring collectively to plant life.

folk lexicography
An encyclopedia of the important categories and relations in a bio-cultural system.

form class
In transformational grammar, a class of words that can be substituted in a sentence and still preserve grammaticality.

formalists
People who believe that you can analyze traditional economies with mathematical (formal) economic methods, just like market economies.

fossil
The hardened remains of an animal or plant after the organic material has been removed.

fraternal polyandry
The cultural practice of a woman marrying multiple husbands who are brothers.

free ridership
The problem that occurs in groups of a size larger than seven members when one or more of the members fails to contribute his or her share and thereby gets a "free ride."

function
The contribution an object or a process makes to the operation of a system.

g

gene
The unit of heredity.

gene flow
The process by which genes enter and leave a gene pool as a result of migration.

genetic code
The amino acids determined by various triplets of RNA nucleotides.

genetic distance
The dissimilarity or "distance" between two groups as measured by the different frequencies of the alleles of the two gene pools.

genetic drift
A class of mechanisms that change gene frequency in a random, stochastic manner.

genetic father
The man who actually engaged in the act of sexual intercourse that led to the conception of a particular child.

genetic mother
The woman who actually engaged in the act of sexual intercourse that led to the conception of a particular child.

genetics
The science of heredity.

genetrix
The woman who is socially recognized to have borne a particular child.

genitor
The man who is socially recognized to have engendered a particular child.

genotype
The combination of genes an organism possesses.

genus
A group of two or more related species.

geographical race
A taxonomic group of populations occupying a certain geographical range and displaying similarities in their genetic structures.

grain
The degree of variegation of ecological outputs in a specified habitat.

h

habitat
The place or locale occupied by a population.

hemoglobin
The oxygen-carrying molecules of the blood.

heredity
The process by which the characteristics of parents are transmitted to those of offspring at the moment of fertilization.

heterozygote
A genotype in which different alleles of the gene are found at a locus on the two chromosomes of a pair.

homeostasis
The maintenance of a steady state by specific mechanisms of internal regulation.

homeostatic
Describing a system that oscillates around an equilibrium point and is equilibrium-seeking.

homogamy
The cultural practice of marrying someone like oneself: from one's own group, class, or caste.

homozygote
A genotype in which the same form of the gene is found at a locus on each chromosome of a pair.

hypergamy
The practice of women marrying men who are of higher status (and, conversely, of men marrying women of lower status).

hypogamy
The practice of women marrying men who are of lower status than themselves (and, conversely, of men marrying women of higher status).

i

immediate constituent analysis (I/C)
Learning a language by analyzing its sounds and syntax.

incest taboo
The cultural rule that prohibits sexual intercourse with certain classes of relatives.

increasing marginal returns
The situation in which each additional unit of input produces more and more output.

independence
A system is said to be strictly independent when no element or sub-system affects any other.

infanticide
The practice of killing children at birth. It may be overt and institution-alized in the society, or it may be covert and punishable.

infectious disease
A disease that is caused by the presence of a specific organism that

can be transmitted from person to person.

integration
1. The situation in which subsystems in a system are highly dependent.
2. The manner and degree to which social units in a larger system are dependent or tied together by exchange.

intelligence
The ability to learn, to know, and to solve problems.

intensive agriculture
Agricultural practices in which the same land is used over and over again, and much labor is expended in preparing it, and keeping it fertile. *Cf.* extensive agriculture.

j

jati
A caste in India.

l

lactation
The process of milk production by a nursing mother.

lactational amenorrhea
Infertile menstrual cycles caused by lactation.

law of small numbers
The law that states there will be greater statistical variability in small populations than in large ones.

local race
A biologically identifiable population living in the midst of a geographical race, yet maintaining their distinctiveness by isolating mechanisms.

m

malnutrition
A state of dietary deficiency that leads to nutritional stress (not just a lack of food).

Malthusians
People who believe that population will inevitably rise to the carrying capacity of the biocultural system (after economist Thomas Malthus).

mandible
The lower jaw.

mapping
The rule in totemism that associates a particular animal or natural event with a particular subgroup or tribe.

marginal return
The extra production produced by adding one *more* unit of input (say, labor).

marginality
The state of being at the edge of society, i.e., out of the mainstream.

mater
One's social, not necessarily genetic, mother.

matrifocal family
A family made up of a mother and her children. (Sometimes wrongly called "absent-father" families.)

matrilineage
A group recruited on the basis of their ties through women.

matrilineal extended family
A family made up of a couple, their married daughters (and grandchildren by these daughters), and their unmarried children of both sexes.

matrilocal
Describing a society in which a married couple sets up residence with the woman's kinspeople.

maxilla
The upper jaw.

maximization of subjective utility
Getting the most of the things that you want.

mechanical solidarity
Durkheim's phrase to describe the kind of solidarity that exists in a society where very little exchange takes place because the household forms are self-sufficient.

mediation
Putting an idea or category between two opposed ideas or categories so that it acts as a go-between for the oppositions.

melanin
Granules of pigment just under the surface of skin which give the skin its characteristic color.

mode of biocultural integration
The way that the cultural, biological and ecological clusters (and their subsystems) are tied together so as to handle stress. There are three modes:

1. biocultural equilibrium
2. unstable biocultural equilibrium
3. the downward spiral

morpheme
A minimal unit of meaning.

morphology
In linguistics, the study of how morphemes go together to form words and compound words. (Do not confuse this with morphology as it is used to refer to the form of animals and humans.)

morphophonemics
The study of how sound changes create new meanings.

mortality rate
The average number of deaths for people, usually of a certain age group.

Mousterian
A Middle Paleolithic tool tradition particularly identified with Neanderthal populations.

mutation
A change in the structure of a gene caused by some external agent.

n

natural selection
An evolutionary process in which the better adapted genetic variants are transmitted in greater proportion to the next generation.

natural symbol
A symbol that stands in an obvious relation to the thing it symbolizes. *Cf.* arbitrary symbols.

need
A biologically based requirement for life itself. *Cf.* want

neophobia
Fear of something new.

nonagnates
People who are not members of the patrilineage.

nonfraternal polyandry
The cultural practice of a woman marrying multiple husbands who are not brothers.

nuclear family
The family consisting of a socially defined mother, father, and children.

nuclear incest
Incest with a member of the nuclear family (mother-son, father-daughter, or brother-sister relations).

numeraire
An accountant's scale to measure the value of different bundles of commodities.

o

object relations
In Freudian theory, mature sexual relations outside the family.

Oedipal conflict
In Freudian theory, the ambivalence ("love/hate") that the maturing son feels toward his father. It peaks around age 4.

off-stage drama
The processes in the social and physical environment that are going on without our realizing it. Slow undetectable environmental degradation is an example of an off-stage process.

on-stage drama
The drama of everyday life, of which we are conscious and aware. It includes our own view of what we are doing, in our own terms and opinions. *Cf.* off-stage drama

opposition
A logical device that creates a world of binary symbols (i.e., divided in two).

organic solidarity
Durkheim's word to describe the social solidarity that comes about when there is a good deal of exchange between social units and a complex division of labor.

ownership
The restriction of rights of access to the means of production to one individual (or corporation); same as private ownership.

p

paleoecology
The science that seeks to determine the environments that existed in the past.

paleolithic
The "Old Stone Age," beginning with the earliest evidence of tool-making and lasting until populations began to make the transition to a more sophisticated technology.

paleontology
The science that studies the life that existed in the distant past.

paradigm
1. The systematic way that words change to give different meanings. One example is the conjugation of Latin *ama-*.
2. The semantic structure that happens when every dimension partitions the whole semantic field.
3. The items of a commutable set (hat, toque, ski cap, etc.).
4. The associations that come with all the items of a set of symbols.

paradigmatic rules
The rules that identify the members of a paradigmatic set; similar to the rules for writing harmony in music.

parallel cousin
The child of the sibling of the same sex as the linking parent (in other words, father's brother's child, or mother's sister's child).

pariah group
The lowest group in a society, or any group that is marginal to the society.
See marginality.

pater
The person who is socially defined to be the moral father of a child.

patrilateral parallel-cousin marriage
The cultural practice that favors the marriage of a person to his or her father's brother's child.

patrilineage
A social group recruited on the basis of one's relationships through males.

patrilineal extended family
A family consisting of a couple, their married sons (and grandchildren by these sons), and their unmarried children of both sexes.

pebble tools
The earliest recognizable stone tools made by hominids.

percussion
A technique of stone tool-making in which flakes are knocked off a flint core.

phenotype
The results of the interaction between one's genotype and the environment.

phone
A linguistic sound that can be discriminated by an expert.

phoneme
That bundle of sounds (phones) that are discriminated by the local people in their language.

phonology
The study of the sound system of a language.

plasticity
The extent to which the phenotype of an individual can be modified by the environment, usually over a long period of time.

polyandry
The practice of a woman marrying plural husbands.

polygyny
The practice of a man marrying plural wives.

population
A group of individuals that form a breeding unit.

population density
The number of people per unit of area (square mile, or square kilometer).

population genetics
The part of genetics dealing with the study of population gene pools.

population pressure
The pressure that is placed on resources when population density increases.

private ownership
Restricted ownership to a person or a group.

protoculture
Those animal behaviors that foreshadow true human culture.

pseudocyesis
False pregnancy with all the signs of a normal pregnancy but without any fetus.

pure production strategy
In agriculture, a practice in which only one technique is used and very few crops are grown; (in general) the use of a single technique for food-getting.

r

racism
A false doctrine that maintains that, because of their biology, members of one race are superior to members of another.

radical empiricist
A person who believes that the world is the same and appears the same to all people everywhere.

radiometric dating
The determination of the antiquity of some past fossil by analyzing the amount of radioactive decay.

rebus writing
An early type of writing in which the sounds of objects that are pictured suggest words and phrases.

recessive
Describing an allele that is not expressed in a heterozygous genotype.

ribonucleic acid (RNA)
A protein/acid compound that transfers genetic information from the cell nucleus into proteins.

risk aversion
1. When the risk gets large, we become more unwilling to play the game.
2. When the stakes get bigger, we are more unwilling to play the game.

savanna
A treeless, grassy plain.

sawah
The Indonesian rice paddy.

sexual dimorphism
Differences between males and females in biological traits besides those of the primary reproductive system.

sicklemia (sickle-cell anemia)
An inherited disease in which the body's hemoglobin molecules are deficient in the capacity to carry oxygen, resulting in profound anemia.

sign
The signal with a fixed referent; signs can refer to only one thing. *Cf.* symbol.

site
In archeological studies, a place where human activity occurred.

slash-and-burn
Swidden agriculture.

social stratification
The existence in a society of different status groups.

socialization
The process whereby children are turned into social animals with culture.

sociobiology
A school of biological scientists who believe that human social behavior is biologically rooted.

species
A group of organisms that breed freely among themselves but are prevented from breeding with other species.

state
A complex human society characterized by social stratification and governed by a ruling class.

stochastic evolution
Evolution by random statistical change.

structure
The arrangements of the parts of a system in relationship to each other.

subsistence
The ways in which the members of a group make a living.

substantivists
People who believe that you cannot analyze traditional economic systems with modern (formal) methods.

swidden
Slash-and-burn agriculture. The larger trees and undergrowth are cut down and final clearance is accomplished by burning everything.

symbol
Something that stands for something else.

symmetric alliance
A system of exchange in which each side reciprocates with the other.

synesthesia
Experiencing with many senses at the same time, such as hearing, feeling, and seeing music.

syntagmatic rules
The rules for stringing symbols (and paradigms) together; similar to the rules for writing melody in music.

syntax
The rules for stringing together morphemes to create well-formed utterances.

taxonomy
The scientific naming of animal and plant populations; also refers to a classification of living forms.

teknonymy
The practice of tracing kinship through children.

terrestrial
Living on the land.

territoriality
The tendency of the populations of a species to defend a particular geographical range.

totemism
The belief that associates some animal or other "natural event" with a subgroup or tribe for the purposes of classification.

uncertainty
The degree of variability in ecological outputs.

unidimensional
Defined by one dimension.

uniformitarianism
A geological theory that the earth's surface changes slowly at a steady rate.

usufruct
1. The right to use or enjoy the produce from some productive resource.
2. Ownership derived from the fact that the owner is using some resource.

v

vagina dentata
A belief in an emasculating spirit with a toothed vagina; often associated with male hostility toward women.

value
The importance attached to an object or an idea by a society.

w

want
A culturally defined desire. *Cf.* need.

Whorfian
A person who believes that thought is determined by language (after Benjamin Lee Whorf).

wolf child
See feral child.

y

yunta
A yoke of oxen (the word is Spanish).

z

zombie
A dead person who appears to be alive.

References

a

Adams, J. B.
1957. "Culture and Conflict in an Egyptian Village." *American Anthropologist* 59:225–235.

Adams, R. M.
1960. "Early Civilizations, Subsistence, and Environment." In *City Invincible,* edited by C. H. Kraeling and R. M. Adams. Chicago: Oriental Institute, University of Chicago.

Allan, W.
1965. *The African Husbandman.* New York: Barnes and Noble.

Allison, A.
1955. "Aspects of Polymorphism in Man." *Cold Spring Harbor Symposia on Quantitative Biology* 20:239–255.

Ardener, E.
1961. "Social and Demographic Problems of the Southern Cameroons Plantation Area." In *Social Change in Modern Africa,* edited by A. Southall. London: Oxford University Press.

————.
1970a. *Kingdom on Mount Cameroon: Documents for the History of Nuea, 1844–1898.* West Cameroon Government Press.

————.
1970b. "Witchcraft, Economics and the Continuity of Belief." In *Witchcraft: Confessions and Accusations,* edited by M. Douglas. London: Tavistock.

Ardener, E.; Ardener, S.; and Warmington, H. G.
1960. *Plantation and Village in the Cameroons; Some Economic and Social Studies.* London: Oxford University Press.

Ardrey, R.
1966. *Territorial Imperative: A Personal Inquiry into the Animal Origins of Property and Nations.* New York: Atheneum.

————.
1961. *African Genesis: A Personal Investigation into the Animal Origins and Nature of Man.* New York: Atheneum.

Armillas, P.
1971. "Gardens on Swamps." *Science* 174:653–661.

b

Baily, K. V.
1966. "Protein Malnutrition and Peanut Foods in the Chimbu." In *An Integrated Approach to Nutrition and Society,* edited by E. H. Hipsley, p. 2. New Guinea Research Unit Bulletin Number 9. Canberra: Australian National University.

Baker, P.
1969. "Human Adaptation to High Altitude." *Science* 163:1149–1156.

Barth, F.
1975. *Ritual and Knowledge Among the Baktaman of New Guinea.* New Haven, Conn.: Yale University Press.

Basso, K. H.
1976. "Wise Words of the Western Apache: Metaphor and Semantic Theory." In *Meaning in Anthropology,* edited by K. H. Basso and H. Selby. Albuquerque: University of New Mexico Press.

Bates, D.
1936. *The Passing of the Aborigines: A Lifetime Spent Among the Natives of Australia.* New York: G. P. Putnam.

Beals, R.
1970. "Gopalpur, 1958–1960." In *Being an Anthropologist,* edited by G. D. Sprindler. New York: Holt, Rinehart and Winston.

Berlin, B., and Kay, P.
1969. *Basic Color Terms; Their Universality and Evolution.* Berkeley: University of California Press.

Berlin, B.; Breedlove, D. F.; and Raven, P. H.
1968. "Covert Categories and Folk Taxonomies." *American Anthropologist* 70:290–299.

Berndt, R. M.
1962. *Excess and Restraint: Social Control Among a New Guinea Mountain People.* Chicago: University of Chicago Press.

Berreman, G.
1959. "Caste in India and the United States." *American Journal of Sociology* 4.

Binford, L. R.
1968. "Post-Pleistocene Adaptations." In *New Perspectives in Archaeology,* edited by S. R. Binford and L. R. Binford. Chicago: Aldine Publishing Co.

Birdsell, J.
1953. "Some Environmental and Cultural Factors Influencing the Structuring of Australian Aboriginal Populations." *American Naturalist* 87:171–207.

Bordieu, P.
1971. "The Berber House or the World Reversed." In *Mélanges Offerts à Claude Lévi-Strauss,* edited by J. Pouillon and P. Maranda. Paris: Mouton.

Boserup, E.
1965. *The Conditions of Agricultural Growth.* Chicago: Aldine Publishing Co.

———. 1970. "Population Growth and Food Supplies." In *Population Control,* edited by A. Allison. Baltimore, M. D.: Penguin Books.

Boyd, W. C.
1950. *Genetics and the Races of Man: An Introduction to Modern Physical Anthropology.* Boston: Little, Brown.

———. 1963. "Four Achievements of the Genetical Method in Physical Anthropology." *American Anthropologist* 65:243–252.

Brace, C. L.
1973. "Sexual Dimorphism in Human Evolution." In *Man in Evolutionary Perspective,* edited by C. L. Brace and J. Metress. New York: John Wiley and Sons.

———. 1964a. "A Nonracial Approach Towards the Understanding of Human Diversity." In *The Concept of Race,* edited by A. Montagu. London: The Free Press of Glencoe.

———. 1964b. "The Fate of the 'Classic' Neanderthals: A Consideration of Hominid Catastrophism." *Current Anthropology* 5:3–43.

Braidwood, R. J., and Howe, B.
1962. "Southwestern Asia Beyond the Lands of the Mediterranean Littoral." In *Courses Toward Urban Life,* edited by R. J. Braidwood and G. R. Willey. New York: Viking Fund Publications in Anthropology no. 32.

Brues, A. M.
1977. *People and Races.* The Macmillan Series in Physical Anthropology. New York: Macmillan and Company.

Buchbinder, G., and Rappaport, R. A.
1976. "Fertility and Death Among the Maring." In *Man and Woman in the New Guinea Highlands,* edited by P. Brown and G. Buchbinder. American Anthropological Association Memoir no. 8.

Burling, R.
1970. *Man's Many Voices: Language in Its Cultural Context.* New York: Holt, Rinehart and Winston.

Burton, M. L.; Brudner, L. A.; and White, D. R.
1976. "A Model of the Sexual Division of Labor." Manuscript. Irvine, Cal.: University of California Press.

c

Calhoun, J. B.
1962. "Population Density and Social Pathology." *Scientific American* 206:139–148.

Centerwall, W. R.
1968. "A Recent Experience with Measles in a 'Virgin Soil' Population." In *Biomedical Challenges Presented by the American Indian,* edited by J. V. Neel. Washington, D.C.: Pan American Health Organization.

Chagnon, N.
1968a. "The Cultural Ecology of Shifting (Pioneering) Cultivation Among the Yanomamo Indians." *Proceedings of the VIIIth International Congress of Anthropological and Ethnological Sciences* 3:249–255.

———. 1968b. *Yanomamo: The Fierce People.* New York: Holt, Rinehart and Winston.

Chase, A.
1971. *The Biological Imperatives. Health, Politics and Human Survival.* New York: Holt, Rinehart and Winston.

Chayanov, A. V.
1966. *The Theory of the Peasant Economy.* Homewood, Ill.: Richard D. Irwin (American Economic Association).

Childe, V. G.
1936. *Man Makes Himself.* London: Watts and Company.

Clark, Sir W. L.
1960. *Antecedents of Man: An Introduction to the Evolution of the Primates.* Chicago: Quadrangle Books.

Cockburn, A., ed.
1967. *Infectious Diseases: Their Evolution and Eradication.* Springfield, Ill.: Charles C Thomas.

Coe, M. D., and Flannery, K. V.
1964. "Microenvironments and Mesoamerican Prehistory." *Science* 143:650–654.

Colson, E.
1954. "Ancestral Spirits and Social Structure among the Plateau Tonga." In *International Archives of Anthropology.* London: Oxford University Press.

Coon, S.; Garn, S. M.; and Birdsell, J. B.
1950. *Races: A Study of the Problems of Race Formation in Man.* Springfield, Ill.: Charles C Thomas.

Crawford, M. H.
1973. "The Use of Genetic Markers in the Study of the Evolution of Human Populations." In *Methods and Theories of Anthropological Genetics,* edited by M. H. Crawford and P. C. Workman. Albuquerque, N.M.: University of New Mexico Press.

d

Darwin, C.
1967. *On the Origin of Species* (facsimile of first 1859 edition). New York: Atheneum.

Davenport, W.
1960. *Jamaican Fishing: A Game Theory Analysis.* New Haven, Conn.: Yale Publications in Anthropology no. 59.

Dawkins, R.
1976. *The Selfish Gene.* New York: Oxford University Press.

Deetz, J. F.
1967. *Invitation to Archaeology.* Garden City, N.Y.: The Natural History Press.

Denison, N.
1968. "Sauris: A Trilingual Community in Diatypic Perspective." *Man* 3:578–592.

Desmond, A.
1962. "How Many People Have Ever Lived on Earth?" *Population Bulletin* 18:1–18.

Dixon, R.
1923. *The Racial History of Man.* New York: Charles Scribner's Sons.

Dobzhansky, T.
1962. *Mankind Evolving: The Evolution of the Human Species.* New Haven, Conn.: Yale University Press.

Doll, R.
1973. "Monitoring the National Health Service." *Proceedings of the Royal Society of Medicine* 66: 729–740.

Dollard, J.
1937. *Caste and Class in a Southern Town.* New Haven, Conn.: Yale University Press.

Douglas, M.
1966. *Purity and Danger.* London: Routledge and Kegan Paul.

————.
1968. "Pollution." In *International Encyclopedia of the Social Sciences,* edited by D. L. Sills. New York: Macmillan.

DuBrul, E. L., and Sicher, H.
1954. *The Adaptive Chin.* Springfield, Ill.: Charles C Thomas.

Durkheim, E.
1965. *The Elementary Forms of the Religious Life,* translated by J. W. Swain. New York: Free Press.

Eiseley, L.
1961. *Darwin's Century.* New York: Doubleday and Co.

ElGuindi, F.
1976. *Religion in Culture.* Dubuque: Wm. C. Brown Company Publishers.

Epstein, T. S.
1962. *Economic Development and Social Change in South India.* Manchester, Eng.: Manchester University Press.

————.
1967. "The Economics in Anthropological Analysis." In *The Craft of Social Anthropology,* edited by A. L. Epstein. New York: Tavistock Publishers.

Evans-Pritchard, E. E.
1940. *The Nuer: A Description of the Modes of Livelihood and Political Institutions of a Nilotic People.* Oxford: The Clarendon Press.

Fagan, B. M.
1977. *People of the Earth.* Boston: Little, Brown and Co.

Fischer, A.
1972. "History and Current Status of the Houma Indians." In *The American Indian Today,* edited by S. Levine and N. O. Lurie. Baltimore, Md.: Penguin Books.

Flannery, K. V.
1965. "The Ecology of Early Food Production in Mesopotamia." *Science* 147:1247–1256.

————.
1976. *The Early Mesoamerican Village.* New York: Academic Press.

Freud, S.
1939. *Moses and Monotheism.* New York: Vintage Books.

Frisancho, A., and Baker, P. T.
1970. "Altitude and Growth: A Study of the Patterns of Physical Growth of a High Altitude Peruvian Quechua Population." *American Journal of Physical Anthropology* 32:279–293.

Garn, S. M.
1971. *Human Races.* 3rd ed. Springfield, Ill.: Charles C Thomas.

Garn, S. M., and Coon, C. S.
1955. "On the number of races of mankind." *American Anthropologist* 57:996–1001.

Geerking, S. D.
1969. *Biological Systems.* Philadelphia: W. B. Saunders Co.

Geertz, C.
1963. *Agriculture Involution: The Process of Ecological Change in Indonesia.* Berkeley: University of California Press.

Goodall, J.
1972. *In The Shadow of Man.* New York: Dell Publishing Co.

Goodenough, W. H.
1955. "A Problem in Malayo-Polynesian Social Organization." *American Anthropologist* 57:71–83.

Gorman, C. F.
1971. "The Hoabinhian and After: Subsistence Patterns in Southeast Asia during the Late Pleistocene and Early Recent Periods." *World Archaeology* 2, no. 3:300–320.

Gough, K.
1959. "The Nayars and the Definition of Marriage." *Journal of the Royal Anthropological Institute* 89.

Griffin, J. E.
1978. "The Origin and Dispersion of American Indians in North America." In *Origins and Affinities of the First Americans,* edited by W. S. Laughlin. New York: Gusdan, Fischer, Publishers.

Hardesty, D.
1976. *Ecological Anthropology.* New York: John Wiley and Sons.

Hardin, G.
1968. "The Tragedy of the Commons." *Science* 162:1243–1248.

Harris, M.
1974. *Cows, Pigs, Wars, and Witches: The Riddles of Culture.* New York: Random House.

Harrison, G. A.; Weiner, J. S.; and Reynolds, V.
1977. "Human Evolution." In *Human Biology,* edited by G. A. Harrison, J. S. Weiner, J. M. Tanner, and N. A. Barnicot. 2nd ed. Oxford: Oxford University Press.

Harrison, G. A.; Morton, R. J. and Weiner, J. S.
1959. "The Growth in Weight and Tail Length of Inbred and Hybrid Mice Reared at Two Different Temperatures." *Philosophical Transactions* 242:479–516.

Haviland, W. A.
1970. "Tikal, Guatemala, and Mesoamerican Urbanism." *World Archaeology* 2:186–198.

Heider, K.
1969. "Anthropological Models of Incest Laws in the United States." *American Anthropologist* 71:693.

Heller, J.
1961. *Catch-22.* New York: Simon and Schuster.

Herskovits, M. J.
1952. *Economic Anthropology: A*

Study in Comparative Economics.
New York: Alfred Knopf.

Hiernaux, J.
1964. "The Concept of Race and the Taxonomy of Mankind." In *The Concept of Race,* edited by A. Montagu. London: The Free Press of Glencoe.

Hopkins, D.
1967. *The Bering Land Bridge.* Stanford, Cal.: Stanford University Press.

————.
1978. "Landscape and Climate of Beringia During Late Pleistocene and Holocene Time and Implications for Human Populations." In *Origins and Affinities of the First Americans,* edited by W. S. Lauglin. New York: Gusdan Fischer, Publishers.

Horton, R.
1962. "The Kalahari World-Views: An Outline and Interpretation." *Africa* 32:197–219.

Howard, W. D.
1972. "Growing up Hunting: Ethnography of a Rural Bow and Arrow Gang." In *The Cultural Experience,* edited by J. P. Spradley and D. W. McCurdy. Chicago: Science Research Associates.

Howells, F. C.
1951. "The Place of Neanderthal Man in Human Evolution." *American Journal of Physical Anthropology* 9:379–416.

Howells, W. W.
1973. "Measures of Population Distance." In *Methods and Theories of Anthropological Genetics,* edited by M. H. Crawford and P. L. Workman. Albuquerque: University of New Mexico Press.

Howlett, P. R.
1967. *A Geography of Papua and New Guinea.* Camden, N.J.: Thomas Nelson and Sons.

i

Itani, J.
1972. "A Prelimary Essay on the Relationship Between Social Organization and Incest Avoidance in Nonhuman Primates." In *Primate Socialization,* edited by F. E. Poirer.

j

Jolly, A.
1972. *The Evolution of Primate Behavior.* New York: Macmillan and Company.

Jolly, C. J.
1970. "The Seed-Eaters: A New Model of Hominid Differentiation Based on a Baboon Analogy." *Man,* N. S. 5:5–27.

Jones, J.
1972. *Prejudice and Racism.* Reading, Mass.: Addison-Wesley.

k

Kappel, W.
1977. "Alternative Adaptive Strategies in Three Mexican Communities." Unpublished Ph.D. dissertation, University of Arizona.

Kardiner, A.
1939. *The Individual and His Society.* New York: Columbia University Press.

Katz, S. H.; Hediger, M. L.; and Valleroy, A.
1975. "The Anthropological and Nutritional Significance of Traditional Maize Processing Techniques in the New World." In *Biosocial Interrelations in Population Adaptation,* edited by E. S. Watts, F. E. Johnston, and G. W. Lusker. Chicago: Aldine Publishing Co.

Kaufman, I.; Peck, A. C.; and Tagiuri, C. K.
1954. "The Family Constellation and Overt Incestuous Relations between Father and Daughter." *American Journal of Orthopsychiatry* 24:266–271.

Kramer, M. J.
1975. "Legal Abortion Among New York City Residents: An Analysis According to Socioeconomic and Demographic Characteristics." *Family Planning Perspectives* 7:128–137.

l

Lancaster, J.
1975. *Primate Behavior and the Emergence of Human Culture.* New York: Holt, Rinehart and Winston.

Larson, L.
1973. "Archaeological Indications of Social Stratification at the Etowah Site, Georgia." In *In Search of Man,* edited by E. L. Green. Boston: Little, Brown and Co.

Laszlo, E.
1972. *The Systems View of the World; The Natural Philosophy of the New Developments in the Sciences.* New York: G. Braziller.

Laughlin, W. S.
1963. "Eskimos and Aleuts: Their Origins and Evolution." *Science* 142:633–645.

Lea, D. A., and Irwin, P. G.
1967. *New Guinea: The Territory and its People.* Melbourne, N.Y.: Oxford University Press.

Lee, D.
1938. "Conceptual Implications of an Indian Language." *Philosophy of Science* 5:89–102.

Lee, R.
1968. "What Hunters Do for a Living, or, How to Make Out on Scarce Resources." In *Man the Hunter,* edited by Richard Lee and I. DeVore. Chicago: Aldine Publishing Co.

————.
1969. "!Kung Bushman Subsistence: An Input-Output Analysis." In *Contributions to Anthropology: Ecological Essays,* edited by D. Damas. Ottawa, Ont.: Natural Museums of Canada Bulletin 230.

————.
1972a. "!Kung Spatial Organization: An Ecological and Historical Perspective." *Human Ecology* 1:125–147.

————.
1972b. "Population Growth and the Beginnings of Sedentary Life Among the !Kung Bushmen." In *Population Growth: Anthropological Implications,* edited by B. Spooner. Cambridge, Mass.: MIT Press.

Lee, M. M.
1969. "Magnitude and Pattern of Compensatory Growth in Rats after Cold Exposure." *Journal of*

Embryology and Experimental Morphology 21:407–416.

Leonard, J. N.
1973. *The First Farmers.* New York: Time-Life Books.

Lerner, I. M., and Libby, W. J.
1976. *Heredity, Evolution, and Society.* 2nd ed. San Francisco: W. H. Freeman and Company.

LeVine, R.
1963. "Gusii Child Rearing." In *Six Cultures: Studies in Child Rearing,* edited by B. B. Whiting. New York: John Wiley and Sons.

Levi-Strauss, C.
1963. *Structural Anthropology,* translated by C. Jacobson and B. Schoepf. New York: Basic Books.

————.
1969. *The Elementary Structures of Kinship.* Boston: Beacon Press.

Lindzey, G.
1967. "Some Remarks Concerning Incest, The Incest Taboo and Psychoanalytic Theory." *American Psychologist* 22:1054.

Little, M., and Morren, G.
1976. *Ecological Aspects of Human Variation.* Elements of Anthropology: A Series of Introductions, edited by F. Johnston and H. Selby. Dubuque: Wm. C. Brown Company Publishers.

Livingstone, F. B.
1958. "Implications of Sickle Cell Gene Distribution in West Virginia." *American Anthropologist* 60:533–562.

————.
1962. "On the non-existence of human races." *Current Anthropology* 3:279–281.

Loomis, W. F.
1967. "Skin-Pigment Regulation of Vitamin-D Biosynthesis in Man." *Science* 157:501–506.

Lorenz, K.
1966. *On Aggression,* translated by M. K. Wilson. New York: Harcourt, Brace and World.

Lyell, C.
1830. *Principles of Geology.* London: J. Murray Publishers. Vol. 1, 1830; vol. 2, 1832; vol. 3, 1833.

m

Malcolm, L.
1970. *Growth and Development in New Guinea—A Study of the Bundi People of the Madang District.* Madang: Institute of Human Biology.

Malinowski, B.
1924. *Sex and Repression in Savage Society.* Boston: Beacon Press.

Malson, L.
1972. *Wolf Children and the Problem of Human Nature.* New York: Monthly Review Press.

Malthus, T. R.
1926. *An Essay on the Principles of Population as it Affects the Future Improvement of Society with Remarks on the Speculations of Mr. Godwin, M. Condorcet and Other Writers (1798).* Facsimile of the first edition. New York: Macmillan and Company.

Mangelsdorf, P. C.; MacNeish, R. S.; Gallinat, W. C.
1964. "Domestication of Corn." *Science* 143:543–545.

Mann, A. E.
1975. *Some Paleodemographic Aspects of the South African Australopithecines.* University of Pennsylvania Publications in Anthropology, no. 1. Philadelphia: Department of Anthropology, University of Pennsylvania.

Maybury-Lewis, D.
1968. *The Savage and the Innocent.* Boston: Beacon Books.

Mayer, E.
1963. *Animal Species and Evolution.* Cambridge, Mass.: Harvard University Press.

McClung, J.
1969. *Effects of High Altitude on Human Birth.* Cambridge, Mass.: Harvard University Press.

McHenry, H., and Giles, E.
1971. "Morphological Variability and Heritability in Three Melanesian Populations." *American Journal of Physical Anthropology* 35:241–253.

McMahon, B.; Kovar, M. G.; and Feldman, J. J.
1972. *Infant Mortality Rates: Socioeconomic Factor.* Vital and Health Statistics, series 22, number 14. Washington, D.C.: U.S. Government Printing Office.

Mead, M.
1935. *Sex and Temperament in Three Primitive Societies.* New York: W. Morrow and Company.

Meggitt, M. J.
1965. *The Lineage System of the Mae-Enga of New Guinea.* New York: Barnes and Noble.

Middleton, J.
1954. *Lugbara Religion: Ritual and Authority among an East African People.* London: International African Institute.

Molnar, S.
1975. *Races, Types and Ethnic Groups: The Problem of Human Variation.* Englewood Cliffs, N.J.: Prentice-Hall.

Montagu, A.
1960. *An Introduction to Physical Anthropology.* 3rd ed. Springfield, Ill.: Charles C Thomas.

Moynihan, D.
1965. *The Negro Family: The Case for National Action.* Washington, D.C.: U.S. Government Printing Office.

Murdock, G. P.
1967. *World Ethnographic Atlas.* Pittsburgh: University of Pittsburgh Press.

Murdock, G. P., and Provost, C.
1973. "Factors in the Division of Labor by Sex: A Cross-Cultural Analysis." *Ethnology* 12:203–225.

n

Nadel, S. F.
1955. "Two Nuba Religions: An Essay in Comparison." *American Anthropologist* 64:661–679.

Napier, J. R., and Napier, P. H.
1967. *A Handbook of Living Primates; Morphology, Ecology and Behavior of Nonhuman Primates.* London: Academic Press.

Nash, M.
1958. *Machine Age Maya: The Industrialization of a Guatemalan Community.* Chicago: University of Chicago Press.

Needham, R.
1962. *Structure and Sentiment.*
Chicago: University of Chicago
Press.

Neel, J. V.
1971. "Genetic Aspects of the
Ecology of Disease in the American
Indian." In *The Ongoing Evolution
of Latin American Populations,*
edited by F. A. Salzano. Springfield,
Ill.: Charles C Thomas.

Neel, J. V., and Chagnon, N. A.
1968. "The Demography of Two
Tribes of Primitive Relatively
Unacculturated American Indians."
*Proceedings of the National
Academy of Science* 59:680–689.

Neel, J. V., and Ward, R. H.
1975. "Village and Tribal Genetic
Distances among American Indians
and the Possible Implications for
Human Evolution." *Proceedings of
the National Academy of Science*
65:323–330.

Nei, M., and Roychoudhury, A. K.
1972. "Gene Differences between
Caucasian, Negro, and Japanese
Populations." *Science* 177:434–435.

Nketia, J.
1963. *Drumming in Akan Communities of Ghana.* Edinburgh:
Thomas Nelson and Sons.

o

Oliver, S. C.
1962. *Ecology and Cultural Continuity as Contributing Factors in
the Social Organization of the Plains
Indians.* University of California
Publications in American Archeology and Ethnology 48 (1).

Olson, M.
1965. *Logic of Collective Action;
Public Goods and the Theory of
Groups.* Cambridge, Mass.:
Harvard University Press.

Oxnard, C. E.
1969. "Evolution of the Human
Shoulder: Some Possible Path-
ways." *American Journal of Physical Anthropology* 30:319–332.

p

Patterson, T. C.
1973. *America's Past: A New
World Archaeology.* Glenview, Ill.:
Scott, Foresman and Company.

Picardi, A. C., and Siefert, W.
1976. "A Tragedy of the Commons
in the Sahel." *Technology Review*
78:42–51.

Pilbeam, D. R., and Simons, E. L.
1965. "Some Problems of Hominid
Classification." *American Scientist*
53:237–259.

Pospisil, L.
1963. *Kapauhu Papuan Economy.*
New Haven, Conn.: Yale University
Press.

Potter, R. G.
1963. "Birth Intervals: Structure
and Change." *Population Studies*
17:160–162.

Price, B. J.
1971. "Prehispanic Irrigation
Agriculture in Nuclear America."
Latin American Research Review
6:3–60.

r

Rappaport, A.
1969. *House Form and Culture.*
Englewood Cliffs, N.J.: Prentice-
Hall.

Rappaport, R. A.
1974. "Obvious Aspects of Ritual."
Cambridge Anthropology 2.

————.
1971. "Flow of Energy in an
Agricultural Society." *Scientific
American* 225:116–132.

————.
1968a. "Maring Marriage." In
Pigs, Pearshells and Women, edited
by R. M. Glass and M. J. Meggitt.
Englewood Cliffs, N.J.: Prentice-
Hall.

————.
1968b. *Pigs For the Ancestors:
Ritual in the Ecology of a New
Guinea People.* New Haven, Conn.:
Yale University Press.

Redfield, R.
1962. *The Papers of Robert Redfield.* Vols. 1 and 2, edited by R.
Redfield. Chicago: University of
Chicago Press.

Rensch, B.
1960. *Evolution Above the Species
Level.* New York: Columbia
University Press.

Richards, A.
1932. *Hunger and Work in a
Savage Tribe; A Functional Study
of Nutrition Among the Southern
Bantu.* London: G. Routledge and
Sons, Ltd.

Roberts, D. F.
1968. "Genetic Effects of Population Size Reduction." *Nature* 220:
1084–1088.

Robinson, J. T.
1963. "Adaptive Radiation in the
Australopithecines and the Origin
of Man." In *African Ecology and
Human Evolution,* edited by F. C.
Howell and Bourliere. Viking Fund
Publications in Anthropology no.
36, edited by S. Tax. Chicago:
Aldine Publishing Co.

Rogers, E. S.
1972. "The Mistassini Cree." In
Hunters and Gatherers Today,
edited by M. G. Bicchieri. New
York: Holt, Rinehart and
Winston.

**Romney, A.K. and D'Andrade,
R. G.**
1964. *Transcultural Studies in
Cognition.* Washington, D.C.:
American Anthropological
Association.

Rosen, S. I.
1974. *Introduction to the Primate.*
Englewood Cliffs, N.J.: Prentice-
Hall.

Rubin, J.
1968. *National Bilingualism in
Paraguay.* The Hague: Mouton.

Ryan, W.
1967. "Savage Discovery: The
Moynihan Report." In *The Moyni-
han Report and the Politics of
Controversy,* edited by L. Rain-
water and W. L. Yancey.
Cambridge, Mass.: MIT
Press.

s

Sahlins, M.
1976. *The Use and Misuse of Biology.* Ann Arbor: University of
Michigan Press.

Salisburg, R. F.
1962. *From Stone to Steel.* Melbourne, Australia: University of
Melbourne Press.

Scholl, T. O.; Odell, M. E.; and Johnston, F. E.
1976. "Biological Correlates of Modernization in a Guatemalan Highland Municipio." *Annals of Human Biology* 3:23–32.

Segner, L., and Collins, A.
1967. "A Cross Cultural Study of Incest Myths." Manuscript. Austin: University of Texas.

Service, E. R.
1975. *Origins of the State and Civilization: The Process of Cultural Evolution.* New York: W. W. Norton.

Simpson, G. G.
1963. "The Meaning of Taxonomic Statements." In *Classification and Human Evolution,* edited by L. Washburn. Viking Fund Publications in Anthropology no. 37, edited by S. Tax. New York: Wenner-Gren Foundation for Anthropological Research.

Smith, C. U. M.
1976. *The Problem of Life: An Essay in the Origins of Biological Thought.* New York: John Wiley and Sons.

Smith, J. M.
1969. "The Status of Neo-Darwinism." In *Towards a Theoretical Biology,* edited by C. H. Waddington. Chicago: Aldine Publishing Co.

Smole, W. J.
1976. *The Yanomamo Indians.* Austin: University of Texas Press.

Snow, C. E.
1948. *Indian Knoll Skeletons of Site Oh 2.* The University of Kentucky Reports in Anthropology, volume IV, number 3, part II. Lexington: University of Kentucky Press.

Spielman, R. S.
1974. "Differences Among Yanomamo Indian Villages: Do the Patterns of Allele Frequencies, Anthropometrics, and Map Locations Correspond?" *American Journal of Physical Anthropology* 39:461–480.

Spielman, R. S.; daRocha, F. J; Weitkamp, L. R.; Ward, R. H.; Neel, J. V.; and Chagnon, N. A.
1972. "The Genetic Structure of a Tribal Population, the Yanomamo Indians: VII. Anthropometric Differences Among Yanomamo Villages." *American Journal of Physical Anthropology* 37:345–356.

Spielman, R. S.; Migliazza, E. C.; and Neel, J. V.
1974. "Regional Linguistic and Genetic Differences Among Yanomamo Indians." *Science* 184:637–644.

Spradley, J. P., and McCurdy, D., eds.
1972. *The Cultural Experience.* Chicago: Science Research Associates.

Spuhler, J.
1963. "The Scope for Natural Selection in Man." In *Genetic Selection in Man,* edited by W. J. Schull. Ann Arbor: University of Michigan Press.

Steegman, A. T.
1970. "Cold Adaptation and the Human Face." *American Journal of Physical Anthropology* 32:243–250.

Stern, J. T.
1970. "The Meaning of 'Adaptation' and Its Relation to the Phenomenon of Natural Selection. In *Evolutionary Biology,* vol. 4, edited by T. Dobzhansky, M. K. Hecht, and W. C. Steere. New York: Appleton-Century-Crofts.

Stini, W. A.
1975. "Adaptive Strategies of Human Populations under Nutritional Stress." In *Biosocial Interrelations in Population Adaptation,* edited by E. S. Watts, F. E. Johnston, and G. W. Laske. The Hague: Mouton.

Stross, B.
1976. *The Origin and Evolution of Language.* Dubuque: Wm. C. Brown Company Publishers.

Suggs, R. C.
1960. *The Island Civilizations of Polynesia.* New York: Mentor Books.

Swedlund, A., and Armelagos, G.
1976. *Demographic Anthropology.* Dubuque: Wm. C. Brown Company Publishers.

Szathmary, E. J. E.
1978. "Blood Groups of Siberians, Eskimos, Subarctic and Northwest Coast Indians: The Problems of Origins and Genetic Relationships." In *Origin and Affinities of the First Americans,* edited by W. S. Laughlin. New York: Gusdan Fischer, Publishers.

t

Tax, S.
1952. *Penny Capitalism.* Chicago: University of Chicago Press.

Textor, R.
1967. *A Cross-Cultural Summary.* New York: Human Relations Area Press.

Thomas, R. B.
1973. *Human Adaptation to a High Andean Energy Flow System.* Occasional Paper in Anthropology no. 7. University Park, Pa.: Department of Anthropology, the Pennsylvania State University.

Tobias, P. V.
1975. "Long or Short Hominid Phylogenies? Paleontological and Molecular Evidences." In *The Role of Natural Selection in Human Evolution,* edited by F. M. Salzano. New York: American Elsevier Publishing Co.

Toffler, A.
1970. *Future Shock.* New York: Random House.

v

Valero, H.
1971. *Yanomamo: The Narrative of a White Girl Kidnapped by Amazonian Indians,* as told to E. Biocca. Translated by D. Rhodes. New York: E. P. Dutton.

Vayda, A. P.
1961. "Expansion and Warfare Among Swidden Agriculturalists." *American Anthropologist* 63:346–358.

von Koenigswald, G. H. R.
1976. *The Evolution of Man.* Rev. ed. Ann Arbor: University of Michigan Press.

w

Walker, A., and Andrews, P.
1973. "Reconstruction of the Dental Arcades of *Ramapithecus wickeri.*" *Nature* 244:313–314.

Ward, R. H.
1972. "The Genetic Structure of a Tribal Population, the Yanomamo Indians: V. Comparisons of a series of genetic networks." *Annals of Human Genetics* 36:21–43.

Washburn, S. L., and DeVore, I.
1961. "Social Behavior of Baboons and Early Man." In *Social Life of Early Man,* edited by S. L. Washburn. Viking Fund Publications in Anthropology no. 31, edited by S. Tax. New York: Wenner-Gren Foundation for Anthropological Research.

Watson, J. D.
1968. *The Double Helix: A Personal Account of the Discovery of the Structure of DNA.* New York: Atheneum.

Watson, O. M., and Graves, T. D.
1966. "Quantitative Research in Proxemic Behavior." *American Anthropologist* 69:971–985.

Weiner, J. S.
1977. "Human Ecology." In *Human Biology,* edited by G. A. Harrison, J. S. Weiner, J. M. Tanner, and N. A. Barnicot. 2nd ed. Oxford: Oxford University Press.

Westermarck, E.
1922. *The History of Human Marriage.* London: Macmillan and Co.

Whiting, J.; Kluckhohn, R.; and Anthony, A.
1958. "The Function of Male Initiation Ceremonies at Puberty." In *Readings in Social Psychology,* edited by E. Maccoby, T. M. Newcomb, and L. Hartley. 3rd ed. New York: Henry Holt and Co.

Whorf, B. L.
1956. *Language, Thought, and Reality; Selected Writings,* edited by John B. Carroll. Cambridge, Mass.: Technology Press of Massachusetts Institute of Technology.

Wilson, E. O.
1975. *Sociobiology: The New Synthesis.* Cambridge, Mass.: Belknap Press of Harvard University Press.

Wittfogel, K. W.
1957. *Oriental Despotism: A Comparative Study of Total Power.*

New Haven, Conn.: Yale University Press.

Wolf, A.
1966. "Childhood Association, Sexual Attraction and the Incest Taboo: A Chinese Case." *American Anthropologist* 68:883–898.

Wolpoff, M. H.
1968. "'Telanthopus' and The Single Species Hypothesis." *American Anthropologist* 70:477–493.

Workman, P. L.; Blumberg, B. S.; and Cooper, A. J.
1963. "Selection, Gene Migration and Polymorphic Stability in a U.S. White and Negro Population." *American Journal of Human Genetics* 15:71–84.

Credits

The Natural History of Man by J. S. Weiner. Universe Books, New York, 1971. **145,** From *Humankind Emerging,* edited by Bernard G. Campbell. Copyright © 1976 Little, Brown & Co., Inc. Reprinted by permission. Photograph, Dorothy Mann, Courtesy of Transvaal Museum. From *Interpreting the Evolution of the Brain,* Human Biology 35(3):277, 1963, by Harry J. Jerison by permission of Wayne State University Press. Copyright © 1963 Wayne State University Press, Detroit, Michigan 48202. Courtesy of University Museum, University of Pennsylvania, Philadelphia. **146,** From *The Natural History of Man* by J. S. Weiner. Universe Books, New York, 1971. **148,** Photo Alan Mann, Courtesy of Transvaal Museum. Photo Alan Mann. From *Origins of Man,* John Buettner-Janusch, 1966. **150,** From *The Fossil Evidence for Human Evolution,* 2nd Ed., by W. E. LeGros Clark. The University of Chicago Press. Copyright © 1964. **154,** From *The Fossil Evidence for Human Evolution* by W. E. LeGros Clark. The University of Chicago Press. Copyright © 1955. **155,** From *Mankind in the Making* by William Howells. Copyright © 1959, 1967 by William Howells. Used by permission of Doubleday & Company, Inc. **156,** Courtesy Dr. Ronald Singer, University of Chicago. **158,** Fine Line Illustrations, Inc.

7

168-169, From *Anthropology* by William A. Haviland. Copyright © 1974 by Holt, Rinehart & Winston. Reprinted by permission of Holt, Rinehart & Winston. **171,** Oldowan Pebble Tools—Trustees of the British Museum (Natural History) from *Man the Toolmaker,* 4th ed. by K. P. Oakley, 1959, and the University of Chicago Press. **173,** Oldowan Pebble Tools—Trustees of the British Museum (Natural History) from *Man the Toolmaker,* 4th ed. by K. P. Oakley, 1959, and the University of Chicago Press. **174,** Acheulian Tools— From *People of the Earth,* by Brian M. Fagan. Copyright © 1977 Little, Brown & Co., Inc. Reprinted by permission. Soan Chopping Tools—Trustees of the British Museum (Natural History) from *Man the Toolmaker,* 4th ed. by K. P. Oakley, 1959, and the University of

Chicago Press. **176,** Trustees of the British Museum (Natural History) from *Man the Toolmaker,* 4th ed. by K. P. Oakley, 1959, and the University of Chicago Press. **177,** "Trustees of the British Museum (Natural History)" from *Man the Toolmaker,* 4th ed. by K. P. Oakley, 1959, and the University of Chicago Press. **179,** Denise de Sonneville Bordes, "Upper Paleolithic Cultures in Western Europe," *Science* 142(3590):350, 1963. **180,** Venus Figurine—From the Photographic Collections of the University Museum, University of Pennsylvania, Philadelphia. Cave Painting—R. Gates from Frederic Lewis.

8

189, Courtesy of J. Mellaart. **190,** Fine Line Illustrations, Inc. **192,** Map—Fine Line Illustrations, Inc. Implements from Ur—From the Photographic Collections of the University Museum, University of Pennsylvania, Philadelphia. Implements from Gordion—Courtesy, Gordion Excavations Turkey, University Museum, University of Pennsylvania, Philadelphia. **194,** Fine Line Illustrations, Inc. **202,** Ban Chiang Burial. C. 1500 B.C.; socketed bronze axe and bronze bracelet. Northern Thailand Archaeological Project, University Museum—Thai Fine Arts Department. **203,** From the Photographic Collections of the University Museum, University of Pennsylvania, Philadelphia. **205,** Rebus and pictograph—Fine Line Illustrations, Inc. From the Photographic Collections of the University Museum, University of Pennsylvania, Philadelphia. The Peabody Museum of Ethnology, Harvard University, Salem, Massachusetts. Calculator—Courtesy Monroe, The Calculator Company, Morris Plains, N.J. Model 1430. **206,** Tikal Project, University Museum, University of Pennsylvania, Philadelphia. Calendar—Courtesy, Field Museum of Natural History, Chicago. Tikal Project, University Museum, University of Pennsylvania. **207,** Copyright Leslie Wong from Contact Press Images, Inc. Editorial Photocolor Archives (Chinese Script). Photo by B. K. Lathbury. **208,** Photo by B. K. Lathbury. **209,** Courtesy of Pan American Airways. Editorial Photocolor Archives (#421A-26). Photo by Gregory Possehl (Mohenjo-daro).

9

220, From *Understanding Evolution,* 3rd ed., by E. Peter Volpe, 1977, Wm. C. Brown Company Publishers. **221,** From *Understanding Evolution,* 3rd ed., by E. Peter Volpe, 1977, Wm. C. Brown Company Publishers. **224,** From F. E. Johnston, *Microevolution of Human Populations,* Prentice-Hall, Englewood Cliffs, N.J., 1973. **225,** From Victor A. McKusick, *Human Genetics,* 2nd edition, Prentice-Hall, Englewood Cliffs, New Jersey, 1969. **227,** Fine Line Illustrations, Inc. **231,** From *Understanding Evolution,* 3rd ed., by E. Peter Volpe, 1977, Wm. C. Brown Company Publishers. **232,** Fine Line Illustrations, Inc. **238,** Courtesy Alabama Museum of Natural History.

10

252, Adapted by Fine Line Illustrations, Inc. from D. F. Roberts, *Climate and Human Variability,* Copyright © 1973 by Cummings Publishing Company, Inc., Menlo Park, California. **254,** Adapted by Fine Line Illustrations, Inc. from D. F. Roberts, *Climate and Human Variability,* Copyright © 1973 by Cummings Publishing Company, Inc., Menlo Park, California. **255,** Eskimo—Photo copyright Leonard Lee Rue III. African—From the Photographic Collections of the University Museum, University of Pennsylvania, Philadelphia. **259,** Fine Line Illustrations, Inc. **262,** From *Integrated Science for Health Students* by T. Randall Lankford, 1976. Reston Publishing Company, Inc.

11

274, Fine Line Illustrations Inc. **276,** Adapted by Fine Line Illustrations, Inc. from Stanley M. Garn, *Human Races,* 3rd ed. Courtesy of Charles C. Thomas, Publisher, Springfield, Illinois. **278-279,** German Man—Photo by Harold Koster. All others—From the Photographic Collections of the University Museum, University of Pennsylvania, Philadelphia. **281,** Table 11.2 from Stephen Molnar, "Races, Types, and Ethnic Groups," Copyright © 1975, *The Problem of Human Variation* p. 70. Reprinted by permission of Prentice Hall, Inc.,

Englewood Cliffs, New Jersey. **282,** Table 11.3 from *The Natural History of Man,* by J. S. Weiner. Universe Books, New York, 1971. **283,** Tables 11.4 and 11.5 from *Human Biology* by Harrison, Weiner, Tanner, & Barnicot, published by Oxford University Press, 1977. **285,**Adapted by Fine Line Illustrations, Inc. from *People and Races* by Alice M. Brues. Copyright © 1977 Macmillan Publishing Co., Inc. Used by permission. **287,** Black Man—Bob Coyle.

12

298, From *The Wild Boy of Aveyron* by Harlen Lane. Cambridge, Massachusetts: Harvard University Press, 1976. **300,** Courtesy, Field Museum of Natural History. **301,** Photograph, Peter Marler. **303,** Squirrels—Bob Coyle. Hippos—WCB *Archives.* Giraffes—Bob Coyle. Dog—Rohn Engh. **309,** Marion Bernstein Editorial Photocolor Archives. **313,** Rick Smolan, Contact Press Images, Inc.,

13

318, Editorial Photocolor Archives. **320,** Mrs. John Jacobson, Freelance Photographers Guild. **321,** Editorial Photocolor Archives, EPA Newsphoto. **330,** Alain Keler Editorial Photocolor Archives (#427A-4). **331,** Courtesy of Warner Communications Company. **332,** Rick Smolan. **333,** Courtesy of *Music Educators Journal.*

14

339, Fine Line Illustrations, Inc. **340,** Fine Line Illustrations, Inc. **344,** Rick Smolan. **352,** Gull—Bob Coyle. Butterfly—Bob Coyle. Airplane— Docuamerica. **353,** Bruce Anspach from Editorial Photocolor Archives (#421A-10). **356,** Rick Smolan.

15

360, Michael Rockefeller. **361,** Alon Reininger from Contact Press Images, Inc. **362,** Woman—UPI. Man— Vivienne della Grotta (#ED-541). **364,** American Museum of Natural History. **367,** Elvehjem Art Center, The University of Wisconsin, Madison. **369,** Adapted from *Zapotec Deviance,* by Henry A. Selby, 1974. The University of Texas Press. **371,** Both photos of Richards—UPI. **376,** From *The Nuer*

by Evans-Pritchard, 1968. Oxford on the Clarendon Press, Oxford University Press. **377,** Fine Line Illustrations, Inc. **380,** Bob Coyle. **381,** Bob Coyle.

16

389, Sorfoto (#900269). **390,** Sedate Religious Ceremony—Religious News Service. Jesus Rally—EPA Newsphoto. **392,** Rohn Engh (#904). **394,** American Kitchen—Camerique (# H-247-23). Indian Kitchen—From James M. Freeman, *Scarcity and Opportunity in an Indian Village,* Copyright © 1977 by Cummings Publishing Company, Menlo Park, California. **395,** Woodfin Camp and Associates. **397,** Fine Line Illustrations, Inc. **399,** I. W. Kelton from FAD. **400,** Woodfin Camp and Associates. **403,** Group—Historical Pictures Service, Chicago (#96-22-196) Pyle. Hanging—Historical Pictures Service, Chicago (#96-22-196) Darley. **407,** Fine Line Illustrations, Inc. **408,** Photo by A. L. Hurrell. **409,** Fine Line Illustrations, Inc.

17

413, UPI. **414,** Courtesy of Austrian Information Service. **415,** Leslie Wong from Contact Press Images, Inc. **417,** Fine Line Illustrations, Inc. **418,** Fine Line Illustrations, Inc. **420-21,** HRS Elizabeth R. II. **424,** Roger Malloch from Magnum. **425,** Sybil Shelton from Monkmeyer (#1888). **428,** Fine Line Illustrations, Inc. **429,** Mato Grosso Family—From the Photographic Collections of the University Museum, University of Pennsylvania, Philadelphia. Mormon Family— Historical Pictures Service, Chicago (96-35-780-1). **431,** The American Museum of Natural History.

18

437, Jim Shaffer. **439,** Fine Line Illustrations, Inc. **440,** Fine Line Illustrations, Inc. **441,** Fine Line Illustrations, Inc. **443,** Fine Line Illustrations, Inc. **445,** Fine Line Illustrations, Inc. **446.** Fine Line Illustrations, Inc. **449,** Fine Line Illustrations, Inc. **450,** Historical Pictures Service, Chicago (# 22-55-101 Ed. VIII). **451,** Historical Pictures Service, Chicago (# 47-55-105-5). **452,** Fine Line Illustrations, Inc. **454,** The Pit—Bern Keating from Black Star. Whites Only—David Margolin from

Black Star (# 12-2). **456,** Gianfranco Gorgoni from Contact Press Images, Inc.

19

464, UPI. **466,** UPI. **467,** Museum of the American Indian Heye Foundation (# 13139). **472,** Bob Coyle. **473,** From Robert Netting, *Cultural Ecology,* Copyright © by Cummings Publishing Company, Inc., Menlo Park, California. **474,** Marjorie Shostak from Anthro-Photo, Woodfin Camp and Associates.

20

488, From *Demographic Anthropology* by Alan Swedlund and George J. Armelagos, copyright © 1976 by Wm. C. Brown Company Publishers. **491,** Bureau of the Census. **492,** United Nations. **495,** Courtesy of Odyssey House. **498,** Fine Line Illustrations, Inc. **499,** Fine Line Illustrations, Inc. **503,** Fine Line Illustrations, Inc. **504,** Michael Rockefeller. **505,** Michael Rockefeller.

21

515, Bob Coyle. **518,** Museum of the American Indian, Heye Foundation (#36063). **521,** From *Land, Labour, and Diet in Northern Rhodesia* by Audrey I. Richards published by Oxford University Press. **523,** From *Yale Publications in Anthropology— Kapauku Papuan Economy,* no. 67 by Leopold Pospisil published by the Department of Anthropology, Yale University, 1963. **524,** Fine Line Illustrations, Inc. **525,** Rick Smolan from Contact Press Images, Inc. **527,** From James M. Freeman, *Scarcity and Opportunity in an Indian Village,* copyright © 1977 by Cummings Publishing Company, Menlo Park, California. **530,** Both—Fred Meyer from Woodfin Camp and Associates. **534,** Courtesy of the Chicago Museum of Natural History.

22

547, Fine Line Illustrations, Inc. **548,** Napoleon Chagnon from Anthro-Photo File. **549,** From William J. Smole, *The Yanoama Indians: A Cultural Geography* by University of Texas Press, 1976. **550,** Napoleon

Chagnon from Anthro-Photo File. **552,** Fine Line Illustrations, Inc. **555,** Napoleon Chagnon from Anthro-Photo File. **556,** Napoleon Chagnon. **558,** Napoleon Chagnon. **559,** Napoleon Chagnon.

23

567, Fine Line Illustrations, Inc. **568,** Reprinted by permission of Yale University Press from *Pigs for Ancestors* by Roy A. Rappaport. Copyright © 1972 by Yale University. **571,** Reprinted by permission of Yale University Press from *Pigs for Ancestors* by Roy A. Rappaport. Copyright © 1972 by Yale University. **572,** Reprinted by permission of Yale University Press from *Pigs for Ancestors* by Roy A. Rappaport. Copyright © 1972 by Yale University. **573,** New Guinea Man—Reprinted from *Adam with Arrows* by Colin

Simpson by permission of Angus and Robertson Publishers, Sidney. **574,** Reprinted by permission of Yale University Press from *Pigs for Ancestors* by Roy A. Rappaport. Copyright © 1972 by Yale University.

24

580, Fine Line Illustrations, Inc. **581,** Fine Line Illustrations, Inc. **584,** Francis E. Johnston. **585,** Alain Keler from Editorial Photocolor Archives (# 421A-3). **589,** Alain Keler from Editorial Photocolor Archives (# 421A-5). **590,** Ginny Lathbury. **591,** Ginny Lathbury. **593,** Ginny Lathbury. **596,** Ginny Lathbury.

Insights

21, Bob Coyle. **62,** Marilyn Phelps. **86,** Courtesy of the American Museum

of Natural History. **88,** Courtesy of the American Museum of Natural History. **114,** Bob Coyle. **159,** From *Humankind Emerging* by Bernard G. Campbell published by Little, Brown and Company, 1976. **183,** Fine Line Illustrations, Inc. **210,** U.S. Department of the Interior-National Park Service Photograph. **227,** Napoleon Chagnon, Anthro-Photo File. **242,** Robert V. Eckert, Jr. **264,** Marla Schafer. **304,** Jean-Claude LeJeune. **354,** UPI. **404,** Fine Line Illustrations, Inc. **469,** Giafranco Gorgoni. **481,** Bob Coyle. **508,** Rick Smolan. **536,** Exchange Floor—Daniel S. Brody. Stock—Courtesy of AT&T. **554,** Napoleon Chagnon. **594,** Photograph © Evelyne and Marc Berheim for Woodfin Camp and Associates. **595,** Photograph © Evelyne and Marc Bernheim for Woodfin Camp and Associates.

Index

Homo habilis, 150-51
Homo sapiens
  appearance of, 154
    Neanderthal, 154-56
      speech and, 159, 300
    spread into the New World, 157-58
Hopkins, D., 158
Horton, R., 401
Houma Indians, 40
Household
  matrifocal, 419
Howard, W. D., 39-40
Howell, F. C., 155
Howells, W. W., 572
Howlett, P. R., 568, 569
Human, distinctiveness of, 52-53
Human biology
  anthropological genetics and, 28-30
  definition of, 28
  human adaptability and, 30
  skeletal biology and, 30
Hunting
  as a social activity, 39-40
  Paleolithic cave paintings and, 44-45
  techniques in the Paleolithic, 175
  territoriality and, 40

i

Incest taboo
  children of incestuous matings, 416
  nuclear family and, 413
  psychological explanations of, 414
  sociological explanations of, 415-16
Indian Knoll Mound, 272
Indus River civilizations, 206
Infanticide, 494
Inheritance
  lineage and, 452
  property, 422
Intellectual performance and malnutrition, 590
Iron Age, 203
Irwin, P. G., 567
Itani, J., 308
Itard, J.-M.-A., 297

j

Jarmo, 193
Jati, 455
Jericho, 197
Johnson, S., 351
Jolly, C. J., 111-12, 141

k

Kanapoi Humerus, 142
Kapauku, 522
Kappel, W., 466, 589
Kardiner, A., 391
Katz, S. H., 261

Kaufman, I., 416
Keller, H., 304-5
Kinship
  Australian Aborigines and, 420-21
  categories of "father" and, 420-21, 422
  categories of "mother" and, 421
  cross cousins, 439
  kin terms, 419
  parallel cousins, 439
  teknonymy, 438
Kofyar, 473-74
Kramer, M. J., 495
Kroeber, A. L., 26
Krogman, W. M., 264

l

Lamarck, J.-B., 76
Lancaster, J., 112
Language
  infrastructure and culture, 328
  productive characteristic of, 326
  structure and, 326
  switching codes in, 334
  transformations in, 327
Larson, L., 167
Laszlo, E., 48
Lea, D. A., 567
Leach, E., 373
Leakey, L., 139
  family of, 126
Leakey, M., 142
Leakey, R., 142
Lee, D., 354
Lee, R., 474
Lenin, 388
Lerner, M., 283
Levallois technique, 176
LeVine, R., 427, 428
Levi-Strauss, C., 379, 404, 448
Lewis, G. E., 139
Libby, W., 283
Lieberman, P., 159
Life
  characteristics of, 49-51
  unity of, 52
Lightfoot, J., 75
Limiting factor, 478
Lindzey, G., 416
Lineage, 439
  agnatic descent, 449
  apical ancestor of, 440
  sublineage and, 452
  uterine descent, 449
Linton, R., 391, 450
Little, M. A., 477
Livingstone, F. L., 258, 275
Loomis, W. F., 262
Lorenz, K., 302
Lothogam mandible, 141
Lyell, C., 75

m

McClung, J., 263
McCurdy, D., 39
McHenry, H., 572
MacNeish, R. S., 193
Mae Enga, 502
Magdelenian people, 26-27
Magic
  causal series and, 401
  escape clause and, 402
Malaria, genetic adaptations to, 258-60
Malcolm, L. A., 569, 570
Malinowski, B., 11, 415
Malthus, T. R., 78, 506
Mammals, characteristics of, 63
Mangelsdorf, P. C., 193
Mann, A. E., 147, 172
Mao Tse-Tung, 388
Marriage
  bilateral cross-cousin, 444
  circular connubium, 447
  endogamous systems of, 439
  homogamy, 437
  hypergamy, 446, 456
  hypogamy, 446
  matrilineal cross-cousin, 446
  patrilateral parallel-cousin, 438
  systems of asymmetric alliance, 446
  wedding and, 436
Maybury-Lewis, D., 442, 443, 448
Mayr, E., 274
Mead, M., 17-19
Meaning
  Anthropology and, 12
  attributes of kin terms and, 343-45
  classification and, 339
  dimensions of, 345
  the monitor and, 339
  radical empiricists, 352
  rules for studying, 341
  taxonomy and, 347
Meggitt, M. J., 502
Menarche, 493
Mendel, G., 60
Mesolithic, 188
Metabolic rate, 252
Microevolution, 90
Minnesota, bow-hunting groups in, 39-40
Mogollon peoples, 195
Molnar, S., 280, 281, 283
Money
  general purpose, 535
  special purpose, 534
Monogenists, 271
Montagu, A., 492
Morphemes, 322
Morren, G., 477
Mortality
  infant, 489, 490
Mousterian, 155, 176-78